W9-CZX-336

The Managing
of Police
Organizations

THE MANAGING

OF POLICE

ORGANIZATIONS

Second Edition

Paul M. Whisenand, Ph.D.

Professor of Criminal Justice
California State University, Long Beach

R. Fred Ferguson, M. S.

Chief of Police
Salinas, California

Prentice-Hall, Inc., Englewood Cliffs, New Jersey 07632

Library of Congress Cataloging in Publication Data

WHISENAND, PAUL M
  The managing of police organizations.

  Includes bibliographical references and index.
  1.–Police administration. I.–Ferguson, Robert Fred,
(date)– joint author. II.–Title.
HV7935.W43–1978   350'.74   77-13640
ISBN 0-13-550731-6

350.74
W576m
1978

Printed in the United States of America

10 9 8 7 6 5 4 3 2 1

PRENTICE-HALL INTERNATIONAL, INC., *London*
PRENTICE-HALL OF AUSTRALIA PTY. LIMITED, *Sydney*
PRENTICE-HALL OF CANADA, LTD., *Toronto*
PRENTICE-HALL OF INDIA PRIVATE LIMITED, *New Delhi*
PRENTICE-HALL OF JAPAN, INC., *Tokyo*
PRENTICE-HALL OF SOUTHEAST ASIA PTE. LTD., *Singapore*
WHITEHALL BOOKS LIMITED, *Wellington, New Zealand*

To our favorite managers—
Joan Whisenand and Marilu Ferguson

CONTENTS

PART TWO:

Role Component Two—External Responsibilities

PREFACE

For the second edition of *The Managing of Police Organizations* we thought it most fitting to ask of ourselves at least three rather gut-level questions: (1) "What's new?", (2) "Who cares?", and (3) "So what?" Trying to answer these questions, in turn, developed the framework for us to revise the material in this book.

To begin with "What's new?", tersely we would respond "Considerable." Let us cite but a few of the more important new topics not available for inclusion in our earlier edition, yet presently impacting police management. First, we now have before us not one but two sets of goals and standards for our police. Specifically, the American Bar Association and the National Advisory Commission on Criminal Justice Standards and Goals have promulgated a large number of comprehensive and challenging goals for our police organizations. Second, the National Commission on Productivity devoted a portion of its study time to an examination of "police" productivity. To this was logically added by others an intensified interest in program evaluation. Third, the *politics* of police management is being more candidly and openly debated than ever before. Fourth, a significant change in direction and emphasis has been placed on collective negotiations, internal inspections, and internal affairs. These subjects (and a few others) are new ones that we have addressed in the pages that follow.

Next, to "Who cares?" We respond hopefully "The same intended reading audience as before." Indeed, we were personally pleased and pleasantly surprised by the acceptance of our first book. Therefore, we have continued to target our efforts toward: police managers, police professionals (possible future managers), criminal justice students (possible future police professionals), and the general citizenry (possible, if not now, police supporters). Since apparently you do care, we would also note that our approach in this instance is intentionally more pragmatic although managerial strategies and techniques are still overtly linked to pertinent theories. Furthermore, two new format elements have been added as aids to our readers—the outlines that precede each chapter and the brief synopses at the beginning of chapters 2 through 16.

Finally, "So what?" or, "What use is the text even if we accomplish our goals?" Basically, the fundamental goal of our text is *to present police management knowledge to knowledgable police managers in order to support them in their commitment to a more efficient and humanistic system of policing.* If the theory and strategies contained in our book prove reasonable, helpful, and applicable we can then feel more comfortable in our belief that effective police managment can and will prevail.

Once again our book awaits your evaluation. After reading its sixteen chapters, you will be in a position to judge, as before, to what extent we have been able to fulfill our stated goal.

We look forward to your assessment.

Paul M. Whisenand, Ph.D.
R. Fred Ferguson, M. S.

The Managing
of Police
Organizations

Chapter One

POLICE MANAGEMENT:
The Role and the Responsibility

Organizational excellence and managerial excellence are one and the same. Consequently, any attempt to improve one automatically involves the other. This book approaches organizational excellence through better management, more specifically, better *police* management. Thus, we focus on the need to increase the manager's understanding of police organizations so that he will be equipped to control and direct them in response to complex human purposes. In terms of concepts, strategies, and skills essential for achieving such managerial abilities, and methods of learning them and then putting them to work, the stage is set. Our text covers the prospects and the need for a modern police management that is capable of directing the modern police organization. *Our major premise is that the police manager is undoubtedly capable of improving his organization so that it can accomplish its particular goals and at the same time meet the needs of its members. Our major hope is that one of the manager's most sought-after goals is within reach; namely, mastery of himself and thereby of his organization.*

We believe that the following three recommendations can aid the reader in getting to the heart of the book: (1) The organization's objectives will probably be attained more effectively by so managing the work and the people that their individual needs are met while on the job. We seek to provide the means for making our opening sentences a reality —organizations can achieve excellence by helping their managers achieve excellence. (2) The book should be read as a study of *managerial* dynamics. It should not be read as a study of *individual behavior*. (3) Please keep in mind that the material is primarily for you—the potential or actual *police manager*. Most of the ideas and strategies presented, however, can also be applied in other organizations.[1]

SELECTED DEFINITIONS

Selecting a definition is similar to picking a winning horse at a race track—everyone has his own choice. As for the terms that are defined in this section, your definition may be as good or better than ours. The primary purpose is, therefore, to create some general agreement as to what

[1]One of the first accounts of the principle of the universality of management is given in a Socratic discourse as recorded (or imagined) by Xenophon, one of Socrates' disciples. It clearly indicates that even in the fifth century B.C. men were aware of or beginning to be aware of the same principles that would apply in the twentieth century when an effective manager of a soap company could also be an effective head of an automobile concern or secretary of defense. For a highly readable text on the development of management theory and practice, see Claude S. George, Jr., *The History of Management Thought* (Englewood Cliffs, N.J.: Prentice-Hall, Inc., 1968).

we mean when certain ideas are discussed. Only those terms central to our thinking are reviewed at this time. Other terms receive consideration in the chapters that focus on their parameters and dynamics.

Let us begin by looking at the term *police*. We use it to identify a particular type of formal organization, and, for our purposes, it is a government organization. Hence, we define *police* as *a formal government organization responsible for enforcing the laws of society and maintaining peace*.[2] Our definition encompasses local (municipal and county), state, and federal policing agencies. It should be noted, however, that our focus is on local police organizations and that we will consider the term *local law enforcement* as being synonymous with the term city and county *police*.

The term *organization*, so prevalent in the above paragraph, is so frequently used in conjunction with the term *management* that the two are often confused. Waldo offers a useful discussion on how to distinguish them:

> *Organization is the anatomy, management the physiology, of administration. Organization is structure; management is functioning.* But each is dependent upon and inconceivable without the other in any existing administrative system, just as anatomy and physiology are intertwined and mutually dependent in any living organism. We are close to the truth, in fact, when we assert that *organization and management* are merely convenient categories of analysis, two different ways of viewing the same phenomena. One is static and seeks for pattern; the other is dynamic and follows movement.
>
> More precisely, organization may be defined *as the structure of authoritative and habitual personal interrelations in an administrative system*.[3] (Italics added.)

Waldo defines *management* as "*action intended to achieve rational cooperation in an administrative system*."[4] The chapters that follow concentrate on the "action" part of the definition. This can also be referred to as the role of the manager, or the behavior that is expected of him in order to achieve universal cooperation. The role is comprised of a variety of functions or processes that the manager must promote and facilitate.

[2]For an excellent discussion of the goals of contemporary local law enforcement, see James Q. Wilson, "Dilemmas of Police Administration," *Public Administration Review*, 28 (September-October 1968), 407–16.

[3]Dwight Waldo, *The Study of Public Administration* (New York: Random House, Inc., 1955), p. 6.

[4]*Ibid.*, p. 7.

More will be said about the manager's role in the subsequent section.

We are now in position to describe *administration* and *administrative system*. They are *formal groupings deliberately constructed to seek specific goals*. And, organization and management serve as the structure and the processes for arriving at the heart of any administrative system—the attainment of goals. *A goal is a desired state of affairs which the administrative system attempts to realize*. The primary responsibility of the police manager is, therefore, to use the organization as a tool for moving the administrative system toward goal attainment. Since administrative goals are so critical, let us examine them more closely.

The goals of a police organization serve many ends. First, *goals provide direction by depicting a future state of affairs which the organization strives to realize*. Second, *goals also constitute a source of legitimacy which justifies the activities of an organization and, indeed, its very existence*. Third, *goals serve as bench marks by which members of an organization and outsiders can evaluate the success of the organization, that is, its effectiveness and efficiency*.

Modern organizations usually have more than a single goal and tend to rank them in order of significance. Let us analyze the preceding sentence in light of our present-day police organizations. You will recall that we cited the two major goals of local law enforcement as law enforcement and order maintenance. While we advocate two basic goals, some lists are a lot longer. More will be said later about the goals of police organizations.

We now examine a concept that is becoming increasingly more important—*the criminal justice system*, or the *administration of criminal justice*. The administration of criminal justice includes the following six processes: law enforcement, prosecution, probation, courts, corrections, and parole. The concept of a criminal justice system is relatively new—it originated in the 1960s. Hence, there is very little literature about it and even less agreement as to its components and parameters.[5] While the phrase *administration of criminal justice* is often used, it is in fact a misnomer. In reality, a loose system of relationships prevails. Ackoff supplied a useful and simple definition of a system when he described it as "any entity, conceptual or physical, which consists of interdependent

---

[5]John P. Kenney describes the system of criminal justice in terms of the voluntary partnership that has been established between the local police agencies and the state in *The California Police* (Springfield, Ill.: Charles C Thomas, Publisher, 1964), p. 111. See also Space-General Corporation, *Prevention and Control of Crime and Delinquency*, report prepared for the Youth and Adult Corrections Agency, State of California (El Monte, Calif.: Space-General Corporation, 1965), p. 14.

parts."[6] Dorsey provided a framework for operationalizing systems theory when he defined a system as

> a bonded region in space and time, within which information and/or energy are exchanged among subsystems in greater quantities and/or at higher rates than the quantities exchanged or rates of exchange with anything outside the boundary, and within which the subsystems are to some degree interdependent.[7]

An extensive vocabulary of systems theories exists and includes such terms as system, boundary, environment, homeostatic-equilibrium, interaction, interdependent, structural-functional relationships, input-output, exchanges, and open versus closed system. In the complete system block diagram (Exhibit 1–1), it is possible to identify the numerous interrelationships within the criminal justice system. The diagram makes it readily apparent that those working in criminal justice are placed in the middle of a system of relationships, out of which they must fashion an operating system that assists in accomplishing the objectives of many involved organizaitons. When local, state, and national law enforcement organizations are viewed as subsystems, it becomes possible to ascertain the basic significance and utility of improving the criminal justice system in total. The Omnibus Crime Control and Safe Streets Act of 1968 is a major step in making what has been called our nonsystem of criminal justice into a *system*.[8]

BASIC CONDITIONS THAT CREATE
THE NEED FOR A "NEW" POLICE MANAGER

From an almost unrecognized position in 1900, *management has risen today to be the central activity of our age and organizational society.* And, as we become increasingly more an organizational society, the importance of effective management also grows.

Management is at one and the same time the determiner of our national progress, the supervisor of our employed, the amasser of our

[6]Russell L. Ackoff, "Systems, Organizations and Interdisciplinary Research," *General Systems,* 5 (1960), 1.

[7]John T. Dorsey, "An Information-Energy Model," *Papers in Comparative Public Administration,* ed. Ferrel Heady and Sybil L. Stokes (Ann Arbor, Mich.: Institute of Public Administration, 1962), p. 43.

[8]For an excellent overview of this act, the government organizations it created, and the direction it has taken in order to improve the criminal justice system, see *1st Annual Report of the Law Enforcement Assistance Administration* (Washington, D.C.: Government Printing Office, 1969).

resources, the guide for our effective government, and the molder of our society. *It is the focal point of our social as well as personal activities, and the way we manage ourselves and our organizations reflects with pertinent clarity what we and our society are in the process of observing.*

By implication or explicit recommendation *the current literature sug-*

Exhibit 1–1.   A general view of The Criminal Justice System

This chart seeks to present a simple yet comprehensive view of the movement of cases through the criminal justice system. Procedures in individual jurisdictions may vary from the pattern shown here. The differing weights of line indicate the relative volumes of cases disposed of at various points in the system, but this is only suggestive since no nationwide data of this sort exists.

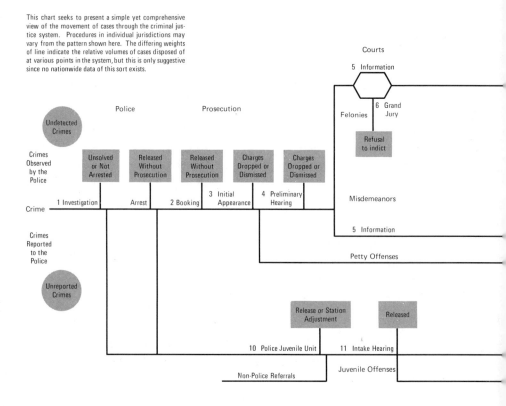

1 May continue until trial.
2 Administrative record of arrest. First step at which temporary release on bail may be available.
3 Before magistrate, commissioner, or justice of peace. Formal notice of charge, advice of rights. Bail set. Summary trials for petty offenses usually conducted here without further processing.

4 Preliminary testing of evidence against defendant. Charge may be reduced. No separate preliminary hearing for misdemeanors in some systems.
5 Charge filed by prosecutor on basis of information submitted by police or citizens. Alternative to grand jury indictment; often used in felonies, almost always in misdemeanors.

Source: **The President's Commission on Law Enforcement and Administration of Justice,** *The Challenge of Crime In A Free Society* **(Washington, D.C.: U.S. Government Printing Office, 1967), pp. 8–9.**

gests to the manager the utility of divergent managerial styles, organization structures and climates, and types of management training. For the behavioral and social scientists who devote their lives to understanding these topics, the apparent contradictions and ambiguities are confusing enough, but for the practicing manager who is responsible for this new

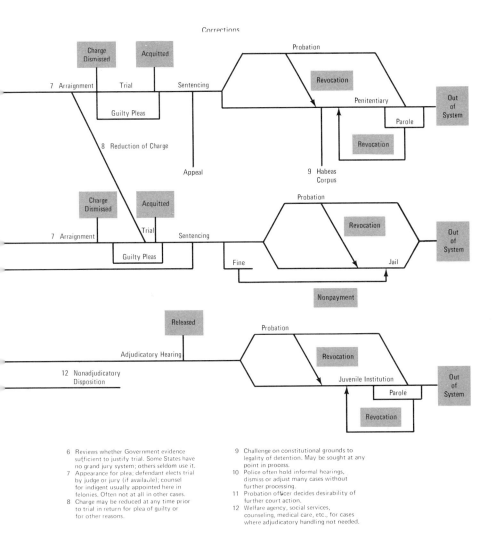

6 Reviews whether Government evidence sufficient to justify trial. Some States have no grand jury system; others seldom use it.

7 Appearance for plea; defendant elects trial by judge or jury (if available); counsel for indigent usually appointed here in felonies. Often not at all in other cases.

8 Charge may be reduced at any time prior to trial in return for plea of guilty or for other reasons.

9 Challenge on constitutional grounds to legality of detention. May be sought at any point in process.

10 Police often hold informal hearings, dismiss or adjust many cases without further processing.

11 Probation officer decides desirability of further court action.

12 Welfare agency, social services, counseling, medical care, etc., for cases where adjudicatory handling not needed.

knowledge as a guide in making organizational decisions, the confusion may at times seem insurmountable. If nothing else is understood, however, the manager is certainly aware that *there is no one best way to manage or organize in all situations.* The need for reducing this confusion is vital for one all-important reason. One of the major causes of management's concern with organizational issues is that the technical, social, economic, and geographical conditions facing their organizations are becoming more diverse and are constantly changing. The police are caught up in such diversity and change. And the police may be more affected by them than are most other organizations in our society. Consequently, effective management is all the more critical to their organizations.

The "new" management that we referred to above is fundamentally and primarily caused by a *boom* (a tumultuous and rapid change from one state of affairs to another).

The Management Implosion and Its Messages

What can we garner from management past and present?[9] First, that management, private and public, went through an accelerated period of worldwide concern beginning in the mid-1940s.[10] In essence, the "boom" was caused by a host of interacting variables paramount of which were: unprecedented growth in organizational size, rapid advancement of technology, intensified economic concerns such as increased productivity, and heightened social concerns such as employee morale. World War II served equally as impetus and fuel to a sharpening focus on the significance of management. The existing plethora of literature and educational/training courses devoted to this subject are irrefutable evidence of a major boom.

Second, as with all booms, the one stimulating management eventually had to end. The mystique about management is now in the process of being erased by the realization that management is not a glittering *panacea,* but rather a *responsibility for performance.* While the amplified period of interest produced much in the way of concepts and techniques, it did not adequately deal with a commitment to *practice*—thus, its demise. Nevertheless, it did position us at a new management vista with proven theories and tools designed to foster the implementation of a discipline—a discipline imbued with *responsibility.*

---

[9]To a large extent this section is extracted from the thinking of Peter F. Drucker, *Management: Tasks, Responsibilities, Practices* (New York: Harper & Row, Publishers, 1974), pp. 11–26.

[10]You should not be deluded into believing that the management boom invented, or for that matter discovered, management. Its roots extend back centuries. For further information see George, *History of Management Thought.*

Third, as already alluded to, the study of management has caused us to recognize that it can be studied as a discipline. Yet, when operationalized, it becomes a practice—a practice that is devoted to performance based on knowledge.

Fourth, the manager cannot operate in a vacuum away from society. He is not a value-free robot. His practice—its theories and techniques—is not the dominant force. Rather, there is an interplay of management concepts and culture values that guide his conduct. Plainly, managing, as compared to the study of management, is a normative art.

The New Management and Its Messages

The management boom is presently dissolving. Out of the residue that remains certain trends have become apparent. First, there are programmatic attempts to interface and harmonize the differing needs and logics of work and the worker. Second, decentralization of responsibility appears to be on the increase. Third, employees are being perceived as valuable resources, rather than humanoid problems, that are to be lead as well as controlled. Fourth, social innovation is being recognized as equal to, if not more important than, technical inventions. Fifth, the manager is being confronted with a better-educated and trained employee. Sixth, knowledge work—of which the police is one form—is surpassing manual skills in size and will continue to expand. Seventh, management (and this clearly applies to most large-scale police agencies) is multicultural and thus spans many differing sets of values and mores. Eighth, management is being assessed in light of its ability to improve our quality of life.

The Messages In Summary

Capsulizing, we can see that in organizations in general and specifically in police organizations there have been recent trends toward:

Expressing considerable interest in management.
Exposing the mystique of management.
Translating the management discipline into a practice.
Defining the practice of management as a normative art.
Integrating the individual with the organization.
Decentralizing managerial responsibility.
Fostering social innovations as well as technical inventions.
Managing a more knowledgeable worker.
Emphasizing knowledge work.
Encompassing heterogeneous cultures.
Being evaluated as it impacts the quality of life.

MANAGEMENT = RESPONSIBILITY

> But these men command my attention and sometimes my admiration
> because they adhere to their codes rigidly in the face of great difficul-
> ties; whereas I observe that many others who have a "higher" morality
> do not adhere to their codes when it would apparently not be diffi-
> cult to do so. Men of the first class have a higher sense of responsi-
> bility than those having, as I view them, the higher ethical standards.
> *The point is that responsibility is the property of an individual by
> which whatever morality exists in him becomes effective in conduct.*[11]

The concept of "responsibility" encompasses three other terms that are
often used to explicate its context and parameters. They are: accountability, morality, and answerability (as in a legal obligation). There are
some people in our society who would not have to inquire as to the meaning of responsibility. They have an intuitive sense of what is meant because they are living it. Hence we can say that they are responsible people! Regretfully, there are a few people who have a lucid understanding
of the concept of responsibility but choose to ignore its practice. The
majority of us, however, find it convenient, and at times necessary, to
turn to specific codes or canons for a definition of our accountability.
Consider, for example, the following standard. Note that it pertains to
the police and their dual responsibility—to the chief and to the public.

Standard 5.1

NEED FOR ACCOUNTABILITY

Since a principal function of police is the safeguarding of democratic processes, if
police fail to conform their conduct to the requirements of law, they subvert the
democratic process and frustrate the achievement of a principal police function. It is
for this reason that high priority must be given for ensuring that the police are made
fully accountable to their police administrator and to the public for their actions.[12]

Responsibility is the power of a particular private or professional code
of ethics to control the conduct of the individual, at times in the presence
of strong contrary desires or impulses. For instance, two people may have
substantially identical codes with respect to a given field of activity, but

[11]Chester I. Barnard, *The Functions of The Executive,* (Cambridge, Mass.: Harvard
University Press, 1938), p. 267.
[12]American Bar Association, *The Urban Police Function* (New York: American Bar
Association, 1973), p. 15.

the code will be dominant with respect to the conduct of one person under adverse immediate conditions, while it will not be dominant with respect to the other under the same or similar conditions. With reference to that code, the first individual is said to be responsible, or to have responsibility or the inherent capacity for responsibility; the second does not.[13]

Since the majority of us possess several, if not many, private and professional codes, it is possible that we may be responsible with respect to some of them and not so with respect to others. We can observe cases in which this appears to be true. For example, persons may be very responsible with respect to national or religious obligations generally (that is, what *they* feel to be obligations), and be quite irresponsible with respect to ordinary social obligations (what *they* also feel to be obligations). But except as to minor codes, it also appears usually true that people who are responsible in one major respect are also responsible in other respects; that is, they possess a general capacity under adverse sentiments and beliefs. The important point here is that persons of high moral *status* (hopefully police managers and supervisors) who are weakly controlled by their code of ethics, are then relatively irresponsible; and vice versa.

To repeat, the capacity of responsibility is that of being firmly governed by codes of ethics—against inconsistent impulses, desires, or interests, and toward the direction of desires or interests that are consonant with such codes. A word for one aspect of this capacity is "reliability," by which we mean that, knowing a person's ethics—that is, being aware of his "character"—we can reasonably predict what he is likely to do or not to do.

In most types of organizations, and this is especially true in police agencies, persons of managerial capacity are assigned initially to positions of low rank. The sense of responsibility is there demonstrated or not. The conditions of these lower-rank positions are those of *relatively* limited ethical complexity. The chief difference between the lower and the higher ranks is not in the *capacity of responsibility* but in the condition of ethical complexity. This is not to say that the higher positions impose more responsibilities, as is often incorrectly said, *but that they do require a greater "sense" of responsibility.*

Who Is Responsible Here?

Let us examine three recently proposed standards. The first talks about the responsibility of the police. Next, the responsibility of the police

---

[13]Drucker, *Management,* p. 280.

chief is posited. Finally, we look at government and society in general as they should relate to their police.

2.2 Major current responsibilities of police.

In assessing appropriate objectives and priorities for police service, local communities should initially recognize that most police agencies are currently given responsibility, by design or default:

(i) to identify criminal offenders and criminal activity and, where appropriate, to apprehend offenders and participate in subsequent court proceedings;

(ii) to reduce the opportunities for the commission of some crimes through preventive patrol and other measures;

(iii) to aid individuals who are in danger of physical harm;

(iv) to protect constitutional guarantees;

(v) to facilitate the movement of people and vehicles;

(vi) to assist those who cannot care for themselves;

(vii) to resolve conflict;

(viii) to identify problems that are potentially serious law enforcement or governmental problems;

(ix) to create and maintain a feeling of security in the community;

(x) to promote and preserve civil order; and

(xi) to provide other services on an emergency basis.

7.8 Authority of police administrator.

A police administrator should be held fully responsible for the operations of his department. He should, therefore, be given full control over the management of the department; and legislatures, civil service commissions, and employee associations should not restrict unnecessarily the flexibility that is required for effective management.

10.2 Responsibility of society and government generally.

The recommendations made in these standards require particular attention at the level of municipal government. Along with the recommendations relating specifically to police agencies, however, it should be recognized that police effectiveness is also dependent, in the long run, upon:

(i) the ability of government to maintain faith in democratic processes as the appropriate and effective means by which to achieve change and to redress individual grievances;

(ii) the willingness of society to devote resources to alleviating the despair of the culturally, socially, and economically deprived;

(iii) the development of effective ways of dealing with drug addiction; and

(iv) the improvement of the criminal justice, juvenile justice, mental health, and public health systems as effective ways of dealing with a wide variety of social and behavioral problems.[14]

[14]American Bar Association, *Urban Police Function*, pp. 9, 20, 25–26, respectively.

Bluntly, the police manager must perform a series of tasks in order to meet his responsibilities and encourage others to do likewise. These tasks combined constitute the *role* of the manager.

RESPONSIBILITY FOR ROLE PERFORMANCE

The main justification for a concern over role performance is a commitment to an improved quality of police services for the citizenry *and* of work environment for the police officer.[15] An identical sense of commitment is also reflected in the "new" public administration writings.[16] At the heart of the new wave of literature is the accusation that public administration as a discipline does not have a sound normative base, hence the belief that its key problem is essentially a "normative gap." Being conscious of this gap, the "new" public administration advocates value consciousness in an area previously self-described as value free and not concerned with policy making. In essence, the "new" public administration movement represents little more than a sharpened sensitiveness to the normative dimension of our administrative settings.

Among the changes which will mold the police service are several which will challenge the police manager personally as a professional: (1) a decline in the public service ethic, (2) erosion of loyalty to an employee's organization, and (3) greater political activism by employees, directed at policy changes.[17] In the face of rapid change, increased complexity, and mounting pressure to produce results, these challenges weaken a manager's ability to meet, *responsibly*, more substantive problems by diverting his time and attention. As a result, at the very time when one can foresee the need for professional leadership in the police service, the base upon which it and professional police service must rest appears to be weakening. The police manager of tomorrow will be sorely tested. Hence, there is no doubt that the future promises to be extraordinarily challenging to those who pursue careers in the police service over the next decade. In many respects, police managers will have to be more adaptable, knowledgeable, patient, tenacious, and perceptive than ever before. Yet they will have new decision-making tools of analysis, information, and

---

[15]An excellent series of articles on the subject of social equity *within* the organization is contained in the *Public Administration Review* 34 (January-Februray 1974): 1–51.

[16]Those interested in a concise examination of the literature see York Wilburn, "Is the New Public Administration Still With Us?" *Public Administration Review* 33 (July-August 1973): 373–78.

[17]This thinking is excerpted from an article by Richard L. Chapman and Frederic N. Cleaveland, "The Changing Character of the Public Service and the Administration of the 1980's," *ibid.*, p. 364.

control. Managing police programs will be even more demanding than it is today, but those challenges can be met if today's police manager takes the lead in anticipating the future and preparing to meet it.

What is needed to break out of the straitjacket of old slogans and old issues, therefore, is managerial *role performance*. This first requires role performance as a control agent. It requires performance that makes the manager's police organization capable of supplying to the community the contribution for the sake of which it exists—police services. But it also requires role performance beyond the immediate mission, beyond controls, in making police work more effective and the worker more achieving, and performance with respect to enhancing the quality of life. If he is to remain—as he should—the manager of human resources, the police manager must accept that he is a "professional" manager. He must accept the moral responsibility of managing—the responsibility of making individual strengths productive and police work satisfying to the employee.

THE POLICE MANAGER'S ROLE

> This year, serious crime is still increasing—up 16 per cent in the first six months, headed toward an estimated record of 10.1 million. And recent surveys indicate these figures show only part of the true picture because most crimes actually committed are never reported— largely because victims feel nothing will be done about them.
>
> Officials see no end to this frightening rise of crime.
>
> The truth is, most officials admit: Nobody really knows what is causing the rise in crime—or how to stop it. . . .
>
> The American public, in a swelling clamor, is demanding some answers. A recent Gallup Poll showed people rank crime as their No. 3 concern—ahead of the energy problem and unemployment, topped only by the high cost of living and dissatisfaction with government. . . .
>
> Spreading throughout this country is a feeling of frustration that borders on despair.
>
> The nation has poured billions of dollars into efforts to improve law enforcement. Local spending has multiplied more than seven times since 1964. Total spending—federal, state, and local—for police, courts, prosecutors, and prisons has shot up from 3.5 billion dollars in 1960 to 14.6 billion this year.[18]

We have included the above quotation at this point to emphasize that the nation's anxiety over crime remains very high. Further, the criminal

[18]"The Losing Battle Against Crime," *U.S. News & World Report,* December 16, 1974, p. 30.

justice system is being equally challenged and criticized in regard to the rate of crime. More specific to our interests here is the role of the police, and thus the police manager, in meeting their assigned responsibilities. The remainder of this section is divided into three parts—beginning with a definition of the concept of a role, then examining a generalized role statement for the police, and ending with a description of the manager's role.

"Role" Defined

In its broadest sense, a *role* comprises the behavior requirements of a position in an organization. Relatedly, the personality is an arrangement of the particular needs and dispositions of the individual. It is interesting to note that some research studies on leadership conclude that the organizational role tends to be a more basic determinant of behavior than does the personality.[19] For our purposes, we will regard an organizational role as a combination of mutually interdependent subroles.[20] One of these, the *institutional role*, is defined as the behavior requirements expected of a person filling a particular position. The institutional role and the organizational position can be easily distinguished by a single term—*behavior*. In other words, a *position* is a static organizational entity that specifies the duties, obligations, rights, and privileges of the present or future incumbent. Once the incumbent assumes a position he is expected to behave according to the specifications. Essentially, the core of position classification is the concept of the position as an abstract entity apart from the employee. From an organizational viewpoint, a position is the smallest administrative unit of an agency.[21] In a position classification

[19]Bernard Berelson and Gary A. Steiner, *Human Behavior: An Inventory of Scientific Findings* (New York: Harcourt, Brace and World, Inc., 1964), p. 343.

[20]This particular scheme is borrowed from Frank J. Jasinski, "The Dynamics of Organizational Behavior," *Personnel* 36 (March-April 1959): 60–67.

[21]Daniel F. Halloran, "Why Position Classification?" *Public Personnel Review* 28 (April 1967): 89. As both explanation and justification Halloran further writes that, "Position classification, and its industrial counterpart, job evaluation, are relatively new concepts. The first application of the position classification principle was in 1909 in the Chicago Civil Service. As a coincidence, the first industrial application of job evaluation was also in Chicago in 1912. The development and application of position classification in the United States as an integral part of the civil service reform movement was in reaction to the excesses of the spoils system and the gross pay inequities that were rampant under it. Position classification served well both management and employees of the public service in the early days of reform. It gave management an orderly administrative plan for the utilization of personnel. To employees it assured equal pay for equal work in place of the erratic and meaningless salary situations which had existed. Because of its impersonal approach to salary, it had an aura of democratic fairness about it which strongly appealed to employees who had become accustomed to seeing favoritism shown in matters of pay" (pp. 89–90).

system an individual employee "fills a position" and achieves promotion by moving from one position to a higher-level position within the organization's structure.

Which role—institutional or social—to emphasize is determined mainly by the manager's value orientation. Although the role adopted most frequently is the one in closest harmony with is value system (more will be said about values in the next chapter), it is untrue that observed behavior is determined exclusively by the response the individual makes to the various roles expected of him. While he may have a clear idea of how he should behave, other influences compel him into a different behavior[22] pattern. Broadly, the demands discussed in an earlier section tend to condition the manager's behavior. More explicitly, the manager's behavior is affected by the police (institution) organization, its technology, its value system, and the chief's boss(es). To some degree all four of these variables combine to shape the actual role that the police manager assumes. *The police organization—its structure and method for gaining compliance, allocating rewards, meeting personal needs, and so on—vastly influences the behavior of a manager.*

The Role of the Police

Before focusing on the manager's role, it is fitting that we examine the role of the police in our society. Although differing in many ways, the following statements establish a nationwide parameter on what we ought to expect from them. (It will be seen that the first three quotations deal with the role, while the latter includes two standards that emphasize the need for a mutual understanding of it.)

> Because only a small part of the activity of the police is dedicated to law enforcement and because they deal with the majority of their problems without invoking the law, a broader definition of their role was proposed. After reviewing briefly what the public appears to expect of the police, the range of activities police actually engage in, and the theme that unifies all these activities, it was suggested that the role of the police is best understood as a mechanism for the distribution of non-negotiably coercive force employed in accordance with the dictates of an intuitive grasp of situation exigencies.

22A series of highly interesting articles pertaining to the subject of city/county administrators and police chiefs can be found in the journal *Public Management* 56 (July 1974): 2–22. Raymond Lee dealt with responsibility and role fulfillment when he wrote, "In theory, the administrator develops general police department policy and the chief oversees day-to-day operations. In fact, the responsibilities are not so clearly defined and it can be argued that effective police administration requires that both individuals become involved in each dimension" (p. 2).

It is, of course, not surprising that a society committed to the establishment of peace by pacific means and to the abolishment of all forms of violence from the fabric of its social relations, at least as a matter of official morality and policy, would establish a corps of specially deputized officials endowed with the exclusive monopoly of using force contingently where limitations of foresight fail to provide alternatives. That is, given the melancholy appreciation of the fact that the total abolition of force is not attainable, the closest approximation to the ideal is to limit it as a special and exclusive trust. If it is the case, however, that the mandate of the police is organized around their capacity and authority to use force, i.e., if this is what the institution's existence makes available to society, then the evaluation of that institution's performance must focus on it. While it is quite true that policemen will have to be judged on other dimensions of competence, too—for example, the exercise of force against criminal suspects requires some knowledge about crime and criminal law—their methods as society's agents of coercion will have to be considered central to the overall judgment.[23]

2.2 Major current responsibilities of police.

In assessing appropriate objectives and priorities for police service, local communities should initially recognize that most police agencies are currently given responsibility, by design or default:

(i) to identify criminal offenders and criminal activity and, where appropriate, to apprehend offenders and participate in subsequent court proceedings;

(ii) to reduce the opportunities for the commission of some crimes through preventive patrol and other measures;

(iii) to aid individuals who are in danger of physical harm;

(iv) to protect constitutional guarantees;

(v) to facilitate the movement of people and vehicles;

(vi) to assist those who cannot care for themselves;

(vii) to resolve conflict;

(viii) to identify problems that are potentially serious law enforcement or governmental problems;

(ix) to create and maintain a feeling of security in the community;

(x) to promote and preserve civil order; and

(xi) to provide other services on an emergency basis.[24]

---

[23]Egon Bittner, *The Functions of the Police in Modern Society* (Chevy Chase, Md.: National Institute of Mental Health, 1970), p. 46.

[24]American Bar Association, *Urban Police Function*, p. 9. We are aware that this citation appeared earlier in this chapter. It is again found relevant for a twofold reason. First, it depicts the ABA's perception of the roles of the police. Second, it implicitly shows the interrelationship of one's responsibility with one's role.

The literature on police behavior reveals widespread agreement that the police officer's role is quantitatively most concerned with the role "Provides Public Assistance," and as a means of achieving the role, "Maintains Order." While no one questions the primary function of the police to maintain order by reducing opportunities for criminal activity and to deter criminal behavior, field studies show that the police spend more time responding to citizen requests for a wide variety of non-criminal services than they do in the pursuit of criminals.

The literature survey also reveals a surprising degree of agreement on the misuse of the term "law enforcement" as applied to the police officer's role. The popular conception of the officer as one who carries out the role, "Enforces Law Impartially," is erroneous. Under-enforcement of the law and the use of wide discretionary power in the making of arrests is described in detail in the literature as a way of life for the police officer.[25] (See Table 1–1.)

Standard   1.5

POLICE
UNDERSTANDING
OF THEIR ROLE

Every police agency immediately should take steps to insure that every officer has an understanding of his role, and an awareness of the culture of the community where he works.

1. The procedure for developing policy regarding the police role should involve officers of the basic rank, first line supervisors, and middle managers. Every police employee should receive written policy defining the police role.

2. Explicit instruction in the police role and community culture should be provided in all recruit and in-service training.

3. The philosophy behind the defined police role should be a part of all instruction and direction given to officers.

4. Middle manager and first line supervisors should receive training in the police role and thereafter continually reinforce those principles by example and by direction of those they supervise.

5. Methods of routinely evaluating individual officer performance should take into account all activities performed within the context of the defined role. Promotion and other incentives should be based on total performance within the defined role, rather than on any isolated aspect of that role.

[25]*Police Officer Role Training Program,* Project STAR, American Justice Institute (Sacramento, Calif., California Commission on Peace Officer Standards and Training, 1974).

TABLE 1-1

Police Roles: Project STAR

Assists Criminal Justice System and
Other Appropriate Agency Personnel

Builds Respect for Law and the
Criminal Justice System

Provides Public Assistance

Seeks and Disseminates Knowledge
and Understanding

Analyzes and Communicates Information

Manages Cases

Assists Personal and Social Development

Displays Objectivity and Professional
Ethics

Protects Rights and Dignity of
Individuals

Provides Humane Treatment

Enforces Law Impartially

Enforces Law Situationally

Maintains Order

Source: *Police Officer Role Training Program,* Project STAR, American Justice Institute (Sacramento, Calif.: California Commission on Peace Officer Standards and Training, 1974).

Standard 1.6

PUBLIC UNDERSTANDING
OF THE POLICE ROLE

Every police agency immediately should establish programs to inform the public of the agency's defined police role. These programs should include, but not be limited to, the following:

1. Every police agency should arrange for at least an annual classroom presentation by a uniformed officer at every public and private elementary school within its jurisdiction.

   a. The content of the presentation should be tailored to the learning needs of the students; however, each presentation should include a basic description of the police role.

   b. Every agency should work through the school to develop a basic study unit to be presented by the teacher prior to the officer's arrival, and every officer assigned to a school visit should be provided with prepared subject matter to be reviewed prior to making his visit.

2. Every police agency with more than 400 employees should, dependent upon securing the cooperation of local school authorities, assign a full-time officer to each junior and senior high school in its jurisdiction.

   a. The officer's assignment should include teaching classes in the role of the police, and serving as a counselor. His assignment should not include law enforcement duties except as related to counseling.

   b. Course content should be developed in cooperation with the schools and should include discussion of the police role, juvenile laws, and enforcement policies and practices relating to juveniles.

3. Every police agency, where permitted by local conditions, should participate in government and civic classes offered in local evening adult schools and community colleges.

4. With agency resources, where available, or in cooperation with employee organizations or local civic groups, every police agency should develop or participate in youth programs including scouting and other athletic or camping activities.

   a. All such programs should be designed to provide officers and young people with the opportunity to become personally acquainted with each other.

   b. Every officer participating in youth programs should be provided with written material describing the objective of the program and its relationship to the police role.

5. Every police agency should accept invitations for officers to speak to business and civic organizations. Efforts should be made to provide speakers in response to every reasonable request and to coordinate the speaker's ability and background with the intended audience. Every opportunity should be taken to describe the police role and the agency's objectives and priorities.

6. Every police agency with more than 150 employees should publish a statement of the police role, the agency's objectives and priorities in filling that role. An annual report should be used for this purpose. In addition, periodic statistical reports on crime, arrests, and property loss due to crime should be disseminated to the public. These reports should include an evaluation of significant trends and other interpretations.

7. Every police agency should inquire into the availability of public service resources from advertising and communication organizations to assist in developing support for the agency and it programs.

8. Every police agency should hold an annual open house and should provide other tours of police facilities and demonstrations of police equipment and tactics when appropriate to create greater public awareness of the police role.[26]

[26]National Advisory Commission on Criminal Justice Standards and Goals, *Police* (Washington, D.C.: U.S. Government Printing Office, 1973). pp. 34, 38–39 respectively.

With the above in mind we are now prepared to proceed with our examination of the manager's role.

Now—The Role of the Police Manager

Two definitions are crucial here. One was discussed earlier, while the second is new. The terms are:

> *Role:* The personal characteristics and behavior expected in a specific situation of an individual occupying a position.
>
> *Task:* An activity to be accomplished within the definition of a specific role associated with a specific position. Different roles or positions may include the same tasks. Performing the tasks is usually considered as one of the principle responsibilities and occupies a significant portion of time of an individual occupying a position.

Police management cannot be defined or comprehended, let alone effectively practiced, except as it relates to the overall mission of the police. Most basically, then, the police manager has a responsibility to perform a role that is in keeping with this mission. In fact, the role of the police manager is the very reason for his presence in a police agency, the determinant of the tasks that he performs, and the seat of his power.

A changing organizational environment and employee has caused management in general to change. We propose that another role ought to be added to the traditional manager's role of an internal coordinative agent. In line with our omnipresent changing organizational world, this new role should be that of an external developer of mutual support.

Let us return to the traditional role for a moment. We did not say, nor did we mean in any way to infer, that the police manager should abrogate his role as a cordinator of human and technical resources. What we are suggesting, however, that to this role we must add one other component. Again, a few of the reasons for doing so are: (1) the continual need for sensing the environment, (2) the changing nature of the community, (3) the fact that more citizens are seeking participation in their government, (4) the growing complexity of police organization and goals, and (5) a deepening concern for an enhanced *quality* as well as quantity of police services.

As a consequence of the above thinking, the police manager's role is presented as a twofold responsibility for (1) coordinating, and (2) building mutual support for the human resources of a police agency in order that they may attain higher levels of goal achievement, and individual need fulfillment.

Chapter Two

MANAGING:
Values and the Art of Achieving Results

In short, value differences are sometimes nothing more than differences in ways of looking at reality. Sometimes they consist of honest differences in opinion about the most effective way to achieve mutually agreed-upon goals. Sometimes they reflect fundamental differences in primary orientation to the world we live in. These differences may be as simple as a preference for the Martins over the Coys; they can be as complex as the choice between egoism and humanitarianism.[1]

It is essential that the group method of decision making and supervision not be confused with committees which never reach decisions or with "wishy-washy," "common-denominator" sort of committee about which the superior can say, "Well, the group made this decision, and I couldn't do a thing about it." Quite the contrary! The group method of supervision holds the superior fully responsible for the quality of all decisions and for their implementation. He is responsible for building his subordinates into a group which makes the best decisions and carries them out well. *The superior is accountable for all decisions, for their execution, and for the results.*[2]

SYNOPSIS

Managers by their very nature are *action-oriented*. They act to achieve *results*. And these results are attained in compliance with a set of *values*. Thus management is value laden. Indeed this is unavoidable. A police manager's value system determines both the "how" and "how much" of results achieved by a police agency. Hence the fundamental import of values.

Nowhere is the manager's set of values more critical than as they relate to his assumptions about people—in this case police people. They can cause him to look upon his personnel with distrust (Theory X), with trust (Theory Y), or according to the situation and the individual (Theory Z). Accompanying the latter two theories is an understanding that each man (manager and subordinate employee) has a set of needs that determine his values. All of us are seeking some form of need fulfillment. And, to a large degree, we seek that fulfillment through our respective jobs.

[1]Robert Boguslaw, The New Utopians: A Study of System Design and Social Change (Englewood Cliffs, N.J.: Prentice-Hall, Inc., 1965), p. 202.
[2]Rensis Likert, *The Human Organization: Its Management and Value* (New York: McGraw-Hall Book Company, 1967), p. 51.

Participative management is a style of managing that attempts to achieve results *and* meet the individual needs of the employee. While originally posited and practiced by private-sector organizations, we now see it being discussed and applied within police agencies. Briefly, the concept advocates that the manager elicit ideas and desires of the employees concerning decisions that will eventually affect them. But, the "buck still stops" with the manager in that the ultimate decision remains his responsibility.

One way of integrating the need for results with human needs is a strategy for action known as management by objectives (MBO). MBO is another business practice that has found its way into public organizations. As a consequence, we now find ongoing MBO programs in our police agencies. While admittedly not an easy process to mount and maintain, MBO has proven itself of considerable merit. That is to say, the obstacles are worth overcoming. MBO is not only a fitting but a necessary capstone for an action-oriented management posture.

MANAGERS: An Action Orientation

If you want to know what makes a competent police manager, ask the man who is one. In most cases he will not be able to tell you. Police managers are, after all, *men of action*; they are too deeply involved in their daily tasks to introspect and contemplate on what makes them tick. To be sure, you do get some high-level generalities and abstractions. Once in a while a police leader does get the time to write or to articulate his ideas at some conference or other. But, in general, all that these utterances produce is a somewhat ambiguous emphasis on such qualities as courage, morality, broad-gauge thinking, and decisiveness—the attributes and symptoms, after all, of any emotionally mature individual and certainly not limited to police managers.

A variety of notions about reasons for a manager's successful behavior as compared with unsuccessful behavior has emerged. Some believe that the better manager is a generalist. This thinking proposes that he does not have to be a technical expert—he can hire specialists to perform these functions. His position, therefore, is to direct organizational activities. Some regard him as a coordinator, bringing divergent views together into an integrated set of goals. Others contend that he is a man who gets things done through others. All these viewpoints suggest that the police manager does not have to know anything—that his main responsibility is to coordinate the work and effort of the management team. In contrast, others see the manager as a man of superior intellect, understanding, and analytical ability who makes the ultimate decisions. He functions at the center of an information network and assesses conditions, and he decides accordingly. Still others see him as a man primarily concerned with maintaining the organization—both the work organization and the decision-making organization. Here the assumption is that if the organization is functioning efficiently and effectively, the manager is performing well. Finally, there are some who see the police manager simply as a figurehead who operates in the public eye and in general represents his organization in important community affairs. Obviously there is some truth in all the above-mentioned ideas about what a police manager does to be effective. We can approach the question more systematically, however, by examining his *values*. To this end Drucker writes.

> Direct results always come first. In the care and feeding of an organization, they play the role calories play in the nutrition of the human body. But any organization also needs a commitment to values and their constant reaffirmation, as a human body needs vitamins and minerals. There has to be something "this organization stands for," or else it degenerates into disorganization, confusion, and paralysis. In a business, the value commitment may be to technical leadership or (as in Sears Roebuck) to finding the right goods and services for the American family and to procuring them at the lowest price and best quality.
>
> Value commitments, like results, are not unambiguous.
>
> The U.S. Department of Agriculture has for many years been torn between two fundamentally incompatible value commitments—one to agricultural productivity and one to the "family farm" as the "backbone of the nation." The former has been pushing the country toward industrial agriculture, highly mechanical, highly industrialized, and essentially a large-scale commercial business. The latter has called for nostalgia supporting a nonproducing rural proletariat. But because farm policy—at least until very recently—has wavered between two different value commitments, all it has really succeeded in doing has been to spend prodigious amounts of money.[3]

Furthermore, according to Chwast, "The social and personal values of

[3]Peter F. Drucker, *The Effective Executive* (New York: Harper & Row, Publishers, 1967), p. 56.

the law enforcement officer strongly condition the quality of service he delivers to different segments of the populace at large."[4]

Underlying all the chapters in this volume is a basic assumption that the values, norms, and ideologies of society are important conditioners of managerial behavior. The effective police manager is the individual who has identified and operates according to a culturally preferred set of values.[5] For example, in modern democratic societies humanitarian behavior is much more desired in management than not. Golembiewski lists five organizational values which should guide human behavior.

1. Work must be psychologically acceptable, nonthreatening.
2. Work must allow man to develop his faculties.
3. The task must allow the individual room for self-determination.
4. The worker must influence the broad environment within which he works.
5. The formal organization must not be the sole and final arbiter of behavior.[6]

Modern students of management, of course, follow Weber in emphasizing the importance of organizational values and norms for understanding the managerial process, but less attention has been paid to the relation of these to the values of the whole society.[7] Implicitly it seems to be assumed that, in the long run, organizational values can continue successfully at odds with societal values. *We firmly believe this assumption is in error.* Moreover, we believe that professional skills, human empathy, and even the values of his organization unit are seemingly not enough to guide the action of the manager in the police department. Police management in our modern world is stagnated and at times threatened by organizational ideologies inappropriate to the goals of the whole society. Even the successful application of human relations knowledge requires identification with the goals of the organization and of the society. The point is the old one that administrative units do not act in isolation, but within a distinct cultural environment. An awareness of societal values and ideology constitute an additional and vital knowledge for *all* police

---

[4] Jacob Chwast, "Value Conflicts in Law Enforcement," *Crime and Delinquency* 11 (April 1965): 152.

[5] For one example, see Everett G. Dillman, "Impact of Culture on Management Practices," *Public Personnel Review* 31 (April 1970): 114–17.

[6] Robert T. Golembiewski, *Men, Management, and Morality: Towards New Organizational Ethics* (New York: McGraw-Hill Book Company, 1965), p. 73.

[7] For details, see H. H. Gerth and C. Wright Mills, *From Max Weber: Essays in Sociology* (New York: Oxford University Press, Inc., 1946).

managers. Boguslaw indirectly implies the central role of values when he writes "The point, of course, is simply that values are not derived either scientifically, logically, or intellectually. They are simply prime factors."[8]

The remaining sections of this chapter deal, in turn, with (1) definitions, (2) the values of management, (3) the manager's value systems, (4) resultant assumptions about the nature of "man," (5) a proposed managerial style, and (6) a proposed managerial strategy.

A FEW BASIC DEFINITIONS

We designate *values* as those sentiments, or ethical principles, regarded as ultimate. Such values cannot be criticized concerning their appropriateness. A society as a whole may affirm certain values as its implicit assumptions, but so, too, do all the myriad of organizations within that society. Commonly, however, administrative units tend to affirm only some of the same values found in the larger society. Their values may be in partial conflict with those of the society and with one another (the learning experience exemplifies such a situation).

Norms are derived from the ultimate values as rules of conduct applicable under specified conditions. The distinction between norms and values is often a vague one in practice. The distinction rests on the assumption that it can be demonstrated that the norm is a rule of conduct derived from an ultimate value.

Ideology is a set of interrelated norms. Therefore, ideology becomes the mode of action for the individual.

POLICE MANAGEMENT AS VALUE LADEN

Among the most oustanding values in American culture of the twentieth century are *progress, efficiency, science, rationality, goal achievement* (effectiveness), and *success*. These values have helped to produce a highly dynamic society—a society in which the predominant characteristic is *change*. More specifically, they have served as both an ideology and a stimulus to action for our police organizations and their managers. By citing the above values, we are not recommending that organizations or managers "fall in line." We simply feel that there may be more appropriate and less appropriate values, and a police manager who would be effective would do well to be aware of such differences. Hence, it is not

---

[8]Boguslaw, *New Utopians*, p. 198.

suggested that the manager adopt the societal ideology as his own; rather, he and his department should attempt to recognize that they must operate within the framework of societal values. It is more than a request to be aware of the "public interest"; it requires the organization and the manager to be aware of the relationship between their actions and societal values.[9]

> If this is the case, it would seem of cardinal importance to examine the nature of police values so as to comprehend better the specific ways in which they affect police work. This is especially imperative since, in dealing with the diverse peoples they encounter, the police might be projecting values which may be either totally or partially inappropriate, or, at least irrelevant to such encounters.[10]

We would be more than a little presumptuous in telling *you*, the police managers, what *your* values are or ought to be. But at the same time we encounter a fairly well recognized general set of managerial values that are either in fact or in fantasy influencing the behavior of many managers today in a variety of organizations. Let us repeat those mentioned earlier:

Progress
Efficiency
Science
Rationality
Success
Goal achievement (effectiveness)

Which is paramount? Well, preferably it would be that of "goal achievement," for the others are dependent on it for their very existence. Hence, "we shall term appropriate an ideology of administration which, if followed by an administrator, yields a high probability of achieving both organizational and societal goals."[11]

The above list is sorely remiss in a critical way—*it fails to indicate the manager's "human" empathy for "humanity"*—humanity in the dual sense of people within (the employees) and outside (the clientele) the organizational boundaries. Consequently, to the list we now add

Human empathy

The literature in support of this managerial value is vast, convincing,

---

[9]For a comprehensive examination of the public interest, see Glendon Schubert, *The Public Interest* (Chicago: The Free Press of Glencoe, 1960).

[10]Chwast, "Value Conflicts in Law Enforcement," pp. 152–53.

[11]Charles Press and Alan Arian, eds., *Empathy and Ideology: Aspects of Administrative Innovation* (Chicago: Rand McNally & Co., 1966), p. 9.

and growing at a rapid pace.[12] Regretfully, some managers approach the values of progress, efficiency, and so forth as being incongruous or, worse yet, in direct conflict with those of a human bent. This is not only wrong, but it can significantly impede goal accomplishment! According to Bennis:

> This is the paradigm: bureaucratic values tend to stress the rational, task aspects of the work and to ignore the basic human factors which relate to the task and which, if ignored, tend to reduce task competence. Managers brought up under this system of values are badly cast to play the intricate human roles now required of them. Their ineptitude and anxieties lead to systems of discord and defense which interfere with the problem-solving capacity of the organization.[13]

In a more concrete manner, he went on to state that a concern for the individual can be put into practice by:

1. Improvement in interpersonal competence of managers.
2. A change in values so that human factors and feelings come to be considered legitimate.
3. Development of increased understanding between and within working groups in order to reduce tensions.
4. Development of more effective "team management," i.e., the capacity for functional groups to work competently.
5. Development of better methods of "conflict resulution" rather than the usual bureaucratic methods of conflict resolution are to be sought after.
6. Development of organic systems. This normative goal, as outlined by Shepard and Blake, is a strong reaction against the idea of organizations as mechanisms, which they claim, has given rise to false conceptions (such as static equilibria, frictional concepts like "resistance to change," etc.) and, worse, to false notions of social engineering and change, e.g., pushing social buttons, thinking of the organization as a machine, etc.[14]

12Obviously a citing of references in this regard would require thousands of pages. For those interested in a short but broad overview of the human factor in organizational settings, see Timothy W. Costello and Sheldon S. Zalkind, eds., *Psychology in Administration: A Research Orientation Text with Integrated Readings* (Englewood Cliffs, N.J.: Prentice-Hall, Inc., 1963); Leonard R. Sayles and George Strauss, *Human Behavior in Organizations* (Englewood Cliffs, N.J.: Prentice-Hall, Inc., 1966); and Edgar H. Schein, *Organizational Psychology* (Englewood Cliffs, N.J.: Prentice-Hall, Inc., 1965).

13Warren G. Bennis, *Changing Organizations,* (New York: McGraw-Hill Book Company, 1966), p. 116.

14*Ibid.,* p. 118.

Three rather obvious though difficult managerial tasks result from the above thinking. Here is what must be done to assure *yourself* that *you* have a comprehensive set of values—organizational and individual. First, recognize that the most vital resource within a police department is its people—sworn and civilian. Second, recognize that these people have social and individual needs that, if met, allow them to experience greater job satisfaction and increased levels of work output. As Argyris puts it:

> In order to experience psychological success, three requirements are essential. The individuals must value themselves and aspire to experience an increasing sense of competence. This, in turn, requires that they strive continuously to find and to create opportunities in which they can increase the awareness and acceptance of their selves and others.

> The second requirement is an organization that provides opportunities for work in which the individual is able to define his immediate goals, define his own paths to these goals, relate these to the goals of the organization, evaluate his own effectiveness, and constantly increase the degree of challenge at work.

> Finally, the society and culture in which he is embedded can influence the individual and the organization. It can influence the individual, through the process of acculturation, to place a high or low value on self-esteem and competence. The process of acculturation, in turn, is a function of the society's norms and values as well as its economic development.[15]

Third, through your position as a manager and your personal capacity for leadership, you must lead the organization in the direction of improved goal achievement and individual happiness. You have a responsibility to yourself, your department, and those who work for you to do both. If you disagree (and we doubt that you do), perhaps it is time to compare your values with those expressed above. Better still, compare your values with those of other managers who you deem to be successful.

The next section discusses how and where managerial values are generated.

VALUE SYSTEMS

What is good for General Motors is good for the Nation.[16]

Societal values, norms, and ideologies vary from place to place and

[15]Chris Argyris, *Integrating the Individual and the Organization* (New York: John Wiley & Sons, Inc., 1964), pp. 33–34.
[16]Attributed to Charles Erwin Wilson while testifying before a U.S. Senate committee, *New York Times*, January 24, 1953, p. 8.

from situation to situation. Even within a society, institutional, organizational, and individual values, norms, and ideologies may differ. But if the police manager is to be effective in his efforts, he must attempt to forge an ideology that will synthesize the values and norms of his organization and society. The values that the manager must cope with are derived from a number of areas or systems. They are societal, historical, institutional, departmental, structural, professional, and personal.

Societal Values

If the police manager functioned like the TV detective of yesteryear, insisting only on "the facts, ma'am," he would be demoted to walking a beat. The most important value system in which the manager operates is that of society. A manager is a creature of our society; he operates in an organization that is a segment of our society; he is part of our ongoing history. He has risen to a key position in one of our most important social institutions. The decisions he makes will have important repercussions throughout society even though he may see them as affecting his own community alone.

Currently there is great concern over the influence of law enforcement, particularly that of large-scale police organizations, on the emerging social character of our urban centers. This is an important value consideration because the ultimate test of the usefulness of any organization lies in the kind of services it provides and the people it produces.

Historical Values

Today's police manager operates not only within the evolving values of our own time but also within a historical framework of past values that have become embodied in our institutions. His forebears were often deeply religious men who saw in work, in organization, and in use of capital the practice of God's will on earth. Formal organizations in this country are in a very real sense the institutional embodiment of the Puritan mind. Even though they may not be consciously aware of the origins of their beliefs, many police managers are deeply convinced of the essential morality of discipline, service, efficient organization, and work. We are not saying this is wrong or right, but merely drawing it to the attention of the reader. (However, if asked, we would be quick to defend such an ethic.) It is therefore important to recognize that the police manager operates in this kind of value environment whether he is aware of it or not. The decisions he makes, whether they come out of his own thinking, the *FBI Bulletin*, or the International Association of Chiefs of Police, all have ethical implications. He may not know it, but as he guides his department in its task of improving laws and maintaining order, he is shaping the history of his community and the nation.

Institutional Values

The police manager is usually aware that he differs from other institutions in our society—religious and educational institutions, unions, government communities, and so on. He may see some of these other institutions as obstacles. Society is characterized, however, by a web of institutions that represents a network of differing values as well as cooperative relationships. Each institution is constantly striving to promote its own values. Each institution, in a sense, views society from its own value system and seeks to universalize its objectives, ideologies, and functions. Moreover, police departments have taken on more functions than they ever dreamed of twenty-five years ago. In fact, most departments today perform the functions not only of law enforcement but also of general community service. Many are now wondering whether all the time being spent by departments in this manner might not better be used to bolster our existing organizations (social welfare, recreation, counseling service, etc.).

This is not the place, however, to enter into arguments about the functions of the various institutions in our society. It is enough to make the point that interinstitutional differences constitute an important environment in which the police manager functions and one with which he must come to grips. He must have a broad understanding of the way a great society runs and the roles and functions of the various institutions that comprise it, and a statesmanlike knowledge of the special values and place of local law enforcement in the "big picture."

Departmental Values

A fourth important value system in which the police manager operates is the culture, or character, of his department. Each police organization has a way of doing things—a set of conventions, customs, and social habits that constitutes its unique character. Managerial development in many police organizations represents a kind of socialization whereby the new officer is taught how this particular department functions—what its philosophy is, what its character is, what kinds of things it will do, what kinds of things it positively will not do, what its policies and common values are.

The difference between the new employee, the fellow who does not know his way around, and the older one is often simply a difference in the degree of socialization that has occurred.

The culture of a department and the understanding that police managers and employees within the organization have of this culture are important controls.[17] As a consequence, determining the character of a police organization, which really means determining who you are, where you are going, and how you operate in this complex world, is likely, and rightfully so, to absorb a great deal of the attention of the management team.

Structural Values

Related to the departmental value system is that of structural values, particularly in its hierarchical character. Every organization is a hierarchical system in which each individual operates within an interacting triad of relationships in which some people are viewed as being in higher positions to him, some as being in lower, subordinate positions, and some as being at the same level. Dealing with these various levels and modifying behavior in appropriate ways in terms of the hierarchical system is one of the important skills of the police manager. He has to learn how to get things done through the boss, how to approach him at the right time, how to avoid getting a definite *no*, how to sell ideas to him, how to motivate him, and so on. The police manager who lacks these skills fails to get much done. Every individual has to be a promoter of ideas; he has to be "selling" all the time.

The manager also has to learn how to deal with subordinates as well as with those at his own level. With his subordinates he has to learn how to sell the sometimes unpopular notion of work and change; he has to learn how to translate organizational values into goals that have meaning to those under him; he has to learn to balance the impersonal values of the organization against the personal values of his people.

Consequently, one of the major problems of police management is achieving some kind of integration of the myriad of values that are being pushed by the various members of the management team and the subordinate personnel. Nothing is more stultifying than the neat balance that some uninspired (or retired on-the-job) managers achieve. We believe that a dynamic imbalance is best. At least there is movement; at least some are motivated and pleased, even if others may be dissatisfied. Perhaps their disaster function will serve as an impetus to "try harder."

17One authority recently focused on the issue of department values. See Herman Goldstein, "Who's in Charge Here?" *Public Management* 50 (December 1968): 305–7.

Professional Values

The police manager also functions within a professional value system. Such values are most obvious in the so-called professions of the medical doctors, engineers, scientists, and others. These men owe allegiance not only to an organization of which they are a part but also to their profession.

Many occupational groups strive for professional status as a kind of way out—a means of achieving the security or recognition that would normally come from their particular organizations. It is suspected that some of these efforts toward professionalization are the result of the employee's not getting this kind of recognition from his organization, or in any event, not getting the degree of recognition he expects. Under such circumstances, a man finds the recognition he needs, the sense of colleagueship and support, the feeling of understanding, of status, and of worth in his professional group.

Even those police managers who do not see themselves as members of professional groups often think of themselves as professionals. A profession is more than a function; it is frequently a way of life. It directs the interests of those engaged in it, shapes their values, determines their relationships with others, and pulls people of similar interests and often similar personalities together and thus enhances the interaction among them. The manager often identifies with his job. He is not merely Captain Blayback, police manager; he is a leader, a controller of resources, a personnel man, an instructor. An attack on his specialty is an attack on him. Moreover, he tends to generalize the special interests and values of his field and wonders why others are so ignorant and so impervious to his philosophy. For example, the police manager is dedicated to goal fulfillment—goal fulfillment with efficiency, rationality, and so forth. The police officer, however, is dedicated to goal fulfillment but usually cares less about efficiency. In other words, the manager would say, "Catch the crook at *so much* cost," while the policeman would say, "Catch the crook at *all* costs." Simply put, the manager is primarily "hung up" on economy, efficiency, and rationality of operation. The police officer continues to focus on getting the job done, "hang the expenses." The reason for renouncing the above thinking is simple, but pertinent—police managers and police practitioners (while members of the same department) possess similar and *dissimilar* values. Thus, we find that police managers and police officers frequently differ in their thinking on not *what* but *how* the job ought to be done.

Personal Values

At this point we have little to offer in the way of advice or comments because personal values are exactly that—personal. The heredity, early learning experiences, and general environment of each of us have caused us to be shaped in certain ways that tend to be reflected in job relationships and task orientation. Sufficient at this point is the knowledge that we—all of us—have certain values. And, by recognizing them, we find that "to thine own self be true" becomes a reality and an invaluable help in solving our daily problems. Although we would welcome the invitation to continue with our analysis of what *you* ought to cherish or value, we feel it not only proper but circumspect to stop here and examine for a few moments our basic assumptions about people—in particular, the people that we manage and, for that matter, the people that manage us. Once we have completed this analysis, we will end the chapter by discussing a management posture and a management program that facilitates achievement—organizational and individual.

McGREGOR AND MASLOW: Dual Hierarchies

Douglas McGregor and Abraham Maslow shared a paramount social value enhancing human happiness. Both dealt with hierarchies—the former, in terms of an organizational setting and in a more prescriptive manner; the latter, in line with the individual and in a descriptive manner. Again, both sages saw fit to conceive their theories in a hierarchical format: the organizational structure, and the human need structure. We begin with McGregor, and end with a brief review of Maslow. Together they provide a foundation upon which an effective management style can be constructed.

McGregor's View of the Organizational Hierarchy: Theory X and Theory Y

In 1960, Douglas McGregor published his definitive text *The Human Side of Enterprise*.[18] In this text, McGregor explores the historical background of organizational development and the assumptions of management styles under which most organizations are managed and develops

[18]Douglas McGregor, *The Human Side of Enterprise* (New York: McGraw-Hill Book Company, 1960).

his famous Theory X and Theory Y. It is important for the manager to learn from the assumptions that follow that a great number of the supervisory and management techniques and tools that have developed down through the ages are built upon the Theory X set of assumptions about how and why people behave as they do in organizational settings. These Theory X assumptions and their resultant practices are slowly being eroded by research and a new set of managers who are beginning to practice the set of contrasting assumptions found under Theory Y. Contrast McGregor's Theory X and Y assumptions as shown in table 2–1. Which

TABLE 2–1

Theory X and Theory Y

Theory X Assumptions	Theory Y Assumptions
1. The average human being has an inherent dislike of work and will avoid it if he can.	1. The expenditure of physical and mental effort in work is as natural as play or rest.
2. Because of this human characteristic of dislike of work, most people must be coerced, controlled, directed, threatened with punishment to get them to put forth adequate effort toward the achievement of organizational objectives.	2. External control and threat of punishment are not the only means for bringing about effort toward organizational objectives. Man will exercise self-direction and self-control in the service of objectives to which he is committed.
3. The average human being prefers to be directed, wishes to avoid responsibility, has relatively little ambition, wants security above all.	3. Commitment to objectives is a function of the rewards associated with the achievement.
	4. The average human being learns, under proper conditions, not only to accept but to seek responsibility.
	5. The capacity to exercise a relatively high degree of imagination, ingenuity, and creativity in the solution of organizational problems is widely not narrowly distributed in the population.
	6. Under the conditions of modern industrial life, the intellectual potentialities of the average person are only partly utilized.

Source: Adapted from McGregor's *Human Side of Enterprise,* (New York: McGraw-Hill Book Company, 1960), chs. 3–4, pp. 15–57.

set of assumptions do you feel police organizations and work groups should practice? Which set of assumptions would you rather have your manager utilize in relating to you in the work group? What managerial assumptions do you think you as a manager would make about your personnel?

In other parts of his definitive explanation of the two opposing sets of assumptions about man in an organizational setting, McGregor states "Theory X is not a straw man for purposes of demolition, but is in fact a theory which materially influences managerial strategy in a wide sector of American industry today."[19]

From this brief overview of McGregor's work we begin to develop a better feel for what is happening in today's emerging organizations—both to the people who direct and control the directions of these organizations and to the people who work in them. In conclusion, we believe that Arthur Kuriloff, writing on the developments and adaptation of these principles into his working environment in the Data Systems Company, aptly captures the results of Theory X orientation and structure in the following statement:

> The organization structure that develops from the assumptions of Theory X is the customary—multilayered, complex. As we all know, it is clogged with communication blocks and distortions as orders and information limp up and down the organizational ladder.[20]

Taking a position on the utility or dysfunction of Theory X or Theory Y quite naturally generates a debate. However, neither position is to any scientific extent axiomatic. In the main, the discussion centers around what each side is disposed toward believing. Reddin proposes a more useful approach in his Theory Z of management.[21] He carefully skirts the ideological poles of either X or Y. Reddin views man as a situationist and thus open to both "good" and "bad."

Theory Z posits that:

Man has a will.
He is disposed toward good and evil.
Situation guides man.
Reason motivates him.
Interdependence is man's primary mode of discourse.
Interaction is man's social unit of importance.
"Objective" best and succinctly describes man's concept of man.

[19]*Ibid.*, p. 35.

[20]Arthur Kuriloff, "An Experiment In Management—Putting Theory Y to the Test," 1971. Unpublished.

[21]This concept is more fully explored in W. J. Reddin, *Mangerial Effectiveness* (New York: McGraw-Hill Book Company, 1970), pp. 189–90.

Maslow's Hierarchy of Needs

Much research has been done by a variety of people into what makes people "turn on" to the work group. Linking the review of McGregor's work above to one other vital concept, we hope to be able to reinforce further the changing style of organization and leadership that we see forming in many police organizations today.

The traditional view of motivation (this, too, growing from history and from assumptions like Theory X) held that the manager or supervisor within the organization could somehow, usually by the use of incentives like fear or money, motivate the employee to work. What we see emerging today is a somewhat different view. This view holds that man has the inherent desire to be involved in what he is doing and that motivational factors are contained *within* himself.

Probably the leading advocate of this concept is Abraham Maslow, a leading industrial psychologist whose lifelong interest was the area of human motivation. In his now well-known development of the "Hierarchy of Human Needs," Maslow demonstrated that man has an insatiable need system that ranges from the most basic up to a level of need defined as "self-actualization."[22] The most important part of Maslow's theory of the "Hierarchy of Needs" is that this need system is present in all men (to varying degrees and strengths), and that when the lowest level of need in the hierarchy is fulfilled, man's desire to move up the hierarchy is heightened—hence these needs serve as a source of motivational force. See exhibit 2–1 which graphically expresses this thinking.

The remaining part of this section focuses on what can be assumed about the nature of man and what these assumptions in turn mean to one's *practice* of management. To begin with, the concept of man over the years has changed from that of a rational-economic robot to one of variegated complexity. Hence we have moved from a point of certainty (pay more and get more output) to one of probabilities (pay more and *maybe* get more output). Man is decidedly complicated and thus should be treated accordingly by other men—in this instance, the police manager. This is critical because it determines (or should do so) his strategy on how best to lead his subordinates. It has always been difficult to generalize about man, and it is becoming more difficult as society and organizations within society are themselves becoming more complex and differentiated. However, we can make the following assumptions and still do justice to this complexity:

[22]Abraham Maslow, *Motivation and Personality*, (New York: Harper & Row, Publishers, 1954).

Exhibit 2–1. The Need Hierarchy

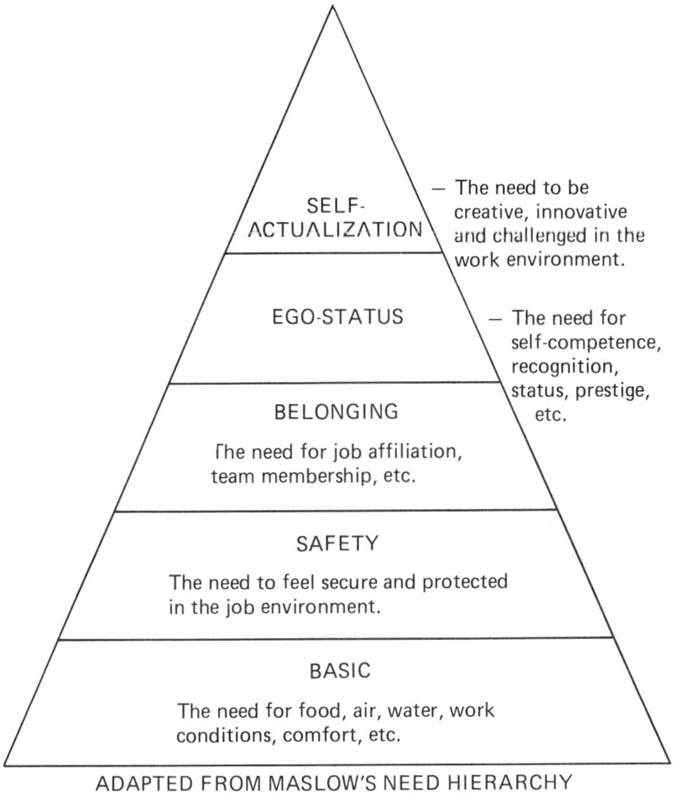

The need to be creative, innovative and challenged in the work environment. — SELF-ACTUALIZATION

EGO-STATUS — The need for self-competence, recognition, status, prestige, etc.

BELONGING — The need for job affiliation, team membership, etc.

SAFETY — The need to feel secure and protected in the job environment.

BASIC — The need for food, air, water, work conditions, comfort, etc.

ADAPTED FROM MASLOW'S NEED HIERARCHY

Source: Adapted from Maslow's Need Hierarchy, Abraham Maslow, *Motivation and Personality*, (New York: Harper & Row, Publishers, 1954), p. 28.

1. Man is not only complex, but also highly variable; he has many motives which are arranged in some sort of hierarchy of importance to him, but this hierarchy is subject to change from time to time and from situation to situation; furthermore, motives interact and combine into complex motive patterns. (For example, since money can facilitate self-actualization, for some people economic strivings are equivalent to self-actualization.)

2. Man is capable of learning new motives through his organizational experiences, hence ultimately his pattern of motivation and the psychological contract which he establishes with the organization is the result of a complex interaction between initial needs and organizational experiences.

3. Man's motives in different organizations or different subparts of the same organization may be different; the person who is alienated in the formal organization may find fulfillment of his social and self-actualization needs in the union or in the informal organization; if the job itself is complex, such as that of a manager, some parts of the job may engage some motives while other parts engage other motives.

4. Man can become productively involved with organizations on the basis of many different kinds of motives; his ultimate satisfaction and the ultimate effectiveness of the organization depends only in part on the nature of his motivation. The nature of the task to be performed, the abilities and experience of the person on the job, and the nature of the other people in the organization all interact to produce a certain pattern of work and feelings. For example, a highly skilled but poorly motivated worker may be as effective and satisfied as a very unskilled but highly motivated worker.

5. Man can respond to many different kinds of managerial strategies, depending on his own motives and abilities and the nature of the task; in other words, there is no one correct managerial strategy that will work for all men at all times.[23]

If assumptions such as the above come closer to the empirical reality, what implications do these have for managerial strategy? Perhaps the most important implication is that *the successful manager must be a good diagnostician and must value a spirit of inquiry.* If the abilities and motives of the people under him are so variable, he must have the sensitivity and diagnostic ability to be able to sense and appreciate the differences. Second, rather than regard the existence of differences as a painful truth to be wished away, he must also learn to value difference and to value the diagnostic process which reveals differences. In conclusion, he must have the personal flexibility and the range of skills necessary to vary his own behavior. *If the needs and motives of his subordinates are different, they must be treated differently.*

It is important to recognize that these points do not refute any of the strategies previously reviewed. We are not saying that adhering to traditional precepts of organization, or being a developer of human resources, or facilitating the work of subordinates is wrong. What we are saying is that any of these approaches *may* be wrong in some situations and with some people. Where we have erred is in oversimplifying and overgeneralizing. As empirical evidence grows, it is becoming apparent that the frame of reference and value system which will help the manager most

[23]These assumptions are derived from Schein, *Organizational Psychology*, p. 70.

in utilizing people effectively is that of the behavioral sciences. If the police manager adopts these values toward man, he will test his assumptions and seek a better analysis—and, if he does that, he will react more appropriately to the varying demands of the situation. He may be highly directive at one time and with one employee but very nondirective at another time and with another employee. He may use pure quantifiable criteria in the design of some tasks, but let a police team completely design another set of tasks. In other words, he will be flexible, and will be prepared to accept a *variety* of interpersonal relationships, patterns of authority, and *psychological contracts*.

PARTICIPATIVE MANAGEMENT

Let us now examine the often debated (usually with vexation if not rancor) concept and practice of participative management (PM). A related subject, that of managing by objectives (MBO), follows. Although the concept of PM is not altogether foreign to contemporary police administration theory and practice, its ethical content has usually been loosely defined. The importance of PM is that the concept of job enrichment that derives from it has a clearly defined ethical content which extends to the structure of and relationships within police agencies. A commitment to PM must not be dependent on empirical evidence showing that participative management leads to utilitarian ends, such as higher productivity or higher commitment of organization members to preestablished organizational objectives. However, it frequently accomplishes this and more. Michael M. Harmon[24] argues (equating "organizational democracy" with PM) that:

> Utilitarianism suggests that the appropriateness of internal organizational democracy (as roughly exemplified by McGregor's Theory Y) is contingent upon empirical evidence which shows that organizational democracy leads to high productivity. The implication of this view is that the autonomy and dignity of organizational members are considerations secondary to efficiency and productivity. Although most of the evidence reported by Likert and others suggests that democratic (or participative) management and high productivity are positively associated, evidence which consistently demonstrated the reverse could, for the utilitarian, justify authoritarianism as an appropriate managerial style."

[24]Harmon fortunately and most effectively transfers Rawl's concepts into the organizational setting. See his article "Social Equity and Organizational Man: Motivation and Organizational Democracy," *Public Administration Review* 34 (January-February 1974), pp. 11–18.

Rawls' theory shifts the basis of the argument from empirical to normative grounds and asserts that the principles of equal liberty and open positions necessarily dictate a normative commitment to internal organizational democracy and participative management. (There is some reason to suspect that the argument about this issue has been a normative one all along, with each side often disguising its ethical posture by a transparent reliance on empiricism.[25]

Participative management strives to accomplish organization objectives by developing its human resources. It is based in a climate of trust and freedom of action that stimulates individual and group growth.

PM recognizes that resident in every individual is a need, a yearning to grow, to solve problems by sensing, searching, testing, and experimenting.[26] It tries to release and channel these creative human energies to realize the individual's potential and the organization's objectives. Its methodology rests on these concepts:

> Involve people in problem solving and goal setting.
> Create climate for learning to occur.
> Enable people to check their performance.
> Mediate conflict openly and constructively.
> Allow people to set challenging goals.
> Provide opportunities to improve the system.
> Provide growth opportunities.
> Recognize achievements and help people to learn from failures.

Management by participation is not soft or laissez faire! *High standards of performance are expected.* External controls and incentives are supplemented by self-imposed controls, enlistment in organizational goals, and self-direction. Under these conditions, authority is delegated and structures flattened and decentralized.

Participative versus authoritarian management can be compared to a car with versus one without power steering. If there is power steering, the car handles with much less energy outlay. Participative management, like power steering, supplies additional creative energy—that of powerful human forces of motivation and attitudes aligned to organizational goals.

Management by participation is indeed a tough-minded managerial style! It is much tougher than the traditional "Authority at the Top" which seeks to avoid confrontation by issuing orders, to avoid personal

[25]*Ibid.*, pp. 15, 17.

[26]This final section is taken with permission from a concept paper prepared by three graduate students. My appreciation is extended to Lee Baca, Michael Graham, and Michael Logue. Two of the authors are middle managers in the Los Angeles Sheriff's Department. Their paper is entitled "Participative Management: A Leadership Style," (February 9, 1972 University of Southern California).

involvement by focusing on production, and to avoid conflict by smoothing the surface. PM is for police managers who feel that understanding, involvement, and commitment proceed from continuing participation in the police agency's daily processes. Further, PM attempts to create an organizational spirit—a vital force—which merges individual drives and goals into a collective will to succeed. The foundation for this *élan vital* is built of enduring interpersonal feelings of mutual trust, caring, respect, and confidence. Significantly, behavioral research findings have repeatedly demonstrated that where a participative climate of mutual understanding and trust exists, other behavior follows, such as:

Increased psychological commitment to objectives

Collective sense of purpose and involvement

High performance standards

Self-discipline and motivation

Increased enjoyment of job

Adaptability to the new and unexpected; feelings that change spell opportunity, and innovation can be fun[27]

Traditional management with its mechanistic mentality condemns many employees to passive activities of a "chewing gum" category. Conversely, participative management strives to promote a climate conducive to self-expression, creativity, and open candid communication. Table 2–2 portrays differences between these two polar styles.

Participative management is, however, no organizational panacea—it cannot transform an ailing police agency into a visible effective enterprise. But it may spark highly useful responses in this age of increasing convolution and flux. Police managers must be aware of its problems as well as its promises. Barriers are to be anticipated due to:

Man's failure to trust in the manager (fear of being manipulated)

The requirement for constant maintenance (energy consuming)

Bureaucratic inhibitions (red tape)

A mandate for effective performance (no buck-passing)

Inability to cope with conflict (let's-not-discuss-it syndrome)

Fear of risk (managerial intolerance to errors)

The situation (PM varies according to the *participants* involved)

In conclusion, PM depends on people and on interactions that increase feelings of trust, caring, and empathy. When people interact in the ways suggested below they enhance an organization's ability to create that vital

[27]This list is derived from miscellaneous reports produced by the National Training Laboratories, Institute for Applied Behavioral Science, Center for Organization Studies, Baltimore, Md., 1970.

TABLE 2–2

Traditional vs. Participative Management Styles

	Traditional	Participative
PRIMARY EMPHASIS	Results and production	Results and people; these two are inseparable. People achieve results and results have meaning only in terms of people
CLIMATE, NORMS, VALUES	Mechanistic Rationality Impersonal power struggles Status-quoism Efficiency	Organic Humanistic Shared responsibility Exploratory Mutual trust Adaptive
INTERACTION BETWEEN UNITS	Moderate	Much, between individuals and groups
COMMUNICATION		
Direction of flow	Down and up	All ways
Acceptance of orders	Accepted but with suspicion	Usually accepted; if not, openly and candidly questioned
Accuracy of communication	"Give the boss the good news"	Accurate
RELATIONS BETWEEN SUPERVISOR/ SUBORDINATE	Impersonal and calculating	Friendly and trusting
TEAMWORK	Little	Substantial
DECISION MAKING	Centered at top	Pushed to lowest possible level
LEADERSHIP	Parent to child; little understanding of the other's problems	Adult to adult; discussion of full problems
GOAL SETTING	Goals set at top orders issued; opportunity to comment may or may not exist	Except in emergencies goals set by group
CONTROLS	External; fear of punishment	Internal; excellence in achievement considered end in itself

Source: Condensed from Rensis Likert, *The Human Organization: Its Management and Value* (New York: McGraw-Hill Book Company, 1967), pp. 4–10.

force or collective will to succeed. Therefore, we would recommend that you:

1. Level with one another. To level means to say what you think is significant, *with the intention of helping the other person to learn from the experience.*[28]
2. Focus on behavior, not the person. Refer to what a person does rather than what you imagine he is.
3. Describe the behavior rather than judge it as good/bad, right/wrong.
4. Think flexibly rather than rigidly. Describe behavior in terms of "more or less" rather than "either-or."
5. Share ideas and information, not advice. This leaves the receiver free to decide for himself.
6. Explore alternatives rather than answers. Attention to alternatives reduces chance of accepting premature incomplete "answers."
7. Be aware of what is going on in the "here and how"; not the "there and then." Information is more meaningful when relayed soon after the fact.
8. Ask questions which help clarify understanding.
9. Seek to be honest, caring, and nonmanipulative with people.

In doing so, we believe you'll be a better, more effective manager—a participative manager!

MANAGEMENT BY OBJECTIVES: "MBO"

Management by objectives requires major effort and special instruments. For in a business enterprise managers are not automatically directed toward a common goal. On the contrary, organization, by its very nature, contains four powerful factors of misdirection: the specialized work of most managers: the hierarchical structure of management; the differences in vision and work and the resultant insulation of various levels of management; and finally, the compensation structure of the management group. To overcome these obstacles requires more than good intentions, sermons, and exhortations. It requires policy and structure. It requires that management by objectives be purposefully organized and be made the living law of the entire management group.[29]

[28]Robert B. Morton, "Leveling: A Method for Communicating Significant Personal Information" (Los Angeles: Center for Training and Development Publication, University of Southern California, 1969), p. 33.
[29]Peter F. Drucker, *Management: Tasks, Responsibiilties, Practices* (New York: Harper & Row, Publishers, 1973), pp. 430–31.

While the literature on MBO is extensive and covers both public[30] and private organizations, the term still remains subject to varying definitions.[31] Peter Drucker first coined the term in 1954 and describes MBO as *a mutual understanding between the manager and his subordinates of what their contribution will be for the organization over a given period of time*. It thus establishes parameters of *self-control* and *common direction*.[32] Moreover, it establishes parameters that target the individual, that target the agency, and that target both in the direction of accomplishing the much to be desired goals.

At this point we will focus on MBO leaving the equally vital subject of goal setting for discussion in the subsequent chapter on planning. While admittedly they should most logically appear in the same context, our arrangement of "role tasks" and baseline materials necessitates the bifurcation.

The Dynamics of MBO

MBO requires a major commitment and effort. For workers seldom "automatically" cooperate, and even more rarely do they cooperate in the pursuit of a common goal. Regretfully, there are many distorting influences. First, the top or middle manager can create dysfunctional situations by egoism or ingrained biases. Also, by merely filtering information up, down, and laterally within the hierarchy, one finds excessive differences in interpretations of the subject matter at hand. Finally, status differentials—whether they be rank, pay, or position based—cause errant decisions on what to do, when, and where.

Are we not at a point where one should ask, "What are the objectives of the police manager?" Each manager, from the chief down to the supervisor, needs clearly spelled out objectives. Otherwise confusion can be guaranteed. These objectives should specify what performance a managerial unit is supposed to achieve. They should indicate what contribution the manager and his unit are expected to make to help other units attain their objectives. Finally, they should detail what contribution the manager can expect from other units toward the attainment of his own objectives. Right from the start, in other words, emphasis should be on

---

[30]For examples of such literature, see Chester A. Newland, "MBO Concepts in the Federal Government," *Bureaucrat* 2 (Winter 1974): 354–61; David S. Brown, "Management by Objectives: Promise and Problems," *Bureaucrat* 2 (Winter 1974): 411–20; and Walter Pudinski, "Management by Results in the California Highway Patrol," *Journal of California Law Enforcement* 8 (April 1974): 194–99.
[31]This thinking is aptly expressed in Bruce A. Kirchhoff's "MBO: Understanding What the Experts Are Saying," *MSU Business Topics*, 22 (Summer 1974): 17–22.
[32]Drucker, *Management*, p. 438.

teamwork and *team* results.[33] These objectives should always derive from the goals of the police agency.

The objectives of every manager should spell out his contribution to the attainment of agency goals in all areas of the police service. Obviously, not every manager has a direct contribution to make in every area. To obtain balanced efforts, the objectives of all police managers on all levels and in all areas should also be keyed to both short-range and long-range considerations. And, of course, all objectives should always contain both the tangible police objectives and such "intangible" objectives as managerial development, worker performance and attitude, and public responsibility. *Anything else is shortsighted and inappropriate.*

Another critical consideration about MBO deals with the question of how the manager's objectives ought to be set and by whom. Most basically, the manager's objectives should be established by the manager in light of (1) his expected contribution to the agency, (2) the expectation of his subordinates, and (3) the expectation of his manager. The manager's own manager has, as he should have, the ultimate purview for approval or rejection. To accomplish all three, a sizable amount of information exchange must occur. Thus, managing supervisors, or supervising police employees, requires special efforts not only to establish common direction but to eliminate misdirection. Mutual understanding can never be attained by "communications down." It can result only from "communciations down, up, and across." It requires the manager's willingness both to listen and to be responsible to employee input.

To be able to control his own performance, a police manager needs to know more than what his objectives are. He must be able to measure his performance and results against the expressed objectives. It should be an axiomatic practice to supply managers with clear and universal measurements in all areas of activity. These measurements need not be rigidly quantitative; nor need they be precise. But they have to be *clear, simple,* and *rational.* They have to be germane and direct attention and efforts to where they should go. They have to be reliable—at least to the point where their margin of error is acknowledged and understood.

Future chapters deal with the concepts of police performance measurement and evaluation. Thus, the crux of the message imparted here as

[33]The concept, and to a lesser extent the practice of team policing is omnipresent in our literature today. It is a reaction to the growing awareness on the part of the police manager that the agency, to be effective, must elicit the participation of the citizen in crime control programs. This latter concern is examined in Richard A. Myren's "Decentralization and Citizen Participation in Criminal Justice Systems," *Public Administration Review* 32 (October 1972): 718–38. In regard to team policing, see the monograph by Lawrence W. Sherman, Catherine H. Milton, and Thomas V. Kelly, *Team Policing: Seven Case Studies* (Washington, D.C.: Police Foundation, 1973).

well as in the remainder of this text is: *Managerial control is best manipulated by directives explicit in a MBO program that concentrates on
one's performance which is constantly measured in relation to the expressed objectives.*

Since the above statement is the underlying thesis of the pages comprising this book, we would recommend that you on occasion return to
this particular page and refresh your memory on the interdependency
of *control, objectives, performance,* and *measurement.*

Each police manager should have the information he needs to measure
his own performance and that of his subordinates and should receive it
soon enough to make any changes necessary for the desired results. And
this information should go to the supervisor as well as his manager. It
should also be reported to the police employee. More complete and accurate information can be a blessing or a curse, depending on how it is
used. The new capability to produce measuring information will make
possible effective self-control; and if so used, it will lead to a tremendous
improvement in the effectiveness and performance of management. But
if this new capability is abused to impose rigid or excessive control on
management from above, the new technology will cause incalculable
harm by demoralizing managers and police officers which in turn tends
to reduce their effectiveness.

MBO: A Basic Assumption and a Philosophy of Management

First, MBO forces the manager and the police officer to exert self-discipline in light of meeting the stated objectives. Indeed, it may well lead to
demanding too much rather than too little. This has been the main criticism leveled against the concept.[34] Yet it remains that MBO is linked to
one's ability to accept self-discipline.[35] A manager must assume that the
vast majority of his subordinates are capable of doing so. *If not, then
MBO will fail!* A manager who starts out with the assumption that people are weak, irresponsible, and lazy will get weakness, irresponsibility,
and laziness. He corrupts. A manager who assumes strength, responsibility, and desire to contribute may experience a few disappointments.
But the manager's *first task is to make effective the strengths of people,*
and this he can do only if he starts out with the assumption that people—
and especially managers and professional police officers—want to achieve.
Above all, the police manager must make this assumption with regard to
the young educated people of today who will be tomorrow's police offi-

[34]Drucker, *Management,* p. 441.

[35]MBO is also directly tied to other programs such as PPB. See Bruce H. Dewoolfson,
Jr., "Public Sector MBO and PPB: Cross Fertilization in Management Systems," *Public
Administration Review* 35 (July-August 1975): 374–380.

cers. They may not know what they mean when they demand to be al-lowed to "make a contribution." But their demand is the right demand. And they are right also that management, as it has been practiced so far in most police agencies, does not act on the assumption that the young educated people want to make a contribution. Police managers need to be subjected—and to subject themselves—to the discipline and the de-mands of MBO.

Second, the police organization is in need of a philosophy of manage-ment and supervision that will give full scope to individual strength and responsibility, as well as common direction to vision and effort; establish teamwork; and harmonize the desires of the individual with the goals of the agency. MBO substitutes for control from outside the stricter, more exacting, and more effective control from inside. It motivates the man-ager and his subordinates to action, not because somebody tells them to do something or talks them into doing it, but because the objective task demands it. They act, not because somebody wants them to, but because they decide that they have to. Finally, this philosophy must permeate the entire hierarchy of the agency. It must apply to every manager, every supervisor, and every employee, whatever his level or assignment.

The Setting of Objectives

The decision to set objectives on the part of a police agency automati-cally presents a major challenge to its entire decision-making process. MBO first requires a series of decisions on what objectives ought to be pursued. Second, an even larger number of decisions are needed to ac-complish them. George S. Odiorne's book provides testimony to this thinking in its title, *Management Decisions by Objectives*.[36] He states that three types of objectives should be rank ordered according to the level of difficulty in their achievement. In order of ascendancy they are:

1. Regular or routine —measured by exceptions from standards ob-jectives.

2. Problem solving —measured by solutions and time established as objectives.

3. Innovative goals —measured by productive changes sought and achieved in time.

Regardless of the type of objective, a singular and common process can be used to set them.[37] Again, the complexity, the challenge, the cer-

[36]George S. Odiorne, *Management Decisions by Objectives* (Englewood Cliffs, N.J.: Prentice-Hall, Inc., 1969).
[37]*Ibid.*, pp. 8–9.

tainty, and the time frame will vary based on the type of objective involved, to wit:

> Is the objective a guide to action?
> Is it explicit enough to suggest certain types of action (alternative)?
> Does it suggest tools to measure and control effectiveness?
> Is it challenging?
> Does it show cognizance of internal and external constraints?

Obstacles to MBO

Much like the "I've got good news and bad news for you, which do you want first?" jokes, we have discussed but one side of MBO—the good news. Now for some bad news. MBO is not without obstacles. As expressed thus far, the advantages are that police managers and supervisors are encouraged to think seriously about their objectives and to try to get them into meaningful and also measurable terms; also, it encourages forecasting, planning, and dialogues between all administrative levels. The disadvantages are that the system is basically foreign to those systems that have developed in both industry and government; most planners fail to see MBO as a system; government sees successful applications of MBO in the private sector as an obstacle; and there is insufficient commitment to MBO among those at executive levels. More specifically, common obstacles include dilution of efforts, crisis management, employer-employee goal divergence, organizational structure, cost inflation, and macro-manpower problems. In addition, limitations to MBO particular to police agencies include organizational structure and basic goals, processes, and economic rewards largely set by statute.

I

ROLE COMPONENT ONE: INTERNAL RESPONSIBILITIES

We have shown how the management function is synonymous with the fulfillment of responsibility. Further, as we learned in the preceding chapter, both one's commitment to managing and, consequently, one's sense of responsibility are strongly influenced by a wide range of sometimes concurring and sometimes conflicting values.

We have now reached the point where it is time to address the components of the police manager's overall role. Again, keep in mind that in order to manage—and therefore to meet our responsibilities—we must act in a particular role. And each role can be divided into components. Additionally each component can be comprised of one or more tasks. For our purposes we found it convenient to divide the police manager's role into two components. Admittedly, however, the two have considerable overlap and in practice are frequently difficult to separate. In any event we hope that our discussion of the tasks that follow is clarified rather than complicated by the approach adopted here.

Very few people actually witness what a manager does. The typical citizen in need of a police service will interact with a police officer and on occasion a police sergeant may be present. Rarely will a citizen communicate with a middle manager (lieutenant or captain). Indeed, only if an incident is very grave or unusual will a citizen, or for that matter a police officer, meet face-to-face with the police chief or sheriff. Naturally this statement is subject to exceptions based on such factors as the size of the agency, the chief's/sheriff's style of managing, etc. You may be thinking at this point "Hey, you're in error! I recently saw our police chief give a speech at a local service club." Or, if you are in the police service your reaction may be "Hey, you're in error! I recently saw my boss at roll call." We will grant you this. But, the fact remains few of us are in a position to observe and thus understand the role expectations of a police chief/sheriff executive.

Because much of what the police manager does is beyond our perception, it should not surprise you to find part I encompassing eleven tasks. Hence, about three-quarters of the manager's total responsibility deals with thinking, activities, issues, and concerns of an internal nature. The tasks that follow are obviously related to the administrative infrastructure. Without their attainment there would be no superstructure, and therefore no police service. To put it another way, police service is inexorably dependent on a delivery system. The manager, in turn, is accountable for developing and maintaining such a system.

Although the chapters that follow are self-explanatory a few comments in respect to the content and format of the chapters are appropriate. First, you will find that many of the chapters are laced with standards elicited from a set of benchmark reports produced by the American Bar Association and the National Advisory Commission on Criminal Justice Standards and Goals. We felt it important to include them (although we are certain that most of you have seen them before) since the police manager is, or should be, concerned for their achievement—standards such as these are fast becoming an integral part of his overriding responsibility. Second, the majority of the chapters conclude with a learning exercise. You may be tempted to ignore them because of disinterest, or lack of time or a group to work with on the exercise. We are convinced that "experiential" learning is an excellent supplement to the more cognitive type. As a consequence, we urge you to engage in a few of the exercises before passing judgment on their worth. Those at the end of chapter 9, in particular, should be interesting. Third, and finally, in some cases we substituted an operationally oriented document. For example, chapter 12 ends with an internal investigations manual. They are not proffered as the "one best way," but rather as paradigms for analysis and discussion.

Significantly, part I closes with a subject so critical to the police manager that his professional existence is contingent on effectively coping with it. This subject is the police officer or deputy sheriff—what can be done to enhance these occupational roles and, as a result, improve the delivery of police services—clearly a critical cornerstone in a foundation of an interlocking set of management responsibilities.

Chapter Three

TASK 1 ORGANIZING:
The Art of Hierarchy

And thou shalt teach them ordinances and laws, and shalt show them the way wherein they must walk, and the work that they must do.

Moreover thou shalt provide out of all the people able men, such as fear God, men of truth, hating covetousness; and place such over them, to be rulers of thousands, and rulers of hundreds, rulers of fifties, and rulers of tens:

And let them judge the people at all seasons: and it shall be, that every great matter they shall bring unto thee, but every small matter they shall judge: so shall it be easier for thyself, and they shall bear the burden with thee. . . .

And Moses chose able men out of all Israel, and made them heads over the people, rulers of thousands, rulers of hundreds, rulers of fifties, and rulers of tens.

And they judged the people at all seasons: the hard causes they brought unto Moses, but every small matter they judged themselves.[1]

Organization is a means to an end rather than an end itself. Sound structure is a prerequisite to organizational health; but it is not health itself.[2]

Standard 5.1

RESPONSIBILITY FOR POLICE SERVICE

Every State and local government immediately should provide complete and competent police service through an organizational structure that most effectively and efficiently meets its responsibility. The government responsible for this service should provide for a police organization that performs the duties described as the police role.

1. Every police agency should provide for access to police service and response to police emergency situations 24 hours a day.

2. Every local government unable to support a police agency and provide 24-hour-a-day services should arrange immediately for the necessary services by mutual agreement with an agency that can provide them.

3. Every police chief executive should establish an organizational structure that will best insure effective and efficient performance of the police functions necessary to fulfill the agency's role within the community. Every police chief executive:

---

[1]Exod. 18:20–22, 25–26.

[2]Peter F. Drucker, *Management: Tasks, Responsibilities, Practices* (New York: Harper & Row, Publishers, Inc., 1974), p. 602.

a. Should, in conjunction with the annual budget preparation, review the agency's organizational structure in view of modern management practices and provide for necessary changes.

b. Should insure that the organizational structure facilitates the rendering of direct assistance and service to the people by line elements. Command of line elements should be as close as practical to the people.

c. Should organize the agency's staff elements to insure that the organizational structure provides for direct assistance and service to line elements.

d. Should limit functional units, recognizing that they increase the need for co-ordination, create impediments to horizontal communications, and increase the danger of functional objectives superseding agency goals.

e. Should establish only those levels of management necessary to provide adequate direction and control.

f. Should define the lines of authority and insure that responsibility is placed at every level with commensurate authority to carry out assigned responsibility.

g. Should not be encumbered by traditional principles of organization if the agency goals can best be achieved by less formal means.[3]

SYNOPSIS

Organizing for action predates recorded history. Paradoxically, while organization itself is clearly not new, we do have "new" organizations—our concept of organizing has undergone a series of iterative changes. From the early beginnings of formal and prescriptive rules we have witnessed a transition to a no "one-best-way" philosophy. Thus, from a highly inflexible set of universal guidelines we find emerging a concern for adaptive and custom-configured structures. In both literature and practice, organizing for action has been influenced by three overlapping eras: classical (principles), neoclassical (human relations), and systems (integrative).

Police organizations are an admixture of all three eras. However, we can observe in them a detectable effort to identify more closely with the systems approach to organizing. Indeed, the term "system" is very much in vogue in the professional police community. A case in point is the frequent reference to the "police delivery system." Complexity, change, and size are three major stimuli for adapting a systems approach. Inherent in an organizational system are adaptivity, temporariness, modularity, openness, and feedback—all critical to police effectiveness. In addition, many police managers are test-

[3]National Advisory Commission on Criminal Justice Standards and Goals, *Police* (Washington, D.C.: U.S. Government Printing Office, 1973), p. 104.

ing their delivery systems with new patterns of integration and specialization such as team policing. If any generalization can be made it is that organizing for police action is, always has been, and always will be in a state of flux.

The chapter concludes with a learning exercise that is designed to assist a police agency in developing a climate of system-wide co-operation and individual goal definition.

ORGANIZATION THEORY: Problem Centeredness

In reading the quote from *Exodus,* above, we see the traditional concepts so familiar to us: selection of personnel based on ability, formation of a hierarchy, delegation, decision making, division of labor, span of control, task specialization, unity of command, and policy determination at the top of the hierarchy. An exhaustive analysis could probably identify other classifiable concepts in the quotation. Even without such an analysis, the great antiquity of most of our traditional ideas about organizational theory and management is vividly illustrated in this remarkable quotation. Traditional organizational patterns, however, are beginning to change, and our experience in local law enforcement reflects some of these changes. Yet the phenomenon known as *organization* is neither understood nor appreciated by most people, even though organizations are among the most important institutions in every part of the world and have a pervasive influence upon almost all human activity. Because of their increasing influence, we find an ever-expanding interest in the whys and wherefores of organizations. It is recognized that organizations are not a modern invention. The pharaohs of Egypt and the emperors of China depended upon organizations for constructing a variety of complex structures, and conscious interest in theories or principles of organization began in ancient Greece.

Organizational theory is *problem*-centered, the problem being how to construct human groupings that are as rational as possible and simultaneously to produce a maximum of individual job satisfaction.[4] There is a record of both progress and regression in the search for the best combination of these objectives. Significantly, the police manager can foster these objectives or detract from them in an attempt to do either one or

[4]Much has been and is in the process of being written about more effective forms of organizing human endeavor. One set of articles in particular is worthy of your attention. See Dwight Waldo, ed., "Organizations for the Future," *Public Administration Review* 33 (July-August 1973): 299–335.

both. He plays a critical role in coordinating human efforts to accomplish organizational goals. This chapter seeks to describe for the police manager the changing aspects of organizational theory and behavior. More specifically, it indicates for the police manager the state-of-the-art and possible future trends in organizing the police structure. Hence, in one sense the chapter is historical, since it deals with the formal side of organization, and in another sense it is contemporary, because much of the historical or classical thinking remains in practice. However, it also reports on a *reaction* and an emerging *synthesis*. The reaction is to those who cannot see beyond the mechanistic doctrine of the traditionalists— it is referred to as the informal side, or human relations in organizational theory. The ultimate synthesis combines these two theoretical concerns— formal and informal—into the much more sophisticated systems theory of organizing.

ORGANIZATION DEFINED

Organizations are social units (human groupings) deliberately constructed and reconstructed to seek specific goals.[5] Corporations, armies, schools, churches, and police departments are included; ethnic groups, friendship groups, and family groups are excluded. An organization is characterized by (1) goals, (2) a division of labor, authority, power, and communication responsibilities in a rationally planned, rather than a random or traditionally patterned, manner, (3) a set of rules and norms, (4) the presence of one or more authority centers which control the efforts of the organization and direct them toward its goals.

In defining organization, it is helpful to define some other concepts frequently confused with it. First, let us again consider management. *Management* is action intended to achieve rational cooperation in an organization. Second, there is *administration*, which is, quite simply, organization and management. The crux or central idea of administration is to deliberately construct a rational plan of human action for goal accomplishment. Third is the much discussed and "cussed" concept known as *bureaucracy*. For those familiar with Weber's work, bureaucracy implies that the unit is organized according to the principles he specified. But many organizations are not bureaucratic. Since many police departments are to a great extent, if not totally, bureaucratic, this concept is covered in more detail later in the chapter. Bureaucracies (1) are organizations that have numerous *formalized* rules and regulations and (2) are among the most important institutions in the world because they not only pro-

[5]Talcott Parsons, *Structure and Process in Modern Societies* (New York: The Free Press of Glencoe, 1960), p. 17.

vide employment for a very significant fraction of the world's population but also make critical decisions that shape the economic, educational, political, social, moral, and even religious lives of nearly everyone on earth.[6] (Chapter 5 discussed the subject of organizational goals. The importance of goals to an organization lies in the realization that they are the main reason for the very existence of the organization.)

ORGANIZATIONAL THEORY: The Formal Approach

By *classical* theory of organization is meant the theory that developed over a number of centuries and finally matured in the thirties. It is exemplified in Luther Gulick's essay "Notes on the Theory of Organization,"[7] in Monney and Reiley's *Principles of Organization,*[8] and in Max Weber's writing on bureaucracy.[9] All these theorists were strongly oriented toward economy, efficiency, and executive control. These values, when combined, create a theory of organization that has four cornerstones—division of labor, hierarchy of authority, structure, and span of control. Of the four, division of labor is the most important; in fact, the other three are dependent on it for their very existence. The hierarchy of authority is the legitimate vertical network for gaining compliance. Essentially, it includes the chain of command, the sharing of authority and responsibility, the unity of command, and the obligation to report. Structure is the logical relationship of positions and functions in an organization, arranged to accomplish the objectives of organization. Classical organization theory usually works with two basic structures, the line and the staff. According to Gulick, both structures can be arranged four ways: purpose, process, people (clientele), and place where services are rendered.[10] The span of control concept deals with the number of subordinates a superior can effectively supervise. It has significance, in part, for the shape of the organization. Wide span yields a flat structure; short span results in a tall structure.

Our approach to classical organization theory is threefold. We first

---

[6]Anthony Downs, *Inside Bureaucracy* (Boston: Little, Brown and Company, 1967), p. 1.

[7]Luther Gulick, "Notes on the Theory of Organization," in *Papers on the Science of Administration,* ed. Luther Gulick and Lyndall Urwick (New York: Institute of Public Administration, 1937), pp. 1–45.

[8]James D. Mooney and Alan C. Reiley, *Principles of Organization* (New York: Harper & Row, Publishers, 1939).

[9]The best-known translation of Max Weber's writings on bureaucracy is H. H. Gerth and C. Wright Mills, trans., *From Max Weber: Essays in Sociology* (New York: Oxford University Press, Inc., 1946).

[10]Gulick, "Notes," p. 33.

deal with rationality and its critical role in a bureaucratic structure. The principal theorist in this case is Max Weber. We then explore the theory that efficiency can be maximized by making management a true science. In this instance, most of our thinking is derived from Frederick W. Taylor. In the third area, best termed *principles*, we turn to the works of Gulick, Urwick, Mooney, and Reiley. Keep in mind that the concepts and developments are not mutually exclusive but overlap a great deal.

Weber : Rationality

Max Weber was a founder of modern sociology as well as a pioneer in administrative thought. Weber probed bureaucracy, here essentially synonymous with "large organization," to uncover the rational relationship of bureaucratic structure to its goals. His analysis led him to conclude that there were three types of organizational power centers: (1) traditional—subjects accept the orders of a supervisor as justified on the grounds that it is the way things have always been done, (2) charismatic—subjects accept a superior's order as justified because of the influence of his personality, and (3) rational-legal—subjects accept a superior's order as justified because it agrees with more abstract rules which are considered legitimate. The type of power employed determines the degree of alienation on the part of the subject. If the subject perceives the power as legitimate, he is more willing to comply. And, if power is considered legitimate, then according to Weber, it becomes authority. Hence, Weber's three power centers can be translated into authority centers. Of the three types of authority, Weber recommended that rational structural relationships be obtained through the rational-legal form. He felt that the other two forms lacked systematic division of labor, specialization, and stability and had nonrelevant political and administrative relationships.

In each principle of bureaucracy described below, Weber's constant concern about the frailness of a rational-legal bureaucracy is apparent. His primary motive, therefore, was to build into the bureaucratic structure safeguards against external and internal pressures so that the bureaucracy could at all times sustain its autonomy. According to Weber, a bureaucratic structure, to be rational, must contain these elements.[11]

1. *Rulification and routinization.* "A continuous organization of official functions bound by *rules*." Rational organization is the opposite of

[11]Max Weber, *The Theory of Social and Economic Organization,* ed. Talcott Parsons, trans. A. M. Henderson and Talcott Parsons (New York: Oxford University Press, Inc. 1947), pp. 329–30.

temporary, unstable relations, thus the stress on continuity. Rules save effort by eliminating the need for deriving a new solution for every situation. They also facilitate standard and equal treatment of similar situations.

2. *Division of labor.* "A specific sphere of competence. This involves (a) a sphere of obligation to perform functions which have been marked off as part of a systematic division of labor; (b) the provision of the incumbent with the necessary means of compulsion are clearly defined and their use is subject to definite conditions."

3. *Hierarchy of authority.* "The organization of offices follows the principle of hierarchy; that each lower office under the control and supervision of a higher one."

4. *Expertise.* "The rules which regulate the conduct of an office may be *technical* rules or norms. In both cases, if their application is to be fully rational, specialized training is necessary. It is thus normally true that only a person who has demonstrated an adequate technical training is qualified to be a member of the administrative staff. . . ."

5. *Written rules.* "Administrative acts, decisions, and rules are formulated and recorded in writing. . . ."

6. *Separation of ownership.* "It is a matter of principle that the members of the administrative staff should be completely separated from ownership of the means of production or administration. . . . There exists, furthermore, in principle, complete separation of the property belonging to the organization, which is controlled within the spheres of the office, and the personal property of the official. . . ."

Weber did not expect any bureaucracy to have all the elements he listed. The greater the number and intensity of the elements an organization possessed, however, the more rational and, therefore, the more efficient would be the organization. His contribution to organizational theory is becoming more recognized and appreciated. Our modern police organizations would find it hard to deny that he has to some degree influenced their structure. Mr. Manager—are you now working in a bureaucratic organization?

Taylorism: Scientific Management

Frederick W. Taylor, production specialist, business executive, and consultant, applied the scientific method to the solution of factory problems and from these analyses established principles which could be substituted for the trial-and-error methods then in use. The advent of Taylor's thinking opened a new era, that of *scientific management*. Taylor probably did not invent the term or originate the approach. Taylor's enormous contribution lay, first, in his large-scale application of the analytical, scientific approach to improving production methods in the shop.[12] Second, while he did not feel that management could ever become an exact science in the same sense as physics and chemistry, he believed strongly that management could be an organized body of knowledge and that it could be taught and learned. Third, he originated the term and concept of *functional supervision.* Taylor felt that the job of supervision was too complicated to be handled effectively by one supervisor and should therefore be delegated to as many as eight specialized foremen. Finally, Taylor believed that his major contribution lay in a new philosophy for workers and management.

Now, in its essence, scientific management involves a complete mental revolution on the part of the workingmen engaged in any particular establishment or industry—a complete mental revolution on the part of these men as to their duties toward their work, toward their fellowmen, and toward their fellow employees. And it involves the equally complete mental revolution on the part of those on the management's side—the foreman, the superintendent, the owner of the business, the board of directors—a complete mental revolution on this part as to their duties toward their fellow workers in the management, toward their workmen, and toward all their daily problems. And without this complete mental revolution on both sides, scientific management does not exist.[13]

Taylor consistently maintained—and successfully demonstrated—that through the use of his techniques it would be possible to obtain appreciable increases in a worker's efficiency. Furthermore, he firmly believed that management, and management alone, should be responsible for putting these techniques into effect. Although it is important to obtain the cooperation of the workers, it must be "enforced cooperation." He emphasizes this point as follows:

> It is only through *enforced* standardization of methods, *enforced* cooperation that this faster work can be assured. And the duty of

[12]Frederick W. Taylor, *Shop Management* (New York: Harper & Row, Publishers, 1911).
[13]Frederick W. Taylor, "The Principles of Scientific Management," in *Classics in Management,* ed. Harwood F. Merrill (New York: American Management Association, 1960), p. 78. A comprehensive account of Taylor's achievements in this field can be found in three basic documents: "Shop Management," a paper presented to the American Society of Mechanical Engineers in 1903; "The Principles of Scientific Management," which Taylor wrote in 1909, when his work was becoming an object of public attention, but which was not published until 1911; and his 1912 "Testimony before the Special House Committee," which consisted largely of a justification of his views in the light of public attack. These three documents have been published in one volume, *Scientific Management* (New York: Harper & Row, Publishers, 1947).

enforcing the adaptation of standards and of enforcing this cooperation rests with the *management* alone. . . .[14]

Taylor prescribed five methods for "scientifically" managing an organization. First, management must carefully study the worker's body
movements to discover the one best method for accomplishing work in
the shortest possible time. Second, management must standardize its tools
based on the requirements of specific jobs. Third, management must
select and train each worker for the job for which he is best suited. Fourth,
management must abandon the traditional unity-of-command principle
and substitute functional supervision. As already mentioned, Taylor ad-
vocated that a worker receive his orders from as many as eight supervisors. Four of these supervisors were to serve on the shop floor (inspector, repair foreman, speed boss, and gang boss) and the other four in the
planning room (routing, instruction, time and costs, and discipline).
Fifth, management must pay the worker in accordance with his individual output.

Ironically, Taylor's general approach to management is widely accepted today in production-oriented business organizations. Scientific
management became a movement, which still has a tremendous influence
on industrial practice. More specifically, it had a major effect on the
reform and economy movements in public administration and thus also
influenced police administration. Its impact on public organizations is
readily apparent at the present time. One can find numerous managers
and supervisors (private and public alike) who firmly believe that if
material rewards are directly related to work efforts, the worker consistently responds with his maximum performance.

Gulick and Urwick: The Principles

While the followers of Taylor developed more scientific techniques of
management and work, others were conceptualizing broad principles for
the most effective design of organizational structure. Luther Gulick and
Lyndall Urwick were leaders in formulating principles of formal organization. Not only did they develop such principles, but Gulick went even
further and defined administration as comprising seven activities.[15] Together these activities spell out the acronym POSDCORB.

[14]Frederick W. Taylor, "Principles of Scientific Management," p. 83.
[15]Gulick's seven elements of administration are drawn from Henri Fayol's list of five:
planning, organization, command, coordination, and control. See Henri Fayol, *General
and Industrial Management,* trans. Constance Storrs (London: Sir Isaac Pitman & Sons
Ltd., 1949), pp. 43–110.

Planning: working out in broad outline what needs to be done and the methods for doing it to accomplish the purpose set for the enterprise;

Organizing: the establishment of a formal structure of authority through which work subdivisions are arranged, defined, and coordinated for the defined objective;

Staffing: the whole personnel function of bringing in and training the staff and maintaining favorable conditions of work;

Directing: the continuous task of making decisions, embodying them in specific and general orders and instructions, and serving as the leader of the enterprise;

Coordinating: the all important duty of interrelating the various parts of the organization;

Reporting: keeping those to whom the executive is responsible informed as to what is going on, which includes keeping himself and his subordinates informed through records, research, and inspection;

Budgeting: all that does with budgeting in the form of fiscal planning, accounting, and control.[16]

The Gulick-Urwick principles deal primarily with the structure of the formal organization. Underlying all their principles was the need for an organizational *division of labor.* In other words, their approach rests firmly on the assumption that the more a specific function can be divided into its simplest parts, the more specialized and, therefore, the more skilled a worker can become in carrying out his part of the job. According to Gulick, any division of labor should be homogeneous, and homogeneity can be achieved if one or more of the following four determinants are used to characterize the type of work each individual is performing:

The major *purpose* he is serving, such as furnishing water, controlling crime, or conducting education;

The *process* he is using, such as engineering, medicine, carpentry, stenography, statistics, or accounting;

The *person* or *things* dealt with or served, such as immigrants, veterans, Indians, forests, mines, parks, orphans, farmers, automobiles, or the poor;

The *place* where he renders his service, such as Hawaii, Boston, Washington, the Dust Bowl, Alabama, or Central High School.[17]

This four-determinant approach is replete with problems. General determinants are difficult to apply to a specific organization because they

16Gulick, "Notes," p. 13.
17*Ibid.,* p. 15.

often overlap, are sometimes incompatible with one another, and are quite vague. For example, when looking at a police organization, it would be difficult not to conclude that the four principles fail to provide a satisfactory guide to division of labor in that organization. Furthermore, it can be seen that these determinants are prescriptive rather than descriptive, that they state how work should be divided rather than how work is actually divided. The planning of the division of labor in a given organization is affected by many considerations not covered by the four principles. The division may be determined by the culture in which the organization is situated, by the environment of the organization, by the availability and type of personnel, and by political factors. Organizations are made up of a combination of various layers which differ in their type of division. The lower layers tend to be organized according to area or clientele, and the higher ones by purpose or process. Even this statement, however, should be viewed only as a probability. In a police organization, all four determinants operate at the same time, and it is their unique mix that makes the department either effective or ineffective.

In addition to Gulick's and Urwick's central principle of division of labor, seven other related principles merit our attention.[18]

1. *Unity of command.* "A man cannot serve two masters."[19] This principle is offered as a balance to the division of labor.

2. *Fitting people to the structure.* People should be assigned to their organizational positions "in a cold-blooded, detached spirit," like the preparation of an engineering design, regardless of the needs of that particular individual or of those individuals who may now be in the organization.[20]

3. *One top executive (manager).* Both Gulick and Urwick strongly supported the principle of one-man administrative responsibility in an organization. Hence they warned against the use of committees or boards.

4. *Staff: general and special.* The classical writers' concern about staff assistance to top management deserves special attention. When management expressed a need for help from larger and larger numbers of experts and specialists, this need immediately raised the question of the relation of these specialists to the regular line supervisors and employees. In this instance, Gulick recommended that the staff specialist

---

[18]This list is in part suggested by Gross. See Bertram M. Gross, *The Managing of Organizations* (New York: The Free Press of Glencoe, 1964), pp. 145–48.

[19]Gulick, "Notes," p. 9.

[20]L. Urwick, *Elements of Administration* (New York: Harper & Row, Publishers, 1943), pp. 34–39.

obtain results from the line through influence and persuasion and that the staff not be given authority over the line. The next question to be answered was that of coordination. Top management would have more people to supervise, since they would be responsible for not only the line but the special staff as well. The Gulick-Urwick answer to this problem was to provide help through "general staff" as distinguished from "special staff" assistance. Significantly, general staff are not limited to the proffering of advice. They may draw up and transmit orders, check on operations, and iron out difficulties. In so doing, they act not on their own but as representatives of their superior and within the confines of decisions made by him. Thus, they allow him to exercise a broader span of control.

5. *Delegation.* Urwick emphasized that "lack of the courage to delegate properly and of knowledge how to do it is one of the most general causes of failure in organization." In larger organizations, we must delegate even the right to delegate.[21]

6. *Matching responsibility with authority.* In this case, Urwick dealt with both sides of the authority-responsibility relationship. It is wrong to hold people accountable for certain activities if "the necessary authority to discharge that responsibility" is not granted. On the other side, "the responsibilities of all persons exercising authority should be absolute within the defined terms of that authority. They should be personally accountable for all actions taken by subordinates." He set forth the widely quoted principle that "at all levels authority and responsibility should be coterminous and coequal.

7. *Span of control.* Again, Urwick asserted that "no supervisor can supervise directly the work of more than five or at the most, six subordinates whose work interlocks. When the number of subordinates increases arithmetically, there is a geometrical increase in all the possible combinations of relationship which may demand the attention of the supervisor."[22]

In review, classical organization theory was built on three interlocking cornerstones: rationality of structure, scientific management, and principles of organization. One way of classifying these three concepts is as follows: First, Weber's writing was primarily descriptive; however, it did indicate that a particular form of organizational structure was preferable. Second, the theories of both Taylor and the Gulick-Urwick team were prescriptive; that is, they expressed the one right way to manage and

---

21*Ibid.,* pp. 51–52.
22*Ibid.,* pp. 45–46, 125.

organize. Interestingly, Taylor's notion of a scientific management, while being purely mechanistic at first glance, is at the same time motivational. Taylor viewed man as a rational-economic animal; hence, the way for management to motivate him is through economic incentives that include improved work methods.

The Consequences

Having considered some of the attributes of the classical approach, we turn now to the present results of its teachings. This historical era lives on in the form of many contemporary formal organizational structures. It keeps those that listen to its tenets constantly gazing at the formal hierarchical jobs, positions, and procedures. Hence operations are stressed over people. Classical organization theory has given rise to not one but four formal structures. Since we live with these structures on a daily basis, it seems worthwhile to discuss them further. The four types of structures that have emerged from the literature are (1) job-task, (2) rank, (3) skill, and (4) pay.[23]

The job-task structure focuses on people working at specialized tasks. There is a division of labor, which in the assembly-line tradition is broken down into the smallest repetitive operations. In small organizations these positions develop rather naturally and are not formalized in writing. As organizations grow and become more complex, two developments usually occur: (1) classification of duties and (2) centralization of the authority to establish new positions. Both these developments provide a basis for establishing a system of position classification. Briefly, position classification is the grouping of positions, according to the similarity of duties and responsibilities, into job categories having identical job descriptions.

The structure of rank involves an officer class, an obvious example being the police. Other examples include the United States Foreign Service and the military. A structure of rank differs from the job hierarchy in that status does not attach to the particular job; a police sergeant is a sergeant whether supervising a patrol unit or conducting an investigation. The job structure emphasizes the duties to be performed, while the concept of rank stresses the personal status, pay, and authority of the incumbents. This is not to say that the latter has no relation to the tasks and level of job responsibility—a police sergeant, for instance, is consid-

---

[23]The remainder of this section is drawn primarily from the work of John M. Pfiffner and Frank P. Sherwood, *Administrative Organization* (Englewood Cliffs, N.J.: Prentice-Hall, Inc. 1960), pp. 66–71.

ered a first-line supervisor; however, some sergeants who spend time in this rank never supervise!

An organization is constructed from a structure of skills. The job descriptions used for personnel administration usually contain a statement of the required training and experience for each position, in addition to the duties to be performed. At or near the top of the organizational structure are the positions demanding the managerial skills of organizing, planning, controlling, and coordinating. In addition to this structure of managerial skills, there is also a hierarchy of professional skills. In any large- or medium-scale police organization we find numerous specialists, such as records analysts, juvenile officers, trainers, researchers, and public information officers. Interestingly, these skills are becoming more concerned with and, in some instances, dependent upon college training. In police organization, the more general positions (patrolman) are frequently broken down into specialized positions (robbery detective, narcotics investigator, juevnile officer, and so forth).

The larger police organizations tend to have a standardized pay structure, often referred to as a compensation plan. Salary and wage administration frequently incorporates some elements of scientific method, using statistical approaches. Consequently, levels of difficulty of positions are established, which helps in the internal comparison of various jobs.

All four of these organizational structures can be found in our police departments.

ORGANIZATIONAL THEORY: The Informal Approach

In the 1920s the classical approach to organization experienced a reaction to its mechanistic prescriptions for managing and organizing. This reaction is commonly referred to as (1) the informal, or human relations, approach or (2) the neoclassical theory of organization. It evolved out of the discovery that within formal organizations man tends to establish informal organizations. This theory emphasized communication, shared decision making, and leadership. The two major assumptions underlying the human relations approach are that (1) the most satisfying organization (for the worker) is the most efficient and (2) it is necessary to relate work and the organizational structure to the social needs of the employee. The informal approach is not without its shortcomings. The reaction to the reaction is discussed in the next section.

The origins of informal theory are usually associated with the Hawthorne studies and, in particular, the writings of Elton Mayo, John

Dewey, Kurt Lewin, and Mary Follett.[24] This theory stressed the affective and the social and was both caused by and a cause of increasing attention of psychology, social psychology, and sociology to contemporary organizations. It "discovered" the small (or face-to-face) group in large organization and, in broad terms, emphasized the notion that formal organizations also have a large informal, that is, social and emotional, component. An *informal organization* includes both the social relations as they naturally evolve from the formal organization and from the needs of the individual workers. In essence, classical organization theory failed to recognize that formal organizations tend to breed informal organizations within them and that in the informal organization, workers and managers are likely to establish relationships with each other which influence the manner in which they carry out their jobs or fulfill their roles.[25] To clarify this point, we look to a highly significant piece of research—the studies conducted by Mayo, Roethlisberger, and Dickson in the Hawthorne plant of the Western Electric Company in Chicago.

The Hawthorne Studies

The Hawthorne studies were conducted during the late 1920s through the mid-1930s. This series of studies (we review only a part of them) produced some important, unexpected findings.[26]

A group of girls who assembled telephone equipment were selected as subjects for a series of studies designed to determine the effect of their working conditions, length of the working day, number and length of rest pauses, and other factors relating to the "nonhuman" environment on their productivity. The girls were located in a special room under close supervision.

As the researchers varied working conditions, they found that each major change was accomplished by a substantial increase in production. When all the conditions to be varied had been tested, they decided to return the girls to their original, poorly lighted workbenches for the

[24]Mary Follett's contribution to neoclassical organization theory is beginning to be better understood and certainly more appreciated. In essence, she developed a theory of human interaction based on the "law of the situation," which means the bringing together of various inputs and acting in accord with their syntheses. An excellent overview of her thinking can be found in Elliot M. Fox, "Mary Parker-Follett: The Enduring Contribution," *Public Administration Review* 28 (November-December 1968), 520–29.

[25]Edgar H. Schein, *Organizational Psychology* (Englewood Cliffs, N.J.: Prentice-Hall, Inc., 1963), p. 27.

[26]A more comprehensive description of these researches can be found in F. J. Roethlisberger and W. J. Dickson, *Management and the Worker* (Cambridge: Harvard University Press, 1939).

usual long working day without rest pauses and other benefits. To the astonishment of the researchers, *output rose again, to an even higher level that it had been under the best of the experimental conditions.* A new hypothesis had to be found. The hypothesis was that motivation to work, productivity, and quality of work were all related to the nature of the social relations among the workers and between the workers and their boss. New groups were created for additional experimentation. The findings of the study can be summarized as follows:

1. The productivity of the individual worker is determined more by his social capacity than his physical capacity.
2. Noneconomic rewards play a prominent part in motivating and satisfying an employee.
3. Maximum specialization is not the most efficient form of division of labor.
4. Employees do not react to management and its norms and rewards as individuals but as members of groups.

The tendency of experimentally chosen groups to show increased productivity and job satisfaction is known as the "Hawthorne effect" and is one of the most widely recognized findings of the social sciences.

In the Hawthorne experiments treatment was the significant factor. The girls selected for the experiment were (1) assigned the best supervisor in the plant, (2) accorded special privileges of genuine importance to them, and (3) *made into a cohesive group* by encouragement of patterns of interaction. Note that the group was created at the beginning of the experiment. Consequently, the group did not hold previously established norms on what its level of production should be. Follow-up studies attempting to achieve similar results failed when the researchers did not create new groups. Essentially, the workers' cohesion around their own norms was too strong to change. Apparently, these researchers forgot the primary lesson contained in the original study—that the level of production is set by social norms (man's social capacity), not by physiological capacities.

Neoclassical Organization Theory after the Hawthorne Studies: The Human Relations Era Continues

In the years since the Hawthorne experiments, a long line of research has added to the evidence that group solidarity and loyalty is associated with productivity, effectiveness, and job satisfaction. Moreover, these experiments have provided a better understanding of organizational leadership, decision making, and communication. In regard to leadership, it has been observed that the leader is able to set and enforce group norms through his particular style of leading a group.[27]

The human relations approach to managing and supervising is still widely accepted in administrative circles. Our fundamental reason for discussing it, however, is that this period in management thinking set the stage for identifying and understanding the informal organization. After man's social capacity was discovered, social scientists began to direct their attention to how such factors as power and expertise operated in a nonformal or informal sense. Thus we see the human relations approach to organization carving out a neoclassical theory, which devoted most of its study to an improved knowledge of the informal organization. John M. Pfiffner and Frank P. Sherwood have most convincingly described not one but five informal organizations that can, and usually do, exist within a formal structure:

> The sociometric network
> The system of functional contacts
> The grid of decision-making centers
> The pattern of power
> Channels of communications[28]

The recognition of and the intense interest in the informal organization was brought about by the weakness inherent in the formal structure. According to Svenson:

> The informal organization is nature's response to management's artificial structuring of an orderly business event. Driven by assumptions about functional division of work, the formal organization splits the natural unity of a business event into segments according to title authority. Informal organization attempts to heal the managerial rupturing by weaving an authority of knowledge about the fracture.[29]

The classical and neoclassical organization theories are in many ways directly opposed to each other. The attributes one theory considers im-

---

[27]See, for example, R. Lippitt and R. K. White, "An Experimental Study of Leadership and Group Life," in *Readings in Social Psychology*, ed. G. E. Swanson, T. M. Newcomb, and E. L. Hartley (New York: Holt, Rinehart & Winston, Inc., 1952), pp. 340–55.

[28]Pfiffner and Sherwood, *Administrative Organization*, pp. 18–27.

[29]Arthur L. Svenson, "Lessons from the Informal Organization," *Systems and Procedures*, 19 (May-June 1968), 14.

portant, the other usually does not mention at all. The two theories do hold one thing in common: An organization's desire for rationality and human happiness could be completely resolved if each theory's particular body of knowledge were utilized. The classical theorists assumed that the most efficient organization would also be the most satisfying one because it would maximize both productivity and the employees' salary. In contrast, the neoclassical theorists assumed that the happier the employees were made through satisfaction of their social needs, the greater would be their cooperation and efficiency. It rejected man as an economic entity and defined him as a social animal.

In summary, both theories said, "Hey, manager and supervisor, follow me and I'll provide you with efficiency and your workers with happiness." Thus they were saying that a perfect balance between organizational goals and employees' needs could be found in their own specific approaches to the problem of organizing and managing. The reason for their different approaches to the utopian dream rests mainly in their view of man—economic versus social.

Before proceeding to the third, or modern, theory, note that there is no sharp discontinuity between the usages of the three theories, that the new is added to and more or less modifies the old rather than displacing it. Classical theory is still very much alive, is widely used, and has its defenders, and while there is now a tendency to regard "human relations" as passé, as associated with certain excess and and naïvetés of the past, there is a massive spillover of concepts, attitudes, and research interests into the modern theory.

ORGANIZATIONAL THEORY: The System (Modern) Approach

> Big fleas have little fleas upon their
> backs to bite 'em;
> Little fleas have lesser fleas
> And so ad infinitum.

The diversity and number of systems is great. The molecule, the cell, the organ, the individual, the group, and the society are all examples of systems. Furthermore, there are communication, information, computer, and hardware systems. In some respects they are alike; however, they differ in their level of complexity and over a host of other dimensions—living, nonliving, or mixed; material or conceptual; and so forth. This section describes the organization, more specifically a police organization, as an open social system. Increasingly, organizations are being considered through a system perspective.[30] The modern organization is thus dominated by the systems approach which, in turn, is itself a set of theories, analytical methods, and plans.

The police manager operates in a system. *A system is any entity, conceptual or material, that consists of interdependent parts.* Certainly this broad definition encompasses a police organization. The primary difference between an organization and a system is that the former has a goal or goals to accomplish, and the latter may not. While we have referred to the police organization as an open social system, it is in reality a mixed social system, since it contains, men, machines, and materials (living and nonliving entities). Moreover, it coordinates (integrates) them in a dynamic manner in order to conduct the work of the system (goal attainment). Consequently, *our idea of an organization is changing from one of structure to one of process.* To foster the view of an organization as a process, or system, this section continues with reasons for the development of a systems approach and its benefits for modern organizational theory. We then consider what is meant by a systems approach. Finally, the characteristics and subsystems of an open social system are described as they relate to a police organization.

Forces toward a Systems Point of View

The reader is perhaps beginning to ask why organizations should be approached as open social systems. The main reasons are (1) the increased complexity and frequency of change in our society, and (2) the limitations of the previously discussed organizational theories, namely, that both the classical and the neoclassical theories viewed an organization as a *closed structure.* Such nearsightedness produces an inability to recognize that the organization is continually dependent upon its environment for the inflow of materials and human energy. Thinking of an organization as a closed structure, moreover, results in a failure to develop a feedback capability for obtaining adequate information about changes in environmental forces and goal accomplishment.

Beyond the more general reasons are specific and compelling ones which cause a police organization to consider itself an open system. These reasons are in terms of the benefits to be derived from such consideration. First, we are beginning to recognize that police organizations are a component of, and positioned within, a system of relationships. And, these relationships are not exclusively confined to a single organizational en-

[30]Perhaps the most outstanding contribution and convincing argument for viewing an organization as a social system is Daniel Katz and Robert L. Kahn, *The Social Psychology of Organizations* (New York: John Wiley & Sons, Inc., 1966). Another example supporting a systems approach to organizations is Stanley Young, *Management: A Systems Approach* (Glenview, Ill.: Scott, Foresman & Company, 1967).

vironment such as a city government. The police agency can be thought of logically as either a system (a single police department) or a subsystem. In viewing the police organization as a subsystem, it is naturally involved in a complex set of interfaces with other subsystems external to its particular organizational boundary, such as the district attorney, parole agencies, and courts. The systems approach effectively helps us to cross boundaries to identify, establish, and make use of significant interrelationships of various organizations. Police departments now undergoing analyses for either of the computer-based information systems are being made more aware of the requirements for external transactions. Second, many police agencies are becoming increasingly aware of the limitations of simplistic research. Organizations and problems in the sphere of law enforcement, as in other fields of endeavor, are seen to exist within a broader system. While the use of a systems approach is new, as a concept it is a product of the past decade. In essence, it has been and remains an attempt to synthesize the research contributions of relevant fields (operations research, educational psychology, etc.). Third, a systems approach provides us with a new perspective on the internal operations and environmental relationships of police organizations. It compels the involved manager or researcher to view the phenomena in an entirely different manner. The solutions arrived at are not likely to be overt in the data or in the stated objectives; yet they must be consistent with existing data and current objectives. Additionally, the available data and theoretical framework are likely to be incomplete and somewhat ambiguous, so that certainty is out of the question. In essence, those who use the systems approach need imagination, judgment, and courage to generate a new perspective. Fourth, the systems approach relies greatly on empirical (hard facts) data. The data of interest to us generally include facts not only on a particular police department but also on the processes, interactions, goals, and other characteristics of all organizations (public and private) that exert an influence on it. Fifth, an important benefit of the systems approach for those in police work is that it is intended to be action oriented. Data are gathered not merely to inform or to describe a relationship, and ideas are evaluated not merely on their cleverness; these activities are pursued because they are instrumental in fulfilling a set of objectives or in solving a problem.

THE POLICE ORGANIZATION AS AN OPEN PARTICIPATIVE SOCIAL SYSTEM

The police organization as an open participative social system provides the point of departure for our forthcoming discussion. All systems possess the following nine characteristics:

1. *Input.* Open systems input various types of energy from their external environment.
2. *Processing.* Open systems process the energy available with an output.
3. *Output.* Open systems output products or services into the environment.
4. *Cyclic Character.* The product or service output furnishes the source of energy for an input and thus the repetition of a cycle.
5. *Arresting of disorganization.* Social systems process and store energy in order to combat the natural trend toward disorganization.
6. *Information input, processing, output, and feedback.* Information is handled much the same as energy. In fact, information can be considered a form of energy.
7. *The steady state.* Open systems seek to maintain a viable ratio between energy input and service output. This state is not to be confused with the *status quo.* A steady state allows for change by constantly adjusting the input and the output so as to achieve a healthy relationship between the two.
8. *Specialization.* Open systems move in the direction of specialization.
9. *Equifinality.* Open systems can reach the same final state from differing initial considerations and by a variety of paths.[31]

In the addition to these nine characteristics, all modern social systems are comprised of the following five subsystems, which enable the total system to accomplish its goals and to survive: (1) operations subsystems to get the work done, (2) maintenance subsystems to indoctrinate people and service machines, (3) supportive subsystems for procurement and environmental relations, (4) adaptive subsystems concerned with organizational change, and (5) managerial subsystems for the direction, coordination, and control of the other subsystems.[32] Obviously, if we were to reshape the present structure of a police organization according to the five subsystems, the result would appear quite different. It would be even more revolutionary when experienced in terms of its new processes—the *new* way of conducting its business. Table 3–1 contains a more detailed explanation of the purpose, functions, and activities of each subsystem.

To the concept of the police organization being an "open" system, we now add one other idea—that of the police department becoming an open and participative organizational structure. The latter idea centers

---

[31]These common characteristics are drawn from Katz and Kahn, *Social Psychology* pp. 19–26.
[32]This typology of subsystems is suggested in *ibid.,* pp. 39–44.

TABLE 3–1

The Subsystems of a Police Organization: Their Purposes, Functions, and Activities

Subsystem	Purpose	Function	Activity
1. Operations Patrol, traffic, investigation, jail, communications, etc.	Efficiency in field operations	Task accomplishment—processing of inputs within the organization	Division of labor: specialization and job standards
2. Maintenance Training, personnel	Maintenance of subsystems: their functions and activities	Mediating between organizational goals and personal needs, indoctrination, and servicing man-machine activities	Establishing operating procedures, training, and equipment maintenance
3. Supportive Community relations	Environmental support for the organization	Exchange with environment to obtain social support	Building favorable image by contributing to the community and by influencing other social systems
4. Adaptive Planning and research	Planned organizational change	Intelligence gathering, research and development, and planning	Making recommendations for change and implementing planned change
5. Managerial Chief of police, staff and subsystem commanders	Control and direction	Resolving internal conflict, coordinating and directing subsystems, coordinating external requirements and organizational resources and needs	Use of authority, adjudication of conflict, increasing of efficiency, adjusting to environmental changes, and restructuring the organization

on increased community involvement through greater decentralization of services. Robert Wood expresses this need and the challenge as follows:

> Our experience in urban administration suggests that one of the critical components in our new urban programs calls for a historical reversal in American administrative doctrine.
>
> Specifically the confrontation now posed is between the several versions of citizen participation that have been foundations in the federal government's urban strategy and the century-old effort in public administration to establish coherent executive structures manned by professionally competent managers. The satisfactory resolution in American political thought is the principal precondition for success in our urban programs. It is on this issue—between effective, purposeful, expert action and widespread public participation—that I focus.[33]

With participation comes a heightened sense representation and reduced apathy and resentment toward an organization.

> But in that century of building professional bureaucracies and executive capacities for leadership, the need for new modes of representation designed to keep pace with new economic, social, and political developments did not arouse equal concern. Partly for this reason, and partly because the burgeoning of large-scale organizations in every area of life contributes to the sensation of individual helplessness, recent years have witnessed an upsurge of a sense of alienation on the part of many people, to a feeling that they as individuals cannot effectively register their own preferences on the decisions emanating from the organs of government. These people have begun to demand redress of the balance among the three values, with special attention to the deficiencies in representativeness.[34]

The movement for representativeness in this generation centers primarily on administrative agencies such as the police. Since administrative agencies have grown dramatically in size, function, and authority—especially in the middle third of this century—this is not surprising. Chief executives, legislatures, and courts make more decisions of *sweeping* effect, but the agencies make a far greater number of decisions affecting individual citizens in *intimate* ways. In them resides the sources of much present unrest; in them, consequently, the remedies are sought.

One type of recommendation for making administrative agencies more representative is traditional—situating spokesmen for the interests affected

[33]Robert C. Wood, "A Call for Return to the Community," *Public Management* 51 (July 1969): 3–4.

[34]Herbert Kaufman, "Administrative Decentralization and Political Power," *Public Administration Review* 29 (January-February 1969): 4.

in strategic positions within the organizations. Frequently, this means nothing more than filling vacancies on existing boards and commissions with appointees enjoying the confidence of, or perhaps even chosen by, those interests. In the case of the controversial police review boards, it involves inserting into administrative structures new bodies, dominated by ethnic minority groups or their friends, to survey and constrain antisocial behavior. Structurally, such plans do not require major modifications of existing organizations, and their purposes could probably be met by changes in personnel at high organizational levels.

Unorthodox, but rapidly gaining acceptance, is the concept of a centralized governmental complaint bureau, with legal powers of investigation, to look into citizen complaints against administrative agencies and to correct inequities and abuses—the office of "ombudsman." The most sweeping expression *of the dissatisfaction over lack of representativeness is the growing demand for extreme administrative decentralization, frequently coupled with insistence on local clientele domination of the decentralized organizations.* Present manifestations of this movement have occurred in the antipoverty program and in education.

The issue of citizen participation is a moral issue—the powerless should have a share of power. It is a legal issue—the right of participation is conferred by law in antipoverty, model cities, and other programs. And it is a practical source—the poor and others of low influence now have enough political power to protect and expand their participatory role.

> In short, "decentralization of administration" is in the air everywhere. While it is sometimes defended on grounds of efficiency, it is more truly justified in terms of effective popular participation in government. Reformers of earlier generations succeeded in raising the level of expertise and professionalism in the bureaucracies, and to a lesser extent, in improving the capacity of chief executives to control the administrative arms of government. Now, people are once again directing their attention to representativeness, and are seeking to elevate it to a more prominent place in the governmental political arena.[35]

The police department's response to the problem of participation and decentralization is under way on a major scale. In general, it can be referred to as *team policing.*[36] Admittedly vague in its meaning to date,

[35]James L. Sundquist, "Citizen, Participation: A New Kind of Management," *Public Management* 51 (July 1969): 9.

[36]For a more comprehensive coverage of this subject see the National Advisory Commission in Criminal Justice Standards and Goals, *Police*, pp. 154–61; and Lawrence W. Sherman, Catherine H. Milton, and Thomas V. Kelly, *Team Policing: Seven Case Studies* (Washington, D.C.: Police Foundation, 1973).

team policing is a sincere and intensive effort to better relate the police department to the community. Essentially, team policing is a vast structural-functional change in local law enforcement. The impetus for team policing rests on the presently recognized ambiguous and transistory nature of the beat officer's relationship with his clientele. No clearly placed responsibility exists for the adequacy of police service in any particular neighborhood. Final accountability is placed only in the chief of police. This is because of the highly centralized command structure (common to all American police departments today), which is primarily organized around time shifts (e.g., 4:00 P.M. to midnight) and includes considerable rotation of full personnel. The beat officer's responsibility is further diminished by the police organization's considerable emphasis on job specialization. Thus, when the beat officer comes upon a crime, he turns over investigation to a detective. If juveniles are involved, the juvenile specialists handle the case from that point. Traffic control activities, too, are handled by functional specialists.

Community-centered team policing attempts to change this situation. This concept seeks transition from a centralized organization to a decentralized one where the beat officer has more responsibility and the citizen has an improved means for participating. The officer will be involved in all police field functions. These can be categorized into three types: *major crime functions* (including the use of patrol strategies and tactics to prevent serious crimes and disturbances, the collection of information on such activities, and the endeavor to apprehend perpetrators); *traffic functions* (including the control of pedestrian and vehicular movement, the investigation of accidents, and the alleviation of congestion when it arises); and *social service functions* (including the pursuit of order and peace-keeping activities demanding use of police advice and authority—control of minor disturbances, intervention in family crises, etc.—as well as activities where assistance rather than authority is required, e.g., aid to injured and elderly persons, and improvement of relations with the community).

The generalist-officer will have total responsibility for these functions on his beat. Further modifications would be made on the basis of such factors as community wishes, evaluation of functional and cost effectiveness of the police teams with regard to a particular function, and evaluation of functional and cost effectiveness of possible alternative agency (or citizen) discharge of the function. To illustrate, thirty police officers and thirty community service officers, directed by a supervisor and lower-level group leaders, might be the best team for a given geographical area. To assist in the impetus of bureaucratic change, it is expected that team members will have distinctive uniforms, automobiles, and equipment. Members of the teams will be allowed to dress in uniform or out of uniform according to the assignment they expect to be on. One team model would provide that team officers and leaders undergo a four-week training program designed to teach needed skills, including family crisis intervention and investigative methods. Members will then be required to live with a family in their beat neighborhood for a few days to learn the values and norms of the local culture.

In addition to police officers and supervisors, a number of integrative or supportive personnel will work on the team. Community service officers are one such possibility. They will attempt to increase police responsiveness to neighborhood concerns and will thus be responsible for handling many of the social service tasks which now fall to the police and are of great importance to the neighborhood. At the same time, they will also work with individual team members in dealing with special problems where the community service officer's experience would be beneficial. A position of community coordinator is also envisioned. This person will develop within the community an understanding of what the police are doing, interpret policy to the community, and, most importantly, assist the community in representing its concerns and interest to the department. The community coordinator will be a resident of the neighborhood hired to assist the community in developing defensive security tactics, community concern, and community action.

In summary, then, the term *team policing* describes an endeavor to increase decentralization in order to enhance the level of citizen participation and acceptance of the police department. Regretfully, space does not permit a more thorough description of the police organization as an open and participative system. Such an attempt would require the writing of another text, in addition to considerable research. For those interested in a start in this direction, see the texts *The Human Organization* and *Organizing Men and Power: Patterns of Behavior and Line-Staff Models*,[37] which suggest new organizational structures fod decentralizing the efforts of employees for greater effectiveness.

COORDINATING THE SYSTEM: Differentiation and Integration

First, there is no one best way for a police department to organize; second, the organizational structure should be directly dependent on the types of decisions that the police personnel must make and on the demands of their environment.[38]

[37]Rensis Likert, *The Human Organization* (New York: McGraw-Hill Book Company, 1967); and Robert T. Golembiewski, *Organizing Men and Power: Patterns of Behavior and Line-Staff Models (Chicago: Rand McNally & Co., 1967).* See also Paul R. Lawrence and Jay W. Lorsch, *Developing Organizations: Diagnosis and Action* (Reading, Mass.: Addison-Wesley Publishing Company, Inc., 1969).

[38]Paul M. Whisenand and R. Fred Ferguson, *The Managing of Police Organizations,* 1st ed. (Englewood Cliffs, N.J.: Prentice-Hall, Inc. 1973), p. 256.

Who would doubt that most police personnel are daily confronted with monumentally complex decisions? And who would doubt that many police organizations are faced with dynamic and uncertain environments where the classical principles of management do not work at all well? Significantly, we qualified the above statements with "most" and "many." The reason is that not all police departments require the same type of organizational structure. In those situations where a department is not confronted by difficult decisions or by a highly diverse environment, the classical approach may be the most effective of all possible approaches, although it is apparently seldom used today.

What does coordination and specialization have to do with the above discussion? Moreover, what does the manager have to do with specialization and coordination? Each question is now furnished with an answer. One brief but vital point of clarification: The terms *specialization* and *differentiation* and, similarly, *coordination* and *integration* will be used synonymously. It is felt that the term *differentiation* is more descriptive of the change created in organizations through specialization. Furthermore, the term *integration* best suggests the interdependency of work units mentioned earlier.

The structure of an organization is based on (1) the division of work into small, single task units, and (2) the coordination of work into a cohesive whole so as to propel it toward its stated goals. A quick glance at the *Municipal Police Administration* provides us with a fairly good notion of how the police service has in many instances "broken up" its organizational structure.[39] In addition to *horizontal differentiation* (work specialization), police organizations are also broken up on a vertical basis (levels of authority): line, supervisor, middle manager, manager, and administrator. Clearly, differentiation is of major degree in most medium- to large-scale police departments. Why? Because the environment and the types of decisions to be made demand it! Hence we are stuck with the need for differentiation. At the same time we become victims of its harmful effects. Stahl alleges:

> In my judgment, the most serious fault in organization life is not the much overworked "interference by staff with the line" but the curse of specialization. I submit that the preoccupation of any specialist, whether line or staff, with the trivia of his profession and his tendency to relate all that goes on about him to the particular orbit of his work assignment, causes more trouble than anything else.[40]

[39]George D. Eastman and Esther M. Eastman, eds., *Municipal Police Administration,* 6th ed. (Washington, D.C.: International City Management Association, 1969).
[40]O. Glenn Stahl, "More on the Network of Authority," *Public Administration Review* 20 (Winter 1960): 36.

Recent research findings show that specialized (differentiated) groups within an organization (1) exhibit less risk-taking behavior ("Don't make any waves!"), (2) are less efficient, and (3) are less productive than non-differentiated groups.[41] And, surprisingly, the emphasis upon integration has received little notice. The principle of specialization has had the lion's share of attention.[42]

Thus far we have seen that differentiation in a police department is on the one hand a necessity and on the other hand—a problem. We need a differentiated structure in order to respond effectively to called-for police services; although, at the same time, differentiation causes the organization to become fragmented, which results in reduced effectiveness. At first sight we appear to have an irresolvable dilemma. Our vehicle for either reducing or eliminating the injurious effects while sustaining the advantages of differentiation is through integrative measures and devices. It is well recognized that high levels of differentiation and integration are naturally antagonisitc states. But, even though antagonistic to each other, both can be achieved and to a high degree! In due recognition of the fact, Lawrence and Lorsch write:

> But this finding still leaves us with a curious contradiction. If, as we have found, differentiation and integration work at cross purposes within each organization, how can two organizations achieve high degrees of both? The best approach to explaining this apparent paradox becomes evident if we consider how organizations might go about achieving both of these states. If organizations have groups of highly differentiated managers who are able to work together effectively, these managers must have strong capacities to deal with interdepartmental conflicts. A high degree of differentiation implies that managers will view problems differently and that conflicts will inevitably arise about how best to proceed. Effective integration, however, means that these conflicts must be resolved to the approximate satisfaction of all parties and to the general good of the enterprise. This provides an important clue to how two of these organizations met the environmental requirements for high differentiation and high integration. These two organizations differed from the others in the procedures and practices used to reach interdepartmental decisions and to resolve conflict.[43]

An off-setting degree of integration is critical for organizational health and effectiveness. Appropriate levels of integration are advantageous for

[41]For details, see Edwin M. Bridges, Wayne F. Doyle, and David F. Mahan, "Effects of Hierarchical Differentiation on Group Productivity, Efficiency, and Risk Taking," *Administrative Science Quarterly* 13 (September 1968): 305–21.

[42]Golembiewski, *Organizing Men,* p. 261.

[43]Paul R. Lawrence and Jay W. Lorsch, *Organization and Management: Managing Differentiation and Integration* (Boston: Harvard University Press, 1967), p. 53.

two reasons. First, intraorganizational conflict is decreased which, in turn, improves the quality of internal communications, group and individual task functions, group and individual problem solving, leadership, intergroup cooperation, and overall efficiency.[44] The following section describes some of the more useful procedures and practices for conflict resolution. Second, under twentieth-century conditions of constant change there has been an emergence of human sciences and a deeper understanding of man's complexity. Today, integration encompasses the entire range of issues concerned with incentives, rewards, and motivations of the individual and the way the organization succeeds or fails in adjusting to these issues. Thus, an integrated organizational structure facilitates the merging of individual needs and administrative goals.

Within the role of a police manager is the often neglected responsibility for integrating the various parts of the organization with one another, and the individual with his organization. The fundamental process establishing and maintaining integration is referred to as *conflict resolution*. The various mechanisms and techniques for resolving organizational conflict must be tailored to the unique conditions existing within the structure. The conditions are, in turn, a product of the organization's environment. Therefore, the police manager must first understand the demands of the environment before he is able to decide how much differentiation and integration is required in his department. Based on this understanding he is in a position to select those conflict resolvers that will furnish the proper balance between differentiation and integration.

The police manager starts by first looking at how much differentiation should exist among the various groupss. As already suggested, this depends upon what internal characteristics each group must develop to carry out planned transactions with its assigned part of the environment. More specifically, it depends primarily upon the extent to which the certainty of information within the various parts of the environment is similar or different. If these parts of the environment (e.g., the community, criminal events, traffic safety, noncriminal services) are fairly predictable in their degree of certainty, the work units will need to be fairly similar in formal organizational practices and members' orientations. If these parts of the environment have quite different or unpredictable degrees of certainty, the units will need to be more differentiated, for example, the information required by the traffic officer is more certain as compared with that needed by the detective.

---

[44]Considerable research evidence shows that structural features that inhibit integration and cooperation produce conflict. For example, see Richard E. Walton, John M. Dutton, and Thomas P. Cofferty, "Organizational Context and Interdepartmental Conflict," *Administrative Science Quarterly* 14 (December 1969): 522–43.

Next, the police manager focuses his attention on two aspects of the integration issue: (1) Which units are required to work together? and (2) How tight is the requirement for interdependence among them? But there is a strong inverse relationship between differentiation and integration. As we have indicated, when units (because of their particular tasks) are highly differentiated, it is more difficult to achieve integration among them than when the individuals in the units have similar ways of thinking and behaving. As a result, when groups in a police organization need to be highly differentiated (as is the case in most medium to large metropolitan law enforcement agencies), but also require tight integration, it is necessary for the organization to develop more complicated integrating mechanisms. The principal organizational mechanism for achieving integration is, of course, the management hierarchy. Downs attests to this fact in his law of hierarchy:

> *Coordination of large-scale activities without markets requires a hierarchical authority structure. This Law results directly from the limited capacity of each individual, plus the existence of ineradicable sources of conflict among individuals.*[45]

Let us repeat our central proposition—how well the police organization will succeed in achieving integration, therefore, depends to a great extent upon how the individual personnel resolve their conflicts.[46] The means of conflict resolution can be divided into *structural* and *behavioral* (in operation they are not mutually exclusive but high interrelated). The former is exclusively determined by the environment—a variable. The latter is determined in part by the environment, and in part is constant for all administrative systems. Both means of handling conflict are critical to those police organizations faced with the requirement for both a high degree of differentiation and tight integration. The structural integrating devices are (1) individual coordinators, (2) cross-unit teams, and (3) whole bureaus of individuals whose basic contribution is achieving integration among other groups. An example of the first device is a single police inspector functioning as a linkage between specialized units such as patrol and traffic. The latter two devices can sometimes be seen in such units as planning and research, and police community relations.

As mentioned above, the pattern of behavior that leads to effective

---

[45]Anthony Downs, *Inside Bureaucracy* (Boston: Little, Brown and Company 1967), p. 52.

[46]There is a large body of research in support of this proposition. See for an example John M. Ivancevich and James H. Donnelly, Jr., "Relations of Organizational Structure to Job Satisfaction, Anxiety, Stress, and Performance," *Administrative Science Quarterly* 20 (June 1975): 272–80.

conflict resolution varies in certain respects depending upon environmental demands, and in other respects is the same *regardless* of variations
in environmental demands. The conflict management factor that varies
with *environmental demands* is essentially power within and among
groups. The power within and among groups means the organizational
level *at which power resides* to make decisions leading to the resolution
of conflict. If conflict is to be managed effectively, this power must be
concentrated at the point in and between the various group hierarchies
where the *knowledge* to reach such decisions also exists. Obviously, this
will vary depending upon the certainty of information in various parts
of a particular environment. The factors that lead to effective conflict
resolution under all *environmental conditions* are (1) the mode of conflict resolution and (2) the basis from which influence is derived. In
police organizations existing in quite different environments we have
found that effective police management occurs when the police personnel deal openly with conflict and work the problem until they reach a
resolution that is best in terms of total departmental goals. In essence,
effective police organizations confront internal conflicts rather than
smooth them over or exercise raw power to force one unit or person to
accept a solution.

In police departments dealing effectively with conflict, one also finds
that the police personnel primarily involved in achieving integration,
whether they be superiors or persons in coordinating roles, need to have
influence based largely upon their perceived *knowledge and competence*.
In other words, they are followed not just because they have formal posi-
tional influence but because they are seen as knowledgeable about the
issues that have to be resolved. Before leaving the subject of conflict, we
want the reader to realize that organizational conflict is inevitable and
not necessarily always harmful. Conflict becomes injurious to the police
department when it is at too high a level, ineffectively handled, and not
tolerated at all. An organization that does not have a certain amount of
internal conflict is not doing anything! To summarize:

> Conflict can have both dysfunctional and functional consequences,
> as Coser (1956) has pointed out. It can lead to heightened morale
> within a subsystem and it can lead to solutions which move more
> in an integrative than a compromise direction. Organizations gen-
> erally develop mechanisms to handle internal struggles and devices
> to dull the sharp edges of conflict. As we have already noted in large
> complex organizations one of the main functions of top manage-
> ment is the adjudication of competing claims and conflicting de-
> mands.[47]

[47]Katz and Kahn, *Social Psychology,* p. 63.

LEARNING EXERCISE

SENSING AND
TEAM BUILDING[48]

Goals

1. To help an intact police agency diagnose its own functioning.
2. To build a cooperative expectation into a police group.
3. To assist a police manager (chief, sheriff, captain) to develop norms of openness, trust, and interdependence among police team members.
4. To help police team members to clarify and evaluate their own goals, the team's goals, and the relation between those two sets of aims.

Group Size. No more than fifteen members.

Time Required. A minimum of three days.

Materials Utilized

1. Sensing Interview Guide (see Exhibit 3–1).
2. Large sheets of newsprint.
3. Felt-tip markers.

Physical Setting. Private room with wall space for posting.

Process

1. Phase 1. *Sensing.* Prior to the team-building meeting, the facilitator interviews each of the team members, privately and confidentially. He indicates to each what his purposes are, what the limits of confidentiality are, and what he is going to do with the interview data. The Sensing Interview Guide may be used and/or adapted in preparation for these interviews.

2. Phase 2. *Data Analysis.* The interview data are analyzed by the facilitator. He may note common themes running through the responses of team members. He prepares a series of posters from the data: a poster of data pertaining to each team member, a poster containing data on the group's process (decision-making patterns, communication phenomena, etc.), a poster displaying goal statements, a poster of team-building meeting objectives, and any other groupings of data which emerge from his analysis.

---

[48]The exercise is taken with permission from J. William Pfeiffer and John E. Jones, *A Handbook of Structured Experiences for Human Relations Training* (La Jolla, Calif.: University Associates Press, 1971), 3: 82–86.

3. Phase 3. *Team-Building.* The team assembles in a room that will permit a minimum of outside interruptions. The facilitator explains the goals of the two-day meeting, and he posts his objectives. Then he posts all of the rest of the interview data, explaining how he analyzed the data. He spends the rest of the meeting facilitating the team's working of the posted data, reinforcing openness, risk-taking, trust, and interdependence. He may suggest a confrontation between the manager and the rest of the members, but he is careful to help the manager to learn how to give and receive feedback nondefensively. The facilitator helps the team members to learn how to observe group process. . . . Decisions made by the group are written on newsprint and posted. The facilitator may wish to urge members to develop contracts with each other for follow-up.

A variation on the sensing strategy described above is the *sensing meeting*. The manager calls a meeting to gather data on his part of the organization. He chairs the meeting, soliciting data and writing them on a chalkboard. The facilitator helps the manager to listen, not to react defensively, and to record the data. The manager then commits himself to a definite course of action in dealing with the data. These meetings may consist of the manager and his immediate assistants, or they may include vertical, horizontal, or diagonal slices of the organization. All subordinates joining the organization within the last year, for example, may be able to point up blind spots in the structure.

Exhibit 3-1.

SENSING INTERVIEW GUIDE

Name_____ Interviewer_____

Date_____ Time_____ to _____

Format ____Face to Face ____Phone Place_____

1. Title (s) of interviewee_____

2. Relation to the team_____

    _____

3. Satisfaction with team's current functioning_____

    _____

4. Goals of the team_____

    _____

    _____

5. Personal goals_____

    _____

    _____

6. How decisions are made_____

    _____

7. Problems of the team right now_____

    _____

    _____

8. Personal problems related to team right now_____

    _____

9. Needed action strategies right now_____

    _____

Exhibit 3–1 (Continued)

10. Feelings about team-building meeting_____

_____

_____

11. Relationships with other team members

    First Name

    1._____(manager/leader/chairman/supervisor)_____

    _____

    2._____ _____

    _____

    3._____ _____

    _____

    4._____ _____

    _____

    5._____ _____

    _____

    6._____ _____

    _____

    7._____ _____

    _____

    8._____ _____

    _____

    9._____ _____

    _____

    10._____ _____

    _____

Exhibit 3–1 (Continued)

11. _____ _____
    _____

12. _____ _____
    _____

13. _____ _____
    _____

14. _____ _____
    _____

15. _____ _____
    _____

12. Other comments_____
    _____
    _____
    _____
    _____

Chapter Four

TASK 2 LEADING:
Leadership Styles

Concern about leadership of police agencies is increasing. Americans are becoming increasingly concerned with crime and their personal safety. The public is looking to the most visible part of the criminal justice system—the police—for leadership. The one individual to whom a State or community looks for professional police leadership is the police chief executive.[1]

SYNOPSIS

Leading in modern police organizations requires, in addition to specific prerequisite skills and experience, a knowledge of modern management theory. Traditionally, law enforcement, like many government agencies, has followed the bureaucratic model with impersonality of interpersonal relations, heavy reliance upon written rules and regulations, and promotions based upon technical competence. In this chapter we have attempted to build a case for taking leave of the bureaucratic model. The leader in his optimum role has become sensitized not only to the organizational needs but to the needs of his subordinates as well. He is aware that subordinates must perceive their work as important and that they must be afforded a measure of autonomy if they are to be self-actualized.

The leader in our model has the ability to move flexibly among seven different leadership styles, making certain that subordinates are aware of the particular style being used.

We suggest that there is support for the theory that current leadership selection methods are in need of modification; that leaders should be competent in the position sought, before promotion; and that provisions should be made to move qualified persons around the system as opposed to the traditional concept that each man must start at the bottom.

The *leader* is not just the purveyor of routine orders, but the one who is capable of bringing order to confusion—in the face of emergency.

In addition to a discussion of the leader we will explore the emerging leadership posture we feel most appropriate for modern law enforcement organizations. This chapter will also cover the various styles of leadership and their applications; the need for sup-

[1]A Report of the Police Chief Executive Committee of the International Association of Chiefs of Police, *The Police Chief Executive Report* (Washington, D.C.: Law Enforcement Assistance Administration, U.S. Department of Justice, 1976), p. 2.

portive relationships; the need for self-actualization and the selection of future leaders.

INTRODUCTION

Leadership is that vague, elusive term used to describe a variety of traits or qualities of persons holding positions of responsibility for the success of any given organization or group. There are, of course, informal leaders in most organizations and groups but those will be covered in chapter 7.

The leaders with whom we are concerned are those formal leaders who hold or aspire to key positions in law enforcement agencies and upon whose abilities the success or failure (or mediocrity) of the organization or unit they command is predicated. The "definition of leadership includes many routine acts of supervision; the essence of leadership, however, has to do with that *influential increment* which goes beyond routine and taps bases of power beyond those which are organizationally decreed."[2]

The police, like other modern organizations, have an ever-growing need for effective, creative leaders at every level. Hierarchical levels are traditionally depicted on organizational charts, which are of course helpful in formalizing areas of leadership responsibility. Charts, however, and their accompanying role descriptions do not necessarily portray the kind of leader who will fill a given position or tell how effective he will be.

Obviously, those persons who fill the leader positions are of vital importance, far beyond their immediate scope of influence, for it is they who set the tone for the present and future health of the organization. Organizational health means the difference between success and failure in the private sectors. In government, the organization can often continue to exist, though unhealthy in the sense that it is not operating in a most efficient manner. This kind of operation does reflect its inadequacy in other ways, however, such as being unable to approach the attainment of desirable or acceptable standards of service.

Granted, many variables can influence the health of organizations, but none are more critical than those of leadership.

While leadership is a variable of organizational health, it, too, is com-

[2]Daniel Katz and Robert L. Kahn, *The Social Psychology of Organizations* (New York: John Wiley & Sons, Inc., 1966), p. 334.

prised of multiple subvariables, some of which will be discussed later in the chapter. Transplanting or superimposing a proven successful leader over an ailing organization in no way insures success. There is a concomitant need to choose the right leader for the particular job.

Pfiffner and Sherwood support this belief with a rather poignant example:

> We have all observed occasions where a change in the leadership has had a pronounced effect on the organization. There is, as one illustration, General Omar Bradley's story of the problem of command in the 90th Infantry Division during World War II. The 90th was brought to Europe by a new division commander who had had no chance to train with it. It was thrown into the Normandy bridgehead and performed miserably. After four days, the division commander was relieved. But a new general and a thorough shakeup of the staff made little difference. The division was floundering so badly that Bradley's subordinates wanted to break it up, sending the men to other units.
>
> However, Bradley rejected the idea. His refusal was at least in part based on his own philosophy of command in the military: ". . . man for man one division is just as good as another—they vary only in the skill and leadership of their commanders." Thus the answer to the 90th's problem was not to destroy the division but to find the right man for command. Bradley's next choice turned out to be such a person. The new commander made exactly 16 changes in the 16,000 man organization. When he left the division a few months later to assume command of a corps, "his successor inherited one of the finest divisions in combat on the allied front."
>
> Bradley's strong conviction that the men at the top make the difference—and his vindication by the performance of the 90th—is rather dramatic testimony that leadership can be an important modifier of organizational behavior.[3]

Obviously, a great deal of information is acquired on career men in the military service. Both predecessors of the successful Ninetieth Division commander had undoubtedly demonstrated successful leadership before their appointment or they would never have been given such a critical assignment, and yet they failed.

This phenomenon is not particularly unusual, for we have all observed successful leaders from the private sector or from other areas of govern-

[3] John M. Pfiffner and Frank P. Sherwood, *Administrative Organization* (Englewood Cliffs, N.J.: Prentice-Hall, Inc., 1960), pp. 348–49.

ment who have been appointed to positions at the presidential cabinet level and have failed. Leadership in itself is not enough—they must be the right leaders.

LEADERSHIP

At this point it seems appropriate to examine the rather elusive term *leadership*, which in itself "is the art of coordinating and motivating individuals and groups to achieve desired ends."[4] As a rule, "leadership" is used to generalize a myriad of qualities, some learned, some inherent, that are brought together in the right combination for the right job. Typically, as small boys imitate their fathers, organizational members with leadership aspirations often strive to "be like" the leaders they admire. While it is possible to learn some aspects of leadership, and to at least partially emulate certain leadership styles, it is our belief that the truly successful leader is a man who *has found himself*, not a man who continutes to "be like" another. Research on the subject of leadership has apparently been unable to isolate any significant number of qualities or traits common to all our successful leaders; no one seems to have discovered an all-encompassing, "sure-fire" formula for guaranteed successful leadership. We do know, however, as mentioned in the introduction, that weak organizations have grown healthy with dynamic leadership and that previously healthy organiztions have crumbled for lack of it.

Furthermore, although a number of our more academically oriented colleagues believe that a successful professional leader can, without regard for his field, be effectively superimposed on any organization, we do not subscribe to this theory.

Although it may be true, to some degree, that a good manager may be able to move about and direct different kinds of organizations, we do not believe this is wholly true in government. Laws that control our operations in government are substantially different from those in private enterprise. The nongovernment management sector has a great deal more latitude, more discretion, fewer regulations to contend with, and most often, greater flexibility. Governmental agencies at all levels are highly complex, but in our opinion none is more so than law enforcement. We doubt the validity of the thought espoused by some learned persons that we could actually bring on board a highly successful lawyer

---

[4]John M. Pfiffner and Robert V. Presthus, *Public Administration* (New York: The Ronald Press Company, 1960), p. 92.

or a good chamber of commerce manager, for example, and have either of them run a police department adequately. We believe that the complexities of modern law enforcement are such that successful police leaders must be reared in the police service.

Different kinds of organizations, even different kinds of policing organizations, call for different kinds of leaders. We could perhaps carry it even a step further and say that different kinds of communities might require different kinds of leadership. This does not imply that one leader would be strong and another weak, but rather, that one kind of community might, for example, require a leader who, in addition to other prerequisite skills, was endowed with particular attributes that permitted him to accomplish some goals on a social plane, while another community might have no such need. There are exceptionally affluent communities within our societies where a police chief would be expected to have deep social commitments or involvements. On the other hand, there are industrialized areas where a police chief would probably have little or no social involvement. Hence, the personality need of these leaders would tend to be different. In leadership, then, personality does appear to play a vital role not only from within the organization but from without as well.

The needs of an organization, the needs of the people themselves, and the product involved all play vital roles in the type of leadership required. Yet "typing" a leader is almost, if not, impossible.

We must again emphasize that few attributes, save perhaps self-confidence and personal commitment to specific goals, can be identified as being held in common by all great leaders, and this is more fully realized when one considers the unique individualities of men like Gandhi and Churchill. It takes many different attributes to make a leader. For example, the late Martin Luther King had certain qualities that made him a successful leader. Yet, when one attempts to equate him with a man like the late General George Patton, there is a full spectrum of difference even though the two men undoubtedly had some traits in common.

We have acknowledged the inability to isolate any significant number of traits common to successful leaders. Davis, however, in discussing successful managers, did list ten traits he viewed as *essential* for success:

1. Intelligence
2. Experience
3. Originality
4. Receptiveness

5. Teaching ability

6. Personality

7. Knowledge of human behavior

8. Courage

9. Tenacity

10. A sense of justice and fair play[5]

While Davis was looking at industrial organizations, we believe that his observations are equally applicable to police leaders.

Actually, Davis identified fifty-six managerial characteristics and traits but doubted that all would be possessed by any single individual.

He did not include *creativity* in his ten basic traits. Perhaps at the time of his study creativity was not a popular term. We believe, however, in light of the complexity of police organizations and the criticalness of the time, that creativity is an essential managerial element. "The creative person is able to be flexible; he can change course as the situation changes (which it always does); he can give up his plans, he can continuously and flexibly adapt to the law of the changing situation and to the changing authority of the facts, to the demand character of the shifting problem."[6]

A CHANGING ART

It is not our desire to develop a treatise on the evolution of management or leadership concepts. Since we are speaking of leadership in a modern police organization, we will confine our remarks to applicable contemporary thought except to acknowledge that an evolutionary process has been taking place since the recorded history of man. In modern times, however, we have not observed the police leadership process evolving at the same rate as the private sector—nonetheless, it is changing.

In law enforcement, as in business, we have tended to be goal oriented. There has been, to oversimplify, a shift from goal to employee orientation, with a blend of both in the private sector. In our opinion, however the police for the most part have remained singly oriented toward the organizational goals. We are not implying that the law enforcement goals are passé. We are suggesting that a more effective leadership posture for modern law enforcement is to be equally concerned with the personal needs of the employee as well as those of the organization.

[5]Ralph Currier Davis, *Industrial Organization and Management* (New York: Harper & Brothers, 1940), p. 32.
[6]Abraham H. Maslow, *Eupsychian Management* (Homewood, Ill.: Richard D. Irwin, Inc., and The Dorsey Press, 1965), p. 192.

Schein, with Maslow and other social scientists, has "come to the conclusion that organizational life has removed meaning from work".[7] They were primarily concerned with industry, but we feel that the same problem is occurring in police departments as they become compartmentalized into highly specialized units. "This loss of meaning is not related so much to man's *social* needs, however, as to man's inherent need to use his capabilities and skills in a mature productive way."[8] Few police officers are assigned to a given area and simply made responsible for certain law enforcement goals there, or are permitted wide latitude as to how those goals are approached. Instead, like those in the factory, policemen's responsibilities tend to be carefully set forth in operation-procedure manuals, breaking the total responsibility into small, measurable segments. We, like the social scientists, are concerned that jobs have become so specialized or fragmented that they neither permit the policeman "to use his capabilities nor enable him to see the relationship between what he is doing and the total organizational mission."[9] An example is the policeman who writes traffic citations "to keep the sergeant off his back" and is unaware of the total traffic safety mission and of how his inputs at the proper time and place could be a significant contribution to the reduction of traffic accidents.

SELF-ACTUALIZED MAN

Schein brings the concept of self-actualization into better focus for us in a discussion of man and his relationship to Maslow's *hierarchy of needs.*

> a. Man's motives fall into classes which are arranged in a hierarchy: (1) simple needs for survival, safety and security; (2) social and affiliative needs; (3) ego-satisfaction and self-esteem needs; (4) needs for autonomy and independence; and (5) self-actualization needs in the sense of maximum use of all his resources. As the lower-level needs are satisfied, they release some of the higher-level motives. Even the lowliest untalented man seeks self-actualization, a sense of meaning and accomplishment in his work, if his other needs are more or less fulfilled.
>
> b. Man seeks to be mature on the job and is capable of being so. This means the exercise of a certain amount of autonomy and independence, the adoption of a long-range time perspective, the development of special capacities and skills, and greater flexibility in adapting to circumstances.

[7]Edgar H. Schein, *Organizational Psychology* (Englewood Cliffs, N.J.: Prentice-Hall, Inc., 1965), p. 56.
[8]*Ibid.*
[9]*Ibid.*

c. Man is primarily self-motivated and self-controlled; externally imposed incentives and controls are likely to threaten the person and reduce him to a less mature adjustment.

d. There is no inherent conflict between self-actualization and more effective organization performance. If given a chance, man will voluntarily integrate his own goals with those of the organization.[10]

Most of the young people being recruited into the police service today have been born since World War II and know little about life in a major depression; their fathers have always been employed, as they themselves; they have been raised in a social affiliative era and have belonged to such organizations since entering elementary school; they are accustomed to being patted on the back for a job well done; and finally, they have enjoyed a greater degree of independence than have the young people of any previous generation. By the time they are recruited into the police service, their basic needs have been met and accepted as a way of life and they have been conditioned to expect a great deal of independence.

We believe that police organizations and police leadership will need to be modified to accommodate the emerging generation of police. We are convinced that some autonomy can be built in at every level and that, with this autonomy, an emphasis on self-actualization can be a most responsible approach to leadership in modern police organizations.

In leaving this area, we should point out that assisting others in self-actualization is much easier when the leader himself is self-actualized, when he is making the best use of his own potential, and when his job has meaning and importance.

LEADERSHIP STYLES

In suggesting that leaders in modern police organizations should be equally concerned with both the organizational goals and the employees' needs, we refrained from referring to this posture or philosophy as a "style." It appears that there are a number of leadership styles, any one of which can be used in conjunction with a particular managerial philosophy. "Consideration of the situation, the followers, and the personality of the leader would be most successful."[11]

Pfiffner and Sherwood, Argyris, Bennis, Etzioni, Schein, and others have recognized and discussed leadership styles in varying degrees. Apple-

---

[10]*Ibid.*, pp. 56–57.

[11]Philip B. Applewhite, *Organizational Behavior* (Englewood Cliffs, N.J.: Prentice-Hall, Inc., 1965), p. 131.

white lists five main styles which are generally representative: authoritarian, democratic, laissez-faire, bureaucratic, and charismatic.[12]

In a more contemporary manner, University of Southern California Professor Terry Polin has suggested seven appropriate styles of leadership, four of which were originally identified by Tannenbaum and Schmidt in their study of boss-centered versus employee-centered leadership.[13] Polin's seven styles are "tells, sells, tests, consults, joins, abdicates, and blocks."[14] Examples of each of these follow.

For the first leadership style, "tells," imagine a large metropolitan police station. The sergeant reports to the station commander that he has just discovered a bomb in the lobby and that it may go off at any moment. The commander quickly calls his staff together and says, "Men, we have a little bomb problem here and I wondered if we could have a discussion to decide what we should do about it." Obviously, no one in an emergency situation such as this expects to have a discussion type of communication. What is wanted is a dictator. At this time the commander had better become an autocrat and say, "Evacuate the area, notify the bomb detail," and so forth.

In the second leadership style, "sells," the sergeant approaches the station commander and inquires, "Do you want the men to wear helmets or their soft hats for the fourth of July parade duty?" There is normally a morale problem when officers are required to wear helmets on hot days. On the other hand, the commander has information that a radical activist group may take advantage of the large crowd to cause a disturbance. The commander should say, "We will wear helmets," and he should explain why.

In the third leadership style, "tests," the sergeant approaches the commander and says, "We have a vacation problem. Six men with equal seniority have applied for vacation leave at the same time. Normally this wouldn't have created a problem, but this year all personnel have been granted an extra week, and we only have coverage for twelve man-weeks." The commander has two immediate alternatives—he can grant each of the six their normal two weeks, saving one week for a later time in the year, or he can try to get two of them to take vacations in a different time period. In this case he should say to the six, "All of you are entitled to three weeks' vacation this year and all of you have requested the same

---

[12]*Ibid.*

[13]R. Tannenbaum and W. H. Schmidt, "How to Choose a Leadership Pattern," *Harvard Business Review,* 29 (March-April 1958): 36. (*Reprinted in The Journal of Applied Behavioral Science* 6, No. 1) (1970): 7.

[14]Terry Polin, a lecture delivered at the University of California School of Business Administration, 1967.

vacation period. The problem is that we can't cover all of your positions for more than twelve work-weeks. Are there two of you who would just as soon take your three weeks' vacation at a different time?" What he is saying is, "What do you think of the idea?" If they react against it, he is not in the position where he must back down. If the men say that they do not like the idea at all, he can go back to the original two-week plan, scheduling the odd weeks at a later time.

In the fourth leadership style, "consults," there is some selling and some testing; a kind of manipulating. The object is to get the person to buy without telling him to do so. In this situation, the sergeant comes to the commander and says, "On July first we shifted into summer uniforms. I noticed in this morning's paper that the expected high today is going to be an unusually low sixty degrees. What should we do?" In this case the commander should say to the men, "The newspaper indicates that we will probably have sixty-degree weather today. We have two choices: one, to remain in the summer uniform in hope that the weather will warm up; or two, to shift into the winter uniform for this one day. If you would like to remain in the summer uniform, raise your hand." The men are then instructed to wear the uniform that received the most popular vote. This is a sort of, "You tell me what you want."

In the fifth leadership style, "joins," the sergeant comes to the station commander and says, "There is a child vomiting in the lobby. What do you want me to do?" The commander replies, "You handle this yourself." What he is saying is, "I'm no different than any other person in the building. I'm not going to tell you how to clean up vomit. You must handle it yourself. I'm part of the group. I'm joining the group."

In the sixth leadership style, "abdicates," the station commander sees the sergeant coming and he turns quickly and locks the door. What he is saying is, "I do not want to become involved with you."

In the seventh leadership style, "blocks," the station commander may decide that the best way to handle this sergeant is to keep him busy. He gives him so many projects to do that he cannot think of problems for the commander to resolve.

Our position is that no *one* leadership style is sufficient unto itself and that all seven styles are appropriate for law enforcement leaders when utilized at appropriate times.

Telling is most appropriate in those situations requiring immediate action; when any delay is likely to result in negative consequences for the organization and where the leader doing the telling is in the best position, and has the best information, to do so. For maximum effectiveness his subordinates must also be perceptive of the above elements.

Selling is simply recognizing that most people are in a better position to, and are more likely to, support the boss if they understand *why*.

Testing provides the leader with some indication of a decision's likely success *before* he makes it and, at the same time, allows an alternative course of action should the reaction be negative.

Consulting should in reality be separated into several parts, which can be generalized as follows: The first involves situations in which there are two or more appropriate solutions to choose from, any of which is acceptable to the leader. He furnishes the list of solutions and takes a vote, selecting the most popular. An arbitrary decision has been avoided and a high degree of compliance is likely. The second involves the leader's sharing a problem with qualified subordinates; qualified in the sense that the background of each is appropriate to the problem. Each is expected to make contributions to the solution, and when all possible alternatives have been explored, each is polled for his opinion of the best solution, which is finally selected by majority vote. The third and last involves the leader's sharing a problem, in which he has discrete information, with subordinates. He makes it known that he needs their inputs to add to his own information and that using the total data he personally will make the necessary decision.

Consulting has many important facets. It includes a sharing of responsibility, participative management, team building, personal commitment, and developing future leaders. It also assists present leaders in that it broadens their base of influence, provides better solutions, relieves part of the burden of command, and develops future support.

Joining, in a sense, is acknowledging that the boss does not have all of the answers and that in some instances his opinion has no more value than that of any other person in the group. In another way it provides the vehicle, the climate, for decisions to be made at the appropriate level. In law enforcement, as in the military, there is often a tendency to expect decisions to be made, or at least cleared, by the highest-ranking officer present. In these instances, it is important to place the responsibility back down where it belongs.

Abdicating will undoubtedly cause concern for those who believe that they must be available at all times. But an important factor in the development of future leaders, of leaders who are capable of assuming greater levels of responsibility, is the learning of decision-making skills. Every police officer is faced with critical decisions when there is no superior to turn to. Indecisive police officers are a luxury that law enforcement cannot afford. People who learn to make appropriate decisions under nonstress situations are more likely to be effective when emergencies do occur.

Obviously, effective leaders would not abdicate in critical situations where a bad decision might have far-reaching implications. On the other hand, if it is true that people learn by doing, it must also be true that intelligent people learn from their mistakes. We believe it absolutely vital that neophyte decision makers, in addition to being forced to make decisions, be permitted to experience the consequences of inappropriate decisions—in noncritical areas, of course.

Blocking may be perceived as the least acceptable of the seven leadership styles. Nevertheless, at times some subordinates appear to view each new situation as a crisis to share. Verbally telling a subordinate that he was "being bothersome or distracting" could solve the immediate problem more directly. It could also serve to confuse the subordinate in his interpersonal relationship with the leader. Equally important, the subordinate might be diverted at a later time when he legitimately should have sought advice.

As we stated earlier, these seven techniques, while somewhat simplified, are legitimate styles of leadership. The problem, however, as we view it is that many law enforcement leaders continue to rely on a single style, perhaps in the erroneous belief that it is necessary to be consistent.

In our enthusiasm for the use of various leadership styles, we would offer the caution that styles are in a sense games. *It is essential that people be told which game is being played,* for they will not continue to play if they do not understand all the rules, or if the rules are violated.

To illustrate, let us assume that a leader has told his group that he wants their opinion on a certain matter and their decision will be his decision. He takes a vote, only to discover that the group has not voted as he had hoped they would. Since the leader is already committed elsewhere, he sets aside their vote and goes in his own direction. It can be anticipated that the next time he calls his group together, genuinely wanting their help, he will discover they are unwilling to play the game, for they "know" that in all probability he has already arranged things in his own way. Subordinates are quick to perceive when their leader is "conning" them, that he is seeking only their support, not their ideas, and that he will not hesitate to go around them if their decision is not to his liking.

There are times, of course, when a leader will ask his group for their opinions, not for a decision. Under these conditions, the leader should make it very clear that he will take all the information, filter it through his own filtering process, equate it with the information he already possesses, and make the final decision himself. In this way, leadership becomes an important aspect of decision making. Things must get done; decisions help get things done, and leaders must make proper decisions. It is equally important that people in the organization know exactly where they stand in regard to the decision-making process of their leader.

The point here is that people must understand the game that is being played. If confusion tends to develop from time to time over leadership styles, the group will simply not participate, and the manager will not have the kind of supportive subordinate relationships that are an absolute necessity for the dynamic organizations of the present and the future.

It was noted earlier that a successful leader is usually a person who has discovered himself; he is not someone who is content to imitate another. We have avoided referring to this development of self as a "style," although it might legitimately be considered such. Our view is that one can develop, or exhibit, a particular profile and yet freely use a number of different leadership styles, depending upon the circumstances involved. Some contemporary writers refer to this same concept as adaptive, or changing, leadership behavior. Our belief is that adaptive leaders are more likely to be successful than are those who remain inflexible in times of great social change.

Being flexible enough to move within the various leadership styles creates a complete type rather than a one-kind leader. Flexibility connotes a *dynamic leadership* quality that includes sharing, and it removes the individual from the bureaucratic category where leaders tend to make even the most minute decisions.

SUPPORTIVE RELATIONS

In our discussion of the leader we have attempted to build a case for the concept that his very being is predicated upon those who are led. Since leadership is dependent upon followership, some thought must be given to the relationship that exists between the two.

In a strict authoritarian setting, the relationship can be described as one of dominance and submission. A model of this relationship can be observed in those police academies adhering to the "stress-training" concept. The authoritarian tends to be impersonal in his relations with subordinates.

On the other hand, the enlightened leader is concerned with the entire spectrum of interpersonal relations between himself and his subordinates, between the subordinates themselves, and between his group and other affiliative groups as well.

The principle of supportive relationships can be briefly stated as follows:

> The leadership and other processes of the organization must be such as to ensure a maximum probability that in all interactions and all relationships with the organization each member will, in the light

of his background, values, and expectations, view the experience as
supportive and one which builds and maintains his sense of personal
worth and importance.[15]

Studies indicate that leaders who are perceived by subordinates to be
supportive are likely to have high-producing units, that "supervisors with
the best records of performance focus their primary attention on the
human aspects of their subordinates' problems and on endeavoring to
build effective work groups with high performance goals."[16]

To fully appreciate the importance of supportive leadership, we must
return to the theory of self-actualized man. Man has certain personal
needs: safety-security, social and affiliative, ego-satisfaction and self-
esteem, and autonomy and independence, as well as self-actualization.
He must feel that his job is important, and he must have a sense of accomplishment.[17]

In summary, the enlightened leader is aware of the necessity to support his subordinates in their drive for self-actualization. He is supportive
of their needs for autonomy and is especially supportive in assisting them
in reaching both their personal goals and the goals of the organization.

SELECTING FUTURE LEADERS

As our twentieth century grows more complex, there is a concurrent
growth of complexity in our policing organizations as they attempt to
deal effectively with the increasing ambiguities of their ever-expanding
roles. While, obviously, the more suburban-rural communities have not
yet felt the same crush for improved increased police services as have their
central-city cousins, even they are not immune. More effective managers
will be needed to provide the necessary leadership for better-equipped,
better-prepared, better-informed police officers. As observers of this phenomenon called "progress," we are concerned that current traditional
methods of identifying, selecting, and preparing future leaders may no
longer be optimal. Perhaps in light of the methodology employed by
major private business organizations, consideration might be given to a
less bureaucratic approach in selecting the twentieth-century leaders in
law enforcement.

Typically, police organizations have had rigidly formalized promotional criteria. Usually a basic prerequisite to applying for any promo-

---

[15]Rensis Likert, *New Patterns of Management* (New York: McGraw-Hill Book Company, 1961), p. 103.
[16]*Ibid.*, p. 7.
[17]Schein, *Organizational Psychology*, pp. 56–57.

tional examination is certain experience-tenure in the job immediately preceding the one sought. More recently, with the publication of *The Challenge of Crime in a Free Society*, some agencies have added requirements such as specific educational achievements commensurate with the desired position: "The ultimate aim of all police departments should be that all personnel with general enforcement powers have baccalaureate degrees. . . . The long-range objective for high-ranking officers should be advanced degrees."[18]

With the necessary criteria met, candidates are usually required to complete some formalized examination process. When this has been accomplished, the candidates' names appear on a promotional list in a rank ordering of their examination scores.

This procedure may appear all too logical for those who have been reared with the process. We feel, however, that the process creates inherent problems that are fourfold:

1. The process may not necessarily reveal the most promising leaders available.
2. Promotions are typically made before any specific training for the new level of responsibility.
3. Personnel to be promoted are not identified early enough to be afforded the opportunity of prepromotional advanced-level experience.
4. At some point in the process, seniority often becomes a final or tiebreaking criterion.

V. A. Leonard, professor emeritus of Police Science and Administration at Washington State University, expressed his concern as follows:

> Too frequently, it is assumed that the man who has the longest service or, if several are approximately equal on this point, then the man with the best record as a policeman may confidently be expected to be successful in the management of the department as its chief. The fallacy of this procedure is demonstrated by its failure in many American cities. The administration of a police department is a technical undertaking, requiring not only successful experience as a policeman, but also special talent and a number of peculiar skills that are not acquired in the course of ordinary police training and experience.[19]

[18]The President's Commission on Law Enforcement and Administration of Justice, *The Challenge of Crime in a Free Society* (Washington, D.C.: U.S. Government Printing Office, 1967), pp. 109–10.
[19]V. A. Leonard, *Police Organization and Management* (Brooklyn, N.Y.: The Foundation Press, Inc., 1964), p. 46.

In our associations with police administrators, we have not found unanimity in the belief that currently available written examinations are valid except, perhaps, as a method of reducing the number of candidates for the job. As for the interview process, it seems even less dependable. Consideration must be given to the myriad of possible leadership qualities and traits that may be possessed by a candidate in an almost infinite number of combinations. It seems unlikely that even the most perceptive police administrator is capable of making a valid, in-depth evaluation during the brief time frame allowed in the typical "oral."

Choosing leaders on the basis of performance in lesser jobs, popularity, seniority, and written and oral examinations primarily concerned with technical skills is simply not efficient in today's people-oriented world. We are not suggesting that the system be abandoned, but rather that an overhaul is in order.

Certain practices currently employed by private organizations and the military in the search for leaders seem applicable to the selection of law enforcement leaders. We believe they should be explored. While we subscribe to the theory that law enforcement administrators must have a background of "police experience," we do not mean to be limited to the traditional process of beginning everyone in the same way—at the bottom. The thought may hinge on heresy; however, we firmly believe it is possible, even desirable, to initially recruit some police management types by circumventing the normal process. In private business, recruiters canvass universities and colleges for potential management personnel trainees. The selected recruits are then provided special training programs. Beyond simple orientation, they spend little time in routine jobs. Instead, they are exposed to the business of management. As interns and aides, they are thrust, almost immediately, into a world of personnel, budgets, and accumulation and interpretation of decision-making data. Normally, the trainees do not assume any line authority. Rather, they are expected to provide staff service while developing management sense.

Few generals spent their formative years learning how to be a rifleman; the president of General Motors did not work his way up from the assembly line.

It may seem ludicrous to equate the United States Army or a gigantic corporation with a police department, but the point is that law enforcement is simply not that unique.

Another method, one that might be somewhat more acceptable to the traditional thinker, evolves from the concept that every manager, at every level, is, among other things, a *trainer*. One facet of such a function is to train other leaders. We are suggesting that police leaders should assume the responsibility for identifying those men who appear promotable, for placing them in experience-gaining situations, and for literally grooming them for eventual promotion.

Concurrently, the promotional system appears to elevate a man first and *then* determine whether or not he is capable of handling the job. Traditionally he is trained for his new level *after* he has been placed there. Today, in the middle management of law enforcement, the approach appears to have developed, at least in some organizations, a number of frustrated individuals known as the "old guard" who have tended, through no fault of their own, to become sedentary in positions beyond their capabilities. To remain stable and retain their *status quo*, they simply do nothing that will rock the boat. As a result, they frustrate people below and above them. They force managers to devise ways to work around them, and the overall situation becomes most difficult. We believe that management has the responsibility for developing men and *then* for promoting them on the basis that they are prepared to do the job to which they are being promoted rather than on the basis of competency in their current assignment.

ASSESSMENT CENTERS

An impressive, relatively new managerial selection process which we believe has great potential for law enforcement is currently emerging. The technique, called the "Assessment Center" or "AC," had its early beginnings with experiments conducted in the 1930s by Harvard University Professor Henry Murry to utilize a variety of objective, projective, and situational tests which he had developed in order to reach conclusions about the personalities of individuals. Similar techniques were used during World War II by Germany and England and later the United States to identify certain elitists for the military.

Since that time AC experiments have enjoyed varying degrees of success until 1956 when Bell Telephone, in the course of its Management Study, began an assessment center where emphasis was placed on accurately identifying the talents of employees.

Bell System psychologists had become disillusioned with traditional methods such as performance ratings, pencil and paper tests, and the like. Several hundred evaluations were made, and the results kept under lock and key. The psychologists did not want to influence traditional promotional patterns. Follow-up evaluations proved that the judgments of the observers in the Assessment Center had, with nearly pin-point accuracy, identified seventy-eight percent of those who achieved and successfully held middle-management positions as well as ninety-five percent of those who had not advanced.[20] Additionally, the A.T. & T. pilot project refined its techniques and is now utilized in certain specific areas.

In 1972, for the same reasons, we (the authors) began to experiment with the applications of AC techniques in the selection of law enforcement managers and middle managers in the City of Riverside, California. Though the beginnings were rudimentary in terms of where the program is today, the results were accurate and encouraging.

Essentially ACs are situational-based in that the process is customed designed, based on current job analysis and terminal perfomance objectives. ACs are more time consuming than traditional Civil Service tests, lasting from one to three days. ACs are multiphasic since they embody a variety of methods and instruments intended to measure job related skills, knowledge, and abilities.[21]

ACs utilize, in addition to a variety of instruments, various types of group discussion and simulation exercises to identify skills in written and oral communication, leadership, risk taking, flexibility, independence, planning and decisiveness, and other leadership traits.

One of the authors has continued to work with and refine techniques, instruments, and supplemental data and has conducted more than one hundred Assessment Center programs for law enforcement agencies with similar excellent results.

We believe that the use of ACs will continue to grow; that they are a step in the right direction in the search for the most talented police managers.

A CONCLUDING PERSPECTIVE

Laurence Peter in a rather humorous approach to the business of promotions developed what is commonly known as the "Peter Principle."[22] His simple hypothesis is that "In a Hierarchy Every Employee Tends to Rise to His Level of Incompetence."[23] And even more simply, that "the cream rises until it sours."[24]

Peter supports his theory with a number of cases, of which the following is representative:

[20]Robert E. Normandin, "The Assessment Center," *The Rohrer, Hibler & Replogle Journal,* 5, no. 1 (December 1973): 321–32.

[21]Don Driggs and Paul M. Whisenand, "Assessment Centers: Situational Evaluation," *Journal of California Law Enforcement* 10 (April 1976): 33–37.

[22]Laurence J. Peter and Raymond Hull, *The Peter Principle* (New York: William Morrow & Co., Inc., 1969).

[23]*Ibid.,* p. 26.

[24]*Ibid.,* p. 36.

Military File, Case No. 8. Consider the case of the late renowned General A. Goodwin. His hearty, informal manner, his racy style of speech, his scorn for petty regulations and his undoubted personal bravery made him the idol of his men. He led them to many well-deserved victories.

When Goodwin was promoted to field marshal he had to deal, not with ordinary soldiers, but with politicians and allied generalissimos. He would not conform to the necessary protocol. He could not turn his tongue to the conventional courtesies and flatteries. He quarreled with all the dignitaries and took to lying for days at a time, drunk and sulking, in his trailer. The conduct of the war slipped out of his hands into those of his subordinates. He had been promoted to a position that he was incompetent to fill.[25]

Given that many organizations are guilty of contributing support to the Peter Principle, what normal action is taken when the problem is discovered? Peter has an answer for that, too, in what he entitles "The Lateral Arabesque":

The lateral arabesque is another pseudo-promotion. Without being raised in rank—sometimes without even a pay raise—the incompetent employee is given a *new and longer title* and is moved to an office in a remote part of the building.

R. Filewood proved incompetent as office manager of Carley Stationery Inc. After a lateral arabesque he found himself, at the same salary, working as co-ordinator of inter-departmental communications, supervising the filing of second copies of inter-office memos.[26]

While the preceding quotations were undoubtedly written as a spoof, they are entirely accurate in all too many instances. Law enforcement, too, has had its share of taking competent personnel and promoting them to their level of incompetency. And when the incompetencies are discovered, these employees are seldom returned to the proper level. Instead, as in Peter's example, they tend to be laterally transferred to less sensitive areas, where they often continue to be incompetent.

What we are suggesting is that the dynamic, flexible, coping police organization necessary to meet the needs of a rapidly changing society can no longer afford the luxury of the Peter Principle. There appear, on the basis of existing models, to be several ways in which our leadership selection process could and should be improved.

[25]*Ibid.*, p. 24.
[26]*Ibid.*, p. 40.

LEARNING EXERCISE:

DEVELOPING GROUP COMMITMENT:
A STRUCTURED EXPERIENCE[27]

Goals

1. To aid the group and/or organization in studying the degree to which members agree on certain values.
2. To focus on the decision-making norms of the group.
3. To discover the "natural leadership" which is functioning in the group.

Time Required. Approximately one hour.

Materials Utilized. Functions of police unions (associations).

Process. The facilitator announced that the group will engage in an activity to accomplish the goals spelled out above and distributes the ranking forms. The facilitator functions as a timekeeper according to the schedule on the form. One member may function as process observer. After the allotted time, the group discusses the process in which it engaged.

The form is easily revised to fit groups other than police unions. The content may be the goals of the organization or group, characteristics of an ideal leader, desirable characteristics of teachers (principals, ministers, counselors, supervisers, employers, etc.), or any other relevant list. One suggestion might be to conduct a problem census of the organization or group and to use that list as the items to be rank ordered.

When several groups in the same organization (class, institution, etc.) engage in this experience simultaneously, it is sometimes helpful to summarize the rank orders for the several groups on a chalkboard and to have discussion of the agreements and disagreements among the groups.

Functions of Police Unions

Instructions: Rank the following functions of police unions according to the importance you attach to them. Place a "1" in front of the most agreement, a "2" before the second most agreement, etc. You have seven minutes for this task.

After the members of your group have finished working individually, arrive at a rank ordering *as a group*. The group has twenty-five minutes for the task. Do *not* choose a formal leader.

———— 1. Police unions have a cohesive or unifying affect on the police department.

[27]The learning exercise is taken from J. William Pfeiffer and John E. Jones, *A Handbook of Structured Experiences for Human Relations Training* (Iowa City, Iowa: University City Associates Press, 1969), pp. 33–39.

——— 2. Police unions should militate for improved working conditions.

——— 3. A police union is where you develop professional and social relationships that tend to improve the efficiency of the organization.

——— 4. Police unions provide a sense of belongingness to the department.

——— 5. The police union seeks to protect its memberships in the face of authoritarian management.

——— 6. The union is an organization within an organization where one is stimulated to personal growth.

——— 7. Participation in union activities is similar to training for leadership within the police organization.

——— 8. Supervisors should not belong to police unions.

——— 9. Binding arbitration should be fostered between unions and police management.

——— 10. Where they exist, management should in good faith maintain constant communication with the union on matters of mutual interest.

Chapter Five

TASK 3 PLANNING:

The Setting of Goals

Once I was asked to head up a new long-range planning effort. My wife listened to my glowing description of my new job. Next evening she blew the whole schmeer out of the water by asking: "What did you plan today, dear?" Bless her.[1]

While the scope and objectives of the exercise of the government's police power are properly determined in the first instance by state and local legislative bodies within the limits fixed by the Constitution and by court decisions, it should be recognized there is considerable latitude remaining with local government to develop an overall direction for police services. Within these limits, each local jurisdiction should decide upon objectives and priorities. Decisions regarding police resources, police personnel needs, police organization, and relations with other government agencies should then be made in a way which will best achieve the objectives and priorities of the particular locality.[2]

SYNOPSIS

The *concept* of planning has been with local policing since its very inception in the nineteenth century. The *practice* of police planning, however, is just now coming to the fore. We can presently observe some police agencies identifying their goals and creating plans for their eventual attainment. Effective planning includes goal setting, and vice versa. The two are inseparable.

Organizational goals have many functions. They may constitute a definition of the general mission; aid in decision making, information system design, control, motivation, and assignment of responsibility; and serve as an integrating mechanism, and the foundation for planning. The police, like most complex organizations, have multiple goals. In a broad sense the goals of a police agency are law enforcement, order maintenance, and provision of general government services. We, in turn, see police agencies making plans and committing their resources to achieve these goals.

If a goal can be defined as "a desired future state-of-affairs" then what is planning? Planning is first and foremost, as compared to

[1]Robert Townsend, *Up the Organization* (New York: Alfred A. Knopf, Inc., 1970), p. 146.
[2]American Bar Association, *The Urban Police Function* (Washington, D.C.: American Bar Association, 1973), p. 4.

a plan, a dynamic process. It is a process that encompasses a variety of activities and methods. Most importantly, it is a process that gives to an organization the necessary muscle and direction for moving toward the accomplishment of its goal(s). The output of the process are plans that can be generally typed as broad (environmental), limited (tactical), or parochial (internal). Planning is playing an ever greater part in policing because it is pervasively recognized by police managers that *any reduction in crime is inextricably linked to careful and constant planning.*

The remaining sections of the chapter cover the following topics. We first consider the scope and importance of planning. Then based on the logical connection between planning and organizational goals, we turn to an examination of the goals of our local police department, keeping in mind that it is the goals of an organization that underpin any rationale for planning. Third, we will discuss the part (role) that the manager plays in the planning process. Also in this section is a short review of the interdependency existing in planning, plans, and policy formation. Fourth, we will describe one of many structural techniques (as compared with scientific or functional) to enhance the quality and quantity of the end product—the plan(s). Finally, the reader will experience a learning exercise that constitutes a "plan" for planning. More will be said later about the extent and content of the exercise. Let us proceed with our analysis of the goals of a police organization.

PLANNING FOR A PLAN

In this chapter we emphasize *planning* rather than the resultant *plan*. In other words, we are primarily concerned with the process—not the output. Few would doubt the central nature of planning to the management of an organization. Ample evidence—theoretical and practical—is available to show just how vitally important planning is to the overall success of an organization. Of the many authorities who have offered witness to the significance of the planning process, Gardner is clearly an advocate. He writes:

> Every individual, organization or society must mature, but much depends on how this maturing takes place. A society whose maturing consists simply of acquiring more firmly established ways of doing

things is headed for the graveyard—even if it learns to do these things with greater and greater skill. In the ever-renewing society [police department] what matures is a system or framework within which continuous innovation, renewal and rebirth can occur.[3]

Contained in the above statement is a partial reason or purpose for planning: "continuous innovation, renewal and rebirth" of individuals and organizations—in our case *police organizations*. We would add a second part to complete the primary purpose of this management process —*the continuous innovation, renewal, and rebirth of individuals and organizations in order to more effectively accomplish their goals.*

Let us reflect for a few moments on some of the early and not so early writings about planning. First, Sun Tzu wrote in approximately 500 B.C. "Now the general who wins a battle *makes many calculations in his temple ere the battle is fought.* The general who loses a battle makes few calculations before hand. It is by attention to this point that I can see who is likely to win or lose."[4]

Second, and more plainly stated, is the following writing by Cyrus in early Greece: ". . . not to adopt such plans only as you have been taught, but to be yourself a *contriver of stratagems*. . . ."[5]

Similarly on planning we should remember his statement "Consider at night what your men shall do when it is day; and consider in the day how matters may be best settled for the night."[6]

With due regard for space, we jump many centuries to the eighteenth where the value of careful and explicit planning began to be recognized. Although the industrialists of the era did not seem to realize the extent to which planning could be utilized and did not attempt to plan the details of company and office operations as is often done today, at least two planning techniques were successfully used in this period which remains among the most productive: plant location and payback computations. As early as 1759 we find clear evidence of location planning in the Carron Ironworks in Scotland, where "everything, even the site, was planned with a view to the greatest efficiencies of production and transportation in the smelting and casting of irons."[7] Adam Smith, under-

[3]John W. Gardner, *Self-Renewal: The Individual and the Innovative Society* (New York: Harper & Row, Publishers, 1963), p. 5.

[4]Thomas P. Philips, *Roots of Strategy* (Harrisburg, Pa.: Military Service Publishing Co., 1955), p. 23.

[5]J. S. Watson and Henry Dale, trans., *Xenophon's Cyropaedia and the Hellenics* (London: G. Bell & Sons, Ltd., 1898), p. 42.

[6]*Ibid.*

[7]Frederick C. Dietz, *An Economic History of England* (New York: Henry Holt and Company, 1942), p. 34.

standing the need for payback computations, outlined a method for their application in machine acquisition and replacement. His explanation was that "when any expensive machine is erected, the extraordinary work to be performed by it before it is worn out, it must be expected, will replace the capital laid out upon it, with at least the ordinary profits.[8]

It was also during the eighteenth century that, of the five generally accepted functions of management at that time (planning, organizing, staffing, directing, and controlling), several economists began to consider planning as the most important. Laughlin gives the reasoning behind this when he says:

> He who controls a large capital actively engaged in production can never remain at a standstill; he must be full of new ideas; he must have power to initiate new schemes for the extension of his market; he must have judgment to adopt new inventions, and yet not to be deceived as to their value and efficiency.[9]

Some of you might enjoy paraphrasing the above quotation to fit your particular organization. For example, substitute the words *public activity* for "capital," *law enforcement* for "production," and *service* for "market." The Prussian General Carl von Clausewitz appeared to concur with this thinking, since he stressed that careful planning was a necessity for the managing of a large organization, with the first requisite being to define one's goals.[10] Note the last term in the preceding sentence—*goals*. For the general was quick to point out the explicit relationship between planning and an organization's goals. He also emphasized that all decisions must be based on probability, not on logical necessity, as commonly believed at the time. Of course, his idea of probability was not as detailed as our current statistical probability, but the theory of trying to prepare best for what might happen is the same. Of all his pronouncements, perhaps Clausewitz's major contribution to management was that managers should accept uncertainty and act on the basis of thorough analysis and planning designed to minimize this uncertainty.

Finally, it is time that we view the twentieth century and planning as it specifically relates to the police department. Obviously the vast majority of contemporary police managers are in support of more and

[8]Adam Smith, *An Inquiry into the Nature and Causes of the Wealth of Nations* (London: A Strahan and T. Cadell, 1793), 3: 154.

[9]J. Lawrence Laughlin, *The Elements of Political Economy* (New York American Book Company, 1896), p. 223.

[10]For details on his concepts of management, see especially Carl von Clausewitz, *On War* (New York: Barnes & Noble, Inc., n.d.); and *Principles of War* (Harrisburg, Pa.: Military Service Publishing Co., 1832).

better planning. Paradoxically, however, of the hundreds of pages comprising the Crime Commission's *Task Force Report: The Police*, only two dealt with police planning.

> There are two vital needs of police departments which can be served by areawide, coordinated planning. One is crime and modus operandi analysis, which calls for areawide planning because of the regional nature of certain crimes and criminal activity. The other assistance on administrative and operational matters, in which many small departments lack competence and facilities. Both are functions which should be performed on a metropolitan or statewide basis.
>
> Crime analysis is a planning function regardless of the organizational unit in which it is placed. The primary purpose of crime analysis is to study daily reports of serious crimes in order to determine the location, time, special characteristics, similarities to other criminal attacks, and various significant facts that may help to identify either a criminal or the existence of a pattern of criminal activity.
>
> Modus operandi, or method of operation, refers to the criminal's individual peculiarities—his methods, techniques, and the tools he uses in the commission of a crime. Modus operandi analysis is concerned primarily with persons, whereas crime analysis relates principally to events although they are interrelated.
>
> Sound police organization and procedures depend upon good planning. Frequently, the emergency nature of police work and the constant attention that must be given to day-to-day operations do not leave enough time for effective planning. Much planning is done daily in all police operations, but, primarily, it is to serve an immediate need. Most police administrators seek to improve their organizations, but many do not know how or do not have enough time to correct deficiencies in organization and faulty procedures.[11]

While somewhat disappointing, the quotation does provide additional weight—this time by police authorities—to the rapidly rising awareness of the critical organizational requirement for an adequate planning process in local law enforcement. The police are not alone in their recognized absence of a planning mechanism because, in general, organizations engage in opportunistic decision making rather than in planning: rather than explain courses of action that will lead the way to the attainment of their goals (and in some cases identify new goals), they extemporize, handling each crisis as it emerges. Thus the challenge becomes all the more obvious—the police need a process (planning) for generating, on a continual basis, *plans*.

[11]The President's Commission on Law Enforcement and Administration of Justice, *Task Force Report: The Police* (Washington, D.C.: U.S. Government Printing Office, 1967), pp. 77–78.

GOALS: A Future Desired State of Affairs

The managerial role of planning is one of identifying the organizational goals and then creating the policies, programs, procedures, and methods for achieving them. The planning role is essentially one of providing a framework or mechanism for integrated decision making in terms of keeping the organization pliable (yielding to constant renewal and change) and viable (striving toward goal accomplishment).

GOALS: In a General Sense

The goals of an organization serve many uses. Etzioni asserts that

> they provide orientation by depicting a future state of affairs which the organization strives to realize. Thus they set down guide lines for organizational activity. Goals also constitute a source of legitimacy which justifies the activities of an organization and, indeed, its very existence. Moreover goals serve as standards by which members of an organization and outsiders can assess the success of the organization— i.e., its effectiveness and efficiency. Goals also serve in a similar fashion as measuring rods for the student of organizations who tries to determine how well the organization is doing.[12]

The fundamental reason for an organization's existence lies in its goals. Although once the goals are decided upon, organizations frequently generate unforeseen needs (for example, providing job satisfaction to their employees in order to retain them). In such instances, organizations usually reduce their attention on their primary goals in order to handle their acquired needs. At times organizations go so far as to abandon their initial goals and pursue new ones more suited to the organizations' needs. We will return to this and other problems concerning goals in a few moments. First, let us look at what organizational goals are, how they come into being, and their benefits.[13]

What is a goal? "An organizational goal is a desired state of affairs which the organization attempts to realize."[14] The organization may or

[12]Amitai Etzioni, *Modern Organizations* (Englewood Cliffs, N.J.: Prentice-Hall, Inc., 1964), p. 5.

[13]Most of the remainder of this section on organization goals is taken from Paul M. Whisenand, *Police Supervision: Theory and Practice*, 2nd. ed. (Englewood Cliffs, N.J.: Prentice-Hall, Inc., 1976), pp 75–80.

[14]*Ibid.*, p. 6.

may not be able to create this hoped-for image of the future. For example, it is very unlikely that our American police system will ever be able to attain its principal goal of maintaining social order at all times. But if a goal is attained, it ceases to be a guiding image for an organization and is either dismissed or replaced with another. Actually, a goal never exists; it is a state that we seek, not one we have. We should distinguish between *real* and *stated* goals. At times they are one and the same, but we are often able to detect that an organization is moving in a direction different from that expressed as its goal. The reasons for this vary from a lack of awareness that this is happening to hiding the real goal so that it can be more easily achieved. The real goals of an organization are those future states toward which a majority of the organization's resources are committed, as compared with those that are stated but receive fewer resources. The distinction between real and stated goals is crucial because they should not be confused with the important difference between intended and unintended consequences. Real goals are always intended. Stated goals can be intended or not.

How are goals derived? All formal organizations have recognized, usually legally specified, means for creating goals and also for changing them. Regardless of the formal means, in practice goals are usually established in a complicated power play involving (1) organizational subdivisions (groups), (2) individuals, and (3) environmental influences. The outcome of the three-cornered power play provides direction for (1) sharpening and clarifying goals, (2) adding new goals, (3) shifting priorities among goals, and (4) eliminating irrelevant goals. In summary, goal formation is the result of policy making. Policy making involves planning which, in turn, draws upon numerous decision centers in order to reach the final choice—in this case, which organizational goals to retain or modify.

What are the benefits of goals to an organization? We can list at least eight primary benefits which a goal or a set of goals can provide:

1. Presenting the general purpose and ideology of the organization,

2. Guiding and supporting organizational decision making,

3. Developing and maintaining a useful information system,

4. Performing the control function,

5. Motivating the people in the organization,

6. Delegating responsibility,

7. Integrating the activities between the operating subunits within the organization, and

8. *Targeting the planning process.*

Let us continue with a discussion of multiple goals, goal displacement, and goal succession. First, most organizations have *multiple goals*. Argyris's "Mix Model" defines one of the essential properties of organization as "the achievement of goals or objectives."[15] As an illustration, besides apprehending offenders, the police also act to prevent offenses. Interestingly, the latter goal seeks to make the former unnecessary. One final comment in regard to multiple goals—organizations that serve more than a single goal do so more effectively than single-purpose organizations of the same category. The reasons for this are twofold: (1) Serving one goal often increases the achievement of another goal, and (2) there is a much improved recruitment appeal because the nature of the work provides more variety and, therefore, enhanced job satisfaction.

Second, with respect to *goal displacement* we find that the attainment of a goal or goals is vastly increased when goal displacement is kept at a minimum.[16] Briefly, goal displacement happens when an organization substitutes for its legitimate goal some other goal for which resources were not allocated, and which it is not known to serve. Since goal displacement is injurious to the effectiveness of an organization, what can be done to avoid it? Making the goals more tangible is the simple answer, for goal displacement is minimized when goals are tangible. Gross, however, takes exception to the importance of goal tangibility in his "Clarity-Vagueness Balance."

> There is no need to labor the need for clarity in the formulation of an organization's objectives. Precise formulations are necessary for delicate operations. They provide the indispensable framework for coordinating complex activity . . . yet in the wide enthusiasm for "crystal-clear goals," one may easily lose sight of the need for a fruitful balance between clarity and vagueness. . . .[17]

Gross again supports the merit of vagueness by writing:

> If all points on a set of interrelated purpose chains were to be set forth with precise clarity, the result would be to destroy the subordination of one element to another which is essential to an operating purpose pattern. The proper focusing of attention on some goals for any particular moment or period in time means that other goals

[15]Chris Argyris, *Integrating the Individual and the Organization* (New York: John Wiley & Sons, Inc., 1964), p. 150.

[16]*Ibid.*

[17]Bertram M. Gross, "What Are Your Organization's Objectives: A General Systems Approach to Planning," *Human Relations* 18 (August 1965): 213.

must be left vague. This is even truer for different periods of time. We must be very clear about many things we aim to do today and tomorrow. It might be dangerously misleading to seek similar clarity for our long-range goals.[18]

Gross's thinking leaves us in somewhat of a quandary. Should we create tangible goals in order to better accomplish them or vague goals in order to be more flexible? The solution to this apparent dilemma is not perfectly clear. Perhaps it lies in better and more frequent organizational analysis—if an organization will subject its goals to periodic study and evaluation, the opportunity for changing them is improved. Hence, there is less need of vagueness because the tangible goals are kept updated and relevant through the planning process. At the same time, the overall mission or philosophy of an organization can remain vague to facilitate adaptation and innovation. For example, the police philosophy "to protect and serve" leaves considerable room for creating and changing the more tangible goals of a police department.

Third, not only do modern organizations usually have multiple goals and experience goal displacement, but they also tend to find new goals when the traditional ones have been attained or cannot be attained. This latter tendency on the part of an organization is known as goal succession. Therefore, *goal succession* is the replacement of a goal or goals with another goal or goals, or merely the acquisition of new goals. The police organization is a case in point. To the more traditional goals of arresting and recovering stolen property have been added those of maintaining public order. Initially, the newer goals are justified in that they improve the accomplishment of the traditional goals, but they often become equal in importance.

GOALS: In a Police Sense

We can draw from any number of sources for a list of police goals. Most listings contain a strong orientation toward law and enforcement. We approach the police organization as having three basic goals:

Law enforcement
Order maintenance
General government services

Evidently the police are actually functioning in three related but

18Bertram M. Gross, *The Managing of Organizations* (New York: The Free Press of Glencoe, 1964), p. 497.

different ways. The manager is directly involved in the planning for all three.

Law enforcement is clearly the more venerable goal of our policing agencies. In attempting to meet this goal, the police play an integral part—along with the prosecutors, the probation departments, the courts, the parole agencies, and the correctional organizations—in the operation of the criminal justice system. At this point you should note that the police are members of two governmental systems: (1) local government—fire, finance, recreation, personnel, etc., and (2) criminal justice—prosecution, probation, etc.) As the front-end agency in the criminal justice system, the primary responsibility of the police is to initiate criminal action against those who violate the law. This responsibility is well defined by statutes and court decisions and is subject to strict departmental controls. In the fulfillment of this goal, police officers must arrest offenders, recover stolen property, prevent criminal acts, and handle civil disorders.

By *order maintenance* we mean the handling of disputes (or behavior that tends to produce disputes) among people who disagree on what is morally right, on what constitutes misconduct, or on the assignment of blame in a situation. A family quarrel, a street disturbance by teen-agers, and a disagreement in a tavern exemplify community problems that require police intervention. The police are called upon to maintain order (keep the peace) without making an arrest. They must resolve human conflict—a task all of us realize is not easy. First of all, when a policeman intervenes, someone is likely to feel wronged, outraged, or neglected. Though a law may have been broken, as in a husband's assault on his wife, the policeman cannot simply compare a particular behavior with a clear legal standard and then make an arrest if the standard has been violated. For one thing, the legal rule is vague in many order-maintenance cases. "Breach of peace" implies a prior definition of "peace" —a matter on which people commonly disagree. For another thing, even when the legal standard is clear enough, as in an assault, the "victim" is often not innocent (indeed, he may have called for the police because he was losing a fight he started). Thus the question of "blame" may be more important to the participants than the question of "guilt," and they will expect the officer to take this into account. Second, most order-maintenance situations do not result in an arrest; the people involved want the officer to do something that will solve the problem, but they do not want that solution to be an arrest. Third, if there is an offense, it is likely to be a misdemeanor, and thus in most instances the patrolman cannot make an arrest unless the illegality was committed in his presence or unless the victim is willing to sign a complaint. As a result, the officer cannot expect a judge to dispose of the case; he himself must decide on a solution that will make order out of disorder. In due regard for the complexities surrounding order maintenance, Tamm states:

> But the social climate of our times has immensely broadened this concept to where the police find themselves the arbiter between rival social factions, where they find themselves involved in the most delicate problems of human relations in the rapidly changing social structure of our modern society. It is no exaggeration to say that the type of duties normally performed by social workers occupy as much as fifty percent of the long day of both police administrators and line officers.
>
> To meet these demands requires abilities, training, and understanding far beyond what was ever conceived as necessary police characteristics in the not-too-distant past. Today any plan of action must be carefully considered from the standpoint of the human factors involved. . . .
>
> Most police executives recognize this problem and are actively eliminating the basic cause through increased emphasis on sociological training and developing expertise in human relations among the personnel under their supervision.[19]

And according to former Los Angeles Police Chief Thomas Reddin:

> Times change and we must change with time. The policeman of the future will be more effective and will function at a more personal level than in the past. He will be much more sociologist, psychologist, and scientist than his present-day counterpart. He will have many more scientific and technological aids to assist him.
>
> In short, he will utilize space-age techniques of the physical sciences coupled with a type of police work that draws upon the best lessons learned from the social scientists.[20]

The third and final goal—the provision of *general government services* —includes everything else that the police department is asked to do by its clientele. Its personnel must abate nuisances, control traffic and crowds, administer first aid, furnish information, and provide a wide range of other miscellaneous services.[21]

In summary, when relating the goals of a police organization to the two systems that it belongs to we find the following:

[19]Quinn Tamm, *The Police Chief* 33 (November 1966): 6.

[20]Tom Reddin, "The Police, the People, the Future," *Los Angeles Times,* May 19, 1968, Sec. G, p. 4.

[21]People are increasingly referring to the police as a service agency. See Thomas E. Bereal, "Calls for Police Assistance," *American Behavioral Scientist* 13 (May-June and July-August 1970): 681–91.

Law Enforcement	Criminal Justice System
Order Maintenance	Criminal Justice System plus
General Government Services	Local Government System[22]

Of the three goals, which is most important? We will let you, the reader, argue which is more vital. Keep in mind, however, that all three are being served at present. Hence, all three must be *planned for* irrespective of how the argument goes.

THE ROLE OF A PLANNER: Activities, Policy Formation, and Problems

To generate an individual and a collective climate conducive to cooperative participation, every police manager must perform several recognizable roles. He must, for example, decide what the goals of the department are, how they should be accomplished, and when plans should be implemented. Making these decisions involves a conceptual look at needed future action—be it tomorrow or five years from now. It thus requires looking ahead, conceptualizing about the future, and planning today so as to adequately meet the future.

Obviously, planning is, in most instances, not a separate recognizable function. It is usually interlaced with other managerial activities. A police manager does not typically give a directive by mere impulse or reflex. On the contrary, even a casually written or oral communication about needed action may well involve some planning along with the message itself. To reemphasize, *every managerial act, mental or physical,* is inexorably intertwined with planning. Although we are able to conceptually separate planning for the purpose of theoretical discussion and analysis, we must remember that in practice it is neither a distinct nor a separable entity. For analysis, let us theoretically extricate the managerial planning function from the others to see how it is involved in the managing of a police department.

Planning, as a conceptually separate managerial role, consists of looking ahead, "systematically" predicting, and anticipating probable future events and the actions needed to cope with them. Planning may result in nothing more than a simple plan for police employee vacations next year in relation to the variations in the probable workload, or it may

[22]Herman Goldstein, "Police Response to Urban Crisis," *Public Administration Review* 28 (September-October 1968): 420.

produce a plan of action to reduce stranger-to-stranger crime and thus minimize the impact of criminal activity eighteen months hence. Whatever the area of consideration, police managers in the performance of the planning function systematically analyze the problem in light of probable future events and therefore make decisions *now* in order to deal more effectively with a constantly changing environment.

Before discussing some of the problems that are currently harassing the full utilization of a planning vehicle, it seems best to provide a definition to what *we* mean by *planning*. A *plan* (the output of planning) is a rational decision with regard to a course of action. The rational selection of a course of action, that is, the making of a rational plan, includes basically the same procedures as those of any rational decision: Most, and if possible all, the courses of action must be identified, the consequences of each course must be predicted, and the courses having the preferred consequences must be selected.[23] Hence the planning process is comprised of the following activities:

> Analysis of the situation (problem identification)
> *Goal setting (desired future state of affairs)*
> Design of courses of action (alternative approaches to goal attainment)
> Comparative evaluation of consequences (predicting the result of each alternative)
> Final selection of course of action (decision making)

It should be recognized that each of these activities is not only interrelated but actually overlaps the others. Also, all the activities can vary as to the type and the number of scientific tools employed. For example, an analysis of the situation might well include such scientific methods as operations research, mathematical modeling, survey research, and DELPHI and statistical inferences. The enormous data-processing power of a computer can also be used in support of these methods. Now—what is planning? *Planning is a dynamic process that involves a number of activities and methods for generating plans that provide an organization with sustained renewal and change in terms of more effective goal accomplishment.*

A basic problem for police organizations in urban America concerns their policy with respect to planning. Police agencies, once past a critical point in the accumulation of sufficient resources, have grown at an ever-accelerating pace. Through their development, services not available to our citizens a half century ago have become necessities for American

---

[23]An excellent discussion of the relationship between decision making and planning can be found in Amitai Etzioni, "Mixed Scanning—A Systems Approach," *Public Administration Review* 26 (January-February 1969): 3–15.

society. Police services move in many directions: toward improving the physical security of life, toward restoring peace, toward solving community problems, and toward bettering the quality of life. And the rapidity of societal and technological change, and the diversity of existing and potential police services, put a premium upon the anticipation and direction of these changes through systematic planning. "Any [police] organization which does not have a four-, or five-, or ten-year plan is risking destruction or a series of continuing crises in its operations."[24]

The planning process can be operated through two auxiliary or staff functions, one to develop specific alternative courses of action for anticipated changes in the environment, the other to gather predictive indicators about community changes and reactions to police programs. Both of these functions are generally combined in a single staff group or endeavor to the great neglect of the indicator gathering. Guesswork replaces exact knowledge of community trends. The planless extreme is currently illustrated by those universities which lack a planning staff and have been overwhelmed by the tremendous increase in demand for their services (trends that everyone knew about but were not anticipated in building or staffing programs). Many other city departments have been in the same situation, and have not planned for zoning, traffic, water, and sewage services. They are now paying the price for the old policy of day-to-day opportunism—the police are not alone in their lack of planning and plans!

Once the policy question has been answered affirmatively—that is, that there will be in fact a planning process—still another automatically arises. The police manager is confronted with a decision about the levels of detail and comprehensiveness that the planning process should include in the plan(s). In this case, the manager must rely on the process itself to generate significant plans. Hence, the planning process should be capable of handling various levels of complexity and scope. In other words, from the very narrow and highly detailed plans, the process ought to be able to produce those of a broad and general nature. A plan that is overly narrow, or overly broad, frequently fails to meet its intended objectives. Of the two failings, inappropriate broadness is the more common. Such grandiose but impractical plans are actually a *very* common phenomenon, particularly among managers entrusted with long-range planning. For example, "city planners are notorious for designing master plans that call for absurdly unrealistic behavior on the part of other agents (such as massive expenditures on parks and nearly perfect law enforcement).[25] Downs refers to this too broad approach as the *superman syndrome.*

All managers engaged in planning process actions have some incentive for indulging in the superman syndrome. It is much easier to make theoretical assumptions about how others will behave than to negotiate with them and base plans upon what they are actually likely to do. In theory, every manager can assume that others will perform their functions and responsibilities in the way he himself regards as most efficient. The actual behavior of these people, however, will be heavily influenced by their views of what is efficient as well as by self-interest. Both of these elements are often difficult to foresee. Superman planning is intellectually more satisfying than realistic planning. Unfettered by reality, planners can develop far more original, daring, sweeping, and internally consistent visions of what should be done than if they actually have to deal with the disenchantment of conflicting interests in the real world. The superman plans produced by a police department often serve specific functions as targets or aspirations that are in fact unattainable (at least in the time proposed) but nevertheless provide utility to their beholders. For example, planning for the use of a helicopter in routine patrol operations normally contains a statement in the plan that crime *will* decrease by a significant percentage. For the above reasons, superman planning is the great temptation of all managers faced by the immense complexities of attempting to design appropriate maneuvers in policy space. They tend to yield to this temptation in direct proportion to the breadth of their operations and the absence of restraints forcing them to create realistic plans.

THE SETTING OF GOALS

The decision to set goals on the part of a police agency automatically presents a major challenge to its entire decision-making process.[26] Clearly a management-by-objectives program requires a series of decisions on what the goals ought to be pursued. Second, a very large number of decisions are needed to accomplish them. George S. Odiorne's book provides testimony to this thinking in its title, *Management Decisions by*

[25]Anthony Downs, *Inside Bureaucracy* (Boston: Little, Brown and Company, 1967), p. 218.

[26]The number of police agencies that have established goal-setting procedures is decidely on the increase. One example can be observed in *Norwalk Station; Mission and Goals,* (Los Angeles County Sheriff's Department, Los Angeles, California, 1976).

Objectives.[27] Odiorne distinguishes three types of objectives which should be rank ordered according to the level of difficulty in their achievement. In order of ascendency they are:

1. Regular or routine   —measured by exceptions from standards objectives.
2. Problem solving   —measured by solutions and time established as objectives.
3. Innovative goals   —measured by productive changes sought and achieved in time.[28]

Regardless of the type of objectives to be set a single common process can be used to set them. Again, the complexity, the challenge, the certainty, and the time frame will vary depending on the type of objective you are coping with. The objective-setting process consists of seven interrelated activities.

1. Identification of the problem
2. Definition of the problem in specific, operational terms
3. Development of alternative strategies to impact the problem
4. Selection of the appropriate alternative
5. Implementation
6. Evaluation
7. Feedback[29]

Identification of the Problem

At first glance this might appear to be a simple matter but experience has proven it to be quite the contrary. In fact, this step is often the most difficult part of the entire process. Let us examine the following hypothetical example. A lieutenant in a medium-sized police department has the overall responsibility for managing a team of fourteen police officers. In addition, he is responsible for the division's in-service training program and supply requisitioning. He is actively pursuing his own formal education and will soon be awarded his Associate of Arts degree from the local college. The Chief of Police is interested in converting the traditional patrol patterns and assignments to a team policing program. The agency

[27]George S. Odiorne, *Management Decisions by Objectives* (Englewood Cliffs, N.J.: Prentice-Hall, Inc., 1969).

[28]*Ibid.,* p. 8–9.

[29]A most useful and in-depth explanation of this process is contained in an article by Stephen J. Caroll, Jr., and Henry L. Tosi, "Goal Characteristics and Personality Factors in a Management-By-Objectives Program," *Administrative Science Quarterly* 15 (September 1970): 295–305.

has never experienced such an ambitious undertaking and, in fact, is understaffed by approximately four personnel. Since the department utilizes a formal hierarchy, the lieutenant's immediate supervisor is a captain (of which the agency has four). The Chief has selected the lieutenant to research, develop, and present to him a position paper exploring the team policing concept for their agency.

In reviewing this example and placing yourself in our lieutenant's shoes, what would you say is the real problem that he must ultimately address with meaningful objectives? Is it time? personnel? converting the attitudes of the department to accept the change? training? or a combination of all of these? If you selected the last alternative, then you are beginning to understand the difficulty of clearly defining the problem.

When we implied earlier that the entire objective-setting process is an exercise of ordering your thoughts and engaging in "mind expansion," we were referring especially to problem identification. In this most critical step you must carefully determine exactly what the problem is and then write out a concise statement of it.

A variety of techniques are available to assist the manager in this step. These include reflective thinking, analyzing available data, generating new data about the problem, brainstorming, slip techniques, personal observation, or seeking the counsel of someone internal or external to the agency who may have had more experience in similar problems. The critical part, however, remains thinking clearly about the problem and then writing it down in the most specific terms possible. This might require several attempts and the manager is encouraged to keep at the task until he satisfies himself that what he has written is an accurate statement—that it is the *real* problem.

Specific Statement

This step of the process is somewhat similar to the one above; however, it is dealt with separately due to its importance. After considering the advice and cautions offered above, the manager should reflect further on his "objective statement" of the problem. It is often productive for him to use his colleagues and work group as a sounding board to modify, correct, or reinforce his objective statement and to assure himself that what has been written is in fact a specific problem statement amenable to solution and measurement.

Alternative Strategies

In this third step of the process, the manager must develop as *many* alternatives as possible which might offer a solution to the problem. In his first attempt at the exercise he should not disregard any possible alternative. The same techniques we indicated before—ranging from individual thinking to group thinking—can be used. After all of the possible alternatives have been identified, the manager can then proceed to reduce the list to the handful that hold the most promise. Factors that affect his decision to leave an alternative on his list or remove it are almost limitless. A few of the more outstanding include:

Time
Money
Personnel
Political ramifications
Tradition and custom
Attitudes
Skill of the participants

The skill and expertise of the individual and the size of the problem are also factors that influence the choice of techniques used to evaluate each alternative. These range from a simple weighting system to very complex mathematical formulas and system techniques.

Selection of an Alternative

This step of the process is what the manager has been aiming toward from the start. After following the above steps he is finally ready to select the paramount alternative and implement it. One caution deserves to be reinforced here; that is, the best alternative is not always the most feasible one. The manager should be aware of this factor and not become disillusioned that the "number one" alternative cannot be implemented, because of a variety of reasons ranging from money to politics.

Implementation

Following the selection step we are now ready for implementation. In preparing to implement the selected alternative, the manager should have thought through the alternative to the point where he knows who is going to be effected, how they will be effected, and where the alternative will be exercised. In effect, he has a "battle plan" for following through with the selected alternative. This also proves valuable in the last two steps, evaluation and feedback.

Evaluation

There is a growing awareness in the police community of the usefulness of evaluation. It enables the police organization to explain and justify action taken, to fend off criticism of the approach that was taken to the problem, to demonstrate the cost effectiveness of the objective, and to reinforce the value of introducing new techniques and methodologies into the police profession. Here again, a host of techniques are available to the manager to evaluate his program. These range from simple statistical review to esoteric evaluation schemes that were developed by the aerospace industry to evaluate space flights. The selection of the correct technique is also dependent on factors such as the size of the program, the number of people involved, its cost, the geographical area involved, the number of interrelated components in the program, and so on.

Feedback

In the context of this process we are using the term feedback to mean communicating the results of our objective-setting process back to those above *and* below us in the hierarchy. Whether or not the results are favorable or unfavorable, it is imperative that we communicate the results back into our system. This is done for the following reasons:

To keep people informed of results

To lead to refined objectives, one building on the results of the last

To continue the process of constantly refining our ability to effect problems in our work group

To build a data base upon which to base future objectives and decisions

In order to review the theme of this section—"the objective-setting process is critical in the supervisor's role of problem solving"—the following series of questions should be asked of each objective.

Is the objective a guide to action?

Is it explicit enough to suggest certain types of action (alternatives)?

Is it suggestive of tools to measure and control effectiveness?

Is it challenging?

Does it show cognizance of internal and external constraints?

PLANNING FOR PLANNING

Although all the managerial functions are interrelated and the police manager performs each at one time or another, any given phase of organizational activity must begin with planning. As mentioned earlier, planning is the process by which the police department adapts its resources to changing environmental forces and achieves its goals. It is a highly dynamic function and must be carried out effectively so as to provide a *solid* foundation for the remaining managerial activities. The planning function in the police organization can be considered as an integrated decision system which establishes the framework for the activities of the organization.[30] It is the responsibility of management planning to plan an integrated planning system that will enhance organizational performance—in other words, planning for planning.

Managers on all levels of the police organization are engaged in all the basic functions of the management process. As the police manager moves up the organizational structure, however, he will or should spend relatively more of his time planning. At the upper levels there is also an increased amount of time spent on planning for various time periods in the future. Upper management not only should devote most of its time to planning but must be dedicated to the creation of long-range plans. It is the manager's responsibility to define the desired role of the organization in the future, to relate the organization to its environment, and to perceive the goals that the organization can fulfill. No one else within the police department is equipped to define the desired role of the department. Together with an internal definition must come an external one that is derived from the city management, the community, and the related criminal justice organizations. The character of the agency must be established, and its goals must be set forth explicitly as guidelines to decision making throughout the entire police organization. Clear statements of expectations, along with both external and internal premises for planning, help focus the effort of all police personnel toward common objectives. The outcome of effective planning is accurate decision making throughout the department.

In regard to planning, first, the manager must refrain from treating it as an entity in itself. Planning should be geared to obtaining, translating, understanding, and communicating information that will improve the rationality of current decisions that are based upon future expectations. Expectations are developed through the process of forecasting and predicting the future. Much effort is being devoted to refining predictive techniques to enable police departments to forecast their social, political, legislative, and tactical environment. Police agencies are becoming more interested in broad environmental data such as social indicators and are relating departmental services to the overall social community outlook. Second, the police manager must also refrain from acting as if forecasting were planning. While forecasting provides a basis for understanding and formulating expectations, management must go beyond this orientation

[30]Such a system is described in Sherman C. Blumenthal, *Management Information Systems: A Framework for Planning and Development* (Englewood Cliffs, N.J.: Prentice-Hall, Inc., 1969).

stage by developing and implementing action plans designed to optimize the department's total performance. Since these plans themselves may alter the future—not only of the department but of the total environment —forecasts, no matter how rigorously developed, are not complete in themselves. The significance of any forecast resides in its insertion into an *action plan* that is *implemented*.

Three levels of plan. The selected planning process should be capable of generating plans that are targeted toward three levels of complexity:

> The environmental plan—sets forth the broad social, cultural, political and legislative parameters in which the department must operate.
>
> The tactical plan—describes the service demands, criminal justice relationships, and agency-clientele relationships for the particular community in which the department operates.
>
> The internal organization plan—indicates the organizational structure, objectives and policies, and functional relationships which distinguish one department from all others.

PLANNING: Three Standards

The National Advisory Commission on Criminal Justice Standards and Goals devoted a large share of its six publications to the subject of planning. The following standards and supporting commentary deal with one component of the criminal justice system—our police.[31]

Standard 5.3

COMMITMENT TO PLANNING

Every police agency should develop planning processes which will anticipate short- and long-term problems and suggest alternative solutions to them. Policy should be written to guide all employees toward effective administrative and operational planning decisions. Every police agency should adopt procedures immediately to assure the planning competency of its personnel through the establishment of qualifications for selection and training.

[31]National Advisory Commission on Criminal Justice Standards and Goals, *Police,* (Washington, D.C.: U.S. Government Printing Office, 1973), pp. 117, 118, 122–24, 129, 130.

1. Every police agency should establish written policy setting out specific goals and objectives of the planning effort, quantified and measurable where possible, which at least include the following:

    a. To develop and suggest plans that will improve police service in furthering the goals of the agency;

    b. To review existing agency plans to ascertain their suitability, to determine any weaknesses, to update or devise improvement when needed, and to assure they are suitably recorded;

    c. To gather and organize into usable format information needed for agency planning.

2. Every police agency should stress the necessity for continual planning in all areas throughout the agency, to include at least:

    a. Within administrative planning: long range, fiscal and management plans;

    b. Within operational planning: specific operational, procedural, and tactical plans;

    c. Extradepartmental plans; and

    d. Research and development.

3. Every police agency should establish written qualifications for employees assigned specifically to planning activities.

4. Every police agency should provide training necessary for all personnel to carry out their planning responsibilities.

5. If there are planning needs that cannot be satisfied by agency personnel, the police agency should satisfy these needs through an appropriate arrangement with another police agency, another governmental agency, or a private consultant.

Commentary

Extensive planning, administrative as well as operational, is one of the most critical needs of the police today. There are not many police chief executives who disagree with this, but few have taken positive steps to encourage or implement such planning. This failure puts the burden on individual subordinates who must plan for their own operations without administrative direction and support, usually on a crisis basis.

Additionally, the failure of the police chief executive to provide for planning indicates to subordinates that he considers planning to be unimportant, or that he is not interested in how they perform their work. The first tends to encourage the subordinate to adopt the same attitude toward planning; the second lowers morale and efficiency. Neither contributes positively to the effectiveness of agency operations.

When the police chief executive does take steps to establish a planning unit or to assign administrative planning responsibilities, problems can develop if he does not clearly delineate the relationship between the planning unit and other agency personnel. Planning personnel may feel removed from operations personnel and operations personnel may feel they have been relieved of all planning duties.

It should be clear that the police chief executive must provide proper direction and an atmosphere that encourages operational planning throughout the agency. The first step should be the formulation and dissemination of a strong and unequivocal policy statement expressing commitment to planning and to positive change. Providing the necessary organizational structure and staffing for planning—should reinforce commitment; at the same time it prepares the agency to meet its needs.

It should be equally clear that he has a responsibility to provide the organizational structure and the staffing necessary to generate a full spectrum of effective planning for his agency. When a product is primarily the result of personal effort, its quality usually corresponds to the qualifications, training, attitudes, and personality of those who contributed to the effort. Police planning is no exception.

Standard 5.4

AGENCY AND
JURISDICTIONAL PLANNING

Every police agency should immediately identify the types of planning necessary for effective operation, and should assign specific responsibility for research and development, and police agency and jurisdictional planning.

1. Every police agency with 75 or more personnel should establish a unit staffed with at least one employee whose full-time responsibility will be intra-agency administrative planning and coordination of all planning activities for the agency.
   a. The size and composition of this planning unit should be proportionate to the size of the agency and the magnitude of the present and anticipated planning task.
   b. The employee in charge of the planning unit should have no more than one person in the chain of command between him and the police chief executive.

2. Every police agency organized into subdivisions should delineate divisional planning responsibilities and should provide personnel accordingly.
   a. To the extent feasible, divisional planning should be a staff activity performed by the agency's central planning unit. If centralized planning for a division is not feasible, the agency should assign planning personnel to the division.
   b. The agency should assign a specialized section of the central planning unit or a separate specialized planning unit to specialized divisions or to divisions with specialized planning requirements.
   c. The agency should insure coordination of all agency planning efforts.

3. Every police agency with fewer than 75 personnel should assign responsibility for administrative planning and coordination of all planning activities of the agency.

    a. If the magnitude of the agency's planing task justifies a full-time employee, one should be assigned; and

    b. If it does not, this task should be assigned to an employee with related duties.

4. Every police agency should assign responsibility for maintaining close interagency planning.

    a. Interagency planning should be engaged in by police agencies that are geographically close, that regularly operate concurrently within the same jurisdictional boundaries, that participate in a plan for mutual aid, or that logically should participate in any combined or regional police effort.

    b. Where regional police planning agencies exist, every police agency should assign responsibility for planning with those regional police planning agencies whose decisions might affect the assigning agency. This responsibility should include liaison with the established regional planning agency or other representative of the State Planning Agency.

5. Every police agency should participate in cooperative planning with all other governmental subdivisions of the jurisdiction when such planning can have an effect on crime, public safety, or efficient police operations.

    a. Every local governmental entity, in all matters of mutual interest, immediately should provide for police planning with that of other governmental subdivisions of the jurdisdiction.

    b. Every police agency should assign responsibility for such planning immediately. This assignment should include at least the responsibility for joint planning, when applicable, with the local government administrative office, local government attorney's office, finance department, purchasing department, personnel department, civil service commission, fire department, department of public works, utilities department, building inspection unit, street or highway department, parks department, recreation department, planning unit, and health department.

Commentary

Planning can be formal or informal, structured or haphazard, painstakingly thought out or completed on the spur of the moment; whatever its form, planning takes place in every police agency.

The planning needs of each police agency are different, and the needs are not static. Obviously the large agency serving a densely populated urban area has different needs than the small agency serving a sparsely populated rural area. The newly created agency in a jurisdiction of rapid growth will normally have needs different from those of a long-established agency of equal size in a relatively stable jurisdiction.

Both the large urban agency and the small rural agency will find their planning needs changing as a result of changed demography in land use and in the nature, type, or rate of crime. Planning requirements of the agency experiencing rapid growth will change as the growth and expansion within the jurisdiction decelerate; and those of the older agency will change if its once-stable community begins to change. Nevertheless, there are a number of requirements common to all police agencies. If an agency is to fulfill its responsibilities to the community it serves, it must recognize and provide for these common needs as a minimum.

Administrative planning relates to giving direction and providing support—planning that facilitates all operations. It includes long-range, fiscal, and other management planning. Operational planning relates directly to performance—planning for action. It Includes procedural, tactical, and specific operational planning (See Commentary, Standard 5.3).

Every police agency, no matter how simple or complex its needs, should devise its planning program to include each of these types of planning. The program should include all administrative planning required to support the agency's operations, and it should include all operational planning required to insure adequate performance and the achievement of the agency's goals and objectives.

When establishing operational plans, the police agency should examine the activities of community groups and organizations whose activities would be likely to affect police operations. Where appropriate, members of those groups should be involved in the planning of police service that may affect their activity. Included should be social groups, service clubs, civic and political organizations, educational institutions, professional or vocational associations, business groups and labor unions, and any others appropriate.

Research and development is the foundation of progressive planning. Results of research and development, however, are rarely shared by criminal justice agencies and, as a consequence, are often duplicated needlessly. This is perhaps due to the decentralized nature of the system and the lack of effective means of communicating the results. Wherever possible, police agencies should make information relating to research and development projects available to other agencies. In 1958, at a seminar on police planning and research at the University of California, O. W. Wilson identified the need for a national registry to index research conducted by police agencies. Such a registry never materialized, despite the need for one.

Most federally funded projects require that any information developed be available to all agencies upon request. The Law Enforcement Assistance Administration established the National Criminal Justice Reference Service to meet the technical information needs of the criminal justice system. Basic services that are provided without charge include: selective dissemination of information materials tailored to specific user needs; selected distribution of hard copy documents; selected topic digests; current awareness materials; document retrieval indexes; a national criminal justice thesaurus; search and retrieval services; and references and referrals.

It is planned that the service ultimately will have "on-line" capability that will allow users access from remote terminals for interactive searches. This should result in faster, more accurate access to existing documentation.

The police chief executive, of course, has the final responsibility for planning. In small agencies most of the administrative planning, and often much of the operational planning, is done personally by the chief executive. The larger the agency the less personal time the chief executive can devote to planning. Where necessary, he should delegate operational planning to line commanders, and he should delegate administrative planning to staff personnel of a planning unit.

Standard 5.5

POLICE-COMMUNITY
PHYSICAL PLANNING

Every police agency should participate with local planning agencies and organizations, public and private, in community physical planning that affects the rate or nature of crime or the fear of crime.

1. Every government entity should seek police participation with public and private agencies and organizations involved in community physical planning within the jurisdiction.

2. Every police agency should assist in planning with public and private organizations involved in police-related community physical planning. This assistance should at least include planning involving:
   a. Industrial area development;
   b. Business and commercial area development;
   c. Residential area development, both low rise and high rise;
   d. Governmental or health facility complex development;
   e. Open area development, both park and other recreation;
   f. Redevelopment projects such as urban renewal; and
   g. Building requirements (target hardening), both residential and commercial.

Commentary

It has long been recognized that certain physical conditions can contribute to the rate and nature of crimes, and to the fear of crime in given geographic areas. Any experienced police officer can identify high crime risk locations on his beat by noting such factors as poor lighting, weak points of entry to potential crime targets, isolated points of entry (i.e., either concealed or located where no one would normally pass), physical layout of crime target providing concealment, and inaccessibility of areas to police patrol.

Attempting to reduce crime or the fear of crime by regulating physical environment is not new. The pyramids of Egypt, in addition to being monuments to their founders, have complex access ways to prevent theft of items contained within. Moats were built around castles. England, in 1285, enjoyed the protection of the statute of Winchester that required the removal of shrubs along highways where persons could lurk.

In modern times, governments have become increasingly involved in physical and environmental planning. They have enacted building codes and zoning laws while concentrating on structural soundness, economics of land use, aesthetic values, and, very recently, ecology. Concern for public safety has centered around fire safety (fireproof or fire retardant materials, emergency exits, and hydrant placements) with little attention to crime prevention.

But today, when technological assistance is available to increase security—to reduce the potential for crime and thereby reduce both crime and the fear of crime—by the proper design and construction of new (or redesign and remodeling of old) industrial, commercial, residential, recreational, or open space developments, the police agency or its government should not permit the perpetuation of the practice of bolting doors with inadequate locks.

A 1971 report, *A Study of Crime Prevention Through Physical Planning,* prepared for the Southern California Association of Governments by the SUA Division of Dillingham Corporation, pointed out:

> The neglect of crime prevention in the physical planning processes can be explained by: a lack of awareness of the possible contributions which could be made by physical planning and, therefore, the lack of support in the form of codes, policies and manpower; the lack of incentives to include crime prevention measures by insurance companies and underwriters; the lack of a body of knowledge and the education and training efforts to produce personnel skilled in the application of crime prevention in the physical planning processes.

As a part of this study, questionnaires were mailed to 80 large police agencies in the U.S., Canada, and England to ascertain their involvement in crime prevention through physical planning. Of the 47 police agencies responding; only three approved plans for new construction, four approved comprehensive plans, five reviewed or approved zone changes or variances for land use, three reviewed or approved subdivision applications, six reviewed or approved annexation proposals, and six reviewed or approved redevelopment or urban renewal plans. The study went on to show that an incredible 87 to 93 percent lack of formal police agency participation in physical planning has a critical effect on the rate and nature of crime and the fear of crime.

Oscar Newman, a New York architect and city planner, has conducted studies on the relationship of physical design and crime rates in public housing. In his book, *Defensible Space,* published in 1972, Mr. Newman discusses how housing projects can be designed so that all areas of the complex can be easily and frequently observed by tenants, the surrounding community, or police patrols. He has isolated certain variables such as the grouping of dwelling units, the definition of grounds, the design and place-

ment of elevators, doors, and lobbies, and the use of lighting that have a strong influence on crime reduction. His studies indicate that while crime rates in public housing
may not correlate specifically with density (the number of apartment units to the acre),
they do correlate with building type and height. Crime rates were found to be much
higher in high rise buildings over six stories, especially in those designed with a "double
loaded corridor" (one floor consists of a long central corridor with apartments lining
both sides).

LEARNING EXERCISE

LONG-RANGE
PLANNING

Purpose. A long-range plan can be an invaluable operating guide or a useless
piece of fiction. This exercise will enable you to see how well your present
long-range police planning procedures fulfill your managers' expectations.

Process

1. Duplicate the Long-Range Planning Questionnaire (exhibit 5–1) and send a
   copy to each police manager/supervisor in the agency who is explicitedly
   impacted by the long-range plan.
2. When the questionnaires are returned, determine the average score by giving
   five points for an "A" answer, four for a "B," three for a "C," two for a "D,"
   and one for an "E."
3. If the total average is below twenty-five points, which suggest poor long-range
   planning, form a high-powered agency project group to investigate the
   planning process.

Exhibit 5-1.

LONG-RANGE PLANNING QUESTIONNAIRE

The purpose of this questionnaire is to discover how well the present long-term plan is meeting the needs of police managers and supervisors. The results may call for further investigation into the planning process.

Directions. Check the box that is nearest to your present experience.

1. I feel that there is full police top management support for the long-term plan.

A ☐	B ☐	C ☐	D ☐	E ☐
Strongly agree	Agree	Moderately agree	Disagree	Strongly disagree

2. Police top management clearly makes decisions on the basis of the plan.

A ☐	B ☐	C ☐	D ☐	E ☐
Strongly agree	Agree	Moderately agree	Disagree	Strongly disagree

3. Proper agency resources are allocated for police planning.

A ☐	B ☐	C ☐	D ☐	E ☐
Strongly agree	Agree	Moderately agree	Disagree	Strongly disagree

4. The police plan makes good sense to me, personally.

A ☐	B ☐	C ☐	D ☐	E ☐
Strongly agree	Agree	Moderately agree	Disagree	Strongly disagree

5. Good short-term police plans evolve from the long-term plan.

A ☐	B ☐	C ☐	D ☐	E ☐
Strongly agree	Agree	Moderately agree	Disagree	Strongly disagree

6. I feel that those responsible for long-term police planning are capable and well qualified.

A ☐	B ☐	C ☐	D ☐	E ☐
Strongly agree	Agree	Moderately agree	Disagree	Strongly disagree

7. The police agency is ready to change things substantially if necessary.

A ☐	B ☐	C ☐	D ☐	E ☐
Strongly agree	Agree	Moderately agree	Disagree	Strongly disagree

8. I feel a part of the police planning process.

A ☐	B ☐	C ☐	D ☐	E ☐
Strongly agree	Agree	Moderately agree	Disagree	Strongly disagree

Chapter Six

TASK 4
COMMUNICATIONS:
The Movement of Information

I know you believe you understood what you think I said, but I am not sure you realize that what you heard is not what I meant.   *Anonymous*

The primary problems faced by the police in using the computer are not technical but are behavioral and people oriented.[1]

Criminal justice information systems are the target of those most concerned about the possibility of the invasion of privacy. Criticism is leveled at the types of information stored in the systems, the validity of the data, the necessity for the information, the dissemination of the material and the eventual purging or retention of the information.[2]

SYNOPSIS

In communications, quality and quantity alike depend on the capability of the police manager to interact with the personnel and machines under his purview. In essence, our bureaucratic mechanisms function in direct relationship to their communications systems. While most would attest to the necessity of effective communications, most would also concur that "effective" communication is difficult to achieve. Effective communication means effective decisions, and vice versa.

In analyzing the information flow in a police organization one can observe both formal and informal channels being used to transmit data downward, upward, and horizontally. Further, one can see that the channels carry varying volumes and kinds of messages. If properly designed and used, the channels can enhance self-correcting control (cybernetics).

In addition to the human message exchanges we also find machines being involved, especially of late the computer. The vast majority of police and sheriff agencies have either in-house or accessible computer-based information systems. The application areas range from wanted persons to resource allocation. As a consequence, the manager is currently experiencing an opportunity to gain technological assistance in the administration of his agency. In terms of

---

[1]Kent W. Colton, "Computers and the Police: Police Departments and the New Information Technology," *Municipal Year Book 1975* (Washington, D.C.: International City Management Association, 1975), p. 221.

[2]Clarence B. Kelley, "The Right to Privacy is American—But so is the Right to Law and Order," *Trial* 11 (January-February 1975): 23.

operational data, however, the issue of computer security and record privacy has become a dominant concern. Although the issue has been addressed in recent federal legislation, much more remains to be decided. In the meantime, the debate over integrated versus dedicated police information systems continues to plague those that are responsible for system design and implementation decisions.

COMMUNICATION IS THE VEHICLE

Communication is the vehicle for managerial planning, and the police manager is a key person in developing and maintaining effective organizational communications as he interacts with subordinates, peers, superiors, and members of the community. To succeed in this task, he must communicate in many directions for the basic purpose of exerting his influence and control. A large part of our consideration of police management, therefore, deals with the subject of communications. Excellent testimony to the importance of *good* communications is expressed in the following statement:

> But good government [police work] requires more than good people. It requires good management of these good people. And too often, managers tend to spend great time and effort on their program responsibilities and their monetary resources while leaving their people-management responsibilities and opportunities to take care of themselves. This type of imbalance must be corrected.
>
> Our greatest single obstacle is poor communication. We are engaged in a rebuilding of the federal personnel system [police system] to better serve the needs of management and employees in the 70's. But we have to communicate what we are doing and why.[3]

A message system, or in terms of organizational setting a communications system, provides the means by which information, statements, views, and instructions are transmitted through a police organization. Although one often speaks of the "flow" of information, this flow actually consists of a series of discrete messages of different length, form, and content. These messages are transmitted through certain channels (or lines of communication), which make up the communications system or

[3]Robert E. Hampton, "Special Feature–Dialogue for the 70's," *Public Personnel Review* 31 (October 1970): 295.

network. Each message is sent by a transmitter (an individual, a group, a division, a computer) to a receiver or several receivers. It may stimulate action or a reaction in the form of a countermessage or both. Every individual or division in a police organization acts as a sender and a receiver, though not for the same messages. Some individuals, depending on their position in the police organization, send more than they receive; others receive more than they send. Significantly, the manager's day is filled with a heavy volume o͡f transmissions and receptions.

Communications can be viewed as occurring in a variety of ways and, in an organizational sense, at a number of levels—interpersonal, group, and systemic. This chapter discusses both the human and technological components of the communications process.[4]

WHY COMMUNICATE?

Why communicate? First, and most important, a police manager makes decisions (or should be making decisions) based on information received in conjunction with previously developed plans, procedures, or rules. Consequently, the communication process is necessary because the flow of proper information to the decision points throughout the police organization is such a vital requirement for goal accomplishment. In fact, if managing were thought of primarily as decision making and if the decision process were considered essentially a communication process including a network of communications systems, then the act of managing could be witnessed as a communication process. Thus the several concepts—communications, planning, control, information, and decision making—are interwoven. Plainly, the closer we look at influence, control, and planning, the more we become aware of the basic features of information exchange. Wiener aptly writes in support of this thinking.

> Information is a name for the content of what is exchanged with 'the outer world as we adjust to it, and make our adjustment felt upon it. The process of receiving and using information is the process of our adjusting to the contingencies of the outer environment, and

[4]For those interested in information pertaining to the technological aspects of police information systems, see The Presidents Commission on Law Enforcement and Administration of Justice, *Task Force Report: Science and Technology* (Washington, D.C.: U.S. Government Printing Office, 1967); selected articles in S. I. Cohn, ed., *Law Enforcement Science and Technology* II (Chicago: Port City Press, Inc., 1969); National Advisory Commission on Criminal Justice Standards and Goals, *Criminal Justice System.* (Washington, D.C.: U.S. Government Printing Office, 1973); and various research reports published by Search Group, Inc. (Sacramento, Calif.).

of our living effectively within that environment. The needs and the complexity of modern life make greater demands on this process of information than ever before, and our press, our museums, our scientific laboratories, our universities, our libraries and textbooks, are obliged to meet the needs of this process or fail in their purpose. To live effectively is to live with adequate information. Thus, communication and control belong to this life in society.[5]

A police manager communicates so as to send or request information for the making of a decision on the direction and coordination of departmental "resources." Hence, we design communications systems to carry the requisite information for decision making to fulfill the provision of task-oriented direction and coordination.[6] The system may be formal or informal or both, and it may be manual or automated or both. Specifically, then, why does a police manager depend on the quality of a communications system? The answer is that goal attainment is achieved through communications. We find that the system's degree of success is based on its doing five things: (1) providing sufficient information to accomplish assigned tasks—this communication function may be satisfied through a variety of forms, such as periodic training, provision of technical reference manuals, daily coaching, and orders; (2) communicating clarified perceptions and expectations of responsibility—organization charts, job descriptions, work plans, schedules, routes, performance ratings, orders, and other devices may serve this function; (3) facilitating the *coordination* (now and in the future) of men and materials in achieving specific objectives; (4) making possible organizational problem solving (task oriented) and conflict resolution (interpersonal problems); and (5) furnishing general direction not only on what to achieve but also on how to achieve it. Johnson, Kast, and Rosenzweig provide a fitting ending for this discussion when they write "Throughout history the transmission of information has been a key to progress. Efficient communication is important in all fields of human endeavor."[7]

MULTIPLE COMMUNICATION CHANNELS

Various channels of communication are available to the police manager for exchanging information. A communications systems can be categorized into formal and informal channels. We choose to amplify this

[5]Norbert Wiener, *The Human Use of Human Beings: Cybernetics and Society,* 2nd ed. (New York: Doubleday & Company, Inc., 1954), pp. 17–18.
[6]For an excellent description of the relationship between communications and information systems, see Sherman C. Blumenthal, *Management Information Systems: A Framework for Planning and Development* (Englewood Cliffs, N.J.: Prentice-Hall, Inc., 1969).
[7]Richard A. Johnson, Fremont E. Kast, and James E. Rosenzweig, *The Theory and Management of Systems* (New York: McGraw-Hill Book Company, 1963), p. 87.

list by dividing the informal communication channels into three sub-classes: subformal, personal task directed, and personal nontask directed.[8]

Formal Communication Channels

All organizations develop formal communication channels as a response to large size and the obviously limited information-handling capability of each individual. The formal channels comply with the recognized official structure of the organization and transmit messages expressive of the policy nature of authority. Hence, one typically sees formal orders and directives, reports, official correspondence, standard operating procedures, and so on. Those persons who emphasize going through channels are doing so in adherence to the unity-of-command principle within the formal hierarchy.

Rigid compliance with formal channels can be harmful. The injuries are mainly in terms of time, creativity, and experience. First, it takes a long time for a formal message from a police manager in one division to pass to a manager in another division. Second, formal messages are on the record and thus restrain the free flow of thoughts. Third, in practice, a formal communications system cannot cover all informational needs. Informational needs change quite rapidly, while the formal channels change only with considerable time and effort. Therefore, the most urgent need for *informal communication channels is to "plug" the gaps in the formal channels.*

Informal Communication Channels

Although some consider formal communication channels the only way to send information necessary to the functioning of the police organization, this theory is no longer as sacred as it was in the past. Not only are we witnessing an interest in obtaining a better understanding of the informal organization, but along with it has come an awareness of its potential use. This interest and awareness logically leads to a different perspective on the structuring of communication flow. This perspective does not delimit organizationally useful communications to purely formal channels. It encompasses all the social processes of the widest relevance in the functioning of any group or organization. Therefore, we now recognize informal and personal communications as a supportive and frequently necessary process for effective functioning. The unofficial communication channels also become a prime means for researching the

---

[8]This classification is suggested in part by William M. Jones, *On Decisionmaking in Large Organizations* (Santa Monica, Calif.: The Rand Corporation, 1964).

formal organization. In fact, police managers are often expected to seek information through channels not officially sanctioned or recognized.

A large number of informal channels means that formal channels do not fully meet the important communications needs in a police department. Therefore, it is futile for police managers to establish formal channels and expect that those channels will carry most of the messages. The more restricted the formal channels, the greater the growth of informal ones. Although the informal system seeks to fill the gaps in the formal one, the leaders of a police organization can severely curtail the development of the former by simply directing subordinates not to communicate with each other, by physically separating people, or by requiring prior clearance for any communication outside a certain division. In doing so, the number of significant messages is sharply reduced, thus affecting the general effectiveness of the organization.

We next proceed to an analysis of three kinds of informal communication channels. The first two are task, or goal, oriented, while the third is oriented toward the *individual*.

Informal communication channels: subformal.   Subformal channels move those messages arising from the informal power structure existing in every police organization. Every member of the department must know and observe informal standards and procedures about what to communicate and to whom. Such norms are seldom written down and must be acquired by experience and example, a necessity that causes difficulties for newcomers.

Subformal communications consist of two types: those that flow along formal channels, but not as formal communications; and those that flow along strictly informal channels. Both types have the definite advantage of not being official—they can be withdrawn or changed without any official record being made. Therefore, almost all new ideas are first proposed and tried as subformal communicaitons. Would anyone refute the statement that the vast majority of communications in police organizations are subformal?

As mentioned above, subformal channels of communication develop whenever there is a need for police personnel to communicate but no formal channel exists. Formal channels are usually vertical, following the paths of the formal authority structure. Thus, most of the gap-filling subformal lines of communication are horizontal, connecting peers rather than subordinates and superiors. This characteristic is one reason that police managers find subformal channels so vital in their job. Subformal communications supply a way for subordinates from all levels to speak more freely to their superiors—the managers!

While in general it has been shown that subformal channels meet the communication requirements not met by formal channels, they become all the more necessary under certain conditions. First, the greater the degree of interdependence among activities (e.g., patrol and detectives) within the department, the greater the number and use of subformal channels. Second, the more uncertainty about the objectives of the department, the greater the number and use of subformal channels. Third, when a police organization is operating under the pressure of time, it tends to use subformal channels extensively, since there is often no time to use formal channels. Thus, police managers stretch out for information wherever they can get it from whatever channel is necessary. Fourth, closely cooperating sections rely primarily upon subformal communications. Conversely, if the divisions of a police organization are in competition, they tend to avoid subformal channels and to communicate only formally. Obviously, rivalry has significant communications drawbacks (vice vs. detectives). Fifth, subformal communication channels are used more often if departmental members have stable, rather than constantly changing, relationships with each other.

Informal communication channels: personal task directed. A personal task-directed communication is one in which an organization member intentionally reveals something of his own attitude toward the activities of his own organization. While personal, this communication is also targeted toward the goals or activities of the organization. Thus we can refer to it as task directed. It possesses the following characteristics: (1) Task-directed personal channels are nearly always used for informing rather than for directions; (2) before a person acts on the basis of information received through personal channels, he usually varies that information through either subformal or formal channels; (3) the channels transmit information with considerable speed because there are no formal mechanisms to impede its flow; and (4) because task-directed personal messages are transmitted by personnel acting as individuals, they do not bear the weight of the position generating them. To this extent, they differ from subformal messages, which are transmitted by individuals acting in their assigned capacity—but not for the official record!

Informal communication channels: personal nontask directed. As suggested by its title, this form of communication *apparently* does not contain information related to the tasks of the organization. Note the emphasis on the word *apparently*. Paradoxically, this channel may handle information on occasion far more valuable to the achievement of organizational goals than any other channels, including the formal ones. An example of this channel is the manager's learning through a loyal subordinate the reasons for growing job dissatisfaction. A discussion of its characteristics will provide an explanation of its benefits: (1) Non-task-directed channels furnish a vehicle for an individual to satisfy his social needs; (2) this channel provides a way for an individual to "blow off steam" over things that disturb him; (3) non-task-directed channels frequently supply useful feedback normally comprised of unexpected information not obtainable in any other way; and (4) personal channels offer the best medium for a person to become adjusted to his organizational setting (unwritten standards, group values, and "the way we do things here" are conveniently expressed through non-task-directed channels). In conclusion and to reemphasize our contention:

> The efficiency of a large formal organization is sizably enhanced when its own chain of command or decision or communication is tied into the informal network or groups within the organization, so that the network can be used to support the organization's goals.[9]

COMMUNICATIONS: Downward, Upward, And Horizontal

Traditionally, communication flow was viewed as being exclusively downward and identical with the pattern of authority. The pattern of authority provides, of course, the structure of an organization, but almost invariably it is found to represent an overly idealized notion of what the organization is like, or what it should be like, and this is why students of organization theory constantly need to analyze the informal structure for other directions of communication flow. A message can flow in one of three directions: downward, upward, and laterally (horizontally).[10]

Downward

Communications from superior to subordinate are of five types:

1. Specific task directives: *job instructions*
2. Information to produce the understanding of the task and its relation to other organizational tasks: *job rationale*
3. Information concerning organizational *procedures and practices*
4. *Feedback* to the subordinate officer about his performance
5. Information to instill a sense of mission: *indoctrination of goals*

---

[9]Bernard Berelson and Gary A. Steiner, *Human Behavior: An Inventory of Scientific Findings* (New York: Harcourt, Brace & World, Inc., 1964), p. 370.

[10]This particular section is drawn from Anthony Downs, *Inside Bureaucracy* (Boston: Little, Brown and Company, 1967), pp. 235–47.

The first type of message is most often given first priority in police organizations. Instructions about the job of police officer are communicated to the person through direct orders from his manager, training sessions, training manuals, and written directives. The objective is to insure the reliable performance of every individual in the organization. Less attention is given to the second type, which is designed to provide the police officer with a full understanding of his position and its relation to similar positions in the same organization. Many police personnel know *what* they are to do, but not *why*. Withholding information on the rationale of the job not only reduces the loyalty of the member to his organization but also makes the organization rely heavily on the first type of information, specific instructions about the job. Some city and police administrators are in favor of reducing the policeman's behavior to that of a robot; others want to use his intelligence by having him act on his understanding of the total situation. It can be seen, therefore, that the benefits of giving fuller information on job understanding are twofold: If an officer knows the reasons for his assignment, he will often carry out his job more effectively; and if he has an understanding of what his job is about in relation to the overall mission of his department, he is more likely to identify with its goals. Third, information about organization procedures supplies a prescription of the role requirements of the organizational member. Fourth, feedback is necessary to insure that the organization is operating properly. Feedback to the individual about how well he is doing in his job, however, is often neglected or poorly handled, even in police organizations in which the managerial philosophy calls for such penetrating evaluation. Fifth, the final type of downward-directed information has as its purpose to emphasize organizational goals, either for the total organization or for a major unit of it. Consequently, an important function of a police manager is to describe the mission of the police department in an attractive and motivational style.

Upward

Communications about or from subordinates to the police manager are of five types:

1. Information about his *performance* and *grievances*
2. Information about the *performance* and *grievances* of others
3. Feedback regarding organizational *practices* and *policies*
4. Feedback concerning *what* needs to be done and the *means* for doing it
5. Requests for *clarification* of the goals and specific activities

For a variety of reasons, however, there are great barriers to free upward communication. Most prominent is the structure itself. Simply stated, bureaucracies or highly formalized organizations tend to inhibit upward informal communications. Thus, a tremendous amount of important information never reaches the upper-level decision centers. Other factors also adversely affect the upward flow of messages. Managers are less in the habit of listening to their subordinates than of talking to them. And because information fed up the line is often used for control purposes, the manager's subordinates are not likely to give him information that will lead to decisions affecting them adversely. They tell the manager not only what he wants to hear but also what they want him to know. How many of you, readers and managers, have detected this in your conversations with those over whom you exert power? Moreover, is it your fault or theirs?

Horizontal

Communications between people at the same organizational level are basically of four types:

1. Information necessary to provide task *coordination*
2. Information for identifying and defining *common problems* to be solved through cooperation
3. Feedback from coworkers which fulfills *social needs*
4. Information needed to provide *social* (not organizational) *control* for a group so that it can maintain the members' compliance with its standards and values

Organizations face one of their most difficult problems in procedures and practices concerned with horizontal communication. In essence, a working balance must be found between unrestricted and overrestricted communications among coworkers in an organization. Unrestricted communications that are horizontal can detract from maximum efficiency because too much nonrelevant information may be transmitted. At the opposite extreme, efficiency suffers if an employee receives all his instructions from the person above him, thus reducing task coordination. Our position here is that lateral communication is critical for an effective police organization. The type and amount of information that should be circulated on a horizontal basis is best determined by answering the question, Who needs to know and why? An interesting "hang-up" in horizontal communication occurs when people overvalue peer communication and neglect those below and above them. Lieutenants talk only to lieutenants, and captains only to captains. The problem resides in the word *only*, for they should be interacting in all directions.

MESSAGES: Number And Kinds

Communication is expensive! Every message involves time for deciding what to send, time for composing, costs of sending the message (which may consist of time, money, or both), and time for interpreting the message. Not only do messages take time and money, but they can also seriously hamper an individual because they subtract time from his working day. Obviously, the more time a person spends in searching or communicating, the less he has for other types of activity. Every individual has a saturation point regarding the amount of information he can usefully handle in a given time period. If he should become overloaded, he will be unable effectively either to comprehend the information given to him or to use it. All of this means that the particular methods used by a police organization to collect, select, and transmit information are critically important determinants of its success. First we taken a closer look at the number of messages; second, at the kinds of messages.

Number

The frequency of messages in a police organization is determined by six basic factors:

1. The total number of members in the organization
2. The nature of its communications networks (downward, upward, or horizontal)
3. The sending regulations controlling when and to whom messages are sent
4. The degree of interdependence of the organization's various activities
5. The speed with which relevant changes occur in its external environment
6. The search mechanisms and procedures used by the organization to investigate its environment

High message volume usually results in "overloading." Attempts are automatically made to reduce any overloading. Police managers can react to this situation in one or more of the following ways. They can slow down their handling of messages without changing the organization's network structure of transmission rules. *But*, this action will cause the police department to reduce its speed of reaction to events and will thereby lessen its output *Or*, they can change the transmission procedures so that their subordinates screen out more information before sending messages. *But*, this reaction will also reduce the quantity of the department's output. *Or*, they can create more channels in the network to accommodate the same quantity of messages in the same time period. *But*, this reaction will provide more opportunities for message distortion and will be more expensive. *Or*, they can relate tasks within the organization so that those units with the highest message traffic are grouped together within the overall communications system. *But*, this action will reduce the volume of messages sent through higher levels in the network and will facilitate the coordination of effort. *Or*, they can improve the quality of messages in order to reduce the time needed for receiving, composing, and transmitting them. In addition to improving the content and format of the messages, the manager can decide on better methods for handling them.

Kinds

Messages vary in content and form. There are reports, statements, inquiries, questions, accounts, comments, notes, records, recommendations, rejoinders, instructions, and so on.[11] Each message may have a different purpose and may thus lead to a different response. Messages can be transmitted either formally or informally in one of three ways: (1) written communication (2) oral communication in face-to-face meetings of two or more individuals, and (3) oral communication in telephone conversations.

Written messages. Samuel Eilon groups written messages into six categories: routine report, memorandum, inquiry, query, proposal, and decision.

Routine report. A routine report is a message that supplies information as part of a standard operation. A report can be generated in two ways: (1) time triggered—a report called for at set time intervals (for example, a police manager is required to send weekly reports on the activities of his subordinates), and (2) event triggered—a report called for when certain tasks are completed (for example, a report is to be sent when a case is finished, or when certain training has been provided to a manager's subordinates). Remember that in this case the initiative to make a report does not lie with the manager—the circumstances under which a report is issued are clearly specified by organizational procedures; and

[11]Most of this section is drawn from Samuel Eilon, "Taxonomy of Communications," *Administrative Science Quarterly* 13 (September 1968): 266–88.

the manager is required only to determine that the circumstances conform to the specification.

Memorandum. A memorandum also furnishes information, but not as part of a routine procedure. A memorandum can be (1) a *statement of fact*, submitted in response to an inquiry, to assist in evaluating a problem or to prepare plans for action; (2) a *statement that is event triggered*, released when circumstances have changed in an unprescribed manner, calling for some initiative by the sender in drawing attention of others to the change so that a plan of action can be developed; or (3) a *comment*, made in response to some other statement to information or to give a different interpretation of data. This does not mean that all routine reports are devoid of initiative, whereas all memorandums are not. If a memorandum is made in response to a request, then the initiative for generating the memorandum lies with the requesting individual, not with the person who created the memorandum. And although event-triggered routine reports do not call for any initiative to create them, initiative may be exercised in determining their content, while event-triggered memorandums may not call for a great deal of initiative with respect to content. Moreover, the creation of a message containing information (report or memorandum) may include one or several of the following activities: (1) extracting data from records; (2) processing data, including computations and analysis, on a routine basis; (3) collecting data as needed; and (4) processing data as needed. In the case of reports, activities are mainly confined to the first two, while memorandums may include all four.

Inquiry. An inquiry is a message requesting information to aid in evaluating a given problem, usually before making recommendations for action. The response to such a request would be a memorandum, which would involve a statement with the necessary information and an analysis of the data. An inquiry normally includes information not contained in reports, unless the reports are time triggered and the information is needed before the next report is due. Also, an inquiry may meet with a comment, which asks for clarification or points out the difficulties in providing certain information in the time specified.

Query. A query is a message defining the characteristics of a problem and asking for instructions or plans about courses of resolution. A query is often made by a subordinate concerning problems not fully discussed in standing regulations, either because of the novelty of the situation or because of ambiguities or inconsistencies in procedures.

Proposal. A proposal describes a course of action the writer feels should be taken. It can be the result of several exchanges of queries, inquiries, reports, and memorandums. It may be generated by a subordinate, on his own initiative or at the instigation of a manager; or it may be created by a manager seeking to test the reactions of his peers or subordinates. A response to a proposal may take the form of a comment or a counterproposal. The absence of a reaction to a proposal is usually viewed as tacit approval.

Decision. A decision states the action to be taken. This message may be of two kinds: (1) a decision that affects repetitious events—which provides direction on how to handle not only the particular events that caused the discussion before the decision but also similar events in the future, and (2) a decision on an *ad hoc* problem—which does not formally affect future procedures. A decision can take a number of forms. It may start with a request to review the causes for making a decision to resolve certain problems; it may continue by outlining alternative courses of action and explaining the reasons for the rejection of some; it may go on to specify what has been decided and how the decision is to be implemented; and it may then express what feedback is expected to keep the decision maker informed of progress in implementation.

Oral messages.   Oral messages are of two types: meetings (face-to-face) and telephone conversations (ear-to-ear).

Meetings. A meeting is a discussion involving two or more persons. Meetings have four purposes: (1) to provide a vehicle for exchanges to take place quickly, (2) to provide a job environment in which members are stimulated to new ideas by the rapid exchange of views, (3) to lessen the degree of semantical difficulties through face-to-face interaction,[12] and (4) to get the members attending the meeting committed more strongly to given plans or procedures than they would be otherwise.

There are two types of meetings: *routine meetings,* such as those of permanent committees, and *ad hoc* meetings, those called to discuss particular issues. The distinction between a routine and an *ad hoc* meeting is similar to that between a routine report and a memorandum. Like a routine report, a routine meeting can be either time or event triggered, while an *ad hoc* meeting may either be called in regard to a request to consider a particular problem or be event triggered. A meeting can also result from the issuance of any one or several of the messages listed earlier: a report, a memorandum, an inquiry for further information, a request for instructions, a proposal, or a decision. Significantly (as most police managers can attest), a meeting can also fizzle and end inconclusively.

---

[12]The importance of semantics for a manager is explained in Gerald H. Graham, "Improving Superior-Subordinate Relationships through General Semantics," *Public Personnel Review* 30 (January 1969): 36–41.

Telephone Conversations. Most of the remarks made on meetings are relevant to telephone communications. The distinction made earlier between routine and *ad hoc* communications may be useful here. There are, however, some noteworthy differences between these two types of oral messages: (1) A telephone conversation is generally confined to two participants, and (2) it lacks certain unique characteristics of interaction which take place in a face-to-face exchange. (Simply stated, if you want to influence someone—do it in person!)

CYBERNETICS: What's A Cybernetic?

Since the latter part of the 1940s a new technology has taken hold in our modern social organizations, one so new that its significance is just now beginning to be understood. While many aspects of this technology are yet unclear, it has moved into the management scene rapidly, with definite and far-reaching impact on our formal organizations. In this and the next section we first explain and then conjecture about this new technology. We refer to this new technology as *information technology.* Implied in this title is our major concern, communications. Information technology is composed of several related components. One includes the machinery and techniques for processing large amounts of information rapidly. A second component is in the offing, though its applications have not yet emerged very clearly; it consists of the simulation of higher-order thinking. A third component centers around the application of statistical and mathematical methods to decision-making problems; it is represented by techniques like mathematical programming and by methodologies like operations research. A fourth component is the control and communication of information for the purpose of feedback. These last two components frequently use computers. We now focus on the fourth component, *feedback*; later we will discuss the *computer.*

Feedback and cybernetics are often considered as being one and the same. The distinction between them. however, is significant. Certain aspects of communication imply that organizations have a built-in capacity to correct their errors, enhancing their potential for effectiveness. *Cybernetics* (a word coined from the Greek *kybernetes,* "steersman") focuses strongly upon the role of feedback in the learning process. *Feedback* is defined by Norbert Wiener as a means for controlling an organization by reinserting into it the results of its past performance.[13] He further described cybernatics as "the entire field of control and com-

13Wiener, *Human Use of Human Beings,* p. 61.

munication theory, whether in the machine or in the animal."[14] Wiener
explained his rationale for linking communication and control into cybernetics as follows:

> When I control the actions of another person, I communicate a
> message to him, and although this message is in the imperative mood,
> the technique of communication does not differ from that of a mes-
> sage of fact. Furthermore, if my control is to be effective, I must
> take cognizance of any messages from him which may indicate that
> the order is understood and has been obeyed.[15]

Feedback is extended here to mean any information that influences
an organization's or an individual's current action. Cybernetics denotes
both the process by which feedback is furnished (communications) and a
special purpose for feedback (control). The computer fits neatly into this
picture because, by being hooked up with electronic data processing machines, the new communication-control systems are able to respond more
quickly and accurately to changes in a large-scale environment. Hence,
the most obvious impact of cybernetics has been in the acceleration of
technological change through new machines that can replace routinized
mental labor.

EFFECTIVE COMMUNICATIONS: Some Suggestions

The importance of maintaining effective communications is as vital
as it always has been. Every human act or thought within a police organization depends in some way on communication. Although it is a vital
part of every police manager's job, communication remains a highly personal art. Human beings have been communicating with each other by
gestures and signs since the origin of the species, by spoken words for
perhaps half a million years, and by some form of writing for more than
four thousand years. We should be experts at it by now, but unfortunately we are not. The major problem today it not that we are not experts
at communication but that the demands now being placed on human
communication threaten to exceed its capacity. Since communication is
a human activity, even though machines may be used to help man in
"talking," we emphasize a fundamental principle: The effectiveness of
communication tends to be directly proportional to the degree to which
both the sender and the receiver regard and treat each other as "hu-

[14]Norbert Wiener, *Cybernetics* (New York: John Wiley & Sons, Inc., 1948), p. 19.
[15]Wiener, *Human Use of Human Beings*, p. 16.

mans," in the personal context of the event.[16] The following techniques or basics for effective communications should be evaluated and (perhaps) implemented with these thoughts in mind.[17]

Many techniques have been developed whereby police managers may remove or circumvent the blockage at each point in the communication process. The major techniques may be broadly classified in terms of the blockage they remedy. There are five areas where blockage might occur in a communications system: (1) sender—one who initiates a message, (2) message—the device for transmitting information, (3) symbol—the content and format of the information, (4) channel—the means for interchanging messages, and (5) receiver—one who accepts a message. The major techniques for surmounting the impasses are as follows (take note, manager):

Sender blockage	Special positions or units whose function is to disseminate information inside or outside the organizations
	Formal and informal reporting systems
Message blockage	Standards for the preparation of reports
	Summarization of long or complex messages
Symbol blockage	Improved style
	Training in use of special terms
	Visual aids
Channel blockage	Liaison officers and special intermediaries
	Routing, screening, and clearance procedures
	Reeducation of hierarchic levels and number of intermediaries
	Exploitation of informal channels and polyarchic relations
Receiver blockage	More use of face-to-face communication
	Indoctrination in common frame of reference

THE CRITICAL NEED FOR COMPUTER-BASED POLICE INFORMATION SYSTEMS

When analyzing the developments of the last few years in local law enforcement *information processing*, we can quickly observe the growing need for assistance from computer-based systems. Acquisition and use of

[16]Edward E. Marcus, "The Basis of Effective Human Communication," *Public Personnel Review* 28 (April 1967): 111.

[17]For a comprehensive discussion on communications-organization, management, and interpersonal relations, see Lee Thayer, *Communication and Communication Systems* (Homewood, Ill.: Richard D. Irwin, Inc., 1968).

large-scale digital computer and communications systems to cope with these rapidly growing information requirements have been made by some local and state jurisdictions (see the appropriate figure). By examining existing and potential applications of these new information-processing techniques and equipment, we can see that the police agencies have considered two major categories of information processing pertinent to local law enforcement activities.

The first category is termed real-time, on-line information processing and retrieval. This approach is important for providing want, record, identification, or vehicle data to field police officers on a fast basis in order to support them in their operational environment. *Real-time, on-line* means basically that the information system is capable of processing individual inquiries simultaneously with field operational needs. *The second category is termed batch information processing and retrieval.* Batch processing signifies that the processing of information does not occur on demand. Rather, all informational requests or needs are processed within some reasonable time convenient to both the computer facility's capability and the needs of the police. This type of processing includes statistical analysis of "called-for services" for management review and decision making, the retrieval of specific documents or information for the purpose of investigation, analysis of crime patterns, and other processes of analysis deemed important to police management or investigation. The criticality of computer-based information systems being applied to the processing of police information requirements is emphasized as follows:

> Information is the life blood of any law enforcement agency. Name and address files, fingerprint records, location indicators, and intelligence and investigation reports are all examples of data to be found in the files of most local police agencies. Added to these, and of equal use, are the files of prosecutors, probation and parole agencies, and state and federal investigative agencies. In other words, we find that the informational needs of the police department are both interrelated and dependent upon other systems within the administration of criminal justice.[18]

STATE OF THE ART

The purpose of the survey-research information reported below is to show you the pervasiveness and intensity of EDP developments in police departments.

[18]Paul M. Whisenand and Tug T. Tamaru, *Automated Police Information Systems* (New York: John Wiley & Sons, Inc., 1970), p. 1.

For our purposes, we can view an automated police information system as consisting of people, computer equipment and related programs, a dynamic data base, and institutional procedures interacting in a prescribed systems pattern. Logically, it is designed to collect, store, update, and facilitate the automated use of data on a continuing basis. Such data and their processing and analysis are related to both the internal affairs of the criminal justice system or component organizations and the external environment. The multifaceted purposes of such an information system are (1) to meet operational requirements, (2) to provide various summarizing or analytical techniques relevant to the definition of community problems, (3) to assist in the search for program goals, (4) to generate cybernetic data flows for evaluation and control, and (5) to permit the exchange of information among governmental units (other criminal justice agencies and noncriminal justice government organizations) and with the public.

It is important to keep in mind that in the majority of instances a computer-based police information system is interfaced to larger-scale statewide criminal justice information systems (CJIS) and, in turn, linked either through the state or directly to such federal systems as the FBI's National Crime Information Center (NCIC). The following is but one of many standards recently promulgated that pertains to police and criminal justice information systems.

Standard 3.2

STATE ROLE
IN CRIMINAL JUSTICE
INFORMATION
AND STATISTICS

Each State should establish a criminal justice information system that provides the following services:

1. On-line files fulfilling a common need of all criminal justice agencies, including wanted persons (felony and misdemeanor), and identifiable stolen items;

2. Computerized criminal history files for persons arrested for an NCIC-qualified offense, with on-line availability of at least a summary of criminal activity and current status of offenders;

3. Access by computer interface to vehicle and driver files, if computerized and maintained separately by another State agency;

4. A high-speed interface with NCIC providing access to all NCIC files;

5. All necessary telecommunications media and terminals for providing access to local users, either by computer-to-computer interface or direct terminal access;

6. The computerized switching of agency-to-agency messages for all intrastate users and routing (formating) of messages to and from qualified agencies in other States;

7. The collection, processing, and reporting of Uniform Crime Reports (UCR) from all law enforcement agencies in the State with report generation for the Federal Government agencies, appropriate State agencies, and contributors;

8. In conjunction with criminal history files, the collection and storage of additional data elements and other features to support offender-based transaction statistics;

9. Entry and updating of data to a national index of criminal offenders as envisioned in the NCIC Computerized Criminal History file; and

10. Reporting offender-based transaction statistics to the Federal Government.[19]

Exhibits 6–1 through 6–4 are self-explanatory. The data emanates from two field surveys conducted in 1971 and 1974 by Kent W. Colton. The number of responding cities in 1974 were 326. He sagaciously comments that:

> The rate of computer implementation has proceeded at a slower pace than was anticipated in 1971. However, given the fact that the third generation of computers has been commercially available only since the late 1960s, the transition to computer use is proceeding amazingly rapidly. In fact, some constraint is probably favorable; with it may come greater caution, possible skepticism, and increased understanding.[20]

SECURITY AND PRIVACY

As with nearly all technological innovations, police information system and CJIS developments have not been, are not being, nor will they be achieved in the future without grasping every opportunity to turn barriers into results. Of the many barriers to existing and prospective CJIS data, privacy/confidentiality and system security are prominent at the present. These two issues are inextricably connected. Clearly, the privacy and security issues attached to large-scale people-oriented information systems are too complex and lengthy to discuss within a single section of this chapter. The issues range from individual freedom to the need for information on a person's present status and past history in the criminal justice system. In essence, we are dealing with a trade-off relationship between the "need to know" on the one hand and the "right to

---

[19]National Advisory Commission on Criminal Justice Standards and Goals, *Criminal Justice System*, p. 46.
[20]Colton, "Computers and the Police", p. 221.

Exhibit 6–1. Police Computer Use in 1971, 1974, and 1977

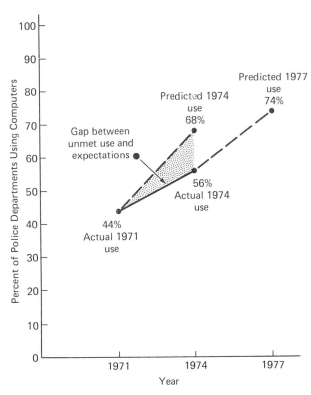

Source: Kent W. Colton, "Computers and the Police: Police Departments and the New Information Technology," *Municipal Year Book 1975* (Washington, D.C.: International City Management Association, 1975), p. 215.

know" on the other. CJIS users are intensely pursuing the building of CJIS locks and keys to preclude errors, misuse of data, and unintentional data change. We need not dwell for long on the possibilities of horizontally linking a CJIS with welfare, IRS, and other personal data bases before we feel threatened. Yet it appears more clearly than ever before that certain vertical systems ought to be linked. Where to start and stop remains the paramount and unresolved issue. This is also discussed in SGI's *Security and Privacy Consideration in Criminal History Information Systems.*[21]

We now turn to a discussion of horizontal file linkages, physical site

---

[21]This 1972 report can also be acquired from Search Group, Inc. (Sacramento, Calif.). See also the Security and Privacy Act of 1974. Another document of significant import is Annette Harrison, *The Problem of Privacy in the Computer Age: An Annotated Bibliography* (Santa Monica, Calif.: The Rand Corporation, 1967).

Exhibit 6–2.   Computer Use by the Police

Twenty four computer applications	Application areas
Warrant file Stolen property file Vehicle registration file	Police patrol and inquiry
Traffic accident file Traffic citation file Parking violation file	Traffic
Personnel records Budget analysis and forecasting Inventory control file Vehicle fleet maintenance Payroll preparation	Police administration
Criminal offense file Criminal arrest file Juvenile criminal activity file	Crime statistical files
Intelligence compilations file Jail arrests	Miscellaneous operations
Police patrol allocation and distribution Police service analysis Traffic patrol allocation and distribution	Resource allocation
Automated field interrogation reports Modus operandi file Automated fingerprint file	Criminal investigation
Computer-aided dispatching Geographic location file	Computer-aided dispatch[1]

[1]Computer-aided dispatch shown in the figures and tables
does not include the tabulations for geographic location
files.

Source: Kent W. Colton, "Computers and the Police: Police Departments and the New Information Technology," *Municipal Year Book 1975* (Washington, D.C.: International City
Management Association, 1975), p. 217.

security, and developments in information privacy. To begin with, many
cities and counties use the terms "vertical," "horizontal," and "sophistication" to describe their information systems. *Vertical subsystems* are a
grouping of components that are reasonably related to common goals and
activities and are arranged in a hierarchical manner to constitute a functional subsystem. Vertical subsystems are, therefore, functional systems.
Illustrative of functional subsystems are police, fire, planning, building,
recreation, finance, and public works. Such functional subsystems and

Exhibit 6–3.   Status of Predicted Computer Use in 1977

Application Area   Percent of Total Computer Use

Application Area	Percent of Total Computer Use
Police Administration	17.5
Traffic	14.8
Crime Statistical Files	17.1
Police Patrol and Inquiry	14.3
Miscellaneous Operations	6.6
Resource Allocation	16.7
Computer-Aided Dispatch	3.7
Criminal Investigation	9.3

0   5   10   15   20   25

Source: Kent W. Colton, "Computers and the Police: Police Departments and the New Information Technology," *Municipal Year Book 1975* (Washington, D.C.: International City Management Association, 1975), p. 221.

components are shown graphically in exhibit 6–5. *Horizontal subsystems* are mechanisms that support automated linking of data within and among vertical functional subsystems. A variety of classifications are available. One frequently used divides the horizontal system into three subsystems, each identified by the kind of information that flows in it; that is, information about people, property, and money. The critical problem in the design of horizontal subsystems is organizing the data in such a way that any current or future requirements for a combination of data, for example, from more than one horizontal subsystem, can be made readily available. *Sophistication* refers to the level of complexity of the data and retrieval requirements. It begins with the least complex level—the automatic data processing techniques employed in the administrative affairs of the municipality. These include personnel, finance, and property accounting; billing and disbursing; registering and licensing; and other routine tasks. The next level of sophistication is the support of operational control in a local government. This includes scheduling, dispatching, allocation, monitoring (for example, traffic control), and command and central emergency vehicle dispatching. Emphasis here is on a rapid response capability, and therefore the on-line, real-time

Exhibit 6–4. Problems Hindering Computer Operation

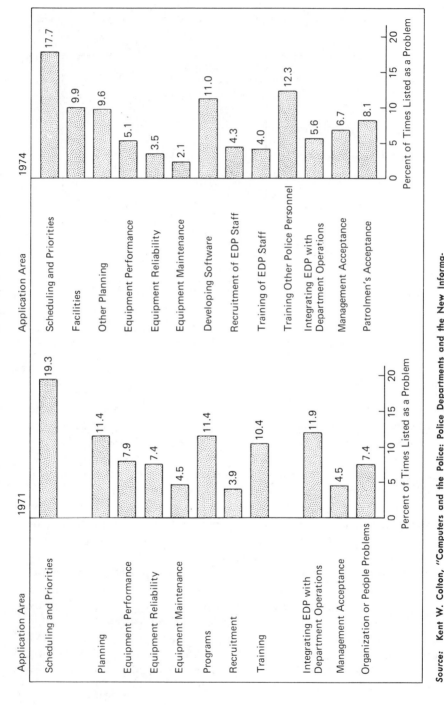

Source: Kent W. Colton, "Computers and the Police: Police Departments and the New Information Technology," Municipal Year Book 1975 (Washington, D.C.: International City Management Association, 1975), p. 222.

Exhibit 6–5.   Horizontal and Vertical Subsystems

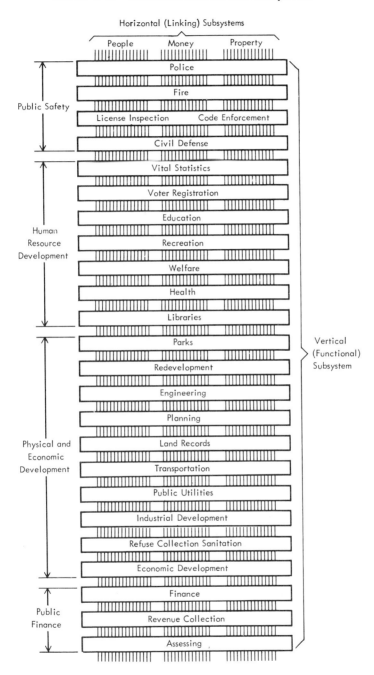

Source: "Request for Proposals No. H–2–70 for Municipal Information Systems," Department of Housing and Urban Development (Washington, D.C.: U.S. Government Printing Office, 1969), p. C–58.

mode is more generally appropriate. A third level of sophistication involves the hardware, software, and files required for planning support.
Here, both batch processing and on-line, real-time modes are important.
Generalized software required includes PERT or CPM for planning and
scheduling, simulation, and statistical analysis programs. The ultimate
level of sophistication is at the policy-making and management level.
Here the requirement is at its fullest development: planning reports,
time- and event-triggered report generation, and controlling administrative processes—in other words, a management information system (MIS).[22]

The next issue, physical site security, is important because those who
seek to destroy or disrupt our society have discovered that when attacking
its formal organizations a "visceral" area is not only more sensitive but
more vulnerable to attack. The area referred to is, of course, the data
processing (DP) center. So far, the reaction to this situation on the part
of DP managers has varied from none at all to rapid hardening of the
potential target site. Apparently the "glass showcase" days for DP centers
are over. We find the older DP facilities being mortared in or moved to a
more secure location. Further, we see many of the new facilities being
buried below ground, with major physical and personnel security methods included in their design and operations.[23] Banks, colleges, cities,
critical industries, and the like are more anxious than ever before about
protecting the physical "life" of their DP centers.

Regarding information privacy, "One of the most studied problems
in American society today is that of the invasion of the right of privacy."[24] In order to focus and amalgamate efforts in this area the Do-
mestic Council Committee on the Right of Privacy was established in
February 1974. The confidentiality of personal information is perhaps
the central privacy issue, and thus the Privacy Committee has devoted
much of its effort to studying information and record-keeping practices.
If an agency or business has information references on an individual,
what responsibility accompanies the stewardship of that information?

The term "information privacy" is often confused with "security."
Information privacy does include all of security as a part of the defini-

[22]An MIS is an information system (usually computer based) that selects, processes,
stores, and furnishes data of interest to management for two purposes and usually in
three modes. The purposes: control (internal) and planning (external). The modes:
time-triggered reports, event-triggered reports, and on demand. The latter two modes
require on-line real-time inquiry-response capabilities.

[23]For an example of one such endeavor, see Paul M. Whisenand, James L. Cline, and
John C. Whisenand, *A Facility Security Analysis of the Data Services Bureau, City of
Los Angeles* (Los Angeles, Calif.: City of Los Angeles, 1970).

[24]Kelley, "Right to Privacy," p. 23.

tion. However, the converse is not true: Security alone, as we normally think of it, is not enough to provide the safeguards needed for information privacy. Information privacy includes the right of individuals to know that recorded personal information about them is accurate, pertinent, complete, up-to-date, and reasonably secure from unauthorized access—either accidental or intentional. Only the very last part of this definition would involve the question of security. Moreover, the concept of information privacy entails the right of the individual to influence the kind, quantity, and quality of information contained in a system in which he or she is readily identifiable. Regardless of whether this information is open to the view of the general public or specifically required to be confidential by law, these privacy guidelines should be observed by all operators and users of information systems.

The privacy of persons named in criminal history records kept by the Federal Bureau of Investigation or federal government–funded criminal justice agencies are now protected under sweeping new regulations issued by the Department of Justice.

> We now find ourselves at a turning point which results from efforts by the federal government to ensure individual rights with regard to criminal justice information. The first provisions of the Department of Justice regulations published in May 1975 pursuant to the Omnibus Crime Control and Safe Streets Act becomes effective on December 16, 1975. All procedures covered under these regulations must be fully implemented by December 31, 1977. The criminal justice community has finally reached the point of no return. Many significant changes will be forthcoming during the next two years particularly with regard to the use and dissemination of criminal history record information and the operation of the systems containing this data. Such issues as an individual's access to his criminal history information, mandatory disposition reporting, and dedicated hardware will soon become the law of the land under these regulations. To accomplish the mandates of the Department of Justice regulations will certainly require more than considerable amounts of planning resources, and most importantly, dedication from all of us in the criminal justice community. The security and privacy concepts of yesterday are about to become the standard operating procedures used by criminal justice agencies in the future. This represents a most significant milestone in the evolution of criminal justice information systems.[25]

[25]Gary D. McAlvey, "Security and Privacy: A Turning Point," *Interface* 1 (September 1975): 2.

The rules will require that the data in criminal records be maintained and disseminated in such a manner as to insure its accuracy, completeness, integrity, and security, while continuing legitimate law enforcement access to the information. Persons named in criminal records will be entitled to review their histories for accuracy, and then have any errors corrected through a set of standardized procedures. Inaccuracies must be corrected by the particular state agency keeping the records, who must then also notify other criminal justice agencies that have previously received erroneous data. Certain specific criminal records have been exempted from the new regulations, including records necessary to the apprehension of wanted persons, original records required by law or custom to be made public, published court opinions, public court proceedings, and records of traffic offenses. In all other cases, however, the new rules will also impose wider restrictions on the dissemination of criminal history information. While the use of this information for criminal justice purposes will remain unlimited, the records will be made available to private agencies only where they perform a necessary function in the administration of justice, or for research purposes, and to other public or private agencies where a statute or Executive Order explicitly refers to criminal conduct and lists requirements or exclusions based on such conduct. State and federal agencies authorized to conduct background investigations into eligibility for security clearances will also be given access to the records. The news media, however, will only be given such facts as are needed to confirm or deny the information in a specific request.

At this point the police manager has probably reached a conclusion: either he has an information privacy problem or he does not. The next logical step, then, is to consider what he can or cannot do about the problem. Basically, he needs to develop a plan for his agency. Specific security implementation plans vary from organization to organization. Each plan is dependent upon myriad variables, such as the size of the organization, the preexistence of security safeguards, the functions performed by the organization, and many others. Therefore, to say that any one plan will fit all organizations would be a fallacy. Nonetheless, there are similarities between programs. The implementation of any privacy program will follow an action plan which shares certain common elements with all other implementation plans. These elements, or steps, form a generalized information privacy action plan. Exhibit 6–6 presents such a plan. You are cautioned, however, that current and in-depth research should be conducted prior to the development or modification of any criminal justice or police information system.

Exhibit 6–6. A Generalized Information Privacy Action Plan

ACTION STEPS

| | 0 | 1 | 2 | 3 | 4 | 5 | 6 | 7 | 8 | 9 | 10 | 11 | 12 | 13 | 14 | 15 | 16 | 17 | 18 | 19 | 20 | 21 | 22 | 23 | 24 | 25 |

Review Information System Requirements

Analyze Confidentiality and Criticality of Data

Assess Vulnerabilities and Risks

Investigate Technological Safeguards

Budget for Information Privacy

Organize for Information Privacy

Establish Individual Accountability

Implement Technological Safeguards

Create Privacy Consciousness Environment

Audit and Optimize Environment

Time Period (Arbitrary Units)

Source: State of Illinois, *Data Security and Data Processing: Executive Overview* (New York: International Business Machines, 1974), p. 22.

LEARNING EXERCISES

ACTIVE LISTENING:
A PARAPHRASING ACTIVITY[26]

Purposes

1. To develop an understanding of the dynamics of being an active listener.
2. To become aware of the barriers that inhibit effective listening in criminal justice groups.

Group Size. A minimum of twelve participants

Time Required. Approximately one hour.

Materials

1. A copy of the Active Listening Topics for Discussion Sheet for each participant.
2. A copy of the Active Listening Observer Discussion Sheet for each observer.

Physical Setting. A room large enough so that dyads may work without distracting other dyads.

Process

1. The facilitator discusses with the group the goals of the activity.
2. Four dyads are formed (two participants each).
3. The remaining group members are assigned as observers to the four dyads.
4. The facilitator distributes the Active Listening Topics for Discussion Sheet to all participants and the Active Listening Observer Discussion Sheet to the observers only.
5. The facilitator gives the following instructions:
   • Each dyad will have a speaker and a listener. The first speaker chooses a topic from the Topics for Discussion Sheet.
   • The listener in the dyad must summarize in his own words what the first speaker discussed. He may not take notes.

26The learning exercise is used with the permission of Michael E. O'Neil and Kai R. Mortensen, *Criminal Justice Group Training: A Facilitator's Handbook* (La Jolla, Calif.: University Associates, Inc. 1975), pp. 24–27.

- The speaker has six minutes to discuss his chosen topic with the listener.
- If the summary by the listener is incorrect, the speaker may interrupt and correct the misunderstanding.
- The observers assigned to each dyad make certain that the listener does not omit, distort, or add to what the speaker has said.

6. After the first topic is discussed, the speaker becomes the listener and the listener becomes the speaker. The above process is then repeated.
7. When each dyad member has had an opportunity to be a speaker and a listener, the facilitator processes the activity with the total group. He conducts a discussion, soliciting comments about communication barriers and active listening from the members.

Variations

1. Dyads can generate their own topics.
2. Triads can be used with one person as the listener, one the speaker, and one the observer.

Active Listening Topics for Discussion Sheet

Each speaker selects one topic from the list below:

1. Probation Subsidy
2. Team Policing
3. Community-Based Corrections
4. Criminal Justice Training
5. Case Management for Prosecutors
6. Security and Privacy—Computer Systems
7. Crime-Oriented Planning
8. Police Response Time
9. Offender-Based Transactional Statistics
10. Plea Bargaining
11. Prisoner Rehabilitation
12. Juvenile Delinquency
13. Juvenile Diversion
14. Public Defender's Role
15. Educational Requirements for Criminal Justice Personnel
16. Police Unions
17. Technology Change in Criminal Justice
18. Crime Prevention
19. Court Calendars

Active Listening Observer Discussion Sheet

Speaker:_____

	Barriers	Additions	Deletions	Comments
Listener:_____				

Speaker:_____

Listener:_____

1. What difficulties did the individuals have in the roles of speaker and listener?
2. Were there barriers that consistently caused communication distortions? What were they? How did they affect communication?
3. Why is it important to paraphrase correctly?
4. What does this exercise tell you about communications that would be useful for your organization?

Chapter Seven

TASK 5
CONTROLLING:
The Use of Authority, Power,

and Influence

The control mechanism in an organization is not a limited, single-purpose invention. Output measures serve the control needs of the organization as a whole, while behavior control serves the quite different needs of the individual manager, who has one subunit to oversee. The use of output measures is largely a result of the demand for quantifiable, simple measures. Paradoxically, output measures are used most when they are least appropriate: in the face of complexity, interdependence, and lack of expertise. Under such conditions, similar to those of low paradigm development in a science (Lodahl and Gordon, 1972), the manager is suspected of poor performance and, as a result, he goes to great lengths to provide evidence of his contributions to the organization. The organization's need for evaluative information is satisfied, but the quality of that information may be low.[1]

SYNOPSIS

In the subsequent pages we endeavor to show that organizations whose managers exercise poor control, or whose control is inconsistent at different levels, tend to have limited organizational effectiveness and, conversely, that organizations whose managers exercise proper control at every level tend to have a higher degree of organizational effectiveness. We also explore three concepts of control: the use of authority, power, and influence, and we hope that all three emerge as legitimate and as having a direct and supportive relationship with each other. It will be obvious that we have leaned strongly toward the integration of the man and the organization. It is our belief that true high-level police organizational effectiveness can be achieved only when each able human component of the organization is encouraged to make use of his personal influences.

INTRODUCTION

Like all organizations which have responsibilities and specific purpose, police organizations must have workable units whose energies are directed toward the achievement of articulated goals. Direction in this instance is used synonymously with control. Control is the ingredient that moves organizations in the desired fashion and without which they are likely

[1]William G. Ouchi and Mary Ann Maguire, "Organizational Control: Two Functions," *Administrative Sciences Quarterly* 20 (December 1975): 568.

to become fragmented. The more complicated the organization and its goals, the more important the aspect of control becomes.

At a time of great social change, when an important issue of every major political campaign is the need for more effective law enforcement, it would be impossible to overstate the need for greater efficiency of police organizations.

And so we must reinforce the theme that organizations in which greater, more responsible control is enacted are likely to experience greater reliability in reaching stated goals. This need for control holds true for any organization but perhaps for none more critically than the modern police organization.

Obviously some organizations in spite of loose controls do provide a modicum of service and do survive their mediocrity. But in the end, loose controls are the harbinger of failure, and sometimes even disgrace. A police organization without proper control may struggle along with few outward signs of crises. The inward signs are, of course, more apparent—absenteeism, employee turnover, inefficiency, apathy towards the public served, and perhaps the most damaging of all in terms of the total police service, dishonesty and general corruption.

We are not suggesting that every policing agency should have controls of the same magnitude. Obviously, a two-man police department is not likely to have the same communication problems as will a department of five or five hundred men and women. As police organizations grow in size, it is proportionately less likely that every member will have a clear understanding and acceptance of organizational goals. More controls will undoubtedly be necessary to insure reasonable goal achievement.

The President's Commission on Law Enforcement and Administration of Justice displayed substantial concern for the internal control of police agencies in its 1967 *Task Force Report: The Police.* Its observations and recommendations are especially relevant to this chapter. The report clearly states the critical need for adequate control. It also defines the methods by which controls or their lack prevent the organization from reaching broader expectations and goals. The following section is drawn from this report.

INTERNAL CONTROLS

It is in the nature of an administrative organization that the establishment of policies to guide the exercise of discretion by individuals is not enough. There is need also for the development of methods for assuring compliance. This requires a system of administrative controls to be applied within an agency.

METHODS OF INTERNAL CONTROL

An analysis of patterns of deviations from appropriate policy standards indicates that such deviations usually fall into three general categories: situations in which an officer violates departmental regulations or policies; situations in which an officer's behavior is considered improper, but does not constitute a violation of existing department policy; and situations in which an officer's behavior is clearly illegal or improper, but is consistent with the routine practice of the particular agency and is generally condoned by its administration.

1. There are a limited number of situations today in which police administrators have issued policy statements to control police conduct. These tend to mirror the requirements of appellate cases as, for example, policies to implement the specific interrogation requirements of the *Miranda* case. Field studies conducted by the commission indicate that such policies, promulgated at the top of the agency, are often disregarded in practice. Occasionally situations may arise in which a failure to adhere to existing policy becomes a source of embarrassment to the top echelons of the police agency, as, for example, if a failure to give the warnings required by the *Miranda* case were to prevent the conviction of a dangerous criminal in a highly publicized case.

The fact that administrative policy for dealing with crime or potential crime situations does not have a very significant impact upon the actions of individual officers appears to be primarily attributable to two factors: the ambivalent attitude which often accompanies the pronouncement of a policy implementing a decision like *Miranda*, and competing influences brought to bear by subordinate command staff who are subject to more immediate pressures from the community they serve.

Top police officials have been quite outspoken in registering their opposition to recent decisions of the U.S. Supreme Court. Personnel within an agency are fully aware of the public pronouncements of their superiors. They recognize that an order which purports to urge compliance with a recent decision is necessitated by the decision and is reluctantly issued by their superior. Without a special effort on the part of the administrator to distinguish between his right to enter into public debate over the wisdom of court decisions and the need for compliance with court decisions, it is likely that departmental policies which simply mirror the requirements of an appellate decision will be largely disregarded.

A somewhat similar situation exists when operating personnel believe that a change in departmental policy reflects a somewhat reluctant effort on the part of the administration to appease some community group that has made a complaint against the department.

In current practice, such departmental policy as exists is but one of a number of competing considerations that influence police actions at the operating level. Tremendous pressures are generated upon the various command levels in a large police agency by community groups—pressures from which such personnel cannot be easily isolated. The desire on the part of a supervisory officer or precinct commander to satisfy a prominent citizen, to meet the demands of a community group on whose support his continued effectiveness and acceptance depend, to obtain favorable publicity, or simply to satisfy his most immediate superior may override any desire he may have to adhere to established policy. Subordinates, in turn, have their eyes upon their superior rather than upon formal pronouncements which come to them in written form. The extent to which they conform with policy formulated at the top levels will be determined, in large measure, by the spirit and tone in which it is communicated to them by their more immediate superiors. Each of the many levels of supervision in a large agency, therefore, constitutes a point at which policies may be diluted or ignored.

2. An entirely different set of problems is raised when an individual officer acts in a manner which none of his superiors would condone, but there is no formulated policy to serve as a basis for discipline or condemnation.

The problems are complicated by the peculiar nature of the police function. Officers are usually spread out about an entire city. They do not have the opportunity for immediate consultation with superior officers when called upon to take action. The danger of mass disorder is always present, and the need for quick decisions often requires that the officer take some form of action before he has the opportunity to acquire all of the facts. It is, therefore, difficult for the police administrator to hold an individual police officer to the same standard one would hold a person who had an opportunity to consult and to think about the matter before acting.

The actions of individual police officers are not easily subject to review. Contacts between police officers and citizens are often contentious, tending to evoke an emotional response on the part of both the officer and the citizen. They occur at times and in locations where others are not present. And an informal code among police officers, which bands individual officers together for mutual support when challenged from the outside, silences fellow police officers who may be the only witnesses to an incident. As a consequence the typical complaint will consist of an assertion of wrongdoing on the part of a citizen and a denial by the officer. There usually is no available basis for corroborating either story. The consequence of continually disbelieving the officer would obviously mean a loss of morale. Hence, the tendency in such cases is for the police administrator to accept the officer's version unless there is some reason to believe the officer is being untruthful.

3. The most complicated situations that arise in current practice are those in which the actions of an officer are clearly illegal or improper but are consistent with prevailing practices of a department. Such practices are commonly found in the police agencies serving large urban areas, where the practices constitute part of the informal response which the police have developed for dealing with problems of a recurring nature. It is, for example, common for police officers to search the interior of a vehicle without legal grounds in high crime-rate areas. It is similarly common for police to search gamblers or arrest known prostitutes without adequate grounds. Since such actions are generally encouraged by superior officers, it is inconceivable that the officer would be administratively criticized or disciplined upon the filing of a complaint. Nevertheless, complaints tend to be processed administratively in the same way as complaints alleging a violation of administrative policy by an officer. As a consequence, the complaint procedure does not serve as a vehicle to challenge and cause a reconsideration of policies which are sanctioned by the department even though not articulated.

PROPOSED IMPROVEMENTS IN METHODS OF INTERNAL CONTROL

Some of the problems of achieving control over the conduct of individual police officers would be simplified if there were a commitment by the police administrator to a systematic policy-formulation process. This would require specific attention to present unarticulated policies which are clearly illegal and as a consequence would create administrative pressure to reject them or develop alternatives rather than assume the indefensible position of formally adopting illegal practices as official departmental policy. The development of adequate policy statements would afford the individual police officers greater guidance with respect to important decisions like the use of force, and the decision to arrest or to search.

But the mere adoption of administrative policies will not alone achieve compliance. This will require "good administration," that is, the use of the whole array of devices commonly employed in public administration to achieve conformity. These include, but are not limited to, the setting of individual responsibility, the establishment of systems of accountability, the designing of procedures for checking and reporting on performance, and the establishment of methods for taking corrective action.

The police administrator currently achieves a high degree of conformity on the part of officers to standards governing such matters as the form of dress, the method of completing reports, and the procedures for processing of citizen complaints. Sleeping on duty, leaving one's place of assignment without authorization, or failing to meet one's financial obligations are all situations against which supervisory personnel currently take effective action.

The success of internal controls as applied to such matters appears to be dependent upon two major factors: (1) the attitude and commitment of the head of the agency to the policies being enforced and (2) the degree to which individual officers and especially supervisory officers have a desire to conform.

The average police administrator, for example, has no ambivalence over accepting responsibility for the physical appearance of his men. He does not wait to act until complaints are received from a third party, He undertakes, instead, by a variety of administrative techniques, to produce a desire in his subordinates to conform. This desire may reflect an agreement by the subordinates with the policy. Or it may reflect respect for their superior, a lack of interest one way or the other, or a fear of punishment or reprisal. Whatever the reason, the officer in a sort of "state of command" does what he is told rather than follow a course of his own choosing.

In sharp contrast, the police administrator is typically ambivalent over the responsibility he has for controlling the activities of his force in the exercise of discretionary power in dealing with crime or potential crime situations. While he views the physical appearance of his men as his concern, he often sees the methods by which the law is enforced as involving matters which are the primary responsibility of others outside the police establishment. This deference may, in part, be attributable to the sharing of responsibilities with other agencies—particularly the courts. Unlike internal matters over which the police administrator has complete control, much of what the police do relating to crime and criminals is dependent for approval upon the decisions of nonpolice agencies.

Strengthening of administrative control requires the creation of the same sense of personal responsibility on the part of the police administrator for the implementation of proper law enforcement policies as he presently has for implementing policies relating to internal matters.

This will require that the administrator be given the education, training, and resources necessary to fulfill the role. It requires also a change in what is expected of police administrators by the public and by those occupying key positions in other agencies in the criminal justice system. Police officials cannot be expected to develop a sense of responsibility, if they are treated like ministerial officers, and excluded from important policy-making decisions, such as those regarding the revision of substantive and procedural laws.

Also required is the development of a professional identification which can serve police officers as a frame of reference within which they can see the importance of their conforming to appropriate law enforcement policies. Blind obedience to orders, such as is currently elicited for some aspects of police operations, is limited in both its values and desirability to purely administrative functions. Personnel called upon to deal with complex problems of human behavior and expected to make decisions on the basis of professionally developed criteria must, themselves, have some form of professional identification as a common basis from which to function.

Professional identification has, for example, been a major element in the rapid development of what are now some of our more highly regarded correctional systems. With training and education in social casework as a prerequisite to employment, operating personnel function from a framework for decision-making which is consistent with and supportive of departmental policies. The whole administrative process is facilitated because both administrators and field personnel are on the same "wave length," talking the same language and supporting the same values.

A somewhat similar development is essential in the police field. Individual police officers must be provided with the training and education which will give them a professional identification consistent with the police role in a free society. Such training and education will equip them to understand the policies of their superiors; make them receptive to efforts to make law enforcement both fair and effective; and enable the officer to take appropriate action in the unpredictable situations not dealt with by even the best efforts at policy formulation.[2]

Private Organizations

Private business organizations have consistently moved ahead of government in recognizing the need and in searching for greater efficiency—control. This is not to say that government and, more specifically, policing

[2]The President's Commission on Law Enforcement and Administration of Justice, *Task Force Report: The Police* (Washington, D.C.: U.S. Government Printing Office, 1967), pp. 28–30.

organizations have not exercised controls, for they have. But apparently there has been and continues to be a primary reliance, almost a preoccupation by many, upon hierarchical authority. We are not suggesting that traditional concepts of authority, responsibility, and accountability be scrapped or bypassed. We are suggesting that the state of the managerial art has progressed to the point that it offers other options and complementing additions.

In recognizing the necessity for more effective controls, private organizations have had at least one built-in motivating factor not shared by government—profit. Private organizations simply cannot continue to exist without profit. On the other hand, we believe that police organizations in the future will be asked to operate at a profit; that is, profit in terms of greater, more efficient services for the people served. Traditionally, police organizations have grown proportionately with the general population. As police goals and expectations have expanded, the growth has become somewhat disproportional. Our belief is that police organizations will not be able to solve tomorrow's problems by simply adding new personnel, nor will there be the dollars to do so. Perhaps, then, it is reasonable to look to business for some of the answers. Granted, there are vast differences between government and private business; however, one theme that we trust will emerge in the following chapters is that the similarities are greater than these differences. If we, the writers and the reader, can agree with this idea, then perhaps we can also agree that many managerial concepts and rules held to be truths by business managers and contemporary writers in that field are applicable to the modern police organization.

George D. Eastman, professor and director of the Institute of Government Research and Services at Kent State University, as editor of *Municipal Police Administration* gave some recognition to this same proposition in his discussion of the principles of organization:

> Students of public and police administration, sooner or later in the course of their studies, are presented with "principles of organization." The principles often are offered as organization dogma and their acceptance taken for granted. Thoughtful people in business, industry, and government, however, have long since questioned their validity. General merit of the so-called principles is not basically at issue; rather, there is a challenge to their universality of application. It would seem appropriate, at this time, to simply identify them as a set of concepts or propositions believed by many to be a basis for sound organization.
>
> Confusion exists in their presentation because some relate to structure and some to process; in the sense of process some could be considered

more meaningfully as matters of administrative action. Nonetheless, an organization structure should assure reasonably that there is provision for:

1. Sound and clear-cut allocation of responsibilities.
2. Equitable distribution of work loads among elements and individuals.
3. Clear and unequivocal lines of authority.
4. Authority adequate to discharge assigned responsibilities.
5. Reasonable spans of control for administrative, command, and supervisory officers.
6. Unity of command.
7. Coordination of effort.
8. Administrative control.

Significantly the organization can only "make provision for" but cannot guarantee anything. It has no life or vitality of its own; it is simply a vehicle for management. As Urwick says, "It is the men and not the organization chart that do the work."[3]

FORMALIZATION AND AUTHORITY

As in police organizations, private organizations tend to formalize their hierarchical structure in the pyramidal shape. Pyramids are convenient in that they clearly signify differences in rank; the higher one's position in the pyramid, the greater one's responsibility and authority. Perhaps private organizations have fewer levels of responsibility within the pyramid, nonetheless there exists the theory of increasing responsibility and authority while conversely the span of control is diminished. The pyramid permits a centralized control over the organization and places the final responsibility and authority in the hands of a single individual.

AUTHORITY

Hampton, Summer, and Webber in their text *Organizational Behavior and The Practice of Management* have described five attributes which exist in an authority system.

[3]George D. Eastman and Esther M. Eastman, *Municipal Police Administration* (Washington, D.C.: International City Management Association, 1969), pp. 20–21.

1. It is caused by, or necessary because of, certain deep-seated forces at work in the organization and in society. These forces are the ones that bring political systems into existence.

2. It is a system in which relatively few (line managers and their specialist staffs) make decisions for relatively many (lower managers, employees).

3. The decisions made are of two types: (a) standing decisions, to be carried out over a period of time by diverse people while they are in effect. In society these are called *laws,* and in the corporation they are called *policies, procedures, programs,* or *methods.* Sometimes, they are called *job descriptions.* Sociologists often lump all of these together and call them "rules" or "work rules." (b) *ad hoc* decisions, which are made by executives either to *interpret* standing decisions or to make certain decisions which are not covered by standing decisions.

4. Decisions, either standing or *ad hoc,* are communicated from managers to subordinates—from relatively few at any level in the organization to relatively many.

5. Certain human motivations tend to cause subordinates to obey or carry out the decisions of management communicated to them . . . there may also be motives to *disobey.*[4]

It becomes clear, then, that authority resides in the position. Superiors in any organization tend to rely on their rank authority to resolve organizational conflict, to change behavior—the superior being identified as the changer, the subordinate the changee. The use of authority to bring about change in behavior is expeditious, to say the least. Unfortunately, authority does not necessarily guarantee the degree or permanence of change.

Organizational heads are commonly held responsible for the formalization of policy that will assist the organization toward its stated goals. In police organizations, authority to bring about desired change is commonly exhibited in the form of general orders and departmental manuals. The following example is extracted from the *Manual of the Los Angeles Police Department:*

> **4/292. Disposing of rewards and gratuities.** When an employee receives a reward or contribution, he shall transmit it to the Commander, Personnel and Training Bureau, for deposit in the Fire and Police Pension Fund.

[4]David R. Hampton, Charles E. Summer, and Ross A. Webber, *Organizational Behavior and The Practice of Management* (Glenview, Ill.: Scott, Foresman and Company, 1968), p. 453.

If an employee is given a check or money order coming within the meaning of this Section, he shall endorse it "Pay to the Order of the City of Los Angeles," followed by his signature as it appears on the face. In addition, he shall complete two copies of the Employee's Report, Form 15.7, which shall be transmitted with the reward or contribution to the Personnel and Training Bureau and shall include the following information:

* Name and address of person giving the reward or contribution.
* Reason for giving reward or contribution.
* Amount of the reward or contribution.[5]

Responsibility with commensurate authority to insure that the regulation is carried out is delegated to subordinates down to the appropriate level. In our opinion, however, it is pure fallacy to assume that the implied authority of the written word has any greater degree of success than that of the spoken word.

Harold J. Leavitt, in his book *Managerial Psychology*, has depicted interesting pros and cons of the use of authority:

From the manager's viewpoint the advantages of authority, especially restrictively used authority, are huge. We have already cited one of them, the control and coordination advantage. There are many others, too.

For one thing, one doesn't have to know much about any particular Joe Doaks to be fairly certain that firing him or cutting his pay or demoting him will strike at some important needs and thereby keep him in line. But one might have to know a good deal about the same employee to find out how to make work more fun for him.

A corollary advantage, then, is simplicity. Authority as a restrictive tool does not require much subtlety or much understanding of people's motives. How simple it is to spank a child when he misbehaves, and how difficult and complicated to distract him or provide substitute satisfactions or to "explain" the situation. Given a hundred children, how much easier it is to keep them in line by punishing a few recalcitrants than to teach them all to feel "responsible." . . .

Restrictive authority has another kind of advantage: speed. A do-it-or-else order eliminates the time consuming dillydallying of feedback. . . .

Employees who expect to be censured whenever they are caught loafing may learn to *act* busy (and *when* to act busy) and also that the boss is an enemy. They are thereby provided with a challenging game

[5]*Manual of the Los Angeles Police Department* (Los Angeles, Calif.: Los Angeles Police Department, 1970), 4 ch. 2, sec. 292.

to play against the boss: who can think up the best ways of loafing without getting caught; a game in which they can feel that justice is on their side and a game they can usually win. . . .

The tenuousness and the self-defeating weakness of reliance on restrictive authority becomes apparent right here. When his authority has been "undermined" by the "sabotage" of subordinates, the superior who has depended on authority is likely immediately to assume that what he needs is *more authority*, because authority is the only tool he knows how to use.[6]

POWER

Although some of Leavitt's examples may appear rather simplistic or basic, his message that authority is an important element of organizational control, of change, is quite clear. On the other hand, Leavitt is just as resolute that reliance upon pure authority leaves the superior with very little reason for security.[7]

In discussing the concept of authority, social scientists Pfiffner and Sherwood observe that authority implies the *right* to command another person, and the subordinate person has the *duty* to obey the command. They make specific note, however, that "the *right* to command does not necessarily connote the *capacity* to command."[8]

Since most law enforcement agencies are developed around the military model, authority in this case does afford a superior the ability to exercise, to a lesser or greater extent depending upon his hierarchical level, control over the subordinate's continued employment, salary increases (merit principle), work hours, assignments, promotions, and infinite other rewards and punishments. The superior does not, however, own the subordinate, nor can he hope for much more than a rather limited control. It is the subordinate, in the end, who makes the decision of whether or not it is worth it; in fact, whether or not he should report for work at all. Authority in a police organization, then, has its limitations.

Power, on the other hand, resides in the person, not necessarily in the position. It may or may not coincide with the official structure of authority. Power in itself is not institutionalized in the sense that one can look to the organizational manual and find out where it resides.[9]

[6] Harold J. Leavitt, *Managerial Psychology*, 2nd ed. (Chicago: University of Chicago Press, 1958), pp. 171–73, 175.
[7] *Ibid.*, p. 180.
[8] John M. Pfiffner and Frank P. Sherwood, *Administrative Organization* (Englewood Cliffs, N.J.: Prentice-Hall, Inc., 1960), p. 75.
[9] *Ibid.*, p. 25.

Conversely, almost every organization or organizational unit has the "person to see."

> It is not unusual for lower participants in complex organizations to assume and wield considerable power and influence not associated with their formally defined positions within these organizations. In sociological terms they have considerable personal power but no authority. Such personal power is often attained, for example, by executive secretaries and accountants in business firms. . . . The personal power achieved by these lower participants does not necessarily result from unique personal characteristics, although these may be relevant, but results rather from particular aspects of their location within their organizations.[10]

It is not unusual for persons to be totally unaware of their own power potential. This normally occurs where the power is deferred. This is to say that the influencing party may be operating at several levels removed from the point of action. Power, simply stated, is the ability to influence behavior.

While we have taken care to emphasize that true power does not necessarily follow hierarchical lines or authoritative positions, the advantage to authoritative figures who also possess concomitant power should be obvious.

The term *power*, perhaps because of its own ominous sound, sometimes connotes being deceitful, or even illegitimate. The reader should bear in mind, however, that the expert, the consultant, exhibits power; that the person whose opinion is respected exhibits power; and that often a person who is simply "liked," who for one reason or another is an attractive person, exhibits power.

Bennis more clearly describes power as falling into five components:

1. *Coercive power,* or the ability of A to reward and/or punish B.
2. *Referent, or identification power,* or the influence which accrues to A because he (or the group) is attratcive, a person whom B wants to like and be liked by—in short, a role model.
3. *Expert power,* or the power that we associate with science and "truth."
4. *Legitimate* or *traditional* power, or power which stems from institutional norms and practices and from historical-legal traditions.

[10]Hampton, Summer, and Webber, *Organizational Behavior,* p. 425.

5. *Value power,* or influence which is gained on the basis of attraction to the values of A.[11]

Pfiffner and Sherwood have defined power as the politics of how things get done.[12] Though not particularly profound, it is important to recognize that in the real political arena, authoritative heads, while occupying a position of relative importance, must rely a great deal upon their knowledge of where the political power lies; otherwise they cannot hope to carry out long-range programs and goals. They can, of course, heroically buck the power, but heroics cannot be relied upon to "get things done." Internal power politics is a part of every organization and police departments are no exception; to deny its existence and to neglect its utilization is foolhardy.

Pfiffner and Sherwood's definition has special meaning when we view power as a component of organization control. Obviously, if the *power* is held by persons other than those in authority, it becomes a matter of political necessity for the authority figures to have access to that power. This becomes especially difficult for the "old guard" type of police manager who simply is not accustomed to "dealing" with subordinates. When an administrator fails to recognize the realities of present-day organizational politics, the result is often a friction-building impasse that causes organizational dysfunction. As we stated earlier, authoritative failure usually results in a drive for more authority which, of course, further complicates the problem.

Practitioners in the field can no doubt conjure up their own nightmarish recollection of examples in which the administrator got himself so far out on a limb that it was finally chopped off. Administrative heads of government tend to back their police managers when the first internal conflicts arise, but history has shown that sooner or later their support wanes.

At this late point the police manager should recognize the political facts of life and change his style, utilizing the power politics of the organization to its best advantage. In many cases where the unswerving managerial style prevails, however, the manager is eventually demoted, retired, fired, or elevated to a state of limbo where he no longer has any influence. There are, of course, those few who have acquired considerable personal power through outside-of-the-organization politics. They seem

[11]Warren G. Bennis, *Changing Organizations* (New York: McGraw-Hill Book Company, 1966), p. 168.
[12]Pfiffner and Sherwood, *Administrative Organization,* pp. 310–11.

to remain almost indefinitely, surrounded by a kind of bureaucratic moat, blindly impeding the organization and its individual elements from reaching optimum goals.

We are in general agreement with contemporaries in the field that authority is an essential component of power, while power itself is not necessarily synonymous with authority. Power and authority are, however, legitimately a part of control.

INFLUENCE

In the following paragraphs we will be using the term *influence* in the most positive sense. Influence in our context then, as an element of control, means giving recognition and support to the hypotheses that people are more likely to do what is desired of them with minimum formal control—supervision—if they are *self-motivated.* To establish continuity with other contemporary writers in the field, the term *self-actualization* will be used synonymously with *self-motivation* throughout the discussion.

Influence, at least effective influence in modern organizations, is not limited to a "top-down" system. Effective managers in the private sector have for some time realized that influence should flow in all directions, at all levels. Contemporary behavioral scientists generally agree that organizations in which subordinates as well as superiors feel a personal sense of influence are most likely to be highly productive. We believe this to be true of modern police organizations as well.

The police manager who has developed modern leadership skills, who has learned to consider the personal needs of his subordinates and has given them a feeling of self-importance, of worth, is likely to have a high-producing unit. *Feedback* is certainly not new to the police manager, but the kind of feedback in which the subordinate's opinion is respected, even solicited, and has direct influence on the organizational operations may well be. This type of subordinate influence, which at times may manifest itself in the form of criticism or at least appear to question the superior's judgment, can be quite threatening, especially if the manager has not gained a proper level of leadership sophistication. Actually, a substantial degree of personal security must always be present for all who participate in the use of influence for organizational effectiveness. This kind of security, together with satisfactory relationships between the manager and the managed, is the cohesiveness that builds effective organizations.

Through research, Rensis Likert in *New Patterns of Management* has verified that high-producing managers build better management systems than do low-producing managers. Likert discovered that a better management system, "while giving the men more influence, also gives the higher producing manager more influence."[13]

Likert's study did not reveal that all high-producing managers use the "influence" concept. Our own experience in police organizations offers some confirmation of this. Highly structured, highly authoritarian, highly bureaucratic, highly goal-centered police management systems can also be high producers. High production is used in this case to denote impressive statistics in the solution of crimes, the repression of traffic accidents, and all the other bench marks traditional with police agencies.

These data, however, do not reveal other important factors, such as employee attitudes, which present themselves in less-measurable ways—excessive, absenteeism, employee turnover, negative discipline, and the like. High production, then, is not necessarily a barometer of organizational health and does not insure the internalization of organizational goals by the employee.

One can expect that subordinates in such a system will operate "by the book." They will tend not to extend themselves beyond what is considered to be their responsibility. Blau and Scott, in their study of formal organizations, were concerned with the results of routinized jobs of certain workers. They discovered that "the contractual bond of nonsupervisory white collar employees to formal organizations normally obligates them to fulfill role prescriptions only in accordance with minimum standards."[14]

Thus the police officer may be producing at a level acceptable to his supervisor, but if Blau and Scott's finding is applicable, he is normally only producing at an acceptable minimum; he has the capacity to do more with proper control—in this case motivation toward self-actualization.

While statistics, or whatever measurement is used to determine organizational effectiveness, may appear encouraging, a careful examination must be made of the more vital signs of organizational health, such as employee morale, tardiness, absenteeism, turnover, and the growing necessity for negative disciplinary measures. If statistics is the game being played, subordinates soon learn to play the game, not unlike an earlier example of learning to "look busy" when the boss is around. True organizational health is more difficult to observe.

[13]Rensis Likert, *New Patterns of Management* (New York: McGraw-Hill Book Company, 1961), p. 58. (For a more complete discussion of *influence* and *performance*, see pp. 44–60.)

[14]Peter M. Blau and Richard W. Scott, *Formal Organizations* (San Francisco: Chandler Publishing Company, 1962), p. 140.

At the beginning of our discussion of *influence,* we incorporated the terms *self-motivation* and *self-actualization.* Our hypothesis is that subordinates are more likely to work harder to achieve organizational goals in the most desirable manner if they are a part of the decision-making process. Self-motivation is fairly simple; if one has a personal stake in reaching organizational goals, he will require less supervision, will be more likely to operate in an acceptable manner, and will sense a deeper feeling of achievement in reaching those goals. Self-motivation can occur from a variety of stimuli. Self-actualization is somewhat different in that it deals with an inner self. Abraham Maslow describes *self-actualization* as referring "to the desire for self-fulfillment, namely, to the tendency for one to become actualized in what one is potentially."[15] Self-actualized, self-motivated people, then, are more likely to be influenced to do what is desired of them because of a personal commitment rather than because of a concern for authority or power.

Since World War II greater emphasis has been placed on attracting high-caliber young men and women into the police services. In 1967 the President's Commission on Law Enforcement and Administration of Justice focused attention on the need for formally educated police officers. "The ultimate aim of all police departments should be that all personnel with general enforcement powers have baccalaureate degrees."[16] High-ranking officers' objectives should be advanced degrees.

We concur with the commission's recommendations but foresee some administrative problems for those organizations that continue to operate with the traditional authoritarian model.

Maslow's theory takes on new and special meaning for police organizations. It appears likely that a better-educated young man will be more critical of the organization and of himself and less likely that he will be content to simply "carry out orders." There is a danger that police organizations and their managers may not recognize the new type of recruit and may not use his *self-actualizing* needs properly. If this occurs, it can be anticipated that retention rate of our brightest resource will sharply decline and today's problems will continue to be tomorrow's.

Reliance upon strict authoritarian controls may continue to insure respectable crime statistics, but as previously mentioned, these may not be a reliable barometer of organizational effectiveness.

[15]Abraham H. Maslow, *Motivation and Personality* (New York: Harper & Row, Publishers, 1954), pp. 91–92.

[16]The President's Commisssion on Law Enforcement and Administration of Justice, *The Challenge of Crime in a Free Society,* (Washington, D.C.: U.S. Government Printing Office, 1967), p. 110.

LEARNING EXERCISE

DEPENDENCY-INTIMACY PERCEPTIONS: A STRUCTURED EXPERIENCE[17]

Goals

1. To focus on participants' relations to authority figures.
2. To focus on participants' relations to each other.
3. To study how these personal dimensions affect group process.
4. To provide instrumented feedback to members on how they are being perceived in the group.

Materials Utilized

1. Dependency-Intimacy Rating Forms. (It is advisable to write in group members' names on the forms in the same order before the session.)
2. Dependency-Intimacy Tally Forms.
3. Pencils.

Process

1. Facilitator gives lecturette on the relationship between group participants' personalities and group development, stressing the centrality of the dimensions of dependency (group participants' orientations to authority, toward the distribution and handling of power, to structure), and intimacy (orientations toward each other, closeness, personalness) .
2. Participants complete the Dependency-Intimacy Rating Form anonymously.
3. The facilitator collects the completed forms and distributes tally forms.
4. The facilitator reads the ratings aloud, and each participant tallies the ratings which he receives. The facilitator redistributes the rating forms randomly.

17The learning exercise is taken from J. William Pfeiffer and John E. Jones, *A Handbook of Structured Experiences for Human Relations Training* (Iowa City, Iowa: University City Associates Press, 1969), pp. 86–88.

5. Participants react to their ratings—how they feel about them, how accurate they feel they are—and are encouraged to solicit feedback on what aspects of their behavior may have elicited the ratings.

6. The group discusses its development in terms of roles that various "types" of participants have played.

Dependency-Intimacy Rating Form

Below are scales on which you are to rate yourself and all of the other participants of your group on two traits, dependency and intimacy. Go through the following steps:

1. Read the descriptions of the two personality traits.

2. In front of the names of the participants, listed below, write the number corresponding to where you would place them on the dependency scale.

3. Then record your rating of each participant on the intimacy scale.

DEPENDENCY

1	2	3	4	5	6

Dependent
Relies on structure,
leader, group, agenda

Independent

Counterdependent
Rebels against
almost all forms
of structure

INTIMACY

1	2	3	4	5	6

Overpersonal
Need to establish close
personal relations with
everyone, to keep the
group on a personal level

Personal

Counterpersonal
Need to keep relations
with others formal and
impersonal and to keep
group interaction for-
mal and impersonal

DEP	*INT*	*Group Member*	*DEP*	*INT*	*Group Member*
___	___	_____	___	___	_____
___	___	_____	___	___	_____
___	___	_____	___	___	_____
___	___	_____	___	___	_____
___	___	_____	___	___	_____
___	___	_____	___	___	_____
___	___	_____	___	___	_____

Name

Dependency and intimacy are not seen as linear dimensions; that is, the extremes of dependency and counterdependency are dynamically close together, as are overpersonalness and counterpersonalness. The person who is conflicted on either dependency or intimacy may display behaviors on both ends of the continuum. He may alternately be dependent and counter-dependent in a stressful situation, even in the same group meeting. The circles below graphically demonstrate the relationship between the extremes of these two dimensions. Tally the ratings which you receive from your fellow group members by marking Xs on the circles.

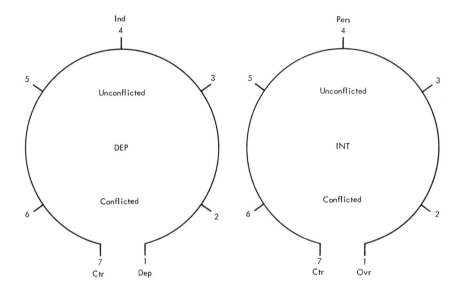

Chapter Eight

TASK 6
DECISION-MAKING:
Where The Buck Stops

It can be argued, however, that the processes of problem-solving and decision-making when carried out by organizations are different from the same processes carried out by individuals in at least one fundamental respect. Organizational decision-making involves both cognitive and social processes. The events that intervene between the identification of a problem (or occasion for decision-making) and a solution or decision are both intra-personal and interpersonal. It is the interpersonal or social aspects of decision-making that are of most direct relevance to processes of leadership. The leader not only makes decisions but also designs, regulates, and selects social systems that make decisions.[1]

SYNOPSIS

Effective managers make effective decisions—or they are not effective managers. Such decisions are not the by-products of charisma but are carefully developed within a logical process which begins with identification of the problem. Following through the process there is the selection of a proper decision and its implementation. Decision without implementation is no decision at all. The final state of the process is feedback, an evaluation of the implementation. The decision maker must know whether or not the action did in fact solve the problem, if it created other problems, or if it needed modification.

Three different decision-making models are discussed: *rational decisions, bounded rationality*, and *heuristic decisions*. Essentially, *rational decisions* are possible when one has access to *all* pertinent information, can trace *every* possible solution to its end, and make a selection from all alternatives based upon the most efficient/economical combination. *Bounded rationality* acknowledges that man's ability to make rational decisions is bounded by certain limitations which include his experiences, his values, and the amount of information to which he has access. *Heurisitc decisions* involve elements of both the other models, adding a most powerful third dimension, the *human* element. The heuristic decision maker is free to internalize all the available data and possible solutions, reflecting this information against his personal experiences, his values,

[1]Victor H. Vroom and Philip W. Yetton, *Leadership and Decision-Making* (Pittsburgh, Pa.: University of Pittsburgh Press, 1973), pp. 4–5.

and his perception of what has been and what is likely to be. He then chooses the decision that he "feels" is the right one.

The chapter next moves to the information-gathering process, which involves formal and informal communication links as well as extraorganizational links, those things going on outside the organization. In addition, consideration is given to the kinds of influence that are likely to affect the decision maker.

The point of the chapter is that effective decision makers do not operate in a vacuum. They are subject to all the elements of organizational, political, community, and personal life. Decisions made within organization or subunit settings are likely to have impact beyond their parameters—the effects of which must be considered before implementation. Implementation is the action part of the decision-making process. It must be monitored through feedback, and modified if need be, to serve identified objectives.

INTRODUCTION

The art of being right in every decision has yet to be mastered. The habit of being wrong—too often—is yet to be tolerated for very long. Every manager in every field is expected to make proper decisions and of course he has some responsibility for the decisions of his subordinates. However, few professions demand so many good decisions and tolerate so few poor ones as does law enforcement. This is as it should be, since law enforcement decisions often effect the lives of citizens. A not uncommon practice is the federal lawsuit alleging that certain law enforcement decisions have been not only bad but a violation of someone's constitutional rights as well. Equally common is a lawsuit of this kind directed at the police manager—as well as his subordinate who actually made the decision. And of course civil rights lawsuits resulting in punitive damages cannot be covered by insurance, and so the penalty for some bad decisions has taken on tones more ominous and personal in the current decade.

It is not enough that the manager is a good *decision maker*. He is responsible for the training, discipline and example from which subordinates learn to make acceptable decisions.

"Decision making is that thinking which results in the choice among alternative courses of action."[2] As we have stated in earlier chapters, it is a primary function of management. Decisions are made at all levels of endeavor, of course, but the administrative decision-making process is set apart, for it provides the basis upon which all other rational organizational decisions are made. The late Los Angeles Chief of Police William H. Parker was concerned about the quality of police decision making when he said:

> All Police Administrators are constantly called upon to make decisions: the wisdom of these decisions will depend, in large measure, upon the information and advice available to them. If decisions are made without proper analysis of facts, or without regard for standard practices developed as the result of research, the chances are that they will be mediocre decisions—and it is the accumulation of mediocre decisions that produces mediocrity in police administration.[3]

In the more contemporary manner of the computer, cyberneticists have a saying: "Garbage in—garbage out." Decisions made on the basis of low quality information: Garbage in—garbage out.

In the preceding chapters on planning, communications, and leadership, we developed a concept of interdependence that included the process of decision making. These several concepts are interwoven.

In this chapter we will focus on an array of decision-making facets, including the rationale of decision making. Again, for reference and validation, we must turn to the literature of business and the social scientists, for modern law enforcement writers have provided little in this area save to acknowledge that it is a process of management. This void is particularly interesting, since it appears that every decision will affect, to some degree, the success or failure, the growth and development, the health, welfare, and prosperity of individuals and organizations. We can think of no other field in which decisions are so open for introspection, so vulnerable to the Monday-morning quarterbacking of politicians and pressure groups and average citizens alike.

SEQUENTIAL STEPS TO EFFECTIVE DECISIONS

Effective decisions are not the result of happenstance but rather are the product of a logical process. Peter Drucker, a leading management

---

[2]Donald W. Taylor, "Decision Making and Problem Solving," in *Handbook of Organizations,* ed. James G. March (Chicago: Rand McNally & Co., 1965), p. 48.
[3]William H. Parker, "Practical Aspects of Police Planning," (Paper delivered at the Sixty-first Annual Conference of the International Association of Chiefs of Police, New Orleans, September 27, 1954), p. 7.

thinker, refers to this process as a series of elements which he systematically arranges into six sequential steps.[4] The steps are as follows:

1. *The classification of the problem.* Is it generic? Is it exceptional and unique? Or is it the first manifestation of a new genus for which a rule has yet to be developed?

2. *The definition of the problem.* What are we dealing with?

3. *The specifications which the answer to the problem must satisfy.* What are the "boundary conditions"?

4. *The decision as to what is "right," rather than what is acceptable, in order to meet the boundary conditions.* What will fully satisfy the specifications *before* attention is given to the compromises, adaptations, and concessions needed to make the decision acceptable?

5. *The building into the decision of the action to carry it out.* What does the action commitment have to be? Who has to know about it?

6. *The feedback which tests the validity and effectiveness of the decision against the actual course of events.* How is the decision being carried out? Are the assumptions on which it is based appropriate or obsolete?

These sequential steps are applicable throughout the chapter and are considered as basic to the process regardless of the model or style used.

DECISION-MAKING MODELS

For the purpose of this chapter we have divided the decision-making process into three models: *rational,* the most formalized and perhaps the most difficult to fully achieve; *bounded rationality,* which takes man's limitations, his frame of reference, into account; and *heuristic,* which introduces the human element. All three are viable and are relevant to the business of effective decisions by law enforcement managers.

Rational Decisions

Decision making in law enforcement, as in other organizations, is the selection of a course of action from two or more alternatives. Sound decisions are more likely to occur (1) when all the variables are clearly understood and when the decision maker (or makers) is privy to all the available related information, and (2) when all possible alternatives have

---

[4]Peter F. Drucker, "The Effective Decision," *Harvard Business Review,* Vol. 53 (January-February 1967): pp. 33–39. Article dervied from his book, *The Effective Executive* (New York: Harper & Row, Publishers, 1966).

been thoroughly explored and narrowed down by a rational elimination process.

Herbert Simon explains that "rational decision-making always requires the comparison of alternative means in terms of the respective ends to which they will lead." He cautions us that "the ends to be attained by the choice of a particular behavior alternative are often incompletely or incorrectly stated through failure to consider the alternative ends that could be reached by selection of another behavior."[5]

One example would be the selection of a crowd control plan. Following Simon's view, it would not be sufficient to select a plan of action on the mere probability that it would satisfactorily meet desired goals. Rational behavior would require that all possible alternatives be explored in terms of the respective ends to which they will lead. "This means that 'efficiency'—that attainment of maximum values with limited means— must be a guiding criterion in administrative decision."[6] The *rational* selection must therefore be made on the basis of which of the available alternatives was the most *efficient/economical* combination. To be efficient without being economical or vice versa would not be considered a rational decision.

Feldman and Kanter refer to a similar though somewhat more complicated model as "comprehensive decision-making," wherein they point out certain inherent limitations. They observe that it is possible to identify and examine all possible alternatives in only the most simple problems. "For even moderately complex problems, however, the entire decision tree cannot be generated."[7] Time, economics, and other constraints prevent the projection of every possible alternative to its ultimate end.

Bounded Rationality

Simon, too, discussed the limitations of rational decision making, not so much in terms of the multiplicity of possible alternatives as in terms of rational man himself. Simon observed that decision-making man was bounded by a triangle of limitations. "On one side, the individual is limited by those skills, habits, and reflexes which are no longer in the realm of the conscious." These take into consideration the physical and mental process developed in one's lifetime. "On a second side, the individual is limited by his values and those conceptions of purpose which

[5]Herbert A. Simon, *Administrative Behavior*, 2nd ed., (New York: The Macmillan Company, 1961), p. 65.
[6]*Ibid.*
[7]Julian Feldman and Herschel E. Kanter, "Organizational Decision Making," in *Handbook of Organizations*, ed. James G. March, pp. 614–15.

influence him in making his decisions." These include his conception of self-worth and his relationship to the total organization. "On a third side, the individual is limited by the extent of his knowledge of things relevant to his job"[8]—not just knowing his job, but what he knows about those other elements of the organization.

In the preceding chapter we discussed the need for man to understand the importance of his job to the total organizational mission. This concept is again reinforced by Simon in his view that man's ability to make rational decisions is bounded by the limitation of his knowledge of the total organization.[9]

The point is that a group of experts, given exactly the same information, considering the rational process, would theoretically reach identical conclusions. In reality, however, as we view Simon's theory, the inherent limitations by which each individual is bounded varies to some degree. The result is that each expert's conclusion may very well be rational in terms of his own perception—but there is a reasonable possibility that all will not have reached identical conclusions.

We have observed, especially in the more authoritarian hierarchical setting such as the police, that failure to make what the "boss" views as a rational decision may result in a withdrawal of support when it is most needed. It is essential that managers have an appreciation of the uniqueness of personal boundaries when viewing the decisions of subordinates.

Heuristic Decisions

In addition to the processes of rational decision making and those of bounded rationality, William Gore identifies what we view as a most potent third process, the "heuristic model."[10] The heuristic model is especially appropriate to the modern police administrator in that it legitimizes a process we sometimes hear referred to as a "gut level decision" and at the same time affords a latitude not recognized in the rational models. Rational systems tend to presume that all the elements of truth are built into the prescribed process—they are codifications of truth in cause-and-effect relationships. These systems enjoy acceptance because they have always worked. But truth and knowledge are transitory things, and if man adheres to his rational systems alone and is mindless of their changing elements of truth and data, then he deludes himself.

The rational process can be seen as one that includes isolating the

8Simon, *Administrative Behavior*, p. 40.
9*Ibid.*
10William J. Gore, *Administrative Decision-Making: A Heuristic Model* (New York: John Wiley & Sons, Inc., 1964).

problem and the almost impossible task of logically identifying all possible alternative solutions from which the best is selected and implemented. Conversely, Gore views the heuristic process as "a groping toward agreements seldom arrived at through logic. The very essence of the heuristic process is that the factors validating a decision are internal to the personality of the individual instead of external to it."[11]

A rational process ultimately involves concrete, here-and-now arrangements that pertain to collective action. Conversely, the heuristic process is an almost verbal process, reaching backward into the memory and forward into the future, touching any number of personalities and people. In addition to using the rational system of cause and effect, the heuristic process takes advantage of the unseen emotional motivations that energize the organizational system.

The heuristic model for administrative decision making, in a way, formalizes the processes used by many. It adds the human dimension. For example, we can put reams of data into a computer and it will respond to certain inquiries with mechanical outputs. The better the data supplied, the more accurate the output will be. Unfortunately, the computer cannot supply the human element, the stuff that one develops in a lifetime of experiences. In the heuristic model, the administrator may also bounce his problem and the gathered data off other management team members (or others) and gain responses based on their combined experiences. Thus armed, the administrator is free to disregard the rational model and make a decision outside the mechanical logic.

We sense that Gore sees heuristic applications as adjuncts to rational models or as alternatives to rational models, depending upon the circumstances. It is simply a case of granting credence to man's proclivity and talent for subjectivity as a viable element in the act of decision making or problem solving.

The heuristic model makes room for effective as well as cognitive input. Thus, what a man *is* becomes a force that conditions the decisions he makes.

AUTONOMY IN DECISION MAKING

The age of modern organizations and enlightened management has brought about the broader sharing of authority and responsibility. There is more autonomy at every level and greater expectations from above and below.

---

[11]*Ibid.,* p. 12.

The degree of autonomy accorded is directly related to a number of factors, not the least of which is the relationship between the various levels in the hierarchy. While it is possible and most often efficient for various levels or subunits to enjoy a measure of autonomy in the decision-making process, the danger of introspection is present. It is absolutely vital that there exist an appreciation for the total organizational goals and policies and for those of the supporting subunits. Decisions made in one unit are likely to have an effect on other units. If units or a collection of units were to become so introspective as to adversely affect other units, the autonomy would by necessity be drastically reduced.

In his study of private organizations, Rensis Likert observed that decisions that might affect subordinates whose interests were not represented in the decision-making process were not likely to be accepted wholeheartedly.[12] He suggests that this is less likely to occur in what he calls "the overlapping group form of organization." (See exhibit 8–1). In the traditional organization, Likert is concerned about the narrowness of influence relationships which are normally one to one, or "man to man."[13] This concept can be more readily understood if the reader

Exhibit 8–1.   The Overlapping Group Form of Organization

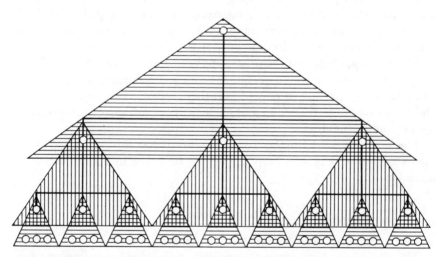

Source: Work groups vary in size as circumstances require, although shown here as consisting of four persons. As illustrated in Rensis Likert, *New Patterns of Management* (New York: McGraw-Hill Book Company, 1961), p. 105.

[12]Rensis Likert, *New Patterns of Management* (New York: McGraw-Hill Book Company, 1961), p. 107.
[13]*Ibid.*, p. 106.

will review his own organizational chart or one of any typical police agency, for it will also convey the lines of communication and influence—one person reports directly to one person.

Likert's diagram of overlapping groups shows that in each group one member holds dual membership in another group and so on; no one individual or group of individuals is mutually exclusive. As one moves up Likert's organizational chart, the superior in one group becomes a subordinate in the next group and has relationships with all others in each group.[14] Likert views this as a "linking pin" concept, which *insures that each group* is able to influence the total organization. (See exhibit 8–2). For example, the field sergeant and his subordinates form a group. The sergeant also holds membership in a second group, made up of other sergeants and one lieutenant. The lieutenant also holds membership in a group of lieutenants headed up by a captain, and so on.

In our view the group overlay and linking pin effects would also reduce the incidence of decisions in any one group being made in a vacuum, without regard for other groups within the organization.

Exhibit 8–2. The Linking Pin

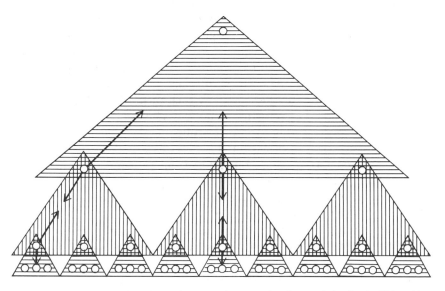

Source: The arrows indicate the linking pin function. As illustrated in Rensis Likert, *New Patterns of Management* (New York: McGraw-Hill Book Company, 1961), p. 113.

[14]*Ibid.*, p. 105.

INFORMATION SYSTEMS

In all three of our decision-making models, two primary factors were present—the identification of the need to bring about some change and the acquisition of enough information upon which to base the selection of a proper decision. Both of these factors are predicated to a great extent upon the flow of information through channels to the point of action.

Formal Channels

In chapter 6 we discussed the multiple channels of communication. These same channels are in fact concurrently information-gathering channels upon which there is absolute dependency by the decision maker. As we stated earlier, the formal channels comply with the recognized official structure of the organization. A great deal of information, both that which has been requested and that which has been discovered independently, travels up these channels. Much of this information is routine, such as monthly reports, logs, and computer printouts, upon which deployment and other operating decisions are made. The degree to which all levels of the hierarchy are sensitized to the nonroutine information that might have value to the next higher level or levels is a limiting factor which determines what independently discovered information is likely to be transmitted up the formal channel. Another common problem is the filtering process through which information must travel. Top managers do not have the time to assimilate each piece of available information. On the other hand, many seemingly sound decisions have been made only to prove unsound later because the decision maker did not have all the necessary information. This is especially disheartening when the information was available but filtered out as being insignificant before reaching the necessary level. Obviously, it is a primary responsibility of management to develop within the total organization a set of values that will reduce this overfiltering process to a minimum.

An especially important addition to the formal information process is the computer. A common unit in the larger police agencies, it is becoming more available to the smaller jurisdictions on a shared-time basis. A major contribution of the computer is that it provides better, more up-to-date information upon which to make operational decisions.

Even the computer, however, with its awesome memory and logic, coupled with the other formal communication links, is not all-seeing or all-knowing. Because of the previously mentioned filtering process and the inflexibility, cumbersomeness, and other limitations of formality, there are serious gaps in the information-gathering process, and these gaps are a factor in Parker's observation of mediocre decisions.

Informal Channels

Since information needs are directly related to decision making, "plugging" the communication gap is in reality plugging the information gap that obviously appears in formal channels.

It is interesting to note that many police administrators appear uncomfortable with the concept of encouraging informal channels of communication—information transmission. This is to say that they have been steeped in the tradition of "unity of command," the proper channels concept. We have observed this philosophy carried to the point where some administrators actually block these types of communication links. In our view, informal communication links are not in any measure a violation of the unity-of-command doctrine. Our belief is that they should be opened up broadly, in a natural manner. The "boss" should at times be available, not in his own forbidding office, but in a place where the lower-level employees are likely to gather informally. This kind of information gathering cannot be ordered; it must occur naturally, for we are not suggesting a running-to-the-boss type situation. In many instances it is not even necessary to acknowledge that information has been received.

If there is acknowledgment, there need not—and should not—be any open evaluation of the information at that point. Any single source of information, especially of that which is received in this manner, is in need of independent validation. A second admonition regarding informal information sources is that the receiver must be sensitive to the message being delivered, not simply to the words being spoken. This is especially true in the identification of organizational problems. Dissatisfaction with such things as working hours, salary, and supervisors may well have nothing whatsoever to do with those issues. It has been our observation, especially in the lower hierarchical levels, that many people have difficulty in saying what they mean, especially if the issues are serious, and especially if they have already been ignored by an immediate supervisor. Instead, their frustrations are voiced in a manner they perceive to be acceptable and noncommitting—"I can't get into trouble for saying it that way." The real message may be that things are not running as smoothly as the boss has been led to believe and he had better begin by initiating the proper action to properly identify the problem.

The point to be made is that the use of informal communication links or channels is legitimate. They are especially important in that they bypass the natural restrictions within the system and provide administration with practical information without requiring commitment or action at that juncture.

In chaper 3 we discussed certain organizational concepts, including authority, hierarchy, and unity of command. We are not now suggesting a disregard for those concepts and principles, for they are an integral part of the decision-making process. It is simply that we do not view the reception of information or even the informal fraternization between the various levels as necessarily leading to a violation of those concepts.

Our belief is that the problems police administrators are most likely to consider will be so critical in terms of the health and operational success of the organization that they must have the best available information upon which to base decisions.

Extraorganizational Communication Links

Information with which to identify problems and develop alternative solutions is being generated outside as well as inside the organization. Earlier we discussed Likert's theory of linking pins and overlapping groups. Application can be readily seen in the membership of the top law enforcement executive in a group composed of city department heads —fire, public works, and the like. Some city managers have gone so far as to design new city halls in which all the various department heads have officers clustered together. There may be any number of motivating factors, but at the top of the list most assuredly is the communication/ decision-making process.

In chapter 4 we observed that in some jurisdictions police leaders will find a need for additional community involvement; we were pointing at a more social aspect. In a purely problem-identification-and-solution sense, we believe that extradepartmental-community communication links are absolutely essential in every jurisdiction. We do not view these links as exclusively important to management, but rather as a total department function. This concept will be explored more fully in chapter 15, "Police and Their Community."

Alert patrolmen and detectives have long pursued the development of informal communication links; for the most part, however, these have been with the world of informers. Their object, as ours, is gathering information with which to identify problems ("Who stole the merchandise?") and the development of alternative solutions ("The best way to catch the thief"). Every seasoned policeman knows that the bulk of solved crimes is cleared in this manner. It logically follows that if the "working cop" is able to develop and use extradepartmental communication links in terms of his assigned departmental goals, police managers should be able to do the same in terms of the broader goals of total organization.

SOME ELEMENTS OF INFLUENCE

Decisions by intelligent leaders are not normally made in a vacuum. In addition to those influences identified by Simon as boundaries, there are others, some of which lend themselves to this discussion. We have chosen to view these influences as elements and have observed that they primarily serve two purposes, which seem on the surface at least to be dichotomous. First, they serve to enlighten the decision maker, providing him with a broader base from which to make rational decisions. Second, and conversely, they tend to restrict the decision-making base by erecting certain parameters or describing the arena in which the decision maker must function.

Legal Elements

For example, legal elements that are often present in the decision-making process of the police administrator are not a concern for his counterpart in the private sector. In the hiring or the discharging of employees, the private sector administrator has much more latitude. His decision can more closely coincide with his perception of the right man for the job. The police administrator, on the other hand, must concern himself with the best individuals from those names appearing on an eligibility list. This type of element is usually covered in ordinances or laws covering personnel practices.

Information Elements

We have been discussing communication links and channels as information-gathering devices. The reason for gathering information is to facilitate the making of sound decisions. The information itself becomes an element of influence. In our experience over the years we have met a number of police administrators who have shunned informal communication links for the very reason that they did not *want* to be influenced. For some, at least, there has been some sinister connotation in the concept of influence. Our view is that the successful administrator must be privy to all forms of information. The weighting he gives it is quite another thing. We are not giving space to the I've-got-influence-at-city-hall huckster, for his lack of validity is obvious. It is simply not feasible, however, to operate a law enforcement organization in a vacuum.

Community Elements

What the police department does affects the total organization (e.g., city government) and ultimately the total community. Community goals, therefore, exert an important influence. (Police departments cannot exist without the community, and vice versa). The jurisdiction may, for example, be a resort community dependent upon visitors for its economy. Within legalistic latitudes, the police department would undoubtedly need to examine its priorities in terms of encouraging rather than discouraging tourist traffic.

An excellent case in point concerns the semiresort city of Newport Beach, California, a favorite vacation community for half a century. Over the years, however, the younger generation began to take more and more latitude. The younger generation visitors are obviously important, as are their older counterparts, for they, too, contribute to the economy by occupying hundreds of the rental units and purchasing services, food, and other commodities. On the other hand, a certain lawlessness was present which had been tolerated for some time. In 1961 Captain James Glavis retired from the Los Angeles Police Department to become the Newport Beach police chief. Chief Glavis was well aware that at least a part of the community looked upon the young people as "good business," and he was also conscious of the need for the establishment and maintenance of good order, not only for the harmony between generations but for general community welfare as well. During the three years following his appointment, Chief Glavis pursued a course of action that was to bring the youthful visitors into line without discouraging their visits. He was able to satisfy the goals of the business community, the residential community, the adult vacationing community, and the police department, and those of the young people as well, through a course of action decided upon, not in a vacuum, but with information inputs from all sectors.

It is not our intent to discuss methodology. Rather, we are reinforcing our hypothesis that political awareness, sensitivity to total community goals in viewing the identification of problems and solutions, need not be a prostitution of the police mission. In our chapter 14 learning exercise we use a classic case study that is pertinent to the discussion at hand and is almost the opposite of Glavis's approach to Newport Beach's problems. In the case study, the chief's tenure was short lived; conversely, Chief Glavis became an institution in Newport Beach.

Family Elements

When one considers all possible influencing elements, their numbers become infinite. For that reason the development of such a list will be left to the reader. We find it impossible, however, to leave this section without some recognition of the most personal of all exterior influences—the family.

Decision makers at every level report for work each day with fluctuating attitudes that seem to be reflected in their total conduct. A suddenly ill child, unexpected out-of-town guests, financial crises, or a wife's wrecking the car are all examples of behavior influences. A test of this is to review a decision made on a previous day, especially one leading to negative action. Our guess is that without the updating of any information, a different course of action may appear more appropriate, especially if home conditions have changed in any way. Grandma may not have been a social scientist, but her admonition to sleep on a decision because "things may look different in the morning" was not based on folklore—they often do.

Our point is that when an employee is hired, the organization is also subject to the influence of his total family unit, a fact that deserves recognition.

Priorities and Timing

Priorities and timing are closely related influence elements. Both include the identification of problems and solutions, and both involve an element of risk. When more than one course of action is called for at the same time, involving the same personnel, priorities must be set. Timing involves the *when* of a course of action and is not necessarily predicated on resources. Every police manager is frequently faced with the problem of appropriately deploying limited personnel in light of conflicting demands for service (e.g., "If you don't slow down the traffic in this area, the blood of our children will be on your hands!" concurrently with, "Daylight burglars are carrying the town away!").

> A decision therefore has to be made as to which tasks deserve priority and which are of less importance. The only question is which will make the decision—the executive or the pressures . . . If the pressures rather than the executive are allowed to make the decision, the important tasks will predictably be sacrificed.[15]

15Drucker, *Effective Executive,* p. 109.

As for timing, it may be prudent to arrest a person running for public office the day after the election instead of the day before, especially if the charges are made by the opposition. Undoubtedly, a few will criticize the delay as having been made for political reasons. On the other hand, the police, rather than the arrestee, will become the focus of general attack if the action is taken the day before. *Everyone* will suspect political overtones.

Sensitivity to the value of proper timing and priorities is a vital component of the decision-making process. Priorities connote a rational compromise between needs and resources. Conversely, timing is not a compromise but rather the maximizing of necessary or desired action while minimizing conflict.

STRATEGIES

In pulling together all the decision-making factors, a suitable strategy must be considered for the particular problem at hand. In some isolated incidents it will be appropriate for a manager to make a decision by himself, as we stated in chapter 4. Autocratic leadership is most appropriate in a crisis situation when an *immediate* decision is necessary for the welfare/survival of the organization. There will be times when the very sensitive nature of the problem will make the decision a lonely one. This is not to say that such decisions are made in a vacuum without considering alternatives. If we subscribe to Simon's theory of bounded rationality, however, it can be seen that the boundaries of a single person are likely to be more restricted than will be the collective boundaries of a group. Therefore, it is our view that the utilization of available human resources in one way or another is likely to produce more effective, higher quality decisions for organizational implementation. How these human resources are used becomes an application of administrative strategy.

Conflict

"I don't want any yes-men working for me" is a frequently heard cliché. In reality many decision makers, even those who use the group process, prefer to avoid conflict. Conflict is undoubtedly viewed by some as time-consuming and dysfunctional. Others simply prefer to "run things" themselves, acting as a sort of chairman of the board, in a most negative sense.

Peter Drucker observes that "the effective decision does not . . . flow from a consensus on the facts. The understanding that underlies the right decision grows out of the clash and conflict of divergent opinions and out of the serious consideration of competing alternatives."[16]

Drucker suggests that subordinates and experts do not express facts but rather opinions when first viewing a problem. He views this as proper, since "people experienced in an area should be expected to have an opinion. . . . People inevitably start out with an opinion; to ask them to search for the facts first is even undesirable."[17] It is from these opinions that facts and alternatives will flow.

> Unless one has considered alternatives, one has a closed mind.
>
> This, above all, explains why effective decision-makers deliberately disregard the second major command of the textbooks on decision-making and create dissension and disagreement, rather than consensus.
>
> Decisions of the kind the executive has to make are not made well by acclamation. They are made well only if based on the clash of conflicting views, the dialogue between different judgments. The first rule in decision-making is that one does not make a decision unless there is disagreement.
>
> Alfred P. Sloan[18] is reported to have said at a meeting of one of his top committees: "Gentlemen, I take it we are all in complete agreement on the decision here." Everyone around the table nodded assent. "Then," continued Mr. Sloan, "I propose we postpone further discussion of this matter until our next meeting to give ourselves time to develop disagreement and perhaps gain some understanding of what the decision is all about."
>
> Sloan was anything but an "intuitive" decision-maker. He always emphasized the need to test opinions against facts and the need to make absolutely sure that one did not start out with the conclusion and then look for the facts that would support it. But he knew that the right decision demands adequate disagreement.
>
> Every one of the effective Presidents in American history had his own method of producing the disagreement he needed in order to make an effective decision. Lincoln, Theodore Roosevelt, Franklin D. Roosevelt, Harry Truman—each had his own ways. But each created the disagreement he needed for "some understanding of what the decision is all about." Washington, we know, hated conflicts and quarrels and wanted a united Cabinet. Yet he made quite sure of the necessary differences of opinion on important matters by asking both Hamilton and Jefferson for their opinions.[19]

[16]*Ibid.,* p. 143.
[17]*Ibid.,* p. 144.
[18]Alfred P. Sloan, Jr., president, General Motors Corporation, 1923 to 1937; chairman of the board, 1937 to 1956.
[19]Drucker, *Effective Executive,* pp. 148–49.

Conflict as a strategy, as can be seen by Drucker's reference to our nation's presidents, is not new. It may, however, be new to many police managers who continue to believe that agreement and harmony are the foundations upon which strength and control are built.

Brainstorming

One of the most constraining factors to effective decision making is the limitation of alternative courses of action. In the process of developing alternatives, there is a tendency to be hypercritical at the wrong point—the inception. This applies to both individual and group decision makers but is more likely to occur in the group process. There appears to be an inherent tendency to "shoot down' 'ideas that do not follow what is considered to be a normal course. Many potentially good ideas fall by the wayside because they are too quickly rejected, not preserved for later consideration. One method of rejection is the verbal "shooting down." Another, equally effective, is no response at all. Without some kind of second, ideas tend to fall flat. Silence in itself is not always rejection. Other group members may be momentarily absorbed in their own thoughts, but the effect is just the same. An idea without support dies.

Dan Pursuit, a professor at the University of Southern California, has for over twenty years been peddling a most effective solution to these problems—brainstorming. In essence, brainstorming is exactly what it sounds like. It is the forcing of ideas off the top of the participants' heads with a complete disregard for validity. None are rejected; all are recorded in writing on a chalkboard or on an easel-held, large newsprint tablet. (We favor the newsprint for all decision-making exercises in that the sheets may be displayed around the room, then preserved for later contemplation).

When the group has run dry, the ideas are gathered together and are grouped under similar headings. One by one they are examined and commented upon without regard for the author. Gradually they are refined until only a workable number remain. Interestingly enough, ideas considered "far out" often become *not* so far out as they are manipulated and built upon.

Another facet of brainstorming is that it permits the nonexpert to become involved, and in the end it might be he who, for the very reason that he *was not* close to the problem, made the important contribution.

Perhaps the phenomenon is not restricted to police organizations, but over the years we have observed that newcomers to the field are not normally encouraged to voice their opinions, especially in group settings. Since decisions are made at all levels, and group decisions are equally valid at both ends of the hierarchy, we view this as a waste of potential power in the decision-making process.

This is especially true today as we see young men and women whose formal education represents a wide variety of fields entering law enforcement. The engineering student is likely to approach a problem in a manner completely different from that of the sociology major, and both may be at odds with the criminologist. Knowledge is power—using the knowledge of others is the harnessing of power.

Risk Technique

In many decision-making sessions, a concept or a course of action is already on the floor. The boss believes he would like to undertake a major deviation from the *status quo* in one manner or another. His staff is called together to examine his "baby." As in Drucker's conflict model, the last thing the boss needs is consensus. What he needs, first of all, is to know the risks involved. An excellent course of action is to impose the risk technique, which amounts to negative brainstorming; no one is permitted to make a positive statement. As in brainstorming, all ideas are recorded without comment and participants are encouraged to go as far out as possible. As each page from the newsprint tablet is filled, it is taped with masking, not cellophane, tape) on the wall to stimulate new ideas and avoid redundancy. Once the group has been drained of negatives, members are free to explore the positive aspects, which, too, are listed and posted. If in the end the negatives are outweighed by the positives in such a manner as to indicate that implementation of the decision should be made, a third set of pages is developed under the heading of "Thing to Do for Implementation."

A side value in preserving these lists is that they can be shared with other subordinate or superior groups. Other groups can be invited to add to each list as it is displayed in sequence. This not only provides broader involvements and utilization of greater resources but also lets others know what other ideas were developed and rejected. A great deal of wheel spinning is avoided in that the implementers are spared the normal reaction of wondering why some other solution was not considered.

All three strategies require the investment of valuable time by a relatively small group, the staff. The payoff comes in the saving of valuable time by a relatively large group, the operating personnel.

IMPLEMENTATION

The most crucial point of every decision is that of implementation. Many excellent decisions fall unproductively by the wayside for lack of decisive action. Decisive action involves risk, commitment, and often some unpleasantness. As Druck observes, "There is no inherent reason why medicines should taste horrible—but effective ones usually do. Similarly, there is no inherent reason why decisions should be distasteful—but most effective ones are."[20] As we stated earlier, timing is important in effective decisions. However, one cannot wait forever.

Examples of "good decision—no action" include a metropolitan police department comprised of a large administrative division in the center of the city, with a number of outlying divisions strategically located geographically to serve the outlying areas. These outlying divisions primarily furnish the patrol function, with most backup functions controlled by the centrally located administrative division. The various divisions operate in areas substantially different from one another in terms of population, industry, economic level, ethnic makeup, and the like. While having some commonality, their problems and needs are for the most part quite different.

The police chief and his staff officers felt that centrally controlling backup functions was not the most efficient use of personnel or the most appropriate answer to regional or area needs. An extensive study was conducted, and at its conclusion, several possible compromise solutions were considered and rejected. The final decision was to decentralize; to create in effect satellite police departments, each complete with all normal services and each responsible to a single regional head—its chief. The plan was to give a great deal of latitude-autonomy to the regional chiefs so that they in turn could be more sensitive to local needs and could react more quickly. They would continue to work within the philosophical framework of the total organization.

All the gathered data, the best judgment of the staff members, and everything in the process apparently indicated the decision for regionalization to be rational in the purest sense of the term. In this, however, as in many plans, the final decision rested with an external body whose members exercised control over the police department, and they were reluctant to move. Perhaps the reasons were political, or perhaps the risk appeared too great. After all, the old program was effective—to some degree.

The best decision in the world is *no decision* if it is not implemented. Wars have been lost and businesses have become bankrupt when the decisions that would have meant survival were at hand but remained for one reason or another unimplemented.

It should be reemphasized that decisions are more effectively implemented when those who must implement them are involved in their making. Typically, implementation is thought of at the physical doing

---

[20]*Ibid.*, p. 157.

level, but it can be seen by our example that there is merit for involvement of those at the ultimate approval level as well.

FEEDBACK

Implementation is the action element of decision making, while *feedback* is the validating or correcting element. Feedback is necessary to determine whether or not the change is being properly carried out, whether or not it is achieving desired results, and what, if any, are the unanticipated side effects. Decisions, or at least changes brought about by decisions, do not always spring forth in full-blown success; often some modification or adjustment may be necessary. With the utilization of prompt feedback, these problems can often be identified and rectified quickly.

Feedback is available in various forms, but Drucker asserts that the most reliable is one's personal observation. "One needs organized information for the feedback. One needs reports and figures. But unless one builds one's feedback around direct exposure to reality—unless one disciplines oneself to go out and look—one condemns oneself to a sterile dogmatism and with it to ineffectiveness."[21]

Few decisions are indefinitely adequate, for organizations are not static. Even implemented decisions that do what they are supposed to do have need for periodic reexamination to be kept current. Feedback is an ongoing process.

LEARNING EXERCISE

PROBLEM-SOLVING: A STRUCTURED EXPERIENCE[22]

Goals

1. To study the sharing of information in task-oriented groups.

2. To focus on cooperation in group problem-solving.

3. To observe the emergence of leadership behavior in group problem-solving.

21*Ibid.*, p. 142.
22J. William Pfeiffer and John E. Jones, *A Handbook of Structured Experiences for Human Relations Training* (Iowa City, Iowa: University City Associates Press, 1969), pp. 26–30.

Group Size. From six to twelve participants. Several groups may be directed simultaneously in the same room.

Time Required. Approximately forty-five minutes.

Materials Utilized

1. Problem-Solving Task Instructions.
2. Information for Individual Group Members (26 cards).
3. Problem-Solving Task Reactions Forms.
4. Pencils.

Physical Setting. Group members are seated in a circle.

Process

1. Problem-solving task instruction sheets are distributed to the group members.
2. After members have had sufficient time to read the instructions sheet, the facilitator distributes the information cards randomly among the members of the group. He announces that the timing begins.
3. After twenty-minutes (or less, if the group finishes early), the facilitator interrupts and distributes the Problem-Solving Task Reaction Forms, to be completed *independently*.
4. The facilitator leads a discussion of the problem-solving activity, on information-processing and the sharing of leadership in task situations. Group members are encouraged to share data from their reaction forms. (The solution to the problem, by the way, is 23/30 wors.)

Problem-Solving Task Reactions Form

Pretend that lutts and mipps represent a new way of measuring distance, and that dars, wors, and mirs represent a new way of measuring time. A man drives from Town A through Town B and Town C, to Town D. The task of your group is to determine how many wors the entire trip took. You have twenty minutes for this task. Do not choose a formal leader.

You will be given cards containing information related to the task of the group. You may share this information orally, but you must keep the cards in your hands throughout.

Information for Individual Group Members

Each of the following questions and answers is typed on a 3 x 5 index card (26 cards). Those are distributed randomly among group members.

How far is it from A to B?
It is 4 lutts from A to B.

How far is it from B to C?

It is 8 lutts from B to C.

How far is it from C to D?

It is 10 lutts from C to D.

What is a lutt?

A lutt is 10 mipps.

What is a mipp?

A mipp is a way of measuring distance.

How many mipps are there in a mile?

There are 2 mipps in a mile.

What is a dar?

A dar is 10 wors.

What is a wor?

A wor is 5 mirs.

What is a mir?

A mir is a way of measuring time.

How many mirs are there in an hour?

There are two mirs in an hour.

How fast does the man drive from A to B?

The man drives from A to B at the rate of 24 lutts per wor.

How fast does the man drive from B to C?

The man drives from B to C at the rate of 30 lutts per wor.

How fast does the man drive from C to D?

The man drives from C to D at the rate of 30 lutts per wor.

Problem-Solving Task Reactions Form

1. Whose participation was most helpful in the group's accomplishment of the task?_____

   What did he/she do that was helpful?

2. Whose participation seemed to hinder the group's accomplishment of the task?_____

   What did he/she do that seemed to hinder?

3. What feeling reactions did you experience during the problem-solving exercise? If possible, what behavior evoked a feeling response on your part?

4. What role(s) did you play in the group as it worked on the task?

Chapter Nine

TASK 7 BUDGETING:

The Allocation of Scarce Resources

Budgetary strategies are actions by governmental agencies intended to maintain or increase the amount of money available to them. Not every move in the budgetary arena is necessarily aimed at getting funds in a conscious way. Yet administrators can hardly help being aware that nothing can be done without funds, and that they must normally do things to retain or increase rather than decrease their income.[1]

SYNOPSIS

In this chapter we discuss the various contemporary forms of budgeting for municipalities and, more specifically, for police organizations. Our intent is not to furnish in-depth information or create instant budgeting experts out of laymen, but rather to provide a brief overview and familiarity with budgeting and, hopefully, to sitmulate the management student to pursue this topic more formally and deeply.

We did, however, enter this discussion with certain biases, based upon experience and observation. For example, we have over the years observed various municipalities attempting to implement innovative budgeting processes only to have legislative bodies reject them, or to request adjunct line-item budgets. Legislators have found the line-item budget easy to understand without a great deal of expertise on the subject, and an excellent control or auditing device (although of funds only).

Legislative bodies are typically more concerned with "How much is it going to cost us?" than "How effective is it going to be?" We have actually observed legislative bodies refuse to participate in sanctioning programs because it is "politically unsound." We believe, however, that this will pass with time and experience.

Frankly, we doubt that there is any rational way to do away with the independent line-item budget in terms of the accounting responsibilities of finance directors and purchasing agents and some state legal requirements. And of course line-item budgets are the building blocks for all other forms.

As for performance budgeting in its present form we don't believe it is practical since it leans heavily on unit accomplishment,

1Aaron Wildavsky, *The Politics of the Budgetary Process* (Boston Mass.: Little, Brown and Company, 1964).

which the police and citizens tend to translate into *quotas*. Nor are planning, programming budgeting systems (PPBS) applicable to law enforcement needs, at least in their current format. Law enforcement must always consider the *human* element—not just what is economically rational in terms of service, but what the citizen feels comfortable with. Thus, the most or only acceptable solution is often not the most economically sound solution. Lastly, PPBS is most expensive and requires an additional staff of experts for which funding cannot logically be expected considering the financial state of most municipalities of the present time.

We do believe that the program (outcomes) budget has great potential. It is relatively inexpensive to implement, though there is an element of training necessary for division and unit heads who participate. It retains the human element; makes good use of the modern management theory of participation; considers the social element of the community; is easily understood by all; and is an excellent audit instrument to determine whether or not programs are achieving what they are designed to achieve.

We also believe that those who espouse the management-by-objectives theory are on the right track and that management by objectives is a necessary facet of program budgeting. Every police department and every element of every police department, regardless of size, should think through and identify rational goals and objectives—and try to meet them.

Lastly, we believe that for most police organizations the rational approach is to amalgamate or *crosswalk* the traditional line-item budget with the program budget. Many are already leading the way in this endeavor. Most attempts are only rudimentary at this point but are improving with each new fiscal budget. Line-item budgets are most useful for auditing the fiscal control; program budgets, for setting goals and working to reach them.

INTRODUCTION

Budgeting is or should be an exciting dynamic process. It is the very hub of all municipal police programs. A preponderance of the police manager's activities are generated by or related to the budget or its process. It appears almost incongruous then that many police managers and middle managers have assumed those critical roles with little or no prior budget preparation or budget execution training or experience. If we believe the experts in the field of finance, and we do, the budget is the very foundation upon which each police agency functions. How then do so many managers rise to such important positions without some preparation in this area? The answer while perhaps logical is not rational. Most budgets in large departments are prepared by separate bureaus with whom field and most staff officers have very little contact. Such bureaus are typically headed and staffed by civilian experts trained in the field of finance. Small department budgets are most likely to be prepared by the department head while the in-between department typically utilizes one middle-management person on a part-of-the-year basis. If fortunate, he may be backed up by one or two civilian staff people who have had some outside training.

Since most police managers at all levels "come up through the ranks" and since a majority of sworn personnel is assigned to field operations, few police officers have the opportunity to work directly with the budget. This is not to say that inputs are not made at the division level for they are. There is, however, a great deal of difference between divisional inputs and the finalized document—its presentation, execution and audit.

Even in those departments with carefully predetermined career ladders that make annual or biannual middle manager reassignments, budget making is an awesome task that precludes regular turnover in its assigned personnel.

If our assumptions are correct, it should come as no surprise that so many budgets are unimaginative, sterile documents that have simply "grown like Topsy". Unfortunately there are budgets that greet each new fiscal year with little or no review to determine existing program values in terms of the most profitable returns for the investment of scarce resources related to departmental goals.

With this hypothesis in mind, we have confined our discussion to the operating budget, briefly covering the history and philosophy of budgeting, various contemporary operating budget styles, and an overview of the budget calendar. We do not intend this as a short course in budgeting, but rather as a stimulus for budding managers to look more deeply into the process in preparation for future budgeting responsibilities. To that end a limited bibliography of "required reading" concludes this chapter.

It is our hope that future police managers will not be content with sterile budgets, but rather will prepare themselves to direct a dynamic budget process that will ensure careful study of existing programs and provide bold, innovative solutions to old and new law enforcement problems. Students who want to follow the capital budgeting process, which was omitted from the following material, will find suitable references in the bibliography.

Origins of Municipal Budgets

As with much United States history, origins of American formalized budgeting systems have their roots in England's Middle Ages and Magna Carta. English budget systems evolved from that time and American budget systems seemed to have evolved from the English. However, Frederick A. Cleveland, pioneer in the field of municipal budgeting, held in 1915 that budget systems did not evolve, but rather:

> It was the uncontrolled and uncontrollable increase in the cost of government that finally jostled the public into an attitude of hostility to a system which was so fondly called "the American system." This growing hostility to doing business in the dark, to "boss rule," to "invisible government" became the soil in which the "budget idea" finally took root and grew.[2]

Since the English form of government and general philosophy is different from that of the United States, it follows that the budget systems will also be different—from the method of assessing and collecting revenues to the method of expenditure and accountability.

In the late 1800s the United States formally took cognizance of the need for formalized municipal budget systems, during which period the National Municipal League drafted a model municipal corporations act. Under the act, mayors were responsible for the direct supervision of the budget system.

Moak and Hillhouse observe:

> In this early period, almost no city of any size in the United States operated under systematic budget procedures. From time to time, appropriations were made to individual departments and agencies; and revenue measures were enacted sporadically, with a view to financing most of these operating expenditures. . . .
>
> This rather haphazard system developed a broad range of critics, interested not only in bringing some order out of the process but also

[2]Lennox L. Moak and Kathryn W. Killian, *A Manual of Techniques for the Preparation, Consideration, Adoption, and Administration of Operating Budgets* (Chicago, Ill.: Municipal Finance Officers Association of the United States and Canada, 1963), p. 6.

in causing offices, departments, and agencies to develop plans for expenditure related to their assigned functions and goals.[3]

In 1906 the New York Bureau of Municipal Research was formed and in 1907 the Bureau released its first report entitled *Making a Municipal Budget.* "The practical outcome of these efforts was the application of a system of budgetary methods in New York City."[4] The Bureau's tenets continue to be the basis for current day budget systems in that they set forth "an objects classification of expenditures . . . designed to systematize the accounting analysis and to standardize the budgetary information within organizational units."[5]

Between 1910 and 1920, many municipal governments throughout the United States had installed some semblance of budgets, a majority of which had some relationship to the New York model.

With the spread of the strong mayor and the manager forms of city government the budget was extensively adopted as an integral part of municipal financing.

Writing in 1915 Lent D. Upson called for an executive budget characterized by the following:

1. An accurate estimate of municipal revenues and a resolution that appropriations be limited to such estimates

2. Appropriation by activities

3. Classification by character of expenditure

4. Inclusion of a salary schedule in the budget

5. Preliminary publication of the budget

6. Separate estimate for each individual fund

7. Scheduling of allotments

8. Preparation of financial reports[6]

These early days saw a great deal of reform and innovation in municipal budgets. With these somewhat revolutionary changes as a base, there appears to have been a gradual evolution of budget system reforms to the present day. In terms of planning, control, and accountability, munic-

[3]Lennox L. Moak and Albert M. Hillhouse, *Concepts and Practices in Local Government Finance* (Chicago, Ill.: Municipal Finance Officers Association of the United States and Canada, 1975), p. 66.
[4]Moak and Killian, *Manual of Techniques,* p. 6.
[5]*Ibid.*
[6]*Ibid.,* p. 7.

ipal finance has taken on an aura of professionalism, particularly since the mid-1940s, and has been in a state of progression to the present time (probably attributed to the post–World War II educational process in addition to other salient elements related to time and progress).

Unfortunately, the same general statement cannot be made for those assigned to the budget function in many localities. It is doubtful that true "professionalism" in finance and budget exists in more than a few municipal police agencies serving populations under 200,000—which appears to encompass a vast majority of American cities.

Certainly we do not suggest, or even believe it advisable, that every person who prepares a police department budget be an expert in *finance* —for there are other equally important priorities. On the other hand, in those departments that, because of size or other restrictions, cannot employ full-time experts, we would hope that special and ongoing budget systems training could be provided. And of course we would hope that in those departments where full-time budget experts are employed, that those responsible managers and middle managers would be afforded adequate professional training in this area. It is important that they be in a position to properly and realistically set goals and audit the products of subordinate experts.

In analyzing the motivation behind the New York Bureau of Municipal Research and its subsequent recommendations for a formal *budget system*, and of those who came after to make important contributions in the same field, three basic facets stand out: (1) the need for responsible and responsive fiscal control; (2) the need to *plan* for immediate and future municipal services in some rational systemized manner; and (3) the need to evaluate existing programs in terms of their efficiency and continuing necessity. Too often municipal budgets have served simply as building blocks, requiring the justification of new programs and personnel each year, but no reevaluation of existing activities.

And finally, it seems to us an irony that New York, who led the way in responsible municipal fiscal budgeting systems, was the focus of fiscal instability in the late 1970s.

THE BUDGET PROCESS

This chapter has been appropriately subtitled, *The Allocation of Scarce Resources.* The resources allocated for a police agency are its life-blood—and are scarce. While police agencies may receive their fair share of funds allocated to all municipal services, they have not been funded for optimum results. Disregarding the state of other departments for the purpose of this chapter, the police have only in rare instances been able to expand in an orderly manner and at a rate commensurate with the general population. Rarely have police managers been able to acquire additional resources on the strength of such factors as the expansion of socioeconomically lower-class neighborhoods, unemployment, rising crime, and all of the other social ills with which they must deal.

Federal funds, once thought to be a panacea, have failed to impact optimally, primarily because guidelines and controls often dictate that they must be spent for purposes other than the solution of local problems. And yet many police managers have grown overly dependent upon federal subsidy that will surely dry up; when that happens funded programs that are meaningful are likely to dry up, too.

Thus, the budget function today has become more critical than ever before and the police manager must place new emphasis on the budget document—since it is the *plan* for the ensuing budget period, hammered out within the framework of existing constraints, finalized and agreed upon by the police manager and the municipal executive and legislative body. The budget document when completed sets forth the programs, projects, services, and activities of the department as well as the resources to support them.

While the requisites and data that eventually culminate in a budget are the inputs of many people from the various sections of a police agency, it is those who prepare and approve the budget who must ask: *What are the areas to be emphasized? How much and what quality of service should be given?* As a plan the budget should be expected to address those and other questions that confront the municipality. And of course *the community* must be emphasized in this process since few are exactly alike in resources or in particular needs.

Identifying Community Needs

Certainly the broad concept of "crime prevention" encompasses a general need for every jurisdiction. Conversely, "crime prevention" is too broad a term to attack without more specific identification. And so there must be a needs assessment based on, for example: the types of crimes; the population makeup—elderly versus youthful, middle class versus lower class; high density versus suburban; distances to be covered; employment and student patterns, etc. Discovering the needs of citizens in a systematic way obviously involves study and analysis. In many cases citizens make their wants known. In others, especially in the lower socioeconomic areas, this may not be so and therefore places the responsibility back on management's shoulders.

In this light, the National Advisory Commission on Criminal Justice Standards and Goals observed that:

> Every police agency should provide for maximum input both within and outside the agency in the development of its goals and objectives. . . . Every police chief executive should require every unit commander to make a periodic review of unit goals and objectives and submit a written evaluation of the progress made toward the attainment of these goals. Annually, in conjunction with the budget preparation, every police chief executive should provide for review and evaluation of all agency goals and objectives and for revisions where appropriate.[7]

Perhaps one of the most difficult aspects of citizen input into the budget document is the political implication. A sufficient number of citizens pressuring their elected representatives in reference to a particular local problem may result in funds being allocated when in fact the problem, in light of other responsibilities, has a very low priority. For example, certain youth-oriented programs may have a great deal of surface appeal when their real value in terms of total community service may be questioned. However, at the risk of irrational inputs, a police agency should, within the legal framework, reflect the needs of the community wherever possible.

Clearly it is not easy to express needs in a rational way. And it is equally difficult to allocate resources to activities and programs in a way that provides assurance that needs will in fact be met.

Responsibility for equitable and effective distribution of resources is, in our society, a political responsibility. When resources are scarce, politicians take refuge in the rhetoric of efficiency and economy. "I am a fiscal conservative" and "Departments can become more *efficient* by becoming more *economical*," really doesn't mean anything except that resources are scarce and your department cannot expect any additional funds this year.

Budget Policy

Prior to budget preparation, instructions are typically sent to departments by the municipal administrative head, setting forth the financial prospect for the coming budget year. Typically efficiency and economy are stressed in requests to "Hold the line," and "Trim the fat." The ad-

---

[7]National Advisory Commission on Criminal Justice Standards and Goals, *Police*, (Washington, D.C.: U.S. Government Printing Office, (1973), p. 49.

ministrator may point out specific problems of needed or unwanted services, but it is *understood* that the police manager is expected, keeping the administrator's personal views in mind, to propose a budget based on that administrator's view of the needs of the citizens served. The administrator will review the proposed budget keeping in mind the views of elected officials and, finally, elected officials will review the proposed budget keeping in mind the values and views of their constituents.

Policies of the administration and legislative functionaries are, in this manner, woven into the budget process, with the result that the finalized budget has not only taken into consideration the needs and constraints of the various community and government levels but has also been agreed upon as a sanction for departmental activities during the ensuing budget period, and as the parameters in which the department must perform.

Prior to budget preparation each year, most municipal administrators direct an executive policy message, or *budget call*, to all department heads. The use of executive budget messages in some form dates back to early budget history.

Moak and Killian observe:

> Today, with the complex organizations and multitudinous functions characteristic of most local governments, it is even more desirable for the chief executive, or the central budget agency acting for him, to transmit to the various operating units a statement of executive policy for the forthcoming budget year. This statement should include an indication as to whether the government will follow a hold-the-line policy on municipal expenses for the forthcoming year or whether retrenchment or expansion, either in general or in specified areas, will be the objective of the administration.[8]

The 1976–77 budget preparation letter directed to the department heads by the City Manager of Phoenix, Arizona, is an excellent model of the executive message. (See exhibit 9–1).

The budgetary function is *process oriented* and as such is not something that begins with the administrative budget message. Rather, it is a dynamic process that is ongoing throughout the course of the entire year.

Just as the budget is process-oriented, so are its three major purposes:

1. Financial Control. This is the traditional and historic purpose to ensure legality, accuracy, and conformity to legislative and administrative mandates as set forth in laws, ordinances, and regulations.

[8]Moak and Killian, *Manual of Techniques,* p. 71.

Exhibit 9–1 (Continued)

		B.R.D. NUMBER
		40
	BUDGET AND RESEARCH DEPARTMENT LETTER	Page 1 of 6
		ISSUE DATE
		January 8, 1976
	SUBJECT	
CITY OF PHOENIX	1976-77 ANNUAL BUDGET PREPARATION INSTRUCTIONS	

THE 1976-77 GENERAL BUDGET OUTLOOK

At the August 1975 Administrative Staff Meeting the need for each department to carefully control its expenditures during the 1975-76 fiscal year was emphasized. The rate of economic recovery from the 1974-75 recession was very uncertain, and the probability of the City's revenue collections meeting budget estimates was unclear. Additional experience with revenue collections is still needed to make budget estimates for next year.

Furthermore, in previewing known financing problems facing the City in the coming 1976-77 fiscal year, the possibility has been discussed that Federal funds available to the City for governmental operations during the current year might not be available next year. Foremost among these Federal funds is Federal Revenue Sharing which is due to expire December 31, 1976, unless re-enacted by the Congress. Also, Federal Public Service Employment funding is now certain only to June 30, 1976, unless, likewise, extended by the Congress.

Budget planning for next year is further complicated by new Federal budget laws which now apparently preclude the Congress from acting on the extension of Federal Revenue Sharing until May 1976. This is after the date by which the City Manager must prepare and submit a proposed budget to the City Council. Consequently, in preparing next year's budget outlook certain assumptions have had to be made on the availability of Federal Revenue Sharing and other Federal funds.

In the course of updating the City's five-year Capital Improvement Program each year, a forecast of general revenues, operating expenses and net amounts available to finance the capital program is routinely made. This very preliminary forecast reveals the largest shortfall of revenues compared to expenditure requirements in recent years, ranging from a "most optimistic" deficit of $11.4 million to a "least optimistic" deficit of $26.9 million. A middle-ground "base forecast" deficit of $17.5 million will be used for budget planning purposes at this time.

The preliminary "base forecast" revenue estimates assume a gradual, steady recovery of the economy reflecting a 7½ percent increase over the current year. This estimate allows for the loss of approximately $1.8 million in anticipated general purpose revenues as a result of the Special Census just completed. This planning forecast assumes that Federal Revenue Sharing will be extended for the whole fiscal year and that Federal Public Service Employment will be extended for at least one-half of the fiscal year to December 31, 1976. Much more information is needed than is available at this time to confirm all resource estimates for actual budget making.

The preliminary "base forecast" expenditure estimates include (1) full-year's costs for deferred hirings and the general employee salary increase in effect for eight months of the current year, plus the Council-approved increase in Fire salaries; (2) full-year's costs for merit salary increases granted during the current year and continuation of merit increases in 1976-77; (3) continuation of the priority categories of Public Service

Exhibit 9—1 (Continued)

Employment positions; (4) increased debt service on existing bonded debt; (5) the cost of operating new facilities and new debt service on planned bond sales; (6) a minimum level of pay-as-you-go capital improvements; and (7) price inflation on all operating expenses at a rate of 7½ percent. This forecast makes no allowance for other supplemental increases for additional personnel or equipment and related costs of any kind.

During the past several weeks the Budget and Research Department has been working with all general fund financed City departments to prepare a more refined budget expenditure forecast for next year. Significant program commitments, if any, requiring expenditure increases are being recorded. And, most importantly, the effect of alternative levels of expenditure reductions on municipal services is being analyzed and documented. In addition, research on alternative revenue increases is being conducted.

Plans are to submit this more thorough study on the 1976-77 General Budget Outlook to the City Council in late February for policy review and guidance in preparing the City Manager's proposed budget. Because of the need for early attention to next year's apparent budget problems, this study must be completed even prior to the time all department budget requests are completed.

Finally, it must be emphasized to all who use these preliminary forecasts, that as time passes and more information becomes available, the budget outlook for next year, as we see it now, may change significantly.

ALTERNATIVE OPERATING BUDGET REQUESTS

In order to know the full consequences of budget decisions that may finally be made to balance next year's budget, departments are again asked to prepare alternative operating budget requests. This is the same technique used by departments in preparing 1975-76 department budget requests, although a slightly modified approach will be used this time as described below.

Departments are to prepare their regular operating budget requests in complete detail following regular Budget Manual procedures. The regular operating budget request includes the base budget request (existing authorized positions including priority PSE positions, commodities and contractual services and replacement equipment at next year's prices) and supplemental budget requests (additional personnel, equipment and related costs).

Using the regular operating budget request as a reference point, departments are asked to consider how they would fashion the most workable budget program at two alternative expenditure levels below their regular base budget request. A description of the regular and two alternative budgets follows:

Alternative Request No. 1 - Regular Request

This alternative includes the normal base budget request as defined above. In addition, necessary supplemental budget requests for previous Council-approved commitments, such as the operation and maintenance of a new City facility, or that which is necessary to meet measurable work load growth are to be included in this alternative request. Regular Budget Manual procedures are to be followed.

Exhibit 9–1 (Continued)

Alternative Request No. 2 - 7½ Percent Base Budget Reduction

This alternative calls for a 7½ percent reduction in the regular base budget request with the following exclusions. The 7½ percent reduction is to be calculated on the department's gross base budget request for 1976-77, excluding debt service. In cases where departments charge work orders to non-general purpose fund activities or projects, these may be excluded from the department's gross base budget before calculating the 7½ percent reduction. This alternative operating budget request requirement applies only to that portion of the department operating budgets financed by General Purpose, Federal Revenue Sharing, Federal Public Service Employment, and Highway User Revenue funds.

That portion of department operating budgets financed with other sources of funds including Water, Aviation, Civic Plaza, Public Housing operating funds and other Federal funding for Transit, LEAP, CETA Manpower Training, Community Development Revenue Sharing, and Federal categorical grants are exempted from this alternative operating budget request requirement inasmuch as these funds are balanced separately.

Current sources of funding for each department is shown on the department program summary page in the current 1975-76 Annual Budget detail document.

Alternative Request No. 3 - 15 Percent Base Budget Reduction

This alternative calls for a 15 percent reduction from the regular base budget request total with the same inclusions and exclusions as in Alternative Request No. 2.

Alternative operating budget requests are to be explained on the budget explanation forms provided. The explanations should list in detail the position reductions, deferred equipment replacement, or other modifications to the regular base budget request to achieve the reduced expenditure levels.

Most importantly, a statement is to accompany each alternative request as to the impact it would have on service levels in objective, measurable terms. Department objectives and measurement criteria, discussed below, should assist in developing service level impact statements.

Service reductions in department objectives and related expenditure reductions are to be listed in priority order for both Alternative Request No. 2 and No. 3.

GOALS AND OBJECTIVES: USE IN PLANNING ALTERNATIVE BUDGET REQUESTS

During the past year, a considerable amount of time has been spent by Budget and Research with each department to further develop a comprehensive set of goals, objectives and measurement criteria.

Measurement of department objective achievement is even more important in a lean year when budget allowances must be curtailed due to economic conditions. The ability to objectively measure the service level impact of the alternative operating budget request called for above, will help identify reductions that will have the least impact on services to the community.

Exhibit 9–1 (Continued)

Page 4 of 6

For convenience, two copies of the goals and objectives form with preprinted data for each department is included in the department's budget packet. The preprinted data indicates the service levels provided by the current 1975-76 budget authorization. Departments are to add the output for each objective measure for the department's regular budget request for 1976-77.

In addition, as part of the alternative operating budget requests, departments are to quote the modified output for department objectives affected by the base budget reductions called for.

BUDGETING FOR EMPLOYEE SALARY ADJUSTMENTS

The City's former cost-of-living pay ordinance has now been replaced by the new Employer-Employee Relations (Meet and Confer) Ordinance recently adopted by the City Council. The ordinance establishes a formalized framework for recognized employee organizations to meet and confer with City Management on wages, hours and working conditions.

Some time will be required in this initial year of the new ordinance to set up the administrative machinery required by the ordinance and set the administrative procedures in motion.

Consequently, there is no firm basis, at this time, for departments to budget for any employee salary increases, with the exception of the Fire Department, which is to budget for the previous Council-approved pay increase, effective July 1, 1976.

Budget allowances for any salary and fringe benefit adjustments will be included as a lump sum salary contingency amount in the City Manager's proposed budget to the City Council.

PUBLIC SERVICE EMPLOYMENT GUIDELINES

Commencing with the 1975-76 Annual Budget, Public Service Employment positions were budgeted in the department to which they were assigned and became an integral part of each department's position authorization, subject, of course, to the continuation of Federal Public Service Employment funding. The exceptions to this budget practice were those Work Experience Program (WEP) positions budgeted in the Economic Security Department but assigned to do special one-time project work in several departments.

When the 1975-76 Annual Budget was adopted, the authorized PSE positions included in the budget were prioritized in four categories to identify those positions the City would plan to continue if and when PSE funding terminated. These priority categories and the number of positions by department are shown in the summary schedules of the 1975-76 Annual Budget detail document, page A-15. The priority categories established were as follows:

Priority I - Positions Essential for Delivery of Police, Fire and Revenue
             Producing Services;

Priority II - Positions Essential for Delivery of All Other Public Services;

Priority III - Positions Required to Sustain All Other Programs at Existing
               Operating Levels; and

Priority IV - Positions Contingent on PSE Funding Levels.

Exhibit 9-1 (Continued)

After the 1975-76 Annual Budget was adopted, final Federal Public Service Employment allocations exceeded the amount budgeted. This made it possible for the City Council to authorize additional PSE positions including supplemental positions which could not be financed in the adopted budget, additional short-term project positions to be terminated when PSE funding expired, and PSE positions to fill regular general fund financed positions as they became vacant to help achieve budgeted salary savings.

The 1976-77 General Budget Outlook discussed earlier included those PSE positions now authorized in priority categories I, II and III in the expenditure requirements fore-cast. All PSE positions now authorized and assigned in each department's budget which fall in priority categories I, II and III should be requested to be continued in department budget requests if the work being performed is essential and the work load warrants continuation of the position.

PSE positions which fall in the lowest priority category IV may be requested to be continued but reauthorization in 1976-77 will be contingent on PSE funding levels. Those PSE positions authorized for short-term projects budgeted in the Economic Security Department may also be continued in 1976-77 if work projects are not yet completed. Departments should notify the Economic Security Department of work projects not completed and the positions that should be continued.

Final recommendations on continuation of Public Service Program positions will be made in the City Manager's proposed budget. Reauthorization and financing of these positions will depend on the level of PSE funding that can be expected and the need to sustain existing operating levels in each of the priority categories.

CAPITAL BUDGETING

The preliminary 1976-81 Capital Improvement Program is still under preparation and is scheduled to be submitted to the City Council in mid-February, which is after depart-ment capital budget requests for 1976-77 are due.

Consequently, the final draft of the 1976-81 Capital Improvement Program last reviewed with the Budget and Research Department should be used as a guide for preparing the 1976-77 Capital Budget requests.

As projected in this draft document, "pay-as-you-go" capital project financing will be severely limited next year; and it is probable that few capital projects can be financed from general purpose funds. Department requests for capital projects financed from the remaining 1970 and 1973 Bond funds and the new 1975 Bond fund should conform as much as possible to those projects scheduled for 1976-77 in the draft 1976-81 Capital Improvement Program.

Departments should be careful, however, to rebudget for carryover projects which are currently financed but which will not be encumbered prior to June 30, 1976.

OTHER INSTRUCTIONS

Special instructions are attached presenting a variety of information to departments who will need to prepare budget requests. Several sections of the Budget Manual have been revised as well as several of the budget forms to reflect the new requirement of Financial Impact Statement on new operating programs and capital projects. All of this information will be discussed at the budget training session scheduled for key depart-ment budget personnel on Thursday afternoon, January 8, 1976.

Exhibit 9–1 (Continued)

Five copies of the department budget request are to be submitted to the Budget and Research Department by the due date announced in City Manager's Letter No. 501. Subsequent distribution of the five copies will be made as follows: (1) City Council, (2) City Manager, (3) Budget and Research (2 copies), and (4) Division of Accounts.

Initial budget reviews, February 9-27, will be conducted concurrently by seven budget review teams from the City Manager's Office and Budget and Research. The dates, times and locations of each department review is attached with these instructions.

CHARLES E. HILL
Budget and Research Director

APPROVED:

JOHN B. WENTZ
City Manager

2. Management Information. In addition to expressing information in financial terms, the modern budget provides data on work units, manpower, motor equipment, and other indicators of services, activities, and tasks. This kind of information shows that work is being accomplished properly in addition to the legal authorization for expenditure of funds.

3. Planning and Policy Implementation. This is the most recent purpose of budgeting, and it has been recognized through performance budgeting, work measurement, policy analysis, the planning-programming-budgeting system (PPBS), establishment of goals and objectives, and other efforts to bring budgeting more closely into the actual planning and carrying out of city work from a management point of view.[9]

It can readily be seen that these three budget functions cannot occur exclusively at the time of formal budget preparation. Budgets should not be *reactionary* (though many are); rather, they should be pro-actionary. Budget systems are ongoing, not just for auditing and regulating expenditures (to see that they are relegated to the authorized tasks and not exceeded) but for other equally important factors.

A continual review of programs is necessary to ascertain that they are *providing* the *services* for which they were designated. Budgets are dynamic, not static systems; if a program is not performing as expected, its design should be modified or, if need be, scrapped in favor of some other important but unfunded project. Some police managers are reluctant to go back through the administrative and legislative processes, though they should not be. The mark of a good manager is to be on top of such things and ready to shift emphasis if the need is indicated. Most administrative and legislative bodies expect and should receive this type of budget management.

Data gathering for new programs, and support or modification of existing programs is an ongoing function. Citizen and employee inputs should be ongoing, as well, so that budget documents represent all of the best available information and not just those data gathered within the constrictions of real-time parameters.

Budget Calendar

The budget calendar is an essential element as was the administration message in the budget system preparation (see exhibit 9–2). Correspond-

---

[9] J. Richard Aronson and Eli Schwartz, eds., *Management Policies in Local Government Finance* (Washington, D.C.: International City Management Association, 1975), p. 63.

Exhibit 9–2

City of Phoenix, Arizona

1976-77 ANNUAL BUDGET CALENDAR

DEPARTMENTS PREPARE BUDGET REQUESTS

January 8	City Manager's Annual Budget Conference Budget Training Session

Department Budget Requests Due

January 30	Small Departments
February 6	Intermediate Departments
February 13	Large Departments

CITY MANAGER'S REVIEW OF DEPARTMENT REQUESTS
AND PRELIMINARY BUDGET PREPARATION

February 9-27	Department Budget Reviews (First Round)
March 11	City Manager's Preliminary Review
March 15-26	Department Budget Reviews (Second Round)
April 1	City Manager's Final Review
April 5 - May 14	Preliminary Budget Document Prepared

CITY COUNCIL REVIEW AND PUBLIC HEARINGS

May 17-21	City Council Preliminary Review
May 24-28	Informal Public Hearings
June 1-4	City Council Final Review
June 15	Publication in Weekly Gazette

CITY COUNCIL ADOPTION

June 29	Tentative Budget Adoption
July 6 and 13	Publication in Weekly Gazette
July 20	Public Hearing and Final Adoption
July 27	Property Tax Levy Adoption

ingly, budget calendars need to be translated into departmental and divisional calendars. Each operating division or unit must work to a specific calendar that meshes with the administrative calendar. To this end, it is imperative that planning and preparation for the budget has been an ongoing function.

There are, however, a number of problem areas connected with year-round preparation—problems such as allotment of time for planning, and allotment of time for employee and citizen contact and feedback. And while employee and citizen inputs are absolutely essential, they are also potentially the most politically difficult to deal with in terms of commitment and implementation. If feedback and ideas are solicited, and subsequently not utilized, the feeling of "Why did you ask me in the first place?" is likely to prevail. On the other hand, if the inputs are utilized but take a year to come to fruition, negative comments are likely to occur. Too many of us equate *idea* with *action*. Push the button and a reward magically appears. The tendency among employees and citizens alike is to expect immediate results.

And so this very vital process of input requires continual reinforcement in the form of explanation of how the budget system operates.

Once the various elements of the department have completed and presented their requests, they are brought together in a formalized meeting to fashion the rough budget document.

Department heads are expected to and must review divisional requests in much the same manner that the executive views all departmental budgets. They must "separate the wheat from the chaff," must consider the supportive data carefully, instilling and developing in division heads the same level of competence expected by the administration of the department head. Erroneous or careless data or deliberate padding will most often lead to exposure and shaky confidence.

> Tradition holds that is should be an orderly, rational process, and most persons do try to keep it that way. Department heads and others, however, are subject to the same psychological stresses that affect other people, and they tend to adopt certain roles in the informal budgetary process. To be more specific, certain department heads deliberately will ask for more than they expect to get. Others will ask for exactly what they want and will not give up a dime without a fight. Occasionally a department head or other administrator may meekly underestimate his requirements, surely a symptom of some kind of incompetence or insecurity.[10]

[10]*Ibid.*, pp. 72–73.

The foregoing, in our opinion, is correct. However, we must rush to the defense of police managers in this regard. Certainly we must recognize that there are some weak police managers who have somehow slipped through the system (or perhaps because of the system). However, police managers, like the rest of the population, tend to *learn* behavior. City administrative heads and legislative bodies that systematically take *x* percent out of every budget on the assumption that "there is so much fat in every budget" invite the overestimate syndrome. As for "meekly underestimated" budgets, administrative heads and legislative bodies who traditionally *have the upper hand*, who typically *second guess* their department heads, breed the insecurity that leads to *presenting the budget the bosses want* rather than the budget that experience and real-time data dictate. Acknowledging that a minority of some less-than-optimum police managers slip by, we submit that the majority of those presenting less-than-adequate budget programs are those who have been tempered by their superiors to operate in this manner.

If we failed to do so at any other point in this book, we must take this opportunity to state clearly that police managers who grow accustomed to compromise before the fact, who in this case do not present programs or budgets that clearly and unequivocally follow the dictates of their conscience, based experience and current data and standards, are clearly programmed for mediocrity, failure, or disgrace—or all three. Decisions that are begun with compromise are likely to be poor decisions and budgets which are compromised *prior* to presentation are likely to be poor and inadequate budgets. Obviously the municipal administrative head and legislative body have discreet information upon which certain budgeting decisions will be made. On the other hand, to present, unknown to them, a compromised budget is likely to culminate in embarrassment and disappointment.

PRESENTING THE BUDGET

The final proposed municipal budget is typically referred to a *budget committee* whose members are selected from the elected governing body. In this manner, the proposed budget can be studied in depth prior to the public hearings. Of course, the remainder of the elected body will be reviewing the proposal independently.

Customarily, the chief executive officer of the government prepares and submits the budget message which accompanies the budget. He may do this in writing or may elect to do so orally in the public hearing. The oral presentation is most often utilized since it permits the chief executive to reach not only the legislative body and attendant citizens but, through the news media, the rest of the community as well.

The *message* typically summarizes the budget and permits emphasis to be placed on special problems and programs.[11]

It is significant to individual departments in that the budget message historically sets the tone for the hearing. The hearing in itself in most municipalities provides the opportunity for the department head, in this case the police manager, to present his budget and any supportive data that he may wish to bring to bear.

Preparation for the hearing is absolutely essential. Alert managers often rehearse the budget preparation process, requiring each division head to rejustify and "prove up" the need for specific requests so that supportive elements can be developed and refined for public hearing presentation.

Supportive data appears in a variety of forms—oral presentation, handout material (chancy since it may not be read or understood), charts, slides, or acetate overlays for the overhead projector. Whatever the style, the primary goal is to present the information in its simplest most direct form. Overly complicated presentations are confusing to both the legislative body and general citizenry. Unfortunately, some of those who do not understand will not openly reveal this and are likely to react negatively. Confused or uninformed citizens are not likely to be supportive.

The timing of the release of budget information is a topic for consideration. There has been a tendency to "leak" budget information to either certain *influential* citizens thought to be supportive of particular new programs, or the news media. Obviously, there is a great deal to be gained by properly informing the news media and citizens alike. However, as with every other facet of police management, municipal executives and elected legislative bodies do not wish to be surprised. It is absolutely essential that public information relating to the budget be released *after* it has been received by those in authority. If the opposite occurs, undesirable built-in resentment and resistance are likely to be the result.

Moak and Killian tell us that the budget presentation (review) should:

1. Result in better informed members of the legislative body as to the policies and work programs currently in force and in prospect.

2. Afford an opportunity for general legislative oversight of the performance of the executive branch of the government. (In conjunction with such oversight, the members of the council will

---

[11]Moak and Hillhouse, *Concepts and Practices*, pp. 90–91.

have an opportunity to become acquainted with the executive officers appearing before them and to reach conclusions as to their competence.)

3. Provide a basis for expansion of community understanding of governmental activities and performance.

4. Permit citizens to voice their views with regard to proposals regarding services and revenues.

5. Permit the legislative body to identify specific weaknesses in the budget which may not have been identified by the chief executive.

6. Establish policies and programs for the following year on both the expenditure and revenue sides of the ledger.[12]

CONTROLLING THE BUDGET

Once reviewed, with necessary revisions made and finally adopted, the budget comes alive and begins to function, setting in motion the amalgamation of funds to programs and programs to planned production or *outputs*. From the point of adoption to the end of its fiscal life, the budget system now becomes an object of control. It is the base from which the police manager determines through regular audit that funds are being properly allocated for authorized functions and not allocated to those for which they were not intended. Additionally, monthly reports should *provide real-time control* on the regular (usually monthly) audit. These reports are vital in predicting and controlling the flow of funds so that the last days of the fiscal year are not fundless, or bloodless, for we have observed earlier that the budget is the department's lifeblood.

Enough emphasis cannot be placed upon the importance of the control-audit function for monitoring not only expenditures but program goal achievements as well. While the predictors used to anticipate and plan programs for modern police organizations are fairly reliable, they are not infallible. As we said earlier, if an audit reveals that a funded program is not producing the expected, desired results, immediate consideration should be given to modifying or scrapping it completely. If the program is scrapped, but the original need still exists, an alternate plan should be developed.

In either case, all deviation from the approved program prior to implementation, must be reported to the municipal executive and the elected legislative body. It is their responsibility to review the revisions

---

[12]Moak and Killian, *Manual of Techniques,* p. 251.

in much the same manner as the original budget with recommendations for further revisions or adoption.

The need to return recommendations for changes to the elected legislative body will of course be predicated upon local laws governing such procedures, as well as specific municipal regulations. Additionally, as we have said before, elected officials do not like to be surprised, and are more likely to be supportive if they are not. That should be reason enough for a modern police manager to keep the proper people informed.

Most budgets will be in need of periodic modifications to keep the funding flow in the proper mode. Inflation and other variables make prediction of certain costs difficult. The bidding process may return surplus dollars to the treasury while an unexpected rise in the cost of fuel oil may effect not only the vehicle-per-mile costs but the cost of electricity, heat, and other items as well. Normally such minor changes are provided for in city charters and state laws and do not necessitate a return to the legislative body. Finance directors have certain latitude in adjusting funds between the various operating accounts.

Again, the *manager* has the responsibility for monitoring his departmental accounts so that neither the finance director or executive is surprised by the accumulation of lopsided account items. Errors and problems discovered and reported as they occur are normally easily rectified. If not reported until the fiscal year end, problems of varying magnitude can be expected.

We are not suggesting that police managers become accountants. There should be subordinates who are experts in this area. Smaller jurisdictions will provide such expertise through its finance department. We are suggesting that police managers need to have a familiarity with monthly accounting reports and with the danger signals obtained therefrom. They should also have some ongoing internal audit system for regular program review and the personal ability to superimpose or interrelate the two audits for purposes covered earlier. In larger, more complicated municipalities audits will need to be summarized by subordinate experts, but the control and breadth of these summaries should be dictated by the manager himself so that his perception of this function is met.

Through accurate audits are discovered some of the basic predictors to be utilized for the preparation of the next fiscal budget—often before the current budget has reached the halfway mark of its life span.

And finally, as Professor Neely Gardner, of the University of Southern California School of Public Administration, so aptly observed:

> Appropriate control processes assure that resources are being utilized in the manner specified in the budget. And, of course, all disburse-

ments should be made according to law. Honesty and integrity must prevail. Therefore systems of accounting, reporting, auditing and inspection are necessary. First, the controls must meet the management needs of the expending agency. Next, they must set standards of performance and fiscal integrity which enable elected officials to keep current with public agency productivity as well as to assure these officials that no "hanky-panky" is occurring. Finally, the control should ensure the public that monies spent are providing the services desired in an efficient and economical fashion.

Ideally, then, the budget provides a fine opportunity to:

1. Understand the needs of citizens.

2. Utilize the knowledge of these needs to develop a plan which will meet the needs.

3. Allocate society's resources in harmony with the fiscal plan.

4. Assure that the public's business will be conducted in an efficient and economical manner.

5. Prepare a budget document which reflects in policies of elected officials in a clear-cut manner.

6. Permits citizens a vehicle for understanding the connection between public expenditure and the rendering of public services.

7. Provide controls that assure that public monies are spent for the purposes intended.

Unfortunately the ideal often remains but a part of administrative folklore. Public managers and elected bodies continue to participate in the annual or biannual budget rituals as if the process were meeting the public purposes of which it is capable. But the reform movement that started in the United States in 1910 has yet a long way to go before it fulfills its promise.[13]

TYPES OF BUDGETS

In present-day government finance, there are five basic budgeting styles or forms. In essence these different styles are only "crosswalking" between different ways of grouping expenditure items. All four are primarily administrative and political instruments and all four spring from the primary tenet that a budget is an instrument to control the allocation of resources through a system that provides needed services in a rational manner.

[13]Neely Gardner, *"Budget and Budgeting to Achieve Public Purpose"* (Unpublished paper, University of Southern California, School of Public Administration, 1976), pp. 5–6.

The five budget forms are:

1. The Line-Item or Object of Expenditure; also referred to as the Traditional Budget
2. The Performance Budget
3. The Planning, Programming, Budgeting System or PPBS
4. The Program Budget System
5. The Zero Base

The Line-Item or Traditional Budget

The line-item budget is so named because its resources are allocated in the budget document line by line. Line-item budgets typically categorize budget items by departments, divisions, or organizational units within the department, listing proposed expenditures under each such categories as:

1. Salaries and wages—with the number of positions allocated for each type of classification assigned to the unit such as police captains, lieutenants, sergeants, police officers, secretaries, and the like
2. Operating expenses—which includes fuel for vehicles, repairs and maintenance, service contracts, telephones, utilities, and the like
3. Equipment—which includes the purchase of new items such as automobiles, motorcycles, weapons, and typewriters
4. Capital outlay—which usually covers those items needed beyond the normal operation and utilized over a wide span of years, such as the acquisition of real property, new building construction, or major remodeling

Typically many line-item budgets also display a series of columns setting forth recent historical data relating to each of the categories listed above. These columns list the amounts budgeted and actual or adjusted figures for several preceding years, including the current operating budget. Thus, comparisons can be made at a glance, by both the legislative body and citizenry.

Some line-item budgets go one step further by displaying separate comparative columns for departmental requests, administrative recommendations, and the legislative approved figures.

Finalized line-item budgets actually provide several sets of data: the budget summary breaks down expenditures and personnel by department; the second set of data sets forth the workload indicators; the third set of data is much more detailed by item and function as set forth previously; the fourth concerns capital outlay. (See examples of the budget summary, workload indicator, line-item budget, and capital outlay in exhibits 9–3, 9–4, 9–5, and 9–6).

Strengths and Weaknesses

There are a number of apparent strengths and weaknesses in the line-item budget. It is primarily an "inputs" type of budget with no real correlation to the end product. There may be a few broad goals attached to the budget format but no real indication of prediction that if *A* is invested *B* will be the result. On the other hand, inputs are made from all divisions and units so that each is offered the opportunity to project its needs. The emphasis, however, is on economy or keeping the cost down, with very little indication as to how this allocation of resources relates to the public need. The primary focus is upon requested increases and on new programs. Old or ongoing programs are rarely questioned.

The line-item budget is, however, simple and easy to understand for both legislator and citizen. Since citizen understanding is essential, this is an important plus, for line-item budgets also encompasses easy to understand accountability.

The understanding, though, sometimes leads to *misunderstanding* as some citizens, armed with their mini-portable adding machines quickly miscalculate the cost of helicopter patrol by the minute, throwing the police manager off his stride during the budget public hearings. As a precaution, the police manager is encouraged to have his own systems analyst present for just such emergencies, if he has one. If not, he is wise to have division heads or *best experts* on potentially controversial programs available.

Gardner points out that, in their simplicity, line-item budgets are based on history—next year's appropriation is based on last year's history, and most of the allocation must be spent whether it is needed or not in order to provide a "base" for next year's request.[14]

Moak and Killian found the following advantages and disadvantages to the traditional or line-item approach:

> Among the advantages of the traditional approach is its relative simplicity. This simplicity makes it possible for comparatively inexperienced but able people to make the system work and to make it work successfully within the limits of the system. Of course, the

[14]*Ibid.*, p. 14.

Exhibit 9-3

BUDGET ESTIMATES FOR FISCAL YEAR 1975 - 1976

Department ___ POLICE ___ Division ___ Activity No ___ 2000 ___ **SUMMARY**

CLASSIFICATION	1973-74 ACTUAL EXPENDITURES	1974-75				DEPARTMENT ESTIMATE	1975-76	
		BEGINNING BUDGET	AMENDED BUDGET	6 MONTHS EXPENDITURES	EST. TOTAL EXPENDITURES		CITY MANAGER RECOMMENDATION	CITY COUNCIL APPROVAL
SALARIES	2,255,640	2,632,310	2,637,390	1,336,141	2,637,390	2,930,805	2,802,090	3,089,740
MAINTENANCE & OPERATION	508,604	436,950	452,205	205,815	452,205	537,510	498,820	498,820
CAPITAL OUTLAY	161,139	131,840	177,040	89,084	177,040	246,535	201,125	201,125
TOTALS	2,925,383	3,201,100	3,266,635	1,631,040	3,266,635	3,714,850	3,502,035	3,789,685

Department functions and objectives:

Repression, prevention, investigation of crime, apprehension of offenders, and recovery of property are the major responsibilities of the department. Accident prevention, control of vehicular congestion and parking, and parking enforcement are secondary responsibilities. Vice control, warrant service, animal control, and regulation of conduct are the other functions performed by the Police Department.

Specific objectives for this fiscal period are to maintain a favorable per capita rate of serious or "Part I Crimes"; proceed with the work of equipping and furnishing the Police facility; continue to work toward obtaining a computer monitored alarm and communications system which will unify Police and Fire Department dispatching and provide the community with a system, utilizing digital signals transmitted through television cable, that will ensure a more rapid response to cases of personal attack or attacks on property; continue to work through the Community Relations program to gain greater citizen participation and cooperation in our efforts to reduce the incidence of crime and criminal attack; continue the extensive education and prevention programs in narcotics and drug abuse and "Child Molest Prevention"; encourage and assist officers to engage in college level career development to improve individual productivity and overall department effectiveness.

Comments:

Salaries:

The salaries portion of this budget ($3,089,740) provides for the transfer of three Emergency Equipment Dispatchers from the Fire Department, merit salary step increases for regular personnel and no additional positions. However, in January 1975, four Police Officers and two Police Clerks I were hired under the federally funded Comprehensive Employment Training Act.

One position of Police Lieutenant is being reclassified to Police Captain. He will command the Traffic Division. The vacated Police Lieutenant position is deleted. One position of Police Officer is being reclassified to Police Sergeant. He will be assigned to the Patrol Division as a field supervisor in order to provide a more realistic level of field supervision. The vacated Police Officer position is deleted.

Four Police Officer positions were added, as authorized and funded under the Comprehensive Employment Training Act. One handles the increased workload in the Planning and Research Unit and works with the vendor in the implementation of the computer aided dispatch system, two were assigned to the Detective Division to investigate crimes against persons and fraud and bunco cases, and one was assigned to the Patrol Division.

One position of Police Clerk I is being reclassified to Police Clerk II. This clerk performs the same functions as the Police Clerk II positions assigned to the Patrol and Detective Division

Exhibit 9-4

CITY OF NEWPORT BEACH

BUDGET ESTIMATES FOR FISCAL YEAR 1976-77

WORKLOAD INDICATORS

Department ___ POLICE ___ Division ___ Activity No. ___ 2000 ___

WORKLOAD INDICATORS	1972-73 Actual	1973-74 Actual	1974-75 Actual	1975-76 Actual	1976-77 Estimated
FELONY CRIMES REPORTED					
Murder	1	1	3	1	2
Rape	6	16	16	26	29
Robbery	21	31	44	33	40
Aggravated Assault	96	73	77	80	86
Grand Theft	403	475	756	741	778
Burglary	1,160	1,586	1,528	1,343	1,477
Grand Theft Auto	226	180	202	233	241
Felony Arrests - Adult	1,020	957	966	825	988
Misdemeanor Arrests - Adult	2,483	2,362	2,517	2,163	2,837
Juvenile Detentions	2,656	3,291	3,843	2,753	4,250
TRAFFIC CITATIONS					
Moving	15,287	18,503	21,517	22,803	24,330
Equipment	5,725	5,925	4,776	6,355	6,952
Parking	68,300	60,512	81,248	97,895	98,728
Citations Issued for Animal Violations	665	1,072	861	1,623	1,600
Animal Impounds	1,588	1,413	1,296	1,377	1,500
Department Civilian Personnel	32	35	42	45	47
Sworn Personnel	115	122	127	127	132
Total Personnel per 1,000 Population	2.60	2.56	2.80	2.73	2.75
Total Sworn Personnel per 1,000 Population	2.04	1.98	2.11	2.01	2.03
Cost per Capita Population	$43.10	$48.74	$54.26	$59.11	$59.96
Field Hours of Patrol Personnel	98,720	96,480	103,364	110,163	119,291

Exhibit 9-4. (Continued)

CITY OF NEWPORT BEACH

BUDGET ESTIMATES FOR FISCAL YEAR 1976-77

Department: POLICE   Division: _____   Activity No. 2000

WORKLOAD INDICATORS

REVENUE SOURCES	1972-73 Actual	1973-74 Actual	1974-75 Actual	1975-76 Actual	1976-77 Estimated
Fines, Forfeitures	513,545	664,602	628,264	710,167	745,000
Dog Licenses	37,362	32,916	36,256	47,853	60,000
Bicycle Licenses, Photocopy, Police Service Fees and Miscellaneous	24,140	22,967	26,696	30,340	28,795
Peace Office Standards and Training (P.O.S.T.)	16,670	62,128	30,980	25,636	28,000
Sale of Property (Auction)	3,588	5,423	9,342	7,298	8,000
	595,305	788,036	731,538	821,294	869,795

Exhibit 9-5

CITY OF NEWPORT BEACH

BUDGET ESTIMATES FOR FISCAL YEAR 1976-77

SALARIES

Department ___ POLICE ___ Division ___ Activity No. ___ 2000 ___

CLASSIFICATION	SALARY RANGE	BUDGETED EMPLOYEES		1975-76		1976-77 DEPARTMENT ESTIMATE		CITY MANAGER RECOMMENDATION		CITY COUNCIL APPROVAL	
		BEGINNING	AMENDED	BEGINNING BUDGET	AMENDED BUDGET	NO	AMOUNT	NO	AMOUNT	NO	AMOUNT
REGULAR											
Police Chief	2430-2954	1	1	33,945	33,945	1	33,815	1	33,815	1	35,580
Police Captain	1951-2371	4	4	107,120	107,120	4	107,540	4	107,540	4	112,915
Police Lieutenant	1677-2038	7	7	163,890	163,890	7	163,370	7	163,370	7	171,540
Police Sergeant	1442-1752	20	21	404,620	404,620	22	443,090	21	424,440	21	445,665
Police Officer	1239-1506	94	93	1,611,905	1,611,905	102	1,735,150	98	1,676,990	98	1,760,855
Policewoman	1239-1506	1	1	17,965	17,695	1	18,110	1	18,110	1	19,015
Systems Analyst	1089-1324					1	17,180	1	12,125	1	14,470
Emergency Equipment Dispatcher	977-1187	10	10	129,255	129,255	10	125,055	10	125,055	10	131,310
Custodial Officer	977-1187	5	5	53,785	53,785	5	55,775	5	55,775	5	64,350
Station Officer	972-1181	1	1	13,580	13,580	1	13,530	1	13,530	1	14,210
Humane Officer	972-1181	4	4	53,310	53,310	5	65,515	5	65,515	6	80,765
Secretary to the Police Chief	907-1102	1	1	12,670	12,670	1	12,620	1	12,620	1	13,250
Parking Control Officer	827-1006	4	4	44,490	44,490	4	44,835	4	44,835	4	47,075
Police Clerk II	803-976	4	4	44,115	44,115	4	44,690	4	44,690	4	46,925
Police Clerk I	743-903	16	16	160,430	160,430	17	172,420	16	163,700	16	171,885
TOTALS											

Exhibit 9-5. (Continued)

CITY OF NEWPORT BEACH

BUDGET ESTIMATES FOR FISCAL YEAR 1976-77

Department POLICE   Division _____   Activity No. 2000   MAINTENANCE & OPERATION

OBJECT NO.	EXPENSE CLASSIFICATION OBJECT TITLE	1974-75 ACTUAL EXPENDITURES	1975-76 BEGINNING BUDGET	AMENDED BUDGET	6 MONTHS EXPENDITURES	EST. TOTAL EXPENDITURES	DEPARTMENT ESTIMATE	1976-77 CITY MANAGER RECOMMENDATION	CITY COUNCIL APPROVAL	OBJECT NO.
10	Advertising and Public Relations	2,412	2,825	2,825	900	2,825	4,255	4,255	4,255	10
11	Automotive Service	124,395	121,700	124,400	57,211	124,400	153,500	137,500	137,500	11
12	Maintenance and Repair of Equip.	7,123	7,980	7,980	3,153	7,980	17,370	14,370	14,370	12
13	Postage, Freight. Express, etc.	5,980	6,000	7,000	5,625	7,000	8,700	8,700	8,700	13
14	Publication and Dues	1,315	1,715	1,715	839	1,715	2,885	2,385	2,385	14
15	Rental of Property and Equipment	26,788	15,805	14,805	6,085	14,805	17,725	15,225	15,225	15
16	Services – Prof., Technical, etc	39,401	49,225	43,825	18,093	43,825	93,030	77,005	77,005	16
17	Travel and Meetings	5,200	4,295	5,195	2,555	5,195	6,335	5,700	5,700	17
18	Utilities	85,071	76,600	91,600	44,059	91,600	96,400	92,400	92,400	18
30	Office Supplies	38,777	37,280	40,780	22,561	40,780	44,700	44,700	44,700	30
31	Janitorial Supplies	628	1,000	1,000	289	1,000	1,000	900	900	31
32	Maintenance and Repair Materials	3,541	1,500	2,500	1,700	2,500	3,000	3,000	3,000	32
33	Special Departmental Supplies	58,485	73,145	73,145	43,419	73,145	83,775	78,775	78,775	33
34	Tools, Instruments, etc.	2,148	2,000	2,000	1,001	2,000	2,500	2,500	2,500	34
40	Special Departmental Expense	3,212	4,000	5,000	2,475	5,000	7,000	6,000	6,000	40
41	Helicopter Maintenance	92,482	90,750	90,750	41,091	90,750	105,100	103,100	103,100	41
50	General Insurance	2,400	3,000	3,000	-0-	3,000	4,500	4,500	4,500	50
	TOTALS	499,358	498,820	517,520	251,056	517,520	651,775	601,015	601,015	

Exhibit 9–5. (Continued)

CITY OF NEWPORT BEACH

BUDGET ESTIMATES FOR FISCAL YEAR 1976-77

SALARIES

Department POLICE   Division _____   Activity No. 2000

CLASSIFICATION	SALARY RANGE	BUDGETED EMPLOYEES BEGINNING	BUDGETED EMPLOYEES AMENDED	1975-76 BEGINNING BUDGET	1975-76 AMENDED BUDGET	DEPARTMENT ESTIMATE NO	DEPARTMENT ESTIMATE AMOUNT	1976-77 CITY MANAGER RECOMMENDATION NO	1976-77 CITY MANAGER RECOMMENDATION AMOUNT	1976-77 CITY COUNCIL APPROVAL NO	1976-77 CITY COUNCIL APPROVAL AMOUNT
SEASONAL PART-TIME											
Police Reserve Officer		1.32	.61	11,055	5,130						
Police Matron	90.00 BW	1	1	1,810	1,810	1	2,350	1	2,350	1	2,350
School Crossing Guard	105.00 BW	2.37	2.37	10,500	10,500	2.60	12,600	2.6	12,600	2.6	12,600
Police Woman	4.80-5.84	.40	.40	4,045	4,045	.40	4,860	.4	4,860	.4	4,860
Police Cadet	2.75-3.25	3.66	3.66	22,560	22,560	4.06	25,740	4.06	25,740	4.06	25,740
Parking Control Officer	4.00-4.86	.92	1.26	8,900	11,940	1.73	14,400	1.73	14,400	2.15	18,000
Librarian	5.83-7.09					.19	2,340	.19	2,340	.19	2,340
Clerk	3.03-3.68					1	6,240	1	6,240	1	6,240
OVERTIME				172,815	187,180		187,200		187,200		196,560
SALARY SAVINGS				(-124,600)	(-130,765)		-0-		(-120,000)		(-126,000)
SCHOLASTIC ACHIEVEMENT				54,000	54,000						54,000
COMPREHENSIVE EMPLOYMENT TRAINING ACT											
Police Officer	1239-1506	(4)	(6)	59,675	95,905	(6)	92,920	(6)	92,920	(6)	97,565
Police Clerk I	743-903	(2)	(2)	17,900	19,655	(4)	37,440	(4)	37,440	(4)	39,310
Emergency Equipment Dispatcher	977-1187	0	(2)	-0-	-0-	(2)	23,470	(2)	23,470	(2)	24,645
TOTALS		181.67	181.30	3,089,740	3,133,040	197.26	3,462,255	189.98	3,251,670	191.40	3,488,020

Exhibit 9-6

CITY OF NEWPORT BEACH

BUDGET ESTIMATES FOR FISCAL YEAR 1976-77

Department _____ POLICE _____   Division _____   Activity No. ___ 2000 ___   **CAPITAL OUTLAY**

OBJECT NO	ITEM OF CAPITAL OUTLAY	1974-75 ACTUAL EXPENDITURE	1975-76 BEGINNING BUDGET	AMENDED BUDGET	8 MONTHS EXPENDITURE	EST. TOTAL EXPENDITURE	DEPARTMENT ESTIMATE AMOUNT	1976-77 CITY MANAGER RECOMMENDATION AMOUNT	CITY COUNCIL APPROVAL AMOUNT	OBJECT NO
90	Office Equipment						5,240	5,240	5,240	90
91	Rolling Equipment						128,650	128,650	137,115	91
92	Shop Equipment						-0-	-0-	-0-	92
93	Equipment, N.O.C.						102,360	83,465	98,675	93
94	Furniture and Fixtures						2,765	2,765	2,765	94
TOTALS		160,878	201,125	181,125	53,083	181,125	239,015	220,120	243,795	

greater the experience and the greater the ability of those to whom the work is entrusted, the better the results are likely to be.

The traditional approach requires a fairly simple system of accounts in which emphasis is placed upon organizational units and object classes of expenditure. The fact that it is largely based upon objects of expenditure makes it easy to develop a system of budgetary accounts that can be applied with great uniformity to the full range of complex activities of the government.

The emphasis upon organizational units and objects of expenditure also has the advantage of using concepts that are easily understood, not only by administrators and executives but also by the members of the legislative body and by interested citizens. Finally, this approach affords certain types of easy statistical comparisons from year to year and from unit to unit of the government.

On the negative side, there are a number of shortcomings of the traditional approach. During the preparation and consideration of the budget, concentration upon organizational units and objects of expenditure tends to forestall a full understanding of the objectives sought to be accomplished under the expenditure authorizations being considered. There is more attention to dollars, units of personnel, and amounts of equipment, materials, and supplies; conversely, there may be less emphasis upon the amount of work which these dollars and other evidences of expenditure are accomplishing.

Because of these factors, measures of performance are more difficult to secure. The administrator at all levels may be relatively uninformed as to what is being done and the cost of the significant units of each operation. Judgment as to the need for expansion or the potentialities for economies is rendered difficult.

In the execution phases of the budget cycle, a central budget office can, by requirement of a rigid adherence to the patterns of expenditure projected in the budget supporting detail, both encroach upon the proper prerogatives of departmental management and produce imbalances between related types of expenditure.

But, the adoption of the traditional approach does not foreclose the use of measures and reporting systems that keep the administrator informed. Thus, within the framework of the traditional approach, much attention can be given to program and performance.[15]

Performance Budget

Performance budgeting as implemented during the 1950s and 60s was a product of the Hoover Commission study and subsequent reports released in 1949. The Commission said, "We recommend that the whole

---

[15]Moak and Killian, *Manual of Techniques,* pp. 12–13.

budgetary concept of the federal government should be refashioned by the adoption of a budget based upon functions, activities, and projects; this we designate a 'performance budget.' "[16]

It was the Commission's intent to place primary emphasis on the public needs, and the required services to answer those needs. This was contrasted to traditional budgets that tended to place more emphasis on equipment and supplies and other specific items rather than on functions.

Significantly for local governments, it was during this same period that computer based data storage and retrieval systems came in vogue. Large municipalities involved themselves in acquiring computers and developing programs. Smaller jurisdictions began to buy time on privately owned computers, primarily for the purpose of employee payrolling and utility billing.

Those who contractually shared computer time soon discovered in payrolling that the primary cost per month was per employee or "address"; that other data could be stored and retrieved for little or nothing extra. Many police departments took advantage of the opportunity and fed into the computer such data as contained in officers' daily logs including arrest and crime reports and traffic citations. This became the base for some attempt at cost accounting and since much of the same data related to performance budgeting, it was natural that efforts be made in some police departments to utilize this relatively new concept.

In its simplest form, a performance budget is a measure of the work process of any agency or unit.

> Expenditures are classified by functions, activities and projects. Budgets are cast in functional terms, and work-cost measurements are developed to facilitate the efficient performance of prescribed activities. The budget is regarded as a work program, the emphasis is on the means, accomplishments to be achieved, the specific activities and work activities are ends in themselves.[17]

Performance budgets, in common with line-item budgets, provide comparative data which may be used by managers, budget analysts, and elected officials on a basis for allocating resources.

For example, if one policeman on one foot beat can effectually patrol a four-square-block area, theoretically that patrolman's activities can be projected over other similar areas to determine the number of patrol-

---

[16]U.S. Commission on Organization of the Executive Branch of the Government, *The Hoover Commission Report,* (New York, Toronto, and London: McGraw-Hill Book Company), pp. 36–37.
[17]Catherine Lovell, *A Very Short Course in Budgeting,* (Unpublished paper, University of California, Riverside Graduate School of Administration, 1975), sec. 2, B.

men needed. Ideally, the data base would furnish other pertinent information which would permit the decision maker to look at alternative methods of delivering services to the same area, such as the patrol car. By utilizing cost accounting and performance data, theoretically managers should be able to rationally select the most effective method of patrol in terms of services delivered per cost dollar.

Unfortunately, this budgeting method requires a large professional staff to sort, store, return, and interpret data. Additionally, it requires a great deal more input from all levels. And, of course, its decisions are based upon the assumption that the data received is correct.

Unfortunately, police officers' logs continue to be completed in broad generalities rather than accurately recorded time frames. Unaccounted for time tends to be lumped under the headings of "other" or "patrol time," because logs are typically *filled out* at the shift's end and events tend to run together, or escape one's memory.

Cost accounting, along with attempts at performance budgeting, began to fade from the police management scene when the data was found to be unmanageable in terms of available staff man hours.[18] As one chief put it, "So I know how much it costs to write the average traffic citation, and whether or not the recipient lived in town, and how much is required to take the average burglary report, but what has that got to do with my traffic problems, and how does it help me solve my burglaries?" (How can I use the information?)

And so, while the tenets of the performance budget are excellent, it appears to most experts in the field that it may be impractical for local government.

To be more specific, we believe that performance budgeting is more practical for those organizations whose production units derive from assembly lines or other work functions that are highly quantifiable, such as paving a certain number of street miles, or sweeping a given number of street miles.

Of course, many police functions are quantifiable. However, while it does not need to be so, quantification often connotes *quotas* and *police quotas* are typically resented by citizen and policeman alike.

Undoubtedly it would be possible to become more efficient in terms of issuing more traffic citations, or arresting more drunks, but unfortunately more citations and drunk arrests may not really benefit the community.

In 1964 Moak and Killian observed:

[18]According to recent observations of Dr. Catherine Lovell, Professor at the Graduate School of Administration, University of California, Riverside, there appears to be a new resurgence of performance budgeting attempts . . . only better.

It must be noted that the growth of performance budgeting has been curtailed by an almost slavish linkage to cost accounting which has led many cities to believe that its installation would be exorbitantly expensive. Some cities have entirely discounted the use of cost accounting because of the variability of the purchasing power of the dollar and use, instead, a man-hour approach to performance budgeting. A major and persistent obstacle to work measurement and performance budgeting, however, is the selection of meaningful work units.[19]

Gardner, in a more contemporary evaluation, believes performance budgeting may make us do better and better those things which are worse and worse for us. Additionally, he observes the following advantages and disadvantages to the system:

Advantages

1. Performance budgets are easy to administer once performance criteria have been agreed upon.
2. Performance budgets possess internal rationality.
3. These budgets involve employees at all organizational levels.
4. Performance budget provides supervisors with useful management information.
5. The performance budget generates data which are useful in creating greater task efficiency.

Disadvantages

1. Performance budgets are a very expensive process.
2. Criteria used may tend to emphasize the measurable rather than the significant.
3. Performance items do not often relate directly to the needs of society.
4. These budgets are short range in scope and are not useful by themselves as planning instruments.
5. Administrators and elected officials do not usually use performance budgets to articulate policy.
6. Performance budgets are not helpful to citizens in making government activities visible.[20]

[19]Moak and Killian, *Manual of Techniques,* pp. 9–10.
[20]Gardner, "Budget and Budgeting," p. 35.

The Planning, Programming, Budgeting System (PPBS)

Management students, especially those involved with municipal finance and budgeting courses will no doubt be exposed to the length and breadth of PPBS. With its roots in earlier planning and programming concepts, developed in its present state by the Rand Corporation, and brought to prominence by the Defense Department in the McNamara era, PPBS rose from obscurity to great prominence, and then dropped off considerably by the late 1960s and early 70s.

> By the mid-1970's it was clear that PPBS was not sweeping through every city in the country—as enthusiasts might have anticipated a decade or so earlier. Neither on the other hand was it totally without influence in the innovative areas of municipal budgeting.[21]

Essentially, according to Lovell,

> In PPBS, the budget is planning oriented; its main goal is to rationalize policy-making by providing data on the cost and benefits of alternative ways of attaining proposed public objectives and other output measurements; to facilitate the effective attainment of chosen objectives. Under PPB the objective itself is variable; analysis may lead to a new statement of objectives. The emphasis is on comprehensiveness and on grouping data into categories that allow comparisons among alternative expenditure mixes.[22]

Primarily, then, PPBS was designed to bring vast amounts of data to bear on the decision-making process with a prominent emphasis on economy and goal achievement. It is certainly rational, even desirable, to provide decision makers with alternatives and to provide for planning and programs beyond the normal budget year (a strong element of PPBS). Unfortunately, PPBS moves away from organizational inputs at all levels and focuses the process in the hands of a group of highly qualified technical people, "preferably with an economics education which is enriched with a knowledge of statistics and computer science."[23]

It was never intended that PPBS remove the final decisions from professional managers and elected legislative bodies. On the other hand, by its very design, systems analysts and other *experts*, without inputs from

[21]Aronson and Schwartz, *Management Policies*, p. 88.
[22]Lovell, *A Very Short Course*, sec. 2, C.
[23]Gardner, "Budget and Budgeting," p. 42.

departmental practitioners or representatives of the social sciences, may very well make erroneous assumptions in the beginning that lead to the development of economically and rationally sound alternatives that, while apparently able to reach identified goals, often lack the human element. *The operation was a success but the patient died.*

Gardner identified the following Planning Programming Budgets System advantages and disadvantages:

Advantages:

1. P.P.B. is likely to be more "needs" oriented than our traditional budgets.
2. It is a budget with a cost-effectiveness thrust.
3. Legislative and administrative policies may be specifically reflected.
4. Citizens and news media provided information on the degree of delivery of expected government services.
5. Planning is greater than in line-item and performance budgets.
6. Government agencies are accountable for ends rather than means.
7. Administrators have a vehicle for improved management.

Disadvantages in the P.P.B. approach for most jurisdictions are:

1. The process requires hard-to-recruit analytical talent.
2. Costs of installing and maintaining the system are high.
3. It is necessary to re-orient and re-focus the accounting system.
4. Over-centralization occurs which:
   a. Creates an elitist system.
   b. Does not provide sufficient opportunity to obtain employee participation and commitment.
5. Provides temptation for over-analysis.
6. Introduces the possibility for making long-term mistakes and extremely costly errors.
7. Involves a higher level of legislative risks.
8. Provides opportunities for special interest groups to apply pressure.
9. There is a danger inherent in failing to meet declared objectives.[24]

The Program or Outcomes Budget System

For the purpose of this section, program or outcomes budgets are the same. Some practitioners, academicians, and critics of the budgetary process prefer the latter in that it avoids confusion with PPBS and dwells on the focus—on outcomes.

[24]*Ibid.,* p. 51.

Actually, program budgeting is far from a standardized form. Many police departments, as well as many municipal governments in toto utilize *programs* to some extent in their budget preparation. A persistent forerunner in this endeavor has been John Wentz, the City Manager of Phoenix, Arizona. Although the Phoenix process has been in a developing stage for several years, we can make some generalizations. The program budget system utilizes a program format budget (as does PPBS).

> But [the budgetary process] does not include elaborate cost benefit analysis. It classifies activities by programs with stated objectives. Choices among programs or objectives are made in the political process. . . . In other words, policy analysis and choices are *separated* from the budgetary process. However, the budget relates proposed expenditures to desired objectives. Expenditures may be grouped in any way necessary to accomplish the desired purposes; exact form is situational.[25]

An appealing facet of the program budget is that it emphasizes community needs and departmental goals and objectives (programs) to satisfy those needs. Accounts are then related to specific programs rather than simply to line-items. The hope for this model is that eventually it will assist legislative bodies in selecting and rejecting programs rather than dwelling on the cost of supplies and equipment. This will be relatively simple in certain city functions such as tree trimming, or rodent control where the focus is on the program, not the equipment and manpower. Police programs that lend themselves to easy application include Youth Diversion, School Resource Officers, Crossing Guards, and the like.

> The outcomes [program] budget is the responsibility of designated program managers working in close cooperation with agency administration. The final version of the budget request is coordinated at the agency level, often with wide participation of program managers [i.e., division and unit heads].[26]

This is especially significant (as contrasted to the PPBS model) in that the important *human element* of modern management is taken into consideration. And of course valuable informational inputs from these levels are likely to "work out the bugs" before programs become a reality—in addition to assuring support at the operational level for new or modified programs.

[25]Lovell, *A Very Short Course*, sec. 2, D.
[26]Gardner, "Budget and Budgeting," p. 53.

Typical program budget submissions provide for:

1. A statement of need.
2. Legal authority for the program.
3. How it originated.
4. Objectives.
5. Work plan.
6. Multi-year program course [when it will start and how long it will go—whether closed or open-ended].[27]

As can be seen above, an important facet of the program budget is that it is easily understood by those who read it as well as by those who must implement it. Perhaps one of the most difficult tasks of a police manager is to work toward citizen understanding of why the police do what they do. Perhaps even more difficult at times is for the lowest man on the totem pole in the police agency to understand why he does what he does. He often issues citations "to keep the sergeant off his back" and arrests drunks because "there isn't anything else to do with them." Another important facet is that program budgeting is relatively inexpensive to formulate and administer in that it requires no great reservoir of *experts* in analysis and economics and as said before, it is easy to understand and to audit both expenditures and accomplishments.

Gardner summarizes the advantages and disadvantages of program or outcome budgets as follows:

Advantages:

1. Wide participation in the budget's preparation.
2. The necessity to constantly sense the environment for emerging needs.
3. Providing a vehicle for managing by objectives.
4. Its focus on social/effectiveness rather than simply cost/effectiveness.
5. Its reflection of administrative and legislative policy.
6. The factor of high accountability to the legislative body and to the people.
7. They are less complicated than P.P.B. and thus within the reach of more jurisdictions.

[27]*Ibid.*

8. That being based on a modified Market Model, Outcomes Budgets are likely to produce greater economizing behavior.

9. Analysis of the budget is a line not a staff function.

10. That budget cycles are equated with the specific needs and nature of each program.

Disadvantages are that:

1. Legislators have to learn to take the risks associated with the advantages.

2. Accounting systems must be revised.

3. It is difficult to formulate meaningful objectives that are sufficiently explicit to manage and budget by.

4. Jurisdictions may be disrupted by a change to programmatic from functional type organizations.

5. Managers may not wish to take the risk of meeting objectives.

6. The different role required of staff may cause dissatisfaction on staff units.

7. Data collection may be costly.[28]

Zero-Base Budgets

Before leaving this section, we wish to alert the reader to a relatively new (in terms of government application) budget form with which he may eventually be confronted. Zero-base budgeting or ZBB is an outgrowth of program budgeting.

> [ZBB is] a sophisticated management tool which provides a systematic method of reviewing and evaluating all operations of the organization, current or proposed; allows for budget reductions and expansions in a planned, rational manner; and encourages the reallocation of resources from low to high priority programs. Because of the nature of the process involved, ZBB also tends to have some important fringe benefits, such as involving more managers in the budgeting process, providing more information and options to decision makers, and establishing a systematic basis for management by objectives and priorities.[29]

[28]*Ibid.*, pp. 63–64.

[29]David W. Singleton, Bruce A. Smith, and James R. Cleaveland, "Zero-based Budgeting in Wilmington, Delaware," *Governmental Finance* vol. 5, no. 3 (Chicago, Ill.: Officers Association of the United States and Canada, 1976) p. 21.

Typical budgets have as a base prior year programs and costs, usually with built-in cost factors for inflation. This base is usually accepted by management and legislative body alike as the place where the budget process begins, with relatively little explanation or justification. New programs, on the other hand, are given much attention and are described in great detail in terms of need, goals, services to be performed, and cost. If more than one new program is proposed, they are priority ordered so the governing bodies can make decisions based upon relevant factors.

ZBB, however, assumes no base whatsoever, except for a few fixed costs over which there is little or no control. Every program, every service performed is broken down into the same detail as are new programs in traditional budgets. Each program or service is ranked in order of relative importance. Theoretically, this not only enables the flushing out of services and programs no longer needed but provides priority updating of those programs that do need to be continued so that service levels can be decided in terms of available resources.

As can readily be seen, ZBB is highly complex and time consuming in relation to the more contemporary approaches to budgeting. At this point it is difficult to predict whether ZBB will be widely adopted in some modified form as it gains more widespread exposure; or toyed with as some laboratory animal; or finally brushed aside as too time consuming, too costly, and too cumbersome for the needs and abilities of most agencies. While some experts have already suggested that ZBB may in fact be too costly and cumbersome for most annual budgets, it might be both practical and beneficial if utilized about every five years.

Suffice it to say that modern managers will want to monitor the progress of ZBB closely.

LEARNING EXERCISE

BUDGET ANALYSIS

All budgets, regardless of format and style, are related to or *crosswalked* with the traditional or line-item budget. The exhibits which follow depict a typical, medium-sized police agency. Included are:

1. Departmental and divisional organization charts (exhibits 9–7 and 9–8)

2. Program and operational objectives

3. Budget summary (exhibit 9–10)

4. Line items by account number and classification exhibit (9–11). All budget data are for one division—administrative services.

The task is for the reader to relate line items to various programs. For example, the objective "continue to explore sources of federal and state aid" would require funds from account number 181 for travel and meeting expenses since the person so assigned must travel to the state capital to meet directly with the Office of Criminal Justice staff as well as attend regional meetings. Some account number 155 postage funds will need to be allocated to this program as will portions of other accounts, and so forth.

The reader will not be completely correct in his estimates but that is not important for purposes of this exercise.

One way to begin to see correlations is to photocopy all exhibits and tape them on a larger sheet—line-item costs beside program objectives. Draw lines from the program objective column to the line-item cost column. Then work up the cost breakdown.

A consideration for the number of personnel you assign to each program will greatly assist in assignment of line-items and dollars. Remember, in the process, goals and objectives are identified first. Secondly, programs are designed to reach the goals and objectives. Thirdly, personnel and nonpersonal costs are estimated for programs. Lastly, program costs are reduced to line items and related to specific account numbers.

Exhibit 9–7.   Police Department Organization Chart

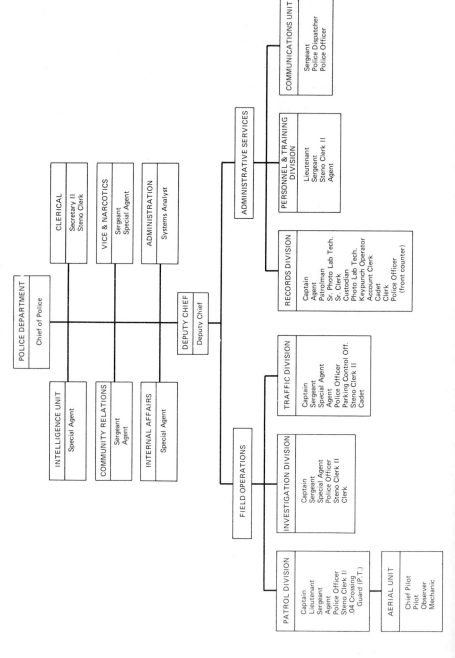

Exhibit 9–8. Administrative Services Division Organization Chart

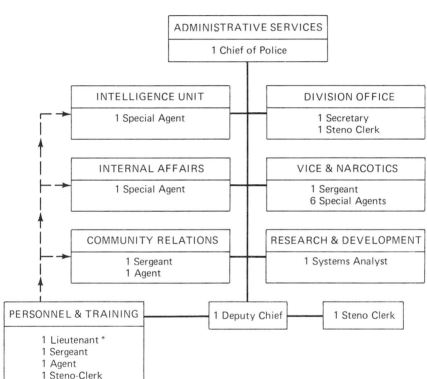

*The Administrative Lieutenant performs functional supervision over the
Intelligence Unit, Internal Affairs Unit and the Community Relations Unit.

Exhibit 9–9. Program Operational Objectives for Administrative Services Division

```
                    PROGRAM OPERATIONAL OBJECTIVES

                    ADMINISTRATIVE SERVICES



   ACTIVITIES:          PROGRAM ADMINISTRATION

   WORK            Planning and Research
   ELEMENTS:
                   Policies and Procedures

                   Fiscal Control

                   Program Coordination

                   Clerical Services

                   Records and Reports

                   Staff Inspections

                          COMMUNITY RELATIONS

                   Community Programs

                   Speakers Bureau

                   Public Information

                   Press Relations



                          SPECIAL OPERATIONS

                   Organized Crime

                   Vice and Narcotics

                   Personnel Investigations

                   Internal Investigations
```

Exhibit 9–9. Program Operational Objectives for
Administrative Services Division (Continued)

PROGRAM OPERATIONAL OBJECTIVES

ADMINISTRATIVE SERVICES

	PROGRAM ADMINISTRATION	COMMUNITY RELATIONS	SPECIAL OPERATIONS
OPERATIONAL OBJECTIVES:	Implement police management and organization study during next 3 years.	Increase participation of line personnel in community relations functions to 3 percent of duty time.	Decrease the incidence of vice and narcotics in the Riverside area.
*CURRENT SERVICE LEVELS	*Implementation underway; dependent on financial resources.	*Currently under 1 percent. (33%)	*Extent of vice and narcotics enforcement limited by present manpower.
	Continue to study new police concepts (i.e., team policing, modified work hours).	Expand safety city program to reach 5,000 children annually.	Increase knowledge of organized crime and subversion activities through improved information analysis.
	*Continuous process.	*Currently making program available to 3,400 annually. (68%)	*Ongoing effort.
	Develop formal staff inspection program.	Conduct a minimum of 15 community relations projects annually.	Investigate all allegations of alleged police misconduct within 5 days.
	*Program currently carried out on an informal basis; formal program to be initiated during 1974–75 fiscal year.	*Currently conducting 10 projects annually. (66%)	*Currently requires an average of 7 days. (70%)
	Continue to explore sources of federal and state aid.	Increase Crime Seminar program for local businessmen to 21 sessions annually.	
	*Continuous process.	*Currently conducting 15 sessions annually. (71%)	

75

267

Exhibit 9—10. Budget Summary

ANNUAL PROGRAM BUDGET   PERSONNEL DETAIL

DEPARTMENT	PROGRAM/SUB-PROGRAM	FUND	
POLICE	ADMINISTRATIVE SERVICES	GENERAL	01-201

POSITION CLASSIFICATION	POSITION QUOTA			ANNUAL SALARY RANGE	AMOUNT REQUIRED 1976-77	FINAL 1976-77
	CUR-RENT	PRO-POSED	FINAL			
FULL TIME PERSONNEL						
Chief of Police	1	1	1	27,024-33,780	37,163	37,163
Deputy Chief of Police	1	1	1	25,561-29,588	28,872	32,625
Lieutenant	1	1	1	19,896-23 28	24,875	24,875
Sergeant (1)	4	3	3	18,048-20,892	65,578	65,578
Academy Training Sergeant (3)	0	1	1	18,048-20,892	20,468	20,468
Special Agent (2)	10	8	8	15,588-18,948	158,909	158,909
Agent	2	2	2	14,844-18,048	37,174	37,174
Systems Analyst	1	1	1	16,296-19,812	19,478	19,478
Rangemaster	0	1	1	9,912-12,048	9,126	9,126
Secretary II	1	1	1	10,512-12,768	12,555	12,555
Steno Clerk II	3	3	3	8,640-10,512	30,397	30,397
Sub Total	24	23	23		444,595	448,348
Less Vacancy Factor					-3,271	-4,483
Total					441,324	443,865
CETA PERSONNEL						
Clerk Typist			1			-0-

(1) One sergeant positions transferred to Uniform Services.

(2) Two special agent positions
transferred to Investigative
Services.

(3) Academy training sergeant position reimbursed by RCC.

ACCOUNT DETAIL

CODE	ACCOUNT CLASSIFICATION AND DETAIL	CURRENT 1975-76	PROPOSED 1976-77	FINAL 1976-77
	PERSONAL SERVICES			
1	Salaries and Wages - Regular	438,348	441,324	443,865
2	Salaries and Wages - Temporary and Part Time			
10	Salaries and Wages - Extra Pay (Overtime, Night Shift Premium, Holiday, Sick Leave Payoff, etc.)	58,137	50,793	50,793
91	Compensation Insurance	14,280	6,270	6,332
92	Health Insurance	7,850	7,310	7,310
93	Life Insurance	522	415	415
94	Retirement - PERS	103,852	95,849	98,124
95	Retirement - OASDI	3,019	3,207	3,207
	TOTAL	626,008	605,168	610,046

Exhibit 9–10. Line-Item Budget (Continued)

City of Riverside ANNUAL PROGRAM BUDGET			ACCOUNT DETAIL	
DEPARTMENT POLICE	**PROGRAM/SUB-PROGRAM** ADMINISTRATIVE SERVICES	**FUND** GENERAL		01-201
CODE	**ACCOUNT CLASSIFICATION AND DETAIL**	**CURRENT BUDGET 1975-76**	**PROPOSED BUDGET 1976-77**	**FINAL BUDGET 1976-77**
	NON-PERSONAL EXPENSE - Continued			
181	Travel and Meeting Expense - Continued Community Relations and various community meetings - Local - Chief of Police and Deputy Chief of Police 160			
	California Peace Officers' Assn., All Committee Conference - Sacramento - Chief Of Police 234			
	Office of Criminal Justice Planning Meetings - Sacramento - Deputy Chief of Police 253			
	Community Relations Officers 200 Intelligence Officers 140 Misc. Local Intelligence Meetings 60 Personnel and Training 90 Planning and Research 97			
182	Services - Professional, Technical and Other Funds used for undercover work and intelligence operations	18,000	9,500	9,500
187	Sundry Expenses Training funds fully reimbursed by Peace Officers Standards and Training (P.O.S.T.)	25,000	60,000	60,000
	TOTAL	84,722	104,752	104,752
	EQUIPMENT OUTLAY			
822 -1 -2	Machinery and Equipment Pistol, 9 mm Shredder, paper	3,750	25) 5,050 1) 421	25) 5,050 1) 421
	TOTAL	3,750	5,471	5,471
	TOTAL BUDGET REQUIREMENTS	714,480	715,391	720,269

Exhibit 9–10.   Line-Item Budget   (Continued)

City of Riverside **ANNUAL PROGRAM BUDGET**			**ACCOUNT DETAIL**

DEPARTMENT	PROGRAM/SUB-PROGRAM	FUND	
POLICE	ADMINISTRATIVE SERVICE	GENERAL	01-201

CODE	ACCOUNT CLASSIFICATION AND DETAIL	CURRENT BUDGET 1975-76	PROPOSED BUDGET 1976-77	FINAL BUDGET 1976-77
	NON-PERSONAL EXPENSE			
111	Telephone 17 lines @ $372/mo plus toll charges	4,860	5,152	5,152
122	Equipment Rental	4,800	-0-	-0-
145	Central Communications	3,900	-0-	-0-
149	Sublet Repair Repair by outside firms for 8 unmarked police vehicles @ $600/ea, 15,000 miles/year ea.	2,356	4,800	4,800
151	Advertising, Printing and Binding Education material, handouts covering bicycle safety, crime prevention, narcotics and other public awareness programs.	700	200	200
152	Periodicals and Dues Membership - American Polygraph Assn. 40 Calif. Polygraph Assn. 30	112	70	70
154	General Office Expense Magnabelts for dictating machines, tablets, paper, pens, typewriter ribbons and other office supplies	182	223	223
155	Postage Approximately 30,769 mailings	3,000	4,000	4,000
163	Motor Fuels and Lubricants Gasoline and oil for 8 unmarked police vehicles	3,556	4,800	4,800
168	Special Departmental Supplies Supplies for Community Relations meetings 733 Purchase and rental of films 1,500 Polygraph supplies 306 Range supplies and field emergency equip. 10,901 Two recording tapes 300 Drug identification kit and replacement Valtrox 60	15,742	13,800	13,800
181	Travel and Meeting Expense International Assoc. of Chief's of Police - Miami Beach - Chief of Police 586

League of California Cities - Chief of Police - San Francisco - Chief of Police   232

California Peace Officers' Assn. - Anaheim - Chief of Police   155 | 2,514 | 2,207 | 2,207 |

Exhibit 9–10. Line-Item Budget (Continued)

City of Riverside ANNUAL PROGRAM BUDGET			DEPARTMENT SUMMARY		
DEPARTMENT	PROGRAM/SUB-PROGRAM	FUND			
POLICE	ADMINISTRATIVE SERVICES	GENERAL			01-201
CLASSIFICATION			CURRENT BUDGET 1975-76	PROPOSED BUDGET 1976-77	FINAL BUDGET 1976-77
PERSONAL SERVICES			626,008	605,168	610,046
NON-PERSONAL EXPENSE			84,722	104,752	104,752
EQUIPMENT OUTLAY			3,750	5,471	5,471
CAPITAL IMPROVEMENTS					
GROSS BUDGET REQUIREMENTS			714,480	715,391	720,269
LESS: DEPARTMENTAL CREDITS					
NET BUDGET			714,480	715,391	720,269
TOTAL MAN YEARS (FULL TIME AND PART-TIME)			24	23	24

The Administrative Services Subprogram includes the offices of the Chief of Police, Personnel and Training Section, Planning and Research Section, Vice and Narcotics Section, Special Investigation Unit, and the Community Relations Section. The responsibilities of the subprogram include: Total administration of the department through the offices of the Chief of Police, using a team management approach and effective leadership styles; coordinating all personnel and training activities with the department; developing policy and procedures through research, studies and crime pattern analysis; enforcement of all laws and regulations for the control of drugs, narcotics, prostitution, gambling and obscene matter; investigation of all official matters, gang activities and organized crime movement; coordinating community programs, public information and other human relations functions.

One additional sergeant would be hired as a police academy training sergeant, responsible for coordinating all peace officer training at the academy. All salary, benefits and equipment costs will be reimbursed to the City by Riverside City College. One civilian rangemaster will be hired, thereby releasing one uniformed officer for field duty. Non-Personal Expense reflects an increase due to a new directive that the department show a true amount needed in the P.O.S.T. reimbursed training account. This year the account will reflect a $60,000 amount, rather than the $25,000 in the 1975-76 budget. The Equipment Outlay category reflects an increase due to the need to purchase handguns. Ninety percent of the cost of the weapons will be returned to the City through the officer's purchase option. Additionally, a portable paper shredder is requested under this category.

Final Budget Changes

Added CETA personnel to the "Final" position quota.

Chapter Ten

TASK 8
POLICE PRODUCTIVITY:
Evaluation and Measurement

State and local governments are challenged to provide more effective police services at a time when the growing desire for public safety is surpassed only by the increase in police costs. For a police department to create one or more round-the-clock posts actually requires adding five officers to the force at a cost that may exceed $80,000 a year. To place an officer in a police car with a partner 24 hours a day may exceed $175,000 in annual costs to the community.

These costs are reflected in the growing nationwide expenditures for police services. In response to the mounting fear of personal harm, loss of property, and public disorder in recent years, municipal police expenditures increased 70 percent from $2.1 billion in 1967 to $3.5 billion in 1971. Total Federal, State, and local expenditures for police services reached $6.2 billion in 1971, a 20 percent increase over the previous year. Those funds went principally to cover the compensation for over 530,000 law-enforcement officers employed full-time in over 10,000 public police agencies at all levels of government.

These fiscal facts of life have forced many communities to recognize that the demand for more police services cannot be met simply by expanding the police force. Rather, police departments must learn to use more effectively the personnel and other resources currently available to them. That means increasing their productivity.[1]

SYNOPSIS

We currently find that elected local government officials and civil service administrators, as well as schools of criminal justice, other academic institutions, the federal government, and national professional associations have expressed a heightened interest in the issue of local government productivity. (As far back as 1928 the National Committee on Municipal Standards developed means of measuring

[1]Report of the Advisory Group on Productivity in Law Enforcement on *Opportunities for Improving Productivity in Police Services* (Washington, D.C.: National Commission on Productivity, 1973), p. 1.

the effectiveness of government services). Indeed, an interest in increasing productivity in police services is being widely and strongly voiced. Basically, augmenting police productivity denotes an endeavor to achieve greater levels of performance per unit cost. Since the police deal with people there is a profound concern not only for *quantity* but, as well, for the *quality* of the services provided. Improving productivity involves five functions: establishment of objectives, assessment of progress, search for better operating methods, experimentation, and implementation.

The concept of productivity naturally embodies the function of work measurement. It is our belief that existing police measures are limited in scope. Typically only a very small part of what our police do is counted and reported. And seldom are the figures compared to the goals of the agency. We would propose that the means of achieving a barometer on work accomplished as related to that planned is via the creation of a crime analysis unit. Such a unit should be held responsible for counting and assessing activities and recommending optimal patterns of human resource deployment to reduce crime.

Subsequent to an intensified concern over the rate and types of crime, a genuine hope for an effective attack on its constant threat and actual harm has arisen in both aware citizens and dedicated police managers. To this end, we now observe an accelerated commitment to the evaluation of ongoing police programs. It is because of evaluative efforts that we can reasonably anticipate an improved rationale for the allocation of scarce resources within the police system.

To "evaluate" a certain phenomena is a most challenging activity for us. Far too often, because of the complexity involved, certain deficiencies tend to surface. Half-hearted designs, insufficient data, fear of failure, and lack of expertise are omnipresent problems. To overcome them, the manager must take into consideration a number of factors relative to the accuracy of evaluative designs. Critical, among others, are type of evaluation, program design, program size, choice of evaluators, and data reliability.

The fundamental steps comprising *evaluation planning* for the *implementation of a project* are:

Quantify the objectives and goals.

Determine a quantifiable objective/goal relationship.

Develop evaluation measures.

Develop data needs considering requirements, constraints, and reporting.

Determine methods of analysis

Further, the police manager and his assigned project leader alike must share in the responsibility for project evaluation. Jointly they should be alert to: goal specificity, evaluation measures, data requirements, data analysis, and milestone reporting. This responsibility, on their part, is linked to present and pending decisions pertaining to the allocation of resources for improving our capability to fight crime.

Any attempt to evaluate a police agency or any one or more of its operating programs quite logically leads us to the issue of measurement. Regretably, the measurement of police service activities and results is fraught with ambiguity—i.e., what ought to be measured? Some agencies have accepted the challenge and are taking action. We have observed that early results are more often promising than not. Three indicators found worthy of measuring are amount and percentage of fiscal resources spent on police services by type, extent of volunteer manpower used, and amount of skill training. The challenge of measuring police work is being approached by many of us as an opportunity to improve the productivity and thus the overall effectiveness of our police delivery system.

In determining the most logical order in which to discuss the topics of evaluation, productivity, and measurement we played the "chicken or egg" game without conclusive results. In essence, we opted in favor of a pragmatic or technical approach. Thus you will initially encounter a broad discussion of *productivity*. Next, we sharpen the focus slightly to the point of looking at police program *evaluation*. Finally, we examine in more finite terms work *measurement*. Together, we *can* view the three phases as being interdependent. *More importantly, we should view them as being the very raison d' etre for our police.*

PRODUCTIVITY: An Issue

The biggest drag on overall productivity advances is not in manufacturing but in the service field, which employs more than 60% of the nation's workers and is hard to automate. Simply measuring—

much less improving—the productivity of policemen, pilots, teachers, or symphony conductors is far tougher than assessing the output of an assembly-line worker.[2]

Increasing this nation's productivity has been given top priority among economists, elected leaders, businessmen, and others who share an interest in our economic well-being.[3] Indeed, most look upon improved productivity as a means of avoiding the constant threat of inflation and unemployment. To this end, in 1970 the National Commission on Productivity was established. Because public employment has been growing sharply in relation to that in private industry, the Commission was charged with looking into productivity in the public as well as the private sector. In 1970, nearly one out of every five wage and salary workers was a government employee, and eighty percent of all public employees worked for state and local governments.[4] Projecting the current trends of government growth and decentralization of federal programs inherent in the revenue-sharing concept, experts foresee continued sharply rising expenditures and employment at the state and local levels. Thus a basis was laid for examining the opportunities for enhancing the productivity of public service employees.

Because a large share of the local government revenue is expended on police services, the Commission established in 1973 an Advisory Group to support them in conducting a study of ways to increase the productivity of our police. In order to enhance creditability and relevance, the Advisory Group was selected from a cross section of progressive police administrators, criminal justice planners, and academicians, as well as representatives from relevant professional and funding organizations. The Advisory Group wisely recognized the diversity of police and sheriff departments and the uselessness of trying to prescribe solutions which could be universally applied. Each department within our country is unique. Local conditions vary, governments are structured differently, community priorities respond to local needs, and expectations of the

---

[2]"Troubling Dip in Efficiency," *Time,* June 3, 1974, p. 71.

[3]A case in point is seen in the 1974 International Conference of the International Personnel Management Association whereby one full day was devoted to the following topics:

Productivity—Organizational and Motivational Aspects.
Productivity and Costs—The Budget and Budget Cycle.
Productivity and Organizational Effectiveness.
Productivity—The Technology of Its Measurement.
Productivity—Case Studies in the Public Sector.
Productivity—Bargaining Productivity in the Public Sector.

[4]*First Annual Report* (Washington, D.C.: National Commission on Productivity, 1972), pp. 13–14.

police agency are diverse. Indeed, productivity analysis is in part a response to that diversity, recognizing as it does the requirement for each government and police manager to respond individually to special local needs.

Productivity tools for the public sector in general, and for police services in particular, are in their infancy. Because of the complex factors involved, these efforts are not likely to reach maturity in the near future. Nevertheless, even though the state of the art is obviously imperfect, this fact *must not* deter police managers from experimenting with new techniques, tactics, and tools designed to raise productivity. The days of the police chief or sheriff being able to cite an increased crime rate as sole justification for additional resources are rapidly coming to an end. Policy makers, in conjunction with budget analysts, are asking in many cases, "What will we get for our money; i.e., how much more productive will you be?" The traditional response of "We don't know because we can't measure noncrime," is not only begging the issue but in error today. Through the use of victimization studies, many cities are now able to predict their actual crime rates as compared to only those crimes brought to their attention.[5] *Productivity* and the associated function of work *measurement* are upon us and will be with us from now on. (Interestingly, one local police agency has tied salary increases for their police officers to their productivity.[6]

Costs: Police and Crime

The figures in the excerpt that follows are intended to concisely and cogently alert you to the apocalyptic dimensions of crime in our nation. Since there will be more current statistics by the time this text is in print, we would suggest that for your own interest you compare the data below with the newer information.

"We're not winning the battle against crime. If anything, we're losing ground. . . ."

Between 1960 and 1973, the number of serious crimes reported to the FBI increased 158 per cent to a one-year's total of 8.6 million.

Murder jumped 116 per cent.

Forcible rape went up 199 per cent.

[5]For one example, see the Law Enforcement Assistance Administration, *Advance Report: Crime in Eight American Cities* (Washington, D.C.: U.S. Government Printing Office, 1974).

[6]In this instance the city is Orange, California, and the productivity factor centers on crime rates.

Robbery more than tripled—up 256 per cent.

Auto theft rose 183 per cent.

Crimes of violence—the kind that most terrify people—leaped 204 percent. . . .

Officials see no end to this frightening rise of crime. The truth is, most officials admit: Nobody really knows what is causing the rise in crime or how to stop it. . . .

The nation has poured billions of dollars into efforts to improve law enforcement. Local spending has multiplied more than seven times since 1964. Total spending—federal, state and local—for police, courts, prosecutors and prisons has shot up from 3.5 billion dollars in 1960 to 14.6 billion this year.[7]

It is police who have been given the major share of the money, equipment, and reinforcements that have been pumped into our nation's attack on crime. In the last seven years, the number of police officers—federal, state and local—has been increased by almost one third: up from 339,000 in 1967 to a total of 445,000 now. Further, nationwide spending on police has almost tripled in the same period: up from $3 billion in 1967 to $8.6 billion this year. (See exhibit 10–1).

Police have tried new techniques, added sophisticated electronic equipment and upgraded the education and training of their officers.

Then why, many people ask, haven't police been able to stop crime's rise?

Talk to police authorities and other law-enforcement experts around the country and you find widespread agreement on these answers:

Police efficiency in catching criminals has improved. More are being arrested than ever before.

Nobody, including the police, has yet found the answer on how to prevent crime.

Police—no matter how efficient they become—can never solve the crime problem alone.

"The reason," says James Q. Wilson, professor of government at Harvard and a recognized authority on law enforcement, is this:

"Crime is beyond the control of police. The courts, the prosecutors' offices, the correctional agencies—that's where the big changes have to be made.

[7]"The Losing Battle Against Crime In America," *U.S. News & World Report*, December 16, 1974, p. 30.

Exhibit 10–1. The Costs of Our Police

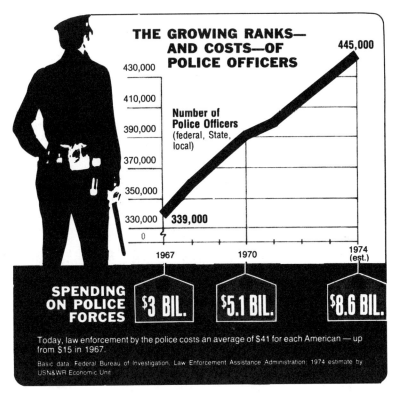

THE GROWING RANKS— AND COSTS—OF POLICE OFFICERS

Number of Police Officers (federal, State, local)

445,000

339,000

1967   1970   1974 (est.)

SPENDING ON POLICE FORCES $3 BIL. $5.1 BIL. $8.6 BIL.

Today, law enforcement by the police costs an average of $41 for each American — up from $15 in 1967.

Basic data: Federal Bureau of Investigation, Law Enforcement Assistance Administration; 1974 estimate by USN&WR Economic Unit

Source: **U.S. News & World Report, December 16, 1974, p. 43.**

"Until some big gains are made there, I doubt we'll ever know what difference improvement in the police really makes in fighting crime."[8]

Granted, the cost of policing does not come cheap. Let us now place the $8.6 billion figure into another perspective. We will now view the cost of our police as but one among many costs of crime. One study puts the total crime bill in the nation in 1974 at close to $90 billion. (See exhibit 10–2). A similar survey in 1970 showed a cost of $51 billion. That is an increase of 73.4 percent in just four years. Even in this era of rising prices, that is frightening inflation.

Break down the crime bill according to the nation's population, and you find it figures out to an average of about $420 for every man, woman,

[8]"What The Police Need to Do a Better Job," *ibid.,* p. 43.

Exhibit 10-2. The Cost of Crime

NEARLY $90 BILLION A YEAR

Estimates of economic impact of crime per year—

TOTAL TAKE BY ORGANIZED CRIME FROM ILLEGAL GOODS AND SERVICES

$37.2 BIL.

Gambling	$30.0 BIL
Narcotics	$5.2 BIL
Hijacked goods	$1.5 BIL
Interest from loan sharking	$0.5 BIL

CRIMES AGAINST PROPERTY AND BUSINESS
(excluding organized crime)

$21.3 BIL.

Embezzlement, fraud, forgery	$7.0 BIL
"Kickbacks" paid by businesses	$5.0 BIL
Unreported business thefts	$5.0 BIL
Robbery, burglary, theft, shoplifting	$3.0 BIL
Vandalism, arson	$1.3 BIL

OTHER CRIMES

$9.5 BIL.

Homicides, assaults (loss of earnings, medical costs)	$3.0 BIL.
Drunken driving (wage loss, medical costs of victims, property damage)	$6.5 BIL.

LAW-ENFORCEMENT COSTS

$14.6 BIL.

Police (federal, State, local)	$8.6 BIL
Penal system	$3.2 BIL
Court system	$2.8 BIL

PRIVATE CRIME-FIGHTING COSTS
(cost of services and equipment)

$6.0 BIL.

TOTAL CRIME EXPENSE $88.6 BIL.

Source: Estimates by USN&WR Economic Unit, based on data from Government and industry

and child in the United States. Usually, when people think of the costs of crime, they think first of the money spent on law enforcement—for police courts and prisons. That has gone up from $8.6 billion in 1970 to $14.6 billion this year. But it still is *less than one sixth of the total crime bill.*

> By contrast: Organized crime now takes more than 37 billion dollars out of American pockets yearly—up from 19.7 billion four years ago. Most of the racketeers' "take" is from illegal gambling. A big chunk comes from narcotics.
>
> Crime against business and property cause losses of 21.3 billion dollars, from "white collar" crimes such as embezzlement, fraud, forgery, kickbacks and thefts, or from vandalism and arson. This is another big increase—up from 13.1 billion dollars in 1970.
>
> *Costliest crimes.* Together, organized crime and business and property losses account for almost 2 out of every 3 dollars in the national crime bill.
>
> Homicides and assaults—although they exact an unaccountable price in human lives and suffering—cost only 3 billion dollars. Drunken driving takes a larger toll in dollars—6.5 billion in lost wages and medical costs of victims, and in property damages. This combined toll of 9.5 billion is also up sharply—from 4.1 billion in 1970.
>
> Another rising cost of crime is in spending by businesses and private individuals to provide for themselves the protection that law-enforcement agencies appear unable to provide. This spending has gone up to 6 billion dollars from 5.5 billion in 1970.[9]

What is to be concluded from the above data? First, and we think that you would agree, crime is expensive. Next, it will probably become even more costly (inflation aside). Finally, there will be enhanced commitment of funds to combat crime. *And, along with this commitment will be an attached expectation of our criminal justice system (CJS) agencies—improved productivity.* Police managers beware!

Police Productivity: A Multiview

To increase productivity means to get a greater return for a given investment. The concept is frequently used in reference to the production of goods; e.g., more agricultural products, automobiles, or tons of steel per man-hour. Specialists differ over the precise definition of the term "pro-

---

[9]"A High Price Tag that Everybody Pays," *ibid.*, p. 32.

ductivity," but it is generally assumed to be a ratio of "output" (or what results from an activity) to "input" (or the resources committed to an activity). To put it another way,

> Productivity improvement is among the practical approaches govern-
> ment is taking to achieve its objectives of effectiveness, efficiency,
> and economy. The concept of productivity improvement focuses on
> whether the right things are being done and whether they are being
> done without wasting valuable resources.[10]

In general, higher police productivity means keeping the police department's budget constant and improving performance, or keeping performance constant and reducing the size of the budget. Also, productivity gain can also mean increasing the budget but improving performance at an even higher rate. The concept of productivity, nonetheless, cannot simply be transferred in a theoretical form from the economics of production to the operations of a state or local police department. Thus, we propose that increasing productivity in police services be viewed in the four ways discussed below.[11]

First, *increasing police productivity means improving current police practices to the best level known, to get better performance without a proportionate increase in cost.* This means doing the things that are considered to be a necessary part of police work, but doing them as well or efficiently as the best current practices permit. For example, officers assigned to patrol spend a great deal of time on such activities as filling out unnecessarily long reports, or on activities that are important but that would require less time if better coordinated, such as the long hours spent waiting to testify at a trial.

Second, *increasing police productivity means allocating resources to activities which give the highest return for each additional dollar spent.* A police agency carries out a wide range of activities, many of which are non-crime-related and most of which are essential to its overall capability and its responsibility to the public. Beyond a given scale, however, expanding certain activities will give the agency less value than initiating or expanding others. For example, experiments already in progress tend to support the contention of some criminal justice analysts that random patrol has a limited effect in deterring criminals. Thus, it may be possible to take, say, ten percent or more of the patrol force off random patrol without a significant negative effect and shift those officers to activities

---

[10]*Personnel News* 40 (September 1974): 1.
[11]For those interested in reviewing the other two areas see Advisory Group on Productivity, *Opportunities for Improving Productivity.* The remainder of this section draws upon much of this report for information pertinent to police productivity.

that focus on preventing crime such as "hardening" likely crime targets (e.g., improved building security) that may provide a higher payoff.

Third, *given the uncertainties of police work, increasing productivity means increasing the probability that a given objective will be met.* The professional police officer—from the chief to the patrol officer—must continually assess the likelihood that a given event may happen, and consequently he becomes more skillful at increasing the probability that each activity will result in useful accomplishment, the more productive the overall operation will be. The clearest example of increasing the probability of achieving intended impact is having personnel assigned when and where crime is highest or calls for service are heaviest. Casual observation can indicate the "when and where" in general terms; careful analysis of available data can more accurately pinpoint probable times and places of crime occurrence, thereby significantly increasing the likelihood of placing officers where they are needed.

Fourth, *increasing productivity in the police service means making the most of the talents of police personnel.* Sworn officers are more qualified and as a result more expensive than ever before. This means that they are (or should be) capable of higher performance, that economy requires they be used more effectively, and that they expect to be treated with greater respect and intelligence. Examples of better human resource development and management abound and can be expected to become increasingly important to police managers. They may include making patrol officers responsible for following through on investigations, permitting successful police officers to avoid promotion but yet receive a higher salary and prestige as a functional specialist, and developing alternative career paths for professional police officers.

The Process of Productivity

Obtaining a greater return for the revenue dollar spent is definitely not a "one-shot" activity. It is an ongoing, long-term process that should be an integral part of police management. The path to productivity improvement includes five steps.

One: Establishment of Objectives. Ideally each police agency establishes its goals in conjunction with the political and professional leadership of its government and the people they serve. It then proceeds to identify intermediate objectives, the achievement of which will contribute to the attainment of the broader goals. Regretfully, in practice, the process of setting objectives is often reversed. Instead of determining the mission of the department and then organizing to accomplish it, more often the apparent aims of ongoing activities are described and are built into departmental goals. It is important that the different levels of objectives be systematically related and understood. (This subject is explained in a subsequent section).

Two: Systematic Assessment of Progress.   Police management needs to know how well (or poorly) it is doing in meeting its objectives. Most police chiefs, sheriffs, mayors, or county supervisors have some intuition about how their police force is doing; for example, good, better than before, about the same, not quite up to par, or, it appears that we have a problem. But, in today's police work, *effective assessment requires more precise measurement.* This is not to say that all assessment must be derived from quantified information, but we are proposing that without more reliable measures it is very difficult to determine how much better or worse a particular unit, strategy, or piece of equipment works.

Three: Search for Improved Operating Methods.   The many improved operating methods, types of equipment, and ideas being used in certain police agencies could and should be made known to, and transferred to other jurisdictions. While numerous journals, conferences, and other communications media provide information on innovative and improved methods, unfortunately some are not presented fully or clearly enough to be usable by busy police managers. Often the most valuable ideas come from within an agency, but people familiar with staff and line problems either are not asked for suggestions for improvement, or are asked to address themselves to the wrong questions. Similarly, nonpolice agencies within the same government, such as management analysis staffs, are to often ignored.

Four: Experimentation.   Most police managers are cautious, and perhaps rightly so, when it comes to doing something different. "Innovation" can result in a price many police departments cannot afford. However, neither can they afford to hold to the status quo while their surroundings change. We believe that a balanced approach to risk taking is needed. It is important to recognize that useful information often comes from the idea that *did not work* as expected. Managers must also learn how to take reasonable and controlled risks. Experiments should be designed in such a form as to make evaluation possible, to determine whether or not they are successful, as well as why and by what margin of quality or cost they are inferior or superior to existing methods, techniques, equipment, and ideas. In addition, those who eventually are to apply a new idea or tool should be involved with its development and testing.

Five: Implementation.   A new method that has been tested and proven feasible now remains to be implemented. At this point, the sense of caution and resistance to change that it might have met from agency leadership now extends throughout the department, the government, and the citizenry as well. Abating this resistance requires the participation of those groups at the experimentation stage, as well as thorough preparation, patience, cooperation, close monitoring of the innovation, and clear accountability.

EVALUATION: A Challenge

The ideal organization would be self-evaluating. It would continuously monitor its own activities so as to determine whether it was meeting its goals or even whether these goals should continue to prevail. When evaluation suggested that a change in goals or programs to achieve them was desirable, these proposals would be taken seriously by top decision-makers. They would institute the necessary changes; they would have no vested interest in continuation of current activities. Instead they would steadily pursue new alternatives to better serve the latest desired outcomes.

The ideal member of the self-evaluating organization is best conceived as a person committed to certain modes of problem solving. He believes in clarifying goals, relating them to different mechanisms of achievement, creating models (sometimes quantitative) of the relationships between inputs and outputs, seeking the best available combination. His concern is not that the organization should survive or that any specific objective be enthroned or that any particular clientele be served. Evaluative man cares that interesting problems are selected and that maximum intelligence be applied toward their solution. While he often does have strong social preferences, his central commitment is to solving problems in the right way.[12]

As increasing sums of money have been infused into criminal justice programs, the need for evaluation guidelines has become more apparent. Evaluations are used at all levels of administration of criminal justice programs, from the Law Enforcement Assistance Administration (LEAA) and State Planning Agencies (SPAs) through local criminal justice coordinating councils and individual agencies. They are useful for a number of purposes: to determine whether to continue, stop or modify a program; to determine whether local funds should be used to support the program after its experimental phase; or to decide whether the program should be promoted in other jurisdictions. Information obtained from evaluations can lead to

---

[12]Aaron Wildavsky, "Evaluation As An Organizational Problem" (Paper delivered at the American Society of Public Administration Convention, New York, March 24, 1972), p. 1.

general principles and guidelines to assist local administrators in setting their priorities for testing and implementing new programs.[13]

When our attention was directed in the mid–1960s to crime as a great social ill, it seemed natural to most of us to question the vitality of the criminal justice system (CJS), and in particular the police. The reported deficiencies primarily centered on either an absence of sufficient resources, or their inadequacy, or both. It seemed reasonable, therefore, to furnish the police, courts, and corrections agencies with additional resources to work with. So municipal, county, and state budgets for criminal justice functions and especially the police have risen, and most important, new federal agencies were created—the most prominent being the Law Enforcement Assistance Administration (LEAA) with funds to massively and rapidly inject into our CJS. As a consequence, now and in the coming years, police and sheriffs departments, along with other elements of the CJS will be spending increased millions of dollars to reduce crime.[14] Indeed we find such funding support and increased attention to crime problems has encouraged local law enforcement agencies to initiate action-oriented programs which could not have been mounted without federal assistance. Thus, innovations have been and are being tested in the state and local agencies comprising the CJS, in all types of their activity.

Basically, this section describes a methodology for planning and evaluating police programs. The term evaluation is defined as "the process of determining the value or amount of success in achieving a predetermined objective. It includes at least the following steps: Formulation of the objective, identification of the proper criteria to be used in measuring success, determination and explanation of the degree of success, recommendations for further program activity."[15] An elaboration of this definition will follow. In turn, it will explicate the elements of each of these steps, the problems in carrying them out, and the way they relate to the context of police programs. It is concerned with police programs, especially those with relatively short-term results. You will find the concepts discussed are not new; many of the problems and procedures have

[13]Michael D. Maltz, *Evaluation of Crime Control Programs* (Washington, D.C.: U.S. Government Printing Office, 1972), p. 1.

[14]This section is the result of an eclectric process whereby numerous resources were drawn upon. Prime among the many were two in particular: Maltz, *Evaluation of Crime Control Programs*, and Ellen Albright et al., *Criminal Justice Research: Evaluation in Criminal Justice Programs, Guidelines and Examples* (Washington, D.C.: U.S. Government Printing Office, 1973).

[15]Edward A. Suchman, *Evaluative Research* (New York: Russell Sage Foundation, 1967), p. 28.

been discussed by others in different contexts. What "newness" there is resides in the fact that they are, or can, and should be applied to police programs.

The guidelines proposed herein are directed primarily at two *user* audiences. First, they are designed to give the evaluative researcher an understanding of the characteristics of police operations and data that can affect evaluations. Second, they should give the police manager an insight into the intricacies, requirements, and problems of evaluations, without getting too involved in technical and statistical matters. Further, it is noted that this section contains information and recommendations on what is to be either counted or measured during the evaluation process.

Finally, we can readily see that the police, perhaps more than any other public agency today, are experimenting with a variety of new technologies, techniques, and theories. It is up to each agency that implements a program to develop the evaluative information on how and how well it worked. It is apparent that the potential value of each program will not be exposed if the program is not evaluated or if its evaluation is kept isolated from similar evaluations in other jurisdictions. It is through the evaluative process that you and I can generate reliable answers to the question "What are we accomplishing with our money and efforts?" Hence, we observe questions about effectiveness—and the money with which to try to answer them—coming more and more frequently from each of hundreds of funding and planning agencies. Coincidentally, those who are supplying funds are not the only ones concerned with the question of effectiveness. On the contrary, we see that the public, academicians and the media are inquiring as to what is being achieved by the police in its pursuit of crime reduction. Of equal importance:

> The police themselves are asking more and more questions. And not just because they are being pressed by others, although that is a fact to which they are responding, but because they themselves need and want to know some answers. Why are so many supposedly smart people telling us to do so many conflicting things? If people think we ought to do this job, why don't they support us when we try? Maybe we should worry less about improving our efficiency and more about whether we're doing the right things? But how do we know that any particular new thing we might want to do would make people fear crime less, or help us more, or be more satisfied with our service? How would we know which of the things we now do could be stopped without affecting crime, or fear? If we don't know that, how do we know it would be wise or safe to change? How do we find these things out without taking reckless and foolish risks? Who can help us?

An increasing number of police are working hard on those last two questions as they are keys to all others. To the first of these, police leaders are saying: Let's try it out and see. Let's test it. We'll try it for a while and keep it, if it works. We'll try it in one area first and then adopt it department-wide, if it works. What they are saying isn't new, but in today's setting, with all these pressures to *know* what we're doing and what works, it takes on a new meaning. It means experiment and measure. We know it's tough, they say, but it's the way to go.[16]

Deficiencies In Program Evaluation

We find that, in general, the fundamental reason for performing an evaluation is to *assist* in making the best decision. Plainly, police agencies need to determine which programs are effective, so they will know which should be continued or modified. Similarly, a criminal justice planning and funding agency must determine whether the program should be supported after the evaluative phase. Such an agency must, in turn, determine the best way to allocate our money among competing problem areas, and among different programs focused on the same problem area. Many of the past evaluations, we have learned of late, were inadequate for these purposes. Worse yet, in many instances there were not any evaluations conducted. There are many reasons for no or malapropos evaluations. First in such cases the agency may feel that the evaluation is superfluous—another nonsensical bureaucratic demand, thus not requiring serious consideration. Second, many evaluations are based on insufficient data sources. It is assumed by many of us that since police records are extensive they must also be adequate; that somewhere within the vast files are all of the right data necessary for the evaluation. When these are not found, as is typical, the evaluator tends to lean on the existing data, rather than search for more pertinent information. Third, the evaluations are overtly ignored and rejected. Fourth, there is at times a lack of expertise in those assigned to perform the evaluation. The rapidly increasing budgets of our police agencies, joined with the decline of funding in other sectors of government, has brought about a surge of individuals and firms ready to take on such work, but with inadequate background in evaluating police activities. Although experienced in performing research and conducting projects, we find that most have little knowledge of peculiarities of our police agencies. Conversely, many of the evaluations are performed by practitioners in police agencies who

[16]Joseph H. Lewis, *Evaluation of Experiments in Policing: How Do You Begin?* (Washington, D.C.: The Police Foundation, 1972), p. 4.

have little training in program evaluations. (While these evaluations may be weak in methodology and may have limited validity, they at least express an understanding of the problem!)

The sections that follow provide recommended corrective action relative to the problem areas described above. The proposed guidelines are intended as a general "cookbook" of evaluations that can be used by an evaluator turning to the appropriate page and following the recipe. It will provide a framework for conducting evaluations, but not all specific kinds or on all specific levels of sophistication. Finally, regardless of the extent of the evaluation performed, we should remain alert to the potential shortcomings of the evaluation in order to avoid reaching unsubstantiated conclusions and, as a consequence, making *expensive mistakes*.

EVALUATION PREPLANNING: Preliminary Considerations

Types of Evaluation

The type of evaluation used most often has its basis in social science research.[17] Primarily, this theory seeks to determine the relationship between two or more variables. For example, if we manipulate the independent variable (the dosage of a drug, let us say), the effect on the dependent variable (pulse rate) is determined, while all other variables and conditions (food intake, mobility) are held constant, constrained, or otherwise accounted for. It is assumed that the dependent variable does not influence the independent variable. This assumption on our part is true in determining the effect of a drug on a population of white mice. However, it is by far more complex in determining the impact of, say, "team policing" on crime. We can design an evaluation plan in the former case in a straightforward manner. The number of mice can be determined to the degree of accuracy (or level of confidence) desired. Experimental and control samples, both drawn from a population with known characteristics, are given the drug and a placebo, respectively; or many experimental samples may be used to determine the effect of different dosages of the drug. The outcome of the experiment on each mouse is determined, and statistical tests are given the data to determine the outcome.

Although more sophisticated in form, the same model can be used in evaluations of complex police programs. Experimental groups (team

---

[17]There are many excellent texts devoted to an explication of social scientific theories and methodologies. One particularly commended to the attention of the interested reader is Fred M. Kerlinger, *Foundations of Behavioral Science Research* (New York: Holt, Rinehart and Winston, Inc., 1973).

units) and control groups (traditional units) can be selected and observed over a given period of time by the researchers or by those taught by the researchers. We can analyze the results for their statistical significance. However, because we are dealing with human subjects, complications arise. The degree of success may have nothing to do with the efficacy of the program, but only with the way it was introduced or with the personal predilections of the officers involved.

In a police program, we may determine it impossible to categorically classify variables as dependent and independent, since they may affect and be affected by each other. Furthermore, because of the difficulty in ascertaining why we behave the way they do, a number of intervening variables may go undetected. Paradoxically, police programs designed to reduce crime may have their most direct effect on the behavior of the general public toward the police, which in turn affects the crime rate.

Evaluations are not always, nor should they be, restricted to our analysis of objective crime data; they can also include subjective considerations and perceptions.[18] These subjective evaluations can be of major benefit to us in explicating statistical analyses of the results of the program. They are especially helpful in assessing why and how a program worked, and whether a statistical figure is actually evidence that the program was successful. Interviews of participating police agency personnel and residents of the area in which the program is constructed are usually used to furnish this data. They can give the evaluator fresh insight into the actual program operation.

Essentially there are two evaluation types, referred to as "internal" and "external" evaluations. The words "internal" or "external" refer to whether the evaluation is conducted of the program's means or its ends. An internal evaluation of a crime prevention program involving the use of, for example, school resource officers would include an analysis of juvenile delinquency and *how* the program was effective in preventing juvenile crime, or *why* it was successful in one area and not in another. The external evaluation would focus only on the effectiveness of the program in achieving its ends; i.e., reducing juvenile crime rates or solving crimes, not on how or why or the conditions under which the results were achieved.[19]

---

[18]There are numerous research methods, such as projective techniques, that lack objectivity but are most useful in discovering or confirming the existence of predicted relationships among the research variables. An outstanding book on this subject is Eugene J. Webb et al., *Unobtrusive Measures* (Chicago, Ill.: Rand McNally & Company, 1966).

[19]The documents by the National Advisory Commission on Criminal Justice Standards and Goals make repeated mention of the importance of evaluation. For example, note the sections devoted to this subject in The National Advisory Commission on Criminal Justice Standards and Goals, *Criminal Justice System* (Washington, D.C.: U.S. Government Printing Office, 1973).

Program Design as it Relates to Evaluation

Connecting program activities to final outcomes is not an easy task. Statistics cannot substitute for a logical connection between the effect produced and the conditions which produced it. For example, after observing the recent increase in *police manpower* concurrent with the increase in *crime rates,* we could well conclude that the former caused the latter. Discovering the actual relationships between cause and effect in crime prevention programs is made n ore frustrating by the elusive nature of the population being "treated": the offenders. We cannot develop reliable statistics on the effect of the program on their behavior. Ironically, a program may deter half of the offenders from committing crime while it motivates the other half into becoming more criminally active. A causal connection may be inferred if, say, a reduction in the crime rate is accompanied by an increase in clearances. Even this inference should be verified by determining how the program contributed to the arrests. The reasons for believing that "Program *A* caused Result *B*" should be specified. Saying, "I don't know how it worked, but it worked and that's all that matters," may satisfy the local administrator for a short time, but it will be of no use in estimating the usefulness of the program under changed circumstances of time, place, or tactics.[20]

In most instances where a police program has been implemented a bureaucratic thread does exist which implies the evaluation design for the overall program. This design should be well in mind before the program is activated. The following outline can be used, in most cases, *to link the evaluation design to the operational problem being addressed.*

> *What is the crime problem addressed*—its nature, its extent and importance, statistics relating to its occurrence, existing information about offender characteristics and tactics which affect the type of program proposed.
>
> *What are the present operations*—how the problem is currently approached, deficiencies in the method.
>
> *What are the program operations*—how the program will operate, how the present deficiencies will be eliminated by the program, anticipated reactions of offenders to the program, how these reactions will affect the program.

---

[20]Possibly two of the most provocative program designs and evaluation to be reported during the 1970s are discussed in the article by Richard Chackerian, "Police Professionalism and Citizen Evaluation: A Preliminary Look" *Public Administration Review* 34 (March-April 1974): 141–48; and *The Kansas City Prevention Patrol Experiment: A Summary Report* (Washington, D.C.: The Police Foundation, 1974). Of special interest are a series of articles critiquing the Kansas City report. See *The Police Chief* 42 (June 1975): 20–45.

What are the evaluative data—sources of required data and their suffi-
ciency, problems in using these data sources, ways in which data reliability may be affected, steps taken to insure uniform data quality and
reliability.

What are the anticipated impasses—problems which might occur, assumptions which have not been verified, conditions which may change.

In some cases it is very difficult for us to explain the logical connection between the problem and the proposed solution—an operational
program. This is especially true when dealing with intuitive assumptions
on the part of experienced police officers about the behavior of potential
offenders and their probable reactions to new programs. "Gut feelings"
are difficult to translate into cold logic yet most important for us to comprehend, allow for, and assess. The final report of the program evaluation
must contain an analysis of this a priori justification of the program. In
summary, then, an operational program design must contain a justification for its implementation (the problem), and a recommended means for
its evaluation.

Choice of Evaluator

As you recall, evaluation considerations related to the choice of a evaluator were mentioned earlier—lack of familiarity with police procedures
on the part of outside evaluators, lack of research expertise by in-house
evaluators. An associated issue is the nature of the relationship between
the evaluator and the program being evaluated, and between the evaluator and the agency conducting the program. However, *the* most important determinants of the objectivity of the evaluation is the attitude of
the heads of the police agency conducting the program. Most will want
an objective evaluation of the program, a few may feel threatened and
want the program to be proved a success regardless of its merits. In the
latter case the evaluation will be of questionable value. On the other
hand, the program evaluator may have preconceived notions about the
merit of the program that would distort his evaluation. He may be a
fervid proponent of the program, or of a competing one. His professional
pride may be affected by the outcome. These factors do not necessarily
preclude unbiased evaluations. However, if they are not compensated
for by the evaluator, the findings may be open to question despite their
validity and reliability.

An outside evaluator is usually considered more impartial than one
selected from within the agency. The outsider does not (normally) have
prior prejudices based on long association with the agency, and can
judge the program on its merits. An evaluation performed by in-house
personnel is (usually) not free of these preconceptions nor free of the

influence of the agency administrators. Outside evaluators are not without their disadvantages. They start without sufficient knowledge of the agency's workings; time must be spent getting them to a point where they can contribute to the evaluation. We find that a "symbiotic" relationship can develop between an agency and an outside evaluator dependent on funds from the agency, in which objectivity is discarded in the interest of maintaining a mutually supportive relationship. Finally, one of the primary responsibilities of a police manager is to evaluate the efforts of his agency. Hence, the agency should develop expertise in this area. If expertise is lacking in the agency, consultants should be retained with the requisite qualifications.

Data Sufficiency and Reliability

The evaluation tactics we are recommending at this time cannot be fulfilled unless sufficient data are developed during the program evaluation. These data will allow an assessment of the amount of resources expended in the program, and how *efficiently* and *effectively* these resources were used. They include the types of personnel assigned to the program, the number of man-hours of each actually spent on the program, the type and cost of special equipment and other inputs employed in the program, and the way each of these resource elements were used. Yet, another data-related problem concerns the ability of the program personnel. For example, the more competent police officers may be pulled off an experimental program to deal with an emergency situation, to be replaced by fewer or less competent officers. (These personnel shifts must be documented in the evaluation report.) Additionally, an effort should be made to monitor the data collected for the evaluation on a continual basis, to make sure that the data is reliable and valid throughout the evaluation.[21]

EVALUATION PLANNING: Programmatic Steps

Evaluation planning provides police program managers with information for (1) assessing the potential value of projects and programs, and (2) blueprinting the evaluation efforts and requirements. Evaluation planning consists of the following five steps:

[21]Most commercial businesses submit their books to external audit as a quality control check on their own bookkeeping. We believe that police managers should also consider this practice, for routine operations as well as for the evaluation of special programs. In support of this proposition, see the monograph by Peter B. Bloch and Cyrus Ulberg, *Auditing Clearance Rates* (Washington, D.C.: The Police Foundation, 1974).

1. Quantify established goals and objectives.
2. Establish quantified goal/objective relationship.
3. Identify evaluation measures.
4. Determine data needs.
5. Determine methods of analysis.

   Let us examine each step more closely.

Quantify Goals and Objectives

The first step for those of us involved in evaluation is to quantify the program goals and project objectives. (Remember that a program such as crime prevention is typically comprised of a set of projects which are more precise in nature.) We should quantify the goals and objectives in terms of a measureable level or levels of achievement. For example, a quantified program goal and two possible project objectives for the program and projects could be as follows:

> Program goal—reduce auto thefts by twenty percent in two years.
> Project (1) objective—identify the major dealers in handling stolen automobiles in three months.
> Project (2) objective—increase the arrest rate of criminal offenders that steal automobiles by ten percent in one year.

Establish Goal/Objective Relationships

The second step is for us to show, whenever possible, the quantifiable relationship between (1) the project objectives, and (2) the program goals. The purpose of this step is to supply the way for assessing the contribution of an individual project to a program goal and an individual program to the total mission of the police agency. Crime statistics, special studies, reports, and any other items that would reveal a relationship should be used.

To illustrate the construction of a quantifiable relationship between the police mission and a program goal, consider that the police, courts, prosecution, defense attorneys and other elements of the law enforcement and CJS of a city perceive that an estimated fifty percent of the city's stranger-to-stranger crime and burglary are drug related (.50 × 8000 incidents/year = 4000 incidents/year). Furthermore, suppose that these perceptions are confirmed by studies and statistics from other similar cities. If the drug program goal of habilitating 400 known drug abusers in two years was met, then crime and burglary would be reduced. The amount of the reduction would depend on the number of habilitated drug abusers who were involved in crime and burglary and the per capita number of criminal incidents. For example, if eighty percent of the habilitated drug abusers committed an average of two crimes and/or burglaries per person (.80 × 2 incident/abuser × 400 abusers = 640 incidents), then meeting the program goal would reduce such crime by four percent (320 incidents/year ÷ 8000 incidents/year) and represent an eighty percent (604 ÷ .05) contribution toward meeting the National Impact Goal.

Next, to illustrate the construction of a quantified relationship between a program goal and a project objective assume a survey of methadone maintenance treatment centers showed that such treatment is fifty-five percent effective (that is, forty-five percent of those treated would continue to use heroin). These statistics indicate that if 500 of the city's heroin abusers were to receive methadone maintenance treatment, then 275 (500 × .55 = 275) of the city's drug abusers would be habilitated. The result is that Project 1 would contribute approximately sixty-nine percent (275 ÷ 400) towards the achievement of the program goal. We may find that these relationships are not as easily formulated as suggested by the drug project/program illustrations. For example, the relationships are predicated upon the identification of drug abusers (a) who are known to the authorities, (b) who are also criminals, and (c) who are criminals primarily to support their drug habit. These data may not be readily available.

Evaluation Measures

The third planning step is to develop evaluation measures for each project and program. Two types of measures are used for assessing levels of achievement: measures of efficiency and measures of effectiveness. Measures of efficiency indicate how well a program is executed in accordance with its plan—in terms of time, allocation of manpower and equipment, program activities, and funds expended. Examples of efficiency measures are (1) average response time to reach the scene of a crime (e.g., a command and control program), and (2) the allocation of resources for the performance of program activities vis-à-vis the results attained (i.e, cost/benefit considerations). We find that measures of effectiveness, on the other hand, are deployed to evaluate the impact of program activities upon the target problem. They are intended to be "end" rather than "means" oriented. That is, they relate to what is ultimately desired, not the way in which it is attained. Examples of effectiveness measures are rates which expose the incidence of target crimes or recidivism. Significantly, we believe that the primary emphasis should be on using measures of effectiveness.

Data Needs

The fourth step is, in essence, comprised of three subroutines each of which is critical to the reliability of the evaluation design. In order of discussion they are data element identification, data element definition, and reporting systems specification. Our first consideration should be that of data element identification. For individual projects and programs the data requirements and constraints will be identified by the agency's unit. Additional data elements may be expressed by other agencies' national evaluations of selected projects and programs. These data elements can be either quantitative or qualitative in value (e.g., crime statistics or a description of a project's environment). The explicit definition of data elements is the second item that must be considered, especially when these elements are (1) common to several projects and programs and/or (2) to be used in the other jurisdictions, and (3) difficult to collect, process, or control.

Third and finally, we must specify how and when the data will be reported to the evaluators. Before we can do this several important items must be identified. These are:

> The organizations involved in gathering and receiving the data
> The sequence of the data flow
> The data frequency requirements

The organizations involved in a single reporting system are often comprised of several local agencies, e.g., police department, the regional planning unit, the state planning agency, the state attorney general, LEAA, and other branches of the federal government. Each of these organizations may have different requirements as to when the data are needed. For example, we find that data could be collected daily by the local agency, reported monthly to the regional planning unit, and quarterly to LEAA. Hence, agreements between organizations may be needed to secure the required data. If the data were required in one form but were being collected in another, procedural changes will have to be negotiated.

Methods of Analysis

The last planning step is to select the analytical methods that are to be used for evaluation and to establish the management procedures needed to execute the analysis. The selection of an analytical method is highly dependent on each project and program. It is highly unlikely that one method of analysis will accommodate all projects and programs since the projects and programs typically vary over a number of dimensions.

Data analysis is a multiphased function. We find that it is a process that is to be performed frequently throughout the project or program evaluation period. Key points for us to consider are:

> It is a good practice to schedule an evaluation analysis on a periodic basis. In this way, project or program process can be continually appraised for management monitoring and directing purposes.
>
> The natural implementation of the project or program itself may generate certain milestones. Evaluation analysis should be performed at these natural review points to assess the past performance and determine the future direction of the project or program.
>
> Critical events both within and outside of the project or program should generate an evaluation analysis, e.g., the starting of a non–Impact Program project (directed toward the same target population as an Impact Program project) that also can reduce stranger-to-stranger crime and burglary. The purpose of this analysis is to establish a new reference point for future project and program analysis.
>
> To determine the outcome of the project or program there should be an analysis at its completion.

There are four primary purposes for analysis, each of which is discussed below.

1. Success level determination. We need to ascertain the degree of project or program success (i.e., *effectiveness*) in meeting objectives or goals during their implementation and at their conclusion. Interim success levels, therefore, should be stated in evaluation components, as well as overall effectiveness measures.

2. Management needs for monitoring and direction. Program/project management must be provided with the information needed to make decisions regarding problems in program implementation, modification and redirection, and continuation:

> *How should problems in implementation be identified and resolved?* The evaluation component should ideally contain a list of problems that may develop during implementation and the method that is planned for their resolution.
>
> *When and how should a project or program be modified or redirected?* The conditions under which we find that a project or program may need to be modified should be spelled out as part of the evaluation component. A discussion of the evaluation measures to be used and how the project or program may be changed also should be included. An essential ingredient of any evaluation design is to describe the possible courses of action that may be initiated if project objectives or program goals are not being achieved.

When should the question of project or program continuation be considered? The evaluation component should contain a discussion of how the results of the analysis will be used to determine project or program continuation. Continuation is of concern when project/program success levels fall outside acceptable tolerances, when interim evaluation reports failure at the end of the implementation period, or whenever subjective judgment indicates the anticipated impact goals will not be met. In the evaluation component, all three of the above questions should be resolved within the context of the particular project or program, with specific *milestones* indicated when the question of continuation will be considered.

3. Contribution to the next level of evaluation. We must assess the contribution made by projects to programs and by programs to the overall police mission. (This use of evaluation satisfies the requirement to measure the actual contribution discussed under *Establish Goal/Objective Relationship.*)

4. Diagnostic. Here we focus our attention on the reasons for the level of success achieved, and encompasses a quantitative analysis of the implementation and results of projects and programs. In addition, diagnostic evaluation of programs requires of us the measuring of the relative contributions of each of its constituent projects. This determination calls for us to analyze the project results within programs, how well each achieved its objectives and the effect on program success.

Evaluation Monitoring

Quite simply, the monitoring of an evaluation effort denotes a "quality control" function whereby the integrity of the function described above is sustained throughout the program and the composite projects. Program monitoring is best operationalized at the moment that the program/project is implemented. Usually it entails the following tasks:

On-site observations
Time-triggered reporting
Exception-to-the-norm (event-triggered) reporting
As determined to be necessary
Conference sessions
Milestone (progress) review

Monitoring is, most logically, custom-fitted to the evaluation strategy. And, as mentioned earlier, the evaluation strategy is best tailored to the program under scrutiny. We can look at monitoring as being much like driving an automobile. One driver arrives at his destination without any dents in the fenders of his vehicle. Another arrives with numerous scratches and dents in the car. Relating the simile to evaluation and the monitoring of evaluation, we can infer that the first driver engaged in constant and alert monitoring while the latter did not.

In Conclusion

We have now covered some general evaluation principles. And, we have traced and postulated the processes which should be followed in the evaluation of police programs, from the program's initial conceptualization to its transfer from limited experimental basis to a full-scale operational mode. As expected, deficiencies in the available data present significant problems in any evaluations design, but they *are not insurmountable.* Monitoring the data quality, more careful analysis of the data, and the collection of additional data will assist in minimizing the problems. However, we should plan these steps from the beginning of the program to achieve maximum benefits. In performing an evaluation it is important to maintain strong liaison with the groups within the police agency that are affected by the program. This will assist us in discovering problems while they are still incipient, and will ease the transition of the program from the experimental phase to the operational phase and to other governmental jurisdictions. Finally, the theories we initially used to justify the program should be tested and verified during the course of the evaluation. In order to promote the greatest benefit, the tools of evaluative research should be applied realistically with due recognition of the unique characteristics of police program evaluations.

MEASUREMENT: A Technique

> *Measures now used by police tend to be internally rather than externally generated; are used more to punish failure rather than to reward success; are used for inter-individual rather than inter-unit comparisons; ask how much and not how well; tend to be situationally specific rather than dealing with generalized competence (such as how well a man relates to the public or uses force) and when situationally specific refer to law enforcement rather than community service or order maintenance, and when not situationally specific involve bureaucratic standards that are often related only indirectly to actual police work.*[22]

The Government is very keen on amassing statistics. They collect them, add them, refer them to the nth power, take the cube root

[22]Gary T. Marx, "Alternative Measures of Police Performance" (Paper delivered at the American Sociological Association Convention, New York, 1973), p. 7.

and prepare wonderful diagrams. But you must never forget that everyone of these figures comes in the first instance from the . . . (village watchman), who just puts down what he damn pleases.[23]

The measurement of police services is definitely not new; in fact, it is probably more familiar to police managers than to many other state and local government officials.[24] Nevertheless, we believe that most police managers would concur that many of the measures currently being applied to police services do not provide information they need to help them evaluate and improve operations. We begin this section with a review of the deficiencies inherent in existing measures. Next, we examine existing and potential data sources that are helpful in providing an enhanced basis for measuring productivity. Finally we will describe two efforts that can be labeled "service analysis."

Limitations Of Current Police Measures

The most common data used today for assessing overall police performance are crime rates—such as compiled in the *Uniform Crime Reports (UCR)* published annually by the Federal Bureau of Investigation.[25] However, because the incidence of crime is a result of many factors unrelated to police activity, crime rates alone provide a very poor measure of police performance. As a consequence, police managers repeatedly voice a need for other measures that more accurately report the amount and type of police activities. The *UCR* has other deficiencies as a police management tool. The most critical of these is the fact that the *UCR* is not a totally reliable reflection of crime. The *UCR* documents only *reported* crime, which, as several "victimization" surveys have shown, is only a fraction of crime actually committed.

Recent surveys of victimization have shown that reported crimes may represent, in some jurisdictions, as little as twenty-five percent, and rarely

---

[23]Sir Josia Stamp. *Some Economic Factors in Modern Life,* (London: P.S. King and Son, Ltd., 1929), p. 258.

[24]For a brief discussion of the history and current trends in local government measurement and productivity see the article by George P. Barbour, Jr. "Measuring Local Government Productivity," in *The Municipal Year Book—1973*. (Washington, D.C.: International City Management Association, 1973), pp. 38–46.

[25]The full title of the latest *UCR* dated August 1974, is *Crime in the United States, 1973—Uniform Crime Reports* (Washington, D.C.: U.S. Government Printing Office). Since it was first published in 1930, the *UCR* has been the only nationwide data source on crimes committed throughout the United States. The report has been improved over the years by refinements in data collection, comparison, and dissemination, and it will undoubtedly continue to be used in the future as an indication of crime rates and police performance.

more than seventy-five percent, of the actual incidence of crime. One reason many types of crime go unreported is the victim's fear of embarrassment, of family or personal involvement, or of retaliation on the part of the offender. In some cases victims failed to report crimes because of lack of confidence in the police. Some hope is offered to us for getting more accurate crime data through victimization surveys (confidential and detailed surveys of scientifically selected samples representative of the population as a whole to detect the true number of crime victims). Scientifically and consistently administered, victimization surveys may provide new measures for assessing crime-control and crime-prevention programs.[26] They may reveal not only the actual incidence of crime but also the reasons why crimes were not reported and the victims' attitudes toward the police and police service. Unfortunately victimization surveys are expensive if conducted properly, primarily because a large sample is needed before the data are valid. Additionally, in the FBI's crime reporting program, data are not published on both offenses and arrests for all categories of crime. The *UCR* identifies "Index crimes," which include the major crimes of murder, forcible rape, robbery, aggravated assault, burglary, larceny of fifty dollars and over in value, and auto theft. It then groups offenses into two categories: "Part I" offenses, which include the Index crimes, and "Part II" offenses, which, while they are lesser crimes, consume much of every police department's time and effort. The *UCR* reports both offense and arrest information for "Part II" offenses. The distinction between major and minor offenses is all the more a problem since many police agencies do not adhere strictly to *UCR* definitions. Some, for example, classify a burglary attempt as a malicious destruction of property, thus demoting it to a "Part II" offense.

In addition to the data contained in the *UCR*, there are several other types of data upon which the police generally rely to help them monitor their workload and evaluate their performance, such as:

> Numbers of arrests by crime category.
> The clearance rate. (As used in the *UCR*, police "clear" a crime when they have identified the offender, have sufficient evidence to charge him, and actually take him into custody. The arrest of one person can clear several crimes, or several persons may be arrested in the process of clearing one crime.)
> The exceptional clearance rate. (Once again using the *UCR* definition, crime solutions are recorded in exceptional instances when some element beyond police control precludes the placing of formal charges against the offender, such as when the victim refuses to prosecute after the

[26]See Anthony G. Turner, "Victimization Surveying—Its History, Uses, and Limitations," Appendix A of National Advisory Commission, *Criminal Justice System*.

offender is identified, or local prosecution is declined because the subject is being prosecuted elsewhere for a crime committed in another
jurisdiction.)

Complaints received from the public about the department or about
specific actions by officers.

Activity measures (called-for services) of field operations.

Workload measures of clerical functions (e.g., number of additions per
month to the fingerprint files).

All of the above data are useful, but they are limited in the amount
and quality of information they supply. One reason that existing data
are not put to better use is that the police mission is multifaceted. The
specific objectives of the force are not always expressed. Nor is it always
definite what some police activities are contributing, or how they relate
to broader department goals. It is difficult for us to know what to measure! Therefore, the initial step to improved measurement is to recognize how the various functions of police work relate to the broader mission of the agency and, in turn, to the goals of state and local government.

Improving the Measurement of Police Services

We find that the measurement of police activities, as is true for most
government organizations, is obscured by the absence of goals and objectives that are easily quantifiable. While there may be consensus on the
broad goals of the police force, we observe that the specific activities that
appropriately fall under the purview of a police agency are subject to
debate.[27]

The Purview of Police Management

Among the variety of services a police agency delivers are the following:

Criminal justice, which includes, depending upon one's definition, the
courts, correctional institutions, probation, parole, and many other

---

[27]Currently one finds two highly reputed sources that deal with police goals and
standards: (1) the National Advisory Commission on Criminal Justice Standards and
Goals, and (2) the American Bar Association. In regard to the latter, the American
Bar Association's Project on Standards for Criminal Justice (which was also approved
by the executive committee of the International Association of Chiefs of Police) ranges
from such general goals as safeguarding freedom and developing a reputation for
fairness, civility, and integrity, to more specific goals such as identifying and apprehending offenders and facilitating the movement of people and vehicles. The Advisory
Group did not attempt to define the overall police goals and functions. Rather, it
decided to focus its attention on selected activities which are of top concern to police
chiefs. The debate over proper police goals no doubt will, and should continue. And
efforts to measure police activity must be attentive to the changing perception of police
responsibilities.

public and private agencies concerned with crime and the criminal offender.

Maintenance of public order.

Emergency response, for fire, accidents, natural disaster, medical emergencies, etc.

Community relations, which affects the community's feeling of confidence in or alienation from the government.

Nonemergency general services. Police are called upon for a variety of non-crime-related tasks which do not fall under the responsibility of any other public agency, or which, because of the twenty-four-hour nature of police duty, befall them when other agencies are closed. These may range from directing a stranger to a historical landmark, to registering bicycles, or to removing the dog manure from a public park.

The relative amount of time and resources a police agency devotes to meeting responsibilities within each of these delivery categories naturally varies from community to community.

Measurement to Underpin Management

Keep in mind that the principal purpose of measurement is to provide sufficiently precise productivity data to enable police managers to: (1) evaluate their agency's performance; (2) identify and diagnose problem areas; and (3) design solutions. But measurement has still other values. For example, measures frequently stimulate constructive thinking—e.g., measurement of crime deterrence requires in-depth analysis of the nature of deterrence—thus increasing the understanding of police activity. Measurement also may serve as a device for linking one activity to another, or one part of the management process to another—e.g., relating resources to output. At the same time measurement per se is not a panacea. In that, it is not a substitute for sound professional judgment; it is meant to assist the manager, *not dictate action to him*. Furthermore, *we emphasize that care must be taken to guard against measures that provoke negative activity*. To use a familiar example, measuring a police officer solely on the basis of arrests made without considering whether or not the arrests are valid, can reward the apprehension of innocent people. Nor should blind acceptance of measures result in meaningless and costly measurement activity. Some measures may require data gathering that is more expensive than its value would justify and thus should be avoided.

There are many types of measures, and as many ways to describe them as analysts have time to devise. Given the state of the art of measuring public services, we need to be concerned with but a few basic distinctions. There are two fundamental types of measures that may be used separately or in combination to provide useful information. They are measures of results (or output) and measures of resources used (or input). Police departments, to date, have been more concerned with measures of resources than with measures of results.[28] The budget gives the most basic measures of what resources are being used for what activities. Resource use might also be measured in terms of man-time, or units of equipment. In turn, results are generally more difficult to define and measure. Traditionally, city and county police agencies have relied upon easy-to-quantify results such as miles driven by a patrol vehicle. Such measures (often referred to as workload) have some use as indicators of intermediate results, but they clearly do not provide an adequate assessment of whether higher level objectives are being met. *A comparison between "results achieved" and "results intended" gives us a simple measure of an agency's effectiveness.*

We can compare result and resource measures in order to indicate productivity. A productivity measure indicates the cost (in money, men, and/or equipment) of accomplishing a given result. You should note that where the results of a smaller division are meaningless to overall departmental goals, the productivity of that division may increase (it gets more results per unit of resource) but with no improvement in the department's overall productivity. Thus, it is essential that *the measurement of individual activities or organization components always be evaluated in the context of overall agency goals and performance.*

Additional Data Sources

We propose that the data currently being collected, processed, and analyzed should be added other categories of information. Examples of such data are presented in tables 10–1 and 10–2.

Gary T. Marx perceptively and convincingly offers three alternative indicators of an agency's performance: (1) how well force is used, (2) the quality of service delivered, and (3) citizens attitudes and behavior. In regard to the first indicator he writes:

> From considering the nature of the arrest, the actions of the person arrested, and the context, the seriousness of the threat to police and others, alternatives available to the use of force, the amount of force used by police and extent of injury and damage, judgments could be reached about how well force was used. Given the complexity of most situations and difficulties of judgment, evaluations of individuals (except in extreme cases) would be based on a number of police-citizen encounters over a period of time, such as each six months.

---

[28]For instance, see Walter Pudinski, "Management by Results in the California Highway Patrol," *Journal of California Law Enforcement* 8 (April 1974): 194–99.

TABLE 10–1

Measurements for Basic Productivity Measurement System,
Police Crime Control

A. Currently available*
   1. Crime rates for reported crimes
   2. Clearance rates relative to reported crimes
   3. Arrests per police department employee and per dollar†
   4. Clearance per police department employee and per dollar†
   5. Population served per police employee and per dollar†

B. Requiring significant additional data gathering*
   1. Crime rates including estimates of unreported crimes from victimization studies
   2. Clearance rates based on victimization studies
   3. Percent of arrests that lead to convictions
   4. Percent of arrests that "survive" preliminary hearings in courts of limited jurisdiction
   5. Average response times for calls for service
   6. Percent of crimes cleared in less than "X" days
   7. Percent of population indicating a lack of feeling of security
   8. Percent of population expressing dissatisfaction with police services

*These (except for A-5, B-7, and B-8) should be disaggregated by type of crime. We recommend initial attention on index crimes.
†Resource inputs should to the extent possible be developed to exclude noncrime control functions such as traffic control.

Source: *Municipal Year Book 1973* (Washington, D.C.: International City Management Association, 1973), p. 39.

Some of the actions taken by prosecutors and the courts can also be seen as rough measures of the extent of police conformity to law or thoroughness of preparation in arrest situations. These include the proportion of those arrested who are charged, proportion of cases actually coming to trial, and those dismissed as a result of the exclusionary rule, entrapment, or inadequate preparation.[29]

Next, concerning emergency services,

Evaluation efforts could be directed at how well the symptoms of the problem in the immediate situation were handled. This would include things such as the quality of the inter-action with citizens, expressed interest in the persons' problems, as well as whether assaults and arrests were avoided. *Some of this information might be gathered*

[29]Marx "Alternative Measures," p. 13.

TABLE 10–2

Minimum Data Requirements for Suggested Police
Productivity Measures

Data	Source*	Generally currently available	Basic data often available but some modifications needed	Requiring significant additional data gathering
Crime control effectiveness-related data†				
1. Annual number of reported index crimes (homicide, rape, burglary, robbery, auto theft, aggravated assault, larceny above $50, and total)	UCR	X		
2. Annual clearance data on each index crime and in total	UCR	X		
3. Estimates of "true" crime rates including unreported crime	Victimization survey			X
4. Estimates of true clearance rates for index crimes including unreported crimes	Victimization survey			X
5. Annual arrests for each index crime	UCR	X		
6. Annual adult convictions associated with each index crime	UCR		X	
7. Arrests for index crimes that pass preliminary hearing in court of limited jurisdiction	Court records		X	
8. Number of days between report of incident and clearance for each index crime	Police records		X	
9. Citizen feeling of security data	Citizen surveys			X
10. Citizen expressed satisfaction with police service	Citizen surveys			X
11. Response time (minutes) between receipt of crime call and police arrival at scene—by crime and whether in progress or not	Police records		X	

TABLE 10–2 (Continued)

Minimum Data Requirements for Suggested Police Productivity Measures

Data	Source*	Generally currently available	Basic data often available but some modifications needed	Requiring significant additional data gathering
Expenditures and manpower data				
12. Police employment for crime-control related activities	UCR local records		X	
13. Police expenditures for crime-control related activities	Local records		X	
Background data				
14. Population: Total, by race, and by age groups (15–24) ..	Census, local reports	X (decennially)	X (other years)	
15. Percent unemployed—by race ..	Census, local reports	X (decennially)	X (other years)	
16. Percent households under $5000 income	Census, local reports	X (decennially)	X (other years)	
Reporting system				
17. Changes made since prior report	Police report	X		
18. Method of data audit or review	Police records	X		
19. Special data gathering procedures	Police records	X		

*UCR refers to the FBI's *Uniform Crime Reports.*
†Though the analysis in this study focused on Index Crimes, full productivity analysis should be expanded to cover other crimes, particularly certain others of special interest to society such as narcotics dealing.

Source: *Municipal Year Book 1973* (Washington, D.C.: International City Management Association, 1973), p. 41.

by random follow-up interviews of a sample of those having contact with police. Taking or encouraging action which helps get at the source of a problem such as (unemployment, alcoholism, housing code violations) in addition to dealing with the symptoms (angry people) ought to be highly rewarded.[30]

Additionally, Marx proposes:

It is important to discover how citizen feelings of security, victimization rates and experiences, reported crime, and various police practices interrelate. Considering these factors *together* gives a far richer and more meaningful assessment than the number of crimes known to police or cleared by arrest or a victimization survey considered separately. One can look at absolute increases and decreases in crime known to police, and in victimization and the ratio between them.[31]

He fittingly concludes:

Yet still another aspect of police change has to do with the reward structure. Without conjuring up wooden images of a reward seeking, punishment avoiding man, if one wishes the restrained use of force, greater police conformity to law, better community relations, and more effective police behavior in conflict and helping situations it is important to structure the job to measure and reward such behavior. Sociologists concerned with social change and understanding inequality in American life could usefully focus more attention on micro-level issues involving selection, training, performance evaluation, civil service, public employee associations, promotion, sanctioning, client-bureaucrat inter-action, and policy formation within police, as well as other public service bureaucracies.[32]

We, in turn, conclude this section with an acknowledgement that there may be other existing and potential measures of productivity not mentioned herein; and the acquisition, processing, and analysis of the potentially meaningful data not now being collected demands considerable effort (in most cases). However, we are quick to defend the requirement for making that effort! As a result, in the following section we proceed with a discussion on how in theory an agency can "tune up" their measuring capability. More importantly, we will briefly examine two theoretical *applications* that are, in fact, currently looking *for* and *at* new measures of police productivity.

30*Ibid.*, p. 16.
31*Ibid.*, p. 26, 27.
32*Ibid.*, p. 33.

"Service Analysis Units": A Strategy for Improving Measurement

The creation of "crime analysis units" within police agencies is under-way and should become more pervasive over the next few years. These units stand to serve as a cornerstone from which improved measurement techniques can be constructed. Of equal if not greater importance is that they also offer a predictive capability for resource planning. In due re-gard for the thinking expressed above, we believe it imperative to broaden the cornerstone to embody crime and noncrime analyses. There-fore, from this point on we will speak in terms of a service analysis unit (SAU).

To begin with, some form of service analysis exists in every police agency. Regretfully, in most agencies the individual officer conducts the analysis of limited crime data (and usually ignores noncrime data) in an informal way. Formal service analysis occurs when a specific unit has been established to collect and analyze all of the available police data and dis-seminate the "distilled" service information to operational user groups.

The operation of a SAU requires several basic elements.[33] These in-clude a definition of goals and objectives, service data input, analysis of service data, service information disseminated as output, and feedback and evaluation. In addition, several fundamental prerequisites must be analyzed. These include formal administrative support, organizational placement, staffing, and a method of guaranteeing the integrity of input service and criminal offender information. Most of the service data col-lected by a SAU is received from the operational units within the agency. This data consists of offense reports, supplemental reports, arrest reports, general service reports, special analysis reports, departmental records, and statistical data. In addition, to this structured data, the SAU should also collect informal data (such as soft intelligence) from other units within the agency. Outside data sources contribute information to the SAU regarding status and records of known offenders, other law enforce-ment agency crime problems, and collateral planning information.

SAUs require the immediate *maintenance* of incoming records and *temporary* data storage. The analysis unit files are *operational* and are based on a *nonduplication* of other departmental records and stored data in the records unit. Thus, a most critical distinction: the SAU and the records unit *are not one and the same*. Indeed, they have major dif-ferences. In general, the former serves as an entry, quality control, and rapid processing checkpoint. While the records unit is responsible for file

[33]Details on crime analysis units and functions can be found in *Crime Data Analysis Handbook* (Sacramento, Calif.: California Crime Technological Research Foundation, 1973).

maintenance (crime description files, known offender files, crime target files, criminal history files, suspect vehicle files, property files, and general service files), and data retrieval. In brief, one is more dynamic, and the other more static in nature. The examples presented in the next few pages are intended to further clarify the differentiation.

A SAU is especially suited to measuring and defining offenses and called-for services with a high probability of recurrence and is directed toward those criminal offenses and services the police are most capable of suppressing or solving. Numerous benefits may be attained in analyzing nearly all types of services; however, the services selected for extensive analysis (usually aggravated assaults) must be based on priority considerations. Naturally, the analysis and measurement of different service categories is dependent upon the information available to the police analyst for extraction, collation, comparison, and correlation. Several informational factors can be considered universal, such as crime type, geographical factors, chronological factors, victim target descriptors, suspect descriptors, vehicle descriptors, and property loss descriptors. However, these universal factors are only variably available when analyzing a specific crime or type of service. Thus, the analysis of a particular crime or type of service presents *specific problems* with *alternate solutions*. In addition to the universal factors, there are a number of factors that may be considered specific to a particular crime or service type. The specific crime or service factors represent the information with which the analyst will usually connect crime or other services by unique characteristics. The suitability of the various crime or service types to analysis typically includes residential and commercial burglary, armed robbery, strong-armed robbery and theft from persons, auto theft, general theft classifications, forgery and fraud, rape and sex crimes, aggravated assault and murder, and a large number of so-called civil matters.

Geographical analysis is the examination of service types to actual location or within prescribed areas. This analysis is performed to identify geographical service patterns and trends. Geographical analysis may be performed utilizing mapping, geo-coding or statistical methods. Specific mapping methods include various manual-visual techniques and computer mapping. In addition to crime type maps, it is recommended that the SAU also maintain known offender and other special maps. Further, the collation and correlation of service analysis data is dependent upon the expertise of the analyst, the analytical techniques utilized, and the availability or retrieveability of data from the records unit. Service analysis is particularly adaptable to correlative listings of possible suspects for certain crimes or listings of services having one or more common dimensions.

One of the most important functions of the SAU is to identify service trends, predictively project service activity, and establish estimated productivity patterns. By effectively analyzing service data the SAU can determine what make these targets more attractive to the criminal or the reason for the type of services being requested.

For the SAU to be effective, the analyzed information must be rapidly disseminated to operational user police groups. Service analysis information can be disseminated by either formal or informal means. The majority of data disseminated by the SAU usually assumes the form of formal structured publications. The publications are tailored to user needs, and function to increase officer awareness and facilitate short-term manpower deployment. Information on service activities is disseminated daily, with weekly and monthly summaries, and on an as-needed basis. These publications take the form of information bulletins, crime summaries, and service analysis reports. Of special importance are service pattern information bulletins, investigative lead reports, and productivity figures.[34] A SAU operation also communicates information to user groups on an informal basis. Informal dissemination of service analysis information occurs during discussions between analysis and operational personnel on the subject of delivered services—past, present, and predicted. (Depending on the volume of data traffic and access to computer hardware, a SAU can significantly increase its analytical and decision-making ability).

A SAU operation can and should be evaluated. First, by utilizing conventional planning techniques, the police manager can estimate to some degree the areas of increased effectiveness that should result from the implementation of a SAU. The SAU activities also require evaluation on a cost effectiveness basis. This can be accomplished mainly by computing costs per output unit and by measuring the amount of user reliance, or number of decisions made.

Now that we have covered SAUs in concept let us see how the concept was developed into practical programs in Columbus, Georgia, and Riverside, California.

Columbus: An Exemplary Case in Point

The Columbus, Georgia, Police Department created a crime analysis unit (referred to hereafter as a SAU) in late 1974.[35] In many respects the SAU can be termed a "now" group—"now" in the sense that it is respon-

---

[34]With the complexities and difficulties surrounding productivity and measurement in the police service one should not be alarmed over resistance to its implementation. This problem is reviewed along with recommended solutions by Walter L. Balk, "Why Don't Public Administrators Take Productivity More Seriously," *Public Personnel Management* 3 (July-August 1974): 318–24.

[35]For those desiring additional information write to the Columbus Police Department, Columbus, Georgia—Crime Analysis Unit.

sible for immediately receiving, processing, and transmitting information from one part of the agency to another. An expanded title that could be legitimately assigned to this new organizational entity is that of "value now unit." All of this is to say that the unit, whatever it may be called, is expected to rapidly move needed information from an entry point to a decision center (or centers).

Briefly, Columbus's SAU processes (1) incoming crime data, and (2) department-wide information. Both serve as the basis for an officers' *Daily Bulletin*. (See exhibit 10-3). This Bulletin provides all field personnel with time-current data on crime and noncrime events, and departmental policy or procedural changes. Also, on an as-needed basis, the SAU will conduct crime research for the Investigative Division.

In many ways this unit can be considered analogous to Lockheed Aircraft's "Skunk Works" which functioned most effectively during World War II. In the main, the Lockheed unit was charged with getting things done irrespective of bureaucratization. Similarly, the SAU can likewise be looked upon as a "do-it-now" group. The personnel are: (1) attending officer watch briefings, (2) generating called-for-services maps, (3) providing public information, and (4) interfacing with the press. Perhaps of greatest import is the report control activity that the unit performs. The SAU serves as the focal and thus critical point of report receipt and processing. Hence *quality control* is a major factor in the life of the SAU. The next section discusses this notion in more detail.

Riverside: Another Exemplary Case in Point

Riverside, California, Police Department (RPD), in an ongoing effort to increase its efficiency, detected that a problem area may exist with police arrest reports.[36] Preliminary observations seemed to indicate that the quality of some police arrest reports may be, in certain cases, inferior. This in turn could cause a problem for the District Attorney's Office which has the responsibility for final disposition of the cases resulting from the police reports. Therefore, a decision was made to conduct a quality control study of police reports to determine the extent and scope of the problem. Again, the underlying hypotheses for the study was that the "quality of police reports which result in or from arrest is directly related to the disposition of these reports by the District Attorney." (For the purpose of their study, quality includes the writing ability of the officer and the legal criteria of the report). The answers sought relate to

[36]Details on this project are contained in a document by Richard L. Hoffman, Allan W. Lynch, and Albert J. Miranda, *A Quality Control Study of Adult Arrest Reports* (Riverside, Calif.: Riverside Police Department, 1975).

Exhibit 10–3. Crime Analysis Report, Columbus Police Department, Columbus, Georgia

SECTION # 1

Beat #2

75007115   ARMED ROBBERY (Bus) KAYO SERVICE STATION, 1103 Ft. Benning Rd.
A. Thurs. 5/22 1130
B. North door to counter
C. 1-B/M/20-25, 5'5" 130-145, lbs., clean shaven, med. hair cut, gold earring in left ear, round face, dark comp. Wearing yellow slacks, white tennis shoes, T-shirt, wool stocking hat, Item stolen Cash $130. -145.00

Beat #5

75007111   BURGLARY (Bus) WYEA T.V., 6140 Buena Vista Rd.
A. ˎ5/22 0225- 0530
B. Metal covering on east window pried loose
C. Money from candy and coke machines and money boxes throughout the store.

SECTION # 2

Beat #6

75007116   BURGLARY (Bus) TERRY'S MARKET, 547 4th Ave.
A. Bet. Wed. 5/21 1930 & Thurs. 5/22 0730
B. Prying off the hinges on the front screen door east.
C. Three (3) lbs. of Pork Loin

Beat #7

75007118   BURGLARY (Bus) PORTIS SNACK BAR, 1254 Cusseta Rd.
A. Wed. 5/21 1200 mid & Thurs., 5/22 0810
B. Removed the wood from roof inside and outside
C. Assorted beer, Unk. amount of change from pin ball machine and rockola machine.

Beat #8

75007086   ARMED ROBBERY AND AGGRAVATED ASSAULT (Bus) DOWNTOWN CAMERA SHOP, 1212 Broadway
A. 5/21/75 1550
B. Subj.   #1, B/M/19, 5'9", mustache, pierced ear, took unk. amount of money, Polaroid SX70 Model 3 camera, (Business loss), $13.00 cash, Timex watch, diamond cluster ring, ladies wedding band, (Employee loss)

SECTION # 4

Beat #16

75007134   BURGLARY (Bus) CHEEK TO CHEEK LOUNGE, 2932 Warm Springs Rd.
A. Thurs. 5/22 0240 & 1015
B. By ripping the boards off the gable end (West) stamping the ceiling through kitchen
C. Assorted change, 4 cases whiskey, 1-100 Piper Scotch, 1-Seagram's V.O., 1-Taaka Vodka and 1-Segram's "7"

STOLEN VEHICLE

75007092   1972 Pont. Gran Prix, 2 dr., red, Gray motor company Tag, Vin/2K57T2-P201275

RECOVERED AUTO

75006994   1973 Ford LTD, Ala./Tag 57-16996, Vin/3U63H118036, blue.

ARREST WARRANTS

15181   Carl Homer Chirco W/M/23 DOB 6/12/52, hair brown, eyes brown, 6! 370 Matheson Dr. Ga/75 FBS-698, 70 Ford, 2 dr., black. . . CONTEMPT OF COURT

15238   James A. Hollins B/M/23 DOB 8/31/51, hair black, eyes brown, 5'10", 165 lbs., 4325 Old Cusseta Rd. Ga./75, GPT-126, 72 Chev., 2 dr., CONTEMPT OF COURT

Exhibit 10–3 (Continued)

15220 Jimmy W. Hutto W/M/27 DOB 4/6/48, hair brown, eyes gray, 5'10", 150 lbs., 6227 Williamsboro Dr. Ga/75 CES-914, 62 Merc., 2 dr., white CONTEMPT OF COURT

15190 Bobby L. Brown B/M/40 DOB 8/16/34, hair black, eyes brown, 6'2", 155 lbs. 3135 Urban Ave. Ga/75 RUE-402, 73 Pont., 2 dr, brown CONTEMPT OF COURT

15203 Evans E. Pitts B/M/54 DOB 11/15/20, hair brown, eyes brown, 5'4", 199 lbs. 4720 11th Ave. Ga/75 BJC-730, Ford Falcon, yellow... CONTEMPT OF COURT

15239 Willie L. Anderson B/M/28 DOB 4/22/47 hair black, eyes brown, 5'4", 183 lbs. 2714 10th St. ..CONTEMPT OF COURT

15245 Kerry V. Blair W/M/20 DOB 6/29/54, hair brown, eyes brown, 5'10", 150 lbs. 1st 29th Eng. Co. Ft. Benning, Ga. TN. 19Cpl2, 71 Dodge, 2 dr...CONTEMPT OF COURT

15293 Robert Lee Johnson B/M/22 DOB 12/21/52, hair black eyes brown, 5'9" 155 lbs. A Co HQ Com. Ft. Benning, Ga. 75/Ga GRM-478, 72 Dodge, 2 dr CONTEMPT OF COURT

15259 Lanny G. Buzbee W/M/24 DOB 8/27/51, hair brown, eyes brown, 5'9", 140 lbs. 3150 Plateau Dr. Lot 902, 75/Fla. 37-W2610, 68 Plym, 2 dr, white...CONTEMPT OF COURT

JUVENILE WARRANT

18249 Steven A. Reed W/M/16, 2234 Dorothy Ave. (He is a runaway and he took his father's car) THEFT OF MOTOR VEHICLE

CANCELLED ARREST WARRANTS

14581 Robert L. Cope B/M/26 DOB 10/4/48..Contempt of Court
Curtis Hurling..Armed Robbery & Aggravated Assault.

MISSING PERSON

75007103 Juanita Hennessey B/G/15 DOB 6/25/60, 5'1", 130 lbs, med. build, fair comp., sandy hair, brown eyes, Wearing navy blue pants, white T-shirt with "Operation Push" writing on front.

THERE WILL BE A MEETING OF THE 937 HUNT CLUB, SUNDAY MAY 25, 1975 at 5:00 PM IN THE DOWNSTAIRS CLASSROOM. ALL OLD MEMBERS ARE URGED TO ATTEND AND ANYONE WISHING TO JOIN.

HOUSE CHECKS

5247 Oxford Dr. -Elben, Lev 5/22 Ret 6/1, lights on in bedroom, 65 Dodge in drive.
7621 Matilda Dr. -Mr. James Stewart, Lev 5/23 Ret 5/26, lights on in bedroom.
300 Crestfield Dr. -Wife is out of town until the 27th of May. Please check.
606-A Farley Homes-Patricia Barnett, Lev 5/23 ret 5/25, lights on front & back.
3214 Melrose Dr. -Lev 5/22 Ret 5/29, brown chev will be there to check at times.

BUSINESS CHECKS

Evergreen Memory Gardens, 4400 St. Mary's Rd, Check often as possible at night. Some stealing Brass Vases & Construction Material Throughout The Cemetery.
Store-Cross Country Plaza-Auburn Ave. Car went through store's front glass window and it is just boarded up. Please watch.

PATROL CHECK

6068 Caprice Cir.Vacant house, fully furnished, including air conditioning units. Owner has a red Pinto, and may be there at times, will call when rented.

the following questions: (1) Does the quality or format of the police report have a direct effect on the dispositions of cases referred to the District Attorney? (2) Does the District Attorney effectively screen reports for quality at the time of initial referral by the police?

Of the 141 cases that were monitored, the RPD released twelve (8.5%) without filing a complaint under the authority of 849bl, 2 California Penal Code (CPC) This section section states:

> b. Any peace officer may release from custody, instead of taking such person before a magistrate, any person arrested without a warranty whenever:
>
> 1. He is satisfied that there are insufficient grounds for making a criminal complaint against the person arrested.
>
> 2. The person was arrested for intoxication only, and no further proceedings are desirable.

The remaining 129 cases were referred to the District Attorney's Office for prosecution. The following breakdown depicts the dispositions of the 129 cases. Ninety-four cases (72.9%) resulted in a conviction. Seventy cases (54.3%) were found guilty of the original charge. Twenty-four cases (18.6%) were found guilty of a reduced charge. Nine cases (6.9%) were referred for drug diversion. In five cases (3.9%) the defendant failed to appear for trial and a warrant was issued.

Six cases (4.6%) were rejected by the District Attorney for the following reasons:

Two—no elements of offense present
One—victim refused to prosecute
One—illegal search and seizure
One—victim unable to identify
One—insufficient evidence

Thirteen (10.1%) of the cases were dismissed by the District Attorney for undetermined reasons which were not available to the researchers. Also, in two cases (1.5%) the defendant was found not guilty by jury trial.

In analyzing the 141 arrest reports the following statistics were revealed: A total of fourteen (9.9%) arrest reports were defective for the following reasons:

Ten arrest reports lacked the necessary elements of the offense.
Four arrest reports lacked the probable cause for the arrest.
Two arrest reports involved illegal search and seizure.
Two arrest reports involved officer overreaction.

It should be noted that in the above fourteen reports, several arrest reports contained deficiencies in more than one area. Of these reports the following pertinent information was noted:

> Two arrest reports were disposed of per 849b1, 2CPC.
> Three arrest reports were rejected by the District Attorney.
> Nine arrest reports were accepted by the District Attorney for complaints and ultimately dismissed by his office.

(In the researchers' opinion the latter nine reports should not have been accepted by the District Attorney for prosecution because of their deficiencies.)

The research findings revealed that there are problem areas involving both the RPD and the District Attorney's Office. The researchers, in turn, recommended the following revised procedures. To begin with, it was discovered that several police arrest reports were rejected by the District Attorney's Office because the reports lacked the corpus delecti of the crime. A possible solution to this problem area may be to require supervisors to approve all arrest reports of officers before submitting them to the District Attorney. If the elements for the crime charged are absent from the report when it is submitted by the officer to the supervisor for approval, the supervisor will note it immediately and return the report to the officer for correction. It is vitally important that errors made by officers in arrest reports be brought to the attention of the officers so that they can correct their writing deficiencies. Feedback concerning errors in arrest reports could be done on an individual basis and by roll-call training to all officers. As a feedback procedure, it was recommended that the RPD investigators who seek complaints from the District Attorney's Office make record of the reasons for rejection of a charge and relay this information via supervisors to the officers.

Additionally it was recommended that the RPD devise a monitoring system which would reveal whether the percent of accurate reports was increasing or decreasing. A suggested system would be to require the investigating officers to keep records on a monthly basis which would express the filing and rejection rate of cases. An increase in the rejection rate of cases would signal the investigator that a potential problem area may be arising. Finally, the research exposed that several cases were accepted by the District Attorney's Office which were deficient and should not have been accepted. Hence it was recommended that the District Attorney's staff be more exacting in the quality of reports that they accept for prosecution.

IN CONCLUSION: Again—A Challenge

Crime heads the list of major concerns among residents of the nation's largest cities, the Gallup Poll reported. In the latest survey, 21% of residents of cities of 500,000 or more cited crime as their community's major problem. Nationally, the figure was 15%. Buttressing this concern, the FBI announced last Monday that crime had risen 18% during the first three months of 1975 over the same period a year ago. That compares with a 15% increase during the first quarter of 1974 over the same period in 1973.

When the survey results are examined in terms of the nation as a whole, crime again emerges as the top problem. The following table [see Table 10–3] compares the views of the nation as a whole with residents of the nation's largest cities.[37]

The quotation above was intentionally selected to serve as a lead-in to a final comment relative to the concept and practice of improved productivity. In regard to *productivity*, quantitative measures can take an

TABLE 10–3

Major Concerns of Citizens

	National	Largest Cities
Crime	15%	21%
Unemployment	11	11
Transportation	9	7
High cost of living	5	5
Education	5	6
High taxes	4	4
Drugs	4	4
Poor housing-slums	4	5
Unsanitary conditions	4	3
Ineffective police	3	3
Other problems	36	34
No opinion	6	5

Source: Los Angeles Times, October 11, 1976, PI, p. 3.

37"Crime Top Urban Issue, Poll Finds," *Los Angeles Times*, October, 1976.

endless variety of forms. At some future date it will be useful to establish a more precise system and language of public service measurement. For the time being, these simple distinctions should suffice. The critical thing is to formulate quantitative measures that provide better information to management, and to constantly be alert to what those measures are and are not exposing. To conclude:

> If any accurate generalization can be derived from the jumble of conflicting data on urban administration it is that every mayor and city manager has a deep and abiding interest in the productivity of the local police. If a citizen must select a single indicator of the effectiveness, responsiveness, and general character of the incumbent administration, the conventional wisdom is that in most cases it will be police performance. Whether or not the chief executive has the legal or traditional authority to affect policy administration, he knows that his store of political capital—whether he conceives of it as a personal asset or as the support necessary to exert effective leadership—is greatly influenced by the public's perception of police productivity.[38]

LEARNING EXERCISE

EXPLORING POLICE
PRODUCTIVITY

Purpose. This exercise is designed to assist police managers and supervisors discover how well they share a common understanding of the purpose and function of a particular police task.

Process

1. Ask a police manager or supervisor to write down what he expects from one of his colleagues or police officers over the next six months and the data or evidence to be used to judge performance.

   This is not simply a formal management-by-objectives approach, because it deals with feelings as well as facts. A good way for the police manager/supervisor to begin his statement of expectations is with the following words: "I expect that you will. . . ."

   For example, a typical statement would be "I expect that you will produce a quarterly report that suggests concrete methods to improve our police delivery

[38]Edward K. Hamilton, "Police Productivity: The View From City Hall," in *Readings On Productivity In Policing*, ed. Joan L. Wolfle and John F. Heaphy (Washington, D.C.: The Police Foundation, 1975), p. 11.

system. I will judge this as being successful if, as a result of your suggestions, we achieve a savings in the public dollar outlay or an improvement in our agency service."

2. Independently, the colleague or police officer produces a list of his own expectations in relation to himself and his superior, and makes a request for the support and resources he needs. Here the form of words is "I expect that I will. . . ."

3. Both individuals meet to share their expectations and requirements. It is necessary for each person to understand the other's point of view and to see what is significant to him or her. Then there needs to be a form of bargaining such as the following:

"If I am expected to do this, then I will need these resources."
"I will give this much time toward this police aim."
"We really need to check this out before we can go forward."
"Can this realistically be accomplished?"
"Yes, I feel committed to this point."

4. Both police personnel work on the problems until they are resolved. A number of sessions may be needed.

Chapter Eleven

TASK 9
POLICE ASSOCIATIONS
AND UNIONS

320

SAN FRANCISCO—Striking policemen ignored a court order to return to work here Tuesday as Mayor Joseph L. Alioto shuttled from one closed-door meeting to another in an effort to settle the walkout.

The Board of Supervisors late Tuesday afternoon made a new offer to the Police Officers Assn. It was described by sources as a very minimal increase in the 6.5% wage boost offer that had been made earlier.

Negotiations between the board and strikers continued late into the night, but City Hall sources said they did not expect a settlement until at least today.

Though there were sporadic incidents of violence and extensive traffic jams, the city remained relatively quiet on the second day of the strike. As attempts continued to get the police back to work, firemen and transit workers were on the verge of joining the walkout. Firemen were voting Tuesday and today on whether to strike. Transit workers already have voted to go out at 12.01 a.m. Thursday.

Alioto, attempting to act as a mediator, brought the Board of Supervisors and the Police Officers Assn. together late Tuesday afternoon. The mayor said he made a proposal both sides were considering, but he would not elaborate.

Gerald Crowley, president of the association, declared after the meeting, however, that there was "no definite proposal. . . . Several ideas were discussed."

He also said association attorneys had advised him that the court order for policemen to return to work was unconstitutional. He provided no specifics.

Police officials said about 85% to 90% of the 1,935-member force were observing the walkout. Sergeants, lieutenants and plainclothes detectives were handling only emergency calls such as homicides, robberies or burglaries in progress. . . .

City Atty. Thomas O'Conner obtained a temporary restraining order Tuesday morning from Superior Judge Robert Drewes directing the strikers to return to work and forbidding them to picket. But the order appeared to have little or no effect on either the strike or the picketing, which continued at the Hall of Justice and at nine district stations.

Drewes set a hearing for September 2 on the city attorney's request for a preliminary injunction to stop the strike. O'Conner's petition maintains that the strike is illegal and threatens "the preservation of peace and safety."[1]

Invoking emergency powers, he gave the strikers just about what they wanted over the unanimous objection of the city-county's Board of Supervisors, which normally sets municipal salaries. As a consequence, every city in the land has become more vulnerable to strikes against the public safety.

The national hazard is implicit in a statement in Washington, D.C., by the president of the 180,000-member International Conference of Police Associations. Edward J. Kiernan said in an interview that policemen, buoyed by the apparent success of the strike in San Francisco, will be more likely to participate in labor action in the future, despite laws prohibiting such strikes or court orders enjoining them—as in San Francisco. This is indeed, a very dangerous position to be taken by public employes sworn to enforce the law. It has been encouraged by Mayor Alioto's arbitrary action.[2]

SYNOPSIS

Police unions are here now and will remain with us in the future. Additionally they are on the increase in terms of both number and power. In many instances they are challenging the police manager's authority and responsibility for administering his agency. The days of the arbitrary, authoritarian, and unilateral management style are on the wane. Concurrently, the time of police unions or associations has arrived in mass and in force. Basically the stage has been set for management-labor relations—relations that, in turn, can vary from being highly mutually supportive to being highly laden with conflict.

Police unions are actively pursuing the promulgation of a police employee "Bill of Rights." Careful observers are at the same time seeking to integrate the elusive concept of "Professionalization" with these "Rights." It is held by some that a well-designed career package can accommodate both. Others believe that employee rights

[1]Daryl Lembke and William Endicott, "Striking San Francisco Police Defy Order to Return," Los Angeles Times, August 20, 1975.

[2]"Dire Alioto Sell-Out" (editorial), The Oregonian, August 23, 1975, pt. 1, p. 16.

and police professionalization are inherently antagonistic and unable to coexist in the same organizational setting.

Although the police manager is having his attention drawn to employee rights, he must not ignore his responsibilities lest they be eroded to the extent that they become a fantasy rather than a reality. Of the many management responsibilities, one is paramount. Simply, yet so critically, it is the safeguarding of the manager's *right* and *capability* to fulfill his multifaceted responsibilities.

A BRIEF PERSPECTIVE ON THE POLICE EMPLOYEE MOVEMENT

The distinction between unions and associations as they relate to the police service becomes daily less clear. At the same time, their import, influence, and number increase on a daily basis.[3] The days of complete police management discretion in the field of labor relations are gone forever. So too is the era in which the chief/sheriff could simply delegate responsibility for the labor-management relations program to departmental personnel. Police employees not only want a greater piece of the action in terms of higher salaries and benefits, but they also seek more influence and control over their work environment. These desires and demands are reflected in the growth of public sector union membership.

Surveys conducted by the International City Management Association show that in cities over 10,000 population more than two-thirds of the municipal work force belongs to, or is represented by, a union or association. These figures are even higher in the largest communities surveyed. The degree of organization varies by region of the country as well with the highest organization in northern cities. The same survey showed that three-fourths of the cities sampled with populations over 25,000 and 50 percent of the cities under 25,000 deal with at least one labor organization.

[3] Three texts worthy of your attention follow. The first is more generic in format, while the latter two concentrate on the police field: Robert T. Woodworth and Richard B. Peterson, *Collective Negotiation for Public and Professional Employees: Text and Readings* (Glenview, Ill.: Scott, Foresman and Company, 1966); John H. Burpo, *The Police Labor Movement: Problems and Perspectives* (Springfield, Ill.: Charles C Thomas, Publisher, 1971); and Hervey A. Juris and Peter Feuille, *Police Unionism: Power and Impact In Public Sector Bargaining* (Lexington, Mass.: Lexington Books, 1973).

This trend is enhanced in part by state action. At least 30 states have enacted legislation relating to public sector labor relations, and now there is increasing pressure for a national law to provide a full measure of bargaining rights for public sector employees. Three states now permit public employees, with the exception of police and fire, to strike, and at least two states provide for "final offer" arbitration for police and fire employees.[4]

The trend clearly is toward increased union and association representation at the local level and a strengthened union position as it relates to management in the labor-management process. Employer-employee conflicts (grievances) cost money! In many instances, a lot of money. Sometimes a grievance can be settled in a five-minute discussion between a police manager and the police officer. Sometimes a grievance may take months or even years, involve many people in numerous meetings and end up in arbitration, in court, or as a *strike* which threatens the safety of our citizens. The immediate response may well be "Do not permit the police to strike!" But

> Public employes cannot be prevented from striking. Time and again, public workers have defied court edicts, ignored legislative limitations, rejected public appeals, and walked off their jobs to enforce their demands for more money or improved working conditions. And the strikers have included vital security workers such as firemen, sanitation engineers and police. . . .
>
> On its essentials, there is broad agreement. Public workers should not be denied the protections of collective bargaining, and inevitably those protections will include the right to strike. But it is in everyone's interest to prevent strikes that jeopardize public health and safety. The broad agreement has disintegrated in the past over the means of preventing certain kinds of public-worker strikes. But the new legislation under consideration in Sacramento offers a constructive solution that is gaining increasing support. We like it.
>
> Under terms of the new legislation, mediation and, if necessary, factfinding would be mandatory. These provisions are likely to settle most disputes. In the face of deadlock, however, employes would be able to proceed to a strike. But a special state employe relations agency could, at that point, appeal for court intervention. And, if the court determined that public health and safety were jeopardized by the proposed strike, the court could prohibit the strike. That step would then impose on the government and employes acceptance of the fact-finding recommendation that had emerged in the media-

[4]Donald Borut and William H. Hansell, Jr., "The Role of the City Manager in Labor Relations," *Public Management* 55 (July 1973): 2.

tion procedures. In other words, the affected government and the employes would be bound by a decision that both would know in advance.[5]

From the material quoted above and the data contained in table 11–1 we can see the existing potential for severe problems emanating from police management-labor disputes.[6]

TABLE 11–1

Public Employee Strikes:
Developing an Effective Management Strategy

Year	No. of strikes	Man-day loss (thousands)
1960	36	58
1961	28	15
1962	28	79
1963	29	15
1964	41	71
1965	42	146
1966	142	455
1967	181	1,300
1968	254	2,600
1969	411	7,500
1970	412	2,000
1971	329	901
1972	375	1,300

Source: Chicago Tribune, October 27, 1974.

POLICE EMPLOYEE "BILL OF RIGHTS"

For decades the police officer has been informed and repeatedly reminded of his responsibilities to the community, to the agency, to management, and to his coworkers. The union movement in the police serv-

[5]"Should Public Employes Strike?" (editorial), *Los Angeles Times*, January 27, 1975.
[6]Note the following astute advice on this front, for the *supervisor* as well as the police manager: "A thorough understanding of how to deal effectively with public employee strikes may well be the best preventive measure public managers can take. Managers should not spend time theorizing about the why of public employee strikes, rather they should proceed on the assumption that strikes will occur and that public managers must know how to react rationally, whether the strike is legal or illegal." "Management Employee Relations Service," *Personnel News* 41 (February 1975): 14.

ice has focused on another "R," that of one's *rights*. Previous chapters have alluded to an officer's right to expect a facilitative work environment, job enrichment, and the like. In this instance we find the police employee organization attempting to formalize such rights as well as others of a protective nature in management-labor contracts. In fact, many collective bargaining contracts negotiated after 1970 contained a "Policeman's Bill of Rights," a document extending broad protections to police officers during disciplinary matters and more specifically internal investigations.[7]

Since the supervisor normally is the first to be confronted with recognizing and dealing with the rights of a police officer, further consideration of this concept seems most pertinent. To this end, Raymond C. Davis, Chief of the Santa Ana Police Department promulgated a Departmental Order that began as follows:

> In recognition of the fact that employees, when possible, should know what they can expect from their superiors, this Bill of Rights has been prepared to clarify some of the questions that could arise when actions of members of this department must be evaluated by superior officers.
>
> We must certainly be mindful of the rights of citizens and our need to respect the individual dignity of all men and at the same time the official administrative position of this department is to assure all employees that their rights shall also be clearly respected.
>
> It is hoped that the detailed description of the following administrative position in regards to the police Employee Bill of Rights will be helpful to all Santa Ana Police Employees.[8]

Exhibit 11–1 presents the substance of the Order. Clearly the adoption of such a policy has major ramifications for the use of managerial controls and leadership. Moreover, it will be the effective manager that maintains his right to manage while simultaneously respecting the rights of those that he manages. If a proper balance is negotiated between the two then conflicts will be minimal; if not, then antagonisms will be prevalent. Thus once more we visualize the police manager in a role of resolving conflicts by judiciously interfacing two sets of varying rights.

---

[7]For additional information and recommendations on this subject see John H. Burpo, "The Policeman's Bill of Rights," *The Police Chief* 39 (September 1972): 18–24. Further, see State of California Assembly Bill 301 which legislates a police officer's Bill of Rights as of January 1977.

[8]This quotation and exhibit 11–1 derived from Raymond C. Davis, Departmental Order 26, Police Employee Bill of Rights, Santa Ana Police Department, August 24, 1973.

Exhibit 11–1. Bill of Rights

SANTA ANA POLICE DEPARTMENT

POLICE EMPLOYEE BILL OF RIGHTS

1.0 The security of the City of Santa Ana, its citizens, plus the integrity and reputation of the Santa Ana Police Department, depends to a great extent on the manner in which Police Officers of this Department perform their varied and difficult duties. The performance of such duties involves those members in all manners of contacts and relationships with the public.

    1.1. Out of such contacts and relationships may arise questions concerning the actions of members of the Department. Such questions require prompt investigation by superior officers designated by the Chief of Police or other competent authority.

    1.2 To ensure that such investigations are conducted in a manner conducive to good order and discipline, meanwhile observing and protecting the individual rights of each member of the Department, the following rules are hereby established:

2.0 The interview of any Department member shall be conducted at a reasonable hour, preferably when the member is on duty and during daylight hours, unless the urgency of the investigation dictates otherwise. If such interview occurs during off-duty time of the member being interviewed, the member shall be compensated for his off-duty time in accordance with regular Department procedures.

    2.1 The interview shall take place at a location designated by the investigating officer, preferably at the Santa Ana Police Department facility building.

    2.2 The member being interviewed shall be informed of the name and rank of all persons present. Should a member, during the investigation, be directed to leave his assigned post, his Watch Commander or Section Commander shall be notified immediately.

    2.3 The member being interviewed shall be informed verbally of the nature of the investigation, name and address of all complaining parties, before the interview commences. The member should be informed of his right to make notes.

    2.4 The interview session shall be for a reasonable period of time, depending upon the seriousness of the investigation. Unless the Chief of Police directs otherwise, a period of two (2) hours shall be the maximum time allowed for any one session of interview.

    2.5 Reasonable rest periods shall be allowed within the two (2) hour period. Time shall be provided for personal necessities, meals, telephone calls, etc., as are reasonably necessary.

    2.6 The member being interviewed shall not be subjected to any offensive or abusive language, nor threatened with dismissal or other disciplinary action. Nothing herein is to be construed as to prohibit the interviewing officer from informing the member that his conduct can be the subject of disciplinary action should he refuse to obey a lawful order from the ranking officer. No promise of reward shall be made as an inducement to answering any question. The member being interviewed shall be asked questions by and through no more than two (2) investigators. The member shall not be subject to visits by the press or news media, without his express consent, nor shall his home address, phone number or photograph, be given to the press or news media, without his express consent.

Source: Raymond G. Davis, Department Order 26, Police Employee Bill of Rights, Santa Ana (Calif.) Police Department, August 24, 1973.

Exhibit 11-1 (Continued)

2.7 When the member being interviewed is under arrest, or is likely to be placed under arrest as a result of the interview, he shall be informed of his constitutional rights prior to the commencement of the interview.

2.8 At the request of a member under arrest, and prior to any interview, the member shall have the right to be represented by counsel of his choice, who may be present at all times during such interview.

The attorney shall not participate in the interview, except to counsel the member. The member may request a postponement of the initial interview, to contact an attorney of his own choosing. The interview may not be postponed more than 24 hours, with allowances being made for week-ends and holidays.

2.9 When a member is being interviewed in a non-criminal matter for violation of departmental rules, regulations, or orders he will not be advised of his rights, nor will he be allowed the presence of counsel during the interview. The member shall answer, truthfully, all questions concerning the investigation posed to him by the interviewing officer. When the member refuses to answer such questions, he will be informed that his refusal to answer can become the subject for disciplinary action.

2.10 When a member is being interviewed in a non-criminal matter, and there is a likelihood that the interview may reveal criminal conduct on the part of the member, the member shall be advised of his constitutional rights prior to the commencement of any interview. The member shall be advised that, if he does not waive his rights, the results of the interview cannot and will not be used against him in a criminal court of law. However, he will be required to answer all questions, to assist in the administrative process. When a member is interviewed and does waive his rights, he shall be informed that the results of the interview can be used by the Department in both administrative and criminal actions, if the accusations are proven.

2.11 No tape recording will be made of the interview, without prior advisement. There will be no "off-the-record" questions during a recorded interview.

3.0 No member of this Department shall be compelled to submit to a Polygraph examination, on a complaint, without corroborating evidence in a non-criminal matter, unless the complaining party is requested and submits to a Polygraph examination beforehand. Should the complainant refuse or fail the examination, the member will not be asked or compelled to submit to the examination. If the complaining party passes the examination, showing truth in his complaint, or if there is sufficient corroborating evidence, the Chief of Police may order the member to submit to the examination. Failure to comply can become the basis for termination for insubordination.

3.1 In criminal matters under investigation, the member shall be advised of his right to accept or reject the Polygraph examination. Should the member elect to refuse the examination, he may be ordered to take the examination by the Chief of Police, as an aid in the administrative investigation. Failure to submit may be the cause for disciplinary action. The member will be informed that the refusal to submit to the Polygraph examination cannot and will not be used against him in a criminal court of law. Should the member waive his rights and elect to take the Polygraph examination, he shall be informed that the results of the polygraph examination or any information derived from the examination may be used by the department in both administrative and criminal actions.

Exhibit 11-1 (Continued)

3.2 In criminal matters, when a member refuses to submit to a Polygraph examination, after being ordered to do so by the Chief of Police, disciplinary action may be suspended, unless the member is under arrest, until the final court disposition of the matter, or the member may be terminated for insubordination. The disposition of the disciplinary action against the member, if any, shall rest with the Chief of Police.

3.3 A member may at any time request a Polygraph examination.

4.0 The member shall read, and be allowed to sign and date, any document having reference to the results and/or disposition of an investigation, prior to its being placed in the member's personnel file.

5.0 Any disciplined member has the right of appeal available to employees in the Civil Service Rules and Regulations as provided in Article X, Section 1008, of the Santa Ana City Charter.

6.0 Nothing contained herein shall preclude or prohibit any member from pursuing civil litigation for false and/or malicious complaints.

7.0 City owned desks, lockers, storage space, rooms, offices, equipment, work areas, and vehicles, are the sole property of the City of Santa Ana and subject to inspection at any time deemed necessary by the Chief of Police or other competent authority. Private property can be stored in areas mentioned above, however, privacy shall not be expected. No one who is not acting in his official capacity shall be authorized the search of areas assigned to others.

8.0 Any telephone call made or received on a department phone is the business of the Chief of Police and not confidential to him or his authorized agents. Due to the very nature of the complex problems that face law enforcement and the need for accuracy in reporting, those using police telephone lines could reasonably expect security could take the form of monitoring and/or recording incoming or outgoing calls.

9.0 Except when on duty, or when acting in his official capacity, no member shall be prohibited from engaging in political activity, nor shall he be denied the right to refrain from engaging in political activity unless prohibited by City of Santa Ana regulations or by federal or state law.

10.0 This document shall not be construed to supercede, in part or in whole, any civil service rules and regulations or any section of the Rules and Regulations for the City of Santa Ana Police Department.

11.0 In the event that any section, subsection, or other portion of this Bill of Rights should be found to be unconstitutional, illegal, or otherwise invalid, the remainder of the Bill shall continue in full force and effect.

UNION IMPACT ON POLICE PROFESSIONALIZATION

The term *profession* refers to an abstract ideal model, which occupations strive to achieve because the attainment of professional status brings with it several rewards.[9] Some of these rewards are monetary but more important, professional status involves a great deal of autonomy in the way in which the occupation carries out its work; i.e., knowledge is assumed to be so specialized that only members of the profession can deal authoritatively with problems in their jurisdiction. The process of *professionalization* is the achievement of professional status—the extent to which an occupation has achieved the ideal state. We believe that the degree of professionalization can be measured by observing three scales: (1) the extent to which the locus of specialization is occupational as opposed to individual or organizational; (2) the extent to which the occupation stresses the process by which ends are achieved as well as the ends themselves (and the extent to which the reward structure emphasizes process over product); and (3) the extent to which there exists a body of intellectual knowledge which can be codified and transmitted abstractly. Applying these measures to the police service, we found that the police are still at the beginning of the professionalization process and that it is not clear whether professionalization is the most effective way to achieve the goals of a police agency.

We have defined professionalization as the process of achieving the ideal state of a profession. This is not the definition being used generally in the police service. Rather, we found two other definitions which serve as the object of professionalization efforts: the first is the *struggle for professional status*; the second is the desire for a *professionally led department*.

A professionally led department is one in which efficiency and managerial rationality are emphasized to the exclusion (or attempted exclusion) of politics. The struggle for professional status involves the quest for the trappings of professionalism; e.g., autonomy, professional authority, the power to determine the character and curriculum of the training process.

In many instances police unions have systematically frustrated management's quest for professional status. The actions of these unions regarding advanced education, lateral transfer, development of a master patrolman classification, and changes in recruitment standards have been

---

[9]This section is drawn from a monograph by Hervey A. Juris and Peter Feuille, *The Impact of Police Unions: Summary Report*, (Washington, D.C.: U.S. Government Printing Office, 1973), pp. 7, 8.

essentially negative and, from management's point of view, clearly counterproductive. Police unions appear to see advanced education and master patrolman proposals as wedges to obtain more money for all their members whereas management sees them as a way of rewarding individual achievement. Both of these can be classified under the quest for status rather than professionalization because in each case it has yet to be shown that the proposed move would, in fact, lead to increased professionalization. Lateral entry, on the other hand, would represent a move toward increased professionalization in that increased mobility would help to shift the locus of specialization from the organization to the occupation. Here, however, in most cases the unions and management have been opposed and where management was in favor, the union was opposed. The question separating management and the unions on changes in entry requirements is whether such changes should be viewed as *lowering* standards (union position) or introducing the concept of *flexible* standards so as to better meet the goals of the agency (management).

The potential impact of the police union movement may be greatest in achieving the professionalization of police supervisory and managerial personnel. To the extent that unionization will drive a wedge between police officers on the one hand and the sergeants, lieutenants, and captains on the other, and force a recognition of their different responsibilities within the department, this realization may open the door to the type of specialization prerequisite to the professionalization of management in police agencies. However, we are not terribly optimistic in this regard, since many unions strongly prefer to have police officers and the superior officer ranks in the same bargaining unit and union. The following quotation clearly expresses the dilemma existing over police unions and police professionalization.

> It is possible to envision a situation in which the future shape of law enforcement teeters precariously between a trend toward professionalization, on the one hand, which should be encouraged by substantially increased salaries, a larger role in decision making and increased social status, and a trend toward unionization, on the other, fed by continued social alienation, undiscriminating public demands for tax reduction and cost cutting, and resistance by shortsighted, efficiency-oriented police leadership to the granting of substantial rewards and recognition for becoming "professionalized."
>
> The power of union organization could replace the appeal of increased education as a means to improve the lot of rank and file. A socially dangerous isolation of rank-and-file officers could be the result of their seeking refuge in politically active "antiliberal" unions. An occupational group which exercises the legal power of physical coercion, even to the point of decisions about the life and

death of citizens, must not be forced into alienation, either from the public they are supposed to protect and serve, or from those officially responsible for their supervision and control.

The data generated by this study should at least give cause for serious reflection and further study. If the public desires a professional police force, chiefs must be encouraged to treat their officers as professionals when, and if, they in fact achieve the qualifications, standards, and competencies associated with professionalism. Police officers cannot be encouraged to become more professional on the one hand and continue to be treated like functionaries on the other, when, and if, they have attained a level of professionalism.[10]

STANDARDS

Recently proposed standards concerning police employee organizations comprise this section. As you will see they relate in differing degrees of relevancy to the police manager's role. All pertain to four basic premises. The first is that police, like other employees, have a proper collective interest in the conditions of their employment. The second is that police work is so vital to democratic government that there must be limitations upon the right of police to take collective action, limitations which may not be applicable to less vital professions. The third is that the policeman, as an individual, particularly the patrolman, has a legitimate interest in law enforcement policy making and ought to have some opportunity to contribute to it. The fourth premise is that the policeman has political rights which ought, however, to be exercised in ways which do not compromise his ability to render effective police service which commands community confidence and support. The following standards are excerpted from two benchmark reports.[11]

Part VI

POLICE UNIONS AND
POLITICAL ACTIVITY

6.1   Collective interest of policemen and limitations thereon.

   (a) Policemen have a proper collective interest in many aspects of their job such as wages, length of work week, and pension and other fringe benefits. To imple-

[10]Terry Cooper, "Professionalization and Unionization of Police: A Delphi Forecast on Police Values," *Journal of Criminal Justice* 2 (Spring 1974): 33, 34.
[11]American Bar Association, *The Urban Police Function* (Washington, D.C.: American Bar Association, 1973) and The National Advisory Commission on Criminal Justice and Standards and Goals, *Police* (Washington, D.C.: U.S. Government Printing Office, 1973).

ment this interest, the right of collective bargaining should be recognized. However, due to the critical nature of the police function within government, there should be no right to strike. Effective alternatives to the right to strike, such as compulsory arbitration, should be made available as methods by which policemen can pursue their collective interest; and model procedures governing this important matter should be developed.

(b) The right of police to engage in collective action, however, should be subject to the following limitations.

(i) The preservation of civilian control over law enforcement policy-making requires that law enforcement policy not be the subject of collective bargaining.

(ii) The need to preserve local control over law enforcement and over the resolution of law enforcement policy issues requires that law enforcement policy not be influenced by a national police union.

(iii) The maintenance of police in a position of objectivity in engaging in conflict resolution requires that police not belong to a union which also has nonpolice members who may become party to a labor dispute.

(iv) The achievement of proper control by the police administrator over his department requires that collective action not interfere with the administrator's ability effectively to implement the policies and objectives of the agency.[12]

Standard 18.1

THE POLICE EXECUTIVE
AND EMPLOYEE RELATIONS

Every police chief executive should immediately acknowledge his responsibility to maintain effective employee relations and should develop policies and procedures to fulfill this responsibility.

1. Every police chief executive should actively participate in seeking reasonable personnel benefits for all police employees.

2. Every police chief executive should provide an internal two-way communication network to facilitate the effective exchange of information within the agency and to provide himself with an information feedback device.

3. Every police chief executive should develop methods to obtain advisory information from police employees—who have daily contact with operational problems—to assist him in reaching decisions on personnel and operational matters.

[12]American Bar Association, pp. 171–72.

4. Every police chief executive should provide a grievance procedure for all police employees.

5. Every police chief executive should have employee relations specialists available to provide assistance in:
   a. Developing employee relations programs and procedures;
   b. Providing general or specific training in management-employee relations; and
   c. Collective negotiations.

6. Recognizing that police employees have a right, subject to certain limitations, to engage in political and other activities protected by the first amendment, every police agency should promulgate written policy that acknowledges this right and specifies proper and improper employee conduct in these activities.

7. Every police chief executive should acknowledge the right of police employees to join or not join employee organizations that represent their employment interests and should give appropriate recognition to these employee organizations.[13]

Standard 18.2

POLICE EMPLOYEE ORGANIZATIONS

Every police employee organization should immediately formalize written policies, rules, and procedures that will protect the rights of all members and insure that they can remain responsible to their oath of office.

1. Every police employee organization should place in writing the scope of its activities to inform all members of their organization's programs and their representatives' activities.

2. Every police employee organization should adhere to rules and procedures designed to insure internal democracy and fiscal integrity. These rules and procedures should include:
   a. Provisions to protect members in their relations with the police employee organization;
   b. Standards and safeguards for periodic elections;
   c. Identification of the responsibilities of the police employee organization officers;
   d. Provisions for maintenance of accounting and fiscal controls, including regular financial reports;
   e. Provisions for disclosure of financial reports and other appropriate documents to members, regulating agencies, and the public; and

[13]National Advisory Commission, *Police,* p. 445.

f. Acknowledgment of responsibility to the governmental entity legally charged with regulation of such employee organizations.[14]

Standard 18.3

COLLECTIVE NEGOTIATION PROCESS

Every police agency and all police employees should be allowed, by 1975, to engage in collective negotiations in arriving at terms and conditions of employment that will maintain police service effectiveness and insure equitable representation for both parties.

1. Legislation enacted by States to provide for collective negotiations between police agencies and public employees should give equal protection for both parties and should include:

    a. Provisions for local jurisdictions to enact specific rules for the collective negotiation process;

    b. Procedures to prevent either party from circumventing the collective negotiation process;

    c. Provisions for police agency retention of certain unrestricted management rights to insure proper direction and control in delivering police services;

    d. Provisions to prohibit police employees from participating in any concerted work stoppage or job action; and,

    e. Procedures that require adherence to the collective negotiation legislation by all parties.

2. Every police chief executive should insure that he or his personally designated representative is present during all collective negotiations involving the police agency, and that he is allowed to protect the interests of the community, the police agency, and all police employees.

3. Every police agency should insure that all police employees receive training necessary to maintain effective management-employee relations. This training should include:

    a. Sufficient information to provide all employees with a general knowledge of the management-employee relations process;

    b. Specific instructions to persons who represent the police agency in the collective negotiation process; and

    c. Specific instructions to enable every supervisory police employee to perform his duties under any collective negotiation agreement.

[14]*Ibid.*, p. 454.

4. Every police chief executive should encourage employee organizations to provide training to enable their representatives to represent members in the negotiation process adequately.

5. Every police chief executive should establish administrative procedures to facilitate the police agency's operation under any collective negotiation agreement.

6. Every police chief executive should recognize that in the collective negotiation process the problems of unit determination, areawide negotiation, and impasse procedures are largely unresolved and that little guidance is currently available in these essential areas.[15]

Standard   18.4

WORK STOPPAGES
AND JOB ACTIONS

Every police chief executive should immediately prepare his agency to react effectively to neutralize any concerted work stoppage or job action by police employees. Any such concerted police employee action should be prohibited by law.

1. Every State, by 1976, should enact legislation that specifically prohibits police employees from participating in any concerted work stoppage or job action. Local legislation should be enacted immediately if State prohibitive legislation does not currently exist.

2. Every police agency should establish formal written policy prohibiting police employees from engaging in any concerted work stoppage or job action.

3. Every police agency should develop a plan to maintain emergency police service in the event of a concerted employee work stoppage.

4. Every police chief executive should consider the initiation of internal disciplinary action, including dismissal, against police employees who participate in a concerted job action or work stoppage. Among the many disciplinary alternatives available to the chief executive are actions against:
   a. All participating employees for violating prohibitive legislation and policy;
   b. Individual employees when their individual conduct warrants special action;
   c. Only those employees who encouraged, instigated, or led the activity; and
   d. None of the participating employees; however, criminal or civil action may be sought for violations of legislative prohibitions.[16]

15*Ibid.*, p. 457.
16*Ibid.*, p. 465.

A POLICE MANAGER'S "BILL OF RESPONSIBILITIES"

> Once a union has been recognized, the police administrator must be prepared to give more time to labor relations generally and to the union in particular. Additionally, if the relationship is to be harmonious, the police administrator must work to develop a rapport with employee representatives. This is done by openhanded dealing, with an attitude of acceptance—not by fear, not by tricky dealings, not by trying to get rid of the organization (or its leaders). The point for the chief to keep in mind is that its (the union's) members are still his employees.[17]

From the police manager's perspective, the growing omnipresence and power of police unions need not be perceived as a "loss," but rather can be viewed as a restructuring of a relationship that may, in fact, provide benefits for the proper management of our cities. For example, unions have been able to remove political influence by insisting on job tenure provisions and in some cases merit promotion. The grievance procedure, which is a standard part of a union contract, forces management and supervisory employees to discuss problems openly as they occur, rather than to permit festering sores to develop within the police agency which can lead to serious problems in the future. Union stewards can be trained properly to assist supervisory personnel in spotting potential problems in terms of sick leave abuse, unsafe working conditions and practices, and other employee-related problems which can develop and cause long-range harm to the agency. For the police chief and sheriff, then, the issue is not how to resist and fight the organization of police employees nor, conversely, to actively promote the unionization of police employees. The issue is to identify and effectively address his role in a changing labor-management relationship. The following discussion revolves around some general considerations that shape the ground the police manager must travel in his role as an assumer of responsibility. The "turf" is quite obviously that of police employer-employee relations. The "travel" is in terms of his overall role as a manager. We start with a "posture."

Responsibility 1: Management "Unit Determination"—A Posture

This entire text could easily be devoted to a discourse on whether the supervisor should be identified as line employee, management, or independent. Ordinarily, we would argue that the supervisor is a separate,

[17]Mollie H. Bowers, "Police Administrators and the Labor Relations Process," *The Police Chief* 42 (January 1975): 55.

third party that acts as an intermediary between the top (the police manager) and the bottom (police employees) of an organizational pyramid.
However, in this instance, and in this instance only, we feel the supervisor should be—though typically is not—positioned with management.
Therefore, from this point forward let us think of the police supervisor
as a member of *management* in terms of his responsibilities.

Responsibility 2:   Personnel Benefits

Police personnel, like other workers, seek equitable economic benefits
and enriched job conditions. They continually pursue increased salary,
compensation for overtime work, improved pension provisions, quality
health insurance, uniform allowances, and guaranteed pay. Increasingly
we see them displaying an interest in their working hours; routine and
safety equipment; vacation and holiday provisions; health benefits; deployment policy; promotion procedures; internal discipline; and many
other job areas not previously cited by police personnel.

The police manager must always analyze his employees personnel benefits and working conditions in relation to other law enforcement agencies and to other public employees.[18] Some issues may be beyond his
authority if they are controlled by legislation or civil service regulations;
he can, however, initiate action to make needed changes. If he does not
assume this responsibility, some other person or group may!

Responsibility 3:   Internal Communications

Every police manager should establish an effective exchange of information within his agency. In an upward sense he should know what his
employees want, how they feel, and he should act on this information.
Downward, he should inform all his employees of his views and the
planned activities of the agency. This two-way exchange of information
can minimize rumors and facilitate implementation of many agency policies and programs. Additionally, it is essential that the police manager
obtain agency reaction to his policies, procedures, and programs. It cannot be assumed that employees are knowledgeable on all subjects; the
manager should constantly ascertain what they *do know* and what they
would *like to know*.

---

[18]The majority of the thinking expressed in this and following sections is excerpted
from The National Advisory Commission on Criminal Justice and Standards and
Goals, *Police*, pp. 447–64; and, John A. Hanson, "How to Bargain in the Public Sector,"
Public Management 57 (February 1975): 15–18.

Responsibility 4: Participative Decision Making

Some police managers abjure employee participation in the decision-making process, while others encourage it. Participation in this context means assistance. It usually means, also, improved decisions. Participation or assistance, to be successful requires a high degree of compatibility on the part of the involved parties; a recognition by employees that final decisions must rest with the top police manager; and encouragement of both formal and informal involvement of the police employee and the manager. This does not occur easily. Years of noninvolvement and resistance must be overcome. Fortunately, the problem is being resolved in many jurisdictions.

Responsibility 5: Grievances

An "employee grievance" is an employee's complaint that he believes he has been treated unjustly by the police agency or one of its members. A system that permits police employees to resolve their grievances fairly and expeditiously can operate within existing police organizational structures *without* the need for an employee organization. The lack of a grievance system will be one of the first issues raised by any employee organization. A grievance system may be viewed as a mechanism for maintaining or increasing employee moral and as another channel of internal communication. With an effective grievance system, the police manager can receive valuable feedback that is useful in pinpointing organizational problems.

A major problem with the grievance system is caused by the supervisory/middle-management level of police agencies. In some cases the supervisor or middle manager fails to make a decision on the issue at hand and, instead, refers it to the next higher level. Police chiefs and sheriffs should establish and enforce the amount of responsibility that lower-level managers should assume on grievances. Moreover, the police supervisor and middle manager should be required to apply his knowledge and trained skills in early problem solving. The supervisor and middle manager in many cases can avoid problems that, in retrospect, should not have occurred in the first place. Police managers should make training in grievance handling an integral part of the supervisor's and middle manager's training program. This training should emphasize: (1) the interpretation of contract language, past practice, and precedent; (2) the importance of documenting the facts as the basis for management's position in grievance proceedings; (3) the desirability of settlement at the

lowest possible level as means of minimizing costs and antagonism between the parties; and (4) skills in responding to grievances both orally
and in writing.

Responsibility 6:   Use of Specialists

Few police managers have expertise in employee relations, employee
organization activities, and collective negotiations. Hence, many seek
management-employee specialists for counsel in the field of employee
relations. Specialists are available in the private employment field and
more are becoming available to public agencies.

Responsibility 7:   Political Rights (First Amendment)

Police employees, as public employees, have been proscribed specifically
from activity in political management and campaigns through local legislation and the 1939 Federal Hatch Act. Most police managers, police
authorities, and police employees, until the last several years, have con-
curred that politics should be kept out of police agencies or the police
out of politics. However, the law is vague on bipartisan or nonpartisan
elections where police employees seek such local offices as member of the
schoolboard or city council. The law suggests (the First Amendment of
the Bill of Rights is but one case in point) that the burden of proof
will be on the police agency to show that the agency is adversely affected
by such political activity.

Responsibility 8:   Formation of and Right to Join an Employee
Organization

The right to organize police employee associations or unions is protected
by the First Amendment to the U.S. Constitution and has been reiterated
in several court cases. Indeed, some chiefs and sheriffs have found that
employee organizations can assist in improving the agency's effectiveness.
While recognition of an employee's right to join an organization is important, the manager also has the responsibility to protect the rights of
those police who *do not* want to join the organization.

Several police employee organizations now propose the requirement
that membership be a condition of employment and thus seek this agency
shop condition during their negotiations with their police agencies. Several court cases, however, support the police officer who does not want
to join police employee organizations.

Responsibility 9:   Organized Labor and the Law

Police management consistently has opposed affiliation of police employee organizations with organized labor. In 1969 the IACP Special Committee on Police Employee Organizations identified four reasons why it thought police employees should not affiliate with organized labor: (1) There would be a threat of a strike, a common tool of the organized labor union; (2) this group would eventually become involved in decision making for the policy agency subordinating public safety to membership interests; (3) it would inhibit police professionalism; and (4) the union would be interested primarily in personal financial betterment, rather than advancement of social and professional goals.

Added to these are the arguments that affiliation with organized labor would encourage police participation in partisan politics and compromise the neutrality of police employees in maintaining order during disputes. *The courts which have struck down regulations that prohibit this affiliation, have done so following consideration of these arguments.*

Responsibility 10:   Collective Negotiation and the Law

Generally, state and local public employee relations legislation is confusing, contradictory, and often incomplete in its coverage of employees.[19] Yet one can detect a growing trend toward legislation requiring mandatory negotiations, particularly for public safety employees.

Laws establishing collective negotiation for public employees have withstood legal attacks on their constitutionality. Courts have been favorable to statutes that reflected careful study and use of the experience of both public and private employee relations programs. At the same time, local jurisdictions should be allowed to establish specific rules for the collective negotiation process. Negotiation involves money and policy formulations that are usually responsibilities of the local government and the individual police agency.

Prime consideration should be given to the establishment of a date for the negotiation process, consistent with the budget cycle of the agency, which allows a reasonable time for negotiations. Further, because two basic issues are in contention—salaries and working conditions—many jurisdictions are making the negotiation for each issue separate: *salaries*

19A brief overview of the state of the art in management-labor negotiations is contained in Carlton Lewis, "State Regulation of Local Government Labor Relations," *Public Management* 57 (February 1975): 7–9.

are negotiated with the local government and working conditions with the police agency.

Exclusive recognition of the organization that represents the majority of the employees involved in the negotiation process is essential to an effective program. Negotiation between more than two parties could result in excessive conflict and prevent settlement. It is generally agreed, however, that the local jurisdiction and police agency should allow representatives of a limited, reasonable number of minority group employees to be heard prior to the actual negotiation process. Police employee organizations usually are willing to negotiate in good faith; however, sometimes they *resort to political circumvention and external pressures when the negotiation seemingly does not satisfy their objectives (an "end run"* to the city council). For effective negotiation, such circumvention must be avoided.

Collective negotiation must not compel unnecessary or unreasonable concession on the part of police management. The ability of the police to supply police services must not be affected by collective negotiation. *The state legislation that establishes collective negotiation for police employees should also define the parameters of negotiable issues and make provisions for dispute resolution on these issues. Regrettably,* however, it appears that police management still is negotiating issues that should be prohibited from negotiation. *Police management must be resolute on the nonnegotiability of restricted management rights!*

Responsibility 11:   Management Involvement

Because public employee organizations in the past usually dealt directly with local government in the areas of personnel benefits, police managers were not involved. Collective negotiation has changed that situation. Police managers who do not involve themselves in the negotiation process *could find their management capability seriously restricted!*

Responsibility 12:   Training and Understanding

Effective management-employee relations, particularly with collective negotiation, require that all police employees have a general knowledge of the program, and that managers and employees directly involved in the process have specific training and information. The most effective time to dispense such general information is during basic police training for sworn employees, introductory orientation training for nonsworn personnel, and routine annual training for other line and management employees. A police agency and an association or union should be represented by a team of experts in personnel, budgetary, and field operations.

Such representatives should be designated long before negotiations begin and should be given as much training, experience, and information in the area of collective negotiations as the agency and association can support.

Responsibility 13:   Keeping the Agreement Alive

The most critical ingredient in the maintenance of effective management-employee relations programs and collective negotiations is what transpires within the police agency after the negotiation process. The public, and many police managers and local governmental officials, look upon collective negotiation as an annual (or less frequent) activity that once concluded can be ignored until the next negotiation period. In reality, the process continues after the formal negotiation period ceases because interpreting the contrast is a *continuous process*. Line supervisors usually will interpret it themselves in relation to their specific problems; however, interpretation of complex clauses and operational adherence to the contract generally is the responsibility of the agency's trained representatives or the local jurisdiction's personnel agency.

When new operational orders that affect areas subject to negotiation, or that are part of the existing contract are drafted, they should be made available to a representative of the employee organization prior to implementation. The assistance of the organization during the drafting of an order can be very helpful. If the employee organization is not involved in this process, it may attempt to block the order's promulgation.

Responsibility 14:   Resolving Unresolved Issues

The three unresolved areas essential to the collective negotiation process are *unit determination, area-wide negotiations,* and *impasse procedures*. To begin with, one of the most perplexing problems facing police collective negotiations is to determine an appropriate division of employees into representative units. The principal issue in dispute has been the definition of supervisor and management employee and whether these persons should be included in a bargaining unit including first level employees, or in a separate unit, or in no unit.

Area-wide negotiations present several problems. Most local governments, police agencies, and police employee organizations are reluctant to grant a share of their authority to another group. The strongest aspect affecting consolidation is that local governments represent the *revenue base* and are typically unwilling to consolidate that base to serve regional needs. Additionally there are significant differences between central city and suburban police service levels and personnel systems.

Impasse resolution procedures are activated when collective negotiations collapse and the parties are unable to mutually resolve the disputed area. In the private employment sector, a strike by employees or lockout by the employers is frequently the result.[20] But for the police service, such a result is both inappropriate and highly dangerous. The public employment sector, therefore, has sought other procedures. Impasse procedures usually begin with mediation, then fact-finding, and finally arbitration.[21] Arbitration is a quasi-judicial process involving hearing both sides, reviewing the evidence and supportive material, and obtaining related material from other sources in making a decision on an appropriate agreement. The form of arbitration ranges from voluntary or compulsory entry into the process, to advisory or binding application of the ultimate decision. In the public sector, to date, the tendency has been to have a three-man arbitration panel with one representative from each side sitting with a neutral third party.

Arbitration to settle disputes in the determination of the collective negotiation agreement is a relatively new procedure even in the private sector. Its primary purpose in the public sector is to resolve disputes and preclude a police work stoppage—in itself a doubtful hope. Whatever the procedure developed, it must fit the needs of the local situation and, to be effective, must emanate from a consensus of the local government, police agency, and police employees. *The community that will be served by the results must also be involved because ultimately it must bear the cost.*

Responsibility 15: To Safeguard Responsibilities

We conclude at this point with the following recommendations for all police chiefs and sheriffs:

Safeguard your officers' *rights,* but at the same time make certain they fulfill their *responsibilities.* Thus to the "Police Officer's Bill of Rights" should be attached a "Police Officer's Bill of Responsibilities."

Safeguard your *rights* in order that you can fulfill your *responsibilities.* Thus define your rights and responsibilities and *do not* bargain them away.

Safeguard your integrity and power base. Thus bargain in good faith, but be constantly alert for and prepared to combat political chicanery.

---

[20]A field research study on impasses (conflicts) and their community-wide implications is examined in Thomas A. Kochan, George P. Huber, and L.L. Cummings, "Determinants of Intraorganizational Conflict in Collective Bargaining in the Public Sector," *Administrative Science Quarterly* 20 (March 1975): 10–23.

[21]For further information see Charles M. Rehmus, "Binding Arbitration in the Public Sector," *Monthly Labor Review* 98 (April 1975): 53–56.

Chapter Twelve

TASK 10
INTERNAL DISCIPLINE:
Monitoring Integrity

The role of the police is best understood as a mechanism for the distribution of non-negotiably coercive force employed in accordance with the dictates of an intuitive grasp of situational exigencies.[1]

5.4 Need for Administrative Sanctions and Procedures.

In order to strengthen administrative review and control, responsibility should formally be delegated to the police for developing comprehensive administrative policies and rules governing the duties and responsibilities of police officers together with procedures and sanctions for ensuring that these duties and responsibilities are met. Police administrative rules and procedures should establish effective investigative, hearing, and internal review procedures for alleged violations. Such procedures should include provisions for handling, monitoring, and reviewing citizen complaints in such a way as to ensure diligence, fairness, and public confidence. In developing such rules and procedures, recognition must be given to the need to conform procedures to administrative due process requirements, to develop means for ensuring impartial investigations, and to keep the public informed of all administrative actions as they are taken.[2]

If the police administrator is more threatened by complaints over the particular behavior of his officers than over crime rates or general police strategy and if he cannot make and enforce policies that prescribe how the officer ought to "handle situations," then the kind of system the administrator develops to defend his organization and to discipline the individual officer will be oriented toward particular kinds of behavior (not general strategies) and toward those elements of police behavior that can be subject to rule. In addition, the defense and control system will confer substantial discretionary power on the administrator to decide whether or not a particular behavior was a violation of a departmental policy even though—indeed, precisely because—that policy is itself ambiguous or equivocal.[3]

SYNOPSIS

Policing his police is a paramount issue and growing concern of today's police manager. Employee misconduct ranges from surly

[1]Egon Bittner, *The Functions of The Police In Modern Society* (Chevy Chase, Md.: National Institute of Mental Health, 1970), p. 46.
[2]American Bar Association, *The Urban Police Function* (Washington, D.C.: American Bar Association, 1973), pp. 163–64.
[3]James Q. Wilson, *Varieties of Police Behavior.* (New York: Atheneum Press, 1973), p. 71.

attitude, to physical abuse, to criminal corruption. Thus, the gravity of opprobious behavior varies over a continuum of activities from improper attitude on the one hand to overt violations of a law on the other. Internal systems of monitoring the integrity of a police agency have been primarily either ineffective or absent. Internal investigative units and procedures have been likewise. Currently the byword in police management is the fulfillment of "responsibility for accountability."

Accountability (once responsibility for it has been assumed) begins with unequivocal policies regarding disciplinary matters. Appropriately, the policies should encompass three overlapping codes of conduct: legalistic, professional, and moralistic. The policies must be lucid, explicit, and enforceable. They, in turn, form a guideline out of which organizational and staffing decisions can be forged. Although the police manager may establish a special internal investigations unit, the responsibility for employee probity must be shared throughout the agency. Only the more severe misconduct problems should be transferred from the concerned supervisor to the special unit.

Internal safeguarding against wrongful behavior most often starts with the receipt of a complaint. Subsequently, it is investigated by a supervisor or internal discipline investigator, and then adjudicated by either the manager or an administrative trial board. Each phase comprises a variety of considerations, options, and steps, all of which entail careful, deliberate, and insightful decisions. A small error can result in exonerating errant personnel or defaming the reputation of honest employees. A viable, fair, and objective internal discipline unit can prevent both from occurring. Other far-reaching and long-term preventative measures are critical to the enduring integrity of the agency. In a few words, this is the one of the two primary responsibilities of the police manager (the other being goal fulfillment).

DISCIPLINE: A System of Accountability

Creation of an internal investigation unit does not relieve command personnel of the need to maintain discipline. On the contrary, it strengthens it by providing assistance to commanders, on request, in the investigation of alleged misconduct of their subordinates. In addition, this investigative unit supervises, for the chief, all disciplinary investigations by commanders.[4]

Alert police managers recognize that they must take steps to strengthen agency review and control of police conduct. Plainly, it is impossible to construct an effective system of accountability (see exhibit 12–1) without a strong and functional mechanism for maintaining behavioral control over police personnel. While the exclusionary rule, criminal and civil actions against police officers, and other external remedies serve as important constraints, the police manager must accept primary responsibility for controlling the vast discretionary power of police officers. Unfortunately some police managers have not yet accepted this challenge, and this is the basic reason why there has been constant pressure for civilian review boards, ombudsmen, and other such external review agencies. Police managers cannot reasonably ignore pressures for formalized review if they want to prove their willingness and ability to assume responsibility for ensuring that their personnel comply with the requirements of law, the security needs of a community, and human social justice. This chapter will concentrate on internal monitoring. However, much of what is discussed here is equally applicable to external review authorities. For those interested, many of the footnotes contain references to various external review concepts and practices.

The promulgation of comprehensive policies and procedures by the police manager, while a necessary first step, is alone insufficient. Much more is required before individual adherence can be anticipated. Hence, the following additional steps should be taken:

> Make overt commitment in voice and deed on the part of police management and supervision to the policies
>
> Intensify training relative to the implementation of policies
>
> Establish a valid and reliable system of accountability
>
> Precisely define approved and wrongful conduct along with commendations for the former and penalties for the latter
>
> Formalize investigative, hearing, and review procedures for alleged violations

Let us for a moment assume that all of these steps have been or are being implemented. One in particular deserves additional explication—that of internal investigative procedures.

The President's Commission on Law Enforcement and Administration of Justice reported in 1967 that there were gross deficiencies nationally

---

[4]O. W. Wilson and Roy C. McLaren, *Police Administration*, 3rd. ed., (New York: McGraw-Hill, Inc., 1972), p. 210.

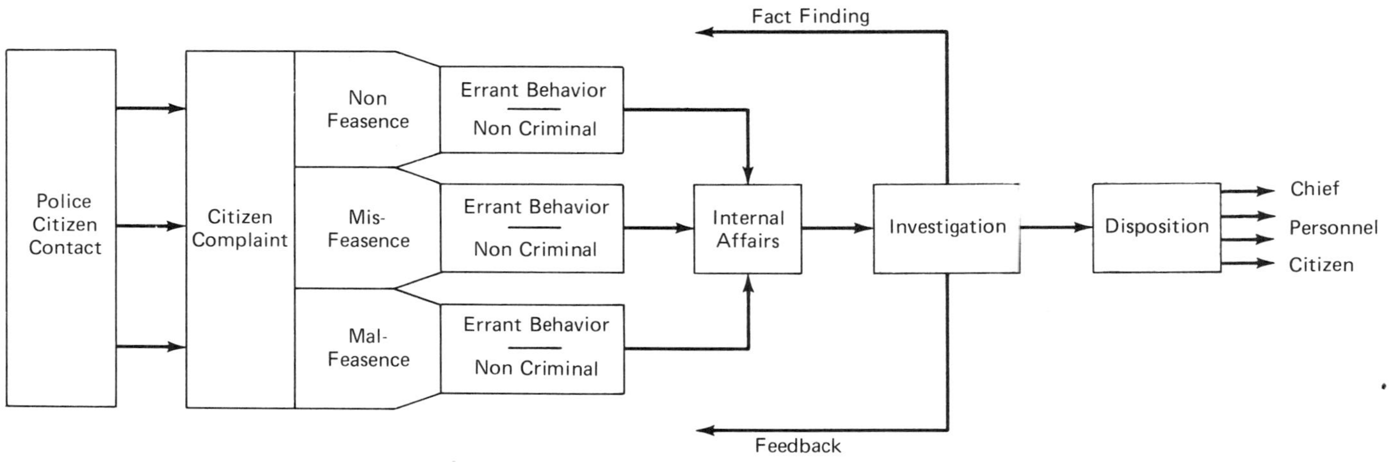

Exhibit 12-1.   Internal Discipline: A System of Accountability

in internal discipline. To this end, the Task Force Report on the Police made several recommendations for improving such procedures.[5]

1. Large to medium-sized police and sheriff agencies should have an internal investigation unit or individual responsible to the chief administrator. The unit should have both an *investigative* and *preventive* role in controlling actions by police officers.

2. Police agencies should make clear that they welcome complaints.

3. Police agencies should reassess their hearing procedures to determine whether they meet appropriate standards of fairness (to the citizen, to the officer, and to the agency).

4. Police agencies should examine penalties to determine whether they are effective in deterring future misconduct and whether they are justified when the nature of the offense is considered.

5. The complainant and the officer should be notified of the decision and of the basis for it. And the public should have access to the facts of the case and the nature of the decision.

6. When an incident has exacerbated tension in an area, it is preferable for the decision to be explained directly to the residents of the area through either the community relations unit, a neighborhood police team, or some other similar procedure.

It is essential that all police managers develop policies, processes, and staff to handle, monitor, and review citizen complaints in a manner which is thorough and which commands the respect of the community as being both careful and equitable. This will be enormously challenging and complex. Officer morale may decline, citizen distrust may increase, and agency effectiveness may suffer for a while as the new commitment is being made to ensure that internal procedures are fair and that complaints are diligently pursued. Nonetheless, it is emphasized that strong internal procedures hold the greatest promise of being the basis for *effective* review and control of police conduct. And, it is with proper police conduct that we will mount and maintain effective police systems for the delivery of much-needed police services.

As long as there are two forms of accounting, one that is explicit and continually audited (internal discipline), and another that is devoid of rules and rarely looked into (dealings with citizens), it must be expected that keeping a positive balance in the first might

[5]The President's Commission on Law Enforcement and Administration of Justice, *Task Force Report: The Police* (Washington, D.C.: U.S. Government Printing Office, 1967), pp. 193–97.

encourage playing loose with the second. The likelihood of this increases proportionately to pressures to produce. Since it is not enough that policemen be obedient soldier-bureaucrats, but must, to insure favorable consideration for advancement, contribute to the arrest total, they will naturally try to meet this demand in ways that will keep them out of trouble. Thus, to secure the promotion from the uniformed patrol to the detective bureau, which is highly valued and not determined by civil service examinations, officers feel impelled to engage in actions that furnish opportunities for conspicuous display of aggressiveness. John McNamara illustrates this tactic by quoting a dramatic expression of cynicism, "If you want to get 'out of the bag' into the 'bureau' shoot somebody." Leaving the exaggeration aside, there is little doubt that emphasis on military-bureaucratic control rewards the appearance of staying out of troubles as far as internal regulations are concerned, combined with strenuous efforts to make "good pinches," i.e., arrests that contain, or can be managed to appear to contain, elements of physical danger. Every officer knows that he will never receive a citation for avoiding a fight but only for prevailing in a fight at the risk of his own safety. Perhaps there is nothing wrong with that rule. But there is surely something wrong with a system in which the combined demands for strict compliance with departmental regulation and for vigorously productive law enforcement can be met simultaneously by displacing the onus of the operatives' own misconduct on citizens. This tends to be the case in departments characterized by strong militaristic-bureaucratic discipline where officers do not merely transgress to make "good pinches," but make "good pinches" to conceal their transgressions.[6]

The remainder of the chapter is divided into four subject areas dealing with internal discipline: policies, organization, processing, and prevention. A procedural manual for internal investigation appears in Appendix B.

DISCIPLINARY POLICIES: Drawing The Lines

When a police administrator declares himself against corruption, he is confronted by questions about his stance. Does he mean an officer should not accept a free cup of coffee? How about a meal? What about a reward sincerely offered for meritorious service? And what about the tip offered by a visiting dignitary to the officer who served as his bodyguard? These are clearly on the periphery of the corruption problem. They are not usually the practices which prompted the administrator to speak out against corruption, nor are they likely

[6]Bittner, *Functions Of The Police,* pp. 57–58.

to be of central concern to those most troubled by the existence of corruption. They cannot, however, be ignored, for they raise several more fundamental questions. Should police be subject to a substantially higher standard of conduct than those in other governmental agencies, the business community, and the private sector generally? Is it preferable to have a departmental policy absolutely prohibiting the acceptance of any gratuity? Or is it desirable to have what some would characterize as a more realistic policy which permits officers to accept minor gratuities offered not to corrupt but in sincere appreciation for a job well done?

Most administrators, at the risk of sounding fanatical, have chosen the first alternative.[7]

While the community may disagree with, or be vague about what constitutes police misconduct, the police cannot. Granted, without community consensus on this subject the problem is a highly perplexing one for our police. Nonetheless, wrongdoing must be *defined* and *policies* must be set by the agency. Lines must be clearly drawn. Essentially these lines should encompass three forms of misconduct: (1) legalistic, (2) professional, and (3) moralistic.[8] The first involves criminal considerations; the second may or may not be criminal in nature but does entail professional considerations; and the third may or may not include professional canons, but does embody personal ethics. Each form of errant behavior is examined further in the following paragraphs. It will be noted that there is a descending degree of clarity or precision with each type of wrongdoing. Conversely, there is an ascending degree of managerial ambiguity on police and procedural violations.

Legalistic Misconduct

This type of misconduct is also commonly referred to as "corruption." The quotation at the beginning of this section basically addresses this form of police malfeasance. Varying degrees and types of corruption exist in all police agencies. Police corruption is an extremely complex and demoralizing crime problem, and it is not new to our generation of police personnel. Police corruption includes: (1) the misuse of police authority for the police employee's personal gain; (2) activity of the police employee that compromises, or has the potential to compromise, his ability to enforce the law or provide other police service impartially; (3) the

[7]Herman Goldstein, *Police Corruption: A Perspective On Its Nature and Control* (Washington, D.C.: The Police Foundation), pp. 28–29.
[8]*Ibid.*, p. 3.

protection of illicit activities from police enforcement, whether or not the police employee receives something of value in return; and (4) the police employee's involvement in promoting the business of one person while discouraging that of another person. Hence, unless an officer's action in such encounters was motivated by a desire for personal gain, the problems raised differ significantly from those raised where personal gain is not a primary objective. Police corruption means, therefore, acts involving the misuse of authority by a police officer in a manner designed to produce *personal gain for himself or for others.* And, this is illegal!

Professional Misconduct

This form of misconduct can range from physical to verbal abuse of a citizen. On the one hand, a criminal or civil violation may have occurred while on the other, agency standards of professional conduct may be at issue. The possibilities for wrongdoing in this instance can fall within two rubrics: the law, and professional conduct "unbecoming an officer." The distinction, again, between this type of wrongdoing and corruption is that no personal gain for the officer or others is involved. The key question is: What conduct is permissible? Hence there is a need for established policies, procedures, rules, and sanctions that explicitly encompass the conduct of police employees. The code of ethics in exhibit 12–2 exemplifies the above thinking.

Moralistic Misconduct

If an officer thinks certain citizens are deserving of aggressive police practices, the likelihood of his behaving aggressively is enhanced—perhaps to the point of overreaction or even physical abuse. Or, if he thinks certain citizens are deserving of no police attention the likelihood of his behaving passively is increased—perhaps to the extent of no reaction—and thus the possibility of corruption occurs. Space does not allow adequate coverage of this subject. Nonetheless, it is at the very crux of other forms of misconduct. Other books on police attitudes should be consulted. Indeed, other books on police attitudes must be consulted since internal discipline will be maintained or not according to one's "attitudes."[9]

[9]The literature and studies dealing with police community relations most often address the subject of police attitudes. One recent study in particular is worthy of perusal, John Van Moanen, "Police Socialization: A Longitudinal Examination of Job Attitudes in an Urban Police Department," *Administrative Science Quarterly* 20 (June 1975): 207–28.

Exhibit 12–2. An Example of a Code of Ethics for Law Enforcement Officers

---

POST Administrative Manual   COMMISSION PROCEDURES C-3

July 1, 1974

Personnel Selection & Standards

LAW ENFORCEMENT CODE OF ETHICS

Purpose

3-1. Code of Ethics: To insure that every officer is fully aware of his individual responsibility to maintain his own integrity and that of his agency, every officer, during his basic training, shall be administered the Law Enforcement Code of Ethics as an oath as prescribed in Section 1013 of the Regulations.

Code of Ethics

3-2. AS A LAW ENFORCEMENT OFFICER, my fundamental duty is to serve mankind; to safeguard lives and property; to protect the innocent against deception, the weak against oppression or intimidation, and the peaceful against violence or disorder; and to respect the Constitutional rights of all men to liberty, equality and justice.

I WILL keep my private life unsullied as an example to all; maintain courageous calm in the face of danger, scorn, or ridicule; develop self-restraint; and be constantly mindful of the welfare of others. Honest in thought and deed in both my personal and official life, I will be exemplary in obeying the laws of the land and the regulations of my department. Whatever I see or hear of a confidential nature or that is confided in me in my official capacity will be kept ever secret unless revelation is necessary in the performance of my duty.

I WILL never act officiously or permit personal feelings, prejudices, animosities or friendships to influence my decisions. With no compromise for crime and with relentless prosecution of criminals, I will enforce the law courteously and appropriately without fear or favor, malice or ill will, never employing unnecessary force or violence and never accepting gratuities.

I RECOGNIZE the badge of my office as a symbol of public faith, and I accept it as a public service. I will constantly strive to achieve these objectives and ideas, dedicating myself before God to my chosen profession . . . . . law enforcement.

Source: Post Administration Manual (Sacramento, Calif.: Commission on Peace Officer Standards and Training, July 1, 1974), p. 31.

Policies: The Written Dos and Don'ts

As stated earlier, the twofold goal of internal discipline is administrative order and employee accountability. As in law, the administration of internal discipline must be based on a firm, formal written foundation.[10] Written policies, procedures, and rules form the standards for police employee conduct and provide redress for the three involved parties: the public, the agency, and the police officer.

The police manager must be intimately involved in the design and monitoring of the disciplinary machinery of his agency. If he fosters a fair and effective system, his decisions will be upheld by reviewing authorities and respected by the personnel comprising his agency. If not, external review will become all the more pervasive, and officer morale all the more curtailed.

Officer conduct must be based on authority that is reasonable and enforceable. Rules should be logical and written in a concise form that every employee can readily understand. Rules of conduct, like the law, are subject to modification. Police managers must constantly monitor their rules and make needed changes.

Rules of conduct can be a cause for litigation, often because they were drafted without legal assistance and in ignorance of administrative law. When such rules are abrogated in a civil action or arbitration, many police agencies fail to update the sections involved. Hence, a police agency must maintain close liaison with its legal unit, legal adviser, or other legal assistance. In addition, records must be kept to identify the background research and sources consulted in drafting policies, rules, and procedures. Finally, employee participation in formulating or revising rules of conduct can be a key to both *acceptance* and *adherence*. The following standard reflects the above thinking and thus serves as the basis for an internal system of discipline.

Standard 19.1

FOUNDATION FOR
INTERNAL DISCIPLINE

Every police agency immediately should formalize policies, procedures, and rules in written form for the administration of internal discipline. The internal discipline system should be based on essential fairness, but not bound by formal procedures or proceedings such as are used in criminal trials.

10This section is based on the National Advisory Commission on Criminal Justice Standards and Goals, *Police* (Washington, D.C.: U.S. Government Printing Office, 1973), pp. 474–76.

1. Every police agency immediately should establish formal written procedures for the administration of internal discipline and an appropriate summary of those procedures should be made public.

2. The chief executive of every police agency should have ultimate responsibility for the administration of internal discipline.

3. Every employee at the time of employment should be given written rules for conduct and appearance. They should be stated in brief, understandable language.

   In addition to other rules that may be drafted with assistance from employee participants, one prohibiting a general classification of misconduct, traditionally known as "conduct unbecoming an officer," should be included. This rule should prohibit conduct that may tend to reflect unfavorably upon the employee or the agency.

4. The policies, procedures, and rules governing employee conduct and the administration of discipline should be strengthened by incorporating them in training programs and promotional examinations, and by encouraging employee participation in the disciplinary system.[11]

ORGANIZATIONAL AND STAFFING CONSIDERATIONS

> Over the past decade there has been considerable sentiment expressed by persons outside law enforcement to establish civilian review boards to investigate or adjudicate allegations against police. Undoubtedly a part of the reason for this has been the tendency of police to avoid making fair and vigorous investigations of wrongdoing within their ranks. What has been described as the "blue veil of protection" has all too often been drawn over police transgressions. There are numerous reasons for it, among them the feeling among police that they are vilified by a growing segment of the public and therefore must band together for self-protection. Some misguided administrators may believe that conducting a vigorous internal investigation is tantamount to admitting failure. The opposite, of course, is closer to the truth.
>
> It is clearly apparent that if the police do not take a vigorous stand on the matter of internal investigation, outside groups—such as review boards consisting of laymen or other persons outside the police service—will step into the void.[12]

In many ways our respect for a policy agency is linked to its preservation of internal discipline. Because the police manager is accountable

---

[11]*Ibid.,* p. 474.
[12]Wilson and McLaren, *Police Administration,* p. 207.

for the conduct of all police agency employees, he should have a direct interface with the internal discipline process. In turn, many agencies have formed internal investigation units to concentrate responsibility for the investigation of misconduct and to give sustained attention to the agency's probity. In a large agency, this unit will be of substantial size. In a medium-sized agency the responsibility may be assigned to a single officer. And, in a smaller agency the police manager or middle manager may assume this responsibility along with other duties. Regardless of who performs the internal investigation function, the fact remains that someone must do so. Otherwise, one can only anticipate support for external review.

Before addressing the organization and staffing of an internal investigations unit, let us examine a few problems that are usually associated with it. Later subsections will recommend tactics for resolving or, at least, reducing their adverse impact on the agency.

Potential Problems

Who's Responsible?   Ironically, many problems occur when a special internal affairs unit is established. In some larger cities and counties there are several levels of investigators. Those at the top check the probity of those assigned to inspect the honesty of those at the bottom—a situation contributing to the paranoia that often pervades an agency. Having a number of hierarchical levels often spreads responsibility to the point where no one except the chief or sheriff feels totally responsible for detecting misconduct.

You May Work For Me!   A major deficiency of special investigative units is one rarely voiced by the police. It is ridiculous to expect officers on special assignment, however honest and dedicated, to investigate zealously the activities of fellow officers who may in the future be their partners or superiors. In other words, "Be careful, you may work with or for me one day."

Head Hunters.   Some police managers are in favor of permanently assigning police officers to an internal affairs unit. However, others are quick to point out that this may intensify the problem of maintaining the unit's effectiveness. Still others contend that officers assigned to investigating errant behavior over a long period of time, like those permanently assigned to vice investigations, eventually lose their value as fair and objective investigators. And, most would fear that such a unit will become an elite squad of "doer's" or "head hunters."

Organizational Location

The hierarchical location of an internal affairs unit or investigator should be within the office (immediate purview) of the chief or sheriff. The importance of this function, plus the constant legal and procedural changes affecting its operation, make it imperative that the top manager is fully aware of its activities. Also, much of the unit's effectiveness is dependent on others in the agency recognizing that it acts as an extension of the manager. In essence it should be perceived as his alter ego. If this is not accomplished then middle managers and those of equal rank to the investigators may resist or ignore the efforts of the unit. In so many words, the internal investigations unit must be next to, and an extension of, the boss.

Policy will determine the shape and scope of the unit. If all complaints are to be processed by the internal affairs officers then it will be a highly centralized and relatively large operation. Unless there are compelling reasons for not doing so, we would recommend that a decentralized model be adopted. Then the severity of the complaint will determine whether the responsible supervisor or the internal affairs officer investigates the alleged breach of ethics. The decentralized model is preferred because (1) the staffing requirement of the unit is minimized, and (2) the immediate supervisor is not relieved of his assumed duty to direct and control his staff. The above recommendations are directed toward resolving the problem of "Who's responsible?" Again, the answer is: The type of complaint determines who will investigate the allegation. Nevertheless, the supervisor has a continuing responsibility for the behavior of his staff.

Staffing

The size of a specialized unit should be determined by the same analytical methods employed for allocating resources to any other specialized function—usually, demands for workload and expertise. Not all members of internal discipline investigation units should be assigned to the normal daytime hours worked by most staff officers. First of all, most incidents causing complaints of police misbehavior do not occur during normal working hours. Also, some persons who have filed complaints consider investigators' visits or phone calls at their place of business during working hours an imposition. Many police officers who may be involved in complaints—whether accused or as witnesses—normally are deployed in other than daytime hours and can be more conveniently contacted while they are on duty. Hence, if the majority of internal affairs investigators are deployed in other than daytime hours, the unit will have greater flexibility and can provide a positive response to external and internal complaints.

Police agencies at times decide that expert assistance is necessary to ensure preservation of evidence and successful preparation of an administrative or criminal case. Thus the internal affairs staff can supplement their number and expertise by eliciting the aid of the local prosecuting attorney. This is important particularly when the complaint of employee misconduct alleges a criminal offense that could result, if proven, in the employee's removal.

It has been repeatedly found that employee participation fosters respect for the internal discipline system. This participation is often accomplished by rotating employees through tours of duty in the specialized internal discipline investigation unit. There should be a maximum length of time, however, for such a tour of duty. Prolonged assignment to this task can impose emotional stress upon employees, alienate them from their coworkers and permanently label them as a "head hunter." It is best that the assignment to the internal affairs unit last from eight to twenty-four months. The preceding recommendations address the second and third problems mentioned above. In turn, the following standard covers the issues discussed in this section.

Standard 19.3

INVESTIGATIVE
RESPONSIBILITY

The chief executive of every police agency immediately should insure that the investigation of all complaints from the public, and all allegations of criminal conduct and serious internal misconduct, are conducted by a specialized individual or unit of the involved police agency. This person or unit should be responsible directly to the agency's chief executive or the assistant chief executive. Minor internal misconduct may be investigated by first line supervisors, and these investigations should be subject to internal review.

1. The existence or size of this specialized unit should be consistent with the demands of the work load.

2. Police agencies should obtain the assistance of prosecuting agencies during investigations of criminal allegations and other cases where the police chief executive concludes that the public interest would best be served by such participation.

3. Specialized units for complaint investigation should employ a strict rotation policy limiting assignments to 18 months.

4. Every police agency should deploy the majority of its complaint investigators during the hours consistent with complaint incidence, public convenience, and agency needs.[13]

COMPLAINT PROCESSING: Receipt, Investigation And Adjudication

The data from Philadelphia strongly suggest that something more than a jurisdictional rearrangement resulted when citizens were offered a mode of redress other than police jurisdiction over all citizen-initiated complaints. Differences in mandate, staffing, organization environment, and ideology resulted in two distinct types of review agencies. The conceptualization of the problem, the ways in which altercations were settled, and the other functions served were markedly different.[14]

Complaints of Corruption. A complaint from a citizen or a police officer is one starting point for detecting corruption and apprehending corrupt officers. Such complaints must be encouraged by informing the public specifically how and where to make complaints and what details are necessary for action. More effective procedures must be established, with strong controls for insuring that complaints get immediately recorded wherever in the Department they may be received. These actions are necessary to mesh with the new departmental procedures for ensuring adequate complaint follow-up.[15]

At first glance the quotations above may appear unrelated. On the contrary, they are very much associated with one other although they are mutually exclusive. The first citation indicates that one jurisdiction found an external complaint review process most rewarding. The second implies than an external review authority may be obviated by a proactive, open, internal mechanism for receiving, investigating, and adjudi-

[13]National Advisory Commission, "Organizational Aspects of Internal and External Review of the Police," *Police*, p. 480.

[14]James R. Hudson, *Journal of Criminal Law, Criminology and Police Science* 63 (Fall 1972): 430.

[15]*Knapp Commission Report: Summary and Principle Recommendations* (New York: Commission to Investigate Allegations of Police Corruption and the City's Anti-Corruption Procedures, August 3, 1972), p. 23.

cating citizen complaints against police conduct. We will concentrate on an internal process. As mentioned before, nonetheless, most of the process can be applied to an external police review agency. We begin with a discussion of the *receipt* phase of complaint processing.

Phase 1. Complaint Receipt

Effective complaint reception procedures provide the police manager with an essential tool for assessing employee performance quality and in measuring public police support. It is also important that *all* instances of employee inefficiency and misconduct be revealed and investigated. Unless the public is convinced that an agency is truly receptive to complaints, it will ignore the system. Additionally, police managers must monitor the procedures for receiving public complaints to ensure that they are not being circumvented and that the initial filing of a complaint alleging employee misconduct is a fast and facilitative process.

Police agencies should develop a form for use in filing a complaint (see exhibit 12–3).[16] Further, police agencies should accept all complaints, whether received in person, by telephone, by letter, or anonymously. The police agency should delineate procedures for employees to follow in processing complaints alleging misconduct. Both supervisory and internal affairs personnel should be equally responsible for receiving complaints.

The person filing a complaint should be given a copy of the report form as a receipt. After the receipt of a complaint, the agency should interview the complainant. This interview provides the complainant with evidence of the agency's concern. Also, it gives the investigator an opportunity to secure additional information such as photographs, medical release statements, and personal observation. Anonymous complaints should not be arbitrarily dismissed. Obviously, a police agency should seek to identify the person giving the information, but reason should indicate the amount of effort expended. An anonymous complaint may be the only clue to the discovery of a dishonest police employee.

All citizens who file a complaint must receive information regarding the results of the investigation. Police agencies that personally contact the complainants and discuss the investigation and adjudication will discover that a better mutual relationship and understanding are fostered. The subsequent standard pertains to the receipt of citizen complaints.

---

[16]A word of appreciation to Raymond C. Davis for use of the Santa Ana (California) Police Department's complaint processing announcement. Incidently, it is printed as a brochure in both the English and Spanish languages.

Exhibit 12–3.   An Example of a Complaint Procedure

WHAT ABOUT MY COMPLAINT?

"The policeman today in every community is an unmistakable symbol not only of the law, but of the entire 'establishment.' Because of this, he is the obvious target for grievances against any shortcomings of our governmental system. The policeman can solve the complex problems of a community only when working in concert with an entire community. The police can, and must, however, recognize their responsibility to serve all the public to the best of their ability. FAIR AND IMPARTIAL LAW ENFORCEMENT WHICH RESPECTS THE INDIVIDUAL DIGNITY OF ALL MEN IS ESSENTIAL and must be accomplished with tact and diplomacy whenever possible, force only when necessary, and then only that amount of force as is necessary."

"As police officers we must professionally and objectively investigate all citizen complaints as expeditiously as possible in order to arrive at all the facts which will quickly clear the officer's name or substantiate the citizen's complaint, whichever is appropriate."

from Department Order 20

Raymond C. Davis
Chief of Police

DOES THAT MEAN THE POLICE DEPARTMENT WANTS COMPLAINTS?

Of course not. A complaint means that someone hasn't done a good enough job. But, we do want to know when our service needs to be improved or corrected.

BUT WILL YOU LISTEN TO MY COMPLAINT?

Certainly. We want to find out what went wrong so that we can see to it that it doesn't happen again.

WHO WOULD INVESTIGATE MY COMPLAINT?

Either a special investigator from the Internal Investigations Section or the officer's boss (Section Commander) would investigate a complaint against an officer.

WELL THEN WHO SHOULD I GO TO FIRST?

You should take a complaint about an officer to his Section Commander. If he isn't there, ask for the on-duty Watch Commander.

BUT I WANT TO TAKE THIS ALL THE WAY TO THE TOP. I WANT THE CHIEF OF POLICE TO KNOW.

And he will. The Chief of Police gets copies of ALL complaints against officers. Each of the officer's superiors is notifies as well.

DO I HAVE TO COMPLAIN IN PERSON?

No. We prefer to talk to you in person; but, we will accept a complaint by telephone or letter if necessary. It won't make any difference in the attention we give it.

I'M UNDER 18; DO I HAVE THE RIGHT TO COMPLAIN?

Yes, just bring one of your parents, guardians or a responsible adult in with you.

Source: Raymond C. Davis, Santa Ana, California, Police Department.

Exhibit 12–3 (Continued)

WILL I HAVE TO WRITE MY COMPLAINT OUT?

We have found it's much easier to investigate a written complaint so we prefer them that way.
If there are valid reasons this can't be done, we'll make other arrangements.

HOW CLOSE WILL YOU REALLY INVESTIGATE?

Very closely! We want to find out where we went wrong. By the same token, if a person makes
a FALSE complaint, we want to find that out and take the appropriate legal action.

DOES THAT MEAN I COULD GET IN TROUBLE FOR COMPLAINING?

Not if what you're telling us is the truth. We're only interested in prosecuting those who make
malicious, false allegations about people. We wouldn't (and couldn't) bring charges against
a person who has acted in good faith.

WHAT WILL HAPPEN TO THE OFFICER?

That will depend on what he did. If his actions were criminal, he would be dealt with like any
other citizen. If they were improper, but not criminal, he will be disciplined by the Chief of
Police.

WILL I BE TOLD HOW THE COMPLAINT CAME OUT?

Yes. You will receive a letter from the Chief of Police telling you the disposition of our investigation.

WHAT ABOUT THE LIE DETECTOR?

In certain cases, where we can't find the truth any other way, you may be asked to take a
polygraph examination. The same is true for our officers.

WHAT IF I'M NOT SATISFIED WITH THE RESULTS OF THIS INVESTIGATION?

We sincerely hope that would never happen. If it did, you could go to the Santa Ana Human
Relations Commission for assistance. You could also contact your representative on the
City Council; or, in some cases, the Orange County District Attorney or the Grand Jury.

Our goal at the Santa Ana Police Department is that you will never need to use the information
contained in this folder. We don't want to fail in our continuing efforts to give YOU the best
possible police service.

Exhibit 12–3 (Continued)

(Ms)
(Miss)
(Mrs.)
MY NAME IS (Mr.) _____

        (first)   (middle)   (last)

I LIVE AT _____

                               AM   AM
MY HOME PHONE IS _____ OR BETWEEN _____ PM AND _____ PM I CAN BE REACHED
AT WORK, PHONE _____ EXT. _____.
MY AGE IS _____ YEARS.

                   (BADGE[s])
                   (OFFICER [s])
I WANT TO COMPLAIN ABOUT (CAR NUMBER) _____
I WANT TO COMPLAIN BECAUSE ON (date) _____
AT (location) _____

               AM   HE
AT ABOUT (time) _____ PM, THEY _____
_____
_____
_____
_____
_____
_____

(attach as many additional sheets as necessary)

I UNDERSTAND, AND IT IS MY DESIRE, THAT THIS COMPLAINT WILL BE INVESTIGATED DILIGENTLY. I
FURTHER UNDERSTAND THAT IF THE INVESTIGATION PROVES THESE ALLEGATIONS TO BE FALSE, I MAY
BE LIABLE TO BOTH CRIMINAL AND CIVIL PROSECUTION. I ALSO UNDERSTAND THAT IN SOME CASES I MAY
BE ASKED TO SUBMIT TO A POLYGRAPH EXAMINATION AS A PART OF THIS INVESTIGATION.

_____   _____
DATE   SIGNATURE

                             _____
                             SIGNATURE OF PARENT/GUARDIAN
                             (if you are under 18 years of age)

Standard   19.2

COMPLAINT
RECEPTION
PROCEDURES

Every police agency immediately should implement procedures to facilitate the making of a complaint alleging employee misconduct, whether that complaint is initiated internally or externally.

1. The making of a complaint should not be accompanied by fear of reprisal or harassment. Every person making a complaint should receive verification that his complaint is being processed by the police agency. This receipt should contain a general description of the investigative process and appeal provisions.

2. Every police agency, on a continuing basis, should inform the public of its complaint reception and investigation procedures.

3. All persons who file a complaint should be notified of its final disposition; personal discussion regarding this disposition should be encouraged.

4. Every police agency should develop procedures that will insure that all complaints, whether from an external or internal source, are permanently and chronologically recorded in a central record. The procedure should insure that the agency's chief executive or his assistant is made aware of every complaint without delay.

5. Complete records of complaint reception, investigation, and adjudication should be maintained. Statistical summaries based on these records should be published regularly for all police personnel and should be available to the public.[17]

Phase 2. Complaint Investigation

The investigation process must be swift, certain, and fair. This means that only the most competent employees be selected and developed to conduct internal discipline investigations. The efforts expended in these investigations must be at least equal to the efforts expended in the investigation of serious crimes. As a consequence, agencies should require specific intensive training for internal discipline investigators and should provide extensive written guidelines on proper investigative and reporting procedures. Additionally, the investigator must employ all reasonable investigative tools and techniques. But he must be careful not to misuse this privilege. In keeping with the principles of investigation, the internal discipline complaint investigator must not be charged with adjudicating the matter.

Police employee associations have recently questioned certain internal discipline procedures, including the duties and rights of employees who are subjects of internal discipline investigations. Most of these duties and rights are recognized by police agencies but they have seldom been put into writing. Police managers should formalize employee duties and rights, then circulate them to all employees.

The majority of substantiated incidents of police employee misconduct are minor departures from agency policies, rules, and procedures. Police agencies usually handle these without difficulty since they ordinarily provide supervisors with a simple and flexible system for reporting and adjudicating these acts of misconduct. Again, whether the internal affairs

[17]National Advisory Commission, *Police*, p. 477.

officer or the supervisor conducts the investigation, it must be fair and
fast. At the same time, both must endeavor to protect police employees
from malicious and false complaints. If a police employee is falsely accused of misconduct with malicious intent, the police agency's best defense is to disclose the investigative results publicly. False accusations
should not be placed in his personal folder. Moreover, those citizens that
are both guilty of false accusations and the violation of a legal statute
should be prosecuted.

Standard 19.4

INVESTIGATION
PROCEDURES

Every police agency immediately should insure that internal discipline complaint
investigations are performed with the greatest possible skill. The investigative effort
expended on all internal discipline complaints should be at least equal to the effort
expended in the investigation of felony crimes where a suspect is known.

1. All personnel assigned to investigate internal discipline complaints should be given
   specific training in this task and should be provided with written investigative procedures.

2. Every police agency should establish formal procedures for investigating minor internal
   misconduct allegations. These procedures should be designed to insure swift, fair, and
   efficient correction of minor disciplinary problems.

3. Every investigator of internal discipline complaints should conduct investigations in a
   manner that best reveals the facts while preserving the dignity of all persons and
   maintaining the confidential nature of the investigation.

4. Every police agency should provide—at the time of employment, and again, prior to
   the specific investigation—all its employees with a written statement of their duties
   and rights when they are the subject of an internal discipline investigation.

5. Every police chief executive should have legal authority during an internal discipline
   investigation to relieve police employees from their duties when it is in the interests
   of the public and the police agency. A police employee normally should be relieved
   from duty whenever he is under investigation for a crime, corruption, or serious misconduct when the proof is evident and the presumption is great, or when he is
   physically or mentally unable to perform his duties satisfactorily.

6. Investigators should use all available investigative tools that can reasonably be used
   to determine the facts and secure necessary evidence during an internal discipline
   investigation. The polygraph should be administered to employees only at the express
   approval of the police chief executive.

7. All internal discipline investigations should be concluded 30 days from the date the complaint is made unless an extension is granted by the chief executive of the agency. The complainant and the accused employee should be notified of any delay.[18]

Phase 3.   Adjudication: Administrative Equity

The adjudicative phase of the complaint process must be unquestionably open and fair.[19] It is at this point that three interests—those of the agency, the community, and the officer—must be weighed to form a single decision which will affect the corporate lives of the first two, and the individual life of the third. For it is here that professional ethics, community values, one's natural rights, and on occasion the law, are congealed. The police manager possesses the main responsibility for ensuring for all involved that ethics, values, rights, and laws are equitably weighed in making a final decision. Again, administrative equity must prevail, and it is the manager that must see to it.

Management Options

The choices a police manager has in adjudicating complaints may make the difference between a system that is equitable and one that is not. If the manager has options he can use in finalizing his decision, he can dispose of charges fairly and precisely. Most agencies use a paradigm which allows the following five options. First, "sustained" indicates that the accused employee committed all or part of the alleged acts of misconduct. Second, "not sustained" indicates that the investigation produced insufficient information to prove clearly or to disprove the allegations. Third, "exonerated" denotes that the alleged act occurred, but was justified, legal, and proper. Fourth, "unfounded" means that the alleged act did not occur. Five, "misconduct not based on the original complaint" denotes the discovery of acts of misconduct that were not alleged in the original complaint. Without the category of "misconduct not based on the original complaint" the number of sustained complaints might be subject to public misinterpretation. The investigation of complaints from the public alleging such acts as excessive force, discourtesy, and dishonesty frequently are not sustained because of lack of sufficient information. During the investigation, however, such acts of misconduct as failing to

---

[18]*Ibid.,* p. 483.

[19]The issue of managerial "fairness" is the subject of a series of articles under the general title of "Social Equity," *Public Administration Review* 34 (January-February, 1974): 1–51.

prepare a report, improperly disposing of property, or some other irregularity, might be discovered. If the complaint simply is classified as sustained it is difficult to know whether the judgment is based upon the original allegation or upon misconduct discovered later.

Additionally, if the charge is sustained or results in proof of misconduct not based on the original complaint then one of the following dispositions can be used.

> Oral reprimand
> Written reprimand
> Loss of time or of annual leave in lieu of suspension
> Suspension up to thirty days (but no longer)
> Removal from service

Management Considerations

Immediate Supervisor. The police manager must ensure that the accused employee's immediate supervisor is consulted in developing the recommendation for the complaint's adjudication. More than anyone else the immediate supervisor should be able to evaluate the overall conduct and performance level of his staff and, if a penalty is indicated, to determine how severe it should be.

Corrective Action. When an internal discipline complaint is sustained, a determination must be made as to a remedy. In a few cases, the misconduct can be attributed to the agency's neglect to provide the employee with proper equipment or training. In some cases it may be a result of inappropriate procedure or policy. Such findings may provide a basis for the police manager to effect changes in procedures. Usually, however, it is the employee's behavior that must be changed. Corrective measures include: retraining, psychological assistance, or reassignment from a particular job classification. Most frequently, disciplinary actions are called for such as reprimand, relinquishment of time, suspension without pay, or, as a last resort, removal. The first question to ask in determining a penalty should be: What will make the employee reliable and productive in the future? Of equal importance is: What effect will this determination have on other employees and on the public?

Legal Assistance. No employee should be compelled to secure legal assistance; if he feels representation is necessary, the agency should provide representation and logistical support equivalent to that afforded the person presenting the agency's case.

Appeals. Appeal procedures above the police manager's decision are available to all concerned. The complainant can appeal to the courts.

Further, many governmental entities are legally empowered to review the practices of the police agency, including its administration of internal discipline. Among these are the civilian police commission, civil service boards, city/county administrators, local legislative bodies, prosecuting attorneys, state agencies, and units of the United States Department of Justice.

Personnel Files. In most police agencies only the internal discipline investigations that are sustained are filed in the accused employee's personnel folder. Some agencies remove the investigations after two or five years if no subsequent complaints are sustained. Retention of investigations not classified as sustained are useful at times in identifying an employee's pattern of conduct. If the findings of these investigations are retained, however, they can be subject to subpoena in a civil case. Since their introduction into evidence might tend to prejudice a jury, the benefits of their retention should be carefully weighed against the possibility of greater liability. If a police administrator decides to retain these records, he should ensure that they are used *only* for future disciplinary matters, rather than personnel evaluation or promotion.

Criminal Violations. Administrative discipline must be neither a barrier to nor impeded by potential criminal prosecution. Police agencies should seek the assistance of prosecuting agencies in cases involving violations of the law. Often justice can be served by the administration of internal discipline; the police agency, however, must not resist or avoid criminal prosecution. The police service must not treat police employees who break the law differently from other citizens in the community.

Statistical Reporting. Some agencies publish an internal statistical report of complaint disposition and a brief description of sustained investigations. Such reports provide a useful vehicle by which the police manager can openly communicate the philosophy and policies of the administration of internal discipline to the police employees. A statistical report, however, should not name the involved employees. Knowledge of the penalty can cause the sanctioned employee unnecessary work problems such as continued alienation, job discrimination, and limited personal advancement.

Morale. Police managers are acutely aware of the effect that disclosure of misconduct has on police morale. They also assume that effective police service depends on high morale. In turn, the officers believe it is essential that they have the support of their manager. The more dangerous police work becomes, the greater the demand will be for blanket support from superiors and the chief. Yet unethical conduct does and will continue to occur in our police agencies. Equitable adjudicatory policies and decisions—along with prevention programs—that are understood by the officers will tend to increase rather than detract from the morale of the agency's personnel.

Another highly important management consideration is whether or not to use an administrative trial board. Because of its prominence, a separate section is devoted to the subject.

Administrative Trial Board

Most medium-sized agencies currently use some form of trial board or administrative hearing. Boards used by smaller agencies generally include persons from other sectors of local government in addition to police employees. Although such boards are time consuming, most police managers and agencies believe they should be an integral element of administering internal discipline. The boards provide a diversity of opinion for the final adjudication, and allow for greater participation in the process by persons involved in the complaint investigation.

The trial board is also useful as a form for discussion of those cases which receive a large amount of public attention and which if adjudicated without a trial board, could cause public distrust. Additionally, trial board procedures allow an accused employee to request a review of the investigation if he feels his position was not represented accurately. However, police managers are finding that most differences in opinion are resolved satisfactorily in a trial board hearing.

> Ideally, the board should consist of five members of the department, with four appointed by the chief and one by the accused officer. The board should have no investigative power and should handle only those cases referred by the internal investigations division or the chief of police. Its jurisdiction should be cases not handled by means of summary punishment, cases directed to the board by the chief, and cases in which the accused requests a hearing, regardless of seriousness.
>
> A board hearing is an administrative proceeding in which evidence and arguments are heard and, based on them, a decision is made. Administrative hearings do not usually require legal formality or adherence to courtroom procedure. Various courts have declared some basic principles governing hearings, however:
>
> 1. The nature of the charge must be made known to the accused.
> 2. The accused must be given reasonable notice of the time and place of the hearing.
> 3. He must be given the opportunity to call witnesses, to cross-examine opposing witnesses, and to testify in his own behalf.

4. He is entitled to have the hearing before those who are to decide the issue.

Of course, if procedures of this kind are specified in civil service laws, he is entitled to have the laws strictly followed.

Although an administrative hearing is quasi-judicial in character and thus need not be strictly formal, it should be conducted in a dignified manner, free of distraction and interruption. The rules for the hearing should be reviewed carefully, so that the accused is fully aware of the items listed above and the rules themselves. The procedure should include provision for opening statements for both the accused and the department advocate, provision for cross-examination, questioning by board members, and other ground rules.[20]

The following standard reinforces and summarizes the above commentary.

Standard 19.5

ADJUDICATION OF COMPLAINTS

Every police agency immediately should insure that provisions are established to allow the police chief executive authority in the adjudication of internal discipline complaints, subject only to appeal through the courts or established civil service bodies, and review by responsible legal and governmental entities.

1. A complaint disposition should be classified as sustained, not sustained, exonerated, unfounded, or misconduct not based on the original complaint.

2. Adjudication and—if warranted—disciplinary action should be based partially on recommendations of the involved employee's immediate supervisor. The penalty should be at least a suspension up to 6 months or, in severe cases, removal from duty.

3. An administrative factfinding trial board should be available to all police agencies to assist in the adjudication phase. It should be activated when necessary in the interests of the police agency, the public, or the accused employee, and should be available at the direction of the chief executive or upon the request of any employee who is to be penalized in any manner that exceeds verbal or written reprimand. The chief executive of the agency should review the recommendations of the trial board and decide on the penalty.

[20]Wilson and McLaren, *Police Administration,* pp. 213, 214.

4. The accused employee should be entitled to representation and logistical support equal to that afforded the person representing the agency in a trial board proceeding.

5. Police employees should be allowed to appeal a chief executive's decision. The police agency should not provide the resources or funds for appeal.

6. The chief executive of every police agency should establish written policy on the retention of internal discipline complaint investigation reports. Only the reports of sustained and—if appealed—upheld investigations should become a part of the accused employee's personnel folder. All disciplinary investigations should be kept confidential.

7. Administrative adjudication of internal discipline complaints involving a violation of law should neither depend on nor curtail criminal prosecution. Regardless of the administrative adjudication, every police agency should refer all complaints that involve violations of law to the prosecuting agency for the decision to prosecute criminally. Police employees should not be treated differently from other members of the community in cases involving violations of law.[21]

PREVENTION OF ERRANT BEHAVIOR

> Each sheriff's department and each city police department in this state shall establish a procedure to investigate citizens' complaints against the personnel of such departments, and shall make a written description of the procedure available to the public.[22]

Usually internal discipline in police agencies is crisis oriented. The majority of police agencies are reactive to employee misconduct. Frequently they do a good job of investigating after the events have occurred; however, they seldom attempt to prevent the causes. Most notably, the basic question police managers should seek to answer concerning employee misconduct is "Why?" Police supervisors must ask themselves "What could have prevented the employee from engaging in this particular wrongful act?" The answer should be made an integral part of the written recommendation for each complaint adjudication. The police manager ultimately responsible for internal discipline should not assume this analytical responsibility alone. It is the responsibility of all employees to seek ways to maintain their self-discipline.

To begin with, the prevention of police employee misconduct is measurably improved by the very existence of a *viable* citizen complaint pro-

---

[21]Assembly Bill No. 1305 (Sacramento, Calif.: Caifornia Legislature, 1973–74 Regular Session), p. 2. Signed by the Governor and effective January 1, 1975.
[22]National Advisory Commission, *Police*, p. 492.

cess and equitable internal investigation policy. It is seen in the quotation above from one state's legislation that the former be accomplished. Predictably the latter will also become a reality. Both can be looked upon as a twofold positive approach to abating errant police behavior. However, more, indeed much more, can and must be achieved in the way of lessening the possibilities that an officer will misbehave.

Policies, programs, and practices intended to either prevent or decrease the possibilities of improper employee behavior are, in many ways, the main themes of this text. The preceding chapter served as one indicator of this posture. Any further discussion at this point would be redundant and far too expansive for inclusion. In summary, a responsible management coupled with a rigorous and consistent set of judicious personnel rules acts as a foundation for prevention. Moreover, this combination must span all facets of the agency from recruitment on through selection, entry-level training, in-service reinforcement training assignments, skilled supervisors, promotional procedures, and so on. What we are saying, then, is that effective management *is* effective prevention. The following standard speaks to this end.

Standard 19.6

POSITIVE PREVENTION

OF POLICE MISCONDUCT

The chief executive of every police agency immediately should seek and develop programs and techniques that will minimize the potential for employee misconduct. The chief executive should insure that there is a general atmosphere that rewards self-discipline within the police agency.

1. Every police chief executive should implement, where possible, positive programs and techniques to prevent employee misconduct and encourage self-discipline. These may include:

   a. Analysis of the causes of employee misconduct through special interviews with employees involved in misconduct incidents and study of the performance records of selected employees;

   b. General training in the avoidance of misconduct incidents for all employees and special training for employees experiencing special problems;

   c. Referral to psychologists, psychiatrists, clergy, and other professionals whose expertise may be valuable; and

   d. Application of peer group influence.

EPILOGUE

The subject of police internal discipline, officer's rights versus management responsibilities, and the maintenance of the overall integrity of operations will undoubtedly dominate the latter half or the 1970s. Indeed, the issues surrounding the policies and practices of controlling organizational behavior will never be fully resolved. A constantly changing work ethic, professional code of conduct, and sense of administrative equity will preclude any final solution to the question of handling wrongs in reference to a standard of what is right. Paradoxically, alleged "rights" on the part of some may not be right when evaluated in light of social justice and organizational effectiveness. As a consequence of this growing importance, we have included in Appendix B a set of recommended procedures for handling internal discipline, or more approximately the failure of an employee to fulfill his/her professional responsibilities. If past is prologue, then the thinking reflected in these investigation procedures should be highly reliable. Further, we would hope to reduce your sense of either frustration or failure by indicating that this nation continues to define and redefine our "inalienable rights" (life, liberty and the pursuit of happiness). Hence, is it any wonder that there are questions constantly outcropping about professional rights and responsibilities.

Chapter Thirteen

TASK 11
JOB ENRICHMENT

Perhaps the single most important reason why job enrichment has been so successful in business is because it attacks the problem of job monotony. With the rising aspirations of workers in our affluent society, the work force is increasingly coming to reject the uninteresting, demeaning, oppressive, and generally undersirable characteristics of some of today's jobs. Job enrichment efforts, then, have succeeded in "Humanizing" jobs—that is, giving more explicit recognition to the notion that man has "higher order" needs, needs for achievement, responsibility, recognition, self-actualization—that are currently being neglected.[1]

Standard 8.2

ENHANCING THE ROLE
OF THE PATROL OFFICER

Every local government and police chief executive, recognizing that the patrol function is the most important element of the police agency, immediately should adopt policies that attract and retain highly qualified personnel in the patrol force.

1. Every local government should expand its classification and pay system to provide greater advancement opportunities within the patrol ranks. The system should provide:
   a. Multiple pay grades within the basic rank;
   b. Opportunity for advancement within the basic rank to permit equality between patrol officers and investigators;
   c. Parity in top salary step between patrol officers and nonsupervisory officers assigned to other operational functions;
   d. Proficiency pay for personnel who have demonstrated expertise in specific field activities that contribute to more efficient police service.

2. Every police chief executive should seek continually to enhance the role of the patrol officer by providing status and recognition from the agency and encouraging similar status and recognition from the community. The police chief executive should:
   a. Provide distinctive insignia indicating demonstrated expertise in specific field activities;
   b. Insure that all elements within the agency provide maximum assistance and cooperation to the patrol officer;

---

[1]Archie B. Carroll, "Conceptual Foundations of Job Enrichment," *Public Personnel Management* 3 (January-February 1974): 35, 36.

c. Implement a community information program emphasizing the importance of the patrol officer in the life of the community and encouraging community cooperation in providing police service;

d. Provide comprehensive initial and inservice training thoroughly to equip the patrol officer for his role;

e. Insure that field supervisory personnel possess the knowledge and skills necessary to guide the patrol officer;

f. Implement procedures to provide agencywide recognition of patrol officers who have consistently performed in an efficient and commendable manner;

g. Encourage suggestions on changes in policies, procedures, and other matters that affect the delivery of police services and reduction of crime;

h. Provide deployment flexibility to facilitate various approaches to individual community crime problems;

i. Adopt policies and procedures that allow the patrol officer to conduct the complete investigation of crimes which do not require extensive followup investigation, and allow them to close the investigation of those crimes; and

j. Insure that promotional oral examination boards recognize that patrol work provides valuable experience for men seeking promotion to supervisory positions.[2]

SYNOPSIS

Designing work so that it concurrently fulfills individual needs and attains organizational goals is of monumental importance to both participants. Since they are interactive either one can either aid or detract from the other. The police manager plays a crucial role in facilitating the two by being responsible for supporting his subordinates. When doing so he normally enriches the subordinate's job and establishes a climate of motivation to accomplish agency objectives. In some situations, and preferably so, the police manager and police officer negotiate a "psychological contract" which informally generates common understanding over a set of mutual expectations.

The first step in a job enrichment program is to adopt a baseline criterion and thereafter have it serve as a referent for determining work values. And, from the defined work values we can build a job-enriching experience—one that certainly includes the support of one's subordinates. Second, we should analyze the job itself. Does

2National Advisory Commission on Criminal Justice Standards and Goals, *Police* (Washington, D.C.: U.S. Government Printing Office, 1973), p. 333.

the design foster an enriching experience? Is it sufficiently flexible to be custom-fitted to the needs of the officer? Third, job enrichment connotes job enlargement. This means that the officer is given greater autonomy as well as increased authority over factors in the job cycle. Improved and expanded training programs are required to facilitate this process. Fourth, job enrichment also means a participative style of managing. Essentially, it seeks to increase the officer's involvement in decisions that affect his organizational life.

Fifth, there must be an expressed individual job satisfaction and team morale in a job enrichment program. The two are related to need fulfillment and can influence (not cause) the varying degrees of job effectiveness. Significantly, the police manager is in a position to influence both. Further, there are some meaningful and easily applied techniques to enable him to do so. Sixth, the mental and physical health of police employees is of vital importance. Psychophysiological stress, of which a police officer receives more than his due share, is dysfunctional to the individual and can affect his performance as a member of the agency. Fortunately, there are proven tactics for coping with stress. Finally, it is recognized that the above components of a job enrichment program are not attainable by mere wishing. Most often, hard decisions and strenuous work is involved. Regardless, job enrichment is "right" because it is supportive of the worker's needs and produces organizationally desired results.

A PSYCHOLOGICAL CONTRACT

Do we not spend considerable time, and expand considerable energy in the accomplishment of organizationally assigned tasks. This is to say, that you and I devote—either willingly or begrudgingly—a lot of our precious "self" to our work. Relatedly, we carry with us at all times a set of human needs that we seek to fulfill. Our work provides, or should provide an opportunity—and a major one—for us to meet our individual needs. And this is the subject that we will focus on in the subsequent pages. We begin by citing assumptions that serve as both framework and guide:

> Human need fulfillment can be attained in one's work—in this case police work.
>
> Individual needs can be integrated with the goals of an organization—in this case a police organization.

The organization has a responsibility for designing the job so that it is as satisfying as is possible to the worker—in this case the police officer.

The manager—in this case a police manager—can play a critical part in integrating the worker's desire to fulfill individual needs with the organization's responsibility for goal accomplishment.

While the assumptions above represent attainable goals, attempts by the organization and by the manager to confirm them will be met with many barriers—in this case we must be prepared to cope with challenges and resolve conflicts.

Based on these propositions, we would strongly argue that the police manager has a responsibility to *support his subordinates* in their fulfillment of individual needs while serving in their role as police officers. Moreover, if the manager desires to be recognized as a leader, then it is imperative that he accept and implement this task. We can conceive of activities he will undertake in providing such support as falling under the rubric of "job enrichment." Therefore, the police manager seeks to enrich the job of police officers in order to support each officer in meeting his human needs while at work. This the officer can and should expect. In turn, the manager can and should expect dedication, compliance, respect, results, and othr organizationally desirable responses from the employee. Thus the requirement for a *psychological contract*.[3]

The notion of a psychological contract implies that the individual has a variety of expectations of the organization and that the organization has a variety of expectataions of him. These expectations not only cover how much work is to be performed for how much pay, but also involve the whole pattern of rights, privileges, and obligations between worker and organization. For example, the worker may expect the company not to fire him after he has worked there for a certain number of years and the company may expect that the worker will not run down the company's public image or give away company secrets to competitors. Expectations such as these are not written into any formal agreement between employee and organization, yet they operate powerfully as determinants of behavior.

The psychological contract is implemented from the organization's point of view through the concept of authority, in that the decision to join an organization implies the commitment to accept the authority system of that organization. As discussed in chapter 3, organizations coordinate their various functions through some kind of hierarchy of authority. Within defined areas a person must be willing to obey the

---

[3]This concept and the remainder of this section is based on the thinking of Edgar H. Schein, *Organizational Psychology*, 2d ed. (Englewood Cliffs, N.J.: Prentice-Hall, Inc. 1970), pp. 12–15, 77–79.

dictates of some other person or some written directives or rules, and to curb his own inclinations, even if they are contrary to the dictates. Authority is not the same thing as pure power. Pure power implies that by the manipulation of rewards or the exercise of naked strength you can force someone else to do something against his will. Authority, by contrast, implies the willingness on the part of a "subordinate" to obey because he *consents*; that is, he grants to the person in authority or to the law the right to dictate to him.

For such consent to be meaningful in a group or an organization, it must rest on a shared consensus concerning the basis of the legitimacy of the authority. That is, a law obtains our consent only if we agree that it is legitimate and right for us to be governed by it. An organization can give meaningful authority to a foreman only if the workers agree that the *system* by which people get to be foreman is one that they will support. It is agreement to the system that permits a worker to tolerate an occasional bad foreman and still take orders from him.

From the side of the worker, the psychological contract is implemented through his perception that he can *influence* the organization or his own immediate situation sufficiently to ensure that he will not be taken advantage of. His sense of influencing the situation is partly the result of his agreement to the basis of consent, his acceptance of the system by which people have come to be in positions of authority; but it also rests on his sense of being able to affect the authority directly and to change his situation in the organization. The mode of influence—whether as a free agent or as a member of a union—is not so important as the worker's fundamental belief that he has some power to influence if from his point of view the psychological contract is not being met. Thus, the organization enforces its views of the contract through authority; the employee enforces his view of the contract through upward influence.

The pattern of authority and influence that will result in any given situation depends in part on the basis of consent. The basis on which we accept the legitimacy of authority can vary from society to society and organization to organization. The sociologist Max Weber first pointed out that the three major bases of legitimacy were tradition, rational-legal organization, and charisma.[4] These ideas are most easily illustrated if we think of whole societies and the political systems that underlie them.

Tradition as a basis of legitimacy implies that the governed grant authority to the ruler in the belief that his position has always been accepted. The clearest example is a monarchy which is supported ulti-

[4]Max Weber, *The Theory of Social and Economic Organization,* ed. Talcott Parsons (Glencoe, Ill.: Free Press and Falcons Wing Press, 1947).

mately by belief in the divine origin and rights of the ruling family and belief in the rightful inheritance of the throne by the oldest male son. Lower levels of authority are accepted to the extent that the king has delegated authority to them. What makes the whole system "right" is the set of beliefs or traditions surrounding the idea of monarchy. The organizational counterpart in our own society would be acceptance of the authority of an owner's son as senior manager, even if workers have questions about his actual ability as a manager. While we rarely see this kind of authority system in operation in our own society, it is still quite common in the political and business institutions of economically less developed countries.

Rational-legal principles as the basis of authority tend to be prevalent in our own society. They underlie the concept of a democracy and the idea of formal organization as outlined above. According to these ideas, power or authority should be assigned on the basis of rational criteria and in terms of procedures embodied in formal laws, contracts, and informal codes. Rational criteria imply that, in order to be given a position of authority, a person should have demonstrated the ability and motivation to fulfill the requirements of the position.

In the political sphere, these principles are expressed in the system of electing officials based on a rational assessment of their abilities, motivation, and prior service. In the organizational sphere, these principles are expressed in the idea of promotion based on merit (ability plus past performance) and in the notion that authority ultimately derives from a person's ability to do *something* better than those under him can do it; in short, his expertness. What the boss is expert at may be quite different from what the subordinate is expert at, as when a manager has under him ten chemists in a research lab. The acceptance by the chemists of their boss's authority rests on their perception that he is a better *manager* than they and that he has achieved his position by legitimate means.

Charisma as a basis for authority occurs in those instances where a very magnetic personality has been able to capture a following through belief in his mystical, magical, divine, or simply extraordinary powers. Political and religious movements often develop around charismatic leaders. They have their counterpart in organizational life in the instances where supervisors or top executives capture the consent of the members purely on the basis of their unique personal qualities. Thus, all of us have at times obeyed orders and followed leaders simply because we trusted them completely and accepted their word as dogma, even if they had neither expertness nor had earned their position by rational-legal means.

Weber did not include in his analysis the purely *rational* basis of authority. By this, we mean the acceptance of anyone who has expert knowledge relating to some goal we are trying to achieve, regardless of his position, personality, or social origin. We accept the authority of the scholar in relation to his field of study, and we accept the authority of the automobile mechanic or the television repairman when we need certain repairs. One of the more difficult organizational dilemmas which frequently arises is when a person in a *position* of authority (based on a rational-legal process) is not perceived as *expert* in relation to the tasks required of that position.

We have inserted this discussion of authority and its bases in order to underline the point that an organization cannot function unless the members of it consent to the operating authority system, and that this consent hinges upon the upholding of the psychological contract between organizaiton and member. If the organization fails to meet the expectations of the employee, and, at the same time, cannot *coerce* him to remain as a member, he will most likely leave. Thus, the problem of motivation and organizational incentives or rewards is best thought of as a complex bargaining situation between organization and member, involving the decision of whether to join, the decision of how hard to work and how creative to be, feelings of loyalty and commitment, expectations of being taken care of and finding a sense of identity through one's organizational role, and a host of other decisions, feelings, and expectations.

A major psychological problem of organizations involves the nature and effects of the psychological contract between the organization and its members. Issues such as the nature of authority, the possibilities of influencing the system, the patterns of motivation and expectations of employees and managers, the incentive systems generated by management, the management patterns that create loyalty and commitment as opposed to alienation and disaffection—all are part of this general problem.

By way of conclusion, we would like to underline the importance of the psychological contract as a major variable of analysis. It is our central hypothesis that whether a person is working effectively, whether he generates commitment, loyalty, and enthusiasm for the organization and its goals, and whether he obtains satisfaction from his work, depends to a large measure on two conditions: (1) the degree to which his own expectations of what the organization will provide him and what he owes the organization match what the organization's expectations are of what it will give and get; (2) assuming there is agreement on expectations, what actually is to be exchanged—money in exchange for time at work; social-need satisfaction and security in exchange for work and loyalty; opportunities for self-actualization and challenging work in exchange for high productivity, quality work, and creative effort in the service of organizational goals; or various combinations of these and other things.

Ultimately the relationship between the individual and the organization is interactive, unfolding through mutual influence and mutual bargaining to establish a workable psychological contract. We cannot understand the psychological dynamics if we look only to the individual's motivations or only to organizational conditions and practices. The two interact in a complex fashion, requiring us to develop theories and research approaches which can deal with systems and interdependent phenomena.

Managers of police organizations must become aware not only of the complexities of human motivation, but of the dynamic processes which occur as the person enters into and pursues a career within an organization. Just as the manner in which a police officer is selected, trained, and assigned influences his image of the organization, so the manner in which he is managed will influence this image. A manager must be aware of the interaction between these various organizational systems and must think integratively about them. For example, if he plans to manage people in a way that will challenge them and provide them with opportunities to use all their potential, he must be careful that the manner in which they are selected, tested, trained, and assigned to their jobs does not undermine the very motivations he wishes to draw on. What this means in practice is that all those members of the police organization who are responsible for the various functions should, together, think through carefully the consequences of the various approaches, and coordinate their activities to accomplish whatever shared goals they have.

We purposely started our discussion of "police" job enrichment with the concept and need for a psychological contract because it theoretically underpins the following material. In addition to the subsequent sections comprising this chapter, you will find that chapters 1 and 2 are highly relevant to any consideration of enriching one's job. Let us now examine the major building blocks out of which job enrichment can be constructed: work values, job design flexibility, job satisfaction and morale, mental and physical health, and implementation techniques.

JOB ENRICHMENT: Work Values

If *justice* is allowed to formulate the fundamental organizational rules it will provide an arena within which all other values can be shaped and realized. John Rawls proposes that there are principles other than justice that have some force, but in respect to them, justice has absolute weight, always deserving priority in cases of conflict.[5] Rawls, in due regard for his profound commitment to justice as *the* paramount value, asserts the *right* should supersede that which is assessed as being *good*. In other words, the theory of justice (that which is right) should be held in higher esteem than utilitarianism.

Defining "ideal" work values is not an easy chore. They can be derived from three primary sources: *Judaeo-Christian theology; the humanistic doctrines of Graeco-Roman philosophy*; and the *peculiarly Western notion of the dignity and worth* of man.[6] And one could reasonably spend a lifetime becoming acquainted in detail with any one of these sources. Fortunately, a ready basis is available. One of the products of the study committee of the Federal Council of Churches was an attempt to think through the Judaeo-Christian moral tradition. Of even greater interest, the effort was part of their series on ethics and economic life. A number of "subordinate goals" relevant to economic life were considered of "great importance." These subordinate goals are summarized in table 13–1.

These goals seem a reasonable enough guide for behavior in general, but they must be further refined for our present purposes since it does not seem that all of these goals could be achieved in police organizations, at least at present. Moreover, there are no clear organizational applications of some of these goals elsewhere.

The Judaeo-Christian ethic will be consistent with the goals enumerated by the study committee of the Federal Council of Churches, then, while it is narrower in scope. Five values comprise that Judaeo-Christian ethic. They are listed below, with the numbers in the parentheses referring to the specific subordinate goals relevant to economic life (tab. 13–1) to which each of the five values contributes:

1. Work must be psychologically acceptable to the individual, that is, its performance cannot generally threaten the individual (1, 3, 8, 10, and 11).

2. Work must allow man to develop his faculties (4, 5, 6, and 7).

3. The work task must allow the individual considerable room for self-determination (3 and 9).

4. The worker must have the possibility of controlling, in a meaningful way, the environment within which the task is to be performed (2, 6, and 9).

---

[5]For those interested in an outstanding discussion of this subject see John Rawls, *A Theory of Justice*, (Cambridge, Mass.: Harvard University Press, 1971).

[6]This and the next few paragraphs are adapted from Robert T. Golembiewski, *Men, Management, and Morality: Toward a New Organizational Ethic* (N.Y.: McGraw-Hill Book Company, 1965), pp. 63–65.

TABLE 13–1

Subordinate Goals Relevant To Economic Life

---

1. *Survival and Physical Well-being (Productivity)*. Each individual should have access to the conditions necessary for health, safety, comfort, and reasonable longevity.

2. *Fellowship.* Each individual should have a variety of satisfying human relationships.

3. *Dignity and Humility.* Each individual should have the opportunty to earn a position in society of dignity and self-respect.

4. *Enlightenment.* The individual should have opportunity to learn about the world in which he lives. He should be able to satisfy his intellectual curiosity and to acquire the skills and knowledge for intelligent citizenship, efficient work, and informed living.

5. *Aesthetic Enjoyment.* The individual should have the opportunity to appreciate aesthetic values in art, nature, and ritual, and through personal relations. Many aesthetic values are attainable through both production and consumption.

6. *Creativity.* The individual should be able to express his personality through creative activities. He should be able to identify himself with the results of his own activity, and to take pride in his achievements, intellectual, aesthetic, political, or other.

7. *New Experience.* An important goal of life is suggested by the word variability, spontaneity, whimsy, novelty, excitement, fun, sport, holiday, striving against odds, solving problems, innovation, invention, etc. Each individual should have opportunity for new experience.

8. *Security.* Each individual should have assurance that the objective conditions necessary for attainment of the above goals will be reasonably accessible to him.

9. *Freedom.* Freedom is the opportunity to pursue one's goals without restraint.

10. *Justice.* The Christian law of love does not imply neglect of the self. The individual is to be as concerned about others as he is about himself—neither more nor less.

11. *Personality.* The preceding goals were stated in terms of the kinds of life experiences we wish people to have. These goals can be translated into the kinds of persons we wish them to be. Goals can then be regarded as qualities of human personality; accordingly, a desirable personality would be defined as one that is favorably conditioned toward the various goals.

Source: Howard R. Bowen, "Findings of the Study," in John C. Bennett et al., *Christian Values and Economic Life* (New York: Harper & Row, Publishers, 1954), pp. 47–60.

5. The organization should not be the sole and final arbiter of behavior; both the organization and the individual must be subject to an external moral order (5, 9, and 10).

This third ethic although incomplete still has several virtues. Thus the values directly infer conduct that has clear applications in both organization structure and supervisory techniques. Moreover, the Judaeo-

Christian ethic is realizable in today's organizations in the sense that approaching the five values can have very favorable consequences for productivity and for employee need satisfaction. However, the five values have only limited, yet growing, empirical support. Together they constitute a *new* theory of organization, management, and supervision.

Traditional organization theory—despite its limitations—has an immense advantage as a frame of reference for this analysis. One need not search for it. Indeed, one cannot avoid it. Almost any textbook on organization or administration is a probable source. Nor is there great disagreement about the properties of this theory. For present purposes, four "Principles" may be emphasized. They prescribe that:

1. Authority should be "one way"; it should flow in a single stream from organization superiors to subordinates.

2. Supervision should be detailed and the span of control should be narrow.

3. The organization of work should respect only the physiological properties of the individual, who is considered a social isolate.

4. Work should be routinized in terms of processes at the lowest levels and organized in terms of functions at the upper levels.

The classical theory calls for a routinized job at the lowest levels, a job whose performance is monitored closely by a manager with a narrow span of control, in an organization in which authority is a one-way relation. The contrast with the Judaeo-Christian ethic could not be more sharp. Additionally, the point here is not merely that the principles were built upon a different ethical set, but that the building was done implicitly and often unconsciously. Space does not permit further discussion of the background, application, or results of the two theories. The Judaeo-Christian ethic is arbitrarily, but with reason, selected as being comprised of the *right* set of work values—the reason being that they are fair.

For the sake of clarity, we believe it best to summarize our basic contention. *In order for job enrichment to be born and remain viable, and hence a supportive work climate established, a new set of work values in line with the Judaeo-Christian ethic must be adopted.* The five values share a common element—that of fairness—or, what is *right* for the worker. Also, it is to be noted that the five values underpin the other ingredients making for job enrichment. Indeed, without work values that are just and fair the material that follows is superfluous.

JOB ENRICHMENT: Job Design Flexibility

Another approach to job enrichment is to design the job to fit the man. Where the typical selection approach is normally based on finding the right man for a given job, the job-design approach is ultimately based on the assumption that work should, from the outset, be explicitly set up to take into account the potentialities, limitations, and interests of the worker. And if the job is not suited for human performance in the first place or if a machine can do the job better, in the interests of overall organizational effectiveness, a person should not be expected or allowed to do it. Adherents of both the flexible design approach and the traditional selection approach are committed to the ultimate assumption that the first requirement to be met is effective task performance. They disagree only on how one best accomplishes this end.

Historically, the selection approach has been embodied in the work of industrial engineers or psychologists doing time-and-motion studies of workers. Time-and-motion studies involve the careful observation of a good or "standard" worker, recording the various moves he makes in performing his job, clocking the amount of time taken by each movement, and constructing a logical analysis of the job. This was done for one or more of the following purposes: (1) structuring the job to make the movements simpler and quicker to do; (2) developing more efficient patterns of movement to be taught to workers so that they can do the job faster and with less fatigue; (3) setting standards for given jobs to be used as a basis for determining pay scales and criteria for the evaluation of any given worker; and (4) developing a complete job description to aid in the process of recruiting and selecting new workers, orienting them to their duties, and training them. In other words, *finding* and *fitting* the man to the job.

Thus, the industrial engineer contributed greatly to the whole "rationalization" of work upon which modern industry depends. Important inventions like the assembly line, the setting of wage scales for jobs based on a rational assessment of the skills and training involved, and the development of machines and work layout which the average person could use efficiently grew partly out of this approach. To a large extent, it helped to replace the potentially biased and fallible judgment of the owner-manager with objective standard procedures in task performance wage administration, and employee evaluation.

At the same time, the classical selection model has proven to have serious limitations and has created some adverse consequences for the effective utilization of workers. These consequences are cited by Chris Argyris. Clearly they are present, in fact prevalent, in our police organizations.

> To the extent that there is an incongruency between the needs of individuals and the requirements of a formal organization, the individuals will tend to experience (1) frustration, (2) psychological failure, (3) short time perspective, and (4) conflict. . . .
>
> In another example Scott and Mitchell agreed with MacKinney, Wernimont, and Galitz that job enlargement does not take individual differences into account. The opposite is the case. Job enlargement increases the variance possible in work and therefore accommodates to a greater range of individual differences. MacKinney, Wernimont, and Galitz raised a straw man when they argue against forcing job enlargement upon everyone. Such a condition is unrealistic. There will be many jobs that cannot be enlarged and thus employees will have no choice. There is a deeper question, however, that goes to the heart of the function of social science research; namely, what kind of a world do we help to design. Let us assume that all jobs could be enlarged. We now have two work worlds; the present with its high routine and the other with less routine. Either world would be coercive in the sense that it makes requirements on employees. If we had the choice, why not opt for the world that is psychologically richer? The authors suggest that employees can cope with this problem by fulfillment outside their jobs. It is ironic that scholars who argue against job enlargement because it has not been proven by a high degree of scientific rigor (Scott and Mitchell, 1972: 279) recommend an alternative for employees that has little empirical support. As has been shown above, the degree of deprivation on the job significantly influences the kind of fulfillment employees seek outside their job.[7]

Thus we see the need for a flexible job design that takes into account the individual as he relates to his work group. Granted the job of the police officer cannot be precisely custom-fitted to the individual characteristics and needs of each person in an agency. But, it is proposed that there are certain parameters within which the job can be *reasonably tailored* to the person.[8] A single and major factor in such "tailoring" is the consideration of job enlargement which we discuss next.

[7]Chris Argyris, "Personality and Organization Theory Revisited," *Administrative Science Quarterly* 18 (June 1973): 144 ,162.
[8]The interest in improved linkings between the worker and his job has not waned in the 1970s. Theoretical and interactive linkages are comprehensively examined by Glen H. Elder, Jr., "On Linking Social Structure and Personality," *American Behavioral Scientist* 16 (July-August 1973): 755–99.

JOB ENRICHMENT: Job Enlargement

One way to define job enlargement is to conceive of it as enlarging the job in such a way that it permits more opportunity for employees to experience jobs that are based on the five work values expressed earlier. Thus, increasing the variety increases the number of abilities used (usually motor or doing abilities). A richer enlargement is to redesign the work so that it enhances opportunity for the employee to experience greater autonomy and control over factors in job content and job context, lengthens the time perspective, and decreases dependence and submissiveness upon the superior. The former is usually called *horizontal* and the latter, *vertical* job enlargement. Optimal enlargement requires that a distinction be made between horizontal enlargement (namely, increasing the number of different things an employee does) from vertical enlargement (that is, increasing the degree to which an employee is responsible for making most major decisions about his work).

Many researchers have concluded that through the design of jobs that permit increased self-regulation, self-evaluation, self-adjustment, and participation to set goals, increases in productivity and positive attitudes have resulted.[9] One should therefore expect that various organaizations would attempt to implement job enlargement programs. For example, we find in an industrial setting:

> Experiments in significant job enlargement are being conducted at Volvo. Gyllenhammar, the new and innovative president of Volvo, was directly involved in the design of a new assembly plant. The work of assembling the cars have been given to teams. Each team has responsibility for its special section of the car (for example, the electrical system, brakes and wheels, and so forth). Within a work team, the members decide the distribution and pace of work. Employees are permitted and encouraged to learn many different engineering skills in order to contribute to their team's effectiveness as well as maintain control over their work environment. It is estimated that the new plant will be more expensive (about 19,000,000 kroner) than the conventional car assembly. The top management decided that the expenditure was worth it because they valued increasing the quality of life within the plants and because they believed that it would lead to a work force with less turnover and absenteeism (Volvo, 1972).[10]

[9] A current list of studies pertaining to job enlargement is contained in Argyris, "Personality and Organ-Theory Revisited," pp. 150–52.
[10] *Ibid.,* p. 152.

More specific to our interests, James Q. Wilson writes:

> Enlarging the job of the patrolman is currently much in vogue for reasons of both morale and effectiveness. Reversing the past tendency to take away from the patrolman various tasks and give them to specialized units (detectives, juvenile officers, community relations specialists, narcotics investigators) should have, in the view of many, the effect of making the patrolman's tasks personally more satisfying and organizationally more effective. The officer will have a wider range of duties, greater freedom in scheduling his own time, and accordingly higher morale; at the same time, he will be able to carry out follow-up investigations on the spot and provide more services to the citizen and provide them without the interruption arising from other radio calls.[11]

The subject of implementing a *police* job enlargement program will close this chapter. We continue here with a more generalized review of its dimensions.

It can be seen that there is a kind of inner logic to job enlargement that tends to force appropriate changes at related points in a flow of work, as is also the case with the classical guidelines. There is a crucial difference. Job enlargement tends to bring together related operations so as to minimize the problems of integrating them. Classical job design tends to fragment related operations. One must choose his inner logic with care, therefore. But integration seems preferable to fragmentation.

Some Qualifiers

This introduction to job enlargement has been painted with a broad brush. A few qualifying features must be stressed lest the reader think that some all-purpose glory road toward greater freedom at lower levels in organizations has been sketched.[12] First, job enlargement is not universally applicable. However, where it can be installed, it should be! Most importantly, it can be and therefore should be applied to police work. Second, job enlargement is not some all-purpose managerial tool. If it is applied by management without enthusiasm and conviction, its chances of success are markedly diminished. If nothing else, job enlargement requires significant changes in *managerial* habits. (Such changes will not be encouraged by lukewarm managerial commitment).

Third, job enlargement is but one element in a situational analysis

[11]James Q. Wilson, "The Future Policeman," in *Future Roles of Criminal Justice Personnel: Position Papers* (Sacramento, Calif.: Commission on Peace Officer Standards and Goals, The American Justice Institute, 1972), p. 18.

[12]This thinking is drawn in part from Golembiewski, *Men, Management, and Morality*, pp. 136–42.

of the particular nature of the work involved, the personalities of the operatives, and the specific changes made in the job and the ways they are made. Volumes of research are required to etch in the details of such situational relations. The trick seems to lie in increasing the worker's control over a work cycle in contrast to, let us say, the introduction of variety into work by rotating individuals through several unit cycles of different work cycles. In the latter case, the employee may feel more estranged from work than ever when the novelty wears off. Relatedly, it may be impossible to assign responsibility for performance when such rotation is relied upon. The situational nature of job enlargement has many ramifications. What might be an effective program for one group of police employees might fail for another group. Experimentation will tell! Finally, job enlargement patently rests upon the effectiveness of the training which supports it and upon the predisposition of the employee to be trained. One-shot efforts will not suffice, for programs of job enlargement tend to develop by successive additions to unit cycles of work. Invariably, enlarged jobs are upgraded in the process, and thus impose increasingly greater demands on the employee. Training must be continuous. Thus the police manager is destined to play a major part in operationalizing a job enlargement program in a police agency.

Two Conclusions

Two conclusions seem reasonable. One, we should not be surprised to find that programs of job enlargement are significant for most employees. The point may seem petty to some since the differences between many enlarged jobs and overspecialized jobs are not that great. However, numerous studies reflect a world of psychological difference between (let us say) jobs with five operations and those with ten. Two, qualifications and all, job enlargement seems a useful managerial technique. This underscores the overly simplistic nature of the claims of universality of the guidelines of classical job design, as well as of the traditional theory of organization from which they derive. Put differently, job enlargement demonstrates that human need fulfillment may be approached without sacrificing the efficiency of police operations, if indeed job enlargement does not lead to significant short-run efficiencies as well as to longer-run effectiveness.

JOB ENRICHMENT: Job Satisfaction And Morale

All of us have, at one time of another, used the terms *satisfaction* or *morale* to indicate our own or others' feelings. And, it is quite likely that we have used both of these terms in an occupational sense. Moreover, either implicitly or explicitly, we have included the notions of "attitudes" and "values" toward a particular job. The above words are seldom defined or dealt with consistently. Added to this lack of precise understanding of terms are some commonly held beliefs, such as that more satisfied people produce more simply because of human nature—but do they? Hence we are heading toward a rather large problem. Is the effort worth it? Our unequivocal answer is yes! The reasons underlying this response will become clear later.

Our problem, to some, may appear quite academic, a matter of semantics. But the problem is not just one of terminology; it involves feelings, emotions, happiness, and organizational effectiveness. Since terminological problems are involved, we spend some time on definitions. Because of the existing confusion between the concepts of job attitudes and job values, let us first consider the term *attitude*. An attitude is the predisposition of an individual to evaluate some symbol or object or aspect of his world in a favorable or unfavorable manner.[13] One develops an attitude concerning an external thing; that is, an attitude has an objective reference. Next is a closely related term, *value*. A value is a personally weighted preference for a thing that has been evaluated. Simply, values express "good," "bad," "should," and "rights." When values are organized into a hierarchical structure, they comprise a value system. Further, values clarify the self-image and, at the same time, mold that self-image closer to the heart's desire. Third is the concept of *personality*. As previously defined, personality is a hierarchical arrangement of the particular attitudes, needs, and values of the individual. Fourth is the term *role*, or *work role*. The reader should recall that a work role is a derivative of the behavior requirements of a position in a formal organization and that it should be viewed as the dynamic aspects of a position, in other words, as a set of functions to be performed by the role occupant.[14] Finally, we come to the most difficult concepts to define—job satisfaction and morale. Unfortunately, there is little standardization in either the meaning or the measures of these two terms. In fact, they are often used interchangeably, "since *satisfaction* means the same thing as *morale*."[15] However, there is ample reason to separate job satiasfaction and morale. They are similar, in that both refer to affective orientations on the part of individuals toward work roles which they presently occupy. The differ-

---

[13]Daniel Katz, "The Functional Approach to the Study of Attitudes," in *Psychology in Administration*, ed. Timothy W. Costello and Sheldon S. Zalkind (Englewood Cliffs, N.J.: Prentice-Hall, Inc., 1963), p. 253.

[14]Victor H. Vroom, *Work and Motivation* (New York: John Wiley & Sons, Inc., 1964), p. 6.

[15]James L. Price, *Organizational Effectiveness* (Homewood, Ill.: Richard D. Irwin, Inc., 1968), p. 150.

ence between the two concepts is that job satisfaction is an individual feeling while morale is a group phenomenon. To put it another way, job satisfaction is the degree of liking that a person has for his work role. Morale is the degree of liking that a group has for its particular work assignment. Before leaving the subject of definitions, it should be understood that positive attitudes toward the job are conceptually equivalent to job satisfaction, and negative attitudes to job dissatisfaction. Findings from recent studies indicate that job satisfaction and job dissatisfaction are located at two different points on a continuum. Between these two points is a very important third point of neutrality (neither pleased nor unhappy).[16] An individual's position on a job satisfaction continuum (or a group's position on a morale continuum) is *determined primarily by the amount of value fulfillment provided by the work role.*[17]

THE RELATIONSHIP OF JOB SATISFACTION AND MORALE TO PRODUCTIVITY AND OTHER ORGANIZATIONAL VARIABLES

To begin, we emphasize that research has established that, "there is in fact no positive correlation between morale, job satisfaction, and high productivity.[18] It was assumed by most in the early days of the human relations movement that a positive relationship existed between morale and productivity. Katz and Heyman's study of morale in U.S. shipyards during World War II indicated morale and job satisfaction to be highly correlated with productivity.[19] Since job satisfaction is definitely related to challenging work calling for skill and responsibility, one can expect that it would also relate to productivity, that is, that higher job satisfaction would be connected to better performance. This prediction would also be made from a theoretical analysis, in which we assume that sincere involvement in work activity would result in greater quantity and better quality of productive work.

[16]See Frederick Herzberg, B. Mausner, and B. B. Snyderman, *The Motivation to Work* (New York: John Wiley & Sons, Inc., 1959).

[17]In support of this contention, Ernest G. Palola and William R. Larson were able to demonstrate that job satisfaction involves not only different work value dimensions, but also different numbers of work value dimensions for varying occupational categories. See Ernest G. Palola and William R. Larson, "Some Dimensions of Job Satisfaction Among Hospital Personnel," *Sociology and Social Research* 49 (May 1965): 205. B. Blai also provides research findings in line with this thinking. See B. Blai, Jr., "An Occupational Study of Job Satisfaction and Need Satisfaction," *Journal of Experimental Education* 32 (June 1964): 383–88.

[18]Albert R. Martin, "Morale and Productivity: A Review of the Literature," *Public Personnel Review* 30 (January 1969): 42.

[19]Daniel Katz and H. Heyman, "Morale in War Industry," in *Readings in Social Psychology*, ed. T. Newcomb and E. Hartley (New York: Henry Holt and Company, 1947), pp. 437–47.

The results of the widely known studies of the Survey Research Center of the University of Michigan destroyed these earlier assumptions. In these studies, of which the one by Kahn is probably the most outstanding,[20] meaningful differences were found between employees in high and low productivity sections on such morale measurements as job satisfaction, employee involvement in the company or participation in company activities, and financial satisfaction. In essence, it was learned that employees could be quite happy with their job and accomplish nothing. Moreover, employees could dislike their work, yet be productive.

The reasons for this failure to confirm the correlation between job satisfaction and productivity are not difficult to find in further analysis. Essentially, three reasons are involved: (1) pride, (2) level of aspiration, and (3) the nature of the work. Let us consider each one in more detail. First, pride in the work group has proven to be the only attitudinal variable showing a distinct relationship to productivity. In Kahn's study there was a significant difference between the ratio of employees in the high and low performance sections who displayed high pride in their work group. The high performance sections indicated a greater degree of pride and loyalty.[21] Second, Morse has suggested that the levels of aspiration of the workers influence the relationship.[22] Workers with higher job involvement were probably setting higher levels of aspiration for themselves and hence reacted more negatively to blocks in their progress than did less aspiring workers. Thus, a job satisfaction measure which does not take into account the aspirations of the worker is an inadequate measure of his degree of job involvement. Third, certain factors have to be present in the work itself before high satisfaction can cause improved productivity, or vice versa. Simply expressed, when tasks are more varied and require more skill, the expected positive correlations do occur. Many jobs have been so thoroughly standardized that individuals have little opportunity to express their talents, with the result that the basic motivation is to maintian an acceptable level of performance rather than to excel. In other words, one's job should be so designed (and this is the rationale behind such things as group decision making and team policing) that the individual can acquire greater need fulfillment through greater productivity.

Hence, an individual's satisafaction with his work and group morale can be linked to high productivity. The so-called link is the quality of

[20]Robert L. Kahn, "Productivity and Job Satisfaction," in *Psychology in Administration,* ed. Timothy W. Costello and Sheldon S. Zalkind (Englewood Cliffs, N.J.: Prentice-Hall, Inc., 1963), pp. 98–105.

[21]*Ibid.*

[22]Nancy Morse, *Satisfactions in the White Collar Job* (Ann Arbor, Mich.: Survey Research Center, 1953).

supervision in the organization. In the preceding chapter, we found that the employee- or group-centered leader was more apt to become a supervisory leader. Pertinent here are the studies which have revealed that group-centered supervisors are higher producers (in terms of group productivity) than production-centered supervisors! The supervisors with the better production records appear to be persons who show in a variety of ways that the individual is important to them, that they understand and appreciate him. The specific characteristics of high production supervisors were that they spent more time on supervision, displayed a closeness to and an identification with the employees, showed personal interest in the employees, both on and off the job, were nonpunitive in their behavior toward the employes, and were accessible for communication with their employees. All of this is to say that the supervisor acted as a leader.

In regard to productivity, we conclude that if all three conditions are met—pride, aspiration, proper job design—the probabilities are very good that high job satisfaction and group morale will cause high productivity. If they are not met then we must abide by the following:

> The overwhelming research evidence to date supports the conclusion that there is no positive correlation between morale, job satisfaction, and productivity. This is not to say that there can not exist high morale and high productivity, but rather that when this is found, variables other than morale or variables interacting with morale are probably responsible for the high productivity.[23]

Another major relationship is that of satisfaction and morale to absenteeism and job turnover. Morse asserts that the "level of general satisfaction may be a predictor of the individual's desire to stay or leave the organization."[24] Further, she relates this does not mean the individual will definitely leave, for this leaving depends upon the state of the labor market. In other words, the worker whose personal needs are satisfied through his work role is more likely to remain in the organization. Moreover, low satisfaction leads to grievances, turnover, absenteeism, and tardiness on the job.

Research has indicated also that morale and job satisfaction differ according to age and skill of the worker. In dealing with age, though, the evidence available suggests that in studying the relationship between age and morale, length of service should be considered. Otherwise, it might be the length of service in the organization that relates to satisfaction, for as the age of the employee increases, usually his length of service with

[23]Martin, "Morale and Productivity," p. 44.
[24]Morse, *Satisfactions*, p. 52.

the company does too. Morse, again, provides an excellent discussion of the age and skill level relationships to morale and satisfaction. "In general, the shorter the time the employee has been with the company the more satisfied he is with his salary and his chances for progress in it."[25] Conversely, the older employees become dissatisfied when their expectations of advancements and salary increases are not met quite so rapidly. All this seems to say that there is a positive correlation between job satisfaction and salary level. It has been shown previously that salary is a component of job satisfaction and morale, but now further analysis is necessary. To begin, skill level is related to job satisfaction and salary— the higher the skill level, the higher the salary. "Therefore, the apparent relationship of salary to job satisfaction is, in fact, indirect. The higher skill level results in greater job satisfaction at *all* age levels."[26] The older employees are more satisfied with the job content because they have, in most cases, acquired the more skilled jobs. Thus, we can expect to find that police supervisors are more satisfied than police officers as a whole because supervisors are generally older and have more highly skilled jobs.

Finally, studies on job satisfaction and morale have either proven or strongly implied that:

1. There is no relationship between worker popularity and job satisfaction (morale).[27]

2. There is no relationship between worker job satisfaction (morale) and in-plant communications.[28]

3. There is a postive relationship between worker job satisfaction (morale) and an increased role in the organizational decision-making processes.[29]

4. There is a negative relationship between worker job satisfaction (morale) and the size of the organization.[30]

---

[25]*Ibid.*, p. 68.

[26]Philip B. Applewhite, *Organizational Behavior* (Englewood Cliffs, N.J.: Prentice-Hall, Inc. 1965), p. 29.

[27]B. J. Speroff, "Job Satisfaction and Interpersonal Desirability," *Sociometry* 18 (January 1955): 69–72.

[28]Dallis Perry and Thomas A. Mahoney, "In-Plant Communications and Employee Morale," *Personnel Psychology* 8 (Winter 1955): 339–53.

[29]Nancy Morse and Everett Reimer, "The Experimental Change of a Major Organization Variable," *Journal of Abnormal and Social Psychology* 52 (June 1956): 120–29.

[30]Sergio Talacchi, "A Critique and Experimental Design for the Study of the Relationship between Productivity and Job Satisfaction," *Administrative Science Quarterly* 5 (June 1960): 309–12. Concerning job attitudes, see Bruce G. Lawson, "Employee Attitude Surveys: An Aid to Administrators," *Public Personnel Review* 30 (April 1969): 97–101.

5. *There is a positive relationship between worker job satisfaction (morale) and the attitudes and behavior of the supervisor.*[31] In case the reader might have forgotten, such a finding is one of the primary reasons for writing this text!

In conclusion, one additional research study is worthy of note in that it has meaning for job enlargement and MBO programs. In fact, if externally valid, Charles P. Ramser's study may be a partial answer to the integration of the manager's role components of *control* and *leadership*.[32] He starts by recognizing that in many situations, employee performance levels have been found to be high, while employee satisfaction levels have been found to be low. In turn, he suggests that high performance may lead to high satisfaction, rather than the reverse. Good performance results in rewards, which lead to employee satisfaction if the work is perceived as interesting and challenging. If the work is not so perceived, then high performance–low satisfaction situations are possible.

Positive Stroking

This section closes with a consideration of various techniques that the police manager may use to increase job satisfaction among his subordinates. Most of the preceding discussion implicitly, and at times overtly, suggests what can be done to improve individual satisfaction and thus group morale. (Certainly Ramser's findings and recommendations are pertinent here.) The following list is, as it stands alone, admittedly incomplete. Further, it may appear sophomoric. Nonetheless, it works! It is predicated on *transactional analysis* which speaks in terms of "positive stroking." To explain, "stroke" is the basic motivation for human survival and enjoyment of life. A stroke is a pat on the back or a word of appreciation. A kick on the shins is also a stroke. Everyone needs some kind of stroking. It is necessary for physical and mental health (which is the subject of the following section). Positive stroking meets one of man's greatest needs. But this need must not only be met but constantly repeated and reinforced. Since it concentrates on the desired rather than on the undesired, it is called positive.

Stroking can also be negative, using forms of discipline and punishment. Because of past experiences many are more accustomed and comfortable with negative stroking than positive stroking. This type of person

---

[31]Morse, *Satisfactions.*

[32]For details of his study see Charles P. Ramser, "Performance, Satisfaction, Effort," *Personnel Administration and Public Personne Review* 1 (July-August 1972): 4–8.

may be provoked into behavior that makes others turn on him (negative stroking). An example is the "bad little boy" who is bad because you say he is bad. However, negative stroking can at best result in acceptable production only on a short-range basis.

Now, what can be done in the way of positive stroking? At the disposal of the supervisor (without any *constraints* or *backing* from management or the organization) are the following techniques:

Listen
Smile
Be approachable
Be friendly
Be sincere
Be forgiving
Be fair
Show interest
Keep a confidence
Look for good and give strokes
Publicize recognition
Involve in decisionmaking
Give constructive criticism
Answer complaints with positive action[33]

JOB ENRICHMENT: Mental And Physical Health

This section will be brief, mainly because the subject of "mental and physical health" for the worker, specifically the police officer, is far too critical to be confined to a single section of one chapter. Chapters, indeed books, on this subject have been and will be written. Hopefully management training will devote time to this subject. The problem is that police work, at times, is a highly stressful job varying from the apprehension of armed criminals to coping with the boredom of early morning patrol.[34] A portion of the answer lies in making the police manager (1) aware that he is responsible for detecting emotional and physical health ailments in his team members, and (2) capable of being *aware!* We do not, nor could we, propose that the police manager serve as psy-

[33]This list appears in the article by Thomas C. Clary, "Motivation Through Positive Stroking," *Public Personnel Management* 2 (March-April 1973): 117.

[34]Obviously emotional stress is not limited to the job of the police officer. Indeed it permeates the entire agency from top to bottom. Consequently police management is no stranger to stress. A most rewarding set of articles on this topic is contained in a series entitled "Tension at The Top," *Public Management* 57 (August 1975): 2-19.

chologist or medical doctor. What we are proposing, nevertheless, is that the manager be perceptually equipped to identify and assist, if necessary, in the resolution of work-related health maladies. Harmon writes that (subsuming participation as a component of job enrichment):

> Chris Argyris makes a similar point about the necessity to increase participation in order to further organizational effectiveness, but places heavy emphasis on the importance of psychological success and positive mental health of organization members. Argyris' central thesis is that pyramidal or hierarchical organizations inevitably produce unintended consequences which drain the organization's long-term productive capacity. Continued reliance on authoritative mechanisms of control, he argues, diminishes the possibilities for organization members to experience psychological success and self-esteem. Argyris argues that the structure of organizations should be arranged so as to induce psychological success for their members on the grounds that the attainment of organizational goals requires it, rather than promoting success-inducing structures as a matter of the individual rights of organization members.[35]

The attitude that employee illnesses must be held in check must start from the top and pervade all levels of the organization down to the first line supervisor. The first line police supervisor is the most critical link in the whole management chain from the standpoint of illness prevention. The police supervisor must be the one to demonstrate management's interest in the general welfare to the employees. Clearly, the police supervisor is the one who influences employee behavior on a day-to-day basis. Regretfully, too often supervisors have come to view employee health as a technical specialty outside their regular supervisory role. A mental/physical health training program must always be designed to aid the supervisor in identifying the early-warning signs of health associated problems. The remainder of this section deals with (1) psychological stress, (2) relevant standards, and (3) fundamental techniques for curbing illnesses.

Psychological Stress

Current research has implicated psychological stress as an important causal agent in such health problems as coronary heart disease, gastrointestinal malfunction, dermatological problems, severe nervous

[35]Michael Harmon, "Social Equity in Public Administration," *Public Administration Review*, 34 (January-February, 1974), 16.

conditions, neurosis, and a number of other physical and mental disorders. Workers in high stress occupations manifest high rates of some of the above mentioned problems, e.g., air traffic controllers.[36]

For a long period of time, the police role has been spoken of as being tension ladden. Further, the media (in particular, television and movies) portrayed the job of a police officer as producing high levels of stress. In the past few years scientific attempts have sought to either confirm or disprove this casual observation. One study of Cincinnati police officers concludes:

> It has been said that the stressors on policemen are not unique compared to working men in general. Many workers list deadlines, complex and frustrating bureaucracies, equipment problems, lack of say, etc. Can we then, in truth, say that the police are in a uniquely high stress occupation? The answer is an unqualified yes. Though policemen face stressors common to other work groups, there is an additional important group of stressors not faced by others. The very heart of being a policeman sets the officer apart from the rest of the community. Groups within society react to the policeman not as an individual but as a stereotype. Even off the job and out of uniform, the policeman must accept prejudice, fear, suspicion, and sometimes open hostility from a large segment of society. Thus, police work becomes one of the few jobs which have a potent adverse effect on the total life of the worker. That is, the policeman's job affects his own personal social life, his family's social life, his children's perception of him as a father, etc. Finally, police work is among those very few occupations where the employee is asked to put his life on the line and when he may face physical danger at any time. These additional stressors not only have a significant impact on their own, but they likely serve to reduce the frustration tolerance necessary for handling other job stressors.[37]

Additionally, Grencik's findings expatiate the above research results by confirming that:

> Stressors in police work emanate not only from immediate job related tasks, but also from family disruptions caused by the job. The irregular and often long hours that beginning patrolmen may be required to work disrupt family life. Research has shown that people who work shift work are more likely to encounter not only family problems, but also various types of medical problems.

[36]William H. Kroes, Bruce L. Margolis, and Joseph J. Hurrell, Jr., "Job Stress in Policemen," *Journal of Police Science and Administration* 2 (June 1974): 145. This subject is covered in greater detail by Walter McQuade in "Watch Your Work." He reports that "There's impressive evidence that the chronic ailments afflicting middle-aged Americans have less to do with fatty diet, cigarette smoking, and lack of exercise than with workaday anger and tension." See *Fortune*, January 1972, pp. 101–42.
[37]Kroes, Margolis, and Hurrell, "Job Stress," pp. 154–55.

In addition, other stressors arise from the nature of police organization within the total criminal justice system and constitute problems
over which the officer has little control. Stresses emanating from the
police organization are likely to include typical kinds of job related
stresses: promotion, career advancement, lack of communication
and/or health and welfare concerns. In addition, officers are likely
to feel that regardless of how well they may do their job, the criminal
justice system itself is so erratic that their own work is really of no
consequence. Other stresses come from the rapidity of social change
and the difficult position in which this places the police officer.
Enforcing the laws of the past in the midst of such rapid change may
be a source of stress to the officer.

With the sources of stress so varied, it is necessary that officers be able
to recognize when to use confrontation as a solution and when to
use avoidance.[38]

The major finding in her research was that those officers who had
prior warning of a potentially stressful situation experienced considerably less stress than those who did not when the adverse conditions were
actually encountered. This finding has numerous implications for the
training and supervising of police personnel. Is it not conceivable that
entry-level and in-service training programs could be so designed to assist
the officer in both anticipating and coping with conditions that can
result in increased tension. Also, is it not conceivable that the police
supervisor can fulfill a similar role as an on-the-job trainer in the early
identification of possible stressful situations. As mentioned earlier, much
can be written about the harmful consequences of job hazards, both physical, psychological, and *psychophysiological*. How to avoid, and if not
avoid then cope with job-related stress on police officers should be a paramount research question of the late 1970s.[39] The following standards
are indicative of this mounting concern for the health and welfare of
our police.

Health Standards

In law enforcement, personnel effectiveness, operational efficiency and
flexibility, and predictability of costs can be greatly improved by institut-
ing nationwide standards governing total health care, income protection,
retirement, and the physiological and psychological fitness of police offi-

[38] Judith Grencik, "Psychophysiological Reactions of Officers to Experimentally Induced
Stress," (Unpublished research report, Los Angeles, California, 1974). This is perhaps
the most definitive study to date.
[39] It would appear national and state legislation will accelerate this trend. For example,
see the series of articles on occupational safety and health in *Trail* 9 (July-August
1973): 12–30.

cers. If police were to adopt reasonable standards relative to the problem areas addressed in the report *Police*,[40] and if the supervisors were trained to implement the standards, millions of dollars would be saved across this country. A few of the more pertinent standards are included below.

Every police agency should require all applicants for police officer positions to undergo thorough entry-level physical and psychological examinations to insure detection of conditions that might prevent maximum performance under rigorous physical or mental stress.[41]

Standard 20.2
CONTINUING PHYSICAL FITNESS

Every police agency should establish physical fitness standards that will insure every officer's physical fitness and satisfactory job performance throughout his entire career.[42]

Standard 20.4
HEALTH INSURANCE

Every police agency should, by 1982, make available a complete health care program for its officers and their immediate families to insure adequate health care at minimum cost to the agency and the employee.[43]

BASIC TECHNIQUES OF JOB SAFETY

Many techniques for achieving job safety are contained or implied in the preceding pages.[44] A few of the more pertinent points in regard to safety are covered again in this section. Not in the following list, however, are the items discussed in the section on physical working conditions. See that particular section again for indicators of "what to do." The last five points below deal with a person's physical and mental health.

1. The first and most important step is to sell yourself on the vital need for the police supervisor to be concerned with his subordinates' safety and mental well-being.

[40]See the National Advisory Commission on Criminal Justice Standards and Goals, *Police* (Washington, D.C.: U.S. Government Printing Office, 1973), pp. 496–514.
[41]From Standard 20.1, "Entry-Level Physical and Psychological Examinations," p. 498.
[42]*Ibid.* p. 501.
[43]*Ibid.* p. 507.
[44]For an easily read and meaningful text in the area of mental health, see Harry Hevinson, *Emotional Health in the World of Work* (New York: Harper & Row, Publishers, 1964).

2. When accidents do occur, investigate carefully and communicate on the basis of facts. Be specific in the analysis, identifying those causes which are still active. Also keep a record on the subordinates.

3. Enforce safety rules! Establish a definite routine to check for violations and take action when safety infractions are found.

4. Instruct the new men. Let them know what has happened in the past, what the most probable causes of accidents are.

5. Let the subordinates help. By listening to them, one may spot new causes for accidents and get suggestions for improvement.

6. Be a good example. Supervisor actions must reflect safety.

7. The supervisor must make every attempt to furnish the police officer with a well-planned and clean working environment.

8. The supervisor should expect (and sometimes encourage) the recital of personal problems whose intensity may interfere with the employee's work. Even in police agencies where psychologists (or psychiatrists) are available for this purpose, it is likely that at least some police employees will prefer talking to their immediate supervisor (depending on their feelings toward him).

9. In our age of anxiety, the police supervisor can provide reassurance—reassurance of the employee's identity, of his existence and functioning as a human being. This is accomplished by recognizing the police employee as a human being, particularly in an age in which personal relationships have a tendency to become impersonal, as, for instance, when people deal with each other on the basis of titles. This dehumanization can be lessened if first names are used instead of titles, social gatherings are encouraged, and so forth.

10. The police supervisor, once having identified a person in need of psychotherapy, should be quick to assist him in seeking out professional help.

11. Use those behaviorisms cited earlier as being manifestations of "positive stroking."

JOB ENRICHMENT: Implementation

"Job enrichment has so far been tried primarily in clerical operations. It would seem, however, to be particularly applicable to knowledge work."[45] Nevertheless

[45]Peter F. Drucker, *Management: Tasks, Responsibilities, Practices* (New York: Harper & Row, Publishers, 1973), p. 276.

None of the beneficial results of job enrichment are achieved without *pain*. The organization practicing job enrichment will have to suffer because it is learning a completely new style of using its human resources. But no learning is without pain. The important thing is that this is constructive pain. John Gardner has stated that, "Most of us have abilities that we have never known we had, simply because the circumstances of our lives never called them forth." Job enrichment is one new method that will call them forth. It holds promise for an exciting future.[46]

What we are driving at in the use of the above two quotations is a threefold proposition: (1) Job enrichment is applicable to the police service; (2) job enrichment is not an easily implemented program; (3) job enrichment, regardless of hurdles, is a *most worthwhile* program. An example of the first point, with definite parallels for the police, is to be found in a recent evaluation of an experimental job enrichment program involving a municipal personnel department. The findings produced evidence that job enrichment does increase the level of job satisfaction and can improve job performance.[47]

The implementation of a job enrichment strategy should be considered a special case of introducing change.[48] As with the introduction of organizational or technological change, the implementation process becomes the real acid test of success. Managerial concepts which have had strong theoretical and experiential underpinnings have failed because due care was not given to necessary implementation requirements.

It is suggested, then, that five steps be followed in implementing the enrichment strategy:

1. Experimentation with the strategy
2. Supervisory coaching in enrichment concepts
3. Identification of jobs to be enriched
4. Implementation of concept
5. Feedback and follow-up on enrichment efforts

LEARNING EXERCISE

JOB SATISFACTION

The following questionnaire can be used to discern one's job satisfaction or group morale. In turn, it can act as an indicator of where management should focus its attention on enriching the job of his staff.

---

[46]Roy W. Walters, "Job Enrichment Isn't Easy," *Personnel Administration and Public Personnel Review* 1 (September-October 1972): 65, 66.

[47]Luis R. Gomez and Stephan J. Mussio, "An Application of Job Enrichment in Civil Service Setting: A Demonstration Study," *Public Personnel Management* 4 (January-February 1975): 49.

[48]For details see Carroll, "Conceptual Foundations," pp. 36–38.

Job Satisfaction Questionnaire

The reader should carefully examine and respond to each question listed below. The over-all numerical score indicates your level of satisfaction. Combining your score with others in the same work group indicates the level of morale present. The police officer and supervisor should find the device of particular interest. In one way, the score is suggestive of how successful the subordinates feel their immediate supervisor is in meeting their personal needs. Where low scores are evident, further analysis of the fifteen items is necessary. Spotting those items that received a low or dissatisfied check should provide to the supervisor a warning sign for remedial action. Corrective action on the part of the supervisor should begin with an examination of the various supervisory techniques described in this text. It should continue through the selection and application of the most appropriate alternatives for the solution. It ends if, after further measurement, the individual's level of job satisfaction has been increased. If not, then back to the drawing board.

Notice that we have provided a space for answering which allows you to show several degrees of satisfaction or agreement. There are no correct answers to these questions, but only answers as you see them.

1. How satisfied are you with the sort of work you are doing?

        1 2 3 4 5

   Very dissatisfied   Very satisfied

2. What value do you think the community puts on your service?

        1 2 3 4 5

     None   Very great

3. In your daily work, how free are you to make decisions and act on them?

        1 2 3 4 5

    Not at all   Very free

4. How much recognition does your supervisor show for a job well done?

        1 2 3 4 5

     None   Great deal

5. How satisfied are you with the type of leadership you have been getting from your supervisor?

        1 2 3 4 5

   Very dissatisfied   Very satisfied

6. To what extent do you get to participate in the supervisory decisions that affect your job?

        1 2 3 4 5

     None   Great deal

7. How closely do you feel you are observed by your supervisor?

        1 2 3 4 5

    About right   Too closely

8. Are you satisfied with the department as it now stands?

                 1   2   3   4   5

    Very dissatisfied   Very satisfied

9. How satisfied are you with your prestige within the city government?

                 1   2   3   4   5

    Very dissatisfied   Very satisfied

10. How satisfied are you with your possibilities of being promoted to a better position?

                 1   2   3   4   5

    Very dissatisfied   Very satisfied

11. How satisfied are you with your present salary?

                 1   2   3   4   5

    Very dissatisfied   Very satisfied

12. How satisfied are you with your status in the community?

                 1   2   3   4   5

    Very dissatisfied   Very satisfied

13. Would you advise a friend to join this department?

                 1   2   3   4   5

       No   Yes

14. Do you receive a feeling of accomplishment from the work you are doing?

                 1   2   3   4   5

    Very dissatisfied   Very satisfied

15. Rate the amount of pressure you feel in meeting the work demands of your job.

                 1   2   3   4   5

    Very dissatisfied   Very satisfied

2

ROLE

COMPONENT TWO:

EXTERNAL

RESPONSIBILITIES

We caution you not to conclude that, because they are discussed last, the tasks comprising the second role component are less important than those you have just completed. In part 2 we present the police chief, the sheriff, and key members of their management team as they function in a more visible manner. You will see how the police manager is responsible for performing operational tasks designed to *integrate* the agency with its surrounding institutions and general milieu. Moreover, as you will be quick to detect, these integrative attempts are, or should be, proactive efforts to build common understanding and mutually supportive relationships. Finally, in a subtle way you will begin to conceptualize and perhaps even identify the manager as a motivational force, endeavoring to apprise others of the inherent value of effective police services, and the sustained need for resources to actuate the administrative delivery system.

A brief statement is in order about the police manager as a politician. In our estimation, controversy over the administrator engaging in politics is academic at best. In fact, our police managers as well as other public administrators often and intentionally become involved in politics. Clearly the elected sheriff must do so. If you will accept our definition of politics as being "the legitimate use of reasonable power in the equitable determination of the allocation of scarce resources," and cast aside for a few moments the venal or demagogic connotations of the term, you should feel more comfortable with the police manager acting in a political manner. Indeed, you may even encourage his active participation.

The final chapter is not intended to serve as a comprehensive or in-depth prognostication of the police manager's emerging future. Rather we hope that it will stimulate the police manager into doing two things: (1) to both realize and accept that he has an obligation to think about the future; and (2) to take action now in order to more successfully meet the demands of tomorrow. In summary, we see the police manager as an alert, predictive, and action-taking individual constantly striving to better meet change.

Chapter Fourteen

TASK 12
THE POLITICS OF
MANAGING

Knowledge of human nature is the beginning and the end of political education.

Henry Adams

SYNOPSIS

"Managing" has been commonly defined as the *art* of coordinating and directing the resources of an organization toward the attainment of its goal(s). "Politics" has not achieved a generally acceptable definition. Indeed, it has a wide normative range starting with a highly positive meaning and ending with a connotation of vileness. When referred to as "politicians" or accused of using politics, we are uncertain whether to smile and respond with a thank you, or to be offended and hostile. We choose to use the word in a nonnormative sense. For us politics means the application of power in determining the allocation of scarce resources. Hence, the questions of how, who, why, and when must be addressed before one is able to say that in a particular situation the use of politics is good or bad—or, how good or how bad.

The message of this chapter is simple but important: police managers function in an administrative, social, *and* political environment. Whether police managers should or not is academic here; the fact remains that they do. And, it is in failing to *sense* the political waters that a police manager can be openly "boiled," or subliminally "frozen." Much of the following discussion, as you will soon discover, poses the dangers, the pitfalls, the problems inherent in the political milieu. As a consequence, we conclude here with the admonition that politics can be good just as well as bad, helpful as well as harmful, and advantageous as well as disadvantageous to the police manager.

THE "POLICE-TICIAN"

It would be difficult, if not impossible, to approach a discussion of the modern police manager's political world without developing at least some historical concern. For law enforcement, while beginning to think of itself as professional, has not yet shaken off the cloak of negative political relationships. "The police, as one of the largest and most strategic groups in metropolitan government, are also likely targets for political patronage, favoritism, and other kinds of influence that have pervaded local governments dominated by political machines."[1]

A chapter such as this would be incomplete without some attention to the negative aspect of politics as it relates to the police manager. Our main thrust, however, is to explore some of the more normal, socially acceptable relationships that may not typically be thought of as political. These are more likely to be found in discussions of interpersonal, collaborative, interdepartmental, interagency, and other similar relationships.

We believe, however, that successful managers must be *politically sensitive and politically astute,* and think in terms of political aspects that relate their offices to the multitude of variables which influence managerial effectiveness. Managers obviously do not operate in a vacuum. All law enforcement agencies have certain common missions that cannot and will not be accomplished by sheer willpower; that can be accomplished only with cooperation. And of course cooperation is more likely to occur when there is an understanding and utilization of the interdependency that exist both within and outside any law enforcement agency.

Police departments obviously depend upon governing bodies for support in terms of policy decisions and resources as well as public support of stated goals and objectives. They are dependent upon their own departmental members to perform tasks in, it is to be hoped, an optimum, but at the very least an acceptable manner, and of course to perform in a fashion that is supportive of the police manager's philosophy and of departmental rules and regulations. Police agencies depend upon other operating departments such as the city attorney, city clerk, public service department, and fire department to provide certain backup or support services. They depend upon other criminal justice agencies, because without their cooperation the police are simply not going to reach stated goals; they will be ineffectual.

It does little good to arrest prostitutes if the district attorney or courts have other priorities, aren't cooperative, or are unaware of the street-level problems as they relate to the overall objective of reducing crime. We are convinced that the "system" would "grind down"—*has* "ground down" in those areas where each part of the justice system operates totally independent of the others.

Police managers cannot ignore the political influence of community groups, nor should they wish to do so. We would hasten to warn at this juncture, however, that there is a history of unsuccessful managers who

[1] The President's Commission on Law Enforcement and the Administration of Justice, *Task Force Report: The Police* (Washington: U.S. Government Printing Office, 1967), p. 208.

have been trapped by a belief that only vocal or *historically* influential groups "need to be reckoned with."

In this chapter we will explore political relationships and strategies with those entities already mentioned, as well as with others such as the news media which continue to present a most prodigious challenge to the police manager.

It is our intention to approach this subject in a humanistic, practitioner fashion. We hope to give a real-world view which the modern manager will wish to expand upon in terms of his own experience. For that reason we have relied heavily upon the experiences of our colleagues both inside and outside the field.

The Laterally Promoted Manager

As we began to focus on the political aspects of the police manager, we discovered that relatively little attention has been directed to those who have moved from one organization to another at the management level. Such practice has become more prevalent in recent years as governing bodies seek ways of bringing about reform or change. This can be seen in some areas as an attempt to *break the hold of politics* in its negative sense, or the recognition that police departments are highly complex organizations which can no longer afford the luxury of promotion on the basis of seniority and popularity without regard for professional leadership ability.

It is our belief that every manager must be politically astute about his relationships with the various groups and organizations with which he must interact. If our observations and beliefs are true for the average manager, they are doubly so for the laterally promoted manager. Therefore, we will continue to make some specific references to this topic throughout the remainder of the chapter. (An excellent example of our hypothesis regarding the lateral manager can be found in the case study which constitutes the learning exercise for this chapter.)

In terms of understanding the "politics" of any given organization, we can reasonably expect that managers who are raised from within will recognize most historical aspects of existing political relationships.

However, it is our observation that managers who are new to existing organizations, even those who have *done their homework*, are for the most part not aware of the total political atmosphere into which they have stepped. Too often, regardless of talent, they are at the mercy of a variety of dichotomous pressures and, in an effort to satisfy one group, they fall into disfavor with another. And of course one must not discount the dysfunction of failing to anticipate the various political pressures that are likely to be brought about by those from within the organization, especially those who believe that the position *should have been theirs.*

This new manager, then, in order to bring about the desired change for which he was hired, must be aware of the political might of his competitors, both within and outside the organization.

In the business of building support, perhaps the number one priority is to locate the disappointed individuals and to begin building bridges with them. Such employees have usually been in the organization for a long period of time and have no doubt built up both support and opposition over the years. They may have even been promised the manager's position, or at least believed that they would have first opportunity. In some cases it is likely that the disappointed person has actually been functioning as an "acting manager" for several months. If so, the transition may be doubly sensitive. To underestimate the power of such people and of their supporters is folly; to attack these people, regardless of the reasons they have been passed over, is likely to bring about innumerable undesirable repercussions. Even casual remarks that can be construed as derogatory are a luxury the new manager cannot afford—for he knows not to whom he is speaking. It can be anticipated that relationships may reveal themselves from time to time in astounding ways.

In observing police organizations that have encountered this situation, the writers have failed to find that any of those passed over were totally incapable of making some valuable contribution to the new manager and to the organization.

We would urge that every effort be made to search out these strengths and assets and to utilize them while publicly acknowledging their existence and value. Conversely, to take the position that "passed-over competitors" were incompetent and totally dysfunctional would be both dangerous and counterproductive. For the most part, faults and weaknesses are not likely to be seen as such by the individuals possessing them nor by their friends and supporters.

In our opinion it is absolutely essential for the new manager to take the personal needs of these "passed-over persons" into consideration. In doing so he creates a situation in which strengths are more likely to surface. Perhaps surprisingly to some, it will be these very persons who *know how to get things done,* to get cooperation. It is they who will know who to approach in other departments or organizations and most often how to make that approach in order to ensure cooperation. As most can attest, even the most necessary functions are rarely accomplished "by the book."

Conversely, if these disappointed persons are treated, by either deed or innuendo, as inadequate failures, problems, or roadblocks, they certainly have all the essentials to become just that.

Our point is this: After many years of service, good or bad, the most demoralizing, disappointing, and often humiliating experience for any aspiring manager is to be identified as inadequate or unwanted. The validity of such decisions may be clear to those who make them but very unclear or at least unacceptable to those who are the object of them.

It can be expected that most passed-over persons will believe that the decision makers were incorrect, that the person *brought in* is a *carpetbagger* who time will show was the wrong man for the job. Given half a reason they may very well work either by commission or by omission to prove this to be true. It can be readily expected that all of their supporters will do the same.

Typically the person passed over will have stature. He will probably have held memberships in a variety of community organizations, will have socialized with and will be admired by many influential citizens who will not be privy to the reasons for which he was passed over. (True reasons for such a move by the persons responsible for the selection are rarely if ever made public.)

These groups and friends can be expected to voice their disapproval and disappointment. They will, in their attempt to console, add fuel to the fire and make it even more difficult for the new manager to build a positive relationship with the person scorned.

New managers will do well to keep the development of a desirable relationship a high priority. Regardless of any coldness or open criticism, they should make every effort to reinforce the positiveness of each contact.

It has been our observation that most laterally promoted managers who have made the smoothest transitions have not only developed an immediate organizational interdependency with those passed over but have also endeavored to establish some social relationship as well. It would appear that the old adage, "The best deals are made on the golf course," may have some application here. We are suggesting neither golf nor "making deals," but rather observing that perhaps the best place to resolve emotional issues such as these is not the office. Too, something done socially is more typically seen as what one *wants to do* as opposed to what one *has to do*.

Suffice it to say that those passed over are often political entities in themselves and should be recognized as such. And like the next entity we will explore, they can offer a great deal in terms of guidance and support—if the new manager moves positively.

A very real secondary danger to the laterally promoted manager is the political polarization of department members away from him. Even in departments where most members believe that an "outside chief" is desirable, there is likely to be a fear or concern for *what is going to happen,* since the outsider is an unknown quantity. News stories about this new manager—after his selection but prior to his arrival—can and often do set off some negative polarization.

Typically the news media is clamoring for the reasons why this candidate was chosen over all others. And just as typically, the hiring authority senses the need to publicly justify its choice and does so in glowing terms.

The second step of this phenomenon is that the news media contacts the newly selected manager for statements as to why he is moving to City X from City Y and what he hopes to accomplish in City X—his goals for the organization and so forth. Few have thought that far ahead and many are caught *flat-footed.* They are not prepared for this sudden focus because they have not operated at the department-head level in the past and are not conscious of the great difference between the impact of a middle manager's open statements as compared to those of the department head.

It makes little difference whether the town has one small weekly newspaper or several large ones, plus radio and television coverage. The impact upon the organization can be less than desirable if the new manager is not prepared for this onslaught. For example, one newly selected chief carefully avoided controversial issues. Instead he dwelt upon such topics as providing more training and educational opportunities for the personnel. He later learned that this was heard by his new department as "He thinks we're a bunch of dummies."

"Who is this stranger who wants to change us?" The new manager can inadvertently bring about the polarization of employees by attempting to initiate change—too quickly—without understanding the history of why things are done in the manner in which they are. To be told that one has been doing it all wrong can be nearly as devastating as being told that one is inadequate. And of course there will always be those who delight in seeing new managers tread on sacred cows for whatever reason.

As was said in Meredith Willson's great musical, *The Music Man,* "You got to know the territory." Suffice it to say that department members do constitute a political entity—one that is vital to organizational goals and managerial effectiveness.

Similar awareness is imperative outside the organization and it should begin with the governing body itself. It is a rarity when the entire governing body is in favor of lateral promotion. Typically, if there were "heirs apparent" there were also supporters among the governing body who were in some movement to *keep the promotion inside the organization.*

It will be important for the newly appointed manager to expeditiously build bridges with these people whoever they are. When this is not done, one can look to regular opposition at the policy-making/funding level. And there will routinely be someone present to exploit *new program* failures. At the local government level this type of bridge building can be exceedingly difficult, especially in the "city manager" form of government. Typically, by city charter, city managers are responsible for hiring and firing department heads, and councilmen or other elected representatives are expressly prohibited from interfering or dealing directly with them (unity of command). Recognizing that such is the case, a new police manager, with the understanding and approval of the city manager, must endeavor to solidify his own position. This means that the police manager must work to build positive interpersonal relationships with council members in a fashion that will not be perceived as threatening to the city manager. And in no manner should these relationships circumvent the city manager's authority.

The cliché "between a rock and a hard place" seems most appropriate to describe the early position often held by new lateral police managers.

The Elected Governing Body

The police manager's relationship with the elected governing body depends somewhat upon the particular form of government. The elected sheriff has a decidedly different relationship with the county board of supervisors as compared to the police manager appointed by the mayor or city council. In the city manager form of government the police manager's relationship is substantially different from that in the commission form of government and so forth. There are, however, certain commonalities and it is those primarily with which we will deal.

Generally speaking, this particular political relationship is one of the more complex because it seems to have more variables. This is to say that in working through the political relationships with other parts of the justice system, the police manager is for the most part dealing with professionals. The system requires certain minimum educational levels in a rather narrow spectrum of fields. The ultimate goals of the system have at least some intrinsic relationship to each other and there is some language commonality. While these are certainly qualified similarities they do at least offer a base.

Conversely, elected officials may spring from a great variety of disciplines and nondisciplines. They may be professionally educated or have no formal education at all. They are neither screened in the qualifying sense that civil servants are, nor for the most part have they met any specific criteria in terms of their elected office, save those requirements of age, residence, and citizenship.

Elected officials may serve on either a part-time or full-time basis; they may be dependent upon their elected position for none, some, or all of their income. And of course, most began their political career at the same level in which they currently serve—while most civil servants work their way up through the ranks, gaining a variety of experiences as they go.

These statements are in no way meant to downgrade elected officials, their background, credentials, or ability, or those qualities that tend to assist candidates in popular elections. They are meant rather to acknowledge a different set of variables that must be taken into consideration.

A city manager once put it this way:

> "When I was manager in a small wealthy town, council members were for the most professional people, chairmen of boards of large corporations, and the like. These men were accustomed to large budgets and understood the business of finance. They didn't spend a great deal of time on small issues but reserved themselves for larger fiscal matters and setting policy guidelines, as they did in their own businesses. Since the town was small my salary wasn't so great, but my wife could have a mink coat and I could have driven a Cadillac without anyone raising an eyebrow—if I could have afforded it. Now I work in a large city with a commensurately larger salary. My city council is larger and while one or two of the council members are professional people, the others are small businessmen—one owning a small gasoline station. Here I could afford a mink coat for my wife and a more luxurious personal car, but these would be viewed as a show of wealth and I would be resented."

In cities where elections of representatives are by district or wards, as opposed to city-wide elections, a great many variables of another kind are likely to be present. Election platforms in fact are variables in themselves. Another variable is the council person/selectman elected by a majority of citizens in his district who have certain vested interests in mind and to whom the candidate has made specific commitments. It can readily be seen that the number of variables developed through the election process itself is likely to be infinite.

Fortunately, most platform commitments involving law enforcement at the local level are publicly announced and open for the manager to consider and deal with. Those concessions that may have been made in private are those more likely to create difficulty for the police manager.

At the extreme end of the spectrum, the behind-the-scenes commitment may be to oust some appointed official, perhaps the police manager himself. In fact, campaign funds may have very well been committed for that specific purpose.

If such a commitment is made by an entire voting block or majority of elected officials, the manager is of course in a most difficult position. It is not unusual for elected officials to enter public office with preconceived ideas relating to law enforcement that may very well be in error. When this occurs, the manager is at a disadvantage but must immediately search for or provide opportunities to bring these beliefs or ideas out in the open where they can be dealt with. Usually citizens without some experience in local government will not be aware of the constraints under which law enforcement people work. They probably will not understand why certain equipment is purchased from a particular manufacturer, or why it is necessary at all. Such issues can normally be clarified through early briefings. Issues concerning enforcement policy, deployment of personnel, budget, and the like will, as a rule, require more explanations and justification—and will in all likelihood be tested with some "expert." Issues concerning the discharge of personnel are likely to be a great deal more complicated. If the elected official has privately committed himself to a course of action, especially to persons who have been instrumental in his campaign, he will find it difficult to change his course. Unfortunately, while such commitments are often made without firsthand knowledge they do ensure that the appointed official is in for a difficult time.

It is important that he discuss the basis for the commitment, and to whom it was made, with the elected official. If there is a basis for the commitment, obviously the manager must change or the attitude or perception of the elected official must be changed if he is to survive.

Poor, incompetent, or corrupt managers should be replaced. On the other hand, many police managers who operate in a perfectly professional manner have found themselves on the verge of being ousted. Those who have survived have taken immediate steps to reinforce their position and have begun an immediate attempt to modify the elected official's ouster commitment.

There isn't any pat way to accomplish the modification. However, the problem is not likely to go away on its own and must be dealt with on a high-priority basis.

Earlier we discussed the political hazards for the laterally promoted manager. It can readily be seen that newly elected officials are the unknowns in much the same manner as the new department was an unknown to him.

It should always be expected that people who have not yet worked together will have formed opinions, both good and bad, with little or no foundation. The majority of elected officials and appointed police managers can and do work together toward a set of common goals. How effectively they do so, however, depends a great deal upon their understanding and appreciation for each other's roles and upon their mutual respect. If elected officials are looked upon as less than qualified by the police manager, or if the police manager is not supported by the elected official, the results will be less than optimum and the general citizenry will not have received the best possible return for its tax dollar.

Perhaps one of the most prevalent issues in the relationship between elected officials and police managers is the officials' need to be kept informed. We have found that most officials are primarily concerned with issues they are likely to be asked about by their constituents. They do not like to be surprised publicly nor do they wish to appear uniformed. In the ward system, an elected official is likely to be much more concerned with an occurrence in his area of influence than with an occurrence in a neighboring sector.

On the other hand, there will probably be unanimity in terms of needs to know on issues that encompass the entire city—for example, the arrest of another public official; the involvement of a policeman in a highly controversial action, such as a fatal shooting in a minority area; major police activity; or local disaster. However, it is not always the magnitude of events that makes them newsworthy but rather who has been touched by them, or their cost, or the anticipated repercussions. It is important for the elected official not only to be knowledgeable but to be knowledgeable first—before he is faced with inquiries of the news media and others.

We are not suggesting that police managers seek sanctions prior to controversial actions that must be taken, but rather that they be sensitive to the elected officials' needs as soon as practical after the action, but prior to a general news release.

There is, of course, a preponderance of police activities many of which can become controversial (such as returning all truant students to school to reduce daytime burglaries, or the carrying of tape recorders by all field personnel) that have no need for instant enactment or confidentiality. In such areas, most managers with whom we have consulted believe it prudent to preinform elected officials. In this way a foundation can be laid for the desirable support while permitting time for feedback that may be beneficial to the police manager.

Most managers find it easier to contact and keep informed those elected officials with whom the manager has already established good lines of communication and mutual respect. That does not relieve the manager of the responsibility to keep all informed equally. One overly

knowledgeable elected official who *drops* police information on the remaining officials can be as damaging or even more so than providing no
information at all. Along these same lines, a close social relationship
with one or two elected officials to the exclusion of the others will have
much the same results. The short-range advantages are far outshadowed
by the long range conflicts.

Elected officials have direct access to several support areas for operating departments. The most obvious is through the budget and then
on a daily ongoing basis through their own public statements in terms
of how they vote or speak out. A third area not to be overlooked is their
access to the electorate. Suffice it to say that new and innovative programs which require broad public involvement can be greatly benefitted
if the electorate respects its elected representatives and they support the
programs.

We hasten to add that all such contacts, notifications, and the like
should always be conducted with sanctions from the person or body to
whom the police manager reports.

It must be understood that mutual respect, support, and open lines
of communication must be developed in a professional manner and in a
positive sense. We are not in any way suggesting a compromise of integrity or principles. We are suggesting that it is proper, when operating
within the framework of good management principles and acceptable
professional police practices to develop positive political relationships
with elected officials.

Police Associations/Unions

In chapter 11, we focused upon police associations and unions. The political aspects of relationships between police managers and associations/
unions, however, was reserved for this discussion.

Many veteran managers find it difficult to accept police associations
and police unions in the representative sense, but the fact is that they
are here to stay. Many veteran managers find difficulty in accepting
changes brought to the management process by police associations and
unions. Some have withdrawn, delegating negotiations, grievance meetings, and the like to subordinates. Others grudgingly go through the
motions of operating within contemporary frameworks—telegraphing
their resentment. A police manager, well educated and with twenty plus
years experience to his credit, is understandably annoyed when he must
sit down and discuss management issues with a four-year veteran patrolman who has not yet qualified for promotion.

The simple truth is that the manager can no longer work as autonomously as he once may have. He must now share some authority, must confer or consult, at least on certain issues concerning working conditions, often with a person or persons who by any previously held standards are not yet qualified to make such decisions.

And of course the manager is being challenged regularly on issues such as grooming standards, rules governing the use of weapons, seat belts, disciplinary procedures, and every other thing imaginable.

As for those who have withdrawn, one can only hope that their administrative subordinates are skillful and sophisticated in the present-day mechanics, the art of working through problems with the association/union representatives. If they are, the manager may somehow survive—until his retirement. If they are not, it is the manager who must shoulder the consequences.

Perhaps acknowledgement of this particular facet as a recognized political relationship is a bitter pill for some. For others who have either associated with unions and therefore the process prior to entering law enforcement or been schooled to the process through academia, the change will not be so great; the change will be more orderly.

In chapter 4 we discussed managerial styles that included shared responsibility in decision making. In reality, what is happening between police management and police unions is an extension of that philosophy though not in a direct sense.

At any rate, a very real political relationship does exist between the police manager and the police association/union. And modern managers should take care to treat the relationship as such. The difficulty is not so much in anticipating the employee organization's strengths and weaknesses and needs, but rather in the shifting relationship and styles as representatives change with annual elections. Like elected officials, the association/union representatives can be expected to run the spectrum in terms of education, background, personal ability, personal goals, sophistication, and the like. Some representatives will be easy to work with, keeping confidences, acting professionally, presenting issues in workable fashion. Others may not have those same attributes and may feel a need to make outlandish statements. "I had to go in and kick the old man's desk to get this or that concession" is not atypical of what may be said, perhaps out of false bravado or simply because it is perceived by that representative as a way to impress his peers and electors. Or he may challenge the manager in front of others, especially large groups. Whatever the basic reason for this type of behavior, an obvious lack of sophistication exists.

It is a wise police manager who recognizes the various strengths and weaknesses of the representatives who confront him. And a wiser one still who has the insight and patience to invest time in counseling and training unsophisticated representatives so that they can accomplish what is needed in a manner acceptable to all concerned, and can experience success without detracting from management. Often these representatives have great long-range managerial potential and lessons learned at this stage can benefit the department in another fashion at a later time.

A political relationship in the true sense does exist, and associations and unions are here to stay.

The Justice System

Two opposite and distinct descriptions tend to surface in discussions of the justice system. One is that the various components are interdependent and operate with some semblance of a system. The second considers the various components to be independent and autonomous. The courts are, of course, the component most likely to be viewed as autonomous— free from influence. The truth is that a variety of relationships exist with even the most autonomous, and of those, the political relationship is perhaps the most delicate.

As we stated earlier, it does little good for a police department to have a drive on illegal prostitution if the prosecutor believes that prostitution prosecution should have a low priority. And of course the prosecutor must have priorities since there are often many more defendants than there are court rooms and judges. To carry it further, the police and prosecutor may set prostitution as a high priority, but if the court does not, a stalemate continues to exist. Examples such as this, where the judge is insulated from the street level, may become very real problems when they reach the point at which regular citizens and businessmen alike are concerned about the downhill trend of a particular city area— and apply pressure on the police.

It may not be the court itself but the probation department that takes a totally different view, especially if it finds that detention facilities are in short supply and makes recommendations to the court that are likely to put the prostitutes right back on the street.

The fact is that, even though each justice system component makes its decisions properly within its own legal framework, there are no assurances that each is working toward a common goal, at least in a manner that is likely to relieve the original problem as seen by the citizen and as interpreted by the police.

Some law enforcement agencies, perhaps through frustration, attempt to change the situation through public castigation. "The D.A. only wants to prosecute cases he knows he can win," "The D.A. doesn't want to try cases—only bargain them away," "The probation department is filled with sociological do-gooders," "The judge is on a rehabilitation kick," and so forth.

Some agencies have encouraged the media to run weekly score sheets on the courts. Most often such tactics have resulted from a history of frustration and public pressure to *do something*. The result of a tactic such as this, or others, or open remarks that are likely to be viewed by the court as discrediting are typically disappointing. Judges, like the rest of us, wish for their efforts to have meaning. Placed in an awkward situation they, again like the rest of us, will need to rationalize and reinforce their actions. The same can be said about all of the other system components—including the police.

The politically astute manager will make certain that he is communicating positively with representatives of the systems components. Offering an explanation of the problem on a personal basis—*without attempting to tell the other party his business*—is much more likely to produce desirable results than will the negative approach.

If those with whom the manager needs to communicate are, for fear of compromise or some other reason, unwilling to develop personal relationships, the same results can often be obtained through representative groups such as the Bar Association. Other excellent intermediaries are the groups of elected officials who make or influence policies, including those regarding finances. These would be identified as legislative bodies. On the local level they would be city councils, mayors, and boards of supervisors.

We are not suggesting pressure tactics. We are suggesting that those bodies, if aware of the broad problem being created, can often talk in terms understandable to all concerned.

It is not always the desire for autonomy nor fear of interference that frustrates effective communication. Often it is the failure to set aside time for meeting with representatives of other criminal justice functions. Police managers tend to become bogged down in day to day activities. Many simply retreat behind their desks in order to grind out work—to meet with people who *need* to see them. Some pride themselves in being on top of *everything*. The problem is that, with only so much time available, many managers tend to operate in a response mode rather than in a planned mode. This leaves little time for sorting out long-range problems, for anticipating the need for change, and for developing important relationships. The tendency for some, in recognizing the need for contact between agencies, is to delegate that function rather than delegating the daily routine problem-solving responsibilities. Managers cannot manage properly if they are tied to desks and telephones and routine appointments that really could and should be handled by subordinates.

If the manager is to develop policy that is responsive to not only organizational needs but system needs and community needs as well, he must have time, and *set aside time*, to do so. He must attend and arrange meetings that will inform him and give him a chance to inform others. He must have time to see firsthand and to discuss firsthand rather than rely on the repairs of others. As in the news media, there are times when something is lost, or undesirable connotations are added, through the written word.

Effective, understanding, responsive relationships between the various parts of the *system* are most likely to occur when the decision/policy makers know and respect each other. This is not to say that certain routine functions should not be delegated to subordinates.

Certainly these are political strategies—but in a most positive sense.

Special Interest Groups (Groups Outside the System)

Throughout this chapter it has been our intent not to focus on the very large or the very small police agency but rather on the median since to a certain extent they typically experience many of the problems of both. And we expected not to find unanimity among police managers on this issue of political relationships or even on whether the area covered here is political at all. Surprisingly, or perhaps not surprisingly, we did find unanimity regarding special interest groups.

Groups formed for specific special interests are often obviously political. Perhaps not so obvious but far from apolitical are the organizations and groups identified as "service clubs," church clubs, women's clubs, men's clubs, lodges, chambers of commerce, and the like. These, while basically not politically oriented, have the capability and history of becoming political when confronted with specific or special interest issues.

Service clubs are traditionally composed of business people and are more likely to become interested or exert pressure on issues that effect business. Parking enforcement was the example most often given. As stated in the section on the laterally promoted manager, these groups are likely to become involved in the selection of a new police manager, or at least attempt to. They also tend to involve themselves in issues such as curfew and loitering, at the bottom end of the spectrum, and high crime rate problems on the other.

One of the problems with special interest groups is that they tend to have "experts" in their membership who may really enjoy some level of expertise, or may enjoy none at all.

In either case, if their area of interest focuses upon the police, it is incumbent upon the management to meet with these groups personally or be adequately represented. In all likelihod, they will be capable of directing some public attention on the topic, attention which can be either positive or negative. If the group perceives the police manager to be evasive or disinterested in their cause, we can anitcipate that they will attack. If, on the other hand, the manager and department are open and helpful, it is more likely that the problem, if it exists, will be portrayed in a more positive manner.

For example, a group centered around a university in a western city was concerned with the erosion of civil liberties. The group strongly opposed the addition of helicopters for police patrol, alleging that helicopter pilots could see into yards, behind fences, and the like, constituting an invasion of privacy.

Though the manager had ample community support to institute the program, he wanted even more support to ensure its continuation after the implementation test period. He called upon the opposition group, inviting representatives to spend time in both a patrol car and the helicopter. Begrudgingly, the opposition group, after orientation experience, publicly stated that they continued to have concern for the erosion of privacy but felt that the helicopter was a necessary police tool in terms of community security.

An excellent example of special interest groups is contained in the case study at the end of this chapter. A subtheme of the study covers the topic of a group formed for one specific role—finding jobs for returning servicemen after World War II. When the need for such a group no longer existed, rather than disband—for they had become recognizable as a group with some community influence—they continued to meet; and they became a *political* influence.

Successful groups tend to remain as groups, though their original emphasis may shift. Membership will usually be in an evolutionary state, which adds to the flexibility of their interests.

In almost every community we visited or contacted we discovered that there existed somewhere an informal leadership group. Some were informal to a degree that they sometimes had no chairman, no set of rules or dues, or even a regularly constituted place or time to meet. Some, though informal in terms of not having any official sanctions, did have regular meetings and an *elected* hierarchy.

Informal leadership began to mean to us those people or groups of people whose opinions are respected and sought after by those who have been elected into formal governing bodies.

The smallest group we discovered met every weekday for coffee in an ancient restaurant, and had done so for some fifty years. There were about ten or twelve seats around a long table, which appeared to be the only membership size limitation, with the exception that the aspirant member had to be *in*. If he was not, he soon "caught on" as we were told, "and left." Those gathering there changed with the years and the character of the community. Traditions remained, including matching smoothly worn silver dollars "to see who paid the check" and passing judgment on most issues before the city council did so. The group undoubtedly had great influence on city matters.

An example of more recent vintage was defeating the new city hall police/fire building proposal—because the city *"didn't need the fancy auditorium."* (The city jail had been condemned by the county grand jury every year for at least twenty-five years, and modern fire equipment could not be housed in the headquarters building. General administrative offices were totally inadequate.)

An interesting aspect of this group was that while they influenced nearly all major—and many trivial—matters for over half a century, no member considered himself to be part of a "pressure group." It is doubtful that they considered themselves a *group* of any kind.

The largest such group that we found met on a regular basis, enjoyed an elected hierarchy, had strict membership rules, and was generally made up of upper class or successful people. Their influence was perhaps more subtle as well as better planned and more official. Endorsements were both openly and privately solicited and, when the group requested any elected or appointed public official to appear before them, the official did so. The setting was one of a breakfast or luncheon with the requested guest as a speaker. There was no doubt, however, as to why one was invited, nor that he was expected to attend. No commitments or oppositions were ever made in front of the speaker but they were forthcoming in a variety of *effective* ways.

Groups made up on the basis of ethnic background have always been present but never more vocal than in current times. Groups formed to gain equal employment, to change employment standards, and to fight social injustices are in proliferation. While some are more active than others, or more effective than others, none can nor should be ignored. Though many lack strong leadership, have never heard of Robert's Rules of Order, and have little or no operating capital, all are very real political forces.

In earlier times, a certain minimum level of cohesiveness and sophistication was necessary in order to consider issues. Such is no longer the case. While it may be difficult to identify leadership, at least in some of the newly emerging groups, their need and right to be heard and to be potentially politically effective is great.

Whether the group is large, highly sophisticated, and enjoys recognition and respect by the total community, or is a small group, newly emerging in a heretofore voiceless section of the city but focusing on real concerns, the police manager's need for communication and credibility is the same. He may feel much more comfortable and productive in meetings with upper-middle-class groups than with groups related to the ghetto and the barrio. However, his preoccupation with one group at the expense of the other is a luxury that he can no longer afford. He cannot ignore the ghetto/barrio any more than he can move with only those groups to the exclusion of older established institutions.

Managers new to core cities or to rural cities that have suddenly grown up will be faced with a continuum of all the social ills of the past, all of the injustices, real or imagined, and all of the local social mores. In bringing about change, they will undoubtedly move too quickly for some and too slowly for others. Old groups that have always attracted the decision maker's attention will find it difficult to share this business of political influence with those not formerly heard from.

> Basic to any agency's political standing in the American system of government is the support of public opinion. If it has that, an agency can ordinarily expect to be strong in the legislative and the executive branch as well. Since public opinion is ultimately the only legitimate sovereign in a democratic society, an agency which seeks first a high standing with the public can reasonably expect to have all other things added unto it in the way of legislative and executive support. Power gives power, in administration as elsewhere, and once an agency has established a secure base with the public, it cannot easily be trifled with by political officials in either the legislative or executive branch.
>
> There are essentially two ways in which public support may be cultivated. The first is by creating a favorable attitude toward the agency in the public at large. The second is by building strength with "attentive" publics—groups which have a salient interest in the agency—usually because it has the capacity to provide them with some significant benefit, or the power to exercise regulatory authority in ways that may be of critical importance to the groups concerned.[2]

In essence, most community groups are either in some fashion influencing policy routinely or occasionally; have vested interests or causes; can and do shift emphasis for a variety of reasons; and do change in membership. Community groups can be supportive or can throw up road blocks. Community groups with common causes often transcend the var-

[2]Francis E. Rourke, *Bureaucracy, Politics, and Public Policy* (Boston: Little, Brown and Company, 1969), pp. 12, 13.

ious societies and levels that comprise a community, and groups that typically concern themselves with the preservation of historical landmarks and other innocuous pursuits can, given the right set of circumstances and without a great deal of effort, be swayed to take up other issues that have direct bearing on law enforcement.

The modern police manager, cognizant of citizen groups, will do well to translate the knowledge into workable form for his subordinates.

In our discussions with managers we found few who were not conscious of the various groups although there was some disagreement as to potential power or effectiveness of certain groups and therefore the degree to which they required attention. In other words, a particular kind of group was likely to be observed differently from one city to another. On the other hand, it appeared that many managers shared common difficulty in transmitting down through the police ranks the need for sensitivity to those groups.

The results of this difficulty or lack of sensitivity at the operating level had at times created undesirable problems for most of the managers interviewed. Where this occurred, almost to a man the managers had been forced to invest many personal hours relieving or attempting to relieve the problems developing out of this insensitivity.

The News Media

The news media will readily be seen as a political entity by most managers. Unfortunately, however, too many managers have not yet developed clear and concise philosophy and policy statements so that their awareness and support can be transmitted to the operating level. Even if the police manager and the publisher understand and support each others needs, very little is accomplished if subordinates do not.

Clearly the news media needs news and the police are involved in activities that are likely to be newsworthy. The media must present interesting and factual information to survive economically and the police need an informed public to be assured of concerned supportive citizens. If the public believes that there are no community problems when in fact there are, they are not likely to support inflationary budgets that call for more policemen and more support services.

Perhaps one of the most refreshing examples of openness with the media and thorough understanding and appreciation of the media's political aspect in this regard occurred in 1957. The City of Downey, California, population about 100,000, had been newly incorporated and was in the process of forming its own police department. Paramount among the sections of a hastily produced operating manual was one dealing with the news media. As new officers were brought on board they were especially indoctrinated with that policy. Simply stated, officers were admonished to expect every aspect of their profesisonal and personal lives to be made public through the media. Every facet of police activity was open to inspection by the media and it was encouraged to report what it saw—whether positive or negative. All disciplinary actions would be made public as would all commendations. All criticism of individual officers and the department as a whole would be made public as would all collective accomplishments and individual achievements.

As the chief use to say to his department, "Damn it all, if you're going to work for the public they have a right to know what you're doing. If you want to continue working for them, it had better be good."

Obviously there have been many changes in the law since 1957. Police agencies are no longer free to release certain types of information lest it prejudice a particular case or violate an individual's right to privacy. On the other hand, working within the legalistic framework, there still remains ample opportunity to develop and maintain a high degree of openness and cooperation.

Obviously there will be times that openness becomes frankness and the resulting backfire may be less than desirable, especially when that frankness doesn't come across in print with the same flavor it had in conversation. When rebuttal or pressure results from one of the faux pas, typical responses are, "I was misquoted," or "My statements were taken out of context," or "In the future I'll tape my comments for my protection."

The hope for such comments is that they will somehow shift the blame to the media. They do not. What they do do, especially if such remarks become a habit, is to jeopardize the political relationships that exist between the police agency and the media.

It is vital that police managers develop and maintain positive political relationships with the news media. Although conditions and situations will at times place each in an adversary roll with the other, the ongoing positive relationship will minimize such things and prevent them from becoming dysfunctional. Movement in this direction is greatly enhanced when both media and police agency understand that each serves the community in its own way. Mutual respect is more essential than mutual admiration.

It should be clearly understood that, as in all interorganizational relationships, certain people within the police group will develop relationships with specific individuals representing the news media. Regardless of the philosophy of either the police agency or the media, every reporter and every policeman will not enjoy a positive relationship—any more than all policemen enjoy positive relationships with all other policemen. Open conflicts are more likely to arise, however, when the police manager appears to be in conflict with the media—or of course where the publisher/editor appears to be in conflict with the police.

The message is then that the manager should set a high and ongoing priority on working towards that desirable relationship—and making certain that his staff and all other department members are conscious of this priority.

Negative/Corruptive Political Relationships

Heretofore, the political relationships we have written about have been positive—positive in the sense that they deal with open, healthy realities of police administration. Broad political relationships will not be new to the modern experienced police manager. It was our intent to simply pull together those which we consider most applicable and label them as they appear from our point of view. However, as we stated at the outset, a discussion of political relationships would not be complete without some attention to the negative side—the corruptive or unhealthy, behind-closed-doors politics. We should add that our use of the terms negative and corruptive politics are at times synonymous.

Public concern for negative political police relationships dates back to the very inception of law enforcement. The thought that power corrupts and that absolute power corrupts absolutely, that there will always be those who live through the misuse of power/influence, is not new. The depression era of the 1920s and 1930s continues to be the setting for movieland stories of police corruption, of payoffs and appointments of entire police departments; of looking the other way while major crime flourished.

Political corruption of course did not leave us with the depression's end. Unfortunately there are still those who prefer to have political control of law enforcement managers and law enforcement managers who knuckle under to that control for reasons of their own, not the least of which may be survival.

One of the greatest police studies of all time, the President's Commission on Law Enforcement and the Administration of Justice (1968) addressed this problem in its *Task Force Report: The Police.*

> *Political Corruption.* . . . . The police are particularly susceptible to the forms of corruption that have attracted widest attention—those that involve tolerance or support of organized crime activities. . . .
> Another form of political corruption—where police appointments are

considered a reward for political favors and police officials are consequently responsive primarily to the local political machine—is still a fairly open and tacitly accepted practice in many small cities and counties. It recurs too, from time to time, in larger cities, though generally in less conspicuous form.

Even in some cities where reforms have ended open political control of the police, policemen who make trouble for businessmen with strong political influence may still be transferred to punishment beats, and traffic tickets may still be fixed in some places through political connections. Honest and conscientious police chiefs often have an extremely difficult time eliminating these practices. . . .

Political Domination. The problem of old-style domination of the police by political machines has attracted the most intensive reform efforts from the police themselves. As a result, the effort to establish independent, professional law enforcement has made considerable headway over the past 30 years. This movement has not been without its own problems, however; the tradition of improper political interference is deep-rooted.

Further, civil service regulations in many jurisdictions have sometimes restricted the reform attempts of honest police executives. In many cities, for example, it is extremely difficult to remove officers who have engaged in serious acts of misconduct.

It is obvious that improper political interference contributes to corruption. Patronage appointments lower the quality of personnel and encourage all officers to cooperate with politicians, even in improper circumstances. Although a man might withstand this temptation for himself, it may be impossible or even pointless for him to separate himself from the practices of his superiors or partners.[3]

Individual investigative bodies such as New York City's Knapp Commission[4] have addressed themselves to specific problems but generally speaking very little has been done or said officially on a nationwide basis.

James Ahern in his book, *Police in Trouble*,[5] has addressed the subject of corruptive politics and the police in perhaps the most direct fashion of any recent author. We would hasten to add that Ahern's book is primarily based upon his experiences over a relatively short period as Chief of the New Haven, Connecticut, Police Department. On the other hand, his account is applicable to negative political observations of other writers and other practitioners. For that reason we have chosen to excerpt the following from his chapter entitled *"Politics and Police."*

[3] President's Commission, *Task Force Report,* pp. 208, 209, 210, 211.
[4] *The Knapp Commission Report on Police Corruption* (New York: George Braziller, Inc., 1972). This is recommended reading for all police managers.
[5] James F. Ahern, *Police In Trouble* (New York: Hawthorne Books, Inc., 1972)

The greatest threat and detriment to fair and effective law enforcement . . . is illegitimate political interference, often intimately connected with corrupt and criminal interference. . . .

Most police chiefs, however, having come up through the ranks of their own departments, alleviate their insecurity—as much as possible —years before they become chiefs. They protect their own, they play politics, and they survive. If they serve in cities where crime machines hold the real power and lubricate police departments with illicit funds, the chiefs function in ways that perpetuate machine power and cut off police from broad democratic controls. . . .

There is nothing more degrading or demoralizing to a police department than the knowledge that every favor or promotion within it is controlled by hack politicians and outright criminals. And there is nothing more nearly universal. . . .

Cities that have recently suffered scandals uncovering the influence of organized crime in politics are not exceptional for experiencing this kind of interference. Newark, Jersey City, and Seattle are exceptional only in that the interrelationships have recently been uncovered. The New Jersey scandals were exposed only because intensive federal investigations run by honest prosecutors intervened at times when corruption had become so widespread as to be impossible to conceal completely. In Seattle, a web of corruption was uncovered that eventually brought indictments of nineteen city officials.

Perhaps the best way to begin an exposition of the way in which police departments are controlled is with the figure around whom the various systems of control revolve: the political boss. Although political bossism was supposed to have gone out of style years ago in the wake of reform efforts that have swept nearly every city at one time or another, most cities are in fact ruled by men or groups of men who function covertly as bosses in much the same way as did the infamous figures of the past.

The primary strength of the boss lies in his political machine. Whether or not he has ever been elected or appointed to public office, the boss is the lynch pin of the machine, the focal point of all its various interconnections.

The machine consists of people who can get votes. It consists of strategically placed people in various communities who can remind voters of their obligations to the machine, who can publicize candidates, who can produce campaign contributions and make sure that people do not forget to go to the polls on election day. It functions as the basic source for candidates for patronage jobs in governmental agencies and can ensure that large groups of people in close-knit communities can be obligated to the machine—whole families through a single job, whole blocks by special favors such as extra police protection or street cleaning, whole neighborhoods by new public-works projects.

Patronage jobs must be approved, however, by the machine's office-holders. If the boss himself holds office, he decides, and he controls the grass-roots organization. They need his political image to survive, because they need a candidate who can win. If the boss does not hold office, he controls those who do to one degree or another, and he functions as "director of patronage." If the boss does not hold office, by definition the candidate who does is so weak that he needs the machine more than it needs him—at least at the outset—and so must give away power to be placed on the party's ticket.

If the political boss has control of the appointments to a city government, he has control over those who hold such appointments. He can replace them or have them replaced, he can embarrass them in various ways, or he can render them powerless by giving real control over their functions to someone else.

This means that political bosses control chiefs of police, who usually serve at the discretion of the mayors under whom they work and who therefore are highly vulnerable. Since bosses also control the boards that administer Civil Service examinations and determine advancement under that system, they are able to subvert Civil Service. Through the chief they can control who is assigned to such vital areas as vice, gambling, and narcotics investigation, and whether the department's Detective Division attempts to combat organized crime. Since they control promotions, the chief owes his to them more often than not, and any deviation from their policies or desires is sure to handicap the career of any officer in the department.

This arrangement assures that the political boss can do numerous favors for politically important people. He can have parking and traffic tickets fixed, he can assure that minor violations of numerous laws—from obstruction of public streets to liquor-law violations—are ignored, and he can deliver extra police protection for favored neighborhoods. He can do a great deal more as well.[6]

As with Ahern, most of what has been written on the subject of negative politics has dealt with the big-city machines and the more bizarre forms of corruption that may not be found in the average community. Or if they do exist there, they probably will not be dealt with at the community level.

But there are negative politicians, cancerous growths of a kind, even in the most model of cities. These are the influence peddlers who rarely seek public offices for themselves—for that would attract the limelight. These are the ones who are content to center their activities in a legitimate business and to gradually develop political muscle at the local level. These are the nice guys who spoil it all in the end by collecting

[6]*Ibid.*, pp. 92, 96, 100, 101.

for their niceness. These are the ones who fancy themselves as king makers—and many of those seeking office believe it, too.

The person who wishes to become a city councilman, a mayor, a
judge, or even to be elected to a state office must have some local support
—a wide variety of support.

The budding police officer who aspires for manager responsibilities
may at times seek to reinforce the selection process through public support by this *king maker*. And it may become difficult for all of those
seeking support to differentiate between legitimate support and that
which has a price tag attached to it.

For *king makers* seldom make *kings* for the simple pleasure of doing
so. While the payoff may not be today or even tomorrow, experience tells
us that there will surely be a day when the mortgage comes due.

Obviously, small-time influence peddlers such as this could not operate
if there were not those in public office who were beholden to them. And
so there exists a vicious circle. As the *peddler* produces results, his influence broadens and his hold becomes very much like a cancerous growth.

Unfortunately, many who solicit and receive support from this type
of person fool themselves into believing that there will be no payoff.
Too many professionals have tarnished their credentials in this manner.
And just as unfortunately, when the tarnished official falls, and he often
does, the *peddler* is still holding court, still respected and still peddling
influence.

Negative politicians, those who are corruptive and decaying, are in
fact a very real facet of the modern police manager's arena. And it will
be the professional, the honest police manager who not only resists them
but exposes them for what they are.

CONCLUSION

Aside from the negative position which we have acknowledged, there
is an exciting side to politics as it relates to the police manager. The
excitement is not the manipulation of people, for that kind of success
is often short lived. It is rather the art of bringing all of the elements and
variables that support the police together in concert so that common
goals can be reached or maximized in the most expeditious, most rational
manner.

Finally, political relationships are not something than can be delegated, but rather they are a trust, a responsibility of the police manager
who must treat them with respect, nurture them, and guard against their
indiscriminate use and abuse so that they may always be utilized in the
most positive sense towards the attainment of organizational goals.

LEARNING EXERCISE

Learning exercises or case studies are especially useful for reexamining an individual's or an organization's values, as noted above, and the following selection attempts to sensitize the reader to this very significant perspective of the job of the police manager. At its best, the approach to police management as an applied social science can simply suggest ways to achieve what it is the manager values by understanding and appropriately manipulating his environment. But if an applied social science provides useful tactics and a working idea of what the world is like, an enormous question remains unanswered: What should the "good" administrative state be? Dealing with immediate subordinates, similar to formulating policy for others, forces the police manager to consider his values and those of others. This requirement cannot be avoided. Therefore, no alternative exists to facing and working through the difficult and frustrating personal and institutional issues of value.[7]

The following learning exercise clearly shows that the problems in police work reside not so much in the statutes or in the tacit norms controlling police management and enforcement as in a "value confrontation" between one form of management (police) and another (city manager).[8] As Sherwood states:

1. Unlike a number of other municipal functions, the *administration* of the police service inevitably involves community value questions. The manager must realize that norms other than efficiency enter into these behavior patterns. It is also of some interest that the manager often enjoys a certain degree of flexibility with regard to his role in these matters; and in this sense his own value system may determine his perception of his responsibilities.

2. The guildism of the police, which is the product of a great many factors, is to be seen in a variety of ways. Even where closed promotions are not prescribed, the community desire for a "local boy" in this sensitive position places important limitations on the manager's ability to deal with the police department as "cleanly" as he can with others. From the standpoint of the theory, these experiences seem to indicate how difficult it is to legislate human behavior. It may suggest the desirability of a more flexible organization structure to permit greater accommodation to the demands of the individual situation.

[7]Robert T. Golembiewski, ed., *Perspectives on Public Management: Cases and Learning Designs* (Itasca, Ill.: F. E. Peacock Publishers, Inc., 1968), p. 10.

[8]Socialization plays a highly influential part in determining how the actor—in this case the manager—is going to behave. It is also the cause of differing values and, therefore, interpersonal conflicts. For a more comprehensive treatment of this subject, see Mark Abrahamson, *The Professional in the Organization* (Chicago: Rand McNally & Co., 1964), pp. 19–20.

3. Finally, it is important for the manager to recognize that simple occupancy of the top of an administrative hierarchy does not automatically accord him the power capacity required to wield effective authority. The municipal government is an open system; power is obtained outside as well as inside the structure. The police chief is one of the most powerful figures in city government, but such informal factors of the authority relationship do not normally appear as a part of traditional council-manager theory.[9]

Basically, the case, a true story, portrays a value conflict situation between two managers—one city and the other police.[10] Secondarily, the emergence of various political factors and strategies broadens the conflict or at least provides entry of variables which have been alluded to in the text.

A CITY MANAGER TRIES TO
FIRE HIS POLICE CHIEF

Frank P. Sherwood

INTRODUCTION

In 1956, the year City Manager Singer fired Police Chief Black, or tried to, the population of the City of Valley had risen to about 25,000.[11] Within a two-hour drive from Los Angeles, Valley was the center of a large citrus farm area. The green orchards which dotted the hillsides south of the city relieved the semi-desert brownness of the landscape. Valley was also the site of a sizable college supported by a Protestant denomination.

For years, going back to World War I, Valley had held a reputation as one of Southern California's most pleasant and peaceful communities. Before 1940 its population had been composed of four main groups: citrus owners, and leaders of associated service firms (packing company owners and managers, and the like); downtown businessmen, realtors, and professionals; the college people; and the Mexican-American laborers. The town had always been heavily and quite seriously Protestant; the Baptist and Methodist congregations were two of the largest groups in the city.

[9]Frank P. Sherwood, "Roles of the City Manager and the Police," *Public Management* Vol. II, (May 1959), 113.

[10]Reprinted with the permission of The Bobbs-Merrill Co., Inc. (ICP Case Series: No. 76, 1955).

[11]The names of persons and local jurisdictions used in this case are entirely fictitious. Because of the author's departure for an overseas assignment, portions of this case—particularly those dealing with the political background—have been prepared by the editor.

The Setting

Railroad tracks running from east to west bisected the community. High ground and hills rose to the south. With the exception of the college, which formed its own little enclave of green lawns and architectural confusion, the area north of the tracks was the poorer part of town. Here the houses were older, the people less well-to-do, less educated. Here one was more apt to find a Democratic voter. Also in this northern section was the Mexican-American community, predominantly Roman Catholic, which tended to be isolated socially from the rest of the city. Rising south of the tracks were the leading hotel, the banks (units of state chains, which appointed the local managers), the City Hall, and the business district. Also to the south was the country club, which had the reputation of being a gathering place for the prestigeful, the old families, and the better-off, although some of the more austere or fastidious among the eligible families chose not to frequent it. Still farther south, up in the hills, were the luxury homes.

By 1956 there had appeared a new element in Valley's population—one that could not be as neatly categorized as those that had been familiar for over forty years. Valley was gradually becoming a "bedroom city." The new people were the product of the rapid growth of the nearby Xerxes metropolitan area. They lived in Valley, but they worked close by in the larger urban centers. These new residents spread throughout the community. Many moved into housing developments on the north side. The wealthier ones erected homes up on the hills. Religiously, the newcomers seemed to include more Catholics and fewer Methodists and Baptists than the pre-existing population. Economically, socially, and politically it was not clear just where they would fit. Although Valley had often been regarded by outsiders as hostile to newcomers who might disturb the peace and order of its settled ways, the newcomers were absorbed without visible eruptions. Up to 1956 observers had not detected any real impact by the newcomers on the politics of the city.

Politically, Valley had always been a city of predominantly Republican voters. Xerxes, the county seat, a railway center with a population three times the size of Valley's, was a Democratic city, and since the mid-thirties the County Board of Supervisors and the county administration had usually been under Democratic control. California state law required non-party local government elections, but most informed people in Valley knew who the infrequent Democratic candidates for the City Council were and whether a Republican or a Democrat had been elected to speak and vote for Valley on the County Board of Supervisors.

By and large, Valley's citizens were not intensely interested in party politics or in city government. From the well-to-do citrus families there had usually come a leading element of support and influence in the Valley Republican organization, but much of the party work and many of the candidates willing to devote time to local government came from the ranks of the more established local businessmen, realtors, and professionals. Some of the downtown businessmen and professionals, meeting regularly and separately for luncheon in different local chapters of six different national service organizations (Rotary, Kiwanis, and the like), some of the country club people, some of the leading laymen in the church congregations, and the (Republican) publisher and editor of the daily *Valley Times* were usually aware of political and governmental events. But beyond this circle were the majority of citizens who seemed uninterested in governmental affairs as long as things ran smoothly and quietly—which up to the 1950s they almost always did.

The "Lemon Street Gang"

Among those who were quite well-informed, an almost legendary element in the city's political history was the Lemon Street Gang. Most people in Valley did not know of its existence, and among those who claimed to, its membership, its political influence, or even its continued existence were often guessed at or disputed. The men alleged to be in the group denied that such a group existed or that they worked together; they were just friends of long-standing and intimate acquaintance. But most insiders believed that the group operated informally and secretly to wield influence in local government and politics.

No hard evidence has been found that the Lemon Street Gang played any part in the events of 1956 that form the subject of this study, but some of the principal participants suspected that the Gang was active behind the scenes.

Actually, the group had started as an informal personal association of a half-dozen Valley war veterans—not sons of high-status families—after they had returned from military service in World War I. They had found it difficult to get jobs and discovered that they were not the only returning veterans who were not well-regarded by potential employers. They resolvd to work togther at influencing affairs in Valley to see that deserving veterans were taken care of, despite the unsympathetic attitudes of Valley's leading citizens and the existing Republican organization. Many of the men who were associated with the group proved to have considerable ability in politics and government. Some were sons of small tradesmen who, in the twenties, were far down from the top of Valley's informal social ladder.

Some members of the group organized a formal veterans organization that spread throughout the county and beyond. One of the leading members became an extremely effective precinct worker for the local Republican organization. The group bargained its voting influence in order to secure jobs for veterans in local and county government. The more jobs it obtained for veterans, the greater its political bargaining power became. Its leaders began to operate increasingly at arms length from the older, more conservative, and more socially established men who acted as leaders of the local Republican organization. Finally, in the middle thirties, one of the leading political figures in the group, dissatisfied with the recognition offered by the county and local Republican organizations, helped secure the election of the first Democrat as County Supervisor from Valley. He stayed on the Democratic side of the fence and formed the first Democratic organization in the city and in the county. During the Depression the political efforts of the Lemon Street Gang to win jobs for veterans were not disturbed by the fact that some were in the Democratic camp and others were Republicans. The members of the group moved below the level where the public tends to pay attention to politics (which in Valley was not deep) to place their protégés, using whatever means their ingenuity could devise. Most often, it was admitted, the men they placed in government jobs proved to have the necessary ability.

The Lemon Street group had its greatest successes in the thirties, when Valley operated under a modified commission form of government, which was then traditional in California. By 1945, some of the leaders in the original group had moved out of Valley to careers in county, state, and even federal government. In the early postwar years the remaining members of the group succeeded in getting the city to set up a veterans bureau with a paid staff. One of the leaders of the group helped to secure necessary Council support for Valley to accept an extensive public housing project, against the inclinations of several local realtors. The group also allegedly secured the appointment of an extraordinarily able and dedicated man to serve as director of the housing project. Some of those who benefited from these projects—including the Mexican-Americans—were alleged to be sufficiently appreciative to vote as the group's leaders suggested when the Lemon Street men wanted to muster support behind some particular local candidate or issue.

The Introduction of a City Manager

The postwar period also brought to Valley a growing pressure from civic-minded citrus families, professionals, and local businessmen in favor of more efficient municipal government under centralized management. A public services director was appointed in 1946 and given many of the powers of a city manager. Under the leadership of Mayor Cassius Bolt, a temperate and respected local businessman who was a deacon in the Methodist congregation, the council-manager plan was adopted by Council ordinance in 1949. Bolt had been moved to devote time to local government by a sense of duty. He took no part in local political party organizations, although, like most respectable people in the city, it was assumed that he voted Republican in state and national contests. Among those strongly supporting the plan was Councilman Antrim Heald, one of the few Democrats ever elected to the Council. Heald was a planing mill owner and a leading figure in the local Democratic organization. Widely-respected, Heald was not connected with the Lemon Street group, although one of the leaders of that group remained active in the Democratic organization and presumably helped to get votes for Democratic candidates.

It was believed by some of the leading supporters of the council-manager plan that during the 1950s the leaders of the Lemon Street group found the existence of a city manager a threat to their continued influence in local government—particularly in the placement of protégés. Hence it was believed by the council-manager adherents that any event that appeared to embarrass the manager or hinder the success of centralized management in local government had been caused by the secret manipulations of the Lemon Street Gang. It appeared to some outsiders that by the mid-1950s the Lemon Street Gang had lost influence and, to some extent, had lost interest in municipal affairs. The movement of some of the group's members to higher echelons of government, the increasing age of those who remained, and the fact that city jobs were no longer as highly sought after as they had been during the Depression were all reasons for less intense involvement in local affairs. But when they wanted to, the remaining Lemon Street men could produce votes and could use extensive personal connections. And there was some evidence that the group was still sufficiently interested to fight selected rear-guard actions against the advance of unsympathetic city managers. Its members still mobilized occasionally to support certain Council candidates who were personally sympathetic, Republican or Democrat. And it resisted efforts of city managers and "good government" supporters who sought to turn certain elective posts such as city treasurer into positions filled by managerial appointment. Whatever it actually did or did not do, whether it was still intensely active or declining in influence and interest, or even whether it still existed as a group, the Lemon Street Gang was still seen in the 1950s as a potent harassing force, working secretly and deviously for patronage and against city manager government. It was seen this way only by those few insiders in Valley who supported manager government and who were sufficiently acquainted with local affairs to have heard of the Gang's alleged activity. Since the friends who reputedly made up the Lemon Street Gang never acknowledged publicly that they worked together, much less had an organization, it was hard to tell just what the truth was.

THE EARLY DAYS OF MANAGER SINGER

Jack Singer became Valley's third City Manager in July 1952. He was a lean six-footer in his mid-thirties who had formerly been manager of a smaller California city. He had become a manager by progressive municipal experience rather than by a university education for the profession. He had once served as an elected town clerk and had become quite an expert in sewage problems. (Valley was about to undertake a sewage project at the time.) Singer heard of the opening in Valley at a district meeting of city managers. Attracted by what he knew of the city, he applied even though the salary offered was below that prevailing in cities of similar size. He was selected.

In talking with his predecessor, Singer found that Valley's council-manager system was reasonably typical for California. As state law prescribed, the City Council had five members elected at large. The Manager served at the pleasure of the Council. At variance with orthodox theory, however, was the Manager's limited power over appointments of department heads other than the City Treasurer and City Clerk, who were elected. In Valley these key administrative appointments were recommended by the Manager but required Council confirmation. Dismissal of these officials was handled the same way. From the Model City Charter standpoint, these requirements represented a significant infringement on the Manager's "right to manage." But Valley's Manager did have considerable discretion in personnel matters because there were no formal merit system, no civil service tenure, no written appeals procedures, no provisions for probationary service. The lack of these formal procedures and regulations broadened the power of the Manager over city employees, but it also placed heavier burdens on him, since he had no laws with which to justify his actions.

Singer's early conversations also yielded some consistent opinions about the style of administration that Valley's leading citizens felt suitable for their town. He was given to understand that Valley had its own quiet ways of community living and that it would not accept as Manager anyone who pushed for changes too strongly or too rapidly. He learned that one of his predecessors had aroused much personal opposition by being too severe in his rigid devotion to efficiency and management principles. He had been gruff with citizens and allegedly had not treated people in a friendly manner. Irritation with him had become so strong that several Council candidates known to oppose him (but not the manager form of government) had been elected. He had thereupon resigned to take another post. Getting on well with people had always been one of Singer's strongest qualities, and he gathered that this had been one of the things that had been given weight in his selection.

Singer came to value highly the advice he received from former Mayor Cassius Bolt who had been instrumental in passage of the Council-Manager Ordinance in 1949. Bolt had retired as Mayor, but he was still well-informed. From Bolt and from Councilman George Simpson, a well-to-do orange grower and real estate man, Singer learned that the manager form of government was safely established in Valley but that it was not immune from attack if a Manager did not perform acceptably.

Councilman Simpson, who had played a considerable part in the hiring of Singer, had lived in Valley most of his life and came from a local citrus-owning family. He was widely respected on all sides as an able, intelligent man. He held all the essentials for full membership in the community: long residence, conservatism, Protestant church affiliation, and prosperity. He had a firm commitment to the manager form of government, and he was critical of some of the men connected with the Lemon Street Gang.

Singer also learned about Hector and Homer Smith, the brothers who were publisher and editor, respectively, of the *Times,* Valley's only daily newspaper. It had to compete for local circulation with the *Xerxes Clarion,* the nearby metropolitan daily that inserted a Valley page in papers delivered there. The Smith brothers had inherited the *Times* from their father. Hector, the publisher was active in Republican politics in the city and the county. Homer, the editor, was nobody's man, but was willing to give advice, orally or editorially, about almost any community matter. The brothers' policy was that any local controversy should be thoroughly aired, if not inflated, in the *Times* more rapidly and more extensively than in the competing Xerxes daily.

The Kelly Affair

According to Singer's comments in 1960, many of the problems of the Valley government of the fifties arose from events of the past. Valley had been like many other small communities—a government of privilege. Building regulations had been winked at for friends; various public utilities, such as street paving and water lines, had been installed to help the "right" people; and other favors had been financed out of public funds. This same general pattern had been found in the Police Department. "I think it is fair to say," Singer said, "that the appointment of Chief Jason Kelly in 1951 marked the first time that the law was *really* enforced in Valley."

Chief Kelly's appointment in 1951 had followed a heated community controversy about the effectiveness of the police. On that occasion hearings before the Council had been held, and the previous Chief had resigned. Some insiders alleged that he had been too susceptible to the wishes of the Lemon Street Gang. There was internal dissension, several policemen had resigned, and, said the *Times,* "public confidence had been shaken."

The new Chief brought a spirit of friendliness to the Valley police operation. "A good-natured Irishman," Kelly, who had retired as a Lieutenant from the force of the city of North Beach, particularly wooed the downtown business community and regularly dropped into the stores of local merchants to exchange pleasantries. When Singer took over as City Manager several months later, he and Kelly became fast friends. They mixed socially and were regular golf competitors at the country club. As Kelly made friends in the community and with top management, his Police Department settled into an easy routine. Kelly himself was not demanding. "There's enough sordidness in police work without making it tough on the boys," he once commented. He joked with his secretary, other girls in the office, and the members of the thirty-man force; and he found little interest or enthusiasm for the paper work of the operation.

Into this good-natured environment, however, trouble finally descended. It came not from the community but from some of the members of the Department, including the Deputy Chief. They criticized the "country club atmosphere," raised questions about the Chief's alleged relationships with his secretary, and charged that he was not giving full time to his job. These accusations were ultimately brought to public attention through two members of the Council in the late fall of 1954. The Chief first resigned, then agreed to stay when City Manager Singer's investigations led him to conclude that the attacks had been inspired by a few men in the Department. And behind these men, Singer felt sure, stood the Lemon Street Gang.

Singer and some councilmen, including Simpson, believed that the men who had instigated the charges against Kelly had been protégés of the Gang. Some of them had consulted with one of the best known members of the Gang about their complaints and about how to present their charges. The two councilmen who had introduced the charges were also believed to be close to the Lemon Street group. One was Joe Rodriguez, the first Mexican-Amreican and the first Catholic to serve on Valley's Council. Born in the Mexican-American section, he had moved to the richer south side. Rodriguez was a complicated person. He had a law degree, had been a school teacher, and was an escrow officer in a large Xerxes firm. Politically liberal, Rodriguez had generally allied himself with the interests of the less well-to-do and the less powerful in the community. Yet he was a registered Republican. Rodriguez' election in 154 had caused some surprise. He had been supported strongly by a principal member of the Lemon Street Gang, who had been a personal friend of his father. Rodriguez had made much in his campaign of the fact that he was a World War II veteran. Soon after his election he became a critic of Manager Singer, whom he considered ineffective and "always doing what the downtown businessmen wanted."

The Councilman who had joined with Rodriguez in introducing the police charges against Chief Kelly was Mayor Crispin Lloyd, believed by Councilman Simpson and some others to have won a Council seat in 1952 because of the support of the Lemon Street Gang. Lloyd worked as a handyman in a local store.

Rodriguez and Lloyd were regarded by some local observers as two council-men who were opposed to domination of city affairs by the Manager or by the well-to-do families of the south side. Often opposed to them were Simpson and Councilman Frank Jones. Jones was one of the largest property owners in the downtown business area. The fifth man on the Council was Ralph Jennings, professor of political science at the local college, whose faculty he had joined in 1949. Jones, Rodriguez, and Jennings had all been elected for four-year terms in April 1954. A Democrat and a liberal, Jennings, like Rodriguez, had run well in the public housing area, but he had received a good number of votes on both sides of town. He supported the council-manager system, but had voted with Rodriguez to elect Lloyd Mayor, while Simpson and Jones had abstained. Jennings saw himself as the "swing man" on the Council, with Rodriguez and Lloyd on one side and Simpson and Jones on the other. Jennings had not heard of the Lemon Street Gang until he became a Councilman. As time went on, he developed an increasing respect for Councilman Simpson, despite the latter's conservatism.

When Manager Singer opposed accepting the resignation of Chief Kelly at the meeting at which Lloyd and Rodriguez introduced the police statement of charges, both councilmen sought to override his suggestion. Nevertheless, the City Manager stood his ground, rejected the Chief's resignation, and stoutly defended Kelly. By a four-to-one vote, the Council went along with the Manager in refusing the resignation.

Shortly thereafter the Deputy Chief was demoted to Lieutenant and at least two other officers were fired. These actions against the individuals who were presumably the central figures in the attack on the Chief caused more disquiet in the community. It could not be ignored by the Council. At the insistence of Lloyd and Rodriguez, joined by a number of citizens including one of the Lemon Street leaders, the Council finally agreed to an investigation. The hearings were closed, but the press was invited and permitted to report in detail. One of the Lemon Street men contributed to pay for a lawyer for the discharged and demoted policemen. A citizens committee was also appointed to play a watch-dog role and insure that procedures at the hearings were fair to both sides.

In the newspapers the community read of (1) the Deputy Chief's withdrawal of his original charges, (2) accusations that some officers had sought to force the Chief's secretary to lie about the closeness of her relationship with her boss, (3) allegations that the Chief's accusers had planned all succession arrangements favorable to themselves once the Chief had been forced to resign, and (4) evidences that the Chief had apparently not run a tight administrative organi-zation. Emotion in the community was very high; the City Manager, his behavior, and the form of government he personified did not escape criticism from the defenders of the discharged policemen. It was clear that Singer had trusted Chief Kelly to run his own department. The Manager had not known much about what was happening in the Police Department until the investigation. (From this point on, he kept a close eye on it.) At the conclusion of the hearings one of the Council members emphasized that the only question with which the legislative body had to deal was whether it had lost confidence in the Manager because of the dismissals and other problems in the Police Department. If so, he should be fired. Otherwise the Council should sustain the Manager. In the vote that followed four councilmen supported Manager Singer. The fifth abstained.

On the surface the police problem was settled. Yet the effects remained. There were people in the community who felt that the prevarications of police officers could cut both ways. Was it not just as possible that the Deputy Chief and the other police officers had capitulated to the Manager and to the other leaders in order to hold their jobs?

Four months after what the *Times* called the "marathon police investigation," Chief Kelly left Valley to accept a position as Chief of Security in a private industrial organization at "twice the pay." His resignation was reluctantly accepted by City Manager Singer as of March 15, 1955, and the Manager's search for a new Chief began.

THE SEARCH FOR A NEW CHIEF

William Black was a retired Lieutenant Commander in the Navy. In the spring of 1955 he was teaching at the University of Southern California, as a one-year replacement for the University's professor of police administration who was in Iran. However, Black did not plan to stay in teaching and was interested in engaging in more active police work. When the Director of the University's Delinquency Control Institute told him about the opening for a Police Chief in Valley, Black was interested. He immediately dispatched a letter to Valley expressing his availability and thus became one of about thirty applicants for the post, which paid approximately $550 a month. The letter in which City Manager Singer acknowledged Black's application reported that there were no major police problems. Particularly striking to Black was the statement that "the present department is in top working efficiency, as the former Chief retired voluntarily to go into private industry." The letter, mimeographed and obviously sent to all applicants, was dated March 23, 1955.

By the time Black had heard about the opening and made his application, City Manager Singer had taken a number of steps to fill the vacancy created by Kelly's resignation. First he reviewed the personnel situation in the Department and decided that none of the officers in the organization "looked too strong." Since he was under no pressure to appoint a local person, Singer determined to recruit a new Chief on a California-wide basis. The absence of a formal civil service system meant that there was nothing to block such a recruiting program. Singer inserted an announcement of the vacancy in *Western City Magazine,* and wrote to a number of cities in California soliciting applications.

Because he recognized the appointment of a new Chief to be one of the most important steps he had taken in his more than four years in Valley, Singer was determined to make the selection system as foolproof as possible. Therefore, he appointed a Screening Board composed of the City Manager, the Assistant Administrative Officer, and the Chief of Police of three different cities in Southern California. Of the thirty applicants for the position, ten were interviewed by this Board at a meeting attended by Singer. Although several chiefs of smaller departments were among those screened, the professor from USC, William Black, was the unanimous choice of the Board. Singer, too, was greatly impressed. Black had strong recommendations from the University. He "interviewed well," and he seemed to be just the kind of person needed to compensate for Kelly's laxity in administrative routine. While the Manager felt some hesitation about Black because he had not had actual experience as a Chief of Police previously, members of the Board agreed that the professor's technical competence outweighed his lack of experience and made him first choice. Singer decided to recommend the appointment, which was tantamount to selection. Council confirmation had become, as in many other centralized management cities, largely perfunctory. Despite all the previous police problems, Council members did not actively involve themselves in the selection process for the new Chief. Jack Singer was being given a chance to run his own show without interference from the Council. Black was "his" man.

The new Valley Chief of Police first heard of his appointment in a telephone call from a reporter on the *Los Angeles Examiner,* asking for a comment. Then Manager Singer called Black to say that he had been hired and to ask when he could start. The date agreed upon was June 13, 1956. After the hiring, Black journeyed to Valley to meet the Council. It was a friendly occasion. As Black recalled, he was particularly impressed with the words of Mayor Crispin Lloyd, who said, "We have made you Chief because we want a firm law enforcement program." It was the kind of statement Black was pleased to hear. It became a charter for his future actions. Crew-cut and muscular, active in amateur wrestling, Black had about his whole being an air of authority. He also had a strong commitment to the professionalization of the police and felt that too frequently police officers themselves failed to pay a proper respect to the important work they had undertaken. He viewed the police function as important to the maintenance of an organized society, as technically demanding, and as requiring the highest moral and intellectual integrity. William Black was now anxious to prove himself equal to the task.

The first day on the job, June 13, Black spent with Manager Singer, who also emphasized that he wanted a rigorous enforcement program. Much of the time on that day was spent in discussing the people in the city government and in the community. Singer for his part believed that he was introducing the newcomer to the mysteries and subtleties of the city government. He was anxious to keep Black from making an early slip. But as Black recalled the talk, the Manager produced a picture of the members of the Department taken in 1954 and talked about each man on the force. Particularly striking to Black was the fact that a number of the men in the photograph were no longer in the city's employment. At this time, he had little knowledge of the Kelly affair, and he was struck by the high attrition rate. Black says he left the meeting somewhat worried. He felt that Singer demonstrated a "suspicion of everyone who was not on his side."

THE RIFT BETWEEN BLACK AND SINGER

William Black was Police Chief in Valley for just a year. Nearly every event during that year was seen and interpreted differently by Black and Singer, and the passage of more years has not made any easier the assembly of a set of facts acceptable to both sides. From the day of their first meeting in June 1955 a gulf widened between the City Manager and his new Police Chief despite the fact that both men had every reason to desire a successful and satisfying relationship.

Singer's Background

Jack Singer was very familiar with the ways of the small town. He had had several years of successful experience as a Manager and as an elected City Clerk. Valley embodied a style of life he accepted, enforced, and understood.

Singer's particular view of the responsibility of the manager seemed to be rooted more in the concept of responding to community expectations and wishes than to hewing rigidly to city manager professionalism. He saw the Manager as the *interpreter* of citizen and Council desires, which he was obliged to satisfy. This orientation, along with his background, led Singer to be more sensitive to the play of forces of power and influence than most city managers might have been. On almost any matter, Singer was acutely aware of his friends and enemies, and of the forces at play. He had, for example, argued strongly and successfully for Council action to carry out more street improvements in the poorer sections of town, and to do it wholly at city expense (with no street assessments), an unusual thing in Valley. On another matter, when a planning officer had aroused protests for pushing a plan some groups thought too rigorous and advanced, Singer had ordered the plan modified so that it was less perfect from a planner's standpoint but more acceptable to those affected. Since his arrival in 1952, Singer had been highly successful in carrying through city planning and capital development programs. He won community approval for such efforts, which were often neglected in other cities of Valley's size.

Within the city administrative hierarchy, Singer believed strongly in the Manager's right to manage. He expected to be held responsible for the functioning of the various departments, and he demanded the authority necessary to meet these obligations. This meant that each department head was distinctly his subordinate and that it was the Manager's prerogative to take whatever fact-finding steps appeared necessary to check on performance in these various units. Nevertheless, the Manager and the employees generally had gotten on well together. On the whole, Singer was proud of the governmental performance of Valley. Despite the events of the previous fall, he did not believe that there was a "mess" in the Police Department, but he knew that the Department was still much in the public eye.

Personally, Singer was happy in Valley. He liked the people and the community. His job, though carrying a compensation somewhat under that paid in other similar-size cities, still returned him a comfortable income. It was a pleasant life which he, his wife, and school-age children enjoyed. He belonged to the country club and to one of the Protestant congregations. Only a very substantial increase in salary could have moved him to another city.

Black's Background

Black's experience and outlook were different from Singer's. His police experience had come in Evanston, Illinois—some of it while studying at Northwestern University. He had had a long career in Navy security. While he had served in the Navy, on the Evanston Police Department, and in academic positions at Northwestern and at the University of Southern California, there nevertheless had been the tangible unifying thread of law enforcement. It was to the profession of law enforcement and its values that Black felt his basic responsibility, not to the city. As he explained later to an interviewer:

> We in police worry so much about how people are going to feel about what we do that we lose sight of our basic responsibility.
>
> In Valley there was a disrespect for the law. Thus the basic problem was the rebuilding of that respect for the laws of the community and the enforcers of those laws; then would have been the appropriate time to worry about public relations. It is also my conviction that in order to engage in law enforcement you must at times be harsh; but that doesn't mean it is ever necessary to be nasty.

This sense of the profession also seemed to permeate Black's perception of the Police Chief's role in council-manager government. As he saw his responsibility, it was to give the community the best possible law enforcement, judged by his professional standards. Political or community squabbles were matters for higher echelons.

Emerging Differences

Chief Black had been on the job only a few days when he began to see things that upset him. Within the Department, he found no written rules and regulations, inefficient procedures, and oddly arranged shifts. When he asked why things were being done in a certain way, Black said the men had no good answer. In addition he felt that morale was poor, the men inadequately trained, and their general appearance not up to his standards. Nor was Black satisfied with the deployment of the men. He found that the small Department was still using two men in patrol cars in the predominantly residential town. To Black this was a particularly indicative sign of ineffective management. Though a lot of old-timers still preferred two-man cars to the one-man variety, Black laid this resistance to a lack of knowledge of modern police doctrine. Thus the use of the old system in Valley not only revealed a great waste of manpower to him; it also meant that the Department had not had imaginative and progressive leadership in the past. For this failure he blamed not only the former Chief but also City Manager Singer.

In the community as a whole the general disregard of the law that was most striking to Black was in the traffic field. (Black's graduate work had made him something of a specialist in traffic problems.) "Nobody paid any attention to stop signs," he recalled. Speed limits were not observed, and there was no selective enforcement in those areas of the city where accidents were most likely to happen. Parking signs and restrictions were not properly obeyed. A good share of the central district's parking spaces were occupied by local merchants and professional people who "nickeled the machines to death."

Black's answer to these problems was tighter enforcement all along the line. He took a personal hand in sharpening procedures and organization, spending the greater part of his first ninety days writing a policy manual, the first the force had had. There were reassignments, new training programs, redesign of forms, and many other changes.

As a result of Black's policies, the men on the force began to hand out an increasing number of citations for parking and traffic violations. The effect of this stringency was magnified when the *Valley Times* began to print a column listing the names and addresses of those who had received tickets. The irritation of citizens at getting citations for driving and parking practices that had previously not drawn police action was exacerbated when their names and offenses were printed in the *Times* for their neighbors and all others to see. Black publicly congratulated the *Times* for initiating the column. As Black's campaign for better parking and traffic enforcement continued, some policemen carried tape measures and allegedly used them when issuing citations for drivers who parked a greater number of inches from the curb than the city ordinance permitted.

The Chief found another practice he opposed: the issuance of special treatment cards or badges to influential citizens. A request for such an item was made shortly after he came on the job, and he discovered that the practice had long been followed in Valley. Badges or cards had been issued since the twenties to large fruit growers to give them some authority in policing their groves, some of which were in remote sections. Black refused to issue more cards and called the others in. "In two months we picked up about 100. I don't know how many more we didn't get," he recalled.

While thus busily engaged, Black found he had no time to follow his predecessor's practice of visiting the merchants in the downtown business section. Nor did he have an interest in doing so. "I personally think the former Chief engaged in these kinds of activities to the detriment of law enforcement in Valley," Black said later. Some of the downtown businessmen were displeased with Black's policy of strict enforcement of parking meter regulations.

Criticism Reaches the City Manager

Criticisms of Black's approach to his new job almost immediately reached City Manager Singer. Irritation was expressed that he was not a friendly, jocular sort. More indignant were those who had run afoul of the new look in Valley's law enforcement activities. Most significant, however, were charges of increasing belligerence and antagonism on the part of police officers. Singer reported that much of the criticism was directed squarely at Chief Black, who was said to have been stopping people himself. He was accused of having an approach to violators which "was sadistic, officious, and out of proportion to the violations committed."12 To these attacks Singer at first paid little attention; but the increasing volume of complaints caused him to move to the defense of the Chief by personally urging press and public leaders to help him across a "difficult period of adjustment."

Much of the difficulty, Singer felt, was that Black had not brought the community along with him. A new regime of law enforcement had suddenly descended on Valley without warning. In Singer's mind it was the Chief's responsibility to "sell" his program. He felt it was a mistake for Black to spend his time in his office. He urged him to invite and accept speaking engagements, which the Chief said he did at the rate of two to three a week. Singer has reported he did not question the policy of firm law enforcement Black had inaugurated.

Even at this early stage, communications between the two men seemed to have been strained by two events. The first had to do with an order issued by Black prohibiting officers from discussing police business with anyone. This, he said, was a standard procedure for most police agencies and was included in his manual of rules and regulations which the City Manager approved. The intent was to keep data on investigations restricted to as few people as possible and was not really directed toward administrative matters. Insofar as the councilmen and the Manager were concerned, Black said he instructed his men to answer any questions but to let him know about such conversations, a procedure he felt was normal for any organization which had a formal chain of command.

12On this point Black has commented: "My officers leaned over backward and were so nice it was almost sickening to watch and listen to. *But* those who had previously talked their way out of arrests or used their influence could no longer do so. When this happened to them for the first time, they reported the officer as belligerent and antagonistic whereas he was nothing of the kind. Several investigations on my part proved this point. In one case an officer said, 'No madam' and 'Yes madam' only. She reported him to Singer as insulting. She treated the incident as a light joke until she saw she was going to get a ticket for a 50 mph violation; then she became indignant and insulting. To the law violator it might appear that the officer was sadistic, officious, and out of proportion to the violation committed, but it is the result of losing the immunity from arrest that caused the great flareup among a small group of special privileged people. With regard to traffic violations, I have seen every type kill an individual; therefore it is proper and justifiable to treat each violation the same, but with courtesy and firmness."

The order was perceived in quite different terms by Singer. Since the Kelly incident of the previous year, Singer had taken a greater interest in the operation of the Police Department and had come to know a number of the policemen. Soon, however, he found that these men refused to talk to him, even those of long acquaintance. He was told Black had issued an order that the men were not to talk to Singer. If they did, they must report the conversation back to the Chief. The order irritated Singer greatly. Yet nothing was ever said to Black, and he did not realize how a directive which he considered routine had antagonized his superior.

At about the same time another incident occurred. In this instance it was Chief Black who felt he had been "used" by the City Manager to avoid political fire. Among his other duties, Black was the city's official poundmaster. It was a nominal title because one man in the employment of the Department did all the work. Up to that time dogs had run relatively free in Valley, and a considerable problem had been created. At the request of the Council, City Manager Singer drafted an animal regulation ordinance and gave it to the Police Chief to introduce at the Council meeting. He said it was within the police responsibility, and the proposed law would perhaps have more acceptance coming from that source. Although he knew that dogs laws were almost always controversial, the Chief agreed, because "I really thought it was a good thing."

Then, "all hell broke loose." The citizens of Valley who had let their dogs run free for many years were up in arms. They accused the Chief of something worse than inhumanity—a hatred of dogs. "I took to riding the streets of Valley with my big setter to prove to people that I really loved animals." After much furor, the effort to pass the ordinance was abandoned. What upset Black was that never during the controversy did the Manager make a major public defense of the proposed ordinance.

Meanwhile, Black was making speeches as the Manager had suggested, but they seemed only to deepen the problem. Members of his audiences charged that the newcomer was too free in his criticism of their community. Although Black declares he had never used the word, a story spread among parents and school officials that he had typified Valley youth as "rotten."[13] His appearances before the local civic associations and clubs, according to the editor of the *Times,* probably did more to destroy his support in the substantial segments of the community than any other single factor.

Singer Gets More Complaints

By fall, three to four months after Chief Black had come to Valley, Singer was getting so many complaints that he had to take them seriously. There were many besides those who complained of harsh personal treatment by police en-

---

[13]Black has commented: "This was one of the false stories spread about town by the 'Hate Black' group. I never said this. Actually the man who started the rumor was never at the speech where it was supposed to have been said. He had been arrested previously for speeding—his first time as a local bigshot and was unable to get the officer to let him go."

forcing traffic violations. A number of middle-class mothers told the Manager that Black's policies were making their children speak of policemen as enemies rather than as friends. They expressed concern that their sons were talking of stoning police cars, and compared this to the pre-Black days when, they said, police in patrol cars would often stop and chat with teenagers, even those who had been in minor scrapes with the law. The mothers attributed the trouble to the tough manner used by the police with teenagers since Black had assumed office.

Another complaint, Singer recalled some years later, had come from the officer who dealt with juvenile delinquents. Several months after Black arrived, this officer reported to Singer that the load of juvenile offenses was rising enormously. This was attributed to the increased stringency of police enforcement.

Singer also received complaints from local insurance men (who were often also realtors and who were one of the occupational groups active in following and influencing city affairs). Black, the Manager recalled later, "had tangled with insurance men who were trying to get the facts on traffic accidents. They needed information for their clients and for their reports to their companies. This sort of information is routinely made available to properly qualified investigators as provided in the Vehicle Code." Black, the insurance men had complained, had arbitrarily decided to withhold some of the data from them. Black's position was that certain items in the reports should be confidential; these were the things he withheld.

Singer also stated later that he had received some reports that Black had had difficulties with other police jurisdictions. The County Under-Sheriff had paid an unannounced courtesy call shortly after Black had arrived in Valley but Black had been too busy to see him. A school safety patrol had taken the number of a private car that had gone through a crossing zone near the high school. The teacher in charge had forwarded the license number to Sacramento. It had turned out to be the number of a car of a member of the force, and this had led to Black being cautioned by a member of the State Highway Patrol. Black had complained to higher headquarters of the Highway Patrol, denying the charge and criticizing the pettiness of the action.

Another complaint, Singer recalled later, came from the parents of two girls of high school age who were exceeding the speed limit in town one night and were chased by a pair of off-duty policemen who were riding in a car with out-of-state license plates. The policemen sought to force the girls' car to the curb. The girls, allegedly not realizing these were policemen, went even faster and drove toward the deserted areas of town before they were stopped. Their girls, the parents complained to Singer, had been frightened almost to the point of hysteria.

These incidents and others arising from tougher parking and traffic enforcement came to Singer with increasing frequency. In the late fall or early winter, Singer recalls, a former Democratic councilman asked him how long he was going to keep the Police Chief. He suggested that if Singer delayed getting rid of Black, the public would force the Council to act. He allegedly told Singer that if Singer waited too long, public resentment might even cost the Manager his own job.

Black's View

If Valley's problem of adjustment to Black was difficult, so was Black's adjustment to it. He saw himself making compromises difficult for a man of his professional background and ethics to accept. There was the failure to book the homosexual son of a prominent citizen. "After the withdrawal of that complaint," he said, "I felt I had a sin on my soul. So far as I know, that man is still walking the streets and is not even registered as a sex deviate. Whatever harm befalls him or others, I will certainly have to assume part of the guilt."

In another instance the wife of a prominent official of a nearby newspaper was charged with hit and run. Black said she had knocked down a brick wall with her auto and left the scene of the accident. Her license number was traced, however; and her attorney came to Valley to make a settlement. Black refused to negotiate. Later that same day, Black said he got a phone call from the City Manager asking him to delay arrest until the following day.[14] By that time the warrant had been withdrawn by the court and the Chief was left powerless in the situation. He never said anything further about it, but he often asked himself what would have happened if the offender had been a Mexican, rather than the wife of a prominent newspaper man. As one observer put it, Black had difficulty learning that there are "somebodies and nobodies" in every community. To that Black has agreed.

In January 1956 occurred the "Mr. X" case, which later received considerable attention because of its relationship to compromise and the community elite. Mr. X was a well-to-do citrus man, over sixty, and long influential in Valley. He had the same last name as one of the councilmen. It was alleged that he was driving drunk, had turned a corner and run head on into another automobile. As Black later reported, "Mr. X was drunk. He did not know who I was that night. He said he would get my job for this. He threw money around the street and said he ran Valley. . . ." Actually the arresting officer had been fearful that he was a councilman and had called both the Manager and the Chief when he got him to the station. Black says Manager Singer took a look in the window, said, "I don't know the man. . . . Do what you want with him." As a consequence the Chief gave the order to "treat him like any other drunk." At midnight an attorney for the drunken man came to the jail and asked to post bond for his release. While it was against departmental policy to free booked people before the following morning, the Sergeant was more aware of the standing of the man in the community than Singer or Black and so released him. Black said later that if he had been at the station, he would not have permitted the Sergeant to take such an action. At any rate, Black said that the next morning at 8:00 he got a call from the City Manager wanting to know

[14]One Councilman disagreed strongly with the Black story. He has noted: "This is Black's version, and an example of giving a sinister import to a fairly simple matter. Black considered any request for information to be an attempt to intervene."

what could be done about the case. According to Black, a city Councilman was reported as interested in seeing that the charges were either reduced or quashed. However, Black told Singer that the case was already out of his hands, charges having been filed, bail posted, and the man released. It was now up to the courts. The Chief thought that Singer was clearly irritated by this departure from routine and indicated he thought the steps had been taken to thwart any "arrangements." The man was found guilty and fined $350. Later, in public hearings, Singer disputed the Black version and called it a "classic distortion." He reported

> I was met in the parking lot and told that—sure enough, the man they held was not Councilman X. I was told also that the "Mr. X" they had in custody had been picked up drunk, abusive, and most certainly in no condition to drive. I told them to lock him up, and I drove home and went to bed. The next morning the man's family, worried and concerned, made inquiries. Among others, they asked Councilman Jones to find out what had happened to the man. Jones asked me, I got the information, and Jones relayed the facts to the family. There was no discussion concerning the disposition or handling of the case. To this day I have never met or talked to— nor could I recognize on the street—the man who was arrested and who—the next morning—pleaded guilty and paid a fine.

An incident occurring in March again dramatized the gulf growing between Manager Singer and his Chief. It involved a relatively minor traffic case in which the wife of a well-to-do professional man was arrested for speeding. Infuriating to her, however, was the fact that the citation was written outside her home. By the next morning she and her husband had called a number of neighbors, with the result that a delegation visited the Manager the following day to urge the Chief's resignation on the grounds that his men were rude and arrogant. "I was called into the City Manager's office," Black later reported, and "he was very much upset. He said he might have to ask me to resign. 'I had a committee visit me,' he went on, 'and they are upset about your enforcement program,'" Black said he thought the charge was probably untrue and asked that he be permitted to talk to the woman before any decisions were made. As a result of a later conversation with the woman, the Chief concluded that she was angry simply because she got a legitimate ticket. He informed Singer that he would take no disciplinary action against the officer. Although the Manager said nothing more, Black felt that his superior was not happy with the decision.

The Peters Case

However, it was the Peters case, which occurred later in March, that caused Singer to decide to dismiss Black. A police car in pursuit of an automobile speeding through town at seventy miles per hour collided with a vehicle driven by elderly Phil Peters, who was thrown on the pavement and killed. The police car was running without flashing light or siren, which was a violation of a state law specifying the use of such equipment "when necessary" in exceeding the speed limit. The police officer, said Black, had fastened his safety belt but had not yet had time to open up the various warning devices on the car. At the Coroner's inquest these facts were laid before the jury; and it was also discovered that the elderly man's driver's license had been suspended two years earlier. The jury concluded the police officer was not guilty of negligence. Valley's insurance carriers, however, did settle any possible claims by making a payment of about $3,000 to the widow.

During the Coroner's inquest on the Peters case, an official in the District Attorney's office told Singer that Black had been angry and had wanted to testify in the hearing that the officer was simply following the policy of the Department. Since such a policy would have been in direct violation of the state law, the official told the Manager, Valley would have been liable for a huge damage suit. This report was a shock to Singer, and a conference with Black on the matter did not ease his mind. As a result the Manager himself issued an order requiring the Department to conform to the state law. Singer later wrote on the importance of this incident to his final decision,

> I maintained hope that Black still could continue as chief and that in time he might come to wear this authority a little more comfortably, both for himself and for the people he was brought here to protect. But suddenly it was demonstrated that the community was actually threatened by the attitudes he held toward his job.
>
> I refer to the tragic death of Mr. Phil Peters out on Brookside Ave. Two conclusions were inescapable concerning the way that Black intended to carry out his job. One had to do with the quality of his judgment, and the other again—with his real attitude toward the citizenry of Valley. Under Black's direct and personal instruction, the police vehicle was violating both the laws of the State of California and the tenets of generally accepted good police practice. And in so doing was creating as great—if not a greater hazard to life and property than was the vehicle being pursued.
>
> Section 454 of the California Vehicle Code provides that whenever conditions required that a police vehicle be operated in excess of legal speed limits that the operator shall use both his red light and siren. Black had ordered that neither be used until the officer had clocked the speeder. Had Black, himself, been driving the fatal police car, he could and should have been booked for manslaughter.
>
> In discussing with him the possible liability the city had incurred by reason of this incident, Black's position was indefensible. The substance of his reaction is covered by the phrase, "Nothing to get ex-

cited about—if you're going to get convictions, you're going to have to take chances and somebody may get killed.[15]

As I sat there listening to him talk, I was forced into the realization that the city could no longer be exposed to the threat imposed by Black's inexperience, bad judgment and his persistent refusal to recognize human considerations in carrying out his job. (Emphasis added.)

Chief Black has disagreed with Singer's understanding of the events surrounding the Peters case. He has denied, in the first place, the truth of the story told by the official of the District Attorney's office to Singer. Furthermore, he has declared he never issued such an order to the Department "For heaven's sake, I certainly knew what the State law was," he has commented. He has pointed out that it was his custom to put all general Department orders in writing and that no such command was ever issued.

At the Coroner's hearing, Black said, the District Attorney had asked the defending police officer, "Do you usually run without a red light?" The man answered, "Yes, as do most other Departments." Chief Black said he was much concerned that his officer was leaving the impression that this was Departmental policy, whereas he was really trying to indicate that practice almost universally did not accord with the state policy. Therefore Black got up and asked the District Attorney, "Would you like to have me tell you what the policy is?" The District Attorney said no, and Black made no further remarks.

Problems of Communication

With so many points of conflict, it would seem appropriate to describe what the Manager did to alert Black to his deficiencies. Even here, however, there is dispute between Singer and Black. The Manager has declared that he tried regularly to counsel Black in meetings occurring two or three times a week and lasting 30 to 45 minutes. The Manager did not feel, however, that the Chief ever really listened with an open or receptive mind. Whenever he raised questions or complaints, Singer said, the Chief either denied them or would retort, "Well, you either want a good law enforcement program or you don't." Furthermore, Singer felt that in their conversations Black never perceived that he might have made a mistake. The Manager kept no record of these conversations and was unable later to indicate precisely what was discussed on the various occasions.

Totally different was Black's perception of his contacts with Singer. He said

[15]Black's comment: "Here is what I really said. 'We could expect further and more deaths in the future if proper enforcement tactics are not carried out.' . . . I never said any such thing [as statement in the text above] to Singer; a man would be crazy to say anything like that. . . ."

that most of their business was not conducted orally but by written memo. The Chief revealed he also felt ill at ease in talking to the Manager because he kept a recording device in his office. The Manager had told him, Black said, that the recorder could be set in operation without a warning signal. Seldom, said Black, did they discuss the way he was performing his job, although in March 1956, after the angry housewife's delegation had paid its visit, Singer had told him, "These people have put so much pressure on me, I am afraid I am going to have to ask you to resign." Yet even in this situation, Black did not feel that he was being given any clear picture of where he might be making his mistakes. This, incidentally, was a point that Black made continually later in the controversy. He said that he had not knowingly disobeyed any of Singer's orders. If he had done the wrong thing, it was only because the Manager had not made clear to him what the policy was.

To some degree, at least, the channels through which City Manager Singer received his information affected communications between the two men. In almost every instance Singer had to rely on reports, rather than firsthand observations. These came from citizens, school officials, realtors, other policing agencies, and some members of the Police Department. It is possible, as Black contended, that these complainants were not in all cases unbiased; and it is also to be noted that the statements from other governmental agencies, such as the schools, could not be verified officially. These people refused to state their accusations publicly, a problem which became quite acute for Singer later in the case. As a consequence it was someone else's word against the Chief's. From Black's perspective, each of these reports meant that he was "called on the carpet" and decisions made before the facts were in. He did not think he was given the backing a subordinate might expect from his chief. The City Manager had so little confidence in him, or was so fearful of a mistake (and Black thought this was the real problem), that the Chief was never given the discretion and freedom from interference the job required.

Except for parking, where Singer did urge some relaxation, the level of enforcement was apparently never raised as an issue between the two men. Nevertheless, Black always felt this was the heart of the problem. He saw himself as a professional law officer—one who put effective law enforcement above all other considerations, and who in so doing, inevitably had to alienate certain segments of the community. That was the price to be paid for a program that benefited the citizenry as a whole. Singer contended, on the other hand, that the problem lay not in *what* was being done but *how* it was being done. "You can have firmness with courtesy," as he put it. The Department led by Black was playing "cop" too much, and people were resentful not so much of the tickets they got as the way they were treated. Thus the grounds upon which Singer based the dismissal were elusive and difficult to pin down. Black's technical competence, industry, dedication, and general ability were not questioned; he was really not charged with insubordination. In Singer's view, Black's sin lay in certain subtle factors of attitude, approach and judgment, that distorted an otherwise sound program.

In his own mind, Singer was certain that dismissal of Black was the only answer. But how effectively could he communicate his reasoning to the City

Council and the public? It was a question that began to answer itself the day William Black was dismissed.

THE LEAK ABOUT BLACK'S DISMISSAL

While the City Council listened to a discussion of a supermarket rezoning issue on the evening of May 1, 1956, Manager Singer's mind was already dwelling on what lay ahead that night. He had made up his mind to dismiss Police Chief Black and to ask the councilmen for their approval.

Singer's timing, which was later criticized, may have been connected with the fact that the April Council elections and the Council's election of the new Mayor were now over.

Singer had been particularly heartened by the April elections for two Council seats. George Simpson, his firm supporter had been swept back into office, and his tireless antagonist, former Mayor Crispin Lloyd, had suffered a humiliating defeat. At the first Council meeting after the election, Simpson had been chosen as the new Mayor. Elected in place of Lloyd was a jeweler from the downtown business center, Andy Carter. He was so new on the Council—and to municipal government generally—that it was unlikely that he would raise any questions. The three continuing members of the Council, who had been elected to four-year terms in 1954, included Jones, the big property owner who usually voted with Simpson, and Jennings, the Democratic college professor, who had proved reasonable and who supported the manager system. That left the third continuing member, Joe Rodriguez, who had opposed Singer on the Kelly affair and who had never masked his disapproval of the Manager and many of his policies. Singer, like Simpson, thought he saw behind Rodriguez and the defeated Lloyd the influences of the Lemon Street Gang.

After the regular meeting Singer asked the five councilmen to go to his office for a closed personnel meeting.[16] Singer's expression, recalled one Councilman, indicated that he had a serious problem on his mind, but none of the legislators knew what it was. After they sat down, the City Manager told them perturbedly that he wanted to fire Police Chief Black. He recounted in some detail the events and complaints that had led him to his decision. "I have tried everything conceivable," he reported. "I have held one conference after another and gotten nowhere. I can see no alternative but to ask Black for his resignation. I want you to know about this and the reasons because I am going to need your support." Singer then suggested that Black be given an opportunity to resign. If he did not, he would be dismissed.

Simpson, Jones, and Jennings had expected that such a recommendation might be coming but had not known when. Rodriguez did ask some questions. Most of the time, however, he stared at the table in front of him. The others were clearly unhappy. "The last thing we wanted," one recalled later, "was trouble in the Police Department." Singer then asked if he had the Council's support. Two or three said "Well, if it has to be, it has to be." There was no

---

[16]Under California law, only meetings of legislators having to do with personnel matters may be closed to the public and press.

formal vote, and Rodriguez did not register his specific disagreement with the tacit decision. Singer went on to say that Black was out of town for the week, and it was important that the meeting be held in strictest confidence until he had had a chance to see him. The Manager did not want it to appear that he was firing the Chief while he was away. There was no further comment on this strategy, and the meeting broke up shortly after midnight.

The newcomer, Councilman Carter, the downtown jeweler, was not taken entirely by surpise. He had noted that "Bill [Black] was never around the community . . . and we had been accustomed to a man that was a part of the town."[17] Carter also said that even in his short tenure he had had a number of complaints about Black's way of doing things. There was more than one manner of arresting a person, the new Councilman said, and Black could not do it "like a gentleman." Nevertheless, it "came as a jolt to me that Black was to be fired. I didn't think he had been given enough of a chance," he concluded.

One Councilman's View

Simpson, Jones, and Jennings had been in close touch with City Manager Singer and were more familiar with the problem. One of them explained his general understanding of conditions at the time of the meeting with Singer in this way:

> After Black was appointed, he began a vigorous campaign of traffic enforcement and put much pressure on the men for arrests. Once he took us Councilmen on a tour of the station and showed us a chart of the number of arrests each officer was turning in weekly. We were given to understand that he expected them to come through with a certain amount each week.
>
> No one was really antagonistic to any part of Black's program. It was the extreme pettiness that got them down, for example, the carrying of a tape measure to check on the distance of cars from the curb. People got to feeling that if they were caught in a violation, they would really get the book thrown at them. Black used to cruise around himself and seemed to take great delight in hauling someone down and giving him a tongue lashing. A prominent minister told me he had gone through this, that Black had started out, "Haven't you got better sense. . . ."
>
> I was getting quite a few complaints, and it got to the point where people were asking, "How long are you going to keep this guy around here?" I think we all tried to defend him, saying we wanted vigorous law enforcement. We either took that position or we said nothing when the complaints were made to us.

[17]Carter meant, presumably, that Black did not socialize much with the downtown merchants in the Kelly pattern. Black lived in Valley in a north side development.

I believe, too, that we were all aware of these problems. Two or three months after Black arrived, I remember encountering Mayor Lloyd, who asked me, "Are you getting a lot of complaints about this new Chief?" I answered I was. Lloyd's comment was, "Jack Singer's really pulled a boner on this guy."

Actually, the Council was not filled in on Singer's day-to-day problems with Black, nor what efforts he was making to solve them. We were aware, however, that the Manager was holding meetings with the Chief in an attempt to straighten him out. As to how he was going about this, I don't think we considered it our problem.[18]

Thus, as of 1:00 A.M. Wednesday, May 2, it appeared that Singer's proposal to dismiss the Police Chief would have the rather strong support of at least three members of the Council. One was disposed to go along with some misgivings, and only one might be in direct opposition. The Manager had not attempted to present a full dossier of facts on Black that night. He had relied on the councilmen's general knowledge of the Chief's behavior and had pointed out that some of the more important causes of dismissal involved information and complaints whose sources could not be publicly identified. There was not a great deal of concern at the time as to whether a good public case for the dismissal would have to be developed. It was apparently hoped that Black would take the easy course and resign.

Any possibility of a tidy handling of the affair, however, reckoned without the reaction of Councilman Rodriguez. Since he commuted to Xerxes, he did not talk often with the other councilmen or with the Manager; and though his colleagues insisted he had been present, he did not remember that the Manager had ever discussed his problems with the Council before. As a consequence, Rodriguez could not escape the feeling that the "whole thing had been caused by a couple of big guys being arrested." Secondly, he was perhaps more mindful than his colleagues of the public response to a dismissal without reasons given. "Personally," he said, "I thought it was only decency that Black be given a chance to speak."

Councilman Rodriguez first made known his strong feelings the next afternoon in a discussion with Mayor Simpson. He said then that he would have "no part in firing Black." The Mayor was conciliatory and unperturbed, Rodriguez recalled. He told Rodriguez, "Black will resign, and that will be all there is to it."

The *Times* Breaks the Story

At 10:00 the next morning (Thursday, May 3) Rodriguez got a call from the *Valley Times*. Was it true, a reporter asked, that Black was being dismissed as a result of the Manager's recommendation to the councilmen at the closed session Tuesday night? The indignant Rodriguez replied, "Yes." (The reporter

[18]Chief Black declares that these charges are essentially untrue.

did not tell Rodriguez where he had gotten his information. Singer and others later suspected that it had come from former Mayor Crispin Lloyd, the Manager's long-time critic, and that Lloyd might have heard of the dismissal originally in personal conversations with Rodriguez, his former ally on the Council.)

The *Times* published the story that afternoon. Councilman Rodriguez was quoted at length:

> The City Manager asked the Council to agree on two proposals. (1) To ask the Chief's resignation and (2) an outright firing backed by the council if the chief refused to resign.
>
> On the basis of the facts presented to us, I cannot see sufficient reason for the move. The reason given was "poor public relations" on the part of the chief, but no particular facts to substantiate these reasons were presented to the council.
>
> I was unaware of any problems in the Police Department until the personnel session last Tuesday, and can say I was definitely shocked.
>
> In my opinion the law enforcement program we now have is commendable in many ways. I understand the morale in the police department is now as high as it ever has been. . . .
>
> Chief Black was highly recommended by the city managers as to background, character, police knowledge, and personality. Now, less than a year later, we are informed things are not as they were supposed to be at that time.
>
> I, for one, do not want to see another upheaval in the police department unless it is for the betterment of the community.
>
> There has been no written report of reasons presented to the council, and I think there should be. I further think that Chief Black should be given an opportunity to have his say.
>
> If the chief has failed in his duties, then the council has the right to know all the facts. Persons reporting unfavorably on his conduct should be identified and the facts investigated. The public and the chief should know what the reasons behind this are.

The *Times* reporter had also telephoned the news to Chief Black, who had been in Los Angeles for the week, serving as an official in the wrestling tryouts for the 1956 Olympic team. The *Times* quoted Black as having said on the telephone:

> For some time I have been well aware that a group of people who I know have been seeking to get me replaced. I wrote a statement to this effect last week, but in view of the fact that I was going to be out of town for seven days, I decided not to release it until I returned.

The *Times* story noted that City Manager Singer and other councilmen had had no comment for the press.

Publication of the story while Black was out of town put the Manager in a disadvantageous position. Rodriguez' decision to talk was viewed by his colleagues and the City Manager as an unpardonable break of confidence. They felt he was basically responsible for the ensuing community conflict. Some erroneously believed at first that Rodriguez had been the person who had first leaked the story to the *Times* reporter. Why had Rodriguez confirmed the report? There were doubtless many reasons: his dislike for Singer and his opposition to the downtown business interests. But perhaps the most important was that he had felt no commitment to his Council colleagues to maintain a silence. He believed that Singer had purposely called the meeting late at night to rush through the dismissal. "I didn't know why they were taking the action, and it was too late to argue. I had to work the next day. I just didn't feel they could bind me to silence in such a casual and arbitrary way."

Some of those on the Manager's side felt that the *Times* should have killed the story and avoided plunging the community into another police controversy. The *Times* publisher later expressed a different view: "This wasn't the dismissal of a clerk-stenographer but just about the most important man in our government. Furthermore, it wasn't a question of *if* he was to be fired but *when*. He had alienated too many important publics in town to last. We were just doing our job." Moreover, some *Times* men pointed out later, the competing Xerxes daily might have published the story first if the *Times* had not.

Singer Sees Black

After Singer received his message from the newspaper, he hurriedly contacted Black, found he was too late, but went ahead and made a date to see the Chief at 4:30 P.M. in Hollywood. By noon he and his assistant were on their way to urge Black to resign.

The call from the *Times* that morning had not surprised Black. The developing pressure, particularly since the Peters case in March, had caused him to set down, before leaving for the Olympic trials, some of the reasons why he believed certain people in the community were trying to have him dismissed. He had written the statement for publication in the *Times* and had personally taken it to the editor. The two men had discussed its content and decided that it would certainly stir things up. But the editor suggested Black "hang on to it for awhile."

When Singer and the Assistant City Manager arrived at Black's Hollywood Knickerbocker suite about 4:00 P.M., little time was lost in getting down to the point. The Chief was shown the proposed resignation, which was typed on City of Valley stationery. Black's name was included, ready for signature. The text was,

> Personal reasons make it necessary that I submit my resignation as Chief of Police of the City of Valley, effective at the earliest possible date.

The Manager explained that it would be better all around if the Chief signed the statement. The city would avoid embarrassment and Black would not have the problem of a discharge on his employment record. Black then asked, "What if I don't sign it?" Then, the Manager said, he would have to institute dismissal proceedings. "What have I done wrong?" Black queried. Singer said there would be no point in such a discussion and urged him to resign. The meeting lasted about 45 minutes, with Black telling the Manager of "20 to 25" improvements that had been made in the Department. He suggested Singer was really submitting to pressure from a small group in the town. Singer said nothing. Ultimately, the Chief declared he would not sign the resignation. He wanted time to consider.

Statements in the Press

The *Times* the next day carried a banner headline that Black had been fired and was demanding a hearing before the Council. Three statements were given prominent display. The first was from City Manager Singer, who said:

> I regret sincerely the extremely unfavorable publicity that has been created by the ill-advised and premature release of information concerning the proposed resignation, or termination, of Chief Black at a time when he was out of town. . . . Because of the premature release of the information it was my desire to contact Chief Black in Los Angeles at his earliest convenience, in order to explain to him that I had no intention to handle the matter behind his back.

> Since Chief Black has decided that he will not submit his resignation, his termination papers are being processed today, because he has not come up to the expectations of the City Manager's office. . . .

> This office and the members of the City Council do not disapprove of a firm law enforcement program and firm police department discipline and there will be no efforts made to change these particular programs in any way.

The second statement was from Chief Black. It said in part:

> I now request a fair and impartial hearing before the City Council during which time the City Manager would have an opportunity to bring his charges and reasons for asking for a resignation or discharge.

> Also, it would give those persons who have charges to make against the Chief [an opportunity] to bring their cases openly before the City Council.

> I would also like to bring before the Council police officers so that they may testify as to the present conditions within the department. I am confident that the good people of this community and the members of the police department are desirous of having an honest and

efficient administration of the police department. I believe that I have given them such an administration.

I came to Valley to do the best job possible in good law enforcement at the request of the City Council and the City Manager. If the City Manager and present Council desired any change in that policy, or wished a new policy, I would have been most happy to have carried them out. . . .

The third statement came from former Mayor Crispin Lloyd, who made two basic points. The first was that the Council shared responsibility with the Manager for the firing of Black. Valley's elected representatives "have, and should have, a part in such decisions." The former Mayor's second point sounded a theme that was to re-echo in most pro-Black arguments throughout the remainder of the controversy: "We either will have impartial law enforcement, or we can again bow to the privileged few." Lloyd continued:

This action was taken without any opportunity for him [Chief Black] to present his side of the story or defend himself in any manner.

To my knowledge, his only crime is the rigid enforcement of our laws—laws, in many cases, made by the City Council. Admittedly, Chief Black has made some mistakes, as will anyone endeavoring to satisfy the public regarding law enforcement.

Valley is growing and the days of Sacred Cows are rapidly passing. These Sacred Cows are the ones making the strongest complaint. . . . Shall we have a chief of police willing to work and enforce our laws, or shall we have a coffee-drinking, hand-shaking figurehead who takes his office and duties with a detached attitude?

With the Lloyd and Black statements, the pro-Police Chief side assumed the offensive. Black hammered at a point that would recur many times. He had done what he was told. Without warning he was now fired and no specific reasons were given. The Lloyd statement represented a blanket refusal to let the Council off the hook. Since the ordinance required the Council to confirm all appointments and dismissals of department heads, Lloyd charged the Council with responsibility for making a full investigation. There was no question, too, but that Lloyd's raising of the fair and equal treatment question was quite a boon to the Black cause. As one Councilman later remarked, "How can you argue against fair and equal treatment? It's like sin and mothers. And the person who accuses you first has the big advantage. All you can do is deny the charge and claim you're not that bad."

On May 4 City Manager Singer appointed the Deputy Chief as acting head of the Police Department and ordered him to continue to follow the policies laid down by his predecessor. Over the weekend the councilmen were mum. Black was still in Hollywood officiating at the wrestling tryouts and due back on Monday. But the newspapers kept the story going.

Pressure for a Public Hearing

From this point on, the telephones in the homes and offices of the councilmen began an intermittent ringing that was not to cease for almost six weeks. The Black affair aroused citizen feeling as no previous civic matter ever had. The volume of telephone calls, sidewalk conversations, and efforts to register opinions with councilmen or their families was unprecedented. And so was the indignation and vituperation with which the citizens communicated their views to their elected representatives. As the Black affair grew hotter, the phone calls came at all hours of the day and night, and before the controversy ended, many of the councilmen felt considerable strain and fatigue.

At the beginning, the extravagant newspaper coverage and the charge that the Manager had acted because some unnamed, but presumably influential, people in Valley did not want tough law enforcement applied to themselves, made the whole affair "look rather sinister," one Councilman recalled. It indicated to him that people were always ready to believe the worst when it came to governmental matters. "Black," this Councilman said,

> was playing the part of the sincere, conscientious Chief who treated everyone fairly and never knowingly did anything wrong. By assuming this role, he made the rest of us seem as if we did not want such a person in the job. Though in my opinion it was never the issue, he made it appear that the real question was whether we wanted to support Singer's attempt to protect his "friends."
>
> There was no question about the impact of this approach. I got calls from constituents saying "We want you to know that we think it is a good thing to have active law enforcement. Lives can be saved that way."

On Monday Mayor Simpson and all the councilmen except Rodriguez declared that there would be no public hearing. "We intend to be firm on this thing," he said. "A public hearing . . . accomplishes little . . . does much harm to the families of the principals involved . . . is too time consuming . . . is very expensive." The situation was different, the Mayor declared, from the "last Police Department flareup. At that time there were some charges of malfeasance in office." In addition to his oral remarks to reporters, the Mayor also issued a rather lengthy statement, which, however, dealt more with the method taken by the Council in arriving at its decision than the reasons. Among the questions Mayor Simpson said he felt people were asking were:

> . . . whether this means a less active law enforcement program; whether the action taken was arbitrary and based on a snap judgment, or whether it resulted from some individual's encounter with local law enforcement officers. To all of these, the answer is definitely NO.

1. All members of the Council and the City Manager have strongly supported the program of vigorous law enforcement and will continue to do so. . . . Good law enforcement, in the long run, is good public relations, not bad. . . .

2. While the Council had not been filled in on all details of existing problems until recently, the Manager informs us that he has discussed them repeatedly, and at length, with Mr. Black . . . the decision to take this action was made slowly and reluctantly. It was no sudden decision, and had no reference to any single specific incident.

3. A number of very fine technical improvements . . . have been made. . . . The problems, without going into unnecessary detail, have apparently been in the area of judgment, personal psychology, relations with other law enforcement agencies, relations with juveniles, etc.

There has been no malfeasance in office, merely a case of resolute incompatibility. It was never intended that the Chief should be dismissed in a manner to prejudice his future employment. . . . Unfortunately the unwise and premature disclosure, before the Manager had a chance to discuss the matter with the Chief, placed both of them in an awkward position. . . .

It is unhappily true that a small group of perennial trouble makers that enjoy behind the scenes activity in our community will seize upon a problem of this sort to exploit community division. Issues should not be decided in that setting. Every effort will be made to handle this fairly and properly, and we ask your patience and confidence. . . . [Emphasis added.]

That same day the *Times* published its first editorial on the "Chief Black Affair." It said that the community was deeply disturbed. Conceding that the Chief had been tactless and had moved too fast in his law enforcement program, the newspaper also noted the furor of the previous few days had revealed that a large number of people considered his performance "vigorous, firm, and impartial."

The majority of the Council and the manager made a mistake in the naive assumption that a highly controversial decision could be made on a Tuesday night, and not leak out before the anticipated Singer-Black conference six days later.

Having made that mistake the council was then unprepared for the public reaction that followed. All members except Joe Rodriguez have been placed on the defensive. They may have excellent reasons for supporting Singer against Black, but the public is unaware of them. They have placed themselves in the position of seeming to have bowed to pressures which they have not explained.

Far more than the council, the people are blaming the city manager. Perhaps it was all right for him to seek council approval of the firing of Black while the chief was out of town for a week. But it doesn't look like fair play to a lot of people.

They are holding the city manager to accountability for his judgment. Only a year ago, they observe, Mr. Singer found Mr. Black to be the best qualified candidate among many. Now he has reversed his opinion and fired the chief.

If he did not like the policies of the Chief of police, then why didn't he issue a different set of instructions, they want to know? Why wasn't Black given a chance to defend himself?

In the first round of the controversy, Mr. Singer has certainly lost, by failing to justify his position publicly. Mr. Black has proved to be an articulate champion of his own position. . . .

What the public wants now is information. . . .

The Council Agrees to Hear Black

Meanwhile, a woman whom Black "had never heard of" began to circulate petitions asking the Council that he be given a hearing. By mid-morning of the first day the lady had obtained 43 signatures, and the *Times* printed each name and address. The petition asked that Black be given a chance to state all the facts "regarding his summary dismissal . . . and present to the people of Valley his admirable record in fulfilling his duty, and the just reasons for his reinstatement." The lady said that people were anxious to sign and some thought that the manner of the firing was "un-American." Although it never came out publicly, the circulation of the petition brought the issue of religion into the controversy. Though Black was a Protestant, the woman circulating the petition was a Catholic and most of the early signatures she obtained were those of Catholics. Hence there was some feeling that the Catholic people, who represented about twenty percent of the population and were growing in proportionate number, were using the problem to secure political power in the community.

Spurred by the newspapers, citizen interest grew in extent and in intensity. It was reported that City Manager Singer's home was visited by a mysterious prowler on Monday night and a rock with a threatening note attached was hurled through his garage window on the preceding evening.[19]

It was becoming increasingly clear to the Council members that their hope of avoiding some kind of public unfolding of the issue would be impossible. Five days after Black had been fired, on May 10, the Council passed unanimously a motion by Rodriguez to allow Black to appear before it at the next regular Tuesday meeting. Mayor Simpson said Black had never really been denied the right to appear at a regular meeting. However, he noted the Council "was,

---

[19]The note said: "You have lost the best chief of police you ever had or ever will have. You have made the worst mistake you ever will make. Now you can live with it. The window is nothing. Just wait."

and still is, against a lengthy drawn out hearing such as we had a year ago."

Thus the Council bowed to a strong public sentiment. Councilman Jennings particularly felt that the Manager's public relations had been poorly handled. He believed that it was necessary under the circumstances for the City Manager to state as "fully and frankly" as possible his reasons for dismissing the Chief. Until this was done, Jennings did not believe the clamor would subside. Jennings had suggested this step to Singer, and Singer had agreed to prepare such a statement. The expectation that the Manager would have such a statement in time for the next Council meeting was one reason why Rodriguez' motion to grant Black "a fair opportunity to speak before the Valley City Council . . ." had been passed unanimously.

Singer Issues His Statement

The day before the Tuesday, May 15, hearing, City Manager Singer issued the statement Councilman Jennings had requested. It was not specific; rather it was an attempt to create the tone that Singer felt was important to an understanding of the reasons for the dismissal. A major portion of the statement follows:

> Tomorrow the former chief of police will have his say.
>
> He has asked why he was discharged. You, the people of this sensitive community, have asked also.
>
> I have been accused of protecting so-called Sacred Cows and yielding to political motives. Am I protecting anyone? Of course. And I fear I must always do so, public hearing or no.
>
> But I offer no protection to Sacred Cows or other vested interests. They not only do not ask my help, they do not need it. They hire legal counsel or go to a higher power than I.
>
> You ask to know why a man who has contributed much to the police administration of this city should be tossed aside. Was not his duty that of enforcing laws? Has he not done it more forcefully than any other chief Valley has had in past years?
>
> Very true. No one has argued that point. We did say, however, that he lacked "good public relations." This meant little to most of you.
>
> What we should have told you was that he lacks something far more important. That precious quality of human kindness . . . a genuine liking for people and an interest in you, as individuals.
>
> More high sounding talk? No, rather the reflection of the forlorn look in the eyes of those who have come away from a visit to the former chief, troubled and humiliated.
>
> These are not people of means and influence. These are people, who, because they lack means and influence, came to me since they had no other place to go. These are the little people. These are the ones who brought the downfall of ex-Chief Black.

They came alone or in groups of two or three. They came apologetically, sometimes a little fearfully. They ask for no favors or relief from violations of the law. They came humbly, asking only for a courteous audience and perhaps an explanation. They had talked with Black. But he had lost himself in the hard printed words of written law. Laws which after all, were made by people, for people —not against people.

Black's downfall came not from a lack of professional knowledge or ability. It came not from any one tangible incident. It came rather from those who spoke softly but from the heart. They cannot step forward and identify themselves "for investigation." They cannot, because they do not even know that their soft words were added month by month to many other soft words, eventually creating a roar which I could no longer ignore. They do not know this, these little people . . . and they never will unless they recognize themselves here.

I did not fire William Black. Nor did the City Council. William Black fired himself.

This was the general situation, the City Manager reported. He went on to say more specifically that there was a "serious, growing friction" between the local schools, the insurance agents, the other law enforcement agencies, and the Valley police, "caused by lack of cooperation or lack of judgment on the part of Mr. Black." Because of their "public positions," however, these agencies and their representatives could not speak openly. Singer concluded:

Yes, other problems exist. In my humble opinion some still should not be discussed. However, you are interested in good government and you have asked, "Why has Black been discharged?"

I have tried to briefly answer this and point out that the step was taken as much to protect the future of the people of this community as for what already occurred.

BLACK DOMINATES THE COUNCIL HEARINGS

Judging by the turnout and the mood of the people at the hearings the next day, Singer's statement had not quieted many citizens who were displeased with the dismissal of Chief Black. Councilman Jennings, who had publicly requested the statement, was not satisfied, either. "You couldn't answer those petition-happy people with high-sounding words. I was well aware of the great difficulties in getting the people who had complained about the Chief to come forward. But . . . I felt we had come to the point where much had to be spelled out and people identified if possible. . . . For example I talked to the school people too. They generally confirmed what the Manager had said to us, but couldn't get the schools mixed up in this. Where did that leave Singer and us?"

The hearings, which began Tuesday, May 15, were "gruesome," as one Councilman put it. Originally scheduled for the Council Chamber in the basement of the City Hall, the appearance of some 300 people forced the removal of the session upstairs to the auditorium. The day was hot, 92 degrees, as some 250 found seats and the others stood around the walls. Chief Black appeared with his attractive wife and teen-age son and daughter. It was a pro-Black audience. Some 1,400 signatures had been obtained on the petitions asking for the hearings, and it looked as if a good number of the signers were present. None of the persons who had previously complained about Black to the Manager could be seen in the audience.

Mayor Simpson was in the chair flanked by all his colleagues except Jennings, who missed the session. The Mayor stated that the proceeding resulted from Chief Black's written request for a public hearing at the regular Council meeting. Black then took the floor and began to read a three-page prepared statement as City Manager Singer sat poker-faced. On this occasion, and in the hearings that followed, the Chief proved to be a highly effective speaker, capable of moving a large audience on his own behalf. Black declared, first, that he was not seeking reinstatement to his position. He said he was still Chief until action had been taken by the Council, "elected to that office to do the will of the majority of the people in keeping with city ordinances." He had refrained from performing his duties since his "illegal" discharge from office because he did not "wish to cause turmoil and upset among the people of Valley." Since no charges had been filed and he had been unable to confront his accusers, Black stated that his dismissal was a violation of the Sixth Amendment of the Constitution of the United States. "I am here to ask the people of Valley to make known to me, through the City Council, the reasons why I should be discharged from the police department," he said, concluding his typewritten statement amidst applause and cheers.

Black then suggested that a motion to restore him to office would be in order. Councilman Rodriguez said, "I so move." But the motion died for lack of a second. Later on Rodriguez tried a second time, but again there was no second.

Black's Speech

No longer reading from notes, Black started a lengthy speech in which he concentrated on four major points: (1) the improvements that he had brought about in the Department ("the first professional administration . . . the Valley police department . . . has ever had"); (2) his insistence on impartial enforcement of the law which had really lost him his job ("it was implied that I would have to adjust to 'the Hill' and to 'the other side of the tracks.' He [Singer] had the wrong man to talk to because I live on the other side of the tracks."); (3) a categorical denial that he failed to co-operate with other agencies ("falsification," he said, producing letters and calling witnesses from the California Highway Patrol and the Valley Police Department); and (4) a view of City Manager Singer as a nice but ineffectual person caught in the squeeze of pressures on his office. (He and Singer "had never had a harsh word" until the current trouble came up.) The witnesses Black called supported his statements, one former officer testifying that he, too, had been warned about the difference between the people on "the Hill" and those "on the other side of the tracks."

At one point in the session Councilman Rodriguez also hurled at Singer the charge that he was not informed equally with the other councilmen about the case. He said he had known nothing of Black's shortcomings before the meeting, and he read from the Manager's Handbook that administrators should "deal frankly with the Council as a unit rather than as individual members."

The meeting ran long over time, but Black was still not finished. The audience by this time was intensely and angrily pro-Black. No one on the Manager's side had commented to any extent. It appeared that the hearings might drag on indefinitely, exactly what the Council had originally sought to avoid. Three of the councilmen—Jones, Rodriguez, and Carter—said that under the circumstances they would not be prepared to vote until "all statements are made." Thus, the Council agreed to convene on Thursday at 3:00 P.M. to continue the hearing. Some young Black supporters moved toward the Manager with jeers as he and the councilmen sought to leave the crowded auditorium, but a newspaper man, fearing violence, headed them off.

The hearing had been a trying experience for City Manager Singer, mindful of the *Times* editorial suggesting that he too was on trial. He had spoken only once when he became angered by Rodriguez' comments, firing back that an example of the Manager's trouble in handling personnel was the hearing, which arose from premature release of information on Black's pending dismissal. "When the end of the meeting came," Singer recalled, "I really felt in physical danger. I'll have to give Black credit. He really stirred up the people in the that room."

Singer Faces a Hostile Audience

On the second day of the hearings the atmosphere was, if anything, even more highly charged with intense pro-Black feeling. The crowd numbered at least 350 persons. "Black's supporters applauded him, and moves they considered fair or favorable to him, and were audibly hostile to City Manager Jack Singer," the *Times* reported. This time City Manager Singer was allowed to speak first by Mayor Simpson, even though Chief Black insisted that he still had the floor and should be allowed to continue.

Singer's delivery was mumbling and ineffective compared to the Chief's oratory. In his remarks the Manager was more specific in treating his reasons for dismissing Black. He stated his version of the problem with the schools, with the insurance agents, of the Peters traffic death, and of failures of co-operation with other law enforcement agencies. Against Black's observation the previous Tuesday that the Manager in Valley had too much power over employees who "lived in fear of their jobs" because there was no formal civil service system, Singer made a spirited statement in defense of the council-manager plan. He said

Mr. Black was familiar with our form of government when he came here. The people of Valley adopted it by vote in 1948. I believe the city has progressed and prospered under it. I feel sorry that Mr. Black believes our form of government has done him an injustice.

I am shocked to learn from Mr. Black that the department heads and the employees of the city government are constantly in fear of losing their jobs. I can only say that in my four years as city manager, I have dismissed but one department head . . . Mr. Black.

Singer declared that he did not propose to "refute, point by point," Black's allegations but called Acting Chief Ken Boyer and asked him about "discriminatory arrests." Boyer, who had been on the force nearly sixteen years, scoffed at the charge, saying he "never heard of it." Black, then getting permission to speak, asked if Boyer was ever present when Singer interviewed new officers. Boyer admitted he was not.

Jennings Sees a Way Out

During the hour or so that the hearings had been under way that day, Councilman Jennings had become increasingly concerned about where the whole controversy might lead. He felt the hearings were getting out of hand and that Black might want several more days to talk about his side of the case. The audience was becoming more inflamed, and no one could see any end to them other than increased passion and community discord. Moreover, Jennings was afraid of what Black would do when he had the chance to reply to the Manager's fumbling remarks. "I felt that Black, clever as he is, would tear into it."

Groping for a way out, Jennings recalled a conversation he had had the previous evening with the Reverened Richmond Jackson, pastor of the State Street Christian Church. The minister, who knew Black well and had provided spiritual guidance to him at times, was much disturbed by the affair. Like others, he felt the violent controversy was beginning to tear the community apart. He had talked to Black as he had to Jennings, about finding some more appropriate basis for mediation. Black had approved of Jackson's proposed intervention.

Jennings asked for the floor. Before asking Jackson to speak, Councilman Jennings first observed that there had been a "welter of charges, and counter charges, which are almost impossible to sort and prove or disprove. . . ." He then continued, "I am concerned by what this does internally to a community and by the problems that arise from it." Declaring that in such an environment the quest for a solution to the problem was futile, Jennings asked for a new approach, which would involve the application of Christian ethics to a social situation. He then asked the Reverened Mr. Jackson to speak.

Everyone was taken by surprise. Jennings himself did not know the details of the proposal Jackson would make.

The minister said the hearing as presently operating was dividing the community. There could be no satisfactory conclusion. He suggested a private conference between Black, Singer, the Council, with a committee of ministers attending. In such an atmosphere perhaps a real "Christian reconciliation" could take place:

> Christian reconciliation that would heal this hurt in the community would be my hope. If invited by the Council, I would be very happy to serve.

For the Jackson statement, the *Times* reported, there was "moderate applause." Councilman Jennings then offered a motion that "this Council invite Mr. Jackson, and four or five other ministers of this community, possibly one of the Catholic priests, in for that kind of a conference." The motion was interrupted from the floor on a point of order on the assertion that Black still had the parliamentary right to speak first. The Mayor said the Chief would be given time, and then Councilman Jennings asked Black for his reaction to the proposal. Actually, of course, Black had already given his approval to Jackson's idea. He later wrote, "I purposely feigned reluctance in not wanting to appear overly-enthusiastic. Jackson felt this was the way to bring Singer to terms. . . ."

According to the *Times,* Black replied:

> "This puts me on the spot. I think it is unfair at this moment." He then interpreted it as a move that would cause him to lose the floor. He said that the city manager had not said anything new in his prepared statement. Then he said he would have to agree that Jackson did have a point.
>
> Looking toward the full-house audience, he said, "I don't know what these people came here to hear. I think they want to know more of what goes on in this community."
>
> This touched off loud applause which continued until the mayor rapped the gravel to restore order.
>
> The Mayor asked Black if he would agree to concluding his remarks in a "reasonable time" and then go "into the personnel session with the ministers. . . ."
>
> Black said Mr. Jackson had an excellent thought, although the proposal came prematurely in the hearing.

Close to "Mob Rule"

Chief Black then resumed his speech. He refuted a number of the points in Singer's statement, talked of a "whispering campaign" by people "who don't have the guts to say those things directly to me." He spoke mainly to the audience, intermittently firing sharply barbed accusations at the City Manager.

At one point cries of "fire Singer" were heard from the audience, as the intensity of feeling brought the affair close to "mob rule." Black concluded, saying, "I am forced to the conclusion that some persons are bringing pressure on some members of the city, or city council, or that they have committed themselves to someone. That is the reason for your stony silence. Whatever shackles are binding you, throw them away." The Chief sat down to loud cheers and long applause.

It was then after 5:00 P.M., and a procedural wrangle began. Mayor Simpson said the Jennings motion had been seconded and was before the house. To Councilman Carter's comment that the motion might lead to interminable hearings, the audience shouted, "Vote now." Soberly Jennings said he still felt that Christian social ethics should be applied, adding that the aim would be "to resolve the problem," but with the Council making the final decision. However, Councilman Rodriguez was cheered loudly when he asked for "one last attempt to settle this question, openly, fairly, justly, here in this open meeting as we were elected to do." He saw no reason why Black and Singer could not get along together, and he asked Jennings to withdraw his motion so he could move "for the last time, that we reinstate Black" But he added he would have to go along with the Jennings motion if there were no other choice.

Jennings said the Jackson approach was the only answer and insisted on his motion. The *Times* then described the final events of the afternoon:

> A call for the question brought shouts of "no, no" from the audience. Rodriguez then defended his colleagues saying that they were in a tough spot and deserved the consideration due to members of a deliberative body.
>
> "If Black would cooperate would Singer forgive and forget?" Rodriguez asked, and sought an answer from each.
>
> Black said, "Yes." Singer said he would prefer the Jennings-Jackson approach and added that Rodriguez was out of order, a motion being before the house.
>
> Jennings, asked if the conference would be open to the press, replied, "Yes—that was included in the motion." . . .
>
> At 5:23 the Jennings motion was put to a roll call vote and was carried unanimously, all members being present and voting.
>
> The hassle involving Black and Singer having been referred, in part, to a committee of ministers, the *Times* inquired about their religious affiliations. Both Black and Singer said they are Protestants.

Although the motion was carried unanimously, the degree of support was not as strong as might have been assumed. Not only was Rodriguez strongly opposed; Mayor Simpson also was unsympathetic to the approach. He did not like the idea of "mixing church and state" and wanted to get "hard-boiled" and make a decision to dismiss the Chief. Since he was chairing the meeting, however, Simpson did not put forth his views aggressively.

Thus, after over five hours of meetings, Black's blistering attacks had so excited the community that the Manager and the Council were now clearly on the defensive. Moreover, Singer felt that the reconciliation proposal had lost ground for his position. As he recalled his uncomfortable feeling later, "This just compounded the already existing community feeling that Black and I were engaging in some kind of personal fight. The real principles were being lost sight of. I should have refused to go along. But how do you object to being prayed over?"

IN A "SPIRIT OF CHRISTIAN RECONCILIATION"

The next noon four Protestant ministers met immediately after lunch and hastily drew up the ground rules for the session, which was to begin in two hours with the Council, the Manager, and the Chief of Police. Besides the Reverend Mr. Jackson, the others were pastors of the First Methodist Church, the First Baptist Church, and the Lutheran Church. They were a completely informal body, nominated by no official process, and participating only to create the atmosphere in which Singer and Black might patch up their differences. When the meeting began, these four were joined by the pastor of Valley's Second Baptist Church (a Negro) and two Catholic priests.[20]

The four Protestants developed three principles, which they suggested should govern the tense conference. These were later accepted by the other clerics.

1. We propose as a basis for our participation in this conference that we are not going to express a judicial opinion as to the right or wrong action of this case, due to our lack of evidence.

2. Having no authority in this government, we are unwilling to be responsible for acts which are of necessity the sole responsibility of the duly elected governing officials.

3. As representatives of some of the religious groups in this community, we are willing to express a concern for the total welfare of the community, and realizing that the final judgment rendered by the Council will leave many persons disappointed, that whatever decision is arrived at by this duly elected Council, it be accepted by the citizens of this community and that we live up to the ideals of brotherhood and understanding through it.

That afternoon, May 18, 1956, all the members of the Council, the ministers and priests, Singer and Black, and members of the press gathered in the small parish house room of the First Evangelical Lutheran Church. The atmosphere

---

[20]Black had a strong basis of support in this last group. He had earlier consulted with the Catholic fathers at the church in the Mexican-American community as to the availability of a good young Mexican-American for police service. The Department had one Mexican-American at the time, and Black had given him a more responsible assignment in traffic. The Chief had also talked to church people in the small Negro community about the possibility of putting on a Negro officer. He felt at the meeting that these representatives of the minority groups were basically in sympathy with him.

was greatly different from the two previous public meetings. "Affirming the presence of God," the group carried on its discussion amicably over a four-hour period. Members of the clergy and the councilmen did the talking. Black and Singer, sitting only two chairs apart, said very little. When they did talk, they spoke quietly and did not argue. Both men, admitting they had made mistakes, stated their grievances in rather general terms. Singer held that the Chief had attacked his honesty, character, and judgment. Black insisted he was fired without specific charges and without an opportunity to confront his accusers.

The councilmen particularly took the opportunity to express their positions and to confront Black with some of their own questions and grievances. Mayor Simpson said that, based on complaints told him, Black had acted unwisely at times, was dogmatic and belligerent in his approach, and rubbed people the wrong way. "These are some of the intangibles," he said. "That's why we tried for a closed hearing right from the start." He said Valley was a "sensitive town."

Councilman Fred Jones, who had said little earlier declared that he heard many compliments for Black's program. However, he had also been kept aware of the difficulties the Manager said he was having. ". . . When Singer said that he could no longer keep Black subordinate, I agreed. . . . If Singer and Black can agree—then Singer must remember he must have assurance from Black that he will submit himself to constituted authority. . . . If we put him [Singer] in a position where every employee went to the people, it would be untenable."

Councilman Andy Carter also took advantage of the occasion to express his criticism of the Chief. He reminded the group that the problem with the insurance agents had not been resolved. Carter then asked:

> If Singer ordered you to work, do you feel in your heart that you could work with the City Manager and the Council? Would you try your best to keep from creating a situation such as we have had? And further, would you throw open your office doors and try to be a likeable citizen?

Black answered, "Yes, sir." Carter then went on:

> We would want to know that you would not only obey orders but do so willingly, not grudgingly. You inferred at the hearing that my idea for downtown parking was to give four hours. It actually was for only two hours in the courtesy parking plan. Suppose it doesn't work? If our local Lions club is willing to furnish the nickels and if the Council does act on it, would you instruct your department willingly to go along with these clubs? Maybe it isn't a good plan, maybe it won't work, but if a civic group wants to do something, and you don't want to, then it would be time to resign.

To this Black responded, "I did not say I was opposed to the plan. I was only trying to point out some things. I will certainly do what the Council asks." The Chief, one Councilman later recalled, "was more humble than I ever saw him."

Among the clerics, the general tendency was to emphasize their community responsibility to the actors in the drama. However, one of the Catholic fathers— he came from the nearby estate of a religious order and at least two councilmen had no idea who had invited him—was particularly vigorous in insisting that a decision be reached that would restore Black to duty. Directing many of his remarks to Manager Singer, the priest was sufficiently scathing to cause one Councilman to suggest that he had been "briefed" by Black supporters. Singer was saved from answering the father's query whether he would put Black back to work "tomorrow morning" by several who said that the purpose of the meeting was not to force a decision on the Manager. Black thought Singer would have reinstated him had he not been interrupted by the ministers.

At 6:00 P.M. the meeting broke up. Black said he thought the meeting had been fair. Singer announced the session was "wonderful" but "some things have gone unanswered which I feel must be answered. I don't think the breach can be healed in four hours. There are some things I must do and some you must do." Then, apparently swept up by the "spirit of Christian reconciliation," Singer added, ". . . I now hold a totally different position than when I first came here. I trust we'll clear up every point. I know I certainly will try." On this basis the two principals decided to meet two days later, Monday, May 21, to search out a possibility of resolving the bitter dispute.

The immediate reaction of the community was enthusiastic. One of the councilmen said he had felt "the presence of God at the meeting. Sometimes I lost the feeling but it kept coming back." A reporter for the Xerxes daily enthusiastically reported that the session "bared some souls" and the "new approach" appeared to offer its own "happy ending." The *Times* also provided a happy version of the affair. Black and Singer were shown together in earnest conversation, and six smiling ministers were posed in another picture. Over the pictures the *Times* ran a bold headline, "Black May Be Restored As Chief."

The Monday Morning Conference

Actually, City Manager Singer did feel that the reconciliation meeting had had an effect on him, not perhaps as great later as he had thought at first. Over the weekend Singer was reasonably certain that Black would be reinstated. "The pressure was terrific," he has said, "and it was clear that the only possible villain in the reconciliation picture would be me if I failed to make peace with Black." His only price for a reversal of his decision, Singer said, was some acknowledgement of human frailty by Black: "If Bill would only say he had made some mistakes and would try to correct things, I thought I could get along."

However, as soon as the pair started talking in City Hall on Monday morning, the City Manager said he realized that Black had not changed. The meeting opened with Singer reviewing some of the problem areas that needed correction. Black took notes. On all the critical issues, however, the Chief refused to concede that he had made any errors. "Actually it was his attitude more than what he said," Singer recalled. "I just had the feeling that if there were going to be any changes made at all, I would have to make them. I couldn't buy that. After about two hours, and when I realized the complete hopelessness of the situation, I just said, 'Well, Bill, I guess that's about all.' " At that time Singer did not indicate to Black that he had no further hope of reconciliation.

According to Black's report of this meeting, the moment he walked into the Manager's office Singer said: "I agreed last Friday to a reconciliation, but since then I have talked to certain people and I am not going along." According to Black, the session from that point on was dominated by Singer, who pointed out problem areas and indicated what he would expect of the Police Chief. However, Black perceived these points as "nothing of real importance—little individual things."

At the conclusion of the session the two men issued a statement to the press. Singer said, "We have covered a great deal of ground regarding our own personal reconciliation and we are now in the process of discussing the problem as it exists as a result of the activities during the past two weeks." Black agreed that Singer's comments were "fair and correct," and they both said they would "probably" meet again that same afternoon to continue discussions. Actually, nothing had been said about a future meeting. There was no conference that afternoon or the next day.

It was the following day (Wednesday) at 11:15 that City Manager Singer made public his decision to oppose the return of Black. He summoned the Chief to his office, as well as press representatives, and made the announcement. Black said only, "O.K." and had no comment for the press. As soon as Singer finished, the Chief left. In a statement written in advance of Singer's official announcement, Mayor Simpson declared that a meeting of the Council would be called to "bring the Black matter to a conclusion at the earliest possible time." However, Councilman Carter was in Monterey for the rest of the week attending a conference for new legislators sponsored by the League of California Cities.

Singer's statement was biting and direct:

> It was proposed that Mr. Black and I might attempt some sort of reconciliation. What sort of "reconciliation" I am not sure. I have met in good faith with Mr. Black. This meeting only made it more clear to me that this issue had nothing to do wtih any personal reconciliation. Reconciliation has nothing to do with the problem of Mr. Black's qualifications to be Police Chief for all the people of Valley.
>
> I have nothing personal against Mr. Black. . . .
>
> Nothing that has happened . . . has in any way changed that condition. It is even more evident to me (and I am sure it is to the people and their Council) that Mr. Black is incapable of being the Chief of Police of the City of Valley. The Council has been able to verify all of the reasons which I gave them in support of my recommendation for dismissal.
>
> It has been, and still is, the responsibility of the Council to act on my recommendation for the dismissal of Mr. Black. I have again notified the Council that I wish their action as soon as possible.

CHIEF BLACK IS REHIRED

By the time Councilman Andy Carter had gotten back to Valley from the Monterey meeting of new city legislators, he was convinced that it would be an error to fire Black. He was deeply disappointed at City Manager Singer's insistence that his action be upheld. With Councilman Jones, he later reported, he went to the Manager's office "with tears in my eyes" and "practically got down on my knees" begging Singer to keep Black on the job.

Finally, Councilman Carter decided that the Council would have to take the initiative itself. He proposed that the City Manager be required by Council action to take back the Police Chief for ninety days. If, in that time, Black failed to work out, it would be agreed in advance that the Council would support the dismissal. Something had to be done, Carter felt, to prevent the complete disintegration of community morale and pride.

(By this time the charges of Black and the leaders of the Black petition movement—charges that the firing on the south side for special treatment—were cutting deep crevices of controversy and suspicion into Valley's customary cohesiveness and orderliness. This was beginning to worry some leading citizens more than the issue of the dismissal of Black.)

Carter frankly admitted that he had changed his mind. Even though he had investigated Singer's charges and felt they had been substantiated, he nevertheless believed that Black's voiced willingness to change at the reconciliation meeting entitled him to another chance.

Excited by the prospect that his compromise would remove the Council from a very uncomfortable hook, Carter consulted with all his colleagues except Rodriguez. He talked with Mayor Simpson for a considerable part of the day. Carter heard the Mayor say he did not think he would "go for it"; but he still felt the Mayor was not completely negative. Actually Mayor Simpson thought he had been arguing against the proposal. He told Carter to see what the others said. "We were in such a turmoil," Simpson recalled, "I didn't want to discourage anybody." While Jones agreed to go along, Councilman Jennings found the idea completely unsatisfactory and reported that his conversation with Carter went something like this:

> *Carter:* "I have talked to George Simpson and I think I have a plan which should be satisfactory to everybody. I will move that Black be reinstated for ninety days. If he doesn't work out in that time, he can be dropped."
>
> *Jennings:* "Andy, do you realize what you're doing? What you are proposing in effect is to fire Singer."
>
> *Carter:* "No, I don't want to do that."
>
> *Jennings:* "You are voting no confidence in the Manager and you are voting to dismiss him."

But Carter protested that his proposal cast no reflection on the Manager and would not affect his position in the least. "While at Monterey," he said, "I came to realize that not only must the councilmen back up their City Manager, but also our City Manager should back up his Council."

Carter Moves a Ninety-Day Trial

The Council meeting was announced late on Monday, May 28. Scheduled for 5:00 P.M., it was 4:00 before the date was given to the public. Nevertheless, about thirty spectators quickly assembled and were present as the deliberations began. Some of them were city employees. Black, who knew nothing of the Carter compromise, later said he thought sure this would be the time when the firing would be made official. Action started quickly when Carter introduced his motion that Black be given another chance and be restored to duty on a ninety-day probationary basis. It was Councilman Jones, sitting next to Carter, who seconded the motion, supported by Rodriguez. The plan had a majority.

Even though the decision was clearly made, it did give most of the councilmen an opportunity to read into the record some of their attitudes toward the whole affair. The most intense was Jones's reaction. The large property owner had been a strong supporter of the Manager. He said he felt that Singer was completely justified in his action. "Black," he said, "has failed from a public relations standpoint. . . . He was abrupt and not well received. . . . Here at home, I've found people have complained. I, too, agreed that Black should go."[21]

Nevertheless, Jones said he was "amazed, actually amazed" that the people who had complained to Singer about Black now refused to come forward and state their positions publicly. This failure had been particularly irritating to the nervous Jones, who had been subjected to anonymous threats and, under the barrage of constant telephone calls, felt himself under terrific pressure. He was, as one of his colleagues said, "boiling mad." As a consequence, Jones said, "I told these people who were against Black that they should come and stand beside me, not behind me. These people apparently haven't felt that this was important enough to stand by Singer. This morning I talked with Singer. I knew his position. He must have the respect of all department heads and employees. I said I'd not ask him to take Black back. I would be willing to take action over his head. . . ." In short Jones was angry enough at the lack of support given the Council by the pro-Singer people in town to put Black back.

The third member of the majority, Joe Rodriguez, was not completely satisfied with the motion. He saw no reason why Black should be placed on probation. "Black," said Rodriguez, "has successfully refuted the charges made." He suggested that if Black went on probation, Singer should too. At this, the *Times* reported, the small pro-Singer audience cried, "No!"

Councilman Jennings also had his say. He read a three-page statement in which he declared that the Police Chief had "handled facts loosely in the

[21]Chief Black says Councilman Jones once told him, ". . . use me as a reference any time."

hearings and artfully managed to give a sinister implication to a number of things which were not sinister and even questionable." Jennings characterized Singer as honest and conscientious. "Independent" investigations indicated that the "Manager did have grounds for his decision"; but both Manager and Council had handled their public relations poorly.

Then Jennings emphasized his underlying theme. By its action, the Council would either support or undermine council-manager government in Valley. He said:

> Realistically, our only choice now is to either confirm the discharge of Mr. Black or perhaps in effect force the resignation of the City Manager and Assistant City Manager (and possibly lose some other valued city employees as well). We are not supposed to decide whether as individuals we would have acted in identical fashion. Reduced to the basic issue, the Council must decide whether it believes the Manager had any reasonable grounds for his action. If he did, we confirm; if he did not, we ask his resignation. Whether or not we might have preferred another approach, it seems clear that he had grounds. I certainly could not honestly and conscientiously conclude that Mr. Singer had no reasonable basis for his decision.

Singer Threatens to Resign

Before the vote was taken, Singer asked for his chance to talk. He said that the "basic facts in the Black case have not been altered. . . . I feel that I must urge the City Council to ratify the recommendation that Mr. Black be terminated." Failing this, he said the Council could order his own termination and accept the responsibility for a decision he did not wish to be "associated with." After applause for Singer's statement died down, the question was called, and Carter's motion for a ninety-day reinstatement passed by a three to two vote. The pro-Singer audience felt the defeat keenly. After the vote, a number of city employees came up to Jennings, two of them women with tears running down their faces. They thanked him for his vote in support of the Manager. One department head, in thanking Jennings, referred to Singer as "the best boss I ever worked for."

Black, quickly shaking Singer's hand after the session, told him, "Jack, I think I can do it. . . ."

"You'll have to do it without me," Singer shot back.

Within an hour after the close of the meeting, both Singer and the Assistant City Manager had submitted their resignations, effective in thirty days. Singer said to obey the order would have put him in an "untenable position." During the month he was still to be on duty, he would take no responsibility for the Police Department. He declared that administrative authority had been badly undermined, that the effect was one of electing a Chief to office by a "small minority of skillfully influenced people," and would result in the creation of an "autonomous police department." Actually, Singer was saying a considerable portion of this for public consumption. He was still hopeful that his departure from Valley might be averted and consequently handed his resignation to the mayor, rather than the City Clerk. If it had been given to the latter, it would have been official. As it was, the resignation simply lay in the Mayor's hands until Singer desired to pass it on to the City Clerk.

The Council decision caused the *Times* to editorialize at considerable length the next day on Singer and his approach to his job. It pointed out that Black had become a symbol of impartial but firm law enforcement and therefore his potential support had not been recognized by the Manager and the Council.

> It was Mr. Singer's ideal of professional conduct, however, that finally put him in an untenable position. He felt that it was only necessary to do what he sincerely believed was right. He did not believe that it was incumbent upon him to justify to the people the correctness of his action. This left many individuals who dealt with the manager's office with the feeling that they were not getting a sympathetic hearing, that the city was being run "by the book." When this same philosophy was applied to the Black affair, it proved to be fatal to the manager.
>
> Black had a large public following—as subsequent events proved—and any plan for his dismissal had to allow in advance for answering to that public. Without that planning, a public clamor ensued and Mr. Singer took the position that it was not up to him to give a prompt and full accounting to anyone other than the five members of the council.
>
> In Utopia it may be possible for city managers to remain silent to the public they serve, but here and now a manager can continue in office only so long as he is understood by the public.

THE PROSPECT OF NO GOVERNMENT

By the next morning the condition of Valley's government approached complete chaos. Not only were the resignations of the two top administrative officials submitted, but Mayor Simpson called in the press at 11:00 A.M. to announce that he was quitting, too. (Jennings had made desperate efforts to dissuade him.) Simpson characterized the previous day's action as "a step backward to ward-heeling days" and said that he and Councilman Rodriguez had "diametrically opposite opinions and standards as to methods and approaches to the solution of city problems." He said he wanted "no part of that system."[22]

Unknown to Simpson, Councilman Jones had also made up his mind to resign. He appeared two hours after Simpson's press conference at the City Clerk's office to make the action official, in contrast to the Mayor's presentation of

[22]Before the Black affair, Mayor Simpson had not given any consideration to resigning from the Council, even though he had been planning a six-week trip to Hawaii for some time. He felt, however, the time had come for a change. "If I couldn't get the job done, we needed some people who could." he said later. A secondary reason, Simpson declared, was his disinterest in "taking any more punishment."

his resignation only to the press. His wife said he had been awake and sick all the previous night. The Councilman declared he could not "take any more of it. I retired from business because of nerves many years ago. . . . My position on the Council has been a lot worse than I thought." That left the city with three councilmen. One was Councilman Jennings, who had applied for a Fullbright Fellowship in The Netherlands the previous September and was expecting to hear at any time about whether he would get it.

Administrative operations, too, were in a state of turmoil. For weeks little work had been done at City Hall. Thirty-five employees signed a statement registering their confidence in the City Manager, and the Planning Director publicly announced he would resign with Singer. In his statement he made an obvious reference to the Lemon Street Gang and its involvement in the situation, saying,

> In the past few years there has developed in Valley a small political group that works under cover—a group that follows the old line— Stir up unrest, grasp any incident to create situations that appeal to the emotions, disorganize government. To create these situations they work through the weakest member of the Council [an apparent reference to Councilman Rodriguez] with the hope of weaving a web dragging the sincere members of the Council into a trap from which it is difficult to extricate themselves. This was demonstrated in the Kelly episode. Fortunately for Valley trying as it was, those undercover artists were sent back to their holes.

> Now the same old strategy is being used—this time they have succeeded in disorganizing city government. However, I believe there is still time for the sincere Councilmen to extricate themselves from the present trap. In spite of the acute proportions to which this grandstand play has developed, I believe the good citizens of Valley will rally and again bring organization out of chaos.

Black's status, too, was up in the air. He had gone back to work. Yet Singer, who was still Manager and still Black's boss, had told the Council he would not take the responsibility of putting Black back on the job. He did not order Black back on the payroll. Insofar as Singer was concerned, Black still was fired. Council confirmation or not, Singer took further steps. He said he had checked with the city's insurance carrier, and there was some question as to the municipality's liability should Black make an arrest or get involved in an accident while driving a public vehicle. Therefore, he ordered that Black do neither of these things.

In the atmosphere of crisis, the *Times* again inserted its editorial voice, suggesting that the council-manager form of government was perhaps at fault.

> In theory, the police department is just another department of government, along with cemetery, streets and water. The manager can supposedly deal with the water superintendent and the police chief alike.

But law enforcement is by its nature a highly controversial sub-ject. . . .

The oldest question in this book is: Who shall police the police? "The City Manager shall." At least that's what the citizens thought who constantly ran to Jack Singer in an effort to make Chief Black change his policies or his ways.

This puts the city manager in the political position of having to interpret the wishes of the people and to supervise the police de-partment accordingly. Political decisions are for elected officers—not appointive ones, and that's where our city managers have found them-selves in hot water that was not of their own choosing.

A Meeting of Some Leading Citizens

It appeared that a resolution of the conflict would depend in great part on the future composition of the Council. Under California law, Council vacancies could be filled by appointment by remaining members without calling an election. It seemed possible, with Jones and Simpson leaving, and Jennings possibly leaving, too, that Valley would soon be governed by an appointive City Council in which Rodriguez and Carter would be the dominant figures. This prospect alarmed a number of citizens in the community: realtors, businessmen, persons active in clubs or church societies, prominent country club members. These persons included men who had formerly been active in city government, but many were persons who had been content to let the Manager and the Council majority run things. They were concerned at the division caused in the community by the Black affair and by the intense controversy provoked by his charges that his dismissal had been the result of not granting lenient treatment to a favored few. Now the Manager was resigning, and it appeared that there would soon be no Council majority. To some appeared the prospect that there would soon be no government at all.

Because of this prevailing feeling of concern and alarm, Vice Mayor Jennings had no difficulty in bringing together on short notice thirty of Valley's leading citizens. They met in the Mayor's office. A *Times* reporter commented later: "I was near the City Hall at lunch time, and within fifteen minutes I noticed people going up the steps. It seemed as if almost everybody who was anybody was going in. . . . These were the people who were accustomed to giving the time and leadership to clubs, church groups, the community chest" and the like. Included in the group were several former councilmen.

During the short session, many of the citizens said they had not realized the pressure under which the councilmen had been operating. They offered greater help for the future and public support for the City Manager. As a result, the group was able to stave off Mayor Simpson's threatened resignation. "As long as we're going to have chaos in city government," Simpson commented, "we should at least have orderly chaos." Councilman Jones, however, had already turned his resignation in to the City Clerk. His resignation was irrevocable, according to the City Attorney's ruling. One vacancy on the Valley City Council remained to be filled.

The Selection of a New Councilman

With the pro-Black citizens still extremely active, it might have been ex-
pected that the appointment of a Councilman to succeed Jones would have led
to a considerable struggle. Black had one solid supporter on the Council in
Rodriguez. Singer had two in Simpson and Jennings. The fourth member,
Carter, the downtown jeweler, had said that Singer had had good reasons to fire
Black but had wanted—and obtained—another chance for the Police Chief.
Thus, the appointment of a new Councilman might have been a close thing.
Despite this, it did not appear that the significance of the impending appoint-
ment was appreciated by the community at large, particularly those on Black's
side.

A few days after the meeting in the Mayor's office, former Mayor Cassius Bolt,
the respected Methodist lay leader and businessman who had been instrumental
in bringing city manager government to Valley in 1949, convened an evening
meeting of leading citizens at his home. Jennings was the only Councilman
invited. (Simpson was out of town.) Present were leading businessmen and
realtors, club leaders, some former councilmen (including the Democratic one),
some leading church laymen, and some substantial citrus men who had taken
an interest in civic affairs. The purpose of the meeting was to find a suitable
person who would be willing to serve on the Council, so that his name might
be suggested for appointment. It had been customary in previous years for groups
of civic leaders to suggest names when vacancies occurred.

Because of the strains and difficulties that the incumbent councilmen were
facing, it was not easy to find someone who was willing to serve. The group, by
design, did not include anyone who was "in opposition" on the Black-Singer
matter. Nor did it include anyone who could not be trusted to work without
publicity. Thus Carter had not been invited, nor had the editor or publisher of
the *Times*. The group was looking, first, for some eligible person who would be
willing to serve. No known supporter of Black would have been considered.
Neither would anyone already publicly committed to Singer.

Several meetings were held before Norman Chandler, manager of the Valley
Citrus Exchange, was selected. Chandler was a former president of the Valley
Rotary Club, a post of respectability in the community. He had once served as
Mayor of the nearby city of Circe. His appointment would have the additional
public relations advantage that he lived on the north side.

Chandler's name was given to Carter, who moved his appointment at the
Council meeting on June 5. The motion was unanimously approved. Rodriguez
had played no role in the filling of the appointment, nor had he or Black's
other supporters done anything to nominate their own candidate. "I didn't see
any point in suggesting anybody, because it was obvious that the other three
would make up their minds together," Rodriguez said. When Carter nominated
Chandler, he said the Council was "full of trouble" but that Chandler was "willing to accept the responsibility." When Chandler was asked if he would like to
come forward to be sworn in, he commented, "No, but I will."

A Police Commissioner?

With the legislative body back to full strength, it was late in the session before the problem of Black's status was raised again. It was not, incidentally, on the agenda. However, Councilman Carter tried to make a motion to restore Black to the payroll and name a Council member as police commissioner; he was interrupted twice. Manager Singer, who had refused to accept responsibility for the Department, pointed out that the ordinance specifically required councilmen to work through the Manager.

Then the City Attorney said that the motion to put Black on the payroll was not necessary. He was still on it until the Council ratified the ouster, a point that was supported by a bulky legal document. Furthermore, said the Attorney, he could not interpret Councilman Carter's motion of the week before because it did not ratify or reject Singer's action. Carter declared he simply wanted to postpone the ratification ninety days.

Carter then said he was much concerned about the exercise of supervision over the Police Department. "I don't want to be police commissioner. I just want Singer to address correspondence to Black as Chief of Police." Singer stated he would resume responsibility and said he had issued a memorandum ordering Black not to drive police cars. However, Black had continued to do so. "There is certainly no indication of any cooperation between Black and my office," the City Manager said.

"Will you direct correspondence to him?" Carter asked.

"I directed this to him and he didn't comply," Singer responded.

The City Manager agreed, however, that he had no alternative but to exercise control over the police. He reiterated that his resignation "still stands under those circumstances. . . ." This statement caused Councilman Rodriguez to ask where the resignation was. (Earlier in the meeting the City Clerk had presented petitions signed by 468 people, asking the Council to accept Singer's resignation.)

The Mayor said he had the resignation . . . but it was not for long. Irked by Rodriguez' question, Singer walked over to Simpson, picked up the resignation, saying, "On second thought I withdraw my resignation and give the Council the opportunity to fire me if they wish!" The Mayor then remarked, "Looks like we're back to status quo. Black is restored to duty for ninety days, and we have no resignation from the City Manager." Shortly thereafter the meeting ended.

As things stood at this point Singer and Black each appeared to have the support of two members of the Council, with Chandler the unknown quantity. While Rodriguez' antagonism to the Manager was long standing, the Manager's refusal to go along completely with the Council's order to reinstate Black had particularly nettled him. "What do you do when the Manager refuses to accept a Council order?" he asked. This intransigence had also irritated Carter, although it was not clear how he would have voted in a showdown. Not even Rodriguez, however, was prepared to force the issue. Little as he would have objected to

Singer's leaving, he realized that the Manager had a "lot of friends in town." He didn't think it wise to press the matter.

Singer Assumes Control of Police

Thoroughly angered, Singer the next day reasserted his control over the Police Department with a vengeance. On the bulletin board was the following order to the Police Chief:

> Until further notice from this office you are to obey the following orders: (1) Any orders from you to the police department, or any of its members, shall first be submitted in duplicate to the office of the city manager for approval. No order or instruction by you shall be effective unless it has such approval. (2) In the absence of the city manager or the assistant city manager you shall submit such orders to the assistant chief of police for approval. (3) In the case of emergency all orders will be issued by the assistant chief of police or that officer who is in charge of the current shift. . . .

In response Chief Black signed and posted the following statement: "Since I am unable by this directive to issue any orders I suggest to all members of the police department that they comply."

Providing his own kind of harassment, Black followed the order scrupulously, sending something for approval to the Manager "every fifteen minutes," with a duplicate to each Councilman. Furthermore, as the *Times* reported, Black's strategy was to suggest three orders covering "certified hot potato issues." He proposed that the Department return to one-man patrol cars instead of the Singer-ordered two-man cars; that a selective enforcement program be reinstituted; and that an officer be reassigned to a regular parking enforcement beat. About the last item, Black commented, "They took the parking patrol man off his beat in May and gave him other duties . . . parking has become commonly improper throughout the city."

To these proposals, the Assistant City Manager responded for Singer with just eight words. "Not approved. Present procedures will remain in effect." The next day Black came back with the same type of proposals, and so the battle went.

A Challenge to the "Old Guard"?

As Black and Singer continued their tug of war, the *Times* on June 7 published an editorial that stirred many in the community. Provocatively titled, "Who Owns Valley?" it fed fuel to Black's claim that he was fired for enforcing the law equitably. The editorial declared:

> What is being challenged is the Old Guard—the people who have been here for decades, if not generations, by the people who have only been here for years (not decades).

This controversy is being waged with symbols. As the elephant is the symbol of the Republican party, City Manager Jack Singer has been cast as the symbol of the Old Guard. As the donkey is the symbol of the Democratic party, Police Chief Bill Black has become the symbol of the challengers. . . .

As the *Times* had noted before the storm ever blew up, Valley was trying to make up its mind as to how much traffic law enforcement it wished to have. As the publication in the *Times* of the weekly "honor roll" of traffic violators showed to all, there were no sacred cows in the book of Bill Black. North side, south side, speeders, and stop jumpers all looked alike to him. . . .

Sympathetic to the Council many citizens interpreted the pro-Black movement as a junior-grade revolution. They did not understand that what was wanted was fair play for all hands. And they began to fan the very flames which they sought to put out.

They used such terribly ill-advised words as "rabble." They implied that only long-time residents are true citizens of Valley and that new-comers are like children—not really entitled to vote. Some who should know better even used epithets which in a bar room would be strong enough to start a free-for-all brawl. . . .

The calm will finally come when the people generally, are con-vinced that equality before law is truly the settled policy. It will quiet when the newer citizens finally demonstrate that they are a constructive force in the community—as they are. It will be history when all of the older residents say—and mean it—that Valley be-longs to everyone who lives in it.

The editorial, penned by the *Times* editor himself, was bitterly criticized. The newspaper was accused of stirring up controversy. City Manager Singer did not feel that these were the real issues, and most of the councilmen were resentful. (However Councilman Simpson did say the community was "sensitive" and Carter that it was "clannish.") On the other hand, the *Times* editorial pro-vided aid and comfort to the Black forces. The point was almost exactly that which Black had been making. The *Times* editorial helped to keep the Black controversy fierce and flaming. This in itself caused the *Times* to be severely criticized by (1) those concerned with the ugly spectacle of a fiercely divided city, and (2) those who supported the Manager.[23]

[23]Asked in 1958 if he had any second thoughts about the editorial, the *Times* editor said he considered it to be generally valid. He reported that there was no question the "somebodys" were treated differently than the "nobodys," as he thought was true in every community. In the editorial he had sought to point out to the "somebodys" that privileges carried responsibilities as well.
One councilman has labeled the editorial "hogwash." The "Old Guard vs. New Guard business was a nice simple answer, but far too simple. . . . I think the *Times* bears a good deal of responsibility for the way this whole thing developed. I don't blame them for breaking the story when they got it. I do blame them for deliberately promoting community divisions with this kind of talk, north versus south, etc."

A few days later Professor Jennings learned that he had received a Fulbright grant. He was to go to The Netherlands for a year, leaving in August. Jennings got the announcement on Saturday, June 9, and immediately informed the newspapers that he would submit his resignation to the City Clerk on Monday. He pointed out that his resignation would not come as a surprise to his colleagues. He had told them the previous September of his application for the grant. "While we shall not be leaving immediately," he said, "I feel it is imperative that a full council be able to consider a replacement in the near future. Beginning soon one or perhaps occasionally two members at a time will be away on vacation."

RESIGNATIONS AND A DISMISSAL

The nearness of summer made it necessary for Valley's Council to settle the Black case quickly. Councilman Carter was to be gone throughout July, and Mayor Simpson had scheduled a trip to Hawaii for six weeks in June and July.

Two days after Professor Jennings had announced his resignation, the Council filled his position. The new appointee was suggested by the same group of citizens (convened by Cassius Bolt) that had put up Chandler. He was a resident of 37 years, Allen Campbell, a former Councilman and a real estate man. (Black said sometime later that of the groups who opposed him, none was so powerful and bitterly antagonistic as the real estate people.) The nomination of Campbell, who by his background certainly seemed to fit the Old Guard mold described by the *Times*, was made by new Councilman Chandler. The nomination was seconded by Carter, and these two were joined by Mayor Simpson in the vote. Councilman Rodriguez was absent because of the death of his father-in-law. If he had been present, however, Rodriguez would not have opposed Campbell's appointment. He had grown up with Campbell, talked to him about Council problems, and privately felt that Campbell might be on his side.

The supporters of Black again did nothing to advance a candidate of their own. It happened that Black was the personal leader and symbol of a new and hastily organized group of people who were not really close to the city government's power centers. As one Councilman recalled, "I had never seen the people who supported Black at a Council meeting before. I think that was the first time they had ever thought about city government." Some of these persons were the new commuters.

The Pressure on Rodriguez

Who could provide the leadership for the Black supporters that would enable them to rival the Council majority? Rodriguez was the most conspicuous possibility. However, there were two reasons why he was not particularly interested in assuming such responsibility. In the first place, he was not as heavily committed to the Black cause as his public utterances might have suggested. He thought the method of dismissing Black was wrong and was prepared to support his opinion with his vote. Having professional responsibilities outside Valley, however, he was not interested in waging the all-out fight necessary to keep Black in his position. "If they had simply taken the vote to dismiss at the public hearing, I would have voted my way and that would have been that," he later commented. "I wouldn't have made a further fight."

Second, Rodriguez himself was feeling tremendous pressures from the other side. "People I had never seen before in the community told me I was public enemy no. 1," he recalled. His wife, a city school teacher, felt a change in her treatment. And the Xerxes land title firm for which he worked was visited by a delegation of Valley's real estate men threatening to withdraw their business unless Rodriguez was dismissed. He was not fired. The firm's President had said, "I won't *ask* you to quit." But there were no salary increases.

That left Black the obvious man to take the leadership. However, he was still an administrative officer of the city. Even though he was involved in one of the biggest political fights of the town's history, this status imposed certain restraints on his behavior. He could not, he believed, engage actively now in a struggle over Council appointments, and he did not.

Singer Resigns

The Black affair was resumed shortly after Allen Campbell assumed his seat on the Council at 2:14 P.M., June 13. City Manager Singer reopened the problem himself when he reminded the Council that Black's status was not yet legally clear. The City Attorney then said that it would be necessary for the Council to take a definite action on the Manager's recommendation of dismissal, either approving or disapproving. He felt that the Carter compromise ought to be rescinded and direct action taken.

Singer then reported to the Council that the situation in the Police Department was "unhealthy" and that a "material split within the Department" was developing. He said two officers would be willing to appear before the Council and that there were rumors six planned to turn in their badges. "I don't enjoy making this request again, nor do I enjoy anything about this whole situation. I do not take this as a stand or a pressure move, but I am seriously concerned with what is happening to the Police Department," he continued. He said that he and the Assistant City Manager were resigning again.

Singer did not feel physically capable of continuing. Furthermore, the controversy was having an effect on his entire family. His child had been threatened in school; and he was not prepared to make further personal sacrifices, though he was still reluctant to leave Valley. In his formal statement, Singer declared that it was "evident" that no effort was to be made to resolve the "personnel problem that exists and becomes more serious with passing of time." He said his work could be of "little effect or benefit under existing circumstances." The Assistant City Manager simply asked that his resignation be effective in thirty days.

However, the request for definite Council action got nowhere. Mayor Simpson declared that any decision would have to await the return of Councilman Rodriguez. Speaking to Singer, Councilman Chandler said he had hoped the Manager would give the Council "a little longer—at least until all the Council members return from their vacations." But Singer said, "I live with this 24 hours a day. The phone is busy all day at the office and doesn't stop even after I go home. I cannot physically or constitutionally live with it any longer." Newly-seated Councilman Campbell said he and others had appreciated Singer's efforts. Would it be possible, he asked, for the Manager to take a month or six-week vacation and let the Assistant assume responsibility? Singer said he wished he could accept but he felt that the budget and other items of business had been delayed too long. Furthermore, he declared that he could not ask the Assistant City Manager to stay. The Assistant, he reported, had been "literally living on dietary supplements and high potency shots—he has not been able to eat or sleep for some time."

Thus the session ended with no decision. This time Singer and his Assistant filed their resignations with the City Clerk.

Black Challenges Singer

Police Chief Black lost no time issuing a statement the next day. He denied that there was a significant split in the Department and said, "Even assuming the accuracy of Mr. Singer's statement, more than eighty percent of my department is solidly behind the policies which I have attempted to institute. . . ." Black went on to say that he had begun again a training program with "police courtesy" a part of the curriculum, had gotten in contact with the president of the local insurance adjusters association to straighten out the records problem, and had attempted to be "co-operative" with the City Manager and "obedient to every order."

The next day, Thursday, Singer was completely discouraged, and he began to clean out his desk at City Hall. During the day he had gotten a phone call telling him his eighth grade daughter had been slapped and roughed up by boys in a school bus coming home on the final day of school.[24] She was near hysteria but uninjured. For Singer this was a final straw. His main interest was simply to get away and forget the whole affair. That included a budget session of the Council, which was scheduled for Friday night. Budget preparation was about six weeks behind schedule, but neither Singer nor his Assistant had any desire to participate further in city matters.

On Friday City Manager Singer did not go up to his office. During the day, however, he was visited at home by a group of citizens, led by new Councilman Allen Campbell. The meeting was relatively brief. Campbell said, "Jack, we

[24]Chief Black says this did not happen. "An investigation by the Assistant Chief . . . showed that this was not the case. Singer's daughter had been one of several children struck on the head by books in the hands of other youngsters celebrating the last day of school. . . . This is an example of the great distortion which took place. . . ."

don't ask for anything more right now. We just want you to be at the Council meeting tonight. That's all. Will you do that?" Singer remonstrated but finally agreed to go to the meeting.

Final Decision

The extent to which the new appointments had been decisive in settling the Black affair was seen at the Council meeting that night. Mayor Simpson was insistent that there be a final resolution of the problem, as he was leaving the next day for his month and a half in Honolulu. No elaborate preparations had been necessary. Simpson, Chandler, and Campbell met briefly before the session, as Mayor Simpson recalls; the principal question was who would introduce the resolution supporting the Manager. Chandler said he would do so. Campbell said he would second. Councilman Carter, who had nominated Chandler and who seconded Campbell's nomination, was not consulted and knew first about the changed outlook when Chandler spoke in Council meeting.

That night the Council Chamber was filled to capacity. Police guards turned away others who sought to enter.

As planned, Councilman Chandler took the initiative. After explaining that he lived on the "north side" and that his interest was in preserving Valley, he declared that he had come to conclude that the real issue, "regardless of who the Manager is," was the council-manager form of government in Valley. He emphasized that he brought little personal emotion to the situation, as he had seen neither the Manager nor the Police Chief before the previous week. Primarily he felt that the council-manager form was worth fighting for, as it was the only kind of government "capable of handling an area that is growing rapidly like Valley is." Chandler reminded the audience that he had served as Mayor in a town operating under the commission form of government, "and you wouldn't want it."

The Council's duty was reasonably clear, Chandler continued. As in a business, the Council held the Manager responsible for the operation of city affairs. As long as the Council had confidence in its Manager, it had the obligation to stand behind his handling of personnel matters. "The Council," he said, "approved the Manager's recommendation before—please, let's have no applause or boos—I think the Council should ratify the Manager's recommendation." He then made the formal motion endorsing the dismissal of Police Chief Black, who was in the audience with his attorney.

The new cut of the Council was indicated when Councilman Campbell, the man who had led the delegation to Singer, took the floor. Declaring his great respect for Councilman Chandler, Campbell went on to say that he too felt the Council had an obligation to back the office of City Manager, regardless of the occupant. He said he recognized the effectiveness of the Police Department's work in protecting "lives and property" in Valley. Yet, Campbell stated, "I don't believe . . . in the Chief of Police telling the Council what to do," an obvious reference to Black's oratory in the earlier hearings. "I'm sure Black is making every effort to do his best, and I believe he's a man who will probably go far— somewhere but not in Valley. . . . I'm going to second the motion." Campbell's second sealed the Police Chief's defeat. Mayor Simpson's vote would give the Singer position a three-to-two majority in the Council.

Before the vote was taken, however, Councilman Carter again stated his feeling that he wanted to keep both the Manager and the Chief. The Council had agreed to dismissal, Carter said, "only if . . . Black failed to mend his ways. So far there has been nothing but improvement," he asserted. The City Attorney again emphasized that the Carter compromise had not been satisfactory in that it neither ratified nor rejected the Manager's action.

Black's attorney then spoke. The lawyer declared that there was no need for Council action, because the Manager had not formally dismissed the Chief but had merely appointed an acting Chief. At the very least, he said, new hearings were required because of the change in the membership of the Council and the new allegations made against Black. The City Attorney responded that since personnel rules in the city were not formalized by law, it was unnecessary for the Manager to follow any specific procedure, and on the same grounds it was not required that the Council hold further hearings. Some of the conflict might have been avoided, the Attorney observed, if the dismissal steps had been spelled out in greater detail. Nevertheless, "we must operate within the framework of these laws."

In the two votes that were taken, the Singer victory was complete. First, the ratification of Black's dismissal was voted by Mayor Simpson and the two new members of the Council; then, by the same majority, the resignations of Singer and his Assistant were refused.

After the meeting, Black commented that "the city government of Valley now consists of Jack Singer."

AFTERMATH

Although the three-to-two decision of the Council marked the end of Black's tenure as Valley's Police Chief, it was almost a year before the issue—and the former Chief—receded from public attention.

Almost immediately after Black's dismissal his supporters began to organize formally a Better Government League, which was to be a "non-profit continuing citizen group." As the president of the League later said, the organization was created as a counter-balance to the "very few" who held political power. The president also said:

> New people have come to our town who owe no allegiance, social or otherwise, to the families long entrenched. A few efforts have been made to right some of the wrongs, but they lacked the proper organization to accomplish anything.

> The incident which triggered the formation of the Better Government League was the dismissal, rehiring and again dismissal of William Black as chief of police. It is not important whether Black

was a good or bad chief—it was the manifest injustice of the whole thing which made a few people band together in an honest effort to bring about a better government. Our name means exactly what it says.

Perhaps the best-known personality in the new League was former Mayor Crispin Lloyd, who was named Chairman of the Board. The membership of the new organization included a number of the newer residents and some older residents who had taken the lead in circulating petitions for Black when his dismissal had first been announced.

The core members of the group had little connection with either of the local political party organizations. Most had taken little part in civic affairs before. One of the members was an automobile salesman; another had a soft-water service route. Several wives were active in the group.

The League embarked on a strenuous program to secure its first objective, "fair treatment" for Black. It retained an attorney to press the case for the deposed Police Chief in the courts. At the attorney's suggestion, the League also went directly to the people by circulating petitions for an initiative election on a civil service ordinance. The ordinance would have established a standard merit system requiring formal charges and procedures for employees, whose dismissal could only be effected on specified grounds. Such civil service protection against discharge was to be conferred on all city department heads who had been in office on May 1, 1956, the day Black's dismissal had first been raised with the Council by the City Manager. The proposed legislation would thus have the effect of putting Black back in office and giving him the job security of civil service rules and procedures.

The ordinance proposed was one modeled after that in operation in Bakersfield, California, whose Chief had taken a special interest in Black's problem. He appeared before the League, explained what he considerd to be civil service advantages, and urged the League membership to push for its adoption. However, it was two months after Black's dismissal before the circulation of petitions finally began. Since direct legislation procedures in California require that fifteen percent of the registered electorate sign petitions for an election on such a proposal, it was anticipated that 1,300 signatures would be needed. Later, the total registrations proved to be 10,456 and 1,569 signatures were necessary. There was hope that the required number could be obtained quickly, inasmuch as about two months were required to arrange for the actual election once the petitions had been certified. However, it was six months later, the middle of January, before the Better Government League finally qualified the measure for an April 2, 1957, ballot.[25]

---

[25]The *Times* published the names of all the signers and made an analysis of their residences. "The Country Club might be considered the center of social status and power in the community," the *Times* editor has said, "and as one moved north from that point, the number of signers picked up from zero proportionally with the distance traveled. There were some modest exceptions, of course, but we were very much struck with the relationship we discovered."

Meanwhile the circulation of the petitions was not lost on the City Council. During August it had the City Manager conduct a secret poll of Valley's 204 municipal employees to find out their attitudes about the Better Government League's proposed ordinance. While the League argued that "the public should decide," the councilmen said the people most concerned were the employees themselves. The councilmen opened the ballots and found that an overwhelming majority of the 174 voting opposed the ordinance. Twenty-nine favored it. Later, a Municipal Employees Association was formed. Its Board of Directors campaigned actively against the proposed ordinance.

In the intervening months, Bill Black played an active role in the initiative campaign. Shortly after his return from a trip East, he made the first of several appearances at the Council, speaking as a "private citizen." He made several efforts to secure the election of new councilmen (to replace the three appointees). He made speeches at Council meetings for the dismissal of City Manager Singer. On one occasion he accused Singer of lying, spreading false rumors, committing felonious acts, and of incompetency. The statement was so hot that the newspapers would not print it for fear of libel. Nevertheless, the former Chief did have many of his statements published in the local press. He was by all odds the most quoted man before the April 2 election. The Manager made no statements on the election. As to the reasons Black stayed in Valley to fight, he said in statements that he did not want to be a "deserter." He continued:

> The Better Government League came into being to promote fair government for the citizens; I did not give birth to the BGL, but I have nurtured it since it came into our midst because it is the tangible expression of the minds of people for impartial government.
>
> A Chief of Police is a public figure; he can do things to improve a city, to help the citizens; that is the reason, and only that, for my remaining in Valley. I am not asking for benefits or privileges; I am asking for myself and the people only the rights guaranteed by the Constitution of the United States. To obtain, guard, and defend these rights, our just heritage, I have stayed in this City.

As long as Black stayed in Valley and carried much of the fight for the passage of the initiative ordinance, it was almost inevitable that opposition should center on him.[26] Two organizations were created specifically to fight the proposal. One, the April Second Committee, included three ex-Mayors in its membership and was well financed. The other, coming into battle later and playing a lesser role, was the Young Guard.

Both groups declared the issue was the former Police Chief and that the proposed ordinance was in his interest and not those of the city employees. The Chief, furthermore, was characterized as a "demagogue." In the frenzied activity, the anti-Black groups did pick up temporarily the support of Councilman Andy

[26]Many people in Valley, incidentally, felt that Black lost a great deal of community support because of his free-swinging political activity. Among these people was Councilman Rodriguez, who did not participate at all in the campaign.

Carter. Friend of Black on both the critical votes in the Council, Carter said a few days before the election that he had changed his mind and was no longer on the side of the former Chief. He said Black's "wild and intemperate utterances" had demonstrated that he was "unfit to lead any City Department, let alone a quasi-military organization such as the Police Department." He would vote against the ordinance, Carter declared, first, because he had no confidence in Black, and second, because "our present form of Council, City Manager government is the best for our city."

By April 2, 1957, the charges and counter-charges were flying thick and fast. Many on both sides were extreme, emotional, and provocative. But there was no question of citizen apathy. The newspapers ran thousands of inches of argument, dutifully quoting any of the principal spokesmen and printing scores of letters, the majority of which seemed to be in opposition to Black. So saturating was Valley's first experience with direct democracy that the *Times* commented on election eve that the experience had been "exhausting." Yet the newspaper also said that the consequence had been a complete discussion of the issues and "nothing like it could have been had in any other way." The editor added that the people were now "ready for the question."

The election brought the largest turnout in the city's history in a purely local contest, with 62 percent of those eligible voting. No other proposition or office was contested. The civil service initiative was defeated 4,312 votes to 3,090, with the Better Government League winning in only one of seven precincts. An analysis of the votes in the city again suggested that, in political terms, the split between the north and the south had some significance. How much of it had been caused by the election campaign and by Black's resistance was impossible to determine. At any rate, one of the north side precincts which had its polling place in a public housing project was the lone supporter of the proposition by a margin of 425 to 319. The initiative's worst defeat occurred in a distinctly south side precinct where the vote was 627 against, 108 for. Another south side precinct registered a four to one vote against, whereas the four other precincts in the city were more evenly divided.

The former Chief's own feeling was that the election occurred too late to provide any accurate index of the nature of his support at the time of dismissal. "If the election had been held within ninety days or so of my final discharge, I think I would have won. As it was, the matter dragged on, and interest and indignation deteriorated," he commented later.

The Court Fight

In the latter part of August 1956, the attorney for the Better Government League obtained a writ of mandate from the Superior Court demanding that Black be reinstated or that a proper hearing be granted. To that the city filed a demurrer. A series of lengthy court actions ended with a decision favorable to the city. Black decided in 1959 "to let the matter drop since it would cost a considerable amount of money to press it further, and, too, one of my ardent [Valley] sponsors passed away . . . her will was never found, yet I took her to her attorney so she could make some changes in it. An interesting and mysterious case well fitting into the intrigues of the community as I so well knew it."

Later Events

Manager Singer's appointee as Acting Police Chief continued in charge of the Department until the defeat of the civil service proposal provided assurance that Black would not be returned to his job. Singer then moved rapidly to select a new Chief. Again he went outside the Department, appointing a man who had been serving as Assistant Chief in a neighboring city of 50,000. Singer said he believed the second recruitment program had yielded a better group of men. As with the Black appointment, a Screening Board was used. This time, however, the Council joined the interviewing sessions and thus participated directly in the selection of William Black's successor.

In June 1962 the new Police Chief was still serving in Valley, and so was City Manager Singer. Things were calm in the Police Department, and the Manager's record of getting along well with city employees—and almost everyone else—was more conspicuous with the passage of six more years.

The Better Government League had disappeared. Following the high point of community conflict over Black in 1956, there had been six changes on the City Council in eleven months, all vacancies being filled by appointment. Chandler became Mayor and proved to be somewhat stronger in his management of Council meetings. When the former Chief made one of his later "private citizen" appearances before the Council to read a lengthy prepared statement, Chandler, after a few minutes, gaveled for silence and told Black to file the rest of his prepared statement with the Clerk. It was the first time that Black's oratory at Council meetings or hearings had been treated this way. Occupying the seat of former Mayor Simpson was the operator of a service station "across from City Hall" who was also a director of the Chamber of Commerce, a member of a Protestant congregation, and a member of the Elks and Rotary. He had been appointed against the wishes of the Better Government League, which, making its first effort to advance a candidate for appointment, had suggested former Mayor Lloyd.

Realtor Campbell, a Rotarian like Chandler and like Simpson's successor, announced his resignation as Councilman in April 1957, after the civil service initiative proposal had gone down to defeat. Council membership had been too great a drain on his time, he said. Campbell emphasized that he was leaving the city in sound condition again and in the hands of three good men in whom he had "all the confidence in the world." Specifically omitted from his statement was the name of Councilman Joe Rodriguez.

Within a week Councilman Rodriguez submitted his resignation. Senior member of the Council by virtue of three years service, Rodriguez said that the pressures directed against him and his family had been too great. "People in Valley, and I suppose other towns as well," he observed, "tend to let a man's actions in the role of councilman influence their relationships toward him as an individual and toward his family. This creates hardship on a councilman's family and affects friendships of long standing." Shortly after his resignation, Rodriguez received a promotion. Appointed to succeed Rodriguez and Campbell were another Mexican-American and a retired resident of the north side. In April 1958 regular municipal elections were held. The Better Government League supported a slate against the appointed incumbents. Its slate was defeated by three to one. Shortly after this, the Better Government League, dwindling in size, became involved in a divisive controversy over a freeway location. By 1962 it no longer existed.

Lasting Scars

Some of the leading supporters of Black in 1956 would carry lasting scars as a result of Valley's most intense civic controversy. It was considered unlikely that the attorney who had acted for the Better Government League would ever develop a substantial practice in the city. The automobile salesman's prominent connection with the pro-Black forces apparently raised the possibility that some citizens would be less inclined to buy cars from his employer, and he lost his job and left town for a time. The pro-Black leader who operated a soft-water service route ran into difficulties at the height of the controversy when one of two south side housewives reported to his employer that they would not let such a man as he enter their homes.

Black himself reported troubles in finding another job. In May 1958 he commented: "I'd be working right now if I had signed that resignation paper at the Hollywood Knickerbocker. Chiefs who have been complete busts on their jobs and have resigned have been appointed in other cities at higher salaries. I know because I have competed against them . . . and lost. I chose to fight something I considered wrong and now no manager wants to touch me." He finally got only a six-months' temporary assignment in a California city of 10,000 to reorganize a small department. The City Manager there later praised his work highly. "He did everything I asked of him, and we had a most pleasant relationship," he said. In 1959 Black accepted a professorship of police science at a state college in the west.

By June 1962 Valley's turbulent days seemed far away. But many leading citizens of Valley still shuddered when they recalled the 1956 controversy about Chief Black. Even to men who had not been strongly active on either side, it seemed in retrospect as if the community and its government had been threatened with disintegration by the intensity of the fight and by the nature of the charges and counter-charges. People who had lived together and accepted one another for years had begun to look at one another with hostility and suspicion, it was claimed. Even the small, comradely reportorial staff of the *Times* had felt the impact of the community's split on the issue, some reporters treating others with the reserve necessary when associating with a member of an enemy force.

Some citizens maintained that the editor and publisher of the *Times* had also felt the whip of public indignation from the affair that the newspaper had had a hand in creating. Originally "playing" the controversy for all it was worth in news value, the *Times* had drawn increasing criticism from the pro-Manager side for irresponsibly encouraging a bitter community dispute that at times had seemed about to lead to outbreaks of violence. The newspaper's treatment of the later phases of the matter had been more subdued, and some former council-men said in 1962 that the editor and publisher had never since sought to whip up unnecessary controversy about governmental affairs.

City Manager Singer believed that some of the leading citizens of Valley had also learned something from the Black controversy—something about the cost of keeping silent on controversial public questions and letting the Manager and the Council bear alone the brunt of running the government. Singer reported in 1962:

> The Chamber of Commerce is now working in active cooperation with the City Council and the City administration, and has stated to the public several times that it would never again allow such a thing to happen in this community. It would stand in support of the City and the administration to prevent a recurrence.

OVERRING
CORRECTION SLIP

Register No.	Cashier	Day	Date

Transaction No. _____

Dept. No.

Rung As: $ _____

Should Be: $ _____

Total Overring $ _____

Manager's Signature: _____

Form No. 556787 NCR Corp.   Order Toll Free 800-5430-8130   In Ohio 800-762-6517

Chapter Fifteen

TASK 13 POLICE AND THEIR COMMUNITY

The issue of "community control" of the police has of late come to dominate any discussion of police-community relations, just as a few years ago such a discussion focused largely on "civilian review boards." The argument is that both better police protection and better police conduct can only be insured by giving neighborhoods control over their own police. In this way, the police will be responsive to the needs of the local citizens—the community will develop both policies for the exercise of police discretion and methods for the restraint or correction of police misconduct.

It is difficult to evaluate this policy since, to a great extent, it is a slogan rather than a program.[1]

SYNOPSIS

One continues to hear the rhetorical query of those policemen who still remain rigidly connected with yesterday's system: "How soon can we get the baloney over with and get back to doing police work?" But who is to say what form modern police work will take? Certainly policemen for decades have shown concern that "some people would like to make us into social workers." Perhaps it seemed so, but most rational people realize that someone must enforce the law; at least enforce it with someone else. And yet one must consider the potential of a Family Crisis Intervention Unit that may reduce felonious assaults and homicides resulting from family disturbances in a high-risk area by as much as twenty-five, fifty, or even seventy-five percent. Who is to say that this is not crime prevention in its purest form? And who can place a true value on taking a youngster for a ride in a police car, or spending an evening with a group in some citizen's home? Is the cop on campus really changing student attitudes, and does it really make any difference whether or not policemen communicate effectively with the community, especially the minority community?

We submit that these questions are not questions at all, for the answers are apparent. These programs are capable of changing attitudes, both within the police service and within the community. The degree of change becomes the challenge for creative police administrators. And that degree of change is decidedly proportional

[1]James Q. Wilson, *Thinking About Crime* (New York: Basic Books, Inc., 1975).

to the philosophical commitment of the administration, coupled with commitment, support, and skills from the highest-ranking officer to the newest recruit.

In this chapter we discuss several models, and there are scores of others with which many readers are familiar. Models are cited, for they are most often examples of successful programs. Models are developed for specific times and places, however, and while these ideas as such are transferable, we suggest that they are seldom applicable in their entirety to other situations without modification.

It is our intent to develop support for the hypothesis that *police-community relations* are the critical link, the difference between cooperation and noncooperation, interest and disinterest, respect and disrespect, and, finally, police success and police failure. We will explore a number of innovative programs and will also approach the question of training which we believe to be most paramount in any community relations program. For in the end it is not the philosophy of a chief alone that will motivate his officers to effective police-community relations, but rather their own understanding of the problem and their own commitment to the program and to the community.

INTRODUCTION

In the time frame beginning with the middle 1950s to the present, this business of police and their community has been in a mode of continuing, albeit slow, philosophical change. Public relations became community relations and the parameters encompassing community relations have been pushed out to accommodate new concepts. Programs have been added and programs have been deleted as agencies searched for magic formulas that would begin to turn back the tide of negativism and lack of confidence in the police. In more recent years, such terms as *physical planning* and *crime prevention* have become synonymous with community relations. Policemen at all levels have found themselves speaking to small neighborhood groups; off-duty police officers work in city recreation programs; and many high schools have full-time officers assigned to them.

It has become quite clear that police agencies will never have sufficient resources to be all things to all people and that priorities will continually need to be examined to ensure that allocations of manpower are determined by the most accurate up-to-date information. Obviously, people from neighborhoods that feel most comfortable with the police are also most likely to be cooperative in assisting the police and each other, and these neighborhoods are likely to require less intensive policing than do other less cooperative areas. To carry this further, it is apparent that socioeconomically lower-class neighborhoods, especially in large metropolitan areas, are less likely to have confidence in the police as compared with the more affluent urban and suburban middle-class neighborhoods, where conflicts are not so likely to occur.

It is a fact of life then that *police community relations* (PCR) for the most part connotes programs designed to bring the police officer into closer, more positive contact with barrio and ghetto dwellers; to reduce conflict so that there is less need for *overpolicing* and to enhance the police officer's image as a protector first rather than *enforcer*.

It is in the ghetto and barrio where officers are more likely to be the focal point upon which the hopelessness and frustration that accompany poverty is openly targeted. "Things are bad for me because of the government. You are the government. Therefore, you are the reason for my problems."

Former centers of powerlessness however are finding and expressing new power through a relatively new idealism that has finally reached down from the university and other formal institutions to the ghetto and barrio. Gang members are now likely to be referred to and refer to themselves as club members or *car club* members though there may not be any cars.

These gangs have found power in that regularly constituted agencies are likely to come to their aid in dealing with the police—after the fact. With this and other social changes, the police have tended to effect a more defensive stance. Institutions and agencies are very quick to take up the cry of *police brutality, overpolicing* and the like, and the police officer feels that he must be ever prepared to defend his actions and the policies of his organization.

The police officer's rhetorical question, "Why can't I enforce the law the same in the poor areas as I do in the rest of the city?" is heard more often as are other equally frustrating queries from street people, who ask no one in particular, "Why do the cops pick on us?"

And so there is good reason to concentrate PCR efforts in the areas of most prominent need, not only with the citizens who live there but with those officers who serve there as well.

This is not to say that the police who serve in white middle-class neighborhoods are free to ignore the problem, for they are not. The relationship that exists between the police and any community served is not to be regarded lightly.

Without the support of its citizens, a city police force, regardless of size, is not likely to be effective.

There has been a tendency in the past at least to identify community support primarily with citizen-police cooperation, with crime prevention, and perhaps even with the absence of verbal and physical assault. However, as we become more conscious of the critical need to attract high-quality young men and women into the police service, as well as retain them, other facets become graphically apparent. The President's Commission on Law Enforcement and Administration of Justice put it this way in its 1967 report:

> Hostility, or even lack of confidence of a significant portion of the public, has extremely serious implications for the police. These attitudes interfere with recruiting, since able young men generally seek occupations which are not inordinately dangerous and which have the respect and support of their relatives and friends.
>
> Public hostility affects morale and makes police officers less enthusiastic about doing their job well. It may lead some officers to leave the force, to accept more prestigious or less demanding employment.[2]

The development of community support through the conscious improvement of police-community relations has shown itself not to be just one more front office idea to take up the field officer's time. Rather, it emerges as a prime target in the survival of not only police departments but entire communities where people can live, work, and play—in confidence and harmony.

The awareness of the importance of a good public image is not new, even to this century. Sir Robert Peel, the father of modern law enforcement, gave recognition in the early 1800s to the concept that the manner in which the police were viewed was likely to influence the degree of cooperation that they were likely to receive. He emphasized as a principle of police organization that "no quality is more indispensable than a command of temper; a quiet determined manner has more effect than violent action."[3]

---

[2]The President's Commission on Law Enforcement and Administration of Justice, *Task Force Report: The Police* (Washington, D.C.: U.S. Government Printing Office, 1967), p. 144.

[3]Attributed to Sir Robert Peel.

In spite of the rich inheritance from Sir Robert Peel and the legion of able police administrators who followed, attempts to gain greater community effectiveness through formalized police-community programs were many decades arriving. While the need for police-community cooperation has been well recognized since those early times, apparently events as drastic as those occurring during the civil unrest of the 1950s and 1960s were needed to bring into focus the critical need for such formalized programs.

POLICE-COMMUNITY RELATIONS VERSUS PUBLIC RELATIONS

Earlier police texts have generally dealt with the relationship between the police and the community as primarily being one of "public relations." One such listed the following as goals for a public relations program:

> *Public Understanding.* This is primarily an educational goal. It presupposes that an informed citizenry is basic to effective law enforcement.
>
> *Public Confidence.* This is primarily a psychological goal. It involves the building of citizen trust and respect for the policemen and police department.
>
> *Public Support.* Such support may take many forms such as compliance with the law, assistance in police investigations, and backing of measures to improve the police service.[4]

These goals are still valid, of course, but it must be recognized that there are major differences in *public relations* as compared with *police-community relations* programs where goals have been formulated as follows:

1. To encourage police-citizen partnership in the cause of crime prevention.

2. To foster and improve communication and mutual understanding between the police and the total community.

3. To promote interprofessional approaches to the solution of community problems, and stress the principle that the administration of justice is a total community responsibility.

4. To enhance cooperation among the police, prosecution, the courts, and corrections.

[4]Institute for Training in Municipal Administration, *Municipal Police Administration*, 5th ed. (Chicago: The International City Manager's Association, 1961), p. 476.

5. To assist police and other community leaders to achieve an understanding of the nature and causes of complex problems in people-to-people relations, and especially to improve police-minority group relationships.

6. To strengthen implementation of equal protection under the law for all persons.[5]

Public relations is essentially a one-way communication program embracing the concept that people are more likely to support those things that they understand. *Police-community relations,* on the other hand, involve two-way communication with the specific intent of bringing about change and modification. This change is desirable on the part of not only the public but the police as well.

The need for an active *public relations* program has not diminished with the formalization of police-community relations. If anything, the priority of its importance to the total law enforcement program is even greater than in earlier years. The police are continually called upon to perform many tasks, the results of which often take on negative overtones, especially when overshadowed by half truths and conjecture by the uninformed or the ill informed. Therefore, much clarification is needed and can best reach the greatest number of people in the most expedient manner through an active public relations program.

It must be recognized, however, that successful organizations are those that are flexible enough to accommodate to changing needs and to change themselves. Recognizing the need for change is the first step in the process, and this recognition is accomplished through feedback. The best feedback is often the most direct, and in this case it involves the bringing together of active members of the police department and active members of the community in a two-way communication situation. Obviously, there is a certain amount of *public relations* in *police-community relations;* a communication of the kind of goals and responsibilities held by the police and the method by which they are most likely to be accomplished. On the other hand, with two-way conversation the police learn something of how they and their actions are perceived and, if they are properly alert, how they can better attain certain goals in a more acceptable manner.

Patrol-level officers and citizens in their own neighborhoods are the two most basic or primary elements in the relationship that exists between the police and the community. Obviously, there are many kinds of policemen and equally numerous publics. Some officers instinctively

[5]Paul M. Whisenand, *Police Supervision—Theory and Practice* (Englewood Ciffls, N.J.: Prentice-Hall, Inc., 1971), p. 277.

know how to communicate effectively in a diversity of situations. And, too, some publics have always respected the police. Numerous studies show, however, that in too many clusters, especially in the lower socio-economic groups and the police who serve them, there is little effective communication and little change by either side to accommodate needs of the other.

PCR: A Recommended National Standard

In 1973 the National Advisory Commission Report on Criminal Justice Standards and Goals focused on this aspect of communication in its report, *Police.*

Standard 1.4

COMMUNICATING WITH THE PUBLIC

Every police agency should recognize the importance of bilateral communication with the public and should constantly seek to improve its ability to determine the needs and expectations of the public, to act upon those needs and expectations, and to inform the public of the resulting policies developed to improve delivery of police services.

1. Every police agency should immediately adopt policies and procedures that provide for effective communication with the public through agency employees. Those policies and procedures should insure:
   a. That every employee with duties involving public contact has sufficient information with which to respond to questions regarding agency policies; and
   b. That information he receives is transmitted through the chain of command and acted upon at the appropriate level.

2. Every police agency that has racial and ethnic minority groups of significant size within its jurisdiction should recognize their police needs and should, where appropriate, develop means to insure effective communication with such groups.

3. Every police agency with a substantial non-English-speaking population in its jurisdiction should provide readily available bilingual employees to answer requests for police services. In addition, existing agency programs should be adapted to insure adequate communication between non-English-speaking groups and the police agency.

4. Every police agency with more than 400 employees should establish a specialized unit responsible for maintaining communication with the community. In smaller agencies, this responsibility should be the chief executive's, using whatever agency resources are necessary and appropriate to accomplish the task.

a. The unit should establish lines of communication between the agency and recognized community leaders and should elicit information from the citizen on the street who may feel that he has little voice in government or in the provision of its services.

b. The unit should be no more than one step removed from the chief executive in the chain of command.

c. The unit should identify impediments to communication with the community, research and devise methods to overcome those impediments, and develop programs which facilitate communication between the agency and the community.

d. The unit should conduct constant evaluations of all programs intended to improve communication and should recommend discontinuance of programs when their objectives have been achieved or when another program might more beneficially achieve the identified functional objective.[6]

THE HANDLING OF POLICE-COMMUNITY RELATIONS PROGRAMS

Police-community relations are handled in a variety of ways depending upon a number of factors, such as the department's size, the available manpower, and the orientation of staff-level officers, especially the chief. And in some departments they are simply not handled at all. The President's Commission on Law Enforcement and Administration of Justice indicated that most police agencies were keenly aware of serious community problems but were slow to institute programs to confront them.[7]

Traditional belief in the police service has been that the *complete policeman* can do and will do all jobs. "Every policeman is a community relations officer" has been espoused by many police administrators. In the organizational structure of the police department, the idea that police-community relations are everyone's job most often leads to the *job* being accomplished by no one. "Although, ideally every man on the force should indeed be a community relations officer, he also has a full-time job of patrol or investigation. What is in effect every officer's business can wind up being no one's business."[8]

We are not indicating that because policemen have other full-time assignments and that because they are busy they are free to ignore their individual and personal role in reducing negative and building positive community attitudes toward the police. Rather, we are observing, along with others, that the importance of community support is too great to be looked upon as simply an adjunct to other duties. Therefore, if a police-

[6]The National Advisory Commission on Criminal Justice Standards and Goals, (Washington, D.C.: U.S. Government Printing Office, 1973), pp. 29–30.
[7]President's Commission, *Task Force Report*, p. 150.
[8]*Ibid.*

community relations program is to be successful, responsibility for its direction, coordination, and implementation must be formalized.

In smaller departments, formalization may be in the form of a single person and in some cases even half of one officer's time. We are aware of the staffing constraints on smaller police departments but still must point out the inherent shortcomings of an assignment that receives only part of a man's time. Generally speaking, there is no equitable way to divide an officer's time in half, for there is no logical way to insure the point at which he can drop one function and pick up another. The probable result will be that at best one of the jobs will suffer, and there is a risk that neither will achieve expectations.[9]

Small police departments typically have had to make do with part-time court liaison officers, part-time pistol range masters, part-time lab men, and so on. Perhaps these have enjoyed a measure of success and could be pointed to as examples of why a part-time police-community relations coordinator might be expected to perform equally well. We would counter with two observations: First, these other functions are close-ended in that they can most often be programmed for a specific time and place. Police-community relations, on the other hand, are open-ended and ever changing, and the coordinator must be available at all times. Second, we would gamble that the other "part-time" jobs are in fact not operating at a desirable level, but rather at an acceptable level, considering other priorities, which of course small departments must always consider. Police-community relations, especially in the more sensitive communities, cannot be considered in the same light. Otherwise, the program will tend to become a lip service program at best.

Some larger departments, more able to specialize, have tended to have one central police-community relations unit that covers all the police divisions, precincts, or area offices, while others have appointed one or more officers in each division. Typically they report directly to the division commander and operate autonomously in terms of the total organization.

Both designs are capable of producing a level of desirable results, but both are restrictive to some degree. The umbrella unit handling all police-community relations from one central point is likely to develop standard programs not properly modified for specific neighborhoods.

> The task of building strong police-community relations is different with each population group. In one case, it may be a matter of translating a general endorsement into concrete assistance to the

---

[9]For an excellent discussion of staffing for effectiveness, we suggest viewing Peter Drucker's training film, *Staffing for Strength* (BNA Films, Division of the Bureau of National Affairs, Inc., Rockwell, Maryland).

police in preventing crime, obtaining adequate salaries, and the like. In minority communities, the effort must begin at a more basic level with a frank exploration of the attitudes and practices which cause hostility on both sides.[10]

A critically important communications problem confronts the police in urban areas with significant minority populations. Those areas have been the scene of civil disorder in recent years, and they often require a disproportionately high percentage of police resources. Inhabitants of those areas frequently feel they have less influence on police enforcement policies and practices than do other city residents. Members of minority groups must be convinced that their police service expectations are known and respected by the police, and that their recommendations are being acted upon.[11]

And too, there is a need for feedback and training by the police-community relations unit to the precinct or division, which may be difficult to achieve since it is not responsible to the area commander.

On the other hand, police-community relations officers assigned to individual precincts or divisions and who are not coordinated by a central unit are likely to produce fragmented programs, some even in conflict with one another.

CENTRAL CONTROL

The necessity for a formal organizational entity's having primary responsibility for police-community relations cannot be overstated. Departments with totally fragmented police-community relations programs have generally not gotten the job done, or the results have not measured up to the investment of manpower and effort.

To realize the best of two worlds, then, it is essential that each division, precinct, or geographical designation have its own police-community relations unit, which in turn has a concomitant relationship to the central or headquarters police-community relations unit. The central unit sets general program guidelines, interprets and translates departmental policy, and generally is responsible for the coordination and communication between all police-community relations units. The individual police-community relations units in turn are expected to transmit programs into action and to adapt them to the individuality of the area served.

The formalization and implementation of a police-community relations unit, or units, does not, however, issue the attainment of necessary

10President's Commission, *Task Force Report,* p. 150.
11National Advisory Commission, *Police,* p. 31.

goals. The President's Commission on Law Enforcement and Administration of Justice observed that

> Too often such units have been regarded by the rest of the department as the sole repository of the responsibility for good community relations. The activities of the units are now well known in other parts of the department and have rarely affected the activities of individual officers or substantially influenced departmental policy in such police activities as field interrogation, recruitment, assignment of personnel, and integrated patrols.[12]

Observation of numerous police-community relations programs has led us to conclude that there must be understanding and support by the departmental majority if such programs are to enjoy a respectable measure of success. In addition, each departmental member must also understand the positive relationship good police-community relations have to his individual job. It appears that this understanding and support is most likely to occur in those departments that involve their regular operational personnel in addition to the police-community relations specialists. Two excellent examples of this philosophy, the Los Angeles Police Department's Basic Car Plan and the Covina Police Department's more modest Coffee Klatch Program, will be discussed later in this chapter. In both cases patrol car officers, through the coordination of the police-community relations unit or cordinator, operate directly with citizen groups in their respective patrol areas or beats and are in the best possible position to relate their philosophy to the real world.

ELEMENTS THAT DETRACT FROM POLICE-COMMUNITY RELATIONS

The very existence of a police-community relations unit surprisingly enough will be threatening to some segments of both the community and the police department. Regardless of the unit's title, regardless of its goals and good intentions, some at least will perceive a sinister or negative motive.

At the community level, there is a need for confidence and freedom of expression. By virtue of his presence, the police-community relations officer will learn a great deal about the community, and rightly so, since his is a training as well as a communication function. Care must be taken, however, to insure that he is not called upon to consciously seek intelligence-type information. Obviously, intelligence is necessary for some departmental operations. On the other hand, "if a community rela-

---

[12]*Ibid.,* p. 151.

tions unit deliberately engages in intelligence activities, many citizens—and particularly those already suspicious of the police—will refuse to participate in its activities."[13]

The point being made is that the formal organization should recognize that sincerity, trust, and mutual respect must exist between the community and the community-relations officer and should make every attempt not to compromise this relationship.

Conversely, the police-community relations officers are bound to learn a great deal about the conduct of other departmental members. If the department in general perceives the police-community relations unit as covert, that is in reality an "internal affairs unit" searching for police misconduct, or at least investigating police misconduct coming to its attention, dysfunctional suspicion will arise.

While the police-community unit is the source of a great deal of information, the information should be primarily utilized for training and bringing about understanding and change in the broadest, most positive sense.

The police-community relations officer must not be placed in a compromising situation in the community. It is only reasonable that he likewise should not be compromised in his own department.

GROWTH AND DEVELOPMENT OF POLICE-COMMUNITY RELATIONS

In recent years we have witnessed a surge of interest in police-community relations programs. This surge has manifested itself in many new experimental and lasting programs that in some cases have literally reshaped the thrust of police agencies. Four factors appear to be major contributors:

1. The 1967 report of the President's Commission on Law Enforcement and Administration of Justice.
2. The 1968 report of the National Advisory Commission on Civil Disorders.
3. Infusion of federal funds through the Law Enforcement Assistance Administration and its local state agency counterparts.
4. The 1973 report of the National Advisory Commission on Criminal Justice Standards and Goals.

The President's Commission on Law Enforcement focused on the general problems of police ineffectiveness. The Commission on Civil Disorders became more specific and more dramatic because of the many im-

[13]*Ibid.*, p. 153.

mediate instances of violent disorder. Together they set the direction; federal funding became the vehicle. Of course all police-community relations programs have not required or received federal funds. Generally speaking, however, it was difficult for most police agencies to justify specific funds for an activity that seemed to have little relationship to the accepted traditional police activity and produced such intangible results.

The National Advisory Commission on Criminal Jusitce Standards and Goals followed along several years later not only to reinforce earlier convictions but to focus on all elements of the criminal justice system and the ways in which they are interrelated. The study of these interrelationships confirmed older, oft-held beliefs, that lack of confidence by the public in any part of the system is likely to result in lack of confidence in all parts. And of course the most visible part of the system is the police. This means that lack of confidence in any part of the justice system is likely to result in lack of confidence in the police.

The continuing national focus on police-community relations has understandably been responsible for much of the current awareness of the need to perpetuate such programs. Implementation of new programs is an almost daily occurrence. With these continuing innovations is the need for control, monitoring, and evaluation so that those programs with real impact are expanded and those which fail to meet expectations are discontinued.

KINDS OF POLICE-COMMUNITY RELATIONS PROGRAMS

Police-community relations programs generally fall into two categories: First and most easily recognized is the formalized police-community relations precinct or area unit. Second is the myriad of support programs, and it is on these programs that this section of the chapter will focus.

Support programs more commonly known by such titles as the School Resource Officer Program (Tucson, Arizona), Ride Along Program (Los Angeles County District Attorney), Bicycle Safety Program (National Safety Council), Crisis Intervention (New York City), Coffee Klatch Program (Covina, California), and Basic Car Plan (Los Angeles, California). Many prefer acronyms, such as P.A.C.E., public anticrime effort (Monterey Park, California). All are vitally important and for a number of reasons, not the least of which is that they tend to involve the greatest number of police officers.

Regardless of the title or the area of special emphasis, each program is aimed at opening communication links with some specific element of the community, and each has an ultimate goal of reducing conflict and obtaining voluntary cooperation and community support. Perhaps the most important single element is that each program places its officers in direct contact with the public in a nonthreatening situation where it is hoped that each will learn something positive about the other. Our own belief is that as police officers become more personally involved in police-community relations programs, the other desirable organizational traits will follow. For example, as we stated in earlier chapters, a man must be "self-actualized," must feel that his work has meaning if he is to reach his potential. If an officer is alienated from those he serves and only uses his job for performing specific assigned functions for eight hours and then escapes back to his own world, he is not likely to perform optimally.

We are reminded of an interview with a veteran eastern police officer who had worked the same particularly difficult ghetto beat for ten years. After listening to his incredible description of a typical tour of duty, we inquired as to how he had retained his stability. His answer was simple. "I just tell myself that I'm a zoo keeper. I go to work in the zoo for eight hours and then I go home." Obviously some people do need to be insulated from man's inhumanity to man, but a policeman who needs to be so insulated is not likely to offer much hope for those he serves. How much more rewarding his job would have been if he could have been personally involved, and how much better for his department had he had a personal mission.

Holyoke: An Example of Involvement and Awareness

Reemphasizing a need for personal development, one looks to the various federal programs that take Americans abroad to assist in the development of other nations. It would be unthinkable to send our representatives on such missions without thorough training and indoctrination in the culture, values, and language of the nation or district to be visited. The reason is obvious; if inadvertently our representatives offend or misunderstand the native culture, they are not likely to be effective in their mission. And yet daily we send white middle-class-oriented police officers into neighborhoods where the culture and the value system are equally foreign and where the language is either completely different or the words are similar but have totally different meanings. Obviously, under these conditions a police officer's effectiveness is severely impaired and he may do irreparable damage to police-community relations. In their 1968 report, the National Advisory Commission on Civil Disorders observed that

If an officer has never met, does not know and cannot understand the language and the habits of the people in the area he patrols, he cannot do an effective job. He deprives himself of important sources of information. He fails to know those persons with "equity" in the community, home-owners, small business men, professional men, persons who are anxious to support proper law enforcement— and thus sacrifices the contributions they can make to maintaining community order.[14]

We would add that he is also likely to unnecessarily offend those people in whose area he patrols and inadvertently turn away the very people he is attempting to serve. It would seem incongruous that any formal police-training program could omit this most elementary base upon which the success of police-community relations is so dependent.

An interesting and viable positive example of this hypothesis was the Holyoke, Massachusetts, Police Team Project. In the Ward 1 Model Cities area of Holyoke, a police team consisting of one captain, two sergeants, and twelve patrolmen, all of whom were volunteers, was responsible for a 235-acre inner-city neighborhood with a population consisting of sixty percent French Canadian descent, twenty-one percent Puerto Rican, and six percent black. This was a storefront operation and the team was located centrally in the area served. The team was a highly sensitized group of men whose members carried and displayed identification credentials printed in both English and Spanish. An important facet of the program design, in addition to its police methodology, was its focus on studies in human relations, with particular emphasis on the language and the traditional culture of those races residing in the team area. The team worked closely with all elements and actively sought advice and assistance of citizens through:

—creating an extremely casual "front" by working out of a storefront office connected to a restaurant, by wearing blazers instead of uniforms and by driving unmarked cars;

—setting up a community relations council made up of six citizens and three police officers who meet regularly and have enlisted a crime and delinquency task force of 17 citizens to carry out the prevention programs agreed upon by the Council. Both citizen groups represent a cross-section of the entire Model Cities area in terms of ethnic, racial and age makeup;

—hiring a Neighborhood Liaison Specialist who communicates the community's information and program needs to the police team and

[14]Otto Kerner, *Report of the National Advisory Commission on Civil Disorders* (Washington, D.C.: U.S. Government Printing Office, 1968), p. 160.

the team's crime control goals to the citizen task force; and then develops innovative programs for uniting the needs and goals of both;

—hiring four community service officers who work side by side with the team and are involved in all law enforcement duties except making arrests (they also represent a cross-section of the community);

—organizing community activities (coffee hours, socials, school lectures, etc.) as a technique to improve police-community relations, to "get the kids off the street," and to improve relations among ethnic and racial groups in the area; and

—working closely with Model Cities representatives who have already developed contacts with citizens since January, 1968.[15]

Upon interviewing team members, we were impressed with the perception and personal depth that had been developed in a relatively short period of time. Simple techniques such as when to sit or when to remove one's coat to reduce tension and unnecessary threat when present in the Puerto Rican household obviously brought amazing results. This was but one example of a myriad of skills relating to cultural awareness that these men had apparently acquired in the early stages of the team project as they began to *understand* their clientele.

Team members worked in plain clothes or blazers. They handled all normal police activities in the model area to conclusion, assuming roles normally reserved for detectives, traffic officers, and the like. The team worked closely with community service officers recruited from the community who had been especially helpful in overcoming language barriers and reducing tension in difficult situations.

The field training in the project was supervised by Professor Raymond Galvin of the School of Criminal Justice, University of Minnesota, and Professor John Angel of the School of Criminal Justice, University of Michigan.

In a March 1971 report the Massachusetts Committee on Law Enforcement and Administration of Criminal Justice stated that

> Although the Police Team has only been training since October and operational since December 1970 it is obvious that it has dramatically changed a few very traditional and sensitive relationships— between police officer and citizen and between patrolman and his superior officers.[16]

[15]Robert H. Quinn, Report by the Committee on Law Enforcement Administration of Criminal Justice, *Holyoke's Police Team: New Roles for Police, Citizens* (Boston: State of Massachusetts, March 1971), p. 1.
[16]*Ibid.*

Before leaving this section we must again look to the Holyoke Model Cities program for an example of positive attitude change. As we have previously stated, members of the most victimized race are apparently the most hostile toward police. Although they are the most victimized, they are also the least likely to report such victimization to the police. In contrast, the Holyoke Team in its 235-acre inner-city model area experienced a sixty-case, or 300 percent, rise in reported crimes in its first three months of existence.[17] (The rise in reported crimes should not be confused with or equated as a rise in actual crimes committed.)

Obviously a new kind of communication, a new feeling of confidence was developing. Perhaps a major factor in the attitude change was the involvement of seventeen citizens of the community who served as a police advisory committee and who had a major role helping the police understand a culture that was so different from their own.[18]

Ride Along Programs

Throughout the country many law enforcement agencies are encouraging young citizens to "ride along" with their policemen during regular duty tours.

The ride along concept was primarily initiated in an effort to improve communication and understanding between youth and the authority structure, especially law enforcement. High school students are given the opportunity to observe firsthand the daily routine of police officers, such as handling calls on narcotics problems, disturbances, and traffic accidents, issuing citations, and writing reports.

A second function of the program is to give officers an opportunity to converse with young people in a nonthreatening situation. Typically, patrol-level officers talk with teen-agers in negative situations, when perhaps neither the policeman nor the teen-ager is at his best, or at least not perceived in the best light. A great deal of understanding can develop in a rather short time under different circumstances. The teen-ager can ask questions about "those other cops," and the policeman can find out that every teen-ager with long hair is not a "wise guy."

Interestingly enough, a number of years before "ride along" became popular, one small West Coast city initiated a similar program. The riders were primarily citizens of all ages who had complained about specific officers' attitudes in traffic cases. The complainants were invited, nearly cajoled, into riding for an afternoon or an evening. Whenever

---

[17]*Ibid.*

[18]The Holyoke program was not refunded. We elected to use it as an example, however, since so many of its points are transferable. Too, lack of funding was not due to any failure on the program's part to reach stated goals, we are told.

possible, they were placed with the officer who had been the basis of the complaint. While the beginning of such rides may have been somewhat traumatic for citizen and officer alike, the results were excellent, most often ending with a much better understanding by both parties and actually bringing about a noticeable behavior change in some officers.

Traditionally, riding in police cars by persons not under arrest had been discouraged for years on the basis of liability or unnecessary time consumption, or simply because of the unwillingness of administrators to take a chance. It appears now that the "ride along" risk is minimal when compared with the gains to be achieved in terms of support for the police.

Family Crisis Intervention

Like the Ride Along Program, Family Crisis Intervention can be classified as a police-community support program. Perhaps somewhat differently in that Family Crisis Intervention provides a much needed service, but beyond that it, too, offers an opportunity for community members to view policemen in a positive nonthreatening role. And policemen in this role learn a great deal about the values and mores of those they serve who may be different from themselves.

In 1967 the original Family Crisis Intervention Unit was implemented by Dr. Morton Bard in the New York City Police Department. The two-year program was accomplished under a Law Enforcement Assistance Administration grant to the City College of New York.

Eighteen highly motivated patrolmen were selected from volunteers for the month-long specialized training. After the training, the members operated in uniform, around the clock, and performed all regular police functions. Their primary responsibility, however, was to respond to family disturbances anywhere in their precinct. They were supported by individual and group professional consultations. An integral part of the program was the utilization of referral agencies.[19]

To deal with family disturbance (crisis) problems realistically and effectively, Family Crisis Intervention Unit officers are expected not only to restore order and prevent injury but also to assist the disputants in finding lasting solutions to their own problems—solutions that will eliminate the need for repeated police involvement. The approach to these disturbances should thus be that of problem solving—usually by referral —and crisis management, and not necessarily that of arrest and prosecution.

[19]Morton Bard and Bernard Berkowitz, *Law Enforcement and Science and Technology,* ed S. I. Cohn (U.S.A.: Port City Press, Inc., 1969), 2: 565–67.

It should be stated that this program has not attempted to develop the police officer as a social worker or a psychologist, but rather to enhance his professional competence as a working policeman. "Police are untrained and ill-equipped to *treat* psychological and social pathology. It is not, moreover, the purpose of this Program to make them so. Officers can be competent, however, to *identify* a vast range of ills—health problems, social hardships, housing problems, employment difficulties and mental illness—all of which, when they lead to turmoil, have been too broadly categorized as 'family disputes.' "[20]

> Intervention in the family fight has been presented as an underrated, rather neglected police function, but one that holds much promise for crime prevention as well as for community mental health and family welfare. Selected and trained police Family Crisis Intervention specialists, supported by other professions, can also gather basic data leading to identification of violence-prone individuals and situations. Such specialists, keenly aware of human sensibilities, may afford a new avenue for improvement in the crucial area of police-community relations.[21]

Since 1967 Family Crisis Intervention Units have been instituted in core cities across the United States as a valid extension of regular police service. The growing number of such programs attests to the support by prominent police chiefs, such as Chief Charles Gain of the San Francisco, California, Police Department, to Dr. Bard's 1967 prediction that "such specialists, keenly aware of human sensibilities, may afford a new avenue for improvement in the crucial area of police-community relations."[22]

The Basic Car Plan—A Large City's Approach to Working Officer Involvement

The Los Angeles Police Department has established a program aimed at "providing more effective police service by establishing a closer relationship between the policeman and the people he serves."[23]

Primarily, the Basic Car Plan is an effort to overcome the anonymity that typically develops between the policemen and the community as officers are rotated and assigned to various districts, various beats, and special details.

[20]*Family Crisis Intervention Program,* Information Bulletin (Oakland, Calif., Police Department, January 18, 1971), p. 1.

[21]Bard and Berkowitz, *Law Enforcement and Science,* p. 567.

[22]*Ibid.*

[23]*Basic Radio Car Plan,* Information Bulletin (Los Angeles, Calif., City Police Department, 1970), pp. 1–5.

The methodology is to establish basic car districts whose boundaries are clearly defined. Nine men, consisting of one lead officer, five senior officers, and three officers with less experience, are assigned to each district. Three of the officers are assigned to each of three watches. Additional cover cars are deployed during peak workload hours and are superimposed on the basic car plan.

The lead officer has primary responsibility for coordinating the activities of those assigned to his basic car district. The nine officers meet on a monthly basis with neighborhood block representatives constituting the basic car area. The purpose of the meeting is to provide valuable dialogue between officers and citizens.

We are especially impressed with this concept in that it tends to "repersonalize" the police service. Policemen have a firsthand opportunity to discover the strong and weak points of their daily activities and to receive the kind of feedback that is likely to produce a more flexible adaptive work style.

The following material is extracted from the Los Angeles Police Department's *Basic Radio Car Plan* information bulletin:

> *Objectives* The Basic Radio Car Plan is a means of attaining the primary police goals of helping society prevent crime by improving community attitudes toward police, providing stability for the Policeman on the street and generating in him a proprietary interest in his "beat," and beter knowledge of the police role.
>
> *Workload study* A Basic Radio Car District profile folder was prepared for each district. Information included is: current crime problems, wanted suspects, crime maps, problem locations, names and addresses of V.I.P.'s living in the district and any other information that would assist the officers in knowing their district. This folder is kept current and passed from watch to watch. The lead officer is responsible for ensuring that the folder is kept current.
>
> *Personnel selection* The selection of officers to participate in the program has been accomplished by utilizing the knowledge of all uniformed supervisors. Personnel selected for assignment to the Basic Car Plan was predicated on many factors: Length of Service, Department Ratings, Reputation, Personality, Personnel Complaints, Partner Compatibility, Education, Hardships, Training Officer Experience.
>
> *Training* Conference leadership training for all personnel assigned to the Basic Radio Car Plan is a necessary factor in the success of the program. Each lead officer and number one senior officer on each watch has attended a three day Conference Leadership Course prepared by Training Division. The remaining team members have had one day of conference, leadership training with follow-up training to be accomplished on the division level.

Selection of community representatives   An integral part of the Basic Radio Car Plan is selecting and organizing the community representatives to meet and effectively communicate with officers. The Division Commander, assisted by the Community Relations Officer, contacted key community leaders to request their assistance in the selection of an Advisory Committee which was composed of residents who represented the Basic Radio Car Districts in the Division. The goals of the committee were to select a representative from each block in the division. The block representatives were organized into groups by radio car district, and regular monthly meetings between the officers and block representatives were established. Divisional detectives, existing Police-Community Councils, entrance oral board members, Community Relations Administration, and other resources were utilized to assist in the selection of community participants. The membership of the community representatives was weighed heavily in favor of bona fide residents of the concerned district.

Monthly meetings   Once each month the nine man Basic Radio Car team meets with the district representatives. The purpose of the meeting is to give the individual citizen and officer an opportunity to participate in mutual discussion concerning police problems. This is facilitated by dividing the meeting into discussion workshops following the general meeting. Each officer acts as a workshop chairman. Supervisory personnel do not normally attend the meetings. Officers wear the basic uniform when participating in the meetings.

The lead officer presides over the meeting and makes the necessary preparations for an interesting and informative program. All resources of the Department are used to accomplish this goal. Specialists (e.g., Detectives, Narcotics Officers, Traffic, etc.) used as resource persons are contacted by the lead officer.

The meeting with the community representatives is preceded by a briefing during which the agendum and program are finalized. The nine radio district team members and the team advisor (Sergeant) attend. The Watch Commanders may also attend.

A debriefing session follows the community meeting, for the purpose of completing an evaluation report. The report is reviewed by the team advisor and several copies forwarded to the Division Commander to be distributed at his discretion. One copy is retained by the concerned "A" Unit team.

It is the responsibility of the lead officer of the Basic Radio Car Unit to maintain direct communication between all team members of his Basic Radio Car on all watches. The lead officer makes himself available for problem discussion with individual team members of his unit on other watches, and to disseminate information received from the team advisor. The lead officer is a coordinator and performs a staff function. He does not act as a supervisor.

A Summary of each lead officer's evaluation is included in the Commander's weekly activities report.[24]

Nothing in the Basic Radio Car Plan detracts from the typical responsibilities of regular supervision. It can be anticipated, however, that the sharing of leadership responsibility with lead officers is likely to have a positive impact on their development as decision makers and as future upper rank leaders.

And, finally, it seems to us that this program genuinely seeks to involve the community in its proper crime prevention role and to consider the personal needs of young officers by offering a greater degree of autonomy and opportunity for self-actualization.

The Coffee Klatch (A Small City's Approach to Working Officer Involvement)

Smaller suburban communities as well as their larger core-city cousins have need to develop viable relationships between the patrolman and the citizens he serves. One city's approach is the "Coffee Klatch."

In Covina, California, each patrolman is responsible for holding at least one Coffee Klatch monthly in some citizen's home located in his assigned beat. The meetings are designed to provide a vehicle for dialogue between policemen and small neighborhood groups of citizens, normally husband and wife teams totaling about twelve people. The meetings are coordinated by a community relations officer, who is also responsible for necessary training and orientation, and for the development of supportive information.

The program is developed around five policemen who are assigned on a twenty-four-hour basis to each patrol beat. Each beat is about one mile square. Basically, the idea is to invite a few couples from a given neighborhood to an informal evening get-together for coffee and conversation, bring into the group the police officer responsible for patrolling that particular neighborhood, and afford him the opportunity to present his department's viewpoints on law enforcement in the community. Over a friendly cup of coffee, the assembled couples are given an opportunity to ask questions, to make known their personal expectations regarding efficient law enforcement, and to air their own gripes about the service.

Getting couples to open their homes and invite neighbors in for the informal coffee klatches proved to be no great obstacle. Original meet-

24*Ibid.*

ings were arranged by members of the Junior Women's Club. Acting as hostesses, they made preliminary arrangements for the initial get-togethers in their own neighborhoods patrolled by Covina officers.

When apprised of a scheduled meeting, the police department arranges for advance delivery of coffee, cookies, and movie projection equipment to the host's home by a police aide (cadet). Everything is in readiness when, at an appointed time, the beat officer, on duty and in uniform, arrives for his coffee klatch session.

The host introduces him to each individual present, and in turn, the officer distributes attractive personal business cards bearing his name and other pertinent information. He encourages each member of the group to call him by his first name, pointing out that it is imprinted on his card.

The officer, armed with up-to-date police information developed for this specific neighborhood, speaks to the guests about the problems and events that are occurring on their street. Through friendly, informal discussion he encourages response from the group.

Next he presents a short movie, which portrays typical home burglaries. He follows with a discussion on crime prevention in the neighborhood, pointing out how each citizen can become personally involved in crime prevention.

The officer talks about his own role in the community. He encourages questions and attempts to answer each one intelligently and sincerely, carefully avoiding negative overtones that might indicate any form of defensiveness on his part.

Offering himself as a personal contact between law enforcement and citizen, the officer invites each individual to call him personally if any future questions or problems arise in which he can assist. He invites comments, including complaints, and makes it clear that he will welcome any opportunity to discuss them. He lets it be known that he is personally concerned about establishing a mutual relationship that will strengthen the sometimes critical feedback procedure, and he promises prompt and correct answers to all future questions, stating that his replies will be fed back no later than the following day.

Before leaving the coffee klatch the officer assures each couple that he will be continuously interested in hearing their suggestions, or their doubts, about his own job performance or that of a fellow officer on the beat. He reiterates that their street is also his street and that their concerns are his as well.

Before taking part in the program, each policeman is given substantial training in communication skills. Special emphasis is placed on the avoidance of defensiveness when receiving negative feedback. It appears that policemen inherently feel the need to defend the actions of other policemen, often without sufficient information but rather based upon some prior personal experience.

This particular portion of the training utilized role playing and the assistance of a local little theater group. The program for developing officers' empathy for people who are different from themselves will not be discussed here but will be thoroughly covered in this chapter's learning exercise case study, for it was an important preparatory ingredient.

In retrospect, the program has not presented the anticipated problems of getting willing participation by the officers. Instead, holding down the number of meetings per officer per month has become a concern, since each klatch represents a substantial investment in time, normally two to three hours. Interestingly enough, it is the officers themselves who are initiating the oversupply of klatches.

Both the Los Angeles and the Covina models tend to maximize the field patrol officers' involvement. Both programs provide a continuing education and development opportunity which in turn gives assurance that as neighborhoods and communities change, the policemen themselves will be changing as well.

PAL: Another role for Police Officers

Police departments have at various times during the past few decades involved themselves with youth recreational and sports-oriented programs. Their longevity was typically oriented to availability of funds and prevailing philosophy (should or should not the police be so involved). In 1967, the San Jose, California, Police Department, following the national organization's format, began its PAL (Police Athletic League) program.

In the beginning PAL's goal was to reduce conflict between under-privileged youths and the police. Early programs such as pool, boxing, and the like were adopted because "gang members liked to do these things." In ten years, San Jose PAL has grown from one police juvenile sergeant, and two or three activities to eighteen regular activities, a police department staff of six, with a volunteer support staff of more than a hundred. Their operating budget has grown from zero to over a quarter of a million dollars annually (half by donation), and from a sand lot and an old building to a half million dollar sports complex (all donated) on seventeen acres donated by San Jose citizens. A million dollar (donated) building is in the planning stages. Sergeant Guido started with a dozen gang members in 1967 and now works with 28,900 San Jose young people, ages six to twenty-one, from all walks of life, on a full-time basis in eighteen formalized programs.

TRAINING FOR POLICE-COMMUNITY RELATIONS STAFF AND
FOR MAXIMUM FIELD SUPPORT

Generally speaking, the key to any police-community relations program is the understanding and enthusiasm brought to it by the police participants. Since these factors are not always present, they must be developed.

It would be unrealistic to expect every policeman to instinctively understand the importance of his role in police-community relations or to have a natural empathy for the various publics he serves. And each public, each population group, represents a different task in building strong supportive relationships. In each of the previously discussed models, special training was an important element of success.

It has been demonstrated in various pre-1965 studies that in most cases police preservice academy training had not devoted sufficient hours to the study of people, of community relations. This void is being dramatically changed in many areas, primarily because of subsidized training programs such as those required by the California Commission on Peace Officers Standards and Training, and similar bodies in other states.

Apparently there is still a need for greater attention to continuing in-service training in this area. Officers assigned specifically to police-community relations units should also have a greatly reinforced training program, for it is they who will set the tone for field officers to follow.

The President's Commission on Law Enforcement and Administration of Justice observed that police-community relations officers "need special training in such fields as the psychology, culture, and problems of minority groups and the poor, the dynamics of crowd behavior, the history of the civil rights movement, and the attitudes of various segments of the public toward the police."[25]

We are in agreement with the commission but would add to their admonition by observing that while classroom-type learning is helpful, police administrators who provide field-learning experiences in the ghetto and the barrio are likely to experience more significant and lasting results. By submerging policemen, who are not acting in their capacity as policemen, into the respective cultures, a great deal of learning will take place that cannot be found in textbooks.

We are reminded of our experience in a recent ghetto workshop in which the participants were predominantly black probation and social workers. An example under discussion was that of poor language under-

[25]President's Commission, *Task Force Report*, p. 156.

standing by a white female elementary school teacher in a totally black school. The young teacher was well motivated and well liked, though somewhat naïve. At the close of class one day, a black fifth grader waited until the students had departed. The youngster approached the teacher stating, "Teacher, the shit's gonna fall." The teacher, taken aback at such language, marched the sputtering youngster off to the *white* principals' office where he spent the next hour, for, after all, "Children shouldn't use such language." The "shit" was indeed going to fall, and did. With some personal risk, but sensing an ally, the black youngster was trying to tell his white teacher that a gang fight was about to take place. A more appropriate reaction by the teacher would have been to inquire, "How big is the pile and where is it going to land?"

The point is, as we stated earlier, the words may be a part of the English language, but that does not guarantee that they will have white middle-class meaning. We are not suggesting that the policeman should alter his vocabulary to a great degree, but he should understand what is going on around him, for an important part of effective communication is *effective listening*. This kind of earthy learning is not easily taught; it must be experienced. A learning program such as this is not without some risks, especially in terms of administrative peer group understanding. The potential for long-range effectiveness, however, should appeal to the more modern creative leader.

Obviously, this submersion into a culture should be supervised by professional trainers, preferably behavioral scientists, who can guide the program and, perhaps more importantly, prepare the participants for the experience.

Familiarity in this type of training has led us to believe that laying a proper foundation for field experiences or real life role playing (sometimes referred to as the "reversal-of-role technique") is likely to bring about a more rapid, more significant transition. The behavioralist continues to play an important role during the training period, which may last for several days, by bringing the participants together from time to time to discuss and share experiences. Finally, the behavioralist must assist the participants in summarizing and evaluating the training experience so that it may be a guide for those who follow.

LEARNING EXERCISE

Altering behavior patterns, actually bringing about dramatic change in attitudes and understanding, is perhaps the most challenging and rewarding aspects of training. In training police officers to be effective, to communicate effectively with *all* of the publics they serve, the challenges becomes even greater when one considers the preponderance of daily negative experiences that must be overcome.

The following learning exercise is a limited case study of such an effort. In it the reader should discover for himself the impact of role playing (or role living) as a training technique. The role playing/living becomes more critical when one considers the emotional risks taken by the participant. He may very well discover heretofore unknowns about his counterpart, or even himself; things he had not considered. This is no sterile classroom from which one goes home at night. Instead, it is what it is, submersion in a true life situation, into a culture totally unlike one's own with a quick vignette of "how it feels."

It should be understood that the program was not welcomed with open arms by the department as a whole and that some participants benefitted more than others. Lastly this program was not seen as a panacea by its creators but rather one rung in a tall ladder. The report follows.

POLICEMEN: AGENTS OF CHANGE
A CRIME PREVENTION REPORT[26]

A wise Sioux Indian once observed that we should not judge a man until we have walked a mile in his moccasins. While the simple truth of this sage advice is still timely, its basic connotation is finding new dimension in the City of Riverside. Men, now emerging from "total immersion experiences," are adding a postscript to the adage: *Do not judge a man's values until you have counted the cockroaches on his sleeping room ceiling, shared his table, rapped with his children, and sampled his culture.* In Riverside, we believe · the postscript is relevant, especially if you happen to be a cop and your beat is the barrio.

If you live in the barrio, at least in our barrio, in relation to the general population you are three times more likely to be feloniously assaulted. You are twice as likely to be sexually assaulted and twice as likely to have your car stolen or damaged by gang violence. You are twice as likely to be arrested for drug abuse and sales and you are much more likely to resist arrest, especially in large gatherings. While you are not likely to receive any bad checks nor be the victim of an armed robbery, your chances of being murdered are twice that of the general population.

As bad as these figures appear to be, we suspect that many barrio residents, for a variety of reasons, fail to report many crimes; that we are only made aware of the iceberg's tip.

In spite of these figures, if you live in the barrio, generally speaking, you are not supportive of the police. Or if you are, you do not display such feelings openly—for a myriad of reasons, not the least of which is fear of retaliation;

[26]R. Fred Ferguson, *Policemen: Agents of Change—A Crime Prevention Report* (Los Angeles, Calif.: Office of the Attorney General—State of California, Crime Prevention Unit, 1975), vol. 2, no. 3, pp. 1–13.

fear for the safety of your family and yourself. Perhaps this is partly so because it is unpopular among the more militant, more vocal young Chicanos to support "la placa"—the cop.

And perhaps even more disconcerting, no one can remember when it wasn't so. Veteran officers and citizens alike swap tales that go back more than thirty years. A collection of old newspaper articles speak to a history of violent barrio gang rivalry (with gangs from other barrios) that frequently resulted in serious injuries, loss of personal property and sometimes death.

Our barrio has had its share of rival "shoot-outs" but more frequently the shots were singularly directed toward a crowd, a car, or an inhabited dwelling. It is true that young men have died as a result of these gunshots, but over the years even more have died as a result of vehicle crashes into trees and parked cars. Although such crashes were often alcohol- related, they were at times helped along, we are told, by one vehicle chasing another "out of our barrio." Impossible to prove, of course, but the evidence is strong.

As might be expected, much of the gang rivalry has ultimately resulted in police involvement. And the involvement has brought its frustrations—for the officer who interviews a young Mexican American lying near death in the hospital: "Sure, I know who shot me—I'll take care of it when I get out of here." You may not get out—at least for a long time." "Then my brother will take care of it! I don't need a cop to take care of me"; and for the detective who puts hours and weeks of work into a felonious assault or homicide investigation, only to have his barrio witnesses melt away on the day of trial. On the other hand, if the witness proves cooperative, there is the officer's concern of providing protection, and the necessity of spiriting the witness and his family away to keep them safe. Generally, however, in the barrio one simply does not break "the code." The system is not to be trusted. In spite of the handicaps, some of our policemen have been moderately successful in their dealings with the barrio inhabitants.

In our city's mile-square barrio of six thousand plus souls, our officers would be hard pressed to identify more than twenty-five young men who seem to foment the negative occurrences in the community. Conversely, however, these twenty-five have the ability to generate five hundred supporters if given the right (or wrong) set of circumstances. While a barrio citizen might telephone for police assistance in a neighborhood disruption, it is not likely he will come forward to support the responding officers. In fact, he may eventually join in the confrontation.

It is easily understood why police officers, even Mexican American officers, do not relish assignment in the barrio. They are frequently subjected to cat calls, thrown rocks and bottles and kids drinking in the barrio park (a prime lead-in to more serious crimes). At night, street lights and sometimes the windows of patrol cars are shot out.

This identifiable twenty-five lawless kid group would be delighted if officers never patrolled in the barrio—and they say so. There may be others who feel the same but we must remind our officers that there are still 6,000 residents to consider, for even the barrio has its "silent majority." Unfortunately, information of this sort is not new to policemen, and the problems are not isolated to one Mexican American barrio in Riverside.

Like barrios throughout the state, Riverside also has its hidden unrecorded population: the illegal aliens—the "wetback"—who compounds the existing barrio problems and creates new ones. The Mexican-American community is often resentful whenever policemen arrest these illegal immigrants. There is a great deal of empathy in the barrio for the "wets" and yet, they are often taken advantage of by many of their more fortunate brothers. They are charged outrageous prices for crowded sleeping rooms. They are exploited by some employers and by some local merchants. When they are the victims of street crimes, they cannot report them—for obvious reasons. As bad as it is though, we are told that life is still better in the barrio than where they came from—better than what they have to go back to. It is obvious that the barrio groups have good reason to mistrust some of the elements of our system, including law enforcement. On the other hand, it has been observed that "to a considerable extent the police are victims of community problems which are not of their making.[27]

As police officers, we are aware of the crime and the inequities that exist in the barrio, and we want to do something about it. Why then are we, for the most part, so unsuccessful?

Much has been written about this phenomena that permeates not only the barrio, but the ghetto and other pockets of lower socioeconomic groups as well.

While such cultures are often different from one another, they do share certain commonalities such as their distrust of government. And, since police are the most visible representatives of government, they have become the focus of this mistrust. Unfortunately, when the actions and words of policemen are negative or perceived to be so, that mistrust is reinforced. Regular enforcement, which is accepted in other parts of the city, becomes a "hassle" or harassment in the minority community. Continued misunderstanding and frustration do, undoubtedly, result in harassment by some officers—and by some citizens.

Modern policemen know that this problem is disfunctional to the process of law and order—that it encourages contempt for the law. Perhaps even more important, they know that it must somehow be stopped.

In 1967, the President's Commission on Law Enforcement and Administration of Justice, in its *Task Force Report: The Police,* observed that "the substantial majority of Americans respect its police force, supports its actions, and looks to it for protection."[28] However, "a significant number of people, largely the poor or members of minority groups, fear and distrust the police. Ironically, this group often has the greatest need for police protection because it usually inhabits the most crime ridden sections of our cities."[29] So it is in our barrio.

Contemporary writers agree that no police force can stand alone, nor be effective without community support. The Los Angeles Police Department expressed it thusly in a department memorandum:

[27]President's Commission, *Task Force Report,* p. 150.
[28]*Ibid.*
[29]*Ibid.*

The mutual advantages of a friendly relationship between the people of a community and their police force should be widely understood and more fully appreciated. The success of a police force in the performance of its duties is largely measured by the degree of support and cooperation it receives from the people it serves. It is of paramount importance, therefore, to secure for this department the confidence, respect, and approbation of the public. The cultivation of such desirable attitudes on the part of the public is dependent upon reciprocal attitudes on the part of this department.[30]

Obviously, attitudes, misconceptions, misunderstandings and misdeeds on both sides have led to the conflict between barrio and youth and the police. Of course, the barrio youth will not admit their part and the policemen have grown weary of "everyone" telling them that it is they that must change to meet community needs. "Why can't I enforce the law in the barrio as I would in any other part of town?" After all—"This is America, if they want to be Americans, let them act like Americans, act like I do." And therein lies the problem.

The United States as a government would not consider sending one of its representatives into any foreign country without specific instructions regarding the mores, values and customs of that country. It is clearly recognized that to do so would be to invite a myriad of continuing problems ranging from ineffectiveness to disaster. The country simply could not afford the "Ugly American" image ,especially in the less affluent countries.

In a foreign country, if one displays contempt for the local culture, one would simply be ejected. But, the barrios are stuck with us—for we have failed to recognize that we have many pockets in our cities, where the mores, the values, the entire social system, is just as different from the typical middle class white community as though it actually was in another country. Oh, we know the language is different enough, that homes often "look funny," that hair and clothing styles are different and that cars are really "jazzed up" so that one knows where they "come from" regardless of where they are observed. We know these things, but what we haven't thought through sufficiently is what the impact of police officers in these "different communities" is, and especially what problems the officers, who were never trained to work there, might evoke.

If we, the reader and the writer, can agree at least in part, with what has been written to this point, then perhaps what follows will make sense in terms of one department's attempt to test a theory that an enlightened policeman is more likely to be a successful policeman.

The City of Riverside is most fortunate to have, in addition to several other establishments of higher learning, the campus of Loma Linda University. Loma Linda does not offer police courses, per se, but it is heavy in the behavioral sciences. Professors Vern Andress (Psychologist), Monte Andress (Social Anthropologist) and Charles Teel (Sociologist), in cooperation with members of the

[30]Los Angeles, California, Police Department Memorandum (1963).

Riverside Police Department, have developed what appears to be a most comprehensive approach to developing policemen's awareness of the Mexican-American (Chicano) subculture.

A study program was initiated with certain specific stated understandings, goals and expectations under the course title: *The Police Officer As An Agent Of Change.*

The philosophy of the Loma Linda Course embraces the theory that the police officer in modern society has roles of a demanding and complex nature. He is called upon to perform and think in ways that require sophisticated knowledge and skills. This knowledge and skill is constantly changing as the changing expectations for police officers takes place within society.

The police officer is often placed, by the expectations of the community, at the interface of confrontations between and within ethnic groups very different from his own. The lack of knowledge of cultures different from his own may increase the volatile nature of these confrontations. This course addresses this problem.

The course exposes the officer to the dynamics of cultures different from his own in order to acquaint him with culture elements that affect the personalities of the people he deals with. The course examines the characteristics of many ethnic groups and presents approaches that may be extrapolated across culture barriers. However, it is directed mainly towards potential police/citizen problems in the Mexican-American (Chicano) community.

The curriculum for the course is planned around learning experiences that include lectures, group participation sessions, films, guest presentations, total immersion (live-in experiences), experiences with the food, music, art, and dance of Mexico, readings and examinations.

The course consists of ten four-hour class sessions. The first week's session is an orientation. Each week thereafter, the students participate in classes as follows: (2) Culture, race and myth, (3) Sensorium; (4) Mexican National character and the Chicanos; (5) Perceived deprivation and violence; (6) Chicano history, politics, and expectations; (7) Life opportunities and ethnicity; (8) Cultural experience: food, art, music and dance; and (9) Total immersion live-in experience. The tenth and final week is devoted to debriefing, conclusions, and a final examination.

Course participants are required to read two texts dealing with the Chicanos and their culture: *Chicanos—Social and Psychological Perspectives* by Nathaniel N. Wagner & Marsha J. Haug; *Chicano—The Evolution of a People* by Rosaldo Calvert Seligmann.

Some interesting observations have already emerged from the series of courses that have proved to be a learning experience for both the instructors and the students. A better understanding of the police problems that are unique to the Chicano community of Riverside has provided depth and restructuring of the course's directions. It is becoming more rigorous and comprehensive as greater challenges are being given to the students. Higher standards of performance are being extracted from the learners, but in a nonstressful way.

The instructors have, at times, felt frustration when the actualization of their goals was elusive. Occasionally, the learners were resistant to concepts that were alien to their thinking. Old deep-seated prejudices surfaced, blocking the acceptance of new ideas and viewpoints. However, there have been compensations, especially when evidence of real personal breakthrough has occurred. These have been moments of great personal insight and growth acknowledged by the officers themselves.

One example of such a breakthrough took place during a class session. One very vocal and resistant officer had stated repeatedly, from deep conviction, that "Chicanos have no values." During the class he came to grips with the concept of the cultural relativity of personal and social values. Deep in thought as the class progressed around him, he finally broke his silence with the observation that now he understood that "Chicanos *did* have values but they were *different*" from his own. He decided that if he could understand their values he could better understand the people. His personal revelation was spontaneous and the entire class benefited.

Still another example was Officer K——. He was vocally resistant to trying to understand barrio culture. He felt the only way to deal with problems in the barrio was with force. He was well known to the Chicano community for his unbending and cold personality. It is apparent that he may have earned the hatred of the Chicano youth who made him the special target of their provocations. Officer K—— enrolled in the course, completed it, and received his grade. Some time later, one of the instructors met Officer K—— while shopping. The officer admitted that at the inception of the class he had totally rejected, both in spirit and content, the information of the class courses. However, with time, he had come to realize that what was presented was true and of practical use to him. He expressed gratitude for the insights provided by the course. An interesting side note to this example was the feedback from one of the barrio leaders; he expressed amazement at the change in Officer K's—— attitude, noting a definite mellowing, and a general improvement of relations between the Chicanos and the police.

The Loma Linda Professors who direct the course are now projecting some changes in the curriculum. They are planning to have the officers spend a session with them in the East Los Angeles barrio. Los Angeles has the largest population of Mexican-Americans in the United States and is second only to Mexico City in numbers of persons of Mexican heritage. On this proposed tour, the officers and their wives will dine, view examples of Chicano street art, music and dancing, and visit the Chicano cultural center at Plaza La Raza. The purpose of this is to steep the students in the Chicano setting in order to catch some of the spirit of the community.

The academic portion of the course is probably not that different from other similar courses. The uniqueness, in addition to the teaching team itself, is probably in the field experiences. The visits to old country Mexican cultural areas have been both enlightening and entertaining—and shared with the participant's spouse. The visits to local Mexican barrios have made a somewhat greater impact.[31]

For example, the policeman participants tour the barrio in a small bus, with

---

[31]Professor Vern Andress, Loma Linda University, Curriculum Review (1975).

one of the officer participants acting as the tour guide. His role is to point out areas of interest and history—from his point of view and from police experiences there. The bus then leaves the barrio and picks up a new tour guide, a native of the barrio, and returns for a second tour. This time the new guide points out areas of interest from *his* point of view. To say that there is a dichotomy would be a gross understatement. At the conclusion of the second tour, the participants withdraw to the classroom to digest the information.

The second and last example is the "graduation exercise." Participation is on a volunteer basis. Officers, one at a time, are immersed into the barrio culture for two nights and three days. They actually become a part of a Mexican-American family, share its beds, its food, its problems, its pleasures and its frustrations.[32] The following excerpts from the participants' diaries reflect the impact of the immersion experiences:

"This memo will reflect three days that the writer (Patrolman Mike Robitzer) spent with a Mexican-American family, beginning December 11, 1974, with the M—— family, who is originally from Mexico. There is a total of fifteen family members, Mr. M——, his wife J——, and seven children are living in the residence. Six other family members still live in Mexico with the possibility of coming to the United States soon.

"Shortly after I arrived, all parties sat around a small table drinking coffee and trying to get to know each other better. It was quite apparent to the writer that there was going to be a communication problem since this officer spoke little Spanish and the M—— family spoke little English. However, with Spanish/English dictionary and a strong desire we plunged ahead. Our seating was quite cramped, since the kitchen was approximately 6 by 10 feet and just about everyone in the family was in there at one time or another during the evening. Mr. M—— brought out family pictures and documents to show me his family as well as his way of life. This lasted until approximately 0030 hours, when it was decided by all that it was time for bed. Tomorrow would be a big day for all parties concerned.

"Mr. M—— then showed me where I was to sleep for the next two nights. I shared a room with the eldest son, F——. The room was dark and cold with only a single light bulb to provide the light. Before getting into bed, I know I counted at least seven cockroaches on the ceiling and the walls of the room though everything appeared clean. As I lay there I wondered which one of the children had to give up his bed for me. I must say it was quite an experience sleeping in a strange house with strange people and my wife and children just a few miles away. I fell asleep wondering how many cockroaches would bite me during the night.

"I awoke early the next morning and found Mr. and Mrs. M—— already up preparing breakfast for the family. I washed and joined the family at breakfast. I noted that the family's eating habits were quite strange and different from mine. The first ones offered food were me, being their guest, and Mr. M——, being the head of the house. Next came the eldest son down to the youngest son. Once all the males in the family had eaten, the females could eat what was

[32]*Ibid.*

left. I might add that I did not eat breakfast, since the menu consisted of orange juice, raw eggs, some type of brownish soup and a cookie. To me, nothing looked appetizing. (I made up for it later at the fantastic dinner prepared by Mrs. M——). I drank coffee and just talked to Mr. M—— about the coming day.

"During breakfast, Mr. M—— showed me a contract he had signed with a Riverside furniture company approximately one month before. In the contract, Mr. M—— had made a $40 down payment, pending credit approval. Mr. M——'s credit was not approved for one reason or another. When he asked for his $40 back, he was told that this was the charge for processing the credit application. Mr. M—— believed that this was wrong but accepted it and did nothing until contact was made with this officer. Again during this conversation, I found communicating difficult; but I could sense an importance about the issue and eventually understood what was being said. I was scheduled to go to school with Mr. M—— and his eldest daughter that morning but knew that sometime during the day I would pay a visit to the furniture store.

"Writer contacted the furniture store manager at approximately 1350 hours. The manager was advised of the situation and told that I felt an injustice had been committed against the family. I advised him that $40 was due back to the family over a month ago and they had not received the money as of this date. The manager began to hem-haw around. Toward the end of the contact with this officer, the manager asked who I was and why I was so concerned about the $40. I advised him that I was a friend but that I was also a police officer and that he, the manager, should do what he thought was best to solve this situation before I left the store. Two minutes later, I had two $20 bills in my hand and was on my way out the door to make contact with Mr. M—— and advise him of what had taken place.

I went straight to the school to pick up Mr. M——. I told him what had happened and gave him the $40. It sounded to me as if Mr. M—— was saying the Rosary all the way home. I could sense that he was extremely happy with the results I had obtained. Mr. M—— told the entire family what had happened at the furniture store and they were as happy as he to find that the $40 had been returned to them. I sensed that the M—— family would have a better Christmas because of this money.

"In closing, I must say that the complete experience with the M—— family was fantastic. I believe that I really know now what it is to be poor but not use the poorness as a crutch to become an undesirable individual as well as family, to be powerless against injustice. The M——'s were a truly poor but proud, hardworking family, which accepted no charity—whose children will never be seen in trouble with authorities. The entire M—— family and their friends were people who I enjoyed being around—people I would enjoy associating with. It was a learning experience that I shall never forget. In my opinion, this experience should be offered to any officer who is willing to put forth the effort, willing to try to promote better community relations with the Mexican-Americans here in the City of Riverside—by developing a better understanding."[32]

[32]Officer Mike Robitzer, Riverside Police Department Training Report (1974).

(It should be understood that Officer Robitzer's method of recovering Mr. M——'s $40, though effective, was questionable to say the least. Proper follow up was done with store owners. The officer was not in any way criticized for his action—he was commended)

"I (Officer Gerry Carroll) was greeted by Mrs. S——, who was cooking chile rellenos. Mr. S—— then introduced me to his children; K—— age 20, M—— age 18, and C—— age 14. We all had dinner in the little dinning room just off the kitchen. The meal was informal and the food was outstanding. While eating dinner, I met a few of the local kids who happened to stop by. All of these kids were in an age group of about 16 to 19. As we ate, we discussed some of the problems the kids felt they were having with the police who worked the area; harassment, etc. J—— suggested that I put one of the kid's hats on and a pair of sunglasses and go out 'LOW RIDING' and find out what the kids were talking about firsthand from their point of view. I was apprehensive about the idea."
("Low Riding"—cruising about the city in a vehicle—most often an older Chevrolet lowered to the limit, with seats nearly on the floor.)

"That evening was spent at a party in the north end of town. I had never heard of the place before and I'm pretty sure none of the other policemen on the department have either. This clubhouse was a garage converted into a recreation room; card table, ping-pong table, dart board, refrigerator (for cold beer), and several pictures of nude Playboy bunnies plastered all over the walls. The crowd at the party consisted of predominantly male Mexican-American youths in the 16 to 21 age group. Forty to fifty subjects were in and out of the party throughout the night, one or two which I recognized as having arrested in the recent past. The ping-pong table, dart board, and card table kept busy all evening, along with the refrigerator opening and closing frequently for the cold beer.

"At first, I was introduced to the whole room of subjects, 'Hey guys, this is Gerry, he's a Policeman on the Riverside Police Department.' Later, as a new person would enter the room, R—— would introduce me simply as 'Gerry,' and then take that person aside and advise him that I was a Police Officer.

"During the whole evening at the party, I couldn't help thinking that this party was very similar to several 'COP' parties that I had been to in the past. At all times, I was treated with great courtesy and was never confronted in any manner. In my opinion, most policemen have a very funny type of humor about them, probably due to the nature of their work, but I found that this group of young people were also very quick witted and never hesitated to make fun of one another, or their race. They also seemed unique in that everybody had a nickname; Bengie, Taco, Slago, etc. I can honestly say that I was treated as a friend. I think that at this point I began realizing that we seemed to have more in common than we have differences.

"Later that night, I had a very unique and very awkward experience. I still have mixed feelings about it. I went out 'Low Riding' in a 1951 lowered beat-up Chevy with a watch cap on my head (no, I wasn't drunk, I don't drink). There were five other people in the car, four males and one female, all twenty years old and younger. Several of the young people in the car complained of being continually stopped by one particular policeman for 'no reason' or simply because this officer knew them and they were 'Low Riders.' They all assured me that if we saw this officer he would stop us for 'no reason.' Before leaving for the ride, I checked the vehicle out for any defects. Everything checked O.K. (he even had a current, valid C.H.P. sticker on that bomb!) We then proceeded to cruise the main drags of the city. Within the first hour, we passed five different patrol cars, but were never stopped. (I was beginning to wonder what was the matter with those guys.) Finally, we cruised through an area where several police cars were parked. Later, I was advised that they were there because there were two burglaries in progress at the same time in that immediate vicinity. Everything was O.K., because we were just passing through on our way home and it looked very doubtful that we would be stopped until the passenger in the front seat stuck his head out the window to look at the helicopter and his straw hat blew off into the street.

"At this point, the driver spun the car around and we went back for the hat, back into the vicinity of the police cars. As the car stopped, the passenger jumped out and ran across the street, picking up his hat. He then jumped back into the car, we spun another U-turn and started to leave the area. At this point, the helicopter put its light on our vehicle (and I knew it was all over . . .) I knew we looked very suspicious and everybody in the car conceded to the fact that they had a good reason to stop us just before the stop was made. As I sat in the rear seat of that old Chevy between two young Chicanos with my watch cap on, watching the red light flashing through the interior of our vehicle, all I could think of was, what's going to happen next . . .? Felony stop . . .? What will the reaction of the officers be if they recognize me . . .? What should I do? I decided to sit tight and play it by ear. Everyone had good identification and everyone was 'clean' (I hoped). I decided that if the officers appeared to recognize me, I would simply identify myself and explain the program. To say the least, I felt I was in a very awkward position and obviously I was!

"By this time, there were about five or six units on the stop or just driving by in what appeared to be stand-by positions. The unit making the stop was a two-man unit. I knew both officers and had actually worked in a radio car with one of them. The officer on the driver's side of the police unit walked up to the driver of our 'Low Rider,' placed his hand on the door handle and, as he began to open the door, he stated to the driver in a low voice, 'get out.' The driver (who was Anglo) stepped out and walked back to the police unit with the officer. I could not hear the conversation. A sergeant then rolled up and started to shine his light in the car at each individual, asking each of us our age. As he shined the light at me, he seemed to hesitate for just a second and then went on to the young man sitting next to me. I knew the sergeant, but really did not know if he recognized me or not. (It was later that I found out that the officers were just about to arrest the driver of the car for curfew when the sergeant walked back to them and advised them that I was in the car.)

"At this point, we were all directed out of the car and were instructed to keep our hands in sight. As we exited the vehicle, I identified myself to the sergeant and advised him that everything was O.K. I then explained the program to him. At this time, the sergeant explained that when he looked into the car he identified me and felt that I was possibly being held hostage. I realize now that it was a difficult situation for all concerned.

"The driver was released, I returned to the car and we left. My emotions at the time of the above stop were of fear, apprehension and that of 'being on the other end of the stick.' That night as I lay in bed looking at the ceiling, I had mixed feelings about the stop. I still do.

"My stay on the east side of town has been a valuable one. I'm going to be working the district for the next six months, and this experience has given me a real feel for the area and the people who live there. It has changed my ideas about policemen working in areas in which they do not live. I believe that it's a real advantage to work in the area you live in. The better (real) understanding of an area a policeman has, obviously the better job he can perform. Overall, this experience has been an educational one for me and hopefully for the people I spent my time with.[34]

"I (Officer Steve Taylor) went to a Mexican bar where a group of Mariachis from Los Angeles had come to have a party. I was introduced to many of F——'s friends who were from Mexico. With the aid of a Spanish/English dictionary, I conversed with several Mexican citizens. Such topics as immigration papers, living conditions in Mexico, living conditions in the United States as Mexican citizens, and attitudes of the police towards 'wet backs' were discussed. We also discussed the 'hassle' that they receive from police agencies, border patrol, etc., and the constant fear of being sent back to Mexico. This party was an extremely jovial one and I was made to feel very welcome and at ease and I sensed that the people I was talking with accepted me as a friend and, therefore, opened up, discussing what I believe to be honest problems as they see them.

"F—— and I went back to his home at approximately 1:00 A.M. and sat in his kitchen drinking coffee and discussing the night's events, his personal experiences with the immigration procedure and his own personal fear of being sent back to Mexico.

"F—— mentioned a burglary in the neighborhood in which it took the police an extremely long time to respond. He wanted to know why the police take so long in acting in the poor areas of town. He said that this is not the first time an incident like this has happened; that it is a constant factor the residents in the poor communities face and, therefore, a lot of people hesitate to call the police for fear they won't take action anyway.

"I then went to bed. It was located in the service porch area of the two-bedroom home. This service porch was enclosed, however, some of the windows were broken. The cover was made up of a drape which did not keep the cold out. While I was in bed, I counted numerous cockroaches and silverfish on the ceiling. It must be noted that it was extremely cold that night.

"Saturday morning started with breakfast. F—— asked if I liked eggs and orange juice. I replied, yes. F——'s wife poured two raw eggs into a small glass of orange juice. This was my breakfast. It was the first time that I have ever had such a breakfast and was a little uneasy about drinking it. However, the thought was worse than the actual taste.

"I spent the morning talking with the family about community problems, the problems the children have at school with the language barrier and the

[34]Officer Gerry Carroll, Riverside Police Department Training Report (1974).

different customs and the attitude towards the police. I found that I had a lot of preconceived ideas that were not correct. Being completely open with the kids a feeling of trust was mutually shared and we had a good rap session.

"We drove to the city-owned property where a charro (slang for horse arena) is being constructed. F—— and I worked approximately three hours on this construction and in doing so exchanged ideas and attitudes with several of the workers. They were Chicanos, 20–25 years, and also several Mexican citizens. Again, the conversation started out awkwardly when these men discovered that I was a policeman. However, when F—— explained that I was a friend living in his home, the tension eased and the conversation became more meaningful.

"Saturday evening F—— and I visited four of his friends to discuss community problems, attitudes toward the police and recommended treatment for the Mexican-Americans by the police. Some of these friends did not have immigration papers and had come from Mexico for work. It was generally stated by all four families that the so-called "wets" were looked down on by the members of the white community and especially the border patrol and the police. These Mexican-born citizens felt as if the border patrol and the police looked on them as inferior. I got the distinct impression that the four families we visited have quite a bit of respect and pride within themselves.

"One particular family we visited has a son who is in the 11th grade. This young man is very outspoken and very antipolice. He blamed the police for most of the problems on the East Side and confused the police with the authority of the government on such problems as housing owned by the government from which people were evicted or forced to leave for nonpayment. This is enforced by the police so, therefore, the police caused the problem.

"All in all, this was a very worthwhile program and I would not hesitate to do the same again at a later date. It is my personal opinion that other officers of this department would profit with meaningful experiences by involving themselves in the same program.[35]

Since its inception in 1974, 46 officers have become a part of the program and are in various stages of experiences. Additionally, 21 officers have also participated in a "Total Immersion Spanish Language Program" offered by the University of California at Davis—in Ensenada, Mexico. Two Community Relations officers work full time to provide new communication links and interpersonal experiences for policemen and barrio youth alike.

It is too early to expect measurable results. We have made some positive observations, are receiving some positive feedback and sense some positive behavioral change. Rocks and bottles are still thrown and policemen continue to have difficulty in dealing with some barrio elements.

We are learning, however, that a few unmanageables do not represent a community and that we do have many friends, people who need us, in the barrio. And, that we are more alike than different.

Lastly, specific needs of the barrio residents have become more apparent from our early assessments of the program. One of these needs, we believe, can be

[35] Officer Steve Taylor, Riverside Police Department Training Report (1975).

filled by expanding our own staff to include an expert in fraud who is also bilingual. Such an expert would be trained to work in the field and assist not only the Mexican-Americans, but also the noncitizens of the barrio, who are subject to exploitation by the larger community and/or their own people. The development of such a staff position is presently under study.

"I looked down the distant road and I saw a rock. As I drew closer, I saw that it was a man. As I drew even closer, I saw that he was my brother."[36]

[36]Author unknown.

Chapter Sixteen

TASK 14
THE POLICE MANAGER
AND THE FUTURE:
Change Agentry

The roaring current of change, a current so powerful today that it overturns institutions, shifts our values and shrivels our roots. *Change is the process by which the future invades our lives, and it is important to look at it closely, not merely from the grand perspectives of history, but also from the vantage point of the living, breathing individuals who experience it.* The acceleration of change in our time is, itself, an elemental force. This accelerative thrust has personal and psychological, as well as sociological, consequences. Unless man quickly learns to control the rate of change in his personal affairs as well as in society at large, we are doomed to a *massive adaptational breakdown.* (Italics added.)[1]

The most common cause of executive failure is inability or unwillingness to change. . . . The executive who fails to understand this will suddenly do the wrong things the wrong way—even though he does exactly what in his old job had been the right things done the right way.[2]

A CONTINUING SYNOPSIS

Yes, a "continuing synopsis"—because how can one delimit an infinite number of probable and possible changes that are and will be confronting the police manager. It appears that two points can be made, however, with a high degree of certainty. First, there will be *change,* and plenty of it in the years to come. Second, required changes will invade our present operations at an ever increasing pace. As a consequence, police managers must either learn to cope with constant and rapid change or expect to experience greater failure. The question is, then, not should we change, but rather in *what* way and *how* can we change in order to maintain an effective system for the delivery of police services to the community both now and in the future.

Based on this thinking, it seems pertinent to conceptualize the police manager as a part-time futurologist and full-time change agent. Hence he is expected, as a part of his organizational role, to be keenly alert for emerging trends and transitions that will affect police work. While clearly responsible for identifying needed change and implementing strategies for bringing it about, the police manager must not act unilaterally. He definitely requires the advice,

[1]Alvin Toffler, *Future Shock* (New York: Random House, Inc., 1970), pp. 3, 4.
[2]Peter F. Drucker, *The Effective Executive* (New York: Harper & Row, Publishers, 1966), p. 58.

assistance, and support of his working team. It becomes, therefore, imperative that he release and at the same time guide the full
energies of his personnel.

Acting in concert can lessen if not eliminate the impact of incoming "future shocks" by preparing people and organizational settings for change. Will Rogers spoke axiomatically when he stated,
"Even if you're on the right track you'll get run over if you just sit
there." Police managers and soon-to-be police managers take heed!

INCREMENTAL CONVOLUTIONS: Decremental Certitude

The crux of our thinking in this section is that increasing complexity
and change results in a decreasing level of sureness so that an ever more
complex future necessitates an ever more complex police manager—one
who can identify incoming changes, make appropriate adjustments, and
thus protect the certitude from which he derives his decisions.

Toffler opened this chapter with an apocalyptic warning about "The
roaring current of change. . . ." He further cautioned us to recognize that
"This is the prospect that man now faces. Change is avalanching upon
our heads and most people are grotesquely unprepared to cope with it."[3]

In summary, Toffler describes the pace of change as being constantly
increased due to an accelerative thrust. This thrust is being forced upon
us through more technology, more knowledge, more transcience, more
diversity, and more novelty in our lives. At the same time while these
forces impact us and our institutions, we should recognize our God-given
limits for adapting to them. Toffler's answer to this problem is not to
impede change but rather to develop strategies for harnessing it.

All right, we have just been challenged to develop strategies for controlling the pace and direction of change. Let us quickly examine some
of the more prominent forces of change that will, if they have not already done so, affect the manager and his police agency. Although most
were covered earlier in greater detail in this chapter we will examine
them in a different light.

Pace

As mentioned in the preceding paragraphs, the accelerative *pace* of
change is to be considered as the paramount force invading our lives.

---

[3] Toffler, *Future Shock*, p. 14.

Role Conflict

It has been scientifically verified that the police officer's role is loaded with conflict. Moreover, the desire for professionalization is increasing the conflict. On the one hand, the police officer is expected to be a law enforcer; and on the other, a maintainer of order. What other profession can you think of that has such an unusual combination of activities that range from crushing crime through order maintenance to community service? Fortunately, the extraordinary demands of the police officer's job are not known to those outside the craft.

Pressures for Centralization and Decentralization

The desire for greater centralization evolves from the police department's need for uniform policy, common standards, and better control. The insertion of technology into the police agency also strengthens the centralizing forces. The growing emphasis on local control, citizen participation, and more effective delivery of police services causes a counter-pressure to decentralize the police function.

Unionization in the Police Service

Unionization of public employees will continue to spread. And, the police will become more involved. In some places, professional associations rather than trade unions are organizing employees and representing them in negotiations with agency management. Hence the form and character of employee organizations within the police service are likely to vary widely. It should be noted that the growth of unionism among the police *and* citizen participation in the processes of public decision making poses double jeopardy to the purview of police managers.

Increasing Citizen Involvement

The involved citizen is the much-sought-after ideal of our democratic society. The current form of citizen participation, however, extends beyond the knowledgeable, voting citizen. We now find citizens regularly challenging government decisions. Clearly, the police who daily provide authoritative, on-the-spot remedies for innumerable situations in American life are being subjected to citizen activism. The police seem to be operating under the old adage, "Damned if you do, damned if you don't." Too much citizen involvement can be dysfunctional to police management and can make it difficult to attract and retain competent professionals. But not enough citizen participation may make the police less than responsive to community needs.

Technological Advancements

Perhaps out of all the conditions requiring change, those of a technological nature are the most tangible. Computer-based information systems, automated communications systems, police aircraft, nonlethal weaponry, laser beam antiintrusion fences, and so forth, are undeniable signs of police technology. Our technological engine is only being warmed up. The next few years should see it be put into gear. Based on the military experience with technology, we can expect to find that (1) the way certain police tasks are performed will change; (2) the training requirements will be modified; (3) the police manager will have to develop a capability for controlling the input, processing, and output of the devices; and (4) the organizational structure will be afforded the opportunity to construct flexible and temporary work groups. The manager can also expect to find (1) an increased need for hardening high risk target sites and systems, (2) citizen apprehensiveness over violations of an individual's right to privacy, (3) the dehumanizing effects of the impersonal machine, and (4) an overreliance on the technician and his technology to solve police problems.

Police Employee Professionalism

It was confirmed earlier that the role requirements of the police officer are most demanding and stressful. Consequently, we either are or should be searching for people who are potentially capable of coping with role conflict. And if we have not already done so, we ought to be retreading those now in the police service so that they will better comprehend the reasons for their dilemma and maybe even make it a workable one. The job of police officer must be restructured in line with a career development scheme that incorporates recurrent education, training, counseling, self-improvement, and a capacity to change. To recruit and retain a person with such a capability for continued professional growth, we must devise a work world that is psychologically richer. Job enlargement, participative management, and an intrinsic reward system are major components of such a job environment. Obviously the unresolved issue of specialist versus generalist looms large at this point. I think the organizational pendulum has swung too far in the direction of the specialist—we have overspecialized. The old boundaries between specialties are collapsing. The police increasingly find that the novel problems can be solved only by reaching beyond narrow specialties. Plainly put, *professional* police employees should be provided the means through their job for meeting higher-order human needs (participation, self-control, self-evaluation, dignity, variety, task identity, and friendship opportunities). Can we expect the professionalization of our police to continue without redesigning our police organizations to accommodate their very presence?

Standards and Program Evaluation

Police work in the 1960s gained a degree of public visibility it had never enjoyed before (or suffered, as the case may be). Such visibility gave rise to police research and "commissionitis." In the main, the output was on-the-shelf documents. We are currently witnessing an attempt to transfer recommended programs into operating realities. Salient examples are the standards proposed by the American Bar Association and the National Advisory Commission on Criminal Justice Standards and Goals. I suspect that there will be a major push-pull effort made by policy makers, fund givers, and police administrators to implement the standards. Simultaneously, you should be aware of a growing emphasis on developing an improved capability to measure the degree to which standards are met. Hence, you will see such terms as *productivity, quantification,* and *program evaluation* being used more frequently. Also, the adoption of standards will mean goal setting and long-range planning. Does anyone doubt that the establishment of standards will not significantly cause changes in the way we organize for the delivery of police services?

FUTUROLOGY: "Star" Gazing

"Foreseeing," "precognizance," "prognosis," "presage," "soothsaying," "clairvoyance," "presentment," "prophesy," and so on are terms that relate to the more generic concepts of foresight and prediction. If the police manager is to deal adroitly with a changing environment, he must plan now for the future—a future that is constantly arriving with new demands, which, if not planned for, may temporarily or even permanently overwhelm his capabilities. Management foreseeability is the very cornerstone of management effectiveness. It is because sustained presaging is critical to prudent coping with change that we have included this section on *planned change*. Planned change, however, is impossible without "telling the future." The manager consequently needs to be, among many other things, a futurologist.

Billions of dollars are being spent on forecasting the direction that our nation will or ought to take. Advanced weaponry, environmental concerns, economic health, foreign relations, and the like have been subjected to major long-range planning efforts. In the recent past, the issue of crime reduction has come to the forefront. We now, in turn, can observe funding and resultant programs dedicated to planning for the future (Law Enforcement Assistance Administration, National Advisory Commission on Criminal Justice Standards and Goals, etc.). One project in particular devoted time to an assessment of the future. We now focus on the premonitions of Project STAR. The prior section discussed currently ongoing changes. STAR presents pending or now arriving changes. In this case we will emphasize those that seem to be more germane to the police service.

Project STAR used selected forecasting methods—expert opinion, time-series trend data, and linear extrapolation of trends—in the analysis of appropriate social trends to identify implications for future roles of criminal justice system personnel and the education and training requirements implied by those trends.[4] The forecasting methods were selected on the assumption that although American society is undergoing major changes, trends that have been in existence for hundreds of years have a high probability of continuing throughout the remainder of this century and, perhaps, well into the next century. Indeed, many of the changes in American society are the manifestations of the long-range trends. Following a literature review of the major long-range trends described by many scholars and social scientists, ten long-range trends or groups of closely related trends were selected for detailed description and analysis of implications for the criminal justice system. The trends selected reflect a consensus of expert opinion on the directions in which American society is moving and have significant consequences for the

[4]Project STAR (Systems and Training Analysis of Requirements) was a collaborative thirty-nine-month effort that began in 1971 and involved many government agencies and private research organizations. Briefly, it sought to identify and describe the roles of operational criminal justice system personnel and, based on this knowledge, develop improved training programs. Most of this section is excerpted from one of its many working documents: Perry E. Rosove, *The Impact of Social Trends on Crime and Criminal Justice* (Sacramento, Calif.: Commission on Peace Officer Standards and Training, American Justice Institute, 1973), pp. 329–49.

criminal justice. Note that some of the trends were discussed earlier. Project STAR prognostications are:

Population growth and change
Industrialization, including the emergence of a "postindustrial" society
Urbanization
Increasingly this-worldly, empirical, humanistic, pragmatic, and utilitarian cultures
Increasing growth of science, empirical knowledge, and technology
Increasing democratization, egalitarianism, and meritocracy
Increasing organization, bureaucracy, integration, and specialization
Increasing economic affluence
Increasing professionalization
Increasing automation of production and information

At numerous places in the Project STAR study it was found essential to note the interdependent relationships of the trends. In many instances the findings pertaining to one trend complement and support findings related to other trends. The end result was a cumulative effect or a compounding of results that could not have been anticipated by dealing with any single trend alone. The reinforcing or inhibiting effects of trends upon one another is seen in exhibit 16–1. For example, what is the probability that the trend toward increasing professionalization will be reinforced by the trend toward a postindustrialized society? The upward arrow in the appropriate cell of the matrix indicates the probability is increased. What happens to that probability if the trend toward increasing automation is also considered? The answer to this question is another upward arrow in another cell of the matrix. It can be seen from the large number of upward arrows that most of the trends are mutually reinforcing. It can also be seen that the probability of population growth is inhibited by most of the other trends. The horizontal lines in the cells indicate no effect of a trend on the probability of another trend.

The Major Finding

The major finding of this study of long-range trends is that despite continuing improvements in American society, as measured by a large variety of economic, educational, and social indicators, *an increase in crime is highly probable in the remainder of the twentieth century*. Continuing population growth, particularly in the young adult category (the category that commits the most serious crimes), urbanization, and residual poverty in the midst of increasing economic affluence are the major factors that lead to this conclusion. Additional factors which contribute to

Exhibit 16–1.   A Cross-Impact Matrix of Social Trends

IF THIS DEVELOPMENT WERE TO OCCUR:	THEN THE PROBABILITY OF:									
	A	B	C	D	E	F	G	H	I	J
A Population Growth and Change		—	↑	—	—	—	↑	—	—	—
B Postindustrialization	↓		—	↑	↑	↑	↑	↑	↑	↑
C Urbanization	↓	↑		↑	↑	↑	↑	↑	↑	—
D Increasingly This-Worldly, Empirical, Humanistic, Pragmatic, Utilitarian Cultures	↓	—	—		↑	↑	↑	↑	↑	↑
E Increasing Growth of Science, Empirical Knowledge and Technology	↓	↑	—	↑		↑	↑	↑	↑	↑
F Increasing Democratization, Egalitarianism, and Meritocracy	↓	↑	—	↑	↑		—	↑	↑	—
G Increasing Organization, Bureaucracy, Integration, and Specialization	↓	↑	—	↑	↑	↑		—	↑	↑
H Increasing Economic Affluence	↓	↑	↑	↑	↑	↑	—		↑	—
I Increasing Professionalization	↓	↑	—	↑	↑	↑	↑	↑		↑
J Increasing Automation of Production/Information	—	↑	—	↑	↑	—	↑	↑	↑	

Source: Perry E. Rosove, The Impact of Social Trends On Crime and Criminal Justice (Sacramento, Calif.: Commission on Peace Office Standards and Training, American Justice Institute, 1973), p. 348.

it are the increasing equality of the sexes and basic changes in attitudes. As our data have shown, there has been a large increase in crime committed by females, particularly among juveniles. The rate of this increase can be expected to continue to rise until women attain almost full equality with men. Basic changes in attitudes may be a reflection of the "sensate" culture referred to by Kahn, Sorokin, and Wiener. This culture is materialistic and utilitarian and reflects an emphasis on the sensory values of wealth, health, bodily comfort, power, recognition, and sensual pleasure.

Subordinate Findings

Following is a list of findings from Project STAR research that are germane to the police.

> Although law enforcement is a critical task performed by the police officer, quantitative studies show that the vast majority of police activity on-the-job is related to some form of social service.

> The organizational emphasis on efficiency and impersonal relationships characteristic of large police departments in urban regions diminishes the opportunities for personal face-to-face relationships between the police officer and the public and contribtues to antagonistic police-citizen interactions.

> A large proportion of police officers who patrol the central cities of urban regions should be demilitarized and should be physically located full-time in urban schools, playgrounds, dance halls, or other facilities frequented by young people. A major responsibility of these officers should be to establish and maintain communication links with young people.

> The demilitarization of the police officer's role should be accompanied by a shift in training of police recruits from the "stress" and authoritarian method of training to the nonstress and nonauthoritarian style. However, police officers assigned to riot control should receive training of a highly disciplined nature.

> The police officer's role will probably be subjected to increasing strain unless criminal codes and statutes are made more compatible with changes in public morality and attitudes related to sexual behavior, public nudity, pornography, and drug use.

> The professionalization of the police officer's role is an essential requirement; the baccalaureate degree will probably become a mandatory standard for recruits and advanced degrees should be mandatory for supervisors, managers, and administrators higher in the police organization.

> Police officers will probably have to become specialists in many different fields as a result of developments in science, technology, and the increasing use of computers.

> While specialization will probably increase, some police officers should possess the capability to function as generalists by being knowledgeable

in two or more specialties, such as police operations and the computer sciences.

Women will probably be increasingly employed by police departments for all types of positions until they achieve full equality with men based on merit.

The varieties of tasks performed by the police officer should be reexamined to determine which tasks may be performed best by women.

Major Issues Associated with the Trends

The analyses of the implications of each of the long-range trends for the criminal justice system served not only to suggest possible future roles and education and training requirements, but also brought out major issues which should be of concern to criminal justice officials and administrators and which will have to be resolved in the future. These include:

1. Assembly-line vs. individualized Justice

2. Adversary vs. fact-finding court procedures

3. Impartiality vs. discretion in law enforcement

4. Social service vs. law enforcement

5. Police efficiency vs. community relations

6. Custody vs. treatment

7. Individual vs. social responsibility for crime

8. Custody vs. education

9. Moralistic vs. pragmatic and rational policies

10. Ivory-tower vs. applied research

11. Technical vs. liberal arts education

12. Racial and ethnic representation vs. educational upgrading

13. Women's rights vs. male dominance

14. Personal vs. impersonal relationships

15. Integration vs. local autonomy

16. Specialization vs. job enlargement

17. Humanitarian vs. hardline policies

18. Informality vs. formality in the juvenile court

19. Election vs. appointment of personnel

20. Centralized data banks vs. individual privacy

21. Independent systems vs. integrated systems

Infinite Changing: Renewal and More Renewal

Most progressive police managers (and police educators) today are deeply concerned with the problem of developing managerial strategies appropriate to the changing conditions. The word *change* is no longer even a buzz word. It has become part of our everyday language. Police are continually working on the problems of how to develop a flexible organization that can move with changing requirements and can be "proactive" (influencing the environment) rather than reactive. Police managers are seeking ways to establish a work climate in which increasingly complex decisions can be made by people with the information, regardless of their location in the organization. Police managers are looking for ways in which increasingly complex technologies can be managed and in which people who have an ever higher sense of freedom and autonomy can be encouraged to want to stay and work in the organization. They are doing all these things (that is, the effective ones are) in addition to fulfilling their more traditional responsibility of organizing for *efficiency*. The search for ways of concurrently increasing collaboration among the members of organizations and at the same time increasing the rationality of decisions occupies many hours of management time and many chapters in management books.

What makes organizations want to change? People, quite obviously. Therefore, it would seem reasonable to make the next inquiry—What makes people want to change? Three things make them want to:[5] One is that they hurt sufficiently. They have invested in the same organization, the same occupation for so long without any psychological rewards that they are finally willing to either drop out or stop trying. They seek relief. They want change.

The second thing that makes people want to change is a creeping form of despair called ennui, or boredom. It is detected in the person who slowly moves through his life repeating "So what?" When he stops, pauses, and shouts "So What?" then you know he is ready for change.

The third thing that makes people want to change is the sudden realization that they can. Many police managers who have shown no particular interest in changing either themselves or their organizations have been exposed to the ideas of self-renewal and organizational development. These ideas have produced an excitement about new possibilities, which has led to even further inquiry and an expressed commitment to change.

[5]This section is drawn from Thomas A. Harris, *I'm OK—You're OK: A Practical Guide to Transactional Analysis* (New York: Harper & Row, Publishers, 1967), pp. 60–61.

To paraphrase Socrates, who held that "the unexamined life is not worth living," we might add that the unexamined organization is not worth basing one's life on. Thus we would propose to you that people—in this case the police—must first begin to examine themselves and change. From this we will find examined, changed, and improved police organizations.

In summary, then, the police manager has an obligation to create a change process that provides his organization with a capability for constant self-renewal. And, at the same time, he must subject himself to the demands of the process.

THREE MANAGEMENT STRATEGIES FOR COUNTERING EPHEMERIALISM

Strategy 1: Organizational Development

To repeat a position taken at the onset of this text—our focus is on the *human* side of the *organization*. Thus, the solutions examined in this section are limited to those activities that "we" can take within our "police organizations" as "police managers" to cope with or control change. Also mentioned earlier, other devices and techniques not only can, but should, be used in sustaining the change process. The two strategies or solutions discussed below contain, however, the majority of the tactics associated with planned human and organizational changes. It is necessary to recognize that there is no one best way to change; rather, the change process needs to be systematically tailored to organizational goals and individual human purposes. Finally, our focus remains on the change process, with little attention given to the outputs. Briefly, the two solutions are organization development (internal orientation) and environmental participation (external orientation).

To begin with, organizational development (OD) is a
planned,
organization-wide,
managed
process
to improve organization *effectiveness*
by either coping with or controlling *change*
with *behavioral science knowledge.*
Again, the threefold mission of OD is to change attitudes and values, modify behavior, and thereby induce change in *people, structure,* and *policies.*

Before describing the tactics, it should be mentioned that OD, while beneficial, is not a panacea for avoiding the crash and crush of change. The omnipresent legal constraints, human resistance to change, procedural habits, and encrusted policies are not easily beaten down. Numerous studies have been, are being, and will be conducted into properties of an organization that either hinder or facilitate change. One study, for example, reported that an organization that had a high degree of job codification was susceptible to programmatic changes. Clearly we cannot separate the individual from his organization or view the organization as comprising some kind of living mass. Hence, we come full circle to once more realizing that any OD effort must be total and must be targeted for both the person in singular form and the persons in corporate form. If nothing else, the above ought to impress upon one that change is difficult to achieve. Moreover, *sustained* change is even more difficult!

The tactics or methods of OD are team development, intergroup relationships, goal setting and planning, and education. In general, the four methods are based on the same set of activities that, in combination, constitute the OD process. The activities and overall process are shown in exhibit 16–2. Remember, the OD process is not the only way to change a police department; however, we do believe it is (in conjunction with the second solution) the most effective means for doing so at the present.

Strategy 2: New Organizational Forms

The preceding solution centers on one or two individuals (the person), on three or more (the group), and on hundreds (the organization). This solution considers the need for new and better ways of organizing the persons who comprise departments so that they will be more adaptive to change. By way of a preface, we wish to inform the reader that we (1) will *not* offer our concept of the one best way to organize for change and (2) do not believe that bureaucracy is dead or dying. In regard to statement one, we will concentrate on the characteristics (not structure) of a flexible organization. Statement two is in answer to those who are having fun with titles. The bureaucracy of yesterday and today was and is a formal organization. Both had or have a set of authoritative relationships, rules, regulations, written policies, rationality, and impersonality. We believe that future organizations will also possess these properties. The manner in which they are established and enforced, however, will be drastically changed. And the frequency with which they change will be extremely fast. We will find ourselves—that is, if we want to be capable of rapid adjustments to environmental demands for changes—creating *temporary* and *open* structures.

Basic Premise: When individuals can meet their own needs while meeting organizational needs, output will be qualitatively and quantitatively best.

An individual's basic needs center around *self-realization* and *self-actualization.* The former involves a person seeing himself as he is in interaction with others, with the goal of increasing the congruence between his intentions and his impact on others. Self-actualization refers to the processes of growth by which an individual realizes his potential.

An individual whose basic needs are satisfied does not seek comfort and security; rather, he *searches for work, challenge, and responsibility.*

An efficient organization will develop an appropriately shifting balance between *institutionalization* and *risk-taking.* The former refers to *infusing with values* the activites of the organization, so as to elicit member support, identification, and collaboration. Risk-taking is necessary in *innovating* more effective ways to deal with existing activities, and in *adapting* to environmental changes in society, market technology, and so on.

An organization's successful balancing of institutionalization and risk-taking will depend upon
—the increasingly complete *use of people* as well as nonhuman resources
—the development and maintenance of a viable balance between *central control* and local initiative
—fluid lines of *communication,* vertically, horizontally, and diagonally
—decision-making processes that solve problems that stay solved without creating other problems.

Satisfaction of both individual and organization needs will be facilitated by, if such satisfaction does not in fact crucially depend upon, *skill and competence in interpersonal and intergroup situations.*

An individual's growth and self-realization are facilitated by interpersonal relations that are *honest, caring, and nonmanipulative.* Hence the reliance on

Organizational "family" teams are exposed to sensitivity training, with the intention of *increasing trust and responsibility* that can be applied directly to solving organizational issues, and with the intention of *decreasing*

Exhibit 16–2. (Continued)

of individuals with no past relationships. Such training is a managed process of gaining experience with attitudes and skills for
inducing greater openness about
positive and negative feelings,
attitudes, or beliefs. Such openness leads to greater trust and reduced risk in communicating in
the "stranger" group, and is intended to suggest possible transfers into other environments.

the risk in being open in interpersonal and group situations.
Skill and competence in interpersonal and intergroup situations can be increased in
sensitivity training groups composed of strangers, but the real
test is the application of such
learning in life-relevant situations. Such application will require that substantial numbers of
organization members learn appropriate interpersonal skills, as
well as that they internalize a set
of values which support and reinforce such learning.

Persons in groups which develop greater openness tend to *identify
strongly* with other members and with the goals of the group.

Groups characterized by strong identification with members and
goals become *increasingly capable of dealing with issues* facing
their members, and hence increasingly *capable of influencing
their environment* in desired ways.

Groups whose members identify strongly and who can influence
their environment are likely to be effective *reinforcers of decisions
about change.* Such groups also can provide *emotional support*
necessary to sustain required changes in the values, attitudes, or
behaviors of their members.

Source: Used with the permission of the *Public Administration Review.* Robert T. Golembiewski,
         "Organization Development in Public Agencies: Perspectives on Theory and Practice,"
         Public Administration Review 29 (July-August 1969): 369.

Strategy 3: Knowledge Management

The prospect for police management in the predictable future is one of
extraordinary difficulty. An exacerbation of crisis in an era of fundamental ideological change and deontological equivocation naturally emphasizes the requirement for foresight, initiative, flexibility, sensitivity,
and equality in the management of our police services. But the underlying need, and resource, of the police manager in this time of accelerated
ephemeralism will be, more than ever before, *knowledge.* For—

Management is knowledge

Knowledge is power

Management is power[6]

This syllogism underscores a major feature characteristic of postindustrial management. Our nation is now a service society—the police being a case in point—and a knowledge technology society. In summary, crux of postindustrial management is the provision of services through knowledge-based, social-technological systems.

The specific types of knowledge more needed at this time concern trends, interactions, and synergistic effects. Technical and procedural expertise, which is well developed among some police managers, *remains a necessary but increasingly insufficient attribute of effectiveness.* The repository of knowledge required for effective management is enlarging by orders of magnitude, and it is doubtful that the current level of sophistication among police managers, or our organizational arrangements for using their capabilities or the knowledge they possess are appropriate for the emerging role tasks.

Do not confuse information with knowledge. For we have an abundance—maybe too much—of the former, with a paucity of the latter. Knowledge is derived from information. Briefly, knowledge is validated and usable information. And, the police manager becomes increasingly involved in the management of information in order that it may eventually become knowledge.

The police manager most needed to lead an agency through continuous transitions should have a broad range of knowledge and personal competence. But very special and uncommon qualities are also required, especially insight, foresight, and the ability to focus. The cost and inconvenience of generating a cadre of such policy-oriented, systems-conceiving managers will appear excessive if measured by traditional criteria. Yet, the failure to attempt it could be one of the most costly mistakes made in the police field.

In conclusion, the management of knowledge may be the most vital factor of managing change toward a police service hopefully more effective, stable, and enduring than the one we now know.

---

[6]This theme and concept is expanded upon by James D. Carrol and Nicholas Henry, eds., "Symposium on Knowledge Management," *Public Administration Review* 35 (November-December 1975): 567–602.

SANGUINE TO THE END: The Continuing Ascent Of Management

The changes and strategies that we have mentioned or hinted about, complex and difficult as they are, are necessary. Our current police and sheriff departments, effective as they have been in the past, constantly court failure. The impersonality of the large police organization, the sharp horns of our immediate dilemma between quality and numbers, the unwillingness of our clients, the citizens, to accept much longer the rigidities of our present police organizations—all combine to force change upon us. *Let us make these changes as they should be made, voluntarily and with careful planning, rather than wait to have them forced upon us, and let us establish a police tradition of not being afraid of something new.*

Either police agencies are closed to the demands for futurity—in which case thought, the fruit of scores of years, is stifled and stillborn in a self-abortive and absurd society—or else an opening exists. We believe that there is an opening. This opening will be explored not by a nameless police management but by police managers within and citizens outside of the organization. The exploration can be made only as dedicated and competent individuals are emancipated from the past and become free to choose either to accept or to reject the organizational values and designs of the past. One conclusion is unavoidable: The police organization cannot change until the people in its employ change. We can base our hope for the future and improved police organizations on the fact that we have seen people change. We have witnessed citizens' greater commitment to improving their police. How this will continue and mature in significance is the good news of tomorrow. Clearly, a viable organizational structure that does not merely cope with but actually accepts and molds complex demands into a highly effective delivery system is at hand. This is our hope. We trust it is yours.

> We are all afraid—for our confidence, for the future, for the world. That is the nature of the human imagination. Yet every man, every civilisation, has gone forward because of its engagement with what it has set itself to do. The personal commitment of a man to his skill, the intellectual commitment and the emotional commitment working together as one, has made the Ascent of Man.[7]

[7]J. Bronowski, *The Ascent of Man* (Boston, Mass.: Little, Brown and Company, 1973), p. 438.

INDEX